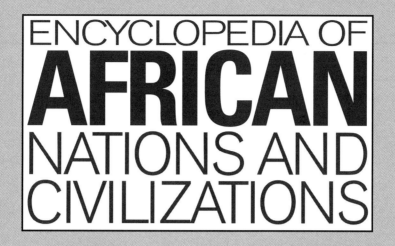

ENCYCLOPEDIA OF
AFRICAN
NATIONS AND
CIVILIZATIONS

ENCYCLOPEDIA OF AFRICAN NATIONS AND CIVILIZATIONS

Keith Lye
and
The Diagram Group

Facts On File, Inc.

Encyclopedia of African Nations & Civilizations

Copyright © 2002 by The Diagram Group

Diagram Visual Information Ltd
195 Kentish Town Road, London, NW5 2JU
e-mail: diagramvis@aol.com

Contributors:	Bridget Giles, John Haywood, Keith Lye
Managing editor:	Denis Kennedy
Editors:	Peter Harrison, Jamie Stokes
Indexer:	Martin Hargreaves
Artist:	Graham Rosewarne
Design and production:	Richard Hummerstone, Lee Lawrence, Chris Owens
Cartography:	Oscar Lobban, Philip Patenall
Picture research director:	Patricia Robertson
Picture researchers:	Catherine Michard, Neil McKenna

Facts On File Inc.
132 West 31st Street
New York NY 10001

Library of Congress Cataloging-in-Publication Data
Encyclopedia of African nations and civilizations/The Diagram Group and Keith Lye.
    p.cm.
    Includes index.
    ISBN 0-8160-4568-2
    1. Africa—Civilization--Encyclopedias. 2. Africa—History—Encyclopedias. I. Lye,
Keith. II. Diagram Group (Firm)

DTI4.E43 2001
960'.03—dc21

                                                                        2001040283

Facts On File books are available at special discounts when purchased in bulk
quantities for businesses, associations, institutions, or sales promotions. Please call
our Special Sales Department in New York at 212/967-8800 or 800/322-8755.

You can find Facts On File on the World Wide Web at http://www.factsonfile.com

Cover design by Cathy Rincon

Printed in the United States of America

EB DIAG 10 9 8 7 6 5 4 3 2 1

This book is printed on acid-free paper

Introduction

Much of what is often referred to as "African history" describes the lives of Arabs or Europeans and their views of the societies they colonized in Africa. Yet African peoples developed many powerful, rich, and sophisticated civilizations that flourished long before—and during—the colonialism of foreign nations. The *Encyclopedia of African Nations and Civilizations* tells the histories of these African civilizations, and their struggle to throw off colonialism, in a highly visual and imaginative way.

The book is organized in three sections, copiously illustrated by line drawings, comprehensive timelines, and numerous maps. These all combine to provide detailed information about occupation by foreign powers, relevant military events and the development of the African peoples. The sections can be read together to reveal a portrait of Africa as a whole, or consulted separately for vital and interesting facts about specific research topics.

Section 1: Africa Today presents an overview of the political and economic status of each of the five main regions of Africa: North, East, West, Central, and Southern. The following information is given for each region: a map showing national borders within the particular region; the areas of individual nations; population density; per capita GNP; official name; capital cities; official language; and currency.

Section 2: Development of the continent focuses on areas of particular relevance to the cultural development of Africa as a whole. An extensive chronology of important events in the history of each nation is followed by special features on such topics as the spread of Christianity and of Islamic beliefs. The historical perspective afforded by the analysis of North African conquests by various colonial powers, and the resistance to them, is complemented by graphic illustrations of the years when independence was achieved, and *coups d'état* in the newly emerging nations. Other topics mentioned in passing in *Section 3* are here dealt with in detail, such as slavery: its economic importance to the colonial powers, the struggle of African peoples to be free from it, and the scars it has left on all touched by the trade.

Section 3: A to Z of Nations and Civilizations is the core of the book, consisting of almost 300 pages. It is presented in alphabetical order so that the history of each civilization, and the emergence of the independent nations from the colonial powers, can be easily found. A wealth of facts and figures is given for each nation, including: a brief history; recent events; indigenous peoples; biographies of the major personalities; and detailed timelines that capture the major events within each nation's recent history, and their leaders since independence. Special features focus on particular events that have had, or will have, far-reaching effects on generations to come, such as the loss of life on both sides in the Anglo-Sudanese and Zulu conflicts, the horrors perpetrated in the Congo, the international tension created by the Suez Crisis, and the inhumanity of the apartheid regime in South Africa.

The *Encyclopedia of African Nations and Civilizations* is unique. The editorial team that worked on the project specializes in the integration of visual forms of information with concise and clear text. This interrelationship of text and images is made even more effective by the care taken in presenting the elements on the page in an attractive, yet coherent, whole. Additionally, the use of two-color artwork, together with the painstaking concern for detail, brings to life the history of the African continent in a way that is, at one and the same time, authoritative, engaging, and exciting.

A concise reference tool for students, researchers and teachers, this book can be used as a companion volume to the *Encyclopedia of African Peoples*, an ethnographic study of more than 1,000 peoples of Africa. This book also gives the general reader an unparalleled overview of the factors which led to the emergence of the nations that inhabit the African continent today, and the ways in which they are developing their independence at the start of the twenty-first century.

Contents

9 **Section 1 Africa Today**

10 North Africa
12 East Africa
14 West Africa

16 Central Africa
18 Southern Africa

21 **Section 2 Development of the Continent**

22 Chronology of Events
Nation-by-Nation
62 Bantu Migrations
64 North African Conquests
68 Spread of Christianity
70 Spread of Islam

72 European Exploration
76 Slavery in Africa
82 Resistance to Colonialism
90 Colonial Occupation and
Independence
92 *Coups d'Etat* in Africa

95 **Section 3 A to Z of Nations and Civilizations**

393 **Index**
394 Index of Personalities
396 General Index

Regions of Africa

This map gives the regions
of Africa used within this book.

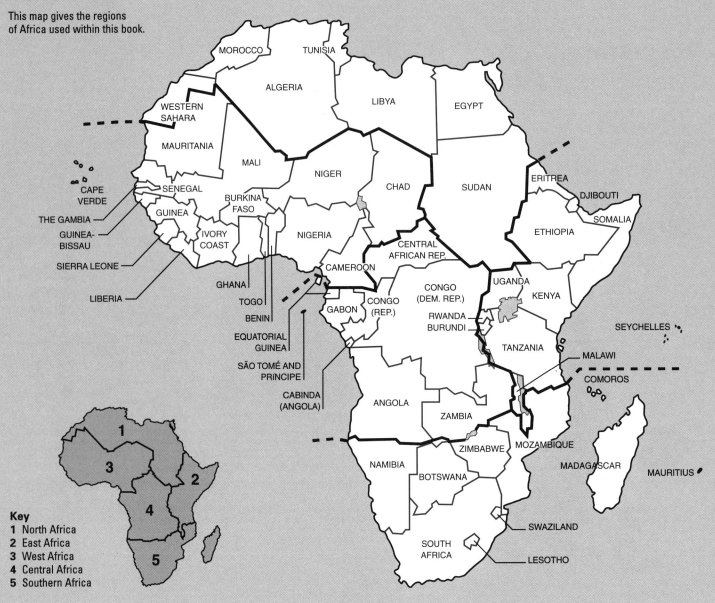

Key
1 North Africa
2 East Africa
3 West Africa
4 Central Africa
5 Southern Africa

SECTION 1

AFRICA TODAY

North Africa

North Africa has played a major part in the history of the continent. The Nile valley was the cradle of the great civilization of Ancient Egypt, while the culture of the entire Mediterranean region was influenced by other civilizations, including those of the Phoenicians, Greeks, and Romans. However, the most important influence on North Africa's modern culture occurred in the seventh century CE with the arrival of the Arabs who introduced their language, Arabic, and their religion Islam. By the nineteenth century, North Africa was poor and, despite uprisings, European colonists took over and exploited the region's resources.

Since independence, the exploitation of natural resources. such as natural gas, and the development of manufacturing industries and tourism, has created countries with economies that are more diverse and stable than those of most nations south of the Sahara. But modern North Africa faces many problems. The resources of the poorest country, Sudan, have been drained by a long civil war, caused by differences between the Muslim north and the mainly non-Muslim south. By the early twenty-first century, no end seemed in sight for this bitter conflict.

Religious issues have affected Egypt and Algeria, where many people support radical Islamic movements similar to those in Iran and other parts of the Middle East. They believe that Islamic fundamentalism

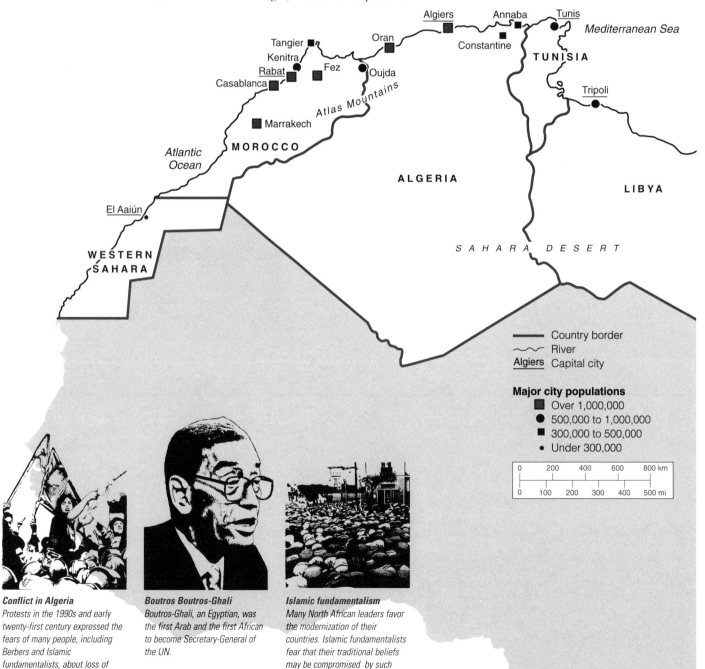

Country border
River
Algiers Capital city

Major city populations
■ Over 1,000,000
● 500,000 to 1,000,000
■ 300,000 to 500,000
• Under 300,000

| 0 | 200 | 400 | 600 | 800 km |
| 0 | 100 | 200 | 300 | 400 | 500 mi |

Conflict in Algeria
Protests in the 1990s and early twenty-first century expressed the fears of many people, including Berbers and Islamic fundamentalists, about loss of their cultural identity.

Boutros Boutros-Ghali
Boutros-Ghali, an Egyptian, was the first Arab and the first African to become Secretary-General of the UN.

Islamic fundamentalism
Many North African leaders favor the modernization of their countries. Islamic fundamentalists fear that their traditional beliefs may be compromised by such modernization.

COUNTRY	OFFICIAL NAME	CAPITAL	LANGUAGE	CURRENCY
Algeria	(al-Jumhuriya al-Jazairiya ad-Dimuqratiya Ash-Shabiya)	Algiers	Arabic	Algerian dinar
Egypt	(Jumhuriyah Misr al-Arabiya)	Cairo	Arabic	Egyptian pound
Libya	(al-Jamahiriyah al-Arabiya al-Libya al-Shabiya al-Ishtirakiya)	Tripoli	Arabic	Libyan dinar
Morocco	(al-Mamlaka al-Maghrebia)	Rabat	Arabic	Dirham
Sudan	(Jamhuryat as-Sudan)	Khartoum	Arabic	Sudanese pound
Tunisia	(al-Jumhuriyah at-Tunisiyah)	Tunis	Arabic	Tunisian dinar
Western Sahara		Laâyoune	Arabic	Peseta

Countries by size (sq mi)	
1 Sudan	967,245
2 Algeria	919,355
3 Libya	679,180
4 Egypt	386,095
5 Morocco (including W. Sahara)	274,460
(without W. Sahara)	171,760
6 Western Sahara	102,700
7 Tunisia	63,360

Populations 1999 (000s)	
1 Egypt	62,655
2 Algeria	29,950
2 Sudan	28,993
2 Morocco	28,238
2 Tunisia	9457
2 Libya	5419
7 Western Sahara	283

Densities (people per sq mi)	
1 Egypt	162
2 Morocco	159
3 Tunisia	149
4 Algeria	32
5 Sudan	30
6 Libya	8
7 Western Sahara	2

Per capita GNP (1999 US$)	
1 Libya	c.6700
2 Tunisia	2090
3 Algeria	1550
4 Egypt	1380
5 Morocco	1190
6 Sudan	330
7 Western Sahara	NA

is the best means of preserving their traditional culture.

In Egypt, attacks on foreign visitors in the 1990s proved a major setback for the valuable and growing tourist industry. In Algeria, civil war broke out after the fundamentalist Islamic Salvation Front was banned after having won a general election in 1991. By the end of the twentieth century, more than 100,000 people had died in the Algerian conflict. Support for Islamic fundamentalism exists in other North African countries, although no major Islamic political grouping has so far developed outside Egypt and Algeria.

The unresolved issue of Western (formerly Spanish) Sahara is a hangover from colonial days. This phosphate-rich desert territory has been occupied by Morocco—for a while jointly with Mauritania—since Spain withdrew in 1975 CE. Saharan nationalists who wanted to found their own nation—the Sahrawi Arab Democratic Republic—set up a government in exile. Recognition of this body from other African countries isolated Morocco, which left the Organization of African Unity (OAU) in protest.

The UN tried to hold a referendum on Western Sahara's future, but it was unable to draw up an electoral register acceptable to both the Saharans and the Moroccan government. By 2001 CE, the prospect of a referendum seemed as remote as ever and some UN officials proposed that Morocco's annexation of Western Sahara should be recognized. In return, they argued, Western Sahara should be granted autonomy within Morocco.

East Africa

Those parts of the Great African Rift Valley which run through Tanzania, Kenya and Ethiopia are rich in fossil evidence of ancient humanlike creatures and many anthropologists believe that human beings first evolved in East Africa. In historic times, when Ancient Egypt was at its most powerful, present-day Somalia may have been the "Land of Punt", from which the Egyptians obtained valuable frankincense and myrrh. Later, the coasts of what are now Kenya and Tanzania were dotted with rival city states which played a major role in early East African trade with Arabia, Persia, India, and even China. However, East Africa is now the continent's poorest region. It lacks the natural resources which have enabled other areas to develop and diversify their economies and most East Africans make their living as subsistence farmers, who make little contribution to the national economy. The farmers are subject to natural disasters, such as droughts, which cause famine and great suffering. Judged by their per capita (for each person) gross national products (GNPs), Ethiopia, Burundi, and Malawi are the poorest countries, though, in the late 1990s, figures were unavailable for Somalia, which was splintered into three parts. With no effective national government, Somalia's economy collapsed. However, hope emerged in 2000, when a transitional Assembly was established in southern Somalia. The secessionist northeast (called Puntland) indicated that it would join a reconstituted Somalia, but the other separatist region, Somaliland (formerly British Somaliland) remained apart, indicating that it wished to remain a separate entity.

Civil war and other conflict has put the economic development of several other countries into reverse. Eritrea, which was united with Ethiopia in 1952 CE, broke away in 1993 CE after a long and bitter civil war. Relations between Eritrea and Ethiopia remained cordial until 1998 CE, when border fighting occurred. It was not until 2000 CE that a peace plan was agreed. Burundi and Rwanda have been rocked by appalling conflict between the two main ethnic groups—the Hutu and the Tutsi. Many refugees fled to escape slaughter, but their numbers caused instability in Zaire (now the Democratic Republic of Congo).

In the former British East Africa, Uganda also suffered much conflict although its neighbors have proved more stable. Tanzania, having embraced more liberal economic policies in the 1990s, is now closer to Kenya, which has always followed free enterprise policies, although it has been held together mainly by autocratic one-party rule. In the 1960s, these three formerly British territories attempted to create an East African Community. But the deep political and economic differences wrecked this chance of pan-African cooperation. However, in 1999 CE, a new pact was signed by Kenya, Tanzania, and Uganda. This aim of this pact was to establish a customs union, a common market, a monetary union, and, ultimately, a political union, which might bring greater prosperity to the region.

Malawi also suffered under the autocratic rule of Hastings Kamuzu Banda, but in 1993, a multiparty system was restored and elections were held in 1994, when Banda was defeated.

Countries by size (sq mi)		Populations 1999 (000s)		Densities (people per sq mi)		Per capita GNP (1999 US$)	
1 Ethiopia	394,895	**1** Ethiopia	62,782	**1** Rwanda	773	**1** Seychelles	6500
2 Tanzania	362,750	**2** Tanzania	32,923	**2** Burundi	621	**2** Djibouti	790
3 Somalia	243,180	**3** Kenya	29,410	**3** Seychelles	512	**3** Kenya	360
4 Kenya	224,900	**4** Uganda	21,479	**4** Malawi	297	**4** Uganda	320
5 Uganda	91,320	**5** Malawi	10,788	**5** Uganda	235	**5** Tanzania	260
6 Malawi	36,315	**6** Somalia	9388	**6** Ethiopia	159	**6** Rwanda	250
7 Eritrea	35,370	**7** Rwanda	8310	**7** Kenya	130	**7** Eritrea	200
8 Burundi	10,745	**8** Burundi	6678	**8** Eritrea	112	**8** Malawi	180
9 Rwanda	10,165	**9** Eritrea	3991	**9** Tanzania	90	**9** Burundi	120
10 Djibouti	8800	**10** Djibouti	648	**10** Djibouti	73	**10** Ethiopia	100
11 Seychelles	156	**11** Seychelles	80	**11** Somalia	39	**11** Somalia	NA

COUNTRY	OFFICIAL NAME	CAPITAL	LANGUAGE	CURRENCY
Burundi	(Republika y'Uburundi)	Bujumbura	French, Kirundi	Burundi franc
Djibouti	(Jumhouriyya Djibouti)	Djibouti	French, Arabic	Djibouti franc
Eritrea	(State of Enitrea)	Asmara	Tigrinya	Birr
Ethiopia	(Itiopia)	Addis Ababa	Amharic	Birr
Kenya	(Jamhuriya Kenya)	Nairobi	Swahili	Kenyan shilling
Malawi	(Republic of Malawi)	Lilongwe	English, Chewa	Kwacha
Rwanda	(Republika y'u Rwanda)	Kigali	Kinyarwanda, French	Rwanda franc
Seychelles	(Republic of Seychelles)	Victoria	English, French	Seychelles rupee
Somalia	(Jamhuriyadda Dimugradiga Somaliya)	Mogadishu	Somali, Arabic	Somali shilling
Tanzania	(Jamhuriya Mwungano wa Tanzania)	Dodoma	Swahili, English	Tanzanian shilling
Uganda	(Republic of Uganda)	Kampala	English	Ugandan shilling

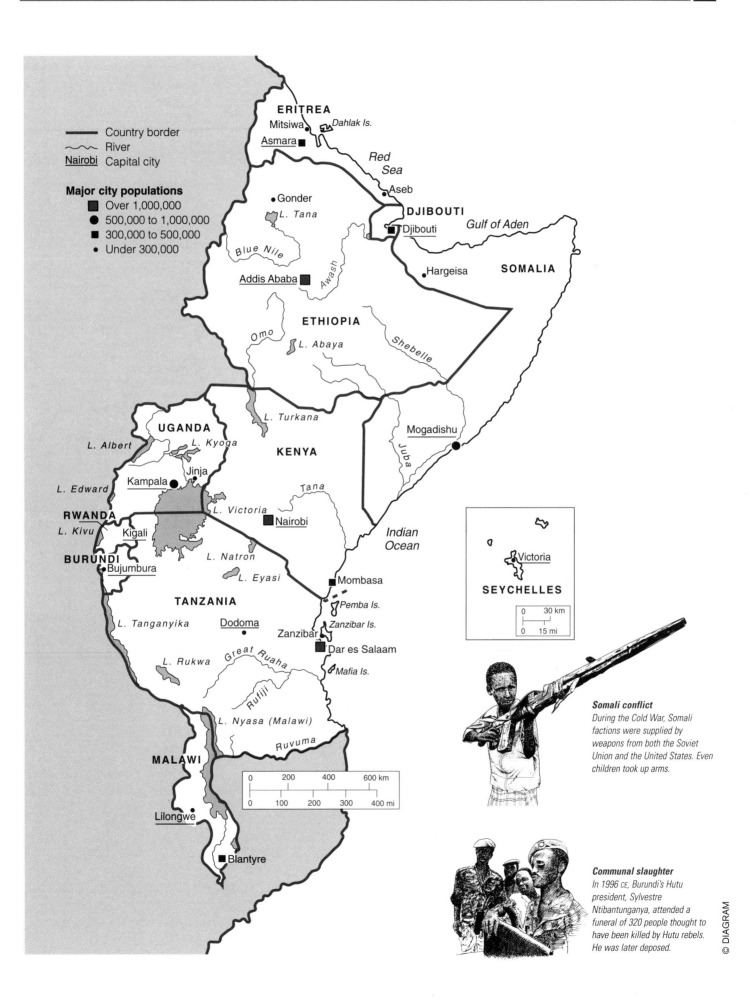

Country border
River
Nairobi Capital city

Major city populations
◼ Over 1,000,000
● 500,000 to 1,000,000
▪ 300,000 to 500,000
• Under 300,000

ERITREA
Mitsiwa • 🌾 Dahlak Is.
Asmara ▪

Red Sea

• Gonder
L. Tana
Aseb
DJIBOUTI
Blue Nile
Awash
▪ Djibouti
Gulf of Aden

• Hargeisa
SOMALIA

Addis Ababa ◼
ETHIOPIA
Omo
L. Abaya
Shebelle

UGANDA
L. Albert
L. Kyoga
L. Turkana

KENYA

L. Edward
Kampala ● • Jinja
RWANDA
L. Kivu
Kigali
L. Victoria
Nairobi ▪
Tana
Mogadishu ●
Juba

BURUNDI
Bujumbura ●
L. Natron
Indian Ocean

TANZANIA
L. Eyasi
Mombasa ▪
Pemba Is.

L. Tanganyika
Dodoma •
Zanzibar Is.
Zanzibar
Dar es Salaam ▪

L. Rukwa
Great Ruaha
Mafia Is.

Rufiji

L. Nyasa (Malawi)
Ruvuma

MALAWI

| 0 | 200 | 400 | 600 km |
| 0 | 100 | 200 | 300 | 400 mi |

Lilongwe

Blantyre ▪

SEYCHELLES
• Victoria

| 0 | 30 km |
| 0 | 15 mi |

Somali conflict
During the Cold War, Somali factions were supplied by weapons from both the Soviet Union and the United States. Even children took up arms.

Communal slaughter
In 1996 CE, Burundi's Hutu president, Sylvestre Ntibantunganya, attended a funeral of 320 people thought to have been killed by Hutu rebels. He was later deposed.

© DIAGRAM

West Africa

West Africa was the home of several great medieval empires, such as ancient Ghana and Mali, whose splendour was recorded by Arab traders and Muslim scholars. But the region was later disrupted by the slave trade and, colonial rule. In 1957, when Ghana was the first black African colony to win its independence, hopes were high that West Africa might unite with the rest of Africa, developing its economy and raising the living standards of its largely impoverished population. However, West Africa's development has been marred in several countries by ethnic and religious conflict, together with economic problems, many arising from fluctuations in the prices for the key export commodities. As a result, many countries have suffered from instability and rule by corrupt and dictatorial one-party or military governments.

Nigeria has also suffered under autocratic and often corrupt military governments. A civilian government was established in 1999 CE, but it faced many problems arising from the country's complex ethnic mix. This petroleum-rich nation is West Africa's giant, accounting for more than half of the region's population. But its gross national product (GNP) per capita (for each person) is below the regional average—partly a consequence of its massive population.

West African nations with lower per capita GNPs than Nigeria include Sierra Leone and Liberia, whose economies have been shattered by civil war, which has spilled over into Guinea. These civil wars have been funded by the plunder of the region's diamond resources—diamonds are smuggled out of Sierra Leone into Liberia where they are used to buy arms. By contrast, Ivory Coast, with its free market economy, is one of Africa's more successful countries. However, it, too, suffered a military coup in 1999, although civilian rule was restored in 2000 CE. By contrast, Cameroon and Senegal have enjoyed stability and their governments have successfully exploited their limited resources.

Execution of an activist
The writer Ken Saro-Wiwa is one of nine Ogoni activists executed by the Nigerian government in 1995 CE. These executions led to the suspension of Nigeria's membership of the Commonwealth.

COUNTRY	OFFICIAL NAME	CAPITAL	LANGUAGE	CURRENCY
Benin	(République du Benin)	Porto-Novo	French	CFA franc
Burkina Faso	(République du Burkina Faso)	Ouagadougou	French	CFA franc
Cameroon	(Republic of Cameroon)	Yaounde	English, French	CFA franc
Cape Verde	(República de Cabo Verde)	Praia	Portuguese	Escudo
Chad	(République du Tchad)	N'djamena	French, Arabic	CFA franc
Ivory Coast	(République de la Côte d'Ivoire)	Yamoussoukro	French	CFA franc
Gambia	(Republic of the Gambia)	Banjul	English	Dalasi
Ghana	(Republic of Ghana)	Accra	English	Cedi
Guinea	(République de Guinée)	Conakry	French	Guinea franc
Guinea-Bissau	(República da Guiné-Bissau)	Bissau	Portuguese	Guinea-Bissau peso
Liberia	(Republic of Liberia)	Monrovia	English	Liberian dollar
Mali	(Republic of Mali)	Bamako	French	CFA franc
Mauritania	(Islamic Republic of Mauritania)	Nouakchott	Arabic	Ouguiya
Niger	(Republic of Niger)	Niamey	French	CFA franc
Nigeria	(Federal Republic of Nigeria)	Abuja	English	Naira
Senegal	(Republic of Senegal)	Dakar	French	CFA franc
Sierra Leone	(Republic of Sierra Leone)	Freetown	English	Leone
Togo	(Republic of Togo)	Lome	French	CFA franc

Countries by size (sq mi)	
1 Chad	495,625
2 Niger	478,695
3 Mali	457,955
4 Mauritania	397,850
5 Nigeria	356,605
6 Cameroon	183,545
7 Ivory Coast	124,470
8 Burkina Faso	105,811
9 Guinea	94,900
10 Ghana	91,985
11 Senegal	75,935
12 Benin	43,470
13 Liberia	42,990
14 Sierra Leone	27,920
15 Togo	21,920
16 Guinea-Bissau	13,945
17 The Gambia	4125
18 Cape Verde	1560

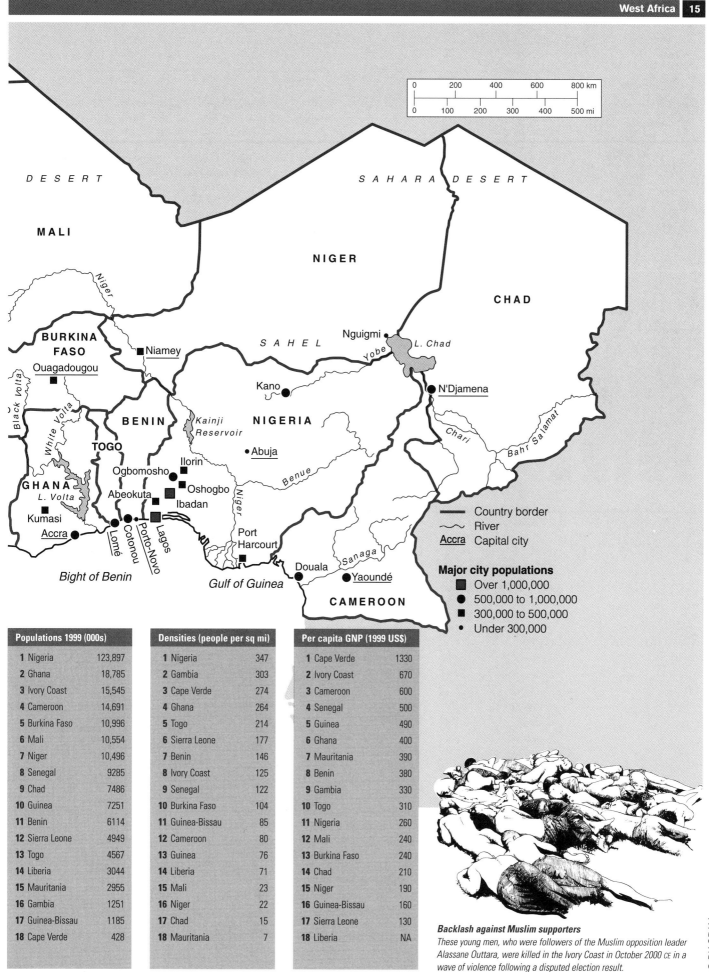

MALI

NIGER

CHAD

D E S E R T

S A H A R A   D E S E R T

0 200 400 600 800 km
0 100 200 300 400 500 mi

BURKINA
FASO

Ouagadougou

■ Niamey

Niger

S A H E L

Nguigmi ● *L. Chad*

Yobe

Kano ●

● N'Djamena

BENIN

TOGO

GHANA
L. Volta

Black Volta
White Volta

*Kainji
Reservoir*

NIGERIA

● Abuja

Ilorin ■
Ogbomosho ■
Abeokuta ■ Oshogbo ■
Ibadan ■

Kumasi ■
Accra ■
Lomé Cotonou
Porto-Novo
Lagos

Port
Harcourt ■

Benue

Niger

Chari

Bahr Salamat

Bight of Benin

Gulf of Guinea

Douala ● *Sanaga*
Yaoundé ●

CAMEROON

Country border
~~ **River**
<u>Accra</u> **Capital city**

Major city populations
■ Over 1,000,000
● 500,000 to 1,000,000
■ 300,000 to 500,000
• Under 300,000

Populations 1999 (000s)	
1 Nigeria	123,897
2 Ghana	18,785
3 Ivory Coast	15,545
4 Cameroon	14,691
5 Burkina Faso	10,996
6 Mali	10,554
7 Niger	10,496
8 Senegal	9285
9 Chad	7486
10 Guinea	7251
11 Benin	6114
12 Sierra Leone	4949
13 Togo	4567
14 Liberia	3044
15 Mauritania	2955
16 Gambia	1251
17 Guinea-Bissau	1185
18 Cape Verde	428

Densities (people per sq mi)	
1 Nigeria	347
2 Gambia	303
3 Cape Verde	274
4 Ghana	264
5 Togo	214
6 Sierra Leone	177
7 Benin	146
8 Ivory Coast	125
9 Senegal	122
10 Burkina Faso	104
11 Guinea-Bissau	85
12 Cameroon	80
13 Guinea	76
14 Liberia	71
15 Mali	23
16 Niger	22
17 Chad	15
18 Mauritania	7

Per capita GNP (1999 US$)	
1 Cape Verde	1330
2 Ivory Coast	670
3 Cameroon	600
4 Senegal	500
5 Guinea	490
6 Ghana	400
7 Mauritania	390
8 Benin	380
9 Gambia	330
10 Togo	310
11 Nigeria	260
12 Mali	240
13 Burkina Faso	240
14 Chad	210
15 Niger	190
16 Guinea-Bissau	160
17 Sierra Leone	130
18 Liberia	NA

Backlash against Muslim supporters
*These young men, who were followers of the Muslim opposition leader
Alassane Outtara, were killed in the Ivory Coast in October 2000 CE in a
wave of violence following a disputed election result.*

© DIAGRAM

Central Africa

The recent history of Central Africa, like that of West Africa, has been marred by instability, civil war and dictatorial governments. In the Democratic Republic of Congo, which was known as Zaire from 1971 until 1997, independence in 1960 was immediately followed by widespread civil conflict and the attempted secession of the mineral-rich Katanga region. The collapse of law and order was only ended when President Mobutu Sese Seko took power and ruled the country as a dictator between 1965 and 1997. Mobutu's repressive policies and corrupt behavior brought him under increasing pressure to restore democracy, but he repeatedly postponed elections. Finally, Laurent Kabila, aided by Tutsis living in the eastern part of the country, formed an army that overthrew Mobutu. Kabila soon fell out with his allies and civil war broke out, with Rwandan and Ugandan troops supporting the rebels, while Angolan, Namibian, and Zimbabwean troops supported Kabila. However, the assassination of Kabila in 2001 raised hopes that his son and successor, Major-General Joseph Kabila, might introduce new initiatives to end the strife.

Since independence in 1975, Angola has endured a long civil war. The main conflict was between the government, which was backed by Communist powers, and National Union for the Total Independence of Angola (UNITA), which was backed by South Africa and Western powers. After the end of the Cold War and the political changes in South Africa, the government began to use revenues from its oil production to finance the war.

Instability and bad government were features of several countries. For example, the people of the Central African Republic (CAR) and Equatorial Guinea lived through years of rule by brutal despots. In 1966 CE, the tyrannical Jean-Bédel Bokassa seized power in the CAR and went so far as to declare himself "emperor" (after his hero Napoleon), changing the name of his country to the Central African Empire between 1976–1979 CE. The CAR has subsequently returned to democracy, though not without difficulty. In Equatorial Guinea, the dictator Francisco Macías Nguema executed and imprisoned thousands of people without trial between 1970–1979 CE. Democratic institutions were later restored, although elections have been marred by allegations of electoral irregularities.

The economic success in Central Africa is Gabon, whose exploitation of petroleum, natural gas, uranium, and various metal ores has made it one of Africa's most successful economies. On the African mainland, only Libya has a higher gross national product (GNP) per capita (for each person). However, most of Gabon's people practise subsistence agriculture and obtain little benefit from the exploitation of their country's natural resources. Gabon's stability was maintained until 1990 CE by one-party rule. One-party systems may produce stability, but they also often foster inefficiency and corruption. In the 1990s, many countries in Africa, spurred on by Western powers, began to restore democratic institutions. For example, in Zambia, veteran leader Kenneth Kaunda, who had served as president since 1964 CE, stood in multiparty elections in 1991 CE and was subsequently defeated.

UNITA rebels
In Angola, following independence, rebels belonging to UNITA mounted a long military campaign against government forces.

Countries by size (sq mi)	
1 Democratic Republic of Congo	905,330
2 Angola	481,225
3 Zambia	290,510
4 Central African Republic	241,240
5 Congo Republic	132,010
6 Gabon	103,320
7 Equatorial Guinea	10,825
8 São Tomé and Príncipe	372

Populations 1999 (000s)	
1 Democratic Republic of Congo	49,776
2 Angola	12,357
3 Zambia	9881
4 Central African Republic	3540
5 Congo	2859
6 Gabon	1208
7 Equatorial Guinea	443
8 São Tomé and Príncipe	145

Densities (people per sq mi)	
1 São Tomé and Príncipe	390
2 Democratic Republic of Congo	55
3 Equatorial Guinea	41
4 Zambia	34
5 Angola	25
6 Congo	22
7 Central African Republic	15
8 Gabon	12

Per capita GNP (1999 US$)	
1 Gabon	3300
2 Congo	1571
3 Equatorial Guinea	1170
4 Central African Republic	290
5 Angola	270
6 São Tomé and Príncipe	270
7 Zambia	230
8 Democratic Republic of Congo	NA

COUNTRY	OFFICIAL NAME	CAPITAL	LANGUAGE	CURRENCY
Angola	(República Popular de Angola)	Luanda	Portuguese	New kwanza
Central African Republic	(République Centrafricaine)	Bangui	French	CFA franc
Congo	(République Populaire du Congo)	Brazzaville	French	CFA franc
Democratic Republic of Congo	(République Democratique du Congo)	Kinshasa	French	New Zaire
Equatorial Guinea	(República de Guinea Ecuatorial)	Malabo	Spanish	CFA franc
Gabon	(République Gabonaise)	Libreville	French	CFA franc
São Tomé and Príncipe	(República Democrática de São Tomé e Príncipe)	São Tomé	Portuguese	Dobra
Zambia	(Republic of Zambia)	Lusaka	English	Kwacha

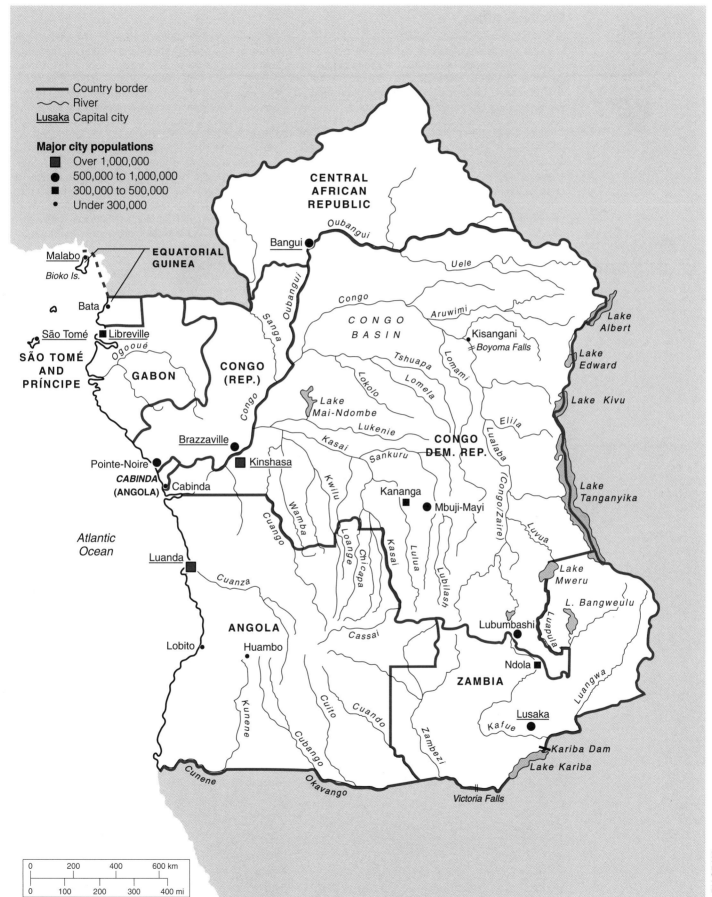

Country border
River
Lusaka Capital city

Major city populations
■ Over 1,000,000
● 500,000 to 1,000,000
■ 300,000 to 500,000
• Under 300,000

CENTRAL
AFRICAN
REPUBLIC

Oubangui

Bangui

Malabo
Bioko Is.

EQUATORIAL
GUINEA

Uele

Bata

Sanga

Oubangui

Congo

Aruwimi

Lake
Albert

São Tomé

Libreville

Ogooué

SÃO TOMÉ
AND
PRÍNCIPE

GABON

CONGO
(REP.)

C O N G O
B A S I N

Tshuapa

Lomami

Lomela

Kisangani
Boyoma Falls

Lake
Edward

Lake Kivu

Congo

*Lake
Mai-Ndombe*

Lokolo

Lukenie

Elila

Brazzaville

Kasai

Sankuru

CONGO
DEM. REP.

*Lualaba
(Congo/Zaire)*

Lake
Tanganyika

Pointe-Noire

Kinshasa

Kwilu

Kananga

Mbuji-Mayi

CABINDA
(ANGOLA)

Cabinda

Cuango

Wamba

Loange

Chicapa

Kasai

Lulua

Lubilash

Luvua

Lake
Mweru

L. Bangweulu

Luapula

Atlantic
Ocean

Luanda

Cuanza

Lubumbashi

Lobito

Huambo

ANGOLA

Cassai

Ndola

Luangwa

ZAMBIA

Kunene

Cuito

Cuando

Zambezi

Kafue

Lusaka

Cubango

Kariba Dam
Lake Kariba

Cunene

Okavango

Victoria Falls

0   200   400   600 km

0   100   200   300   400 mi

© DIAGRAM

Southern Africa

In 1652, Dutch settlers, headed by Jan van Riebeeck, founded a trade settlement on the present-day site of Cape Town. In doing so, they laid the foundations for the "rainbow nation" of modern South Africa, which is now the most powerful and economically developed nation in southern Africa. In the twentieth century, South Africa has dominated southern Africa. It occupied Namibia until 1990 and intervened to support rebel forces in the civil wars in Angola and Mozambique. It also aided the white-minority regime in Rhodesia until that country achieved majority government as Zimbabwe in 1980. One consequence of the bitter struggle by black Zimbabweans to win majority rule occurred in 2000, when the government began to take over white-owned farms without paying compen-

sation, and redistributing the farms to landless black Africans. This policy led to violence and the murder of some European farmers.

South Africa's intervention in the affairs of its neighbors was part of a destabilizing strategy aimed at preserving its system of racial segregation known as apartheid. Introduced in 1948 CE, the apartheid system aimed at dividing the country into separate areas for whites and blacks, although no areas were allocated for the Colored and Asian minorities. The ten areas designated for blacks, which were called Bantustans or "homelands," covered about 13 percent of the country. Four of these fragmented "homelands" were declared to be "independent," although no country other than South Africa recognized their independence. In the late

Nelson Mandela (left)
In office, Mandela pursued a policy of "reconciliation." His aim was to turn South Africa into a compassionate, non-racial society.

Sam Nujoma (left)
Sam Nujoma led the struggle against South Africa's rule over Southwest Africa (now called Namibia). He became Namibia's president in 1990 CE.

Countries by size (sq mi)		Populations 1999 (000s)		Densities (people per sq mi)		Per capita GNP (1999 US$)	
1 South Africa	457,345	**1** South Africa	42,106	**1** Mauritius	1630	**1** Mauritius	3540
2 Namibia	318,262	**2** Mozambique	17,299	**2** Comoros	760	**2** Botswana	3240
3 Mozambique	302,915	**3** Madagascar	15,051	**3** Lesotho	180	**3** South Africa	3170
4 Madagascar	229,345	**4** Zimbabwe	11,904	**4** Swaziland	152	**4** Namibia	1890
5 Botswana	221,950	**5** Lesotho	2105	**5** South Africa	92	**5** Swaziland	1350
6 Zimbabwe	150,660	**6** Namibia	1701	**6** Zimbabwe	79	**6** Lesotho	550
7 Lesotho	11,715	**7** Botswana	1588	**7** Madagascar	66	**7** Zimbabwe	530
8 Swaziland	6705	**8** Mauritius	1174	**8** Mozambique	57	**8** Comoros	350
9 Mauritius	720	**9** Swaziland	1019	**9** Botswana	7	**9** Madagascar	250
10 Comoros	718	**10** Comoros	544	**10** Namibia	5	**10** Mozambique	220

COUNTRY	OFFICIAL NAME	CAPITAL	LANGUAGE	CURRENCY
Botswana	(Republic of Botswana)	Gaborone	English	Pula
Comoros	(Jumhuriyat al-Qumur al Itthadiyah al-Islamiyah)	Moroni	Arabic	Comoro franc
Lesotho	(Kingdom of Lesotho)	Maseru	English, Sotho	Maloti
Madagascar	(Repoblika Demokratika Malagasy)	Antananarivo	Malagasy	Malagasy franc
Mauritius	(State of Mauritius)	Port Louis	English	Mauritian rupee
Mozambique	(República Popular de Moçambique)	Maputo	Portuguese	Metical
Namibia	(Namibia)	Windhoek	Afrikaans, English	Namibian dollar
South Africa	(Republic of South Africa)	Pretoria (administrative) Cape Town (legislative) Bloemfontein (judicial)	Afrikaans, English, Ndebele, North Sotho, South Sotho, Swazi, Tsonga, Twsana, Venda, Xhosa, Zulu,	Rand
Swaziland	(Kingdom of Swaziland)	Mbabane	Swazi, English	Lilangeni
Zimbabwe	(Republic of Zimbabwe)	Harare	English	Zimbabwe dollar

1980s, under pressure from the rest of the world, South Africa began to modify its discriminatory policies. The African National Congress (ANC) leader Nelson Mandela was released from prison in 1990 CE and gradually the nation's discriminatory legislation was dismantled. Mandela was elected president in 1994 CE and the "homelands" were abolished. Mandela's government sought to replace racial discrimination with a policy of "reconciliation" and racial conflict was avoided.

Mandela retired in 1999 CE and was replaced by Thabo Mbeki. Mbeki faced many problems, notably the disparity between the lifestyles of the prosperous whites and the poverty of most blacks. Another huge problem in a country with limited resources to pay for expensive drugs is the high incidence of HIV and AIDS. South Africa has the largest number of people infected by the HIV virus, though Botswana has the highest rate

of infection. Southern Africa has experienced the world's greatest explosion of HIV infection. At the end of the twentieth century, experts have estimated that, on average, nearly one adult in five aged between 15 and 49 is infected with HIV in Botswana, Lesotho, Namibia, South Africa, and Zimbabwe.

South Africa is Africa's most industrialized country, But, because of its impoverished black majority, its average per capita gross national product (GNP) is low by Western standards. Botswana, one of Africa's most politically stable countries, also has a relatively high per capita GNP. Since independence, Botswana has benefited by exploiting its mineral resources, including diamonds. The poorest countries are Madagascar and Mozambique. Their economies are based on subsistence agriculture and they are periodically hit by natural disasters, including heavy flooding.

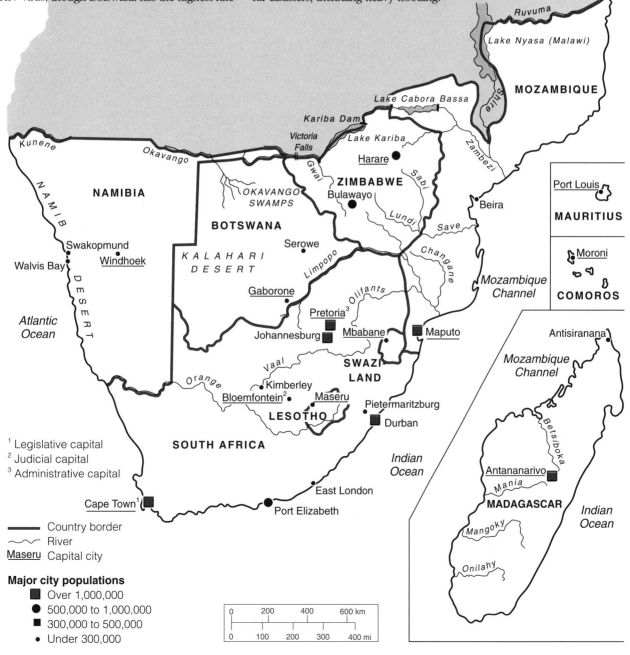

¹ Legislative capital
² Judicial capital
³ Administrative capital

— Country border
〜 River
Maseru Capital city

Major city populations
- ■ Over 1,000,000
- ● 500,000 to 1,000,000
- ■ 300,000 to 500,000
- • Under 300,000

Scale:
0   200   400   600 km
0   100   200   300   400 mi

© DIAGRAM

SECTION 2

DEVELOPMENT OF THE CONTINENT

Chronology of Events Nation-by-Nation

Pre-19th century

Dancing figures
An early example of rock art found in Algeria depicting life in the Sahara thousands of years ago.

Algeria
c.3000 BCE Berbers migrate to the Algeria region
c.000 BCE Phoenicians found colonies on the Algerian coast
c.200 BCE Massinissa establishes the kingdom of Numidia in northern Algeria
105 BCE The Romans defeat king Jugurtha of Numidia
44 CE Numidia is formally annexed by the Roman Empire
432 The Vandals settle on the coast of Algeria
682–702 Muslim Arab conquest of Algeria
1518 The Turkish pirate Barbarossa captures Algiers for the Ottoman empire

Angola
1483 CE Portuguese explorers reach Angola
1490 Portuguese convert king Nzinga Nkuwu of Kongo (in northern Angola) to Christianity
1575 The Portuguese found Luanda as a base for slaving operations
1623–1626 Queen Nzinga of Ndongo in present-day Angola is defeated in a war against Portuguese slave traders
1641 The Dutch drive the Portuguese out of Angola
1648 The Portuguese regain control of Angola from the Dutch

Benin
1625 CE King Dako of Abomey founds the kingdom of Dahomey in present-day Benin

Botswana
c.420 CE Earliest dated evidence of farming and ironworking in Botswana
c.1095 Tswana people migrate to the area of modern Botswana from the north
c.1795 Ngakwetse chiefdom dominates central Botswana region

Burkina Faso
c.1300 CE Mossi kingdom founded in the area of present-day Burkina Faso
c.1450 Mossi establish a capital at Ouagadougou

Burundi
1st millennium CE The Hutu people settle in the Burundi region
14th century The Tutsi invade Burundi and conquer the Hutu

Cameroon
c.200 CE Bantu-speaking peoples, modern Africa's largest linguistic group, originate in Cameroon
1472 CE Portuguese navigator Fernão do Po becomes the first European to visit Cameroon

Cape Verde
1455 CE Cape Verde islands discovered by Portuguese navigators, Alvise de Cadamosta and Antonio Noli
1492 Portuguese planters and their African slaves settle the Cape Verde Islands

Central African Republic
18th century CE The area is in turmoil because of the slave trade and large-scale population movements occur; the Azande and Baya people enter the area from the west

Chad
c.5000 BCE Rock paintings show scenes of hunting and herding in the Sahara desert
c.500 BCE Cattle rearing peoples arrive in the region of Lake Chad
8th century CE Berber peoples from the north migrate to Chad
11th century Kingdom of Kanem begins to develop northeast of Lake Chad under Saifawa's dynasty
c.1100 Islam is introduced to the region by Arab merchants
13th century Kanem merges with the neighbouring kingdom of Bornu
17th century Frequent wars between Kanem-Bornu and its neighbours Baguirmi and Wadai

Comoros
5th century CE Indonesian settlers become the first inhabitants of the Comoros Islands
12th century Muslim traders from East Africa settle on the islands

An armed Portuguese soldier
Firearms were introduced to West Africa during the period 1500–1800 CE, as depicted by this bronze figure from Benin.

Congo, Democratic Republic of
c.800 CE Bantu-speaking ironworking peoples arrive in the Congo region
15th century Kongo kingdom develops in northern Angola and western Congo region
1483 Portuguese navigator Diogo Cão discovers the mouth of the Congo River

16th century Kongolo people found the Luba kingdom in southern Congo region
17th century Lunda empire develops in southern Congo region
18th century Kuba kingdoms develop in central Congo region

Congo, Republic of
1483 CE Portuguese navigator Diogo Cão discovers the mouth of the Congo River

Djibouti
3rd century BCE Ancestors of the Afar people migrate to the Djibouti area from Arabia
825 CE The Afars are converted to Islam
14th century Kingdom of Adal dominates the Djibouti region
1415 Christian Ethiopians kill the Muslim ruler of Saylac (near modern-day Djibouti city)
1527 Ahmed Gran of Adal invades Ethiopia
1543 Ahmed Gran killed in battle with an Ethiopian-Portuguese army
18th century Somali Issa people migrate into the southern Djibouti region

Egypt
639–642 CE Muslim Arabs conquer Egypt
640 Cairo founded as a military base
969–1171 The Shiite Fatimid dynasty rules Egypt
1171 Saladin becomes ruler of Egypt
1250–1517 The Mamluk dynasty rules Egypt
1260 The Mamluks defeat the Mongols at Ain Jalut in Palestine
1517 The Ottoman Turks conquer Egypt
1798 Napoleon invades Egypt

Equatorial Guinea
c.1200 CE Bubi people from the mainland settle Bioko island
1472 Fernão do Po sights Bioko and claims it for Portugal
1777–1778 Portugal cedes its claim to the area to Spain by the treaties of San Ildefonso and Pardo

Eritrea
c 1–975 CE The kingdom of Axum dominates the region of present-day Eritrea

Ethiopia
4.4 million years ago Date of the oldest known humanoid fossils, discovered in the Awash region of Ethiopia
c.1–975 CE The kingdom of Axum dominates northern Ethiopia
c.350 King Ezana of Axum becomes the first African ruler to be converted to Christianity
639–642 Arab conquest of Egypt cuts Ethiopia off from the rest of the Christian world
1137–1270 The Zagwe dynasty rules Ethiopia
1270 Yekuno Amlak overthrows the Zagwe and founds the Solomonid dynasty
1415 Ethiopians kill the Muslim ruler of Saylac (in modern-day Djibouti)
1492 The Portuguese make contact with the Emperor of Ethiopia
1527 Ahmed Gran of Adal invades Ethiopia
1543 Ahmed Gran killed in battle with an Ethiopian-Portuguese army
1557 A Jesuit mission is sent to Ethiopia
16th century Ethiopia fragments into small semi-independent kingdoms
1632 Jesuits expelled for undermining the Ethiopian Orthodox church

Gabon
13th century CE The Mpongwe people settle in Gabon
1472 Portuguese explore the coast of Gabon
c 1800 The Fang begin to settle in Gabon

Gambia
13th–15th century CE The Gambia region is part of the Mali empire
1455 Portuguese set up trading posts on the coast
1618 Portugal sells its rights in the area to England
1642 France sets up a trading post on the Gambia River
1644 The English start buying slaves from the Gambia region
1658 James Island ceded to the Dutch
1661 The English found a trading post on James Island in the Gambia river
1665–1667 England recaptures James Island in the Second Dutch War
1763 Britain expels the French from the Gambia and Senegal region
1765 Britain creates the colony of Senegambia, incorporating parts of Gambia and Senegal
1783 Britain cedes Senegal to France

A mammoth, c.5000 BCE
Rock paintings found in caves show scenes of hunting and herding in the Sahara desert.

Solomon and Sheba
A visit by Sheba, the Queen of Ethiopia, to meet Solomon, the King of Israel in Jerusalem when Israel was at the height of its power in the fourth century BCE.

Ghana

14th century CE Akan people migrate to the Ghana region from the north and establish kingdoms
15th century Kingdoms develop among the Asante people in southern Ghana
1471 Portuguese navigators explore the region which they name the Gold Coast
1482 The Portuguese build a fortress at Elmina ("the mine")
17th century The Akans defeat invasions by the Doma people
1637–1642 The Dutch capture Portuguese bases on the Gold Coast
c.1650–1730 Akwamu empire monopolizes slave-trade routes to the coast
1651 Danes establish trading posts on the Gold Coast
1664 English merchants establish headquarters at Cape Coast Castle

Guinea

11th century CE Guinea region forms part of the Ghana empire
16th century Guinea region forms part of the Mali empire
18th century Kingdom of Futa Djallon develops in western Guinea

Guinea–Bissau

1480 CE Portugal founds trading posts on the Guinea coast
1687 Portuguese found Bissau city as a fortified center for the slave trade

Ivory Coast

1637 CE French missionaries visit the Ivory Coast
1730 Queen Aura Poka of the Asante founds the kingdom of Baule in northern present-day Ivory Coast

Kenya

1st century CE Greek merchants sail to East Africa from Egypt to buy ivory
c.800 Trading towns develop on the East African coast
c.1000 Arab merchants introduce Islam to the East African coast
1498 Portuguese navigator Vasco da Gama reaches Kenya via the Cape of Good Hope
1593 The Portuguese build a fortress at Mombasa
18th century Masai cattle herders migrate into the Kenya region from the north
1729 The Omanis oust the Portuguese from the Kenyan coast

Lesotho

c.300 CE Bantu-speaking farmers, the ancestors of most of southern Africa's modern population, enter the area from the north, gradually displacing the hunter-gatherers living there

Liberia

1461 CE Portuguese merchants arrive and establish a trade monopoly on what they call the Grain Coast (from the grains of local pepper they bought)

Libya

9th century BCE Phoenician settlements founded on the Libyan coast
6th century BCE Tripolitania (western Libya) is part of the Carthaginian empire: Cyrenaica (eastern Libya) comes under Greek control
146 BCE Tripolitania becomes part of the Roman empire
96 BCE Cyrenaica becomes part of the Roman empire
643–647 CE Libya is conquered by the Islamic Arabs
868–972 Libya is independent under the Tulunid dynasty
990–1171 Libya is part of the Fatimid caliphate of Cairo
1551 Libya is conquered by the Ottoman Turks
1711 Libya becomes autonomous under the Qaramanli dynasty

Madagascar

1st–5th centuries CE Madagascar is settled by peoples from Indonesia
10th–13th centuries Muslims from East Africa settle the north of the island
1500 The Portuguese navigator Diogo Dias becomes the first European to visit Madagascar
1506–1507 Portuguese destroy Muslim trading towns in Madagascar
17th century Foundation of the kingdom of Merina
1643 The French found Fort Dauphin in southern Madagascar
1671 The French abandon Fort Dauphin
1680–1720 Madagascar is a important base for pirates
18th century The Sakalava kingdom dominates Madagascar
1787–1810 Merina wins control of most of Madagascar under King Nampoina

Malawi

15th century CE The Maravi (Malawi) kingdom dominates the Malawi region
17th century The Portuguese are the first Europeans to explore the region

A gift from the sultan
This fifteenth-century illustration depicts the gift of a giraffe to the Chinese emperor from the sultan of Malindi, East Africa.

Mali

c.400 CE The earliest city in sub-Saharan Africa develops at Jenne-jeno
c.700–1205 Western Mali region dominated by the Ghana empire
c.1000 Islam introduced into the Mali region by Arab and Berber merchants
c.1240–1450 The empire of Mali is the dominant West African power
1312–1337 Timbuktu becomes a major center of Islamic culture under King Mansa Musa
c.1450–1591 The Songhay empire dominates the Mali region
1493–1528 Songhay empire at its peak under Askia Muhammad
1591 Morocco destroys the Songhay empire

Mauritania

c.700–1205 CE Southern Mauritania region dominated by the Ghana empire
c.1000 Islam introduced into the Mauritania region by Arab and Berber merchants
1448 The Portuguese establish a trading post on the coast of Mauritania
c.1450–1591 The Songhay empire dominates much of Mauritania region
1591 Mauritania is conquered by Morocco

Mauritius

1510 CE The Portuguese discover and explore Mauritius
1598 The Dutch claim the uninhabited island and name it after Prince Maurice of Nassau
1710 The Dutch abandon Mauritius
1715 The French claim the island and name it Île de France
1722 French colonists from Réunion settle and grow coffee, sugar, and spices using slave labor

Morocco

475–450 BCE Carthaginians establish colonies on the Moroccan coast
40–44 CE Morocco becomes part of the Roman empire
682–683 Moslem Arabs from Tunisia raid Tangier and Agadir
702 The Berbers of Morocco submit to the Arabs and accept Islam
711 An Arab and Berber army invades and conquers Spain
788 Idris I Ibn Abdullah breaks away from the Arab caliphate and founds independent Idrisid caliphate of Morocco
859 The world's oldest university founded at Fez
926 The Idrisid caliphate is conquered by the Omayyad emirate of Cordoba
1056 Yusuf Ibn Tashfin founds the Sanhaja Berber Almoravid emirate
1076 The Almoravids conquer Ghana
1085 Yusuf invades and conquers Omayyad Spain
1147 The Almohad dynasty replaces the Almoravids
1269 Marinid dynasty overthrows the Almohads
1415 The Portuguese capture Ceuta
1465 Wattasid dynasty succeeds the Marinids in Morocco
1554 The Saadi dynasty replaces the Wattasids
1578 Moroccans defeat and kill king Sebastian I at Alcazarquivir
1591 Saadi sultan Ahmed al-Mansur captures Timbuktu and overthrows the Songhay empire
1666 Moulay al-Rashid is proclaimed sultan, founding the Alawi dynasty (still in power 1999)

Mozambique

3rd century CE Bantu-speaking herders and ironworkers move into the Mozambique region
12th century Manekweni develops as a center for the Indian Ocean gold trade
14th century Swahili merchants found trading cities at Sofala and Chibuene
1490 The Portuguese navigator Covilhã reaches Mozambique via Egypt and India
1505 The Portuguese sack the Muslim port of Sofala
1508 The Portuguese found the city of Moçambique
1531 The Portuguese begin to extend their control inland along the Zambezi river
1628 Portuguese missionaries convert the Monomatapa (the ruler of the Karanga) to Christianity
1693–1695 The Changamiras attack Portuguese settlements

Namibia

15th century CE Bantu-speaking peoples migrate into the Namibia region
1485 Portuguese navigator Diogo Cão arrives at Cape Cross
1773 The Dutch claim Angra Pequena (Lüderitz), Halifax island and Walvis Bay

Niger

c.1000 CE Tuareg nomads migrate to the Niger region from the central Sahara Desert
14th century Eastern Niger becomes part of the Kanem–Bornu empire

Mansa Musa on his throne
The first European map of West Africa was drawn in 1375 CE, and depicts the Malian king, Mansa Musa. He is shown with a gold nugget in his hand, ready to trade with the Arab merchant riding toward him on a camel.

Mungo Park (1771–1806 CE)
The Scottish explorer who is credited with the discovery of the upper and middle reaches of the Niger river.

© DIAGRAM

15th century The Tuareg state of Aïr develops around Agadez. Western Niger becomes part of the Songhay empire
1515 Aïr is conquered by Askia Muhammad of the Songhay empire
1591 Aïr recovers its independence when Songhay is conquered by Morocco
18th century The Hausa expand into Niger from the south
1735–1756 The Great Drought aids Tuareg expansion at the expense of farmers

Nigeria
500 BCE–200 CE Nok civilization flourishes
11th–12th centuries Hausa settlements develop
14th–17th centuries Kingdom of Benin at its height
16th–17th centuries Kanem–Bornu is powerful

Rwanda
7th–10th centuries CE Hutu farmers migrate to the Rwanda region
15th century The Tutsis invade Rwanda from the north and conquer the Hutus

São Tomè and Príncipe
1470 CE The Portuguese discover the islands of São Tomé and Príncipe
1485 Portuguese colonization begins: sugar cane plantations are created
1522 São Tomé and Príncipe are taken over by the Portuguese crown

Senegal
c.800–1100 ce Senegal region is dominated by the Fulani Takrur empire
c.1240–1400 The empire of Mali dominates the Senegal region
15th–18th centuries The Fulani Wolof kingdom dominates much of Senegal
1445 Portuguese navigators explore the coast of Senegal
1617 The Dutch establish a trading post on Gorée island
1626 The French build a trading post at the mouth of the Sénégal River
1677 The French take over Gorée Island from the Dutch
1763 Britain expels the French from Senegal
1765 Britain creates the colony of Senegambia, incorporating parts of Senegal and Gambia
1783 Britain cedes Senegal back to France. The reformist Islamic kingdom of Futa Toro dominates inland Senegal

Seychelles
1505 CE The Seychelles are discovered by the Portuguese
1742 A French expedition explores the islands
1756 France claims the islands
1770 French planters and African slaves settle on Mahé
1794 The British occupy the Seychelles

Sierra Leone
1460 CE Portuguese navigators explore the coast of present-day Sierra Leone
16th century Ancestors of the modern Mende and Loko peoples arrive in Sierra Leone from the east
1787 Granville Sharp of the Anti-Slavery Society buys land on Cape Sierra Leone for a settlement of freed slaves
1792 The first 400 freed African-American slaves are settled on the site of present-day Freetown

Somalia
c.1400 BCE Egyptian trading expeditions reach the Somali coast
c.750 CE The Somalis settle the north of modern Somalia
920 The Omani Arabs capture Mogadishu
11th century The Somalis convert to Islam
13th century Somali kingdom of Ifat (later Adal) develops in the northwest
16th century The Somalis have settled most of modern Somalia
1506–1542 Ahmed Gran of the Somali kingdom of Adal occupies most of Ethiopia
1543 Ahmed Gran is killed in battle with a Portuguese-Ethiopian army

South Africa
c.300 CE Bantu-speaking farmers, the ancestors of most of South Africa's modern population, enter southern Africa from the north
1488 The Portuguese are the first Europeans to reach South Africa
1652 The Dutch East India Company establishes a supply base at the site of present-day Cape Town
1657 The Dutch East India Company allows some employees to become farmers (boers)
1770 The Boers fight their first war against the Bantu-speaking Xhosa
1795 Britain occupies the Cape Colony

Nok sculpture
The artistic achievements of the Nok Culture (c.500 BCE–200 CE) include superb sculptures such as this terracotta head.

The Coldstream Stone
This quartzite stone was excavated from Coldstream Cave on the southern Cape coast. It was painted 2,000 years ago by a Khoisan artist.

Sudan

c.1700 BCE The kingdom of Kush (Nubia) develops
1504–1492 BCE Kush is conquered by Tuthmosis I of Egypt
712 BCE The Nubians conquer Egypt
671 BCE The Nubians are driven out of Egypt by the Assyrians.
590 BCE The center of Nubian power shifts south to the city of Meroë in central Sudan
c.300 BCE The kingdom of Meroë is at its peak
c.350 CE Meroë is conquered by the Ethiopian kingdom of Axum
c.540 The Nubians are converted to Christianity
652 The kingdom of Makkura repels an Islamic Arab invasion
1317 Islamic Arab nomads conquer the kingdom of Makkura
1505 Alwa, the last Christian kingdom in present-day Sudan, is conquered by African Funj tribes
17th century Funj kingdom is at the peak of its power

Swaziland

c.1 CE Bantu-speaking herders arrive in the Swaziland region
c.1770 Chief Ngwane II leads his Dlamini clan into present-day Swaziland

Tanzania

1st century CE Egyptian and Greek merchants sail to Tanzanian coast to buy ivory and hardwood
695 Prince Hamza of Oman settles at Zanzibar
10th century Bantu-speaking peoples settle in Tanzania region
975 According to tradition, prince Ali bin Sultan al Hassan of Shiraz (Iran) settles at Kilwa
c.1200 Kilwa becomes the first state in sub-Saharan Africa to issue its own coinage
1499 The Portuguese navigator, Vasco de Gama, visits Tanzania on his way to India
1698 The sultanate of Oman wins control of Zanzibar

Tunisia

814 BCE Phoenicians found the city of Carthage near present-day Tunis
c.264 BCE Carthaginian empire at its peak
146 BCE Carthage is conquered by the Roman Empire: all of present-day Tunisia comes under Roman rule
439 ce The Vandals, a Germanic tribe, capture Carthage
534 Carthage is recaptured by the Eastern Roman Empire (Byzantine Empire)
670 The Islamic Arabs invade Tunisia and found the city of Kairouan
698 The Arabs capture Carthage: the city is abandoned in favor of nearby Tunis
800–909 Tunisia becomes independent under the Arab Aghlabid dynasty
909 The Aghlabids are replaced by the Arab Fatimid dynasty
969 The native Berber Zirid dynasty replaces the Fatimids when they move their capital to Cairo
1236–1574 The Hafsid dynasty rules Tunisia
1270 The Eighth Crusade attacks Tunis
1535 The Spanish capture Tunis
1573–1574 The Spanish again occupy Tunis
1574 The Ottoman Turks conquer Tunisia
1705 The *bey* (regent) of Tunis becomes effectively autonomous within the Omani empire

Uganda

c.1600 CE Kingdoms of Bunyoro, Buganda, Ankole and Busoga founded

Zambia

c.1000 CE Bantu-speaking peoples settle in the area of modern Zambia
1514 Portuguese explorers are the first Europeans to enter the Zambia region
1740 The Lunda people invade Zambia from the west
1762 Portuguese traders from Mozambique found a trading post on the border of present-day Zambia

Zimbabwe

5th century CE Bantu-speaking peoples settle in the Zimbabwe region
c.1100 The Karanga people found a state centered on the city of Great Zimbabwe
c.1200 The "Great Enclosure" is built at Great Zimbabwe
c.1400 The Torwa kingdom is founded near present-day Bulawayo
c.1450 Great Zimbabwe is abandoned when it is superseded by the Mwenemutapa kingdom to the north
c.1600 The Rozvi people conquer Torwa and establish the Changamire state

A Carthagian coin
An African elephant, as used by Hannibal in his invasion of Italy during the Second Punic War (218–201 BCE), appears on this coin. Carthage had its own currency from c.400 BCE.

Nyatsimba Mutoto
He was the founder of the Mwene Mutapa dynasty, and ruled from c.1440 to c.1450 CE. A member of the Shona peoples, he conquered territory from the Kalahari desert to the Indian Ocean.

© DIAGRAM

Abd-al-Qadir
He was the leader of Algerian resistance to French occupation of his country in the first half of the nineteenth century.

Dressed for battle
A typical uniform worn by a soldier in the Portuguese artillery in 1807 CE.

King Léopold II of Belgium
In 1885 CE, he laid claim to a large area of land that now lies in the north of the Democratic Republic of Congo.

19th century CE

Algeria
- **1815** US Navy attacks bases of the Barbary Corsairs in Algiers
- **1827** France blockades Algiers
- **1830** The French capture Algiers
- **1834** The first French settlers (*colons*) arrive in Algeria
- **1847** Algerian resistance leader Abd al-Qadir defeated by France
- **1848** Algeria is declared an integral part of France
- **1871** French suppress the Kabylie uprising of Muhammad al-Moqrani

Angola
- **1884** The Portuguese begin to extend their control inland from the coast

Benin
- **1807** Britain outlaws the slave trade, causing an economic crisis in Dahomey
- **1851** France signs a trade agreement with Dahomey

Botswana
- **1801** British missionaries visit the Tswana people
- **1817** The London Missionary Society creates a permanent mission station at Kuruman
- **1830s** Tswana attacked by migrating Kololo and Ndebele peoples
- **1840s** David Livingstone active as a missionary in Botswana
- **1860s** The Tswana seek British protection against their enemies
- **1867–1869** An influx of white prospectors follows the discovery of gold in Botswana
- **1885** With the agreement of King Khama III and other chiefs, Britain declares the Bechuanaland Protectorate
- **1894** Tswana chiefs visit London
- **1895** Tswana chiefs cede land to the British South Africa Company (BSAC) for railroad construction

Burkina Faso
- **1896** France captures Ouagadougou
- **1897** The Mossi kingdom formally becomes a French protectorate

Burundi
- **1897** Burundi becomes part of the German East-African territory of Ruanda–Urundi

Cameroon
- **1884** Cameroon becomes a German protectorate

Cape Verde
- **1876** Slavery is abolished in Cape Verde and the economy begins to decline
- **1879** Portugal separates Cape Verde and Portuguese Guinea, which had been ruled as one territory, into two separate colonies

Central African Republic (CAR)
- **1805–1830** The Baya people settle in the CAR region
- **1889** The French establish an outpost at Bangui
- **1894** The French create the territory of Oubangoui–Shari in present-day CAR

Chad
- **1808** The Hausa invade Kanem–Bornu
- **1822** English explorers Dixon Denham and Hugh Clapperton are the first Europeans to visit Chad
- **1846** The last king of the Saifawas dynasty is assassinated
- **1890** Kanem–Bornu, Baguirmi and Wadai are conquered by the Sudanese leader Rabeh
- **1898** France declares a protectorate over Chad

Comoros
- **1843** France annexes Mayotte
- **1886** France takes control of the rest of the Comoros islands

Congo, Democratic Republic of
- **1868–1881** The Zanzibari merchant Tippu Tip maintains a private slave trading empire in the Congo River Basin
- **1874–1877** Henry Morton Stanley follows the course of the Congo River from its upper reaches to the Atlantic Ocean
- **1878** King Léopold of Belgium employs Stanley to investigate the potential of the Congo region for colonization
- **1884** The Berlin Conference on Africa recognizes the Congo Free State as a private holding of a group of European investors headed by King Léopold

Congo, Republic of
1874–1877 Henry Morton Stanley traces the course of the Congo River, reaching Stanley (now Malebo) Pool, on which Brazzaville now stands, and, finally, the Atlantic Ocean
1875 French explorer Pierre Savorgnan de Brazzaville explores the region
1880 De Brazza reaches Malebo Pool and meets the Bateke King Ilo Makoko; the two sign a treaty making the region north of the Congo River a French protectorate; De Brazza founds a trading post on the site of present-day Brazzaville
1887 Frontiers of the territory are fixed with the Congo Free State
1891 The colony of French Congo is created

Djibouti
1862 France purchases the Afar port of Obock
1881 France establishes a coaling station for ships at Obock
1884 France signs protectorate agreements with the sultans of Obock and Tadjoura
1888 France establishes the colony of French Somaliland
1896 The newly developed port of Djibouti city becomes the capital of French Somaliland
1897 Djibouti becomes the official port of trade for Ethiopia

Egypt
1801 French troops in Egypt surrender to a British and Ottoman army
1805 Muhammad Ali (Ali Pasha) seizes power in Egypt
1859–1869 Construction of the Suez canal
1875 Egypt sells its share in the Suez canal to Britain
1882 Britain annexes Egypt

Equatorial Guinea
1843–1858 Spain conquers the area and establishes the colony of Spanish Guinea

Eritrea
1882–1889 Italy conquers Eritrea

Ethiopia
1855 Emperor Tewodros II reunifies Ethiopia
1867 Tewodros imprisons the British consul
1868 Tewodros commits suicide after a British punitive expedition captures his fortress at Magdala
1889 Emperor John killed fighting the Mahdists of the Sudan: he is succeeded by Menelik II
1896 Menelik defeats an Italian invasion at Adowa

Gabon
1839 France establishes a naval and trading post on the present site of Libreville
1849 A group of freed slaves is settled at the station which is named Libreville (free town)
1875 The Fang have become the dominant ethnic group in Gabon
1883 Libreville becomes the capital of the French colony of Gabon
1885 The Berlin conference recognizes French control of Gabon
1889 Gabon becomes part of the French colony of Middle Congo (now Republic of the Congo)

Gambia
1807 Gambia loses economic importance when Britain abolishes the slave trade
1816 British merchants found Bathurst (now the capital Banjul)
1843 Britain sets up the colony of Gambia
c.1850 Conversion of Gambians to Islam begins
1866–1888 Gambia governed as part of the colony of Sierra Leone
1870–1876 Britain negotiates with France to exchange Gambia in return for concessions elsewhere
1889 Present borders of Gambia agreed by treaty with France
1893 Britain proclaims a protectorate over the interior

Ghana
1824–1826 First British Asante War: Britain occupies the Asante capital, Kumasi
1830–1844 British merchants establish an informal protectorate over the Gold Coast
1850 Britain buys out Danish commercial interests on the Gold Coast
1872 The Dutch withdraw from their trading posts on the Gold Coast
1874 The Second British Asante War: British forces sack Kumasi and the Gold Coast is declared a British colony
1893–1894 Defeated in the Third British Asante War, the Asante accept a British protectorate
1895–1896 The Fourth British Asante War: the British put down an Asante uprising

Guinea
1849 France establishes control of the coast of Guinea

A heavy burden to bear
A Congolese sculpture depicting the plight of Africans forced to carry French colonialists on their shoulders.

An Ethiopian victory
In 1896 CE an Ethiopian army, under the leadership of Menelik II, defeated the Italian invaders at the Battle of Adowa.

The Yam Festival, 1817 CE
An illustration depicting the first day of the Yam Festival that took place at Kumasi, Asante.

© DIAGRAM

1865 Eastern Guinea forms part of Samouri Touré's Mandinke empire
1881 Futa Jalon becomes a French protectorate
1886–1892 France conquers the Mandinke empire
1895 The area of Guinea is incorporated into French West Africa
1898 Samouri Toure is captured by French forces and exiled

Guinea–Bissau

1879 The region becomes the Portuguese colony of Portuguese Guinea

Ivory Coast

1830s French trading posts established along the Ivory Coast
1843 Coastal kingdoms of Aigini and Atokpora ask for French protection against the Asante
1870 France withdraws from the Ivory Coast
1887–1889 France reaches protectorate agreements with many local rulers
1893 France claims Ivory Coast as a colony
1895 Ivory Coast becomes part of the French West Africa colony
1897 Northern kingdom of Kong destroyed by Samouri Toure
1898 Present borders of Ivory Coast fixed after the capture of Samouri Toure

Kenya

19th century Kikuyu farmers migrate into the Kenya region from the south
1849 Johann Ludwig Krapf discovers Mt Kenya
1858 John Hanning Speke reaches Lake Victoria
1861 Control of the Kenyan coast passes to the sultanate of Zanzibar
1886 Britain and Germany reach agreement on their respective spheres of influence in East Africa
1887 A British business group leases the Kenyan coast from the sultan of Zanzibar
1888 The Imperial British East Africa Company is formed
1890 An Anglo-German treaty fixes the southern border of the Imperial British East Africa Company's territory
1895 The British government dissolves the Imperial British East Africa Company and establishes the East Africa Protectorate

Lesotho

c.1818 Chief Moshoeshoe of the Moketeli leads a coalition of peoples into present-day Lesotho to escape the Zulu conqueror Shaka
c.1824 Moshoeshoe unites his followers into the Basotho nation
c.1833 Moshoeshoe invites missionaries to his fortress at Thaba Bosigo near modern-day Maseru
1856–1868 Boers attempt to conquer the Basotho
1868 Basotho appeal to Britain for protection against the Boers
1869 Britain establishes the protectorate of Basutoland
1870 Death of Moshoeshoe
1871 Basutoland comes under the administration of the British Cape Colony (now in South Africa)
1880 The Basotho rebel against British efforts to disarm them
1884 Britain reestablishes control of Basutoland

Moshoeshoe I
The son of a Sotho chief, he founded a wealthy mountain kingdom, known by the name of Basuto (Lesotho), in the 1820s.

Liberia

1816 The American Colonization Society (ACS) buys land along the Grain Coast and founds Monrovia
1822 The ACS settles the first group of freed slaves at Monrovia
1824 The ACS adopts the name Liberia for their settlement
1838 Monrovia joins other settlements on the Grain Coast to form the Commonwealth of Liberia
1841 The US approves a constitution for Liberia: a free-born black Virginian, Joseph J. Roberts, becomes governor
1847 Jul 26 Liberia becomes an independent state: Roberts becomes its first president
1849 Great Britain becomes the first country to recognize Liberia as an independent state after Roberts visits London
1856 Roberts resigns from the presidency
1862 The US recognizes Liberian independence
1871 Roberts returns to power after president Roye is imprisoned for corruption
1876 Death of president Roberts
1885–1892 Liberia's borders demarcated by treaties with Britain and France

Libya

1804 US navy attacks a base of the Barbary Corsairs at Tripoli
1835 Direct Ottoman rule is restored
1843 The puritanical Islamic Sanusiyah movement spreads to Libya

Madagascar
1810 King Radama I outlaws the slave trade
1817 Britain recognizes King Radama as king of all Madagascar
1845 Queen Ranavalona I defeats a British and French invasion and expels European missionaries and traders
1861 Death of Queen Ranavalona: King Radama II gives concessions to a French trading company
1869 The prime minister Rainilaiarivony imposes Protestant Christianity on the Malagasyl
1883–1885 The first Franco-Merina war: Merina cedes Diego Suarez to France
1890 France declares a protectorate over Madagascar
1895 The second Franco-Merina War: France occupies the capital Antananarivo after Merina refuses to submit to French rule
1896 Madagascar is declared a French colony
1897 France deposes Queen Ranavalona III, the last monarch of Madagascar

Malawi
1830s Ngoni and Yao peoples settle in the area of present-day Malawi
1859 The British missionary David Livingstone visits the region and finds it torn by civil wars
1875 The Free Church of Scotland sets up a mission station
1889 The British make protection treaties with local chiefs
1891 The British proclaim the Protectorate of Nyasaland

Mali
1850 Mali area conquered by the Islamic reformer al-Hajj Umar of the Tukulor caliphate
1866 The French begin the conquest of Mali
1895 France wins full control of Mali: it becomes the colony of French Sudan

Mauritania
1858 France begins to extend military control over southern Mauretania
1898 Xavier Coppolani wins the Berber tribes of southern Mauretania over to French rule

Mauritius
1810 The British capture the island and rename it Mauritius
1814 France formally cedes the island to Britain
1833 Britain abolishes slavery in its empire: 75,000 slaves are freed on Mauritius
1835 The first Indian laborers arrive to work on sugar plantations

Morocco
1830 Armed clashes begin on the border of Morocco and French-ruled Algeria
1844 French defeat the Moroccans at Isly
1894 Tribal rebellion in the Rif provokes a Spanish invasion

Mozambique
1832 Portugal outlaws the much abused *prazo* system of land grants
1833 Shoshangane of the Nguni massacres the garrison of Lourenço Marques (now Maputo)
1836 Shoshangane burns Sofala
1851 Portugal begins to subdue the *Bongas* (half-caste chiefs) of the Zambezi valley
1859 Death of Shoshangane
1885 King Gungunhana of Gaza cedes mineral rights to the British South Africa Company (BSAC)
1890 Britain successfully claims inland territories also claimed by Portugal for its central African colonies.
1891 Borders agreed by international treaties
1891–1892 Antonio Enes reforms the administration of Portuguese East Africa
1894 Lourenço Marques is attacked by supporters of Gungunhana

Namibia
1814 The Dutch cede their interests in Southern Africa to the British
1830s Chief Jonker Afrikaner establishes Nama dominance over the Herero people
1861 Death of Jonker Afrikaner
1863–1892 Frequent Nama-Herero wars
1868 German missionaries and farmers settle on the coast
1870 Germans make peace agreements with local chiefs
1876 Britain annexes Walvis Bay
1884 Germany creates the German Southwest Africa colony
1894 Chief Hendrik Witbooi is killed leading a joint Nama-Herero rebellion against the Germans

Niger
1804 Hausa refugees from the Fulani *jihad* flood into Niger
1891 The French begin the conquest of Niger

A French victory
A magazine cover records the defeat of the Merina peoples of Madagascar by French forces in 1895 CE.

Adapting a style
When Christian missionaries came to Namibia in the nineteenth century, Herero women adapted the style of the missionaries' wives' clothing to create styles still followed today.

© DIAGRAM

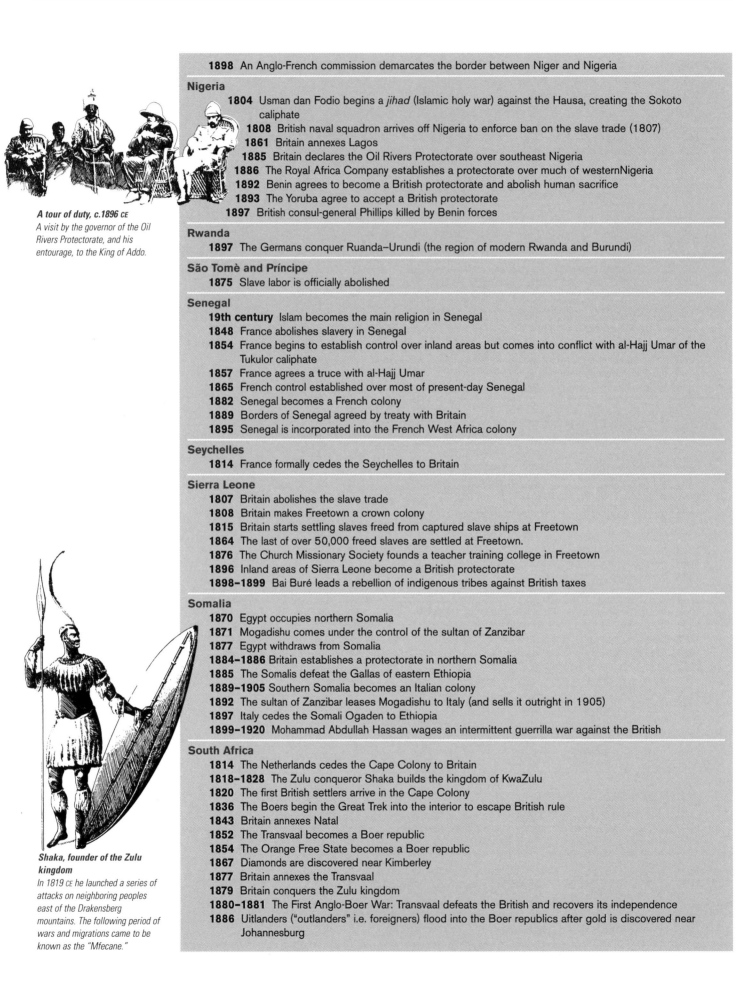

1898 An Anglo-French commission demarcates the border between Niger and Nigeria

Nigeria
1804 Usman dan Fodio begins a *jihad* (Islamic holy war) against the Hausa, creating the Sokoto caliphate
1808 British naval squadron arrives off Nigeria to enforce ban on the slave trade (1807)
1861 Britain annexes Lagos
1885 Britain declares the Oil Rivers Protectorate over southeast Nigeria
1886 The Royal Africa Company establishes a protectorate over much of westernNigeria
1892 Benin agrees to become a British protectorate and abolish human sacrifice
1893 The Yoruba agree to accept a British protectorate
1897 British consul-general Phillips killed by Benin forces

Rwanda
1897 The Germans conquer Ruanda–Urundi (the region of modern Rwanda and Burundi)

São Tomè and Príncipe
1875 Slave labor is officially abolished

Senegal
19th century Islam becomes the main religion in Senegal
1848 France abolishes slavery in Senegal
1854 France begins to establish control over inland areas but comes into conflict with al-Hajj Umar of the Tukulor caliphate
1857 France agrees a truce with al-Hajj Umar
1865 French control established over most of present-day Senegal
1882 Senegal becomes a French colony
1889 Borders of Senegal agreed by treaty with Britain
1895 Senegal is incorporated into the French West Africa colony

Seychelles
1814 France formally cedes the Seychelles to Britain

Sierra Leone
1807 Britain abolishes the slave trade
1808 Britain makes Freetown a crown colony
1815 Britain starts settling slaves freed from captured slave ships at Freetown
1864 The last of over 50,000 freed slaves are settled at Freetown.
1876 The Church Missionary Society founds a teacher training college in Freetown
1896 Inland areas of Sierra Leone become a British protectorate
1898–1899 Bai Buré leads a rebellion of indigenous tribes against British taxes

Somalia
1870 Egypt occupies northern Somalia
1871 Mogadishu comes under the control of the sultan of Zanzibar
1877 Egypt withdraws from Somalia
1884–1886 Britain establishes a protectorate in northern Somalia
1885 The Somalis defeat the Gallas of eastern Ethiopia
1889–1905 Southern Somalia becomes an Italian colony
1892 The sultan of Zanzibar leases Mogadishu to Italy (and sells it outright in 1905)
1897 Italy cedes the Somali Ogaden to Ethiopia
1899–1920 Mohammad Abdullah Hassan wages an intermittent guerrilla war against the British

South Africa
1814 The Netherlands cedes the Cape Colony to Britain
1818–1828 The Zulu conqueror Shaka builds the kingdom of KwaZulu
1820 The first British settlers arrive in the Cape Colony
1836 The Boers begin the Great Trek into the interior to escape British rule
1843 Britain annexes Natal
1852 The Transvaal becomes a Boer republic
1854 The Orange Free State becomes a Boer republic
1867 Diamonds are discovered near Kimberley
1877 Britain annexes the Transvaal
1879 Britain conquers the Zulu kingdom
1880–1881 The First Anglo-Boer War: Transvaal defeats the British and recovers its independence
1886 Uitlanders ("outlanders" i.e. foreigners) flood into the Boer republics after gold is discovered near Johannesburg

A tour of duty, c.1896 CE
A visit by the governor of the Oil Rivers Protectorate, and his entourage, to the King of Addo.

Shaka, founder of the Zulu kingdom
In 1819 CE he launched a series of attacks on neighboring peoples east of the Drakensberg mountains. The following period of wars and migrations came to be known as the "Mfecane."

1895 Cecil Rhodes, prime minister of Cape Colony, organizes the Jameson raid on Transvaal
1899 Transvaal and the Orange Free State declare war on Britain beginning the Second Anglo-Boer War (the South African War)

Sudan

1821 Egypt conquers the Funj
1869 Khedive Ismail of Egypt sends Samuel Baker on an expedition up the White Nile
1873 Baker establishes Egyptian control on the upper Nile and undermines the local slave trade
1874 Ismail appoints the British general Charles George Gordon governor of Sudan
1876 Egypt has control of most of present-day Sudan
1881 Muhammad Ahmad proclaims himself the Mahdi ("messiah") and leads a revolt against Egypt
1885 The Mahdi captures Khartoum after a long siege in which Gordon is killed
1896 Anglo-Egyptian force under Kitchener invades Sudan
1898 Anglo-Egyptians defeat the Sudanese at Omdurman
1898 Fashoda incident: Britain forces a French military expedition to withdraw from Sudan
1899 Joint Anglo-Egyptian government of the Sudan established

Swaziland

1830s British traders and Boer farmers visit Swaziland
1836 Ngwane's successor, Mswati (Mswazi) II, names his people "Swazi" after himself
1865 Mswati II allies with the British against the Boers
1878 Influx of Europeans after gold is discovered in Swaziland
1881 Britain guarantees the independence of Swaziland
1884 The Boer republic of Transvaal guarantees the independence of Swaziland
1888 The Swazi give European settlers conditional self-government
1890 A provisional government of Swazi, British and Boer representatives is formed
1894 Britain agrees that Transvaal should establish a protectorate over Swaziland
1899 The infant Sobhuza II becomes king under a regency

Tanzania

1840 Sultan Sayyid Said of Oman moves his court to Zanzibar
1844 The Anglican Church Missionary Society sets up a mission station in Zanzibar
1848 Johannes Rebmann becomes the first European to see Mt Kilimanjaro, the highest mountain in Africa
1850s Trading caravans from Zanzibar reach as far as the Congo River basin
1858 Richard Burton and John Hanning Speke reach Lake Tanganyika and Lake Victoria
1867 Britain begins a campaign to destroy Zanzibar's slave trade
1871 Henry Morton Stanley meets David Livingstone at Ujiji on Lake Tanganyika
1873 The sultan of Zanzibar abandons the slave trade
1884 German explorer Karl Peters signs treaties with several chiefs in the Tanzania region
1890 The Sultanate of Zanzibar becomes a British protectorate
1891 The German East Africa colony is established

Togo

1884 Germany sets up a protectorate on the coast
1899 The German Togoland colony is created

Tunisia

1869 A financial crisis forces the *bey* to accept Anglo-French financial control
1878 Tunisia is recognized as a French sphere of influence at the Congress of Berlin
1881 Tunisia becomes a French protectorate

Uganda

1840s Arab slave traders begin operating in the Uganda region
1862 John Hanning Speke reaches Buganda during his search for the source of the Nile
1875 Henry Morton Stanley visits *kabaka* (king) Mutesa I of Buganda
1877 British Anglican missionaries arrive in Buganda
1879 French Catholic missionaries arrive in Buganda
1888 *Kabaka* Mwanga is briefly deposed after attempting to drive missionaries from his country
1889 The German explorer Karl Peters agrees a protection treaty with *Kabaka* Mwanga
1890 Anglo-German treaty recognizes Buganda as a British sphere of influence
1894 Buganda becomes a British protectorate and helps the British conquer the rest of Uganda
1896 The British protectorate is extended to Bunyoro, Toro, Ankole, and Busoga
1897 Mwanga is deposed after rebelling against the British

Zambia

1835 Zambia is settled by Nguni people fleeing from Zulu expansion in southern Africa

The Mahdi
The leader of a revolt against Egyptian rule in the Sudan, he is best remembered for his defeat of General Gordon after a long siege at Khartoum in 1885 CE.

The source of the Nile?
British explorer John Hanning Speke reached Buganda in 1862 CE *while engaged in his search for the source of the Nile.*

© DIAGRAM

Cecil Rhodes
The founder of the British South Africa Company (BSAC), he tried to impose British rule throughout Southern Africa.

1855 David Livingstone discovers the Victoria Falls
1889 Cecil Rhodes' British South Africa Company (BSAC) is given responsibility for Barotseland (the area of present-day southern Zambia) by British government charter
1890 Agents of the BSAC take possession of Barotseland
1898 The Ngoni rebel against the BSAC

Zimbabwe
1840s The Ndebele under Mzilikazi conquer the Changamire kingdom and establish a capital at Bulawayo
1888 Cecil Rhodes' British South Africa Company (BSAC) obtains extensive mineral rights from the Ndebele king Lobengula
1889 The BSAC gains responsibility for the Zimbabwe area by a British government charter
1890 The BSAC's Pioneer Column establishes Fort Salisbury on Harare Hill
1893 BSAC forces defeat Lobengula and destroy the Ndebele kingdom
1895 The BSAC territory is named Rhodesia after Cecil Rhodes
1897 Rhodesia is divided into two territories, Southern Rhodesia (now Zimbabwe) and Northern Rhodesia (now Zambia)

1900–1949 CE

Algeria
1902 Algeria's present boundaries established
1923 French deport the nationalist leader Emir Khaled
1943 Ferhat Abbas calls for Algerian independence
1944 French citizenship granted to many Algerians
1945 France deports the nationalist leader Messali Hadj
1947 Algerian Muslims are given limited voting rights

Angola
1921 Portugal gains full control of all modern Angola

Benin
1904 France annexes the kingdom of Dahomey and incorporates it into French West Africa
1946 Dahomey becomes an overseas territory of France

Botswana
1935 Britain rejects a request for Bechuanaland to be transferred to South African control

Burkina Faso
1919 France creates the colony of Upper Volta within the borders of present-day Burkina Faso

Burundi
1916 Belgian troops occupy Ruanda-Urundi
1920 The League of Nations awards Ruanda-Urundi to Belgium as a mandated territory

Cameroon
1914 French and British troops occupy Cameroon
1922 Cameroon is divided between France (75 per cent) and Britain (25 per cent)
1946 Britain and France agree to give their parts of Cameroon self-government or independence
1948 Nationalists in French Cameroon found the People's Union of Cameroon (UPC)

Cape Verde
1920s Cape Verde's economy starts to decline as the number of ships visiting the islands falls

Central African Republic
1920s France develops cotton cultivation, but concessionaires continue to use conscripted labour and opposition to French rule continues into the 1930s
1949 Independence movement founded by Barthélémy Boganda

Chad
1908 Chad becomes part of French Equatorial Africa
1912 Last resistance to French rule ended
1920 Chad becomes French colony with a separate administration
1930 Cotton farming begins in Chad
1935 France agrees to cede the Aouzou strip to the Italian colony of Libya but the agreement is never implemented
1940 Chad is the first colony to declare for the Free French
1946 Chad becomes a French overseas territory

Comoros
1914 France rules the islands from Madagascar
1947 The Comoros becomes a French overseas territory

Congo, Democratic Republic of
1908 The Belgian government takes over administration of the Congo Free State

Congo, Republic of
1903 French Congo becomes known as Middle Congo
1910 Middle Congo becomes part of the colony of French Equatorial Africa
1921–1935 Up to 20,000 African forced laborers die building the Congo–Atlantic Ocean railway
1925 The first roads are built in Middle Congo
1940 Middle Congo supports the Free French in World War II
1944 Brazzaville conference on the future of France's African colonies
1946 French end the practice of forced labor

Djibouti
1917 A railway is completed from Djibouti to the Ethiopian capital, Addis Ababa
1924–1934 Road building program opens up the interior of Djibouti
1946 Djibouti is granted a representative council and a deputy in the French national assembly
1947 Issa nationalists begin a campaign for independence

Egypt
1914 Britain makes Egypt a protectorate
1922 Britain grants Egypt nominal independence
1922 Howard Carter discovers the tomb of Tutankhamun
1923 Egypt becomes a constitutional monarchy
1940–1941 The British defeat an Italian invasion of Egypt
1942 British defeat the Italians and Germans at the battle of El Alamein
1945 Egypt is a founder member of the Arab League
1948 Egypt and other Arab countries invade Israel
1949 Egypt accepts an armistice with Israel

Equatorial Guinea
1900 The borders of Spanish Guinea are fixed by the Treaty of Paris
1936 The colony supports Franco in the Spanish Civil war

Eritrea
1935 Italians use Eritrea as a base for their conquest of Ethiopia
1941 The British expel the Italians from Eritrea

Ethiopia
1916 Emperor Lij Yasu is overthrown after he converts to Islam
1923 Ethiopia becomes a member of the League of Nations
1930 Ras Tafari becomes emperor, adopting the title Haile Selassie I
1931 Haile Selassie gives Ethiopia a written constitution
1935 Italy invades Ethiopia
1936 The Italians capture the capital Addis Ababa
1941 The British drive the Italians out of Ethiopia
1940s Modernization program begun by Haile Selassie continues

Gabon
1910 Gabon becomes a territory of French Equatorial Africa
1940 Gabon supports the Free French in World War II
1946 Gabon is given an elected legislature

Gambia
1902 All of modern Gambia is under British control
1906 Slavery in Gambia is abolished
1945 Gambia gains limited internal self-government

Ghana
1900 The last Asante resistance to the British is extinguished
1901 British protectorate established over northern Ghana
1922 The western part of German Togoland is mandated to Britain by the League of Nations: it is administered as part of Ghana
1925 The first Africans are elected to the colonial legislative council
1947 Kwame Nkrumah organizes a Ghanaian nationalist party

Conscripted soldiers
Many Africans fought in the armies of the European colonial powers at the time of World War II. These soldiers, for example, fought for the Belgian army.

© DIAGRAM

1948 Nationalists riot in Accra

Guinea
1947 Democratic Party of Guinea (PDG) founded to campaign for independence

Guinea–Bissau
1913–1915 "Pacification" wars fought by the Portuguese to quell opposition in the interior
1940s Nationalist demands for independence start to increase

Ivory Coast
1908 Military occupation of Ivory Coast completed
1914–1918 Frequent rebellions as France tries to conscript Africans to fight in World War I
1932 Most of the colony of Upper Volta (now Burkina Faso) is added to Ivory Coast
1944 Félix Houphouët-Boigny and Auguste Denise form the African Farmers Union (SAA),
1946 The African Democratic Union launched to campaign for independence for France's African colonies
1947 Ivory Coast and Upper Volta are separated

Kenya
1901 The British build a railroad from Mombasa to Lake Victoria, opening up the Kenyan highlands for white settlers
1920 The interior becomes the British Crown Colony of Kenya: the coast remains a protectorate, nominally ruled by the sultan of Zanzibar
1944 The Kikuyu and other Kenyan peoples form the Kenya African Union (KAU) to oppose British rule
1947 Jomo Kenyatta becomes leader of the KAU

Lesotho
1910 The Basutoland Council of chiefs and elected representatives is formed
1943 Nine district councils are established as advisory bodies
1944 Britain declares that the Basutoland Council and the paramount chief will be consulted before any legislation is enacted
1946 The traditional courts are reorganized and a national treasury is established

Liberia
1904 President Barclay promotes a policy of cooperation between the Americo-Liberians and the indigenous peoples
1915 Uprising by the indigenous peoples against the Americo-Liberians
1919 Liberia transfers 2,000 square miles of territory to French control
1926 Liberia leases land to the American Firestone Company for rubber plantations
1930s League of Nations investigates domestic slavery in Liberia
1942 Liberia signs a defense agreement with the US
1943 William V. S. Tubman becomes president
1944 Liberia declares war on Germany

Libya
1911 The Turkish-Italian war breaks out
1912 The Ottomans cede Libya to Italy
1922 The Italians recognize the Sanusi leader Sayyid Idris as autonomous emir of Cyrenaica
1923 The Italians gain full control over Tripolitania
1931 The Italians gain full control over Cyrenaica after they capture and execute the Sanusi leader Umar al Mukhtar
1940 The Italians invade Egypt from Libya
1941 German troops are sent to support the Italians in Libya after the British capture Benghazi
1943 The British drive the Italians and Germans out of Libya: Libya comes under Allied military government
1947 Italy abandons its claims to Libya
1949 The UN approves a proposal that Libya should become an independent state

An Italian possession in Libya
Following hostilities between Italy and Turkey in 1912 CE, Cyrenaica became an Italian possession. It ceased to be an official political division in 1963 CE.

Madagascar
1915 A nationalist secret society, the *Vy Vato Sakelika* (VVS), is outlawed
1920 A moderate nationalist movement calling for citizenship rights for the Malagasy is suppressed by France
1940 Madagascar supports the collaborationist Vichy French government
1942 British and South African forces occupy Madagascar
1943 The British hand Madagascar over to the Free French
1945 France gives Madagascar the right to elect an assembly
1947 A pro-independence rebellion breaks out
1948 France crushes the rebellion with the loss of 80,000 lives

Malawi

1915 John Chilembwe leads an unsuccessful rebellion against British rule in which he is killed

1944 The Nyasaland African Congress, the first national political movement, holds its first assembly

Mali

1904 The French Sudan is incorporated into the French West Africa colony

1946 French Sudan is given a legislative council

Mauritania

1902 French authority is effective in most of Mauritania

1920 Mauritania becomes a French colony

1946 Mauritania becomes a territory of the French Union with a legislative council

Mauritius

1918 Immigration of Indian laborers is ended

1948 A new constitution gives votes to a large number of Indians and Creoles

Morocco

1904 Britain recognizes Morocco as a French sphere of influence

1904 Franco-Spanish treaty grants Spain sphere of influence in northern Morocco

1911 German gunboat Panther causes an international crisis when it arrives at Agadir

1912 Mar Treaty of Fez; Morocco becomes a French protectorate

1912 Nov Spanish protectorate established over northern Morocco

1921–1926 Rebellion of Abd el-Krim in the Rif Atlas

1923 Tangier becomes an international city

1930s French settlement in good farming areas

1940 Jun Morocco comes under control of the collaborationist Vichy government following the fall of France in World War II

1942 Nov Operation Torch: Anglo-American landings in Morocco

1944 The Istiqlal (Independence) party is founded

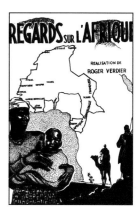

A Moroccan film poster
Published in the 1930s, this poster identifies the areas of northeast Africa that were then under French control.

Mozambique

1920 Mokombe of Tete, the last of the Bongas, is defeated

1921 Portugal introduces the *assimilado* system, which enables some Africans to attain Portuguese citizenship

1926 The "New State" regime introduces protectionist trade and investment policies

1930 Colonial Act encourages Portuguese emigration to Mozambique

Namibia

1904 The Herero rebel against German rule

1907 The Germans crush the Herero rebellion in a genocidal campaign

1910 Walvis Bay enclave becomes part of South Africa

1915 South African troops occupy German Southwest Africa in World War I

1920 The League of Nations mandates Southwest Africa to South Africa

1945 South Africa refuses a request to place Southwest Africa under UN trusteeship

1946 The UN refuses to permit annexation of Southwest Africa by South Africa

1948 South Africa's apartheid policies introduced into Southwest Africa

Niger

1906 The French conquer Aïr; Niger's present borders are demarcated

1917 The French expel most of the Tuareg from Niger after a rebellion

1922 Niger is incorporated into the French West Africa colony

1946 The *Parti Progressiste Nigérien* (PPN) is formed by Hamani Diori

A British protectorate
A stamp issued in 1912 CE when Northern Nigeria was still under British control.

Nigeria

1900 The British government buys out the Royal Africa Company and assumes juridiction over its territory

1902 Britain conquers the Ibo

1903 Britain completes the conquest of the Sokoto caliphate

1914 Britain conquers Abeokuta, the last independent state in Nigeria

1914 Britain forms the colony and protectorate of Nigeria

1918 Abeokuta rebels against British rule

1929 Ibo and Ibibio women protest against British rule

1946 The Richards' Constitution gives Nigerians a role in government

Rwanda

1916 Belgian troops occupy Ruanda–Urundi

1923 The League of Nations mandates Ruanda–Urundi to Belgium

1946 Ruanda–Urundi becomes a UN trust territory administered by Belgium

© DIAGRAM

A German victory
A poster issued by the German forces to celebrate the defeat of the British and Free French forces, who were attempting to gain control of Senegal during World War II.

DAKAR-MERS EL-KEBIR

São Tomè and Príncipe
1909 British and German manufacturers boycott the country's cocoa because of the use of indentured labor

Senegal
1933 Léopold Sédar Senghor and others develop the idea of *négritude* (a primarily literary movement aimed at resistance to French cultural influence)
1940 Senegal supports the collaborationist Vichy French regime
1942 Free French gain control of Senegal
1946 Senegal becomes an overseas territory of France
1948 Senghor founds the Senegalese Progressive Union to campaign for greater autonomy

Seychelles
1908 The Seychelles, formerly a dependency of Mauritius, becomes a separate British colony
1948 Seychelles gets its first legislative council with elected members

Sierra Leone
1924 The first elected representatives join the Sierra Leone legislative council

Somalia
1912 The British build border posts to halt Somali infiltration into Kenya
1936 After Italy conquers Ethiopia, Italian Somaliland is ruled from Addis Ababa
1940 Italy occupies British Somaliland
1941 Britain recaptures British Somaliland and occupies Italian Somaliland

South Africa
1902 Peace of Vereeniging ends the Anglo-Boer war: the Boer republics become British colonies
1910 The Union of South Africa is formed and becomes an independent dominion within the British empire
1912 The African National Congress (ANC) is formed to campaign for black rights
1914 James Barry Munnik Hertzog founds the National Party to promote Afrikaner (Boer) interests
1914 South African forces occupy German Southwest Africa
1920 The League of Nations mandates Southwest Africa to South Africa
1931 Britain grants South Africa full independence
1939 South Africa declares war on Germany at the beginning of World War II
1946 The UN rejects a South African request to annex Southwest Africa
1948 The National Party comes to power under Malan and introduces apartheid

Sudan
1924 Britain expels Egyptian officials from Sudan after they incite an army mutiny
1936 Britain permits Egypt to resume joint control of Sudan
1948 Sudan is granted a legislative council

Swaziland
1902 Following their victory in the Anglo-Boer War, the British take control of Swaziland
1903 Swaziland is declared a British protectorate
1921 King Sobhuza II begins personal rule
1944 The king is granted power to issue legally enforceable decrees

Tanzania
1905 The Maji Maji rebellion against German rule is crushed
1907 Germany has full control of the territory of modern Tanzania
1914–1918 The German commander in East Africa, Gen. Paul von Lettow-Vorbeck, fights a skillful guerrilla war against allied forces throughout World War I
1918 British forces occupy the Tanganyika portion of German East Africa
1919 Disruption caused by fighting in World War I leads to a serious famine
1920 Tanganyika is mandated to Britain by the League of Nations
1926 Legislative councils appointed for Tanganyika and Zanzibar
1930s The Nazi party becomes popular among German settlers in Tanganyika
1945 The first Africans are appointed to the legislative councils
1946 Tanganyika becomes a UN Trust Territory

Togo
1914 British and French troops occupy German Togoland
1922 The League of Nations mandates the western third of German Togoland to Britain, the eastern two-thirds are mandated to France
1946 British and French Togolands become UN trust territories

Tunisia
1920 The *Destour* party calls for the creation of a national assembly

1934 Habib Bourguiba founds the Neo-Destour (New Constitution) party
1940 Tunisia supports the collaborationist Vichy regime after France surrenders to Germany in World War II
1942 German and Italian troops occupy Tunisia
1943 British, US and Free French troops drive the Germans and Italians out of Tunisia

Uganda
1900 Buganda's chiefs sign a treaty accepting British protection in return for freehold rights to their land and other privileges
1904 Cotton is introduced to Uganda and quickly becomes a major cash crop
1921 A colonial legislative council is set up
1925 An education department is set up to provide basic schooling
1926 Uganda's present borders are established
1931 The railroad between Kampala and the Indian Ocean at Mombasa is completed
1945 The first Africans are appointed to the legislative council

Zambia
1900 The BSAC acquires mineral and trading rights from King Lewanika in the area of northern Zambia
1902 Vast copper deposits are discovered at Broken Hill
1909 A railroad links Zambia with the Indian Ocean
1911 Barotseland and other BASC territories are united to form the territory of Northern Rhodesia
1924 The British government takes over the administration of Northern Rhodesia
1927–1939 Rapid expansion of the copper mining industry
1935 Lusaka becomes the capital of Zambia
1940 A general strike by African copper miners achieves major improvements in pay and conditions

The Zambian 'Copperbelt'
This has been one of the largest producers of copper in the world since the 1930s.

Zimbabwe
1900 The BSAC begins to encourage white settlement in Southern Rhodesia
1922 In a referendum, the white settlers vote to become a self-governing colony rather than join South Africa
1923 Southern Rhodesia becomes a self-governing British colony
1930 The Land Apportionment Act divides the land between whites and Africans, much in favor of the whites
1934 The Industrial Conciliation Act restricts African competition in the labor force

1950–1959 CE

Algeria
1954 The National Liberation Front (FLN) begins a war of independence against France
1956–1957 France defeats the FLN in the battle of Algiers
1958 French army rebels and French settlers seize control of the colonial government in Algeria
1959 President de Gaulle of France decides to offer Algeria self-determination

Angola
1956 Pro-independence Popular Movement for the Liberation of Angola (MPLA) is formed

Benin
1958 Dahomey is granted self-government by France

War of Independence, 1954 CE
Armored French troops guard against attacks by the National Liberation Front in Algeria during the War of Independence.

Botswana
1950 Chief Seretse Khama is refused permission to return to Botswana after he marries an Englishwoman while studying in Britain
1956 Seretse Khama given leave to return to Botswana

Burkina Faso
1958 France grants Upper Volta internal self-government

Burundi
1950–1951 The Belgian administration abandons attempts to standardize the languages–Kirundi (in Urundi) and Kinyarwanda (Ruanda) because of popular opposition

Cameroon
1959 French Cameroon is granted internal self-government

Cape Verde
1956 Pro-independence nationalists set up the *Partido Africano de la Independência do Guiné e Cabo Verde* (PAIGC)

Central African Republic
1958 Oubangoui–Shari is granted internal self-government

Chad
1958 Chad is granted internal self-government

Comoros
1958 The people of the Comoros vote in a referendum to retain the islands' status as a French overseas territory which they had achieved in 1947

Congo, Democratic Republic of
1957 Belgians permit the formation of African political parties
1959 Belgium announces its intention to make Congo independent

Congo, Republic of
1958 Middle Congo is granted internal self-government

Djibouti
1958 French Somaliland is granted internal self-government

Egypt
1952 King Farouk is deposed by a military coup
1953 Egypt becomes a republic
1954 Gamal Abdel Nasser becomes president of Egypt
1954 Britain agrees to withdraw its troops from the Suez Canal zone
1956 Suez Crisis: Israel, Britain and France invade after Nasser announces the nationalization of the Suez Canal
1958 Egypt and Syria form the United Arab Republic (UAR)

Equatorial Guinea
1959 Spanish Guinea is reorganized, becoming two provinces of Spain. Its citizens are granted the same rights as Spanish citizens

Eritrea
1952 Under a UN agreement, Eritrea is federated with Ethiopia

Ethiopia
1952 Eritrea is federated with Ethiopia by the UN

Gabon
1957 Gabon is given internal self-government

Gambia
1954 A new constitution is introduced
1959 Further constitutional changes help to prepare Gambia for eventual independence

Ghana
1951 Gold Coast gains full internal self-government
1952 Kwame Nkrumah becomes prime minister of Gold Coast
1956 In a UN sponsored referendum, British Togoland votes for full union with Gold Coast
1957 **Mar 6** Gold Coast becomes independent as Ghana

Guinea
1952 Sekou Touré becomes leader of the PDG
1958 **Oct 2** Guinea rejects French offer of internal self-government and votes for independence: Touré becomes president.

Guinea-Bissau
1951 Portuguese Guinea becomes an overseas province of Portugal
1956 Nationalists form the Partido Africano da Independência do Guiné e Cabo Verde (PAIGC)

Ivory Coast
1950 Under the leadership of Houphouët-Boigny, the RDA begins a policy of cooperation with France
1958 Ivory Coast gains internal self-government

Kenya
1952 The Mau Mau terrorists begin attacks on white settlers and African supporters of British rule
1953 Kenyatta is jailed after he is convicted of being a Mau Mau leader
1956 Mau Mau movement is suppressed by the British
1957 The first Africans are elected to the colonial legislature

Lesotho
1955 The Basutoland Council asks Britain for powers to legislate on internal matters
1956 Basutoland is granted full internal self government

The first president
Jomo Kenyatta became the first president when Kenya acquired independence in 1964 CE.

Liberia
  1955 Despite efforts to diversify the economy, the Firestone Company still accounts for 40 percent of the country's revenue and 7 percent of its exports

Libya
  1951 Dec 24 Libya becomes an independent kingdom of three federated provinces under emir Sayyid Idris al-Sanusi
  1954 Idris grants the US military and naval bases in Libya
  1959 Oil is discovered in Cyrenaica

Madagascar
  1958 Madagascar gains internal self-government

Malawi
  1958 Hastings Kamuzu Banda becomes leader of the nationalist Malawi Congress Party (MCP)

Mali
  1958 French Sudan gains full internal self-government
  1959 French Sudan and Senegal merge to form the federation of Mali

Mauritania
  1955 The Rigaibat are the last Mauritanian ethnic group to be pacified
  1958 Mauritania is granted powers of internal self-government
  1959 Mokhtar Ould Daddah becomes prime minister of Mauritania

Mauritius
  1957 Mauritius gains internal self-government

Morocco
  1953 France deposes the nationalist sultan Muhammad V and replaces him with his uncle, Moulay Arafa
  1955 Independence negotiations begin between France and Morocco
  1956 Mar 2 Morocco becomes independent: Muhammad V is restored
  1956 Apr Spanish zone (except Ceuta and Melilla) and Tangier are restored to Morocco
  1957 Muhammad V exchanges the title of sultan for king

Mozambique
  1951 Mozambique becomes an overseas province of Portugal

Namibia
  1958 The Ovamboland People's Organization is founded

Niger
  1957 A local legislature is set up under the left-wing trade unionist Djibo Bakary
  1958 Despite Bakary's call for a "no" vote, Niger votes to retain links with France

Nigeria
  1954 A new constitution the third in eight years, establishes the Federation of Nigeria, consisting of the Northern, Eastern, and Western regions

Rwanda
  1959 Gregoire Kayibanda forms the Party for Hutu Emancipation (PARMEHUTU)
  1959 Hutu-Tutsi violence breaks out after the mysterious death of King Mutara III

São Tomè and Príncipe
  1953 The Batepa massacre: troops kill hundreds of striking plantation workers

Senegal
  1956 Senegal is granted internal self-government
  1959 Senegal and the French Sudan join to form the federation of Mali

Seychelles
  1958-1959 The country ceases to be self-supporting

Sierra Leone
  1951 Freetown is united with Sierra Leone and the colony is granted internal self-government
  1952 Milton Margai becomes prime minister of Sierra Leone

Senegal
  1959 Senegal joined with Mali to form the Federation of Mali

Somalia
  1950 The UN returns Italian Somaliland to Italy for a ten year period to prepare it for independence

First president (1960–78 CE)
Mokhtar Ould Daddah (left), the first president of Mauritania, is shown here with President Charles De Gaulle of France.

The apartheid regime
During the time that apartheid was
practiced in South Africa, separate
facilities, such as train platforms,
had to be provided for different
races.

South Africa
1953 The Bantu Education Act denies the right of blacks to study at white universities
1955 The ANC's Freedom Charter provokes a government crackdown on leftwing organizations
1956 The Tomlinson Report produces a blueprint for apartheid; it advocates that the 264 scattered reserves for Bantu-speaking people be grouped into Bantustans
1959 The right of Africans to elect white representatives to parliament is removed

Sudan
1951 King Farouk of Egypt declares himself King of Sudan
1953 Britain and Egypt grant self-government to Sudan
1955 The Sudanese parliament votes for independence
1956 Jan 1 Sudan becomes an independent republic
1958 Gen. Ibrahim Abboud becomes president after a military coup

Swaziland
1950 Sobhuza II, then Paramount Chief, is granted increased powers over his people

Tanzania
1954 Julius Nyerere forms the Tanganyika African National Union (TANU)
1958 Tanganyika is granted internal self-government

Togo
1956 British Togoland votes to join Gold Coast (now Ghana)

Tunisia
1955 France grants Tunisia internal self-government
1956 Mar 20 Tunisia becomes independent under the bey of Tunis
1957 Tunisia becomes a republic when the bey abdicates, Bourguiba is elected the first president of Tunisia

Uganda
1953 *Kabaka* (King) Mutesa II of Buganda is exiled to Britain for refusing to support a British constitutional plan
1954 A hydroelectric dam is built at Owen Falls
1955 Mutesa is allowed to return to Uganda after Britain shelves its constitutional plans
1956 Copper mining begins at Kilembe

Zambia
1953 Britain forms the Central African Federation of Northern Rhodesia, Southern Rhodesia (now Zimbabwe) and Nyasaland (now Malawi)
1959 Kenneth Kaunda is jailed for nationalist activities

Zimbabwe
1953 Britain forms the Central African Federation from Southern Rhodesia, Northern Rhodesia and Nyasal and (now Malawi)
1958 The prime minister Garfield Todd is forced from office after he attempts to end segregationist policies

**Protesting against
nuclear tests**
The decision by the French
authorities to test nuclear
weapons in southern Algeria met
with resistance in 1960 CE.

1960–1969 CE

Algeria
1960 Rebellion of French settlers suppressed
1962 July 3 Algeria becomes independent of France after a referendum
1963 Muhammad Ben Bella of the FLN becomes president
1963 Short border war with Morocco
1964 Ben Bella suppresses an attempted military coup
1965 Military coup overthrows Ben Bella; Boumédienne becomes president
1968 Boumedienne survives an assassination attempt

Angola
1961 An MPLA uprising in Luanda is defeated by the Portuguese
1962 Northern Angolan rebels organize the Front for the Liberation of Angola (FNLA)
1966 Southern Angolan rebels form the National Union for the Total Liberation of Angola (UNITA)

Benin
1960 Aug 1 Dahomey becomes a fully independent republic
1960–1972 Frequent changes of government due to military coups

Botswana
1960 Bechuanaland is granted a legislative assembly
1961 Seretse Khama forms the Bechuanaland (later Botswana) Democratic Party (BDP)
1964 A new administrative capital is built at Gaborone
1965 Britain grants Bechuanaland internal self-government
1966 Sept 30 Bechuanaland becomes independent as the Republic of Botswana. Seretse Khama becomes the first president
1967 Diamonds discovered at Orapa
1969 The national assembly re-elects Seretse Khama as president

Burkina Faso
1960 Aug 5 Upper Volta becomes independent: Maurice Yaméogo becomes president
1966 Yaméogo is overthrown by a military coup: Gen. Sangoulé Lamizana becomes president

Burundi
1961 Urundi votes to separate from Ruanda–Urundi and become the independent kingdom of Burundi
1962 July 1 Burundi becomes independent
1966 Burundi becomes a republic

Cameroon
1960 Jan 1 French Cameroon becomes the independent Republic of Cameroon. Alhaji Ahmadou Ahidjo of the UPC becomes president
1961 The southern part of British Cameroons and the Republic of Cameroon combine to form the Federal Republic of Cameroon. Northern British Cameroon votes to join Nigeria
1962 A UPC rebellion is put down by the Ahidjo regime
1966 Ahidjo forms the Cameroon National Union (CNU): all other parties are banned

Cape Verde
1961 Guerrilla warfare breaks out

Central African Republic (CAR)
1960 Aug 13 Oubangoui–Shari becomes independent as CAR: David Dacko becomes the first president
1962 Dacko makes the country a one party state
1966 Gen. Jean-Bédel Bokassa seizes power in a military coup

Chad
1960 Aug 11 Chad becomes independent of France: François Tombalbaye is the first president
1962 Chad becomes a one-party state
1965 Civil war breaks out after northern rebels form the *Front de Libération National du Tchad* (FROLINAT)

Comoros
1961 France grants the Comoros internal self-government

Congo, Democratic Repuclic of
1960 Jun 30 Congo becomes an independent republic under Joseph Kasavubu
1960 July Katanga province secedes
1960 Sept Kasavubu dismisses and jails his prime minister Patrice Lumumba
1961 Lumumba is murdered in Katanga
1963 Katanga is forcibly reunited with the rest of the country
1964 White mercenaries used to suppress widespread rebellions
1965 Gen. Joseph-Désiré Mobutu becomes president after a military coup
1966 Mobutu abolishes the office of prime minister
1967 Mobutu nationalizes the copper mining industry

Congo, Peoples Republic of
1960 Aug 15 Congo becomes an independent republic: Fulbert Youlou becomes the first president
1963 Labor uprising overturns the Youlou government
1964 Congo becomes a one party state
1965 US breaks off diplomatic relations after its consular staff are mistreated
1969 A group of army officers under Capt. Marien Ngouabi seizes power

Djibouti
1967 French Somaliland votes to remain a French territory and is renamed the French Territory of the Afars and Issas

Egypt
1960 Construction begins on the Aswan High Dam
1961 Syria withdraws from the UAR

Sir Sereste Khama
Having founded the Bechuanaland (later Botswana) Democratic party in 1961 CE, he later became its first president upon gaining independence in 1966 CE.

Patrice Lumumba
A former prime minister of Democratic Republic of Congo, he was first jailed by Joseph Kasavubu in 1960 CE, then murdered in Katanga in 1961 CE.

© DIAGRAM

1967 Egypt, Syria and Jordan defeated by Israel in the Six Day War
1968 Aswan High Dam completed

Equatorial Guinea
1968 Oct 12 The country becomes independent as Equatorial Guinea: Macias Nguema becomes the first president

Eritrea
1961 Civil war breaks out between the Eritrean Liberation Front (ELF) and the Ethiopian government

Ethiopia
1961 Eritrean rebels begin a war of independence
1962 Ethiopia formally annexes Eritrea

Gabon
1960 Aug 17 Gabon becomes independent: Leon Mba is the first president
1964 An attempt to overthrow Mba is crushed by French troops
1967 Mba dies in office: he is succeeded by Bernard-Albert Bongo
1968 Bongo declares Gabon a one party state

Gambia
1963 Gambia gains full internal self-government
1965 Feb 18 Gambia becomes independent

Ghana
1960 Ghana becomes a republic: Kwame Nkrumah becomes the first president
1965 The Akosombo dam begins production of hydroelectric power
1966 Nkrumah is ousted by a military coup: Gen. Joseph Ankrah becomes head of government
1969 Ankrah resigns and is replaced by Brigadier Akwasi Amankwa Afrifa who restores civilian rule

Guinea
1961 Guinea expels the Soviet ambassador, accusing him of interfering in its internal affairs
1963 Guinea restores relations with France

Guinea-Bissau
1963 PAIGC begins a war of independence

Ivory Coast
1960 Aug 7 Ivory Coast becomes independent: Houphouët-Boigny becomes the first president
1963 An attempted military coup is defeated

Kenya
1961 Kenya African National Union (KANU) wins elections to a new parliament but it refuses to take office unless its leader Kenyatta is released from jail. Kenya African Democratic Union (KADU) takes office instead
1963 Dec 12 Kenya becomes independent with Kenyatta as prime minister
1964 Kenya becomes a republic with Kenyatta as president. KADU merges with KANU to make Kenya a one party state
1966 A new opposition party, the Kenya People's Union (KPU) is formed
1967 Kenya, Tanzania and Uganda form the East African Community
1969 Kenyatta dissolves the KPU

Lesotho
1960 Basutoland is given its first constitution
1964 The constitution is revised to provide for a constitutional monarchy
1965 In general elections under the new constitution, Chief Leabua Jonathan of the Basutoland National Party (BNP) becomes prime minister. Paramount chief Motlotlehi Moshoeshoe II becomes king
1966 Oct 4 Basutoland becomes the independent kingdom of Lesotho

Liberia
1960 Liberia offers a "flag of convenience" to costcutting ship owners
1964 The US transfers ownership of the port of Monrovia to the Liberian government

Libya
1963 The provinces are abolished as Libya becomes a unitary state
1969 Emir Idris is overthrown by a military coup: Col. Muammar al-Qaddafi becomes head of state and introduces radical socialist policies

Madagascar
1960 Jun 26 Madagascar becomes independent and becomes known as the Malagasy Republic: Philibert

Kwame Nkrumah
He became the first president of the Republic of Ghana upon its independence in 1960 CE, but was later overthrown in a military coup in 1966 CE.

Tsiranana is the first president
1965 Tsiranana is re-elected president

Malawi
1964 Jul 6 Nyasaland becomes independent as Malawi: Banda becomes prime minister
1966 Malawi becomes a one-party state: Banda becomes president

Mali
1960 Jun 20 The federation of Mali becomes independent
1960 Aug 20 Senegal leaves the federation
1960 Sept 22 The independent Republic of Mali is proclaimed: Modibo Keita is the first president
1968 Keita is overthrown by a military coup. Gen. Moussa Traoré becomes head of government

Mauritania
1960 Nov 28 Mauritania becomes independent
1961 Ould Daddah is elected as the first president of Mauritania
1965 Mauritania becomes a one party state

Mauritius
1968 Mar 12 Mauritius becomes independent with Sir Seewoosagur Ramgoolam as prime minister

Morocco
1961 Death of Muhammad V: succeeded by his son, Hassan II
1963 Morocco repels Algerian cross-border raids
1965 Riots in Casablanca lead King Hassan to assume direct rule
1965 Hassan II orders the kidnapping from France and murder of opposition politician Ben Barka

Mozambique
1960 An independence demonstration in Muenda is crushed leaving 500 dead
1961 Front for the Liberation of Mozambique (FRELIMO) guerrilla movement founded to fight for independence
1964 FRELIMO gains control of northern Mozambique
1969 The moderate president Eduardo Mondlane of FRELIMO is assassinated: he is replaced by the Marxist Samora Machel

Namibia
1960 The Ovamboland People's Organization changes its name to South West Africa People's Organization (SWAPO)
1966 The UN votes to end South Africa's mandate in Southwest Africa. SWAPO begins a guerrilla war for independence
1967 The UN appoints a council to oversee Southwest Africa's transition to independence
1968 At SWAPO's request, the UN changes the name of Southwest Africa to Namibia
1969 South Africa ignores a UN ultimatum to withdraw from Namibia

Niger
1960 Aug 3 Niger becomes independent: Hamani Diori becomes the first president
1968-1973 A long drought devastates agriculture

Nigeria
1960 Oct 1 Nigeria becomes independent of Britain
1963 Nigeria declares itself a republic
1966 Military takes over the Nigerian government: Lt. Col. Gowon becomes leader of Nigeria
1967 May 30 Eastern Region under Ojukwu declares independence as Biafra: civil war breaks out

Rwanda
1960 The Hutus win control of local legislature in elections
1961 Ruanda votes to become an independent republic, Urundi to become an independent kingdom (Burundi)
1962 July 1 Rwanda becomes independent. The Hutu leader Kayibanda, becomes president
1965 Kayibanda is re-elected president
1969 Kayibanda is elected to a third term as president

São Tomè and Príncipe
1960 The Committee for the Liberation of São Tomé and Principe is formed

Senegal
1960 Jun 20 The federation of Mali becomes independent
1960 Aug 20 Senegal withdraws from the federation and becomes the republic of Senegal: Senghor is the first president

Hassan II of Morocco
In 1961 CE, Muhammad V of Morocco died unexpectedly and was succeeded by his son, Hassan II.

Lt. Col. Yakubu Gowon
In 1966 CE he led a military takeover of the government, then assumed the leadership of the country during the Biafran (Nigerian Civil) War, which lasted from 1967–70 CE.

© DIAGRAM

1962 The prime minister Mamadou Dia attempts unsuccessfully to overthrow president Senghor
1963 Senghor abolishes the office of prime minister
1966 Senegal becomes a one party state

Seychelles
1964 The Seychelles Democratic Party, which opposed independence for the islands, and the leftwing Seychelles People's United Party are formed

Sierra Leone
1961 Apr 27 Sierra Leone becomes independent with Milton Margai as prime minister
1964 After the death of Margai, political instability sets in
1967 An indecisive general election is followed by a military coup
1968 The military government is overthrown: Siaka Stevens becomes head of government

Somalia
1960 Jun 26 British Somaliland becomes independent
1960 Jul 1 The two Somali territories unite to form the independent Republic of Somalia
1969 President Shermarke is assassinated during a military coup: Maj. Gen. Mohammad Siad Barre becomes president

South Africa
1960 The Sharpeville Massacre: a PAC demonstration in which police kill 69 blacks protesting against restrictive pass laws: the ANC is banned
1961 South Africa becomes a republic and leaves the Commonwealth
1961 The ANC abandons its non-violence policy and forms an armed wing under Nelson Mandela
1962 Nelson Mandela is jailed for sabotage and treason
1966 The prime minister Hendrik Verwoerd is murdered

Sudan
1964 General strike forces the military government to step down. A rebellion breaks out in the Christian southern provinces
1969 Col. Gaafar Nimeiri seizes power after a military coup

Swaziland
1964 The royalist Imbokodvo party wins elections to a newly created legislature
1967 Swaziland is granted internal self-government
1968 Sept 6 Swaziland becomes an independent constitutional monarchy under King Sobhuza II

Tanzania
1961 Dec 9 Tanganyika becomes independent
1962 Julius Nyerere is elected president
1963 Dec 10 Zanzibar is granted independence
1964 Apr 26 Tanganyika and Zanzibar merge to form the United Republic of Tanzania
1965 Nyerere merges TANU with Zanzibar's Afro-Shirazi party to form the Chama Cha Mapinduzi (CCM) party: it becomes the only legal political party
1967 Tanzania, Kenya and Uganda form the East African Community

Togo
1960 Apr 27 French Togoland becomes the independent republic of Togo: Sylvanus Olympio becomes the first president
1963 Olympio is assassinated by rebel army officers who make Nicolas Grunitzky president
1967 Grunitzky is overthrown by a military coup led by Gnassingbé Eyadéma
1969 Eyadéma creates the Rally of Togolese People (RPT) and makes it Togo's only legal party

Tunisia
1961 Fighting breaks out when France attempts to expand its naval base at Bizerte without Tunisian permission
1962 France withdraws from its bases in Tunisia
1963 Bourguiba's Democratic Socialist Rally (formerly the *Neo-Detour* Party) becomes the only legal party
1964 Land owned by Europeans is nationalized

Uganda
1962 Oct 9 Uganda becomes independent: Apollo Milton Obote becomes prime minister
1963 Mutesa II is elected president
1966 Obote dismisses Mutesa and makes himself president under a new constitution
1967 Uganda becomes a republic and the traditional kingdoms are abolished. Uganda, Kenya and Tanzania form the East-African Community

Hendrik Verwoerd
Prime minister of South Africa from 1958 CE, he was murdered in 1966 CE amidst increasing levels of civil unrest. He was popularly known as the "architect of apartheid" for his efforts to enforce the policy.

Julius Nyerere
A leading campaigner for independence from colonial rule, he was elected president of a newly independent Tanzania in 1962.

Zambia
1960 Kenneth Kaunda becomes leader of the United National Independence Party (UNIP)
1961 UNIP is outlawed
1963 Britain dissolves the Central African Federation
1964 Oct 24 Northern Rhodesia becomes independent as Zambia: Kenneth Kaunda becomes president

Zimbabwe
1960 Africans form the National Democratic Party (NDP)
1962 The white supremacist Rhodesian Front (RF) wins control of the legislature in whites-only elections
1963 The Central African Federation is dissolved
1963 The NDP splits into Zimbabwe African Peoples' Union (ZAPU) under Joshua Nkomo and the Zimbabwe African national Union (ZANU) under Ndabaningi Sithole
1964 Ian Smith becomes leader of the RF
1965 Nov 11 Smith issues a unilateral declaration of independence (UDI), illegally proclaiming "Rhodesia" independent
1966 The battle of Chinhoyi begins a guerrilla war by Africans

Kenneth Kaunda
A former leader of the United National Independence Party (UNIP), he became president of Zambia upon its independence in 1964 CE, and served in office until 1991 CE when he was defeated in multiparty elections

1970–1979 CE

Algeria
1970 The French withdraw from their last military base in Algeria
1971 French oil concessions nationalized
1976 Boumedienne introduces a new constitution
1978 Boumedienne dies of a rare blood disease
1979 Chadli Bendjedid of the FLN becomes president after an election in which he is the only candidate

Angola
1974 Portugal announces its intention to withdraw from Angola. Civil war breaks out between MPLA, FNLA and UNITA. Cuban troops arrive to support MPLA, South Africans give aid to UNITA.
1975 Nov 11 Angola becomes independent of Portugal: MPLA unilaterally forms a government at Luanda
1976 The UN recognizes the MPLA as the legitimate government of Angola
1977 Attempted coup by dissidents within the MPLA

Benin
1972 Gen. Mathieu Kérékou becomes president after a military coup
1975 Dahomey is renamed Benin. Marxist-Leninist policies introduced

Botswana
1974 Program of agricultural improvements permits enclosure of grazing land
1977 The first all-weather road between Botswana and Zambia is completed

Burkina Faso
1977 Elections are held under a new multiparty constitution
1978 Lamizana is elected president

Burundi
1972 An unsuccessful Hutu revolt results in about 100,000 deaths

Cameroon
1972 Cameroon becomes a unitary (i.e. non-federal) state
1977 Cameroon becomes an oil exporting country

Cape Verde
1975 Cape Verde Islands become independent of Portugal: Aristides Pereira of PAIGC becomes president

Central African Republic
1972 Bokassa becomes president for life
1976 Bokassa appoints himself emperor and renames CAR the Central African Empire
1979 Bokassa is overthrown by a French supported coup

Chad
1971 Libya begins to support FROLINAT rebels
1972 FROLINAT forces advance to within a few miles of the capital N'Djamena
1973 Libya occupies the Aouzou strip in northern Chad
1975 President Tombalbaye is killed during a military coup: Gen. Félix Malloum becomes president
1979 Efforts to establish a government of national unity end in failure

Gen. Félix Malloum
He became leader of the Supreme Military Council following the overthrow of President Tombalbaye in a military coup in Chad in 1975 CE.

© DIAGRAM

Comoros

1974 Anjouan, Grande Comore and Mohéli vote for independence, Mayotte votes to remain a French colony

1975 Jul 6 The Comoros become independent under president Ahmad Abdullah who is soon overthrown in a coup

1978 President Abdullah is returned to power with the aid of foreign mercenaries

Congo, Democratic Republic of

1970 Mobutu declares the country a one party state

1971 Congo is renamed Zaire, the capital Léopoldville is renamed Kinshasa

1973 Over 2,000 foreign-owned businesses are seized by the government and handed over to Zairians

1974 Mobutu's Popular Revolutionary Movement is made the "sole institution of society"

1976 International Monetary Fund (IMF) backs an economic stabilization plan

1977 Rebellion in Shaba province (formerly Katanga) is put down with French assistance

1978 A second rebellion in Shaba province is put down with French assistance

Congo, Republic of

1970 Congo declares itself a Marxist country and is renamed People's Republic of Congo

1972 President Ngouabi defeats an attempted coup

1977 Ngouabi is assassinated: Col. Jaochim Yhombi-Opanga succeeds

1979 Yhombi-Opango resigns: Col. Denis Sassou-Nguesso becomes president

Djibouti

1977 Jun 27 Afars and Issas become the independent republic of Djibouti after a referendum: Hassan Gouled Aptidon becomes the first president

1979 The Afar Popular Liberation Movement is banned

Egypt

1970 Death of Nasser: Anwar el-Sadat succeeds him as president

1973 Egypt and Syria are defeated by Israel in the Yom Kippur War

1977 Sadat visits Jerusalem to begin Egyptian-Israeli rapprochement

1978 Camp David accords agreed between Egypt and Israel

1979 Egypt and Israel sign a peace treaty

Equatorial Guinea

1970 A one party dictatorship is declared

1979 Lt.-Col. Teodoro Obiang Nguema Mbasango seizes power in a military coup: Macias Nguema is executed

Eritrea

1970 Eritrean People's Liberation Front (EPLF) rbecomes the main Eritrean resistance movement

Ethiopia

1972-1974 Prolonged drought leads to devastating famine

1974 Emperor Haile Selassie overthrown by a military coup: Lt.-Col. Mengistu Haile-Mariam becomes president and adopts Marxist policies

1974 An insurrection breaks out in Tigre province

1975 Haile Selassie dies in prison

1977 Somalia invades the disputed Ogaden region of Ethiopia

Gabon

1973 Bongo is re-elected president and changes his name to El Hadj Omar Bongo

1974 Construction of the Trans-Gabon railroad begins

1975 Gabon becomes a member of OPEC

1977 Gabon supports an unsuccessful military coup in Benin

1979 Bongo is re-elected president in elections in which he is the only candidate

Gambia

1970 Gambia becomes a republic: Dawda Jawara becomes the first president

1970 Development of tourist industry begins

Ghana

1972 Col. I. K. Acheampong becomes head of government after a military coup

1978 Acheampong resigns and is replaced by Gen. Frederick Kwasi Akuffo

1979 Akuffo is overthrown by a coup led by Lieut. Jerry Rawlings. Afrifa, Acheampong and Akuffo are executed and a civilian government is elected

Guinea

1970 An attempted invasion by exiled Guineans and Portuguese troops fails

Yom Kippur War, 1973 CE
Egypt and Syria attacked Israel, hoping to regain territorial borders lost in 1967 CE, but were defeated by Israel within a matter of weeks.

Haile Selassie
Emperor of Ethiopia from 1930 CE until the army deposed him in 1975 CE, he died in prison in 1975. Although he sought to introduce reforms, many felt that the rate of change was too slow.

Guinea-Bissau
1974 Sept 10 Portuguese Guinea becomes independent as the state of Guinea-Bissau: Luiz Cabral is the first president

Ivory Coast
1973 Another attempted military coup is defeated

Kenya
1975 Josiah Mwangi Kariuki, a leading critic of the Kenyatta government, is assassinated
1977 The East Africa Community is dissolved
1978 Kenyatta dies and is succeeded as president by Daniel arap Moi

Lesotho
1970 Chief Jonathan suspends the constitution after early election returns show the BNP is about to lose power

Liberia
1971 Tubman dies: he is succeeded as president by William R. Tolbert
1979 Increase in the price of rice causes rioting against Americo-Liberian political domination

Libya
1973 Qaddafi sets up a system of local, regional and national popularly elected congresses
1973 Libya occupies the Aozou strip in northern Chad
1977 Qaddafi declares Libya a one-party socialist *jamahiriya* ("state of the masses")

Madagascar
1971 An opposition party rebellion in southern Madagascar is crushed
1972 Mass demonstrations force Tsiranana to resign: the army takes power under Gen. Gabriel Ramanantsoa
1975 President Didier Ratsiraka nationalizes foreign-owned business and changes the country's name to Madagascar

Malawi
1970 Banda becomes president for life

Mali
1974 Traoré makes Mali a one party state

Mauritania
1976 Mauritania and Morocco take over administration of Western Sahara (formerly Spanish Sahara)
1978 Ould Daddah is overthrown by a military coup
1979 Mauritania gives up its claim to Western Sahara and withdraws from the territory

Mauritius
1972 A state of emergency is declared because of ethnic tension
1978 The state of emergency is ended

Morocco
1976 On Spanish withdrawal, Morocco and Mauritania partition Western Sahara (formerly Spanish Sahara)
1979 Mauritania cedes its claims in Western Sahara to the Polisario independence fighters
1979 Morocco claims sovereignty over all of Western Sahara and builds a fortified wall through it

Mozambique
1974 Portugal agrees to grant independence to Mozambique
1975 Jun 25 Mozambique becomes independent: Samora Machel becomes president
1976 Mozambique closes its border with Rhodesia (now Zimbabwe). Rhodesia forms the Mozambique National Resistance (RENAMO) to undermine the FRELIMO regime
1977 FRELIMO signs a friendship agreement with the Communist Party of the USSR

Samora Machel
A founder of the FRELIMO independence movement, he became president when Mozambique became independent in 1975 CE.

Namibia
1971 The International Court of Justice declares South Africa's occupation of Southwest Africa to be illegal
1973 UN recognizes SWAPO as the legitimate representative of the Namibians
1975 SWAPO sets up bases in Angola after it becomes independent from Portugal
1977 South Africa announces a plan to make Namibia independent under a white dominated government
1978 SWAPO boycotts South African organized elections

Niger
1971 Uranium mining begins in Niger
1974 Military coup ousts Diori: Seyni Kountché becomes president

© DIAGRAM

Chukwuemeka Ojukwu
He was the leader of Biafra during the Biafran (Nigerian Civil) War which lasted from 1967–70 CE. He went into exile after the failure of the rebellion.

Nigeria
1970 Jan 12 Biafra surrenders, ending the civil war
1975 Gowon is replaced by Gen. Murtala Muhammad in a bloodless coup
1976 Feb Gen. Muhammad is killed in a failed coup attempt: Lt. Gen. Olesegun Obasanjo succeeds as leader
1978 May Obasanjo approves a democratic presidential constitution to go into effect in 1979
1979 Aug Alhaji Shehu Shagari's National Party of Nigeria wins federal elections
1979 Oct Obasanjo resigns: Shagari takes office as president

Rwanda
1973 Kayibanda is ousted by a military coup: Hutu Maj. Gen. Juvenal Habyarimana becomes president
1978 Rwanda becomes a one party state

São Tomè and Príncipe
1975 July 12 São Tomé and Principe become independent: Manuel Pinto da Costa becomes president

Senegal
1970 The office of prime minister is restored by a referendum
1974 Political parties are legalized

Seychelles
1976 Jun 29 The Seychelles become independent: James Mancham is the first president
1977 France Albert René becomes president after a military coup
1979 René's Marxist Seychelles People's Progressive Front (SPPF) becomes the only legal party

Sierra Leone
1971 Sierra Leone becomes a republic with Stevens as president
1978 Sierra Leone becomes a one party state

Somalia
1974 War breaks out between Somalia and Ethiopia over the Ogaden region
1976 Siad Barre sets up the Somali Revolutionary Socialist Party as the only legal political party
1977 Somalia occupies the Ogaden
1978 Ethiopia recovers the Ogaden
1979 Drought results in food shortages

South Africa
1976 Over 600 blacks killed by police during the Soweto uprising

Sudan
1971 Nimeiri becomes president of Sudan
1972 Nimeiri gives the southern provinces an autonomous regional government ending the rebellion
1973 Nimeiri's Sudanese Socialist Union (SSU) becomes the only legal political party

Swaziland
1973 King Sobhuza suspends the constitution and assumes direct rule
1979 King Sobhuza appoints a new legislature but retains the power of veto

Tanzania
1975 Tan-Zam (Tanzania-Zambia) railroad is completed
1977 Internal differences cause the collapse of the East African Community
1978 Tanzania defeats a Ugandan invasion
1979 Tanzanian troops help overthrow the Ugandan dictator Idi Amin

Gaafar Nimeiri
A professional soldier, he seized power in Sudan after a military coup in 1969 CE, and served as president until he himself was deposed in a coup in 1985 CE.

Togo
1974 Eyadéma nationalizes the French-owned phosphate industry
1979 A new constitution is approved; Eyadéma proclaims the third Togolese republic

Tunisia
1975 Bourguiba becomes president for life
1978 A general strike is broken by the army

Uganda
1971 Obote is overthrown by a military coup: Maj. Gen. Idi Amin Dada becomes president
1972 Amin expels 50,000 Asians and confiscates their assets
1978 Uganda invades Tanzania following a border dispute
1979 Ugandan rebels, aided by Tanzanian troops, overthrow Amin's government

Zambia
1970 The Zambian government acquires a controlling interest in the copper mining industry

1972 UNIP becomes the only legal party
1973 The white government of Rhodesia (Zimbabwe) closes its border with Zambia
1975 A railroad from the Copperbelt to the Indian Ocean at Dar-es-Salam (Tanzania) is built with Chinese help

Zimbabwe
1971 Bishop Abel Muzorewa forms the United African National Council (UANC)
1976 Nkomo and Robert Mugabe, the new leader of ZANU, unite to form the Patriotic Front (PF)
1979 After a RF alliance with the UANC fails to bring peace, Rhodesia reverts to colonial status

1980–1989 CE

Algeria
1989 Algeria, Morocco and Tunisia form the Arab Maghrib Union

Angola
1981 South African forces advance 100 miles (160 km) into Angola to support UNITA
1984 FNLA withdraws from military operations
1986 US begins to send aid to UNITA
1988 Cuba and South Africa agree to stop aiding the MPLA and UNITA
1989 MPLA and UNITA agree to a cease-fire

Benin
1989 Marxist-Leninist ideology is abandoned

Botswana
1980 Seretse Khama dies, Dr Ketumile Masire succeeds as head of the BDP
1982 Drought causes serious losses of livestock
1984 The BDP wins the first elections after Khama's death
1985 South Africa withdraws from a non-aggression treaty with Botswana
1986 South African army raid on Gaborone
1987 South Africa blockades the capital Gaborone
1989 South African covert operations against African National Congress (ANC) refugees cause tension

Burkina Faso
1980 Lamizana is overthrown by a military coup
1983 Capt. Thomas Sankara becomes president: he changes the name of the country to Burkina Faso
1987 Sankara is assassinated during a military coup: Capt. Blaise Campaoré becomes president

Burundi
1987 President Jean-Baptiste Bagaza is removed from office in a bloodless coup
1988 A Hutu uprising occurs; about 5,000 people are killed and many flee to neighboring countries

Cameroon
1981 Cameroon and Nigeria dispute the ownership of offshore oilfields; the dispute is resolved by the Organization of African Unity (OAU)
1982 Paul Biya becomes president when Ahidjo retires because of poor health

Cape Verde
1980 Plans for a union with Guinea-Bissau are dropped
1981 PAIGC changes its name to *Partido Africano de la Independência da Cabo Verde* (PAICV)

Central African Republic
1987 Bokassa is imprisoned for murder and embezzlement

Chad
1980 Libya proposes a union between the two countries
1982 Hissène Habré becomes president
1984 Famine due to prolonged drought
1986 FROLINAT-Libyan alliance breaks down
1987 The government establishes its authority in the north, except for the Libyan occupied Aozou strip

Comoros
1989 President Abdullah is assassinated

Congo, Democratic Republic of
1980 Zaire's national debt is rescheduled

Jean-Bédel Bokassa
He seized power in 1966 CE, and served as president until 1976 CE when he proclaimed himself "Emperor of the Central African Empire." He was eventually jailed for murder and fraud, and died of a heart attack in 1996 CE.

1984 Mobutu is re-elected president in elections in which he is the only candidate
1986 CIA uses Zaire as a base for supplying arms to UNITA rebels in Angola
1989 Mobutu visits the US and obtains a loan of $20 million from the World Bank

Congo, Republic of
1988 Conference in Brazzaville paves the way for Namibia's independence

Djibouti
1981 Djibouti becomes a one party state
1988 Ethiopia and Somalia recognize Djibouti's borders
1989 Fighting breaks out between Afars and Issas in Djibouti city and Tadjourah

Egypt
1981 President Sadat is assassinated: Hosni Mubarak succeeds him as president

Equatorial Guinea
1985 Equatorial Guinea joins the franc zone
1987 A single new political party, the Democratic Party of Equatorial Guinea, is formed

Eritrea
1987–1988 EPLF victories end Ethiopian control in Eritrea

Ethiopia
1984–1987 Prolonged drought causes famine on a massive scale
1988 Ethiopia and Somalia sign a peace treaty
1989 Mengistu agrees to hold peace talks with the Eritrean and Tigrean rebels but refuses their demands

Gabon
1982 The opposition National Reorientation Movement is suppressed
1984 Bongo gives France permission to build a nuclear plant in Gabon
1986 Bongo is again re-elected president in elections in which he is the only candidate
1989 Riots follow the murder of Joseph Redjambe, the leader of the Gabonese Progressive Party, in Libreville
1990 Opposition parties are legalized: the ruling Gabonese Democratic party wins the assembly elections

Gambia
1980 Libya is implicated in an attempt to overthrow the government
1981 A military coup is defeated with the aid of Senegal
1982 Gambia and Senegal form the confederation of Senegambia with joint armed forces
1985 Jawara refuses to sign a treaty promoting closer ties with Senegal
1989 The confederation of Senegambia is dissolved after dispute between Gambia and Senegal

Ghana
1981 Rawlings seizes control of the government in another coup: political parties are outlawed
1983 A housing crisis follows the expulsion of one million Ghanaian migrant workers from Nigeria

Guinea
1984 On the death of Touré, the army under Col. Lansana Conté seizes power

Guinea-Bissau
1980 Cabral overthrown by a military coup: Maj. João Bernardo Vieira becomes president
1984 A new constitution creates a National People's Assembly and Council of State

Ivory Coast
1980 An attempted military coup is defeated
1981–1985 An agricultural recession causes rapid growth of the national debt
1983 Work starts on a new capital at Yamoussoukro (Houphouët-Boigny's birthplace)
1987 Economy badly hit by 50 percent fall in the price of cocoa
1989 The largest Christian church in the world is completed at Yamoussoukro

Kenya
1982 A new constitution makes KANU the only legal party
1982 A failed military coup is accompanied by widespread rioting and looting
1987 Islamic fundamentalists demonstrate in Mombasa

Lesotho
1983 South African saboteurs attempt to destroy the country's main power plant
1986 Chief Jonathan is overthrown by a South African-backed military coup. Maj. Gen. Justin Lekhanya becomes head of government

Death of President Sadat
In 1981 CE, he was assassinated by Islamic fundamentalist gunmen in Cairo during a military parade. He is best remembered for his peace initiative that led to the Camp David peace treaty, signed in 1979 CE, which ended the conflict between Egypt and Israel.

Jerry Rawlings
He first seized power in Ghana in a peaceful coup in 1979 CE, but ruled for only 112 days before restoring civilian government. His second coup in 1981 CE lost him some support, but he was eventually elected president in 1992 CE.

Liberia
1980 Tolbert is killed during a military coup: master sergeant Samuel K. Doe of the Khran tribe becomes president
1984 Under US pressure Doe announces a multiparty constitution
1985 Doe and his National Democratic Party win multiparty elections amid allegations of vote rigging
1986 Doe survives an assassination attempt
1988 Doe gives US financial experts coauthority over the national budget
1989 A former Doe supporter, Charles Taylor invades from Ivory Coast

Libya
1980 Qaddafi proposes a union between Libya and Chad
1981 US downs two Libyan jets over the Gulf of Sirte
1986 US aircraft bomb Tripoli and Benghazi in response for Libyan support for international terrorism
1989 Libya joins the Arab Maghrib Union

Madagascar
1982 Ratsiraka is re-elected president
1983 Ratsiraka introduces measures to liberalize the economy

Malawi
1986 Banda refuses to break Malawi's friendly links with South Africa
1987 The Malawi Congress Party wins all 107 elected seats in the National Assembly
1988 South Africa's President P. W. Botha visits Malawi and agrees to reschedule Malawi's debts to South Africa

Mali
1985 Mali fights a five-day war with Burkina Faso over a 25-year dispute concerning the possession of the mineral-rich Agacher Strip; a ceasefire is signed in December
1987 The International Court of Justice rules that the Agacher Strip should be divided between Mali and Burkina Faso

Mauritania
1980 After a long period of political uncertainty, Muhammad Ould Haidalla becomes head of government
1984 Col. Maawiya Ould Taya becomes president in a bloodless coup
1989 Inter-ethnic violence breaks out on the border with Senegal

Mauritius
1982 The Militant Mauritian Movement wins elections and Aneerood Jugnauth becomes prime minister
1983 Jugnauth forms the Socialist Party of Mauritius which wins new elections

Morocco
1987 Hassan II calls on Spain to return Ceuta and Melilla
1989 Morocco joins other North African states in the Arab Maghrib Union

Mozambique
1980 South Africa begins supporting RENAMO after the white government of Rhodesia falls
1984 Mozambique and South Africa sign a non-aggression pact
1986 President Machel is killed in a plane crash, Joaquim Chissano becomes president
1989 Mozambique officially renounces Marxist policies

Namibia
1988 After victories by Angolan-led SWAPO forces, South Africa agrees to make Namibia independent by 1990
1989 South Africa and SWAPO agree a cease-fire

Niger
1983 An attempted military coup is defeated
1984 Nigeria closes its borders with Niger causing economic hardship
1986 Nigeria reopens its borders
1987 On the death of Kountché, Col. Ali Saibou becomes president
1989 Saibou is elected president in elections in which he is the only candidate

Nigeria
1983 Dec Shagari's government is overthrown by a military coup: Maj. Gen. Muhammad Buhari becomes president
1985 Mar The military government expels 700,000 aliens
1985 Aug Buhari overthrown by Maj. Gen. Ibrahim Babangida
1986 Jul 40 students killed in protests against the military government

Samuel K. Doe
A former army master sergeant, he seized power after a military coup in Liberia in 1980 CE in which president William Tolbert was assassinated.

Muammar al Qaddafi
His support for radical movements abroad such as the Black Panthers in the United States, and the Irish Republican Army (IRA) in Northern Ireland, resulted in the bombing of the Libyan cities of Tripoli and Benghazi by the US in 1986 CE.

© DIAGRAM

1988 Mar–Apr Elections for local and national government prepare for return of civilian government

Rwanda
1980 Habyarimana purges the ruling party, PARMEHUTU
1983 President Habyarimana is re-elected unopposed

São Tomè and Príncipe
1988 President Manuel da Costa modifies his government's socialist policies and accepts a reform package from the International Monetary Fund (IMF)

Senegal
1981 President Senghor resigns: the prime minister Abdou Diouf becomes president
1982 Senegal and Gambia form the confederation of Senegambia
1983 Diouf is re-elected to the presidency
1989 Gambia withdraws from Senegambia. Fighting breaks out on the border with Mauritania

Seychelles
1981 A coup attempt by foreign mercenaries is defeated

Sierra Leone
1985 Siaka Stevens retires and hands over his office as president to Major General Joseph Momoh
1987 A coup led by former president Francis Minah fails

Somalia
1980 US is granted the use of a naval base at Berbera
1988 Somalia and Ethiopia sign a peace treaty
1989 Anti-government rioting breaks out in Mogadishu

South Africa
1986 Economic sanctions are imposed on South Africa by the Commonwealth, the European Community and the US
1989 F. W. de Klerk becomes prime minister and begins talks with the ANC

Sudan
1983 Rebellion breaks out in the Christian south after Nimeiri imposes Islamic law throughout the country
1985 Nimeiri ousted by a military coup and the SSU is disbanded
1986 Elections are held for a new legislature, Sadiq al-Mahdi becomes prime minister
1989 Brig. Gen. Omer Hassan Ahmed al-Bashir overthrows al-Mahdi in an Islamic fundamentalist inspired military coup

Swaziland
1982 Death of King Sobhuza after a reign of 82 years
1983 Sobhuza II's son Makhosetive is named heir to the throne
1984 The State University is closed by the government after student protests
1985 Prince Clement Dlamini, leader of the opposition Swazi Liberation Movement, is exiled
1986 Makhosetive is crowned king, assuming the name Mswati III

Tanzania
1981 Tanzanian troops are withdrawn from Uganda
1985 Nyerere retires from the presidency: he is succeeded by Ali Hassan Mwinyi

Togo
1986 An attempted coup by a group of commandos is put down

Tunisia
1982–1986 Tunis is the headquarters of the Palestine Liberation Organization (PLO)
1983 Mass protests follow the withdrawal of government food subsidies
1987 Prime minister Zine el-Abidine Ben Ali removes Bourguiba from office and becomes president in his place
1988 Opposition parties are legalized
1989 Tunisia joins Algeria, Libya and Morocco in the Arab Maghrib Union

Uganda
1980 Obote returns from exile and is re-elected to the presidency
1981 Yoweri Museveni founds the National Resistance Movement (NRM) and starts a guerrilla war against Obote
1985 Obote is overthrown by another military coup: Gen. Tito Okello becomes president
1986 The NRM captures Kampala and overthrows the military government: Museveni becomes president
1986–1994 The National Resistance Council (NRC) serves as Uganda's legislature

Frederik Willem de Klerk
He became president of South Africa in 1989 CE and, under his leadership, the racial policies of apartheid were swiftly dismantled.

Sadiq al Mahdi
The great grandson of the Mahdi of Sudan, he served twice as prime minister before being overthrown in 1989 CE.

Zambia
    1986 Widespread rioting breaks out after austerity measures are introduced by the government

Zimbabwe
    1980 Feb ZANU-PF win British supervised elections: Mugabe becomes prime minister
    1980 Apr 18 Rhodesia becomes independent as the Republic of Zimbabwe
    1982 Mugabe dismisses Nkomo from the government
    1987 Mugabe becomes president
    1988 ZANU and ZAPU formally merge and Zimbabwe becomes a one party state

1990–2000 CE

Algeria
    1990 Fundamentalist Islamic Salvation Front (FIS) enjoys unexpected success in local government elections
    1991 After the FIS wins first round in general elections, the government declares a state of emergency
    1992 President Bendjedid resigns, a military regime is established and Islamic fundamentalists begin a terrorist campaign
    1995 Liamine Zeroual is appointed president
    1996 Algerians approve a new constitution banning political parties based on religion, sex or language
    1999 President Zeroual resigns and Abdulaziz Bouteflika is elected president
    2000 Under an amnesty, large numbers of Islamic militants handed over their arms

Angola
    1990 The MPLA renounces Marxism
    1991 MPLA and UNITA agree a ceasefire
    1992 The MPLA's José Eduardo dos Santos becomes president after multiparty elections. UNITA begins the civil war again
    1993 Peace talks start at Lusaka, Zambia
    1994 New peace agreement signed by the MPLA and UNITA
    1995 UN peacekeeping force arrives to oversee the peace agreement
    1996 Angola joins the Community of Portuguese-speaking Countries
    1997 New government of national unity formed
    1999 Civil war breaks out again between MPLA and UNITA

Benin
    1990 Kérékou's government is dissolved and political parties are legalized
    1991 Nicéphore Soglo becomes president after Benin's first multiparty elections
    1996 Kérékou returns to power as a democratically elected president
    1997 Labor unions protest against the government's economic liberalization measures

Botswana
    1990s Botswana becomes the second largest exporter of diamonds after Russia
    1991 Opposition parties form a united front against the BDP
    1994 BDP wins general elections but with a reduced majority
    1998 Masire retires and Festus Mogae becomes president
    1999 BDP retains power in general elections

Burkina Faso
    1997 Drought devastates agricultural production

Burundi
    1994 Hutu-Tutsi massacres occur when a plane carrying newly elected president Ntaryamira of Burundi and president Habyarimana of Rwanda is shot down over Rwanda
    1996 Burundi expels thousands of Rwandan Hutu refugees
    1991 Political parties legalized

Cameroon
    1992 Biya and the People's Democratic Movement retain power after Cameroon's first multiparty elections
    1995 Cameroon joins the Commonwealth of Nations
    1998 Cameroon and Nigeria take a fishing rights dispute to the International Court
    1994 Cameroon disputes with Nigeria over the oil-rich Bakassi peninsula on the border
    1995 Cameroon becomes the 52nd member of the Commonwealth of Nations

The Fundamentalist Islamic Salvation Front
Muslim fundamentalists, shown here at prayer, won the first round in general elections in Algeria in 1991 and the government declared a state of emergency.

José Eduardo dos Santos
He became president of Angola for the first time in 1979, CE then again in 1985 CE and 1992 CE. In 1994–45 CE he negotiated a cease-fire in the war with South African-backed rebels.

© DIAGRAM

Ange-Félix Patassé
A former prime minister, he became president of the Central African Republic in 1993 CE after defeating the military dictator André Kolingba in multiparty elections.

Cape Verde
1991 Pereira and the PAICV lose power in Cape Verde's first multiparty elections
1996 Cape Verde joins the Community of Portuguese-Speaking Countries

Central African Republic
1992 A multiparty constitution is introduced
1993 Ange-Félix Patassé becomes president after multiparty elections
1996 France helps suppress a military rebellion
1997 President Patassé calls for the withdrawal of French troops amid growing anti-French hostility
1998 A UN force arrives in CAR to replace French troops

Chad
1990 President Habré overthrown by a Libyan supported coup: Gen. Idriss Déby becomes president and promises to introduce democracy
1992 Uprising by supporters of ex-president Habré is defeated with French aid
1993 New legislature appointed to oversee transition to democracy
1994 Libya agrees to withdraw from the Aozou strip after a ruling by the International Court
1996 Déby is re-elected president
2000 Habré is placed under house arrest in Senegal and charged with torture

Comoros
1995 Attempted coup by mercenaries is defeated with French help
1998 Anjouan and Mohéli declare independence from the Comoros: their independence is not recognized internationally

Congo, Democratic Republic of
1990 Mobutu lifts the ban on political parties
1991 Economic problems lead to widespread rioting
1992 A constitutional conference replaces the government with a High Council of the Republic
1993 The president and the High Council appoint rival prime ministers
1994 One million Hutu refugees flee to Zaire from Rwanda
1995 Outbreak of the deadly Ebola virus in Kikwit
1996 Hutu-Tutsi conflict in Rwanda and Burundi spreads to the Tutsi of eastern Zaire
1997 Laurent Kabila overthrows the Mobutu government and becomes president with the support of Tutsi forces: name of the country is changed to Democratic Republic of Congo
1998 Civil war breaks out. Angola, Chad, Namibia and Zimbabwe send forces to support Kabila against rebels supported by Burundi, Rwanda and Uganda

Congo, Republic of
1990 Congo renounces Marxism
1991 Political parties are legalized
1992 A new multiparty constitution is approved by a referendum: the country resumes its old name, Republic of Congo
1993 President Sassou-Nguesso is defeated in elections by Pascal Lissouba
1994 Anti-government urban militias clash with government forces
1997 Sassou-Nguesso seizes power with the support of Angolan troops
1998 The Republic of Congo and the Democratic Republic of Congo begin negotiations for the demarcation of their common frontier

Djibouti
1991 Guerrilla warfare breaks out between the Afars and Issa dominated government forces
1992 President Aptidon introduces a multiparty constitution
1993 Aptidon re-elected in multiparty elections
1994 Afars and Issas reach a peace agreement
1996 Exiled opponents of the Aptidon regime are abducted from Addis Ababa

Egypt
1990–1991 Egypt joins the US-led coalition against Iraq in the Gulf War
1993 15 Islamic fundamentalist terrorists executed.
1997 Islamic fundamentalist terrorists kill 60 western tourists
1999 Hosni Mubarak is re-elected as president

Equatorial Guinea
1992 A multiparty constitution is introduced
1993 The Democratic Party wins 68 of 80 seats in elections
1996 Obiang Nguema is re-elected as president amid allegations of vote rigging
1998 Mass arrests of Bubi separatists on the island of Bioko

Hosni Mubarak
Having survived an assassination attempt in 1995 CE during a visit to Ethiopia, he was reelected as president of Egypt in 1999 CE.

Eritrea
1991 Eritrean and Tigrean rebels overthrow the Ethiopian government
1993 May 24 Eritrea becomes independent: Issaias Afewerki of the EPLF becomes president
1998–1999 Armed clashes along the Ethiopian border

Ethiopia
1990 USSR cuts off economic aid to Ethiopia
1991 Mengistu regime overthrown by Eritrean and Tigrean rebels
1992 The Tigrean dominated Ethiopian People's Revolutionary Democratic Front (EPRDF) forms a transitional government
1993 Ethiopia recognizes Eritrea's independence
1994 A new constitution is introduced giving provinces the right to secede
1995 The EPRDF wins the first elections under the new constitution
1998–2000 Armed clashes along the Eritrean border

Mengistu regime overthrown
The Marxist regime set up by Mengistu Haile-Mariam of Ethiopia in 1974 CE was overthrown by Eritrean and Tigrean rebels.

Gabon
1993 Bongo retains the presidency after he wins Gabon's first multiparty elections
1996 Gabon withdraws from OPEC
1998 Bongo wins presidential elections with 66 percent of the vote

Gambia
1991 Gambia and Senegal sign a reconciliation and cooperation treaty
1994 Jawara overthrown by a military coup: Yahya Jammeh becomes president
1995 An attempt to overthrow Jammeh is foiled
1996 Jammeh wins presidential elections under a new constitution
1997 Multiparty elections for a National Assembly

Ghana
1992 Rawlings is elected president under a new multiparty constitution
1994 A state of emergency is declared following the outbreak of inter-ethnic violence in northern Ghana
1996 Rawlings re-elected president

Guinea
1990 Conté appoints a transitional government to oversee a return to civilian rule
1993 Conté narrowly retains the presidency in multiparty elections
1998 Conté is re-elected president

Guinea-Bissau
1991 The law making the PAIGC the sole political party is abolished
1994 PAIGC wins Guinea-Bissau's first multiparty elections: Vieira retains the presidency
1998–1999 An army revolt disrupts peace in Bissau

Ivory Coast
1990 Mar After tax rises cause rioting, a new multiparty constitution is introduced
1990 Oct Houphouët-Boigny wins the first presidential elections held under the new constitution
1993 Houphouët-Boigny dies and is succeeded by Henri Konan Bédié
1995 Bédié wins presidential elections held under rules that barred his main opponents
1998 CIA announces that Ivory Coast is now a major center for growing and smuggling marijuana
1999 Bédié is overthrown and a military regime is established under General Robert Guei

Lansana Conté
After the introduction of a multiparty system in Guinea in 1991 CE, Conté narrowly retained his presidency in 1993 CE and was re-elected again in 1998 CE.

Kenya
1990 Prodemocracy demonstrations break out in Nairobi and other cities
1991 Under pressure from aid donors, a multiparty constitution is introduced
1992 Moi and KANU win presidential and parliamentary elections held under the new constitution amid allegations of fraud
1995 The anthropologist Richard Leakey founds a new opposition party, Safina
1997 Moi is re-elected president with 40 percent of the vote
1998 A car-bomb explosion outside the US embassy in Nairobi kills 250 people
1998 Kenya, Tanzania and Uganda sign a framework agreement establishing a new East African Community, aimed at creating a common market

Lesotho
1990 The military government forced King Moshoeshoe II to abdicate in favor of his son Letsie III
1991 Lekhanya is forced to resign and is replaced by Col. Elias P. Ramaema
1993 Multiparty constitution introduced. Basotho Congress Party (BCP) under Ntsu Mohehle wins power
1995 King Letsie III abdicates in favor of his father Moshoeshoe II

1996 King Moshoeshoe II is killed in an automobile accident: Letsie III returns to the throne
1997 A dam project is suspended after protests by displaced local inhabitants
1998 Rioting follows a disputed election result and South African troops arrive to restore order

Liberia

1990 Full scale civil war breaks out between Doe's Armed Forces of Liberia (AFL) and two rebel groups, the Independent National Patriotic Front of Liberia (INPFL) and Taylor's National Patriotic Front of Liberia (NPFL)
1990 Sept Doe is killed by the INPFL
1990 Nov West African peacekeeping troops arrive to police a cease-fire
1992 Renewed civil war after the NPFL attack Monrovia
1993 A seven-month ceasefire is agreed
1994 A transitional government fails to end the violence
1995 Charles Taylor is brought into the transitional government
1996 The warring parties sign a peace agreement but fighting breaks out again in Monrovia
1997 Presidential and legislative elections are held: Charles Taylor becomes president
1998 Nearly 480,000 Liberian refugees begin to return home

Libya

1992 UN sanctions imposed on Libya after it refuses to hand over two agents suspected of the 1988 Pan Am Flight 103 bombing over Lockerbie, Scotland
1993 UN tightens sanctions against Libya
1994 The International Court awards the Aouzou strip to Chad
1996 An aqueduct to supply water to desert settlements is completed
1999 Qaddafi surrenders suspects for the 1988 Pan Am bombing for trial at The Hague

Madagascar

1991 President Ratsiraka places Albert Zafy in control of a transitional government
1992 A multiparty constitution is approved by voters at a referendum
1993 Zafy is elected president
1996 Zafy resigns from the presidency after he is impeached by the National Assembly
1997 Ratsiraka returns to power after presidential elections
1998 A new constitution provides for a federal system and increased presidential powers

Malawi

1993 Banda gives up the life presidency and prepares to hold elections
1994 Bakili Muluzi of the United Democratic Front Party becomes president after defeating Banda in multi-party elections
1995 Banda is acquitted on charges of conspiracy to murder four opposition politicians in 1983
1997 Following his death, Banda is given a state funeral

Mali

1991 Traoré is overthrown by a military coup: a transitional military-civilian government is created
1992 Alpha Oumar Konaré becomes president in elections under a new multiparty constitution
1993 An attempted coup to restore Traoré is defeated
1997 Konare is re-elected president

Mauritania

1991 Taya introduces a multiparty constitution
1992 Maawiya Ould Taya is elected president in the first elections under the new constitution
1997 Taya is re-elected president

Mauritius

1992 Mauritius becomes a republic: Cassam Uteem becomes president (a largely symbolic role)
1995 Dr Navinchandra Ramgoolam replaces Jugnauth as prime minister
1997 Uteem is re-elected president

Morocco

1991 Jan–Feb Morocco contributes troops for the liberation of Kuwait
1991 Sept Ceasefire between Morocco and Polisario in Western Sahara
1993 King Hassan opens the world's second largest mosque in Casablanca
1999 UN organizes a referendum on the future of Western Sahara to be held in 2000
1999 Jul 23 King Hassan II dies: succeeded by his son, Sidi Muhammad, who becomes Muhammad VI

Mozambique

1990 Ban on opposition parties lifted
1992 FRELIMO and RENAMO sign a peace agreement

Dr. Hastings Kamuzu Banda
He was appointed the prime minister of Malawi in 1963 CE, and president in 1966 CE. He was voted "president for life" in 1971 CE, but the title was withdrawn upon the introduction of multparty government in 1993 CE. He lost the 1994 CE elections, was cleared of killing four of his former ministers in 1995 CE, and died in 1997 CE.

1994 FRELIMO leader Joaquim Chissano wins the first multiparty presidential elections
1995 Mozambique joins the Commonwealth of Nations
1996 Mozambique joins the Community of Portuguese-speaking Countries
1998 A cholera epidemic kills over 800 people
2000 Central and southern Mozambique devastated by floods

Namibia
1990 Mar 21 Namibia becomes independent: Sam Nujoma, the leader of SWAPO, becomes the first president
1992 Namibia and South Africa agree to joint administration of Walvis Bay
1994 South Africa cedes Walvis Bay to Namibia
1994 Nujoma is re-elected president
1999 Fighting breaks out in the Caprivi Strip as separatist guerrillas clash with Namibian troops

Niger
1991 A national conference strips Saibou of his powers
1992 Niger adopts a multiparty constitution. A Tuareg rebellion breaks out in the north
1993 Mahamane Ousmane is elected president under the new constitution
1994 The government offers the Tuareg a degree of internal autonomy in return for a ceasefire
1996 Military coup ousts Ousmane: Gen. Ibrahim Bare Mainassara becomes president
1997 The government and the Tuareg sign a ceasefire in Algiers
1999 Mainassara is assassinated: Daouda Malem Wanke becomes president

Nigeria
1991 The Nigerian seat of government is transferred from Lagos to Abuja
1993 Jan Interim government takes office under Babangida
1993 Jun Social Democratic Party of Moshood Abiola wins federal elections
1993 Aug Babangida annuls the election result and picks a non-elected civilian government
1993 Nov Government overthrown by military coup of Gen. Sanni Abacha
1994 June Abiola declares himself president and is arrested for treason
1995 Nov Ken Saro-Wiwa and other members of the Movement for the Survival of the Ogoni People executed
1995 Nov Nigeria expelled from the Commonwealth
1998 Jun Death of Abacha: he is succeeded by Gen. Abdulsalam Abubakar
1998 Jul Riots follow the sudden death of Moshood Abiola
1998 Oct Hundreds of villagers killed after a leaking oil pipeline catches fire
1999 Feb Former military dictator Olesegun Obasanjo is elected president
1999 Feb–Aug Ethnic unrest interrupts oil production in SE Nigeria
1999 May Military government hands over power to president Obasanjo
2000 Muslim-Christian clashes occur in the north

Rwanda
1990 The Rwandan Patriotic Front (RPF), a Tutsi rebel movement based in Uganda, begins attacks on the government
1991 A multiparty constitution is introduced after another RPF invasion
1992 Hutu militias forcibly relocate members of the Tutsi minority
1993 Habyarimana repudiates a peace treaty signed by his prime minister and the RPF
1994 Apr President Habyarimana and President Ntaryamira of Burundi are killed when their plane is shot down by Hutu extremists
1994 May Hutu extremists kill 750,000 Tutsi in a campaign of genocide
1994 Jun Despite the genocide, France supports the French-speaking Hutus against the English-speaking RPF
1994 Jul The RPF defeats Hutu forces and forms a government of national unity under a moderate Hutu president and prime minister: two million Hutus flee, most of them to Zaire (now Dem. Rep. of Congo)
1995 The government begins holding war crimes trials
1996 Many Hutus return to Rwanda after attacks on their refugee camps by Zairian Tutu rebels
1998 After being convicted of genocide, 22 Hutus are executed

São Tomè and Príncipe
1990 Da Costa resigns. Miguel Trovoada becomes president after the first multiparty presidential election since independence
1995 Principe is granted autonomy. An attempted military coup is defeated
1996 São Tomé and Principe join the Community of Portuguese-speaking Countries. President Miguel Trovoada is re-elected

Sam Nujoma
He was the founder of the SWAPO resistance movement, and fought against the illegal occupation of Namibia by South Africa. He then became president of the independent state in 1990 CE, and was reelected in 1994 CE.

General Sanni Abacha
He became the head of Nigeria's military government after a military coup in 1993 CE, and served in office until his death in 1998 CE.

© DIAGRAM

Senegal

1991 Renewed fighting on the border with Mauritania
1992 Armed clashes with Casamance separatists in southern Senegal
1993 Diouf is re-elected to the presidency for the third time. A cease-fire is agreed with the Casamance separatists
1995 The Casamance separatists breach the ceasefire
1998 In a visit to Dakar, US president Clinton proposes the creation of an "African peace maintaining force"

Seychelles

1991 Opposition parties are legalized and Marxism is abandoned
1993 René defeats Mancham in the first multiparty presidential elections
1998 René and the SPPF are again re-elected

Sierra Leone

1991 Corporal Foday Sankoh leads an uprising against Momoh
1992 Capt. Valentine Strasser overthrows Momoh and cancels planned elections: Sankoh leads a second uprising
1993 The rebels refuse a government offer of a cease-fire and amnesty
1996 Ahmad Tejan Kabbah of the Sierra Leone People's Party is elected president: he signs a peace deal with Sankoh
1997 Maj. Johnny Paul Koromah ousts Kabbah in a military coup
1998 Troops from Nigeria overthrow Koromah and restore Kabbah to power
1999 A peace agreement is signed and Foday Sankoh becomes vice president

Somalia

1991 The rebel United Somali Congress overthrows the military government and captures Mogadishu. Civil war breaks out between rival clans and in the north the Somali National Movement declares the independent Somaliland Republic
1992 A US-led force arrives to secure the distribution of food aid after famine breaks out
1993 May A UN peacekeeping force is sent into Somalia
1993 Jun Warlord Gen. Mohammad Farah Aidid attacks Pakistani UN peacekeepers
1993 Oct A bungled attempt to capture Aidid leaves 18 US soldiers and hundreds of Somali civilians dead
1994 Mar US troops are withdrawn from Somalia
1995 Remaining UN forces pull out after the peace settlement fails. Aidid pronounces himself president
1996 Gen. Aidid is killed fighting a rival faction
1997 The UN begins a new aid program after southern Somalia is devastated by floods
1998 Rival clan leaders in the south declare their commitment to peace and unity

South Africa

1990 Feb The ANC is legalized and Nelson Mandela is released from prison
1990 Mar South Africa grants independence to Namibia
1990–1991 The government repeals the apartheid laws
1992 A referendum of whites supports reform of the electoral system
1993 Mandela and de Klerk are awarded the Nobel Peace Prize
1994 Nelson Mandela becomes president after South Africa's first all race elections: the ANC forms a government
1999 Nelson Mandela retires as president, Thabo Mbeki of the ANC is elected president

Sudan

1991 Southern rebels split over whether to seek independence or a united secular Sudan
1993 The military appoint al-Bashir president
1995 Sudanese conspiracy to assassinate president Mubarak of Egypt fails
1996 In presidential and parliamentary elections, al-Bashir is re-elected president and the fundamentalist National Islamic Front wins control of the legislature
1997 Rebel Sudanese Peoples Liberation Army makes big gains in the south
1998 Government declares its willingness to hold a referendum on the secession of the south
1998 Aug US missiles destroy pharmaceutical plant at Khartoum in retaliation for bombing of US embassies in Kenya and Tanzania
1999 Sudan and Uganda sign a peace agreement

Swaziland

1992 King Mswati suspends the legislature and rules by decree
1993 For the first time directly elected members of parliament are appointed to the legislature
1995 Democracy protesters from the Swaziland Youth Congress burn down the parliament building

Nelson Mandela
He became the president of South Africa, after winning the first multiracial elections in its troubled history, in 1994 CE. The African National Congress then formed a government. He retired from the presidency in 1999 CE.

1996 A constitutional committee is appointed to consider plans to democratize the country
1997 Labor unions call for the constitutional committee to be dissolved
1998 King Mswati announces a major environmental restoration program

Tanzania
1990 Mwinyi is re-elected president
1992 Opposition parties are legalized
1994 Around 800,000 refugees from ethnic violence in Rwanda and Burundi flee to Tanzania
1995 Benjamin Mkapa of the CCM becomes president after the first multiparty elections
1996 Government expels 540,000 Rwandan refugees
1998 11 killed and 80 injured in Islamic fundamentalist bomb attack on the US embassy in Dar-es-Salaam
1999 Nyerere dies; Tanzania, Kenya and Uganda sign a framework agreement establishing a new East African Community, aimed at creating a common market

Togo
1993 Eyadéma is re-elected under a new multiparty constitution
1994 The RPT forms a coalition government with opposition parties
1998 Eyadéma is re-elected president

Tunisia
1992 The Islamic fundamentalist Nahda party is banned
1994 Islamic fundamentalist political parties are banned from participating in the first multiparty elections. Ben Ali is re-elected to the presidency

Uganda
1993 Uganda's four traditional kingdoms are restored
1994 A Constituent Assembly replaces the NRC
1995 A new constitution is approved extending nonparty government for five years
1995–1996 Terrorist campaign in northern Uganda by the Lord's Resistance Army
1996 Museveni is elected president in nonparty elections
1998 Uganda supports rebel forces in the civil war in the Congo
1999 Uganda Kenya and Tanzania sign a framework agreement to establish a new African Community, aimed at creating a common market. Uganda and Sudan sign a peace agreement

Zambia
1990 Opposition parties are legalized
1991 Frederick Chiluba of the Movement for Multiparty Democracy (MMD) defeats Kaunda in the first multi-party elections
1993 A state of emergency is declared to undermine a campaign of civil disobedience by supporters of UNIP
1996 Chiluba is re-elected president
1997 Kaunda is barred from standing for election after a failed coup attempt

Zimbabwe
1991 Opposition parties are legalized but under conditions which prevent them from campaigning effectively
1992 The Land Acquisition Act provides for government purchase of white-owned lands for redistribution to poor Africans
1996 Mugabe is re-elected president in elections boycotted by opposition parties
1998 Mugabe sends troops to support the government in the Congo civil war
1999 Demonstrations break out over Zimbabwe's involvement in the Congo war

Gnassingbe Eyadéma
He seized power in Togo after a bloodless coup in 1967 CE, set up a sole political party in 1969 CE, and was reelected as president under a new constitution in 1993 CE. An unpopular leader, there have been many attempts to overthrow him.

Bantu migrations (below)
Migrating Bantu settlers brought
with them ironworking, The maps
below show:

1 The probable spread of iron
working c.1500 BCE–300 CE.

2 The probable spread of
metal technology c.300 BCE
–600 CE.

Bantu Migrations

There are three main groups of Black African people: the Bantu, the Nilotes, and the Cushites. These groupings are based on cultural and linguistic similarities. A large number of the hundreds of Central, Southern, and East African languages are Bantu.

The Bantu originated in eastern Nigeria several thousands of years ago. At first, they spread over West Africa and through the equatorial rainforest belt and then, between 500 BCE and 300 CE, eastward and southward into East and Southern Africa. Later migrations–from the south to the east–further dispersed them throughout Africa. The Bantu settlers brought iron working and hoe cultivation with them.

In Southern Africa there are two main divisions of

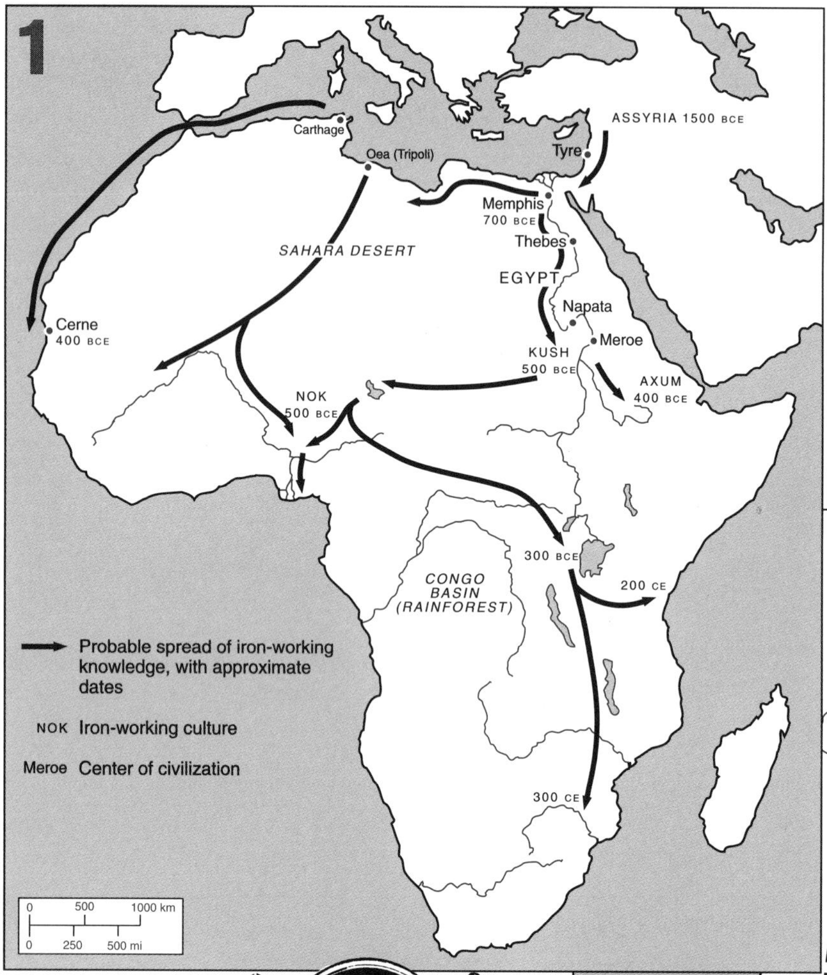

Founder of the Swazi kingdom (below)
The Swazi are descended from a group of Bantu-speaking peoples called the Nguni. King Mswati I, who reigned from 1839–65 CE, is shown here with Swazi chiefs in full ceremonial dress. He created a powerful kingdom when the region was under threat from Portuguese, Zulu, Boer, and British aggressors.

Map 1 labels:
ASSYRIA 1500 BCE
Carthage
Oea (Tripoli)
Tyre
Memphis 700 BCE
Thebes
SAHARA DESERT
EGYPT
Napata
Cerne 400 BCE
Meroe
KUSH 500 BCE
AXUM 400 BCE
NOK 500 BCE
300 BCE
200 CE
CONGO BASIN (RAINFOREST)
300 CE

→ Probable spread of iron-working knowledge, with approximate dates

NOK Iron-working culture

Meroe Center of civilization

0 500 1000 km
0 250 500 mi

Kabaka Mutesa II (right)
The Ganda people, who lived on the northern shores of Lake Victoria, were one of the largest groups in what is now Uganda to establish monarchies. Buganda was ruled by a kabaka (king). Kabaka Mutesa II ruled Buganda from 1939 until 1967 CE. He also served as president of Uganda from 1962 until 1966 when he was dismissed by the prime minister Milton Obote. In 1967 CE, Uganda became a republic. Obote became president and abolished the country's traditional kingdoms.

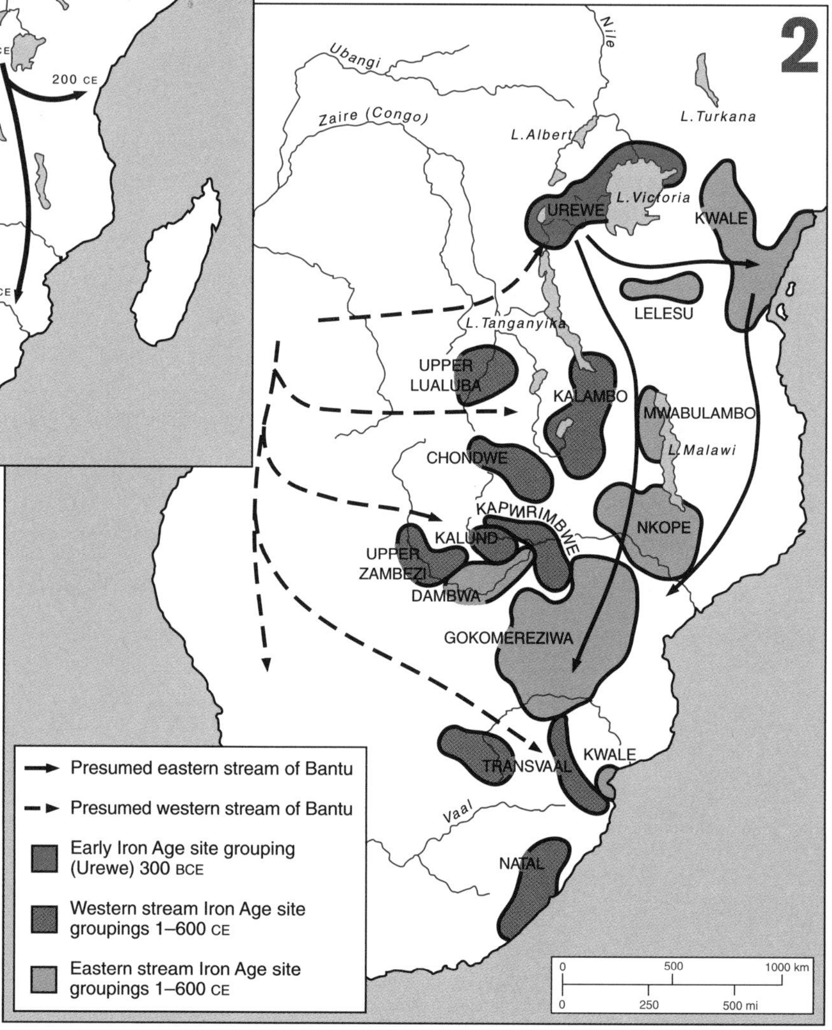

Map 2 labels:
Ubangi
Zaire (Congo)
Nile
L. Albert
L. Turkana
L. Victoria
UREWE
KWALE
LELESU
L. Tanganyika
UPPER LUALUBA
KALAMBO
MWABULAMBO
L. Malawi
CHONDWE
KAPWIRIMBWE
NKOPE
KALUND
UPPER ZAMBEZI
DAMBWA
GOKOMEREZIWA
TRANSVAAL
KWALE
Vaal
NATAL

→ Presumed eastern stream of Bantu

▶ Presumed western stream of Bantu

Early Iron Age site grouping (Urewe) 300 BCE

Western stream Iron Age site groupings 1–600 CE

Eastern stream Iron Age site groupings 1–600 CE

0 500 1000 km
0 250 500 mi

Bantu peoples: the Nguni and Sotho–Tswana peoples. The Bantu peoples were established in Southern Africa by the start of the Common Era, at least thirteen centuries before the arrival of Europeans in the seventeenth century. In East Africa, the larger Bantu groups include the Kikuyu, Ganda, Nyoro, and Nyamwezi.

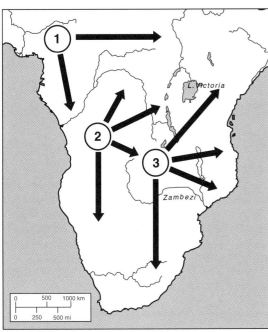

The probable dispersal of bantu languages (above)

This map shows the extent of the dispersal of Bantu languages during the period c. 100 BCE–600 CE. A large number of the hundreds of Central, Southern, and East African languages are Bantu.

1 Primary dispersal area
2 Secondary dispersal area
3 Final dispersal area

Bantu timeline	
Ganda	**c. 1000 CE** Bantu-speakers migrate from Central to East Africa; Ganda settle around northwest Lake Victoria **1500s** Buganda Kingdom expands **c. 1650** Bataka mutiny against authoritarian *kabaka* **1700s** *Kabakas* increase power **1800s** Buganda evolves into centralized monarchy
Kikuyu	**1400s on** Eastern Bantu-speakers migrate into region of present-day Kenya **1500s–1600s** Kikuyu settle southeast of Mount Kenya **1700s–1800s** Period of expansion and migration
Nguni	**200s** The Nguni arrive in Southern Africa. The larger Nguni groups in this area include the Zulu, Swazi, and the Xhosa
(a) Swazi	**200s** Bantu-speaking peoples begin to arrive in Southern Africa **300s–400s** Bantu-speakers reach modern Transvaal (South Africa) **c. 1750** Swazi king, Ngwane II, alive **by 1800** Ngwane kingdom one of most powerful in region (present-day KwaZulu/Natal in South Africa) **c. 1815–1839** Reign of King Sobhuza I over Ngwane kingdom **1816** Ngwane driven north by Ndwandwe kingdom **1819–1839** Mfecane/Difaqane: period of mass migrations and wars
(b) Xhosa	**200s** Bantu-speaking peoples begin to arrive in Southern Africa **300s–400s** Bantu-speakers reach present-day KwaZulu/Natal **1799–1803** Cape-Xhosa Wars I, II, and III: Xhosa-Boer frontier wars **1811–1812** Cape-Xhosa War IV: British drive many Xhosa east of Groot-Vis River
(c) Zulu	**200s** Bantu-speaking peoples begin to arrive in Southern Africa **300s–400s** Bantu-speakers reach present-day Kwazulu/Natal **1787** Birth of Shaka **1816** Shaka becomes Zulu leader **1818–1819** Zulu-Ndwandwe War establishes Zulu supremacy **1819–1839** Mfecane/Difaqane: period of mass migrations and wars
Nyamwezi	**1600s** Nyamwezi settle in present-day area of west-central Tanzania **1800s** Nyamwezi develop trade links with east coast **1860–1870** Mirambo controls Ugowa and begins empire building
Nyoro	**1000s–1300s** Bantu–speakers migrate to lakes region of present-day northwest Uganda **c.1350–c. 1500** Bachwezi dynasty rules over Bunyoro-Kitara Empire **c.1500** Babito rule begins in Bunyoro **c.1550** Bunyoro Kingdom at greatest extent **c.1830** Babito prince founds independent Toro Kingdom
Sotho	**200s** Bantu-speaking peoples begin to arrive in Southern Africa **by 1400** Emergence of Sotho clan **1600s–1800s** Bapedi Empire of Northern Sotho Pedi clan **1819–1839** *Mfecane/Difaqane*: period of mass migrations and wars: Boers colonize Northern Sotho

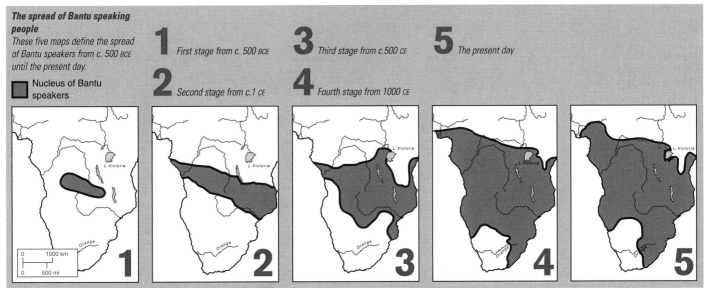

The spread of Bantu speaking people

These five maps define the spread of Bantu speakers from c. 500 BCE until the present day.

☐ Nucleus of Bantu speakers

1 *First stage from c. 500 BCE*

2 *Second stage from c.1 CE*

3 *Third stage from c.500 CE*

4 *Fourth stage from 1000 CE*

5 *The present day*

© DIAGRAM

North African Conquests

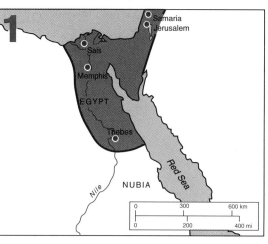

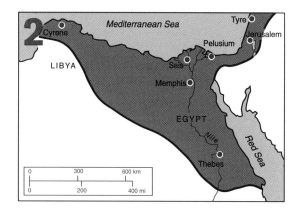

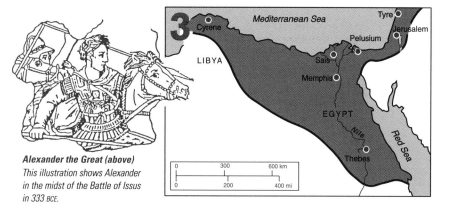

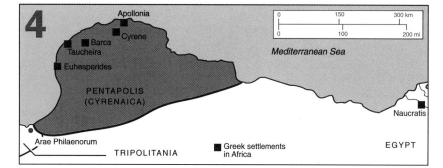

Alexander the Great (above)
This illustration shows Alexander in the midst of the Battle of Issus in 333 BCE.

Assyrian Africa c. 660 BCE

The New Assyrian Empire emerged c. 909 BCE and was the only one of three Assyrian Empires to extend its territory into Africa.

During the seventh and eighth centuries, it expanded southeastward through Syria and Palestine. Nubian-ruled Egypt was conquered during the reign of King Esarhaddon (680–669) in 671. The overthrow of Memphis resulted in the Egyptians having to pay tribute to the Assyrian Empire. The Assyrians formed an alliance with the kings of the indigenous 26th "Saite" Dynasty in order to drive the Nubians out finally in 657.

Egypt was lost to Assyria in 651 because conflict at home, coupled with the long distances involved, made it difficult for the empire to retain its African territory.

In 612, the New Assyrian Empire collapsed as a result of attacks from the Medes and Babylonians.

Persian Africa c. 500 BCE

Following the withdrawal of the Assyrians in 651 BCE, the indigenous 26th "Saite" Dynasty ruled in Egypt until 525. In that year, Cambyses I (525–522), king of the Persians, conquered Egypt and invaded North Africa to just beyond Cyrene (an area known as Libya). He was the first pharoah of the 27th "Persian" Dynasty. The Persians ruled until they were driven out by the Egyptians in 404.

Egyptian pharoahs (28th–30th Dynasties) ruled from 404 until 343, when the Persians invaded Egypt again. This "Second Persian Period" lasted until 332, when the Persian Empire collapsed owing to a series of attacks upon it by Alexander the Great of Macedonia.

Macedonian Africa c. 323 BCE

The Macedonian state emerged c. 350 BCE, under the leadership of Philip II (382–336). After Philip's murder in 336, his son, Alexander III (the Great), took over the leadership. He began an 11-year campaign in the Middle East against the Persians, which led to the formation of the Macedonian Empire in 332.

Alexander swept into Egypt, in 332, and proclaimed himself Pharoah. During a year's stay, plans were made to build the city of Alexandria. In 331, Alexander left Egypt to extend the Macedonian Empire through Persia to India, incorporating Babylon, where he died in 323. After his death, the empire was divided among his generals with Ptolemy claiming Egypt.

Greek Africa c. 321 BCE

The Greek Dorian Empire expanded to include settlements on the North African coast c. 750 BCE It reached its greatest extent c. 550. The Greeks moved westward from Cyrene and founded five cities, between c.630 and the early fifth century, in an area they named Pentapolis (Cyrenaica) on the coast of modern-day Libya. Territorial disputes with the neighboring Carthaginians of Tripolitania were settled c. 321, when it was agreed that Arae Philaenorum, in the extreme east of Tripolitania, should mark the boundary between the two powers.

Ptolemaic Africa c. 250 BCE

Upon the death of Alexander the Great in 323 BCE, his favorite general, Ptolemy, claimed Egypt as his share of the divided Macedonian Empire. In 305, Ptolemy crowned himself King of Egypt and so founded the Ptolemaic Empire. Alexandria was made the capital city, and Ptolemaic rule was extended to Cyrene, Crete, and Cyprus. During his reign, King Ptolemy I founded the Alexandrian library and museum. Under his successor, Ptolemy II (284–246), Egyptian power spread into Nubia and the lighthouse on the island of Pharos was completed.

Cleopatra VII (51–30), Ptolemy XI's youngest daughter, was the last Hellenistic monarch, because the Ptolemaic Empire was absorbed in 30 BCE by the increasingly powerful Roman Empire.

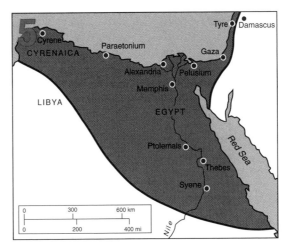

Cleopatra
The last of the Ptolemaic dynasty, she ruled Egypt from 47–30 BCE. The Ptolemies were of Macedonian Greek origin, and ruled Egypt from 304–30 BCE.

Phoenician Africa c. 310 BCE

From the ports of Sidon and Tyre, on the eastern Mediterranean, the Phoenicians began to extend their commercial activities to North Africa about 3000 years ago. The trading posts, which were set up to link the slave, gold, and ivory trade of sub-Saharan Africa with that of the Mediterranean, rapidly became more permanent settlements. Under the leadership of Carthage, the Phoenicians controlled much of the North African coast by 450 BCE.

Phoenician (Carthaginian) border disputes with the Greeks on the North African coast were frequent from c. 400. In 321, it was agreed that Arae Philaenorum would mark the boundary between Carthaginian and Greek territory. This truce lasted only a few years, however. In 310, the Greeks invaded and ruled Carthage, and its immediate hinterland, but were driven out by the Carthaginians in 306.

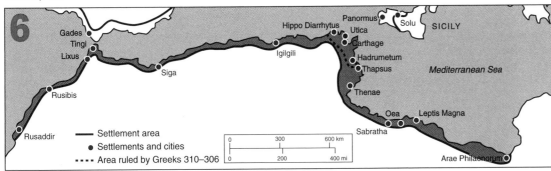

Carthaginian Africa c. 150 BCE

The city-state of Carthage was founded on the North African coast in 814 BCE by Phoenician seamen. With its two excellent harbors and its large fleet of vessels, it grew enormously wealthy through merchant trading across the Mediterranean Sea.

By c. 600, Carthage was self-governing and had become the leading state of the Phoenician western territories. In 264, it fought the first of the three Punic Wars against Rome over the occupation of Sicily. All three wars were lost by Carthage. After the Second Punic War, in 201, the Numidian kingdoms began to encroach on the Carthaginian hinterland and had made significant advances c. 150 BCE. In the Third Punic War, the city itself was defeated, and it became a possession of the Roman Empire.

Hannibal of Carthage
Best remembered as the greatest Carthaginian general ever, it was thanks to his military skills that Carthage came to control most of the North African coast, parts of Spain and Sicily, and Corsica and Sardinia. Their island possessions brought them into conflict with the Romans, and subsequently led to the three Punic Wars.

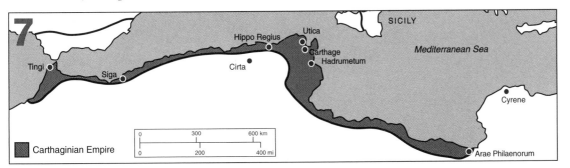

© DIAGRAM

Expanding empires (cont.)
Further empires expanded their territories into North Africa. The maps show the extent of these territories at the following times (CE):

  8 *The Roman Empire, 46*
  9 *The Vandal Empire, 455*
 10 *The Christian Empire, 565*
 11 *The Muslim Empire, 900*
 12 *The European Empire, 1914*

Roman Africa 46 CE

Roman expansion to include North Africa began with the annexation of Carthage in 146 BCE, after the Third Punic War. From this base, the Romans moved eastward, initially leaving the indigenous rulers of Mauretania alone, conquering Egypt in 30 BCE. Rome annexed Mauretania in 42 CE.

The Emperor Diocletian abandoned much of the Northwest African coast (the Maghrib) in the reorganization of the Roman Empire in 285. Internal divisions split the Empire in 395, weakening it, allowing the remainder of the Maghrib to revert to indigenous rule c.430, and to be overrun by the Vandals.

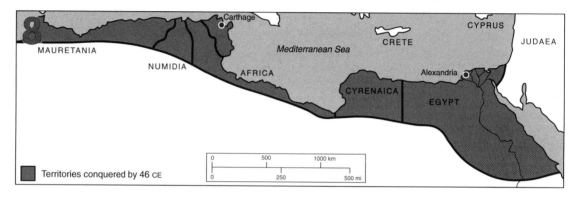

Vandal Africa 455 CE

The Vandals, a Germanic people, moved from northern Europe, down through the crumbling West Roman Empire and into North Africa in 429 CE. Led by their chieftain, Gaiseric, they met with little resistance. By 435, they had taken Hippo Regius and the area surrounding Cirta. In 439, Carthage fell and, by 455, the Vandals had taken all Roman possessions in the Maghrib except Ceuta. The indigenous kingdoms, however, began to encroach upon Vandal territory. This weakened the Vandals, which helped the Byzantine general Belisarius to take their territory for the Byzantine Empire in 533.

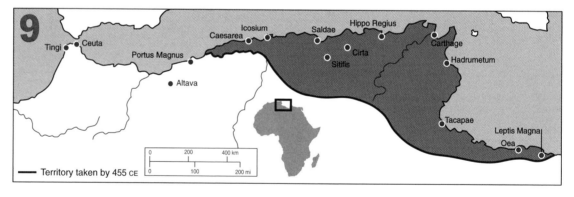

Christian Africa 565 CE

The Maghrib was lost to the Vandals and Berbers during the 430s as the West Roman Empire grew weaker. The East Roman or Byzantine Empire survived the West's eventual collapse in 476 CE. During the reign of the Byzantine Emperor Justinian (527–565), Vandal North Africa was taken by his general Belisarius. The empire was at its greatest extent c.600.

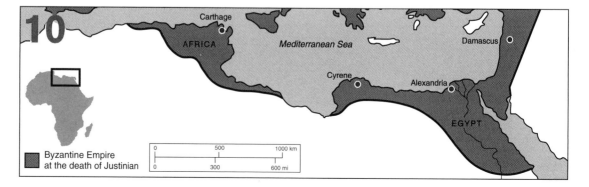

Muslim Africa 900 CE

At the time c.900 CE the Arab Empire in North Africa comprised four distinct groups: the Omayyads (766–1031); the Idrisids, or Shi'ite Idrisids, (789–926); the Aghlabids (801–905); and the Tulanids (868–905). The map (below) combines all four groups to show the extent of the then current Arab Empire.

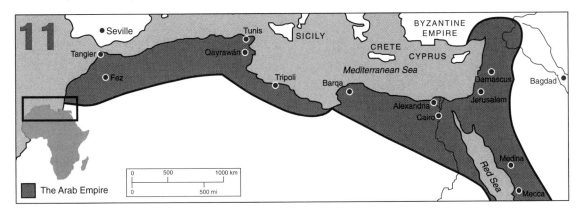

A Muslim dynasty
This gravestone commemorated Sultan Abu Yaqub Yusuf, a king of the Marinid dynasty of Morocco, who reigned from 1286–1307. The inscriptions on the stone are taken from the Koran, the Islamic holy book.

European Africa 1914 CE

The period 1899–1914 CE marked a significant decrease in the power of the Ottoman Empire in Africa, and a rise in the expansion of colonial powers such as Britain, France, Italy, and Germany. The map (below) shows the extent of the territories occupied by these four major colonial powers prior to the start of World War I in 1914.

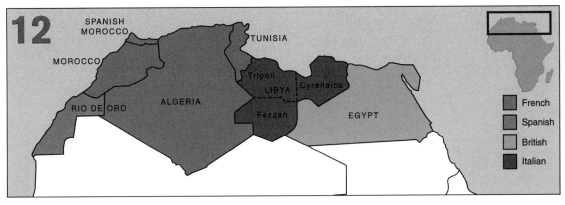

The battle for control of North Africa

The period from the middle of the nineteenth to the start of the twentieth century was marked by frequent disputes between the colonial powers over who controlled North Africa. Four illustrations exemplify the conflicts that arose. First, the French Consul was struck by the *Bey* of Algiers in 1830, which gave the French an excuse to invade, and subsequently colonize Algeria (far left). Second, the Algeciras Conference, 1906, was set up to decide whether or not the French or Germans should have control of Morocco (left). Third, Italy fought Turkey over the territory known as Cyrenaica in North Africa in 1912 (above); and Abbas II, the last Turkish Khedive of Egypt, after whose rule a British protectorate was established (right).

© DIAGRAM

Spread of Christianity

Tradition has it that Christianity was introduced into Egypt and North Africa by the evangelist Mark in 40 CE. It survived many persecutions, but succumbed to the westward march of Islam from 640 CE onwards, when the Arabs began their invasion of North Africa. From 540 CE Christianity spread northward from Axum to the Nubian kingdoms, which eventually succumbed to Islam in the sixteenth century because of Muslim incursions from the north. Christianity continued to flourish, though, in Ethiopia. The nineteenth century saw perhaps the most concentrated effort by the colonial powers to introduce Christianity to the continent of Africa. Coptic, Calvinist and Catholic belief systems had been introduced with limited success into limited parts of Africa before 1800. However, by 1914, Christian missions–both Roman Catholic and Protestant–had been established over the greatest part of the continent.

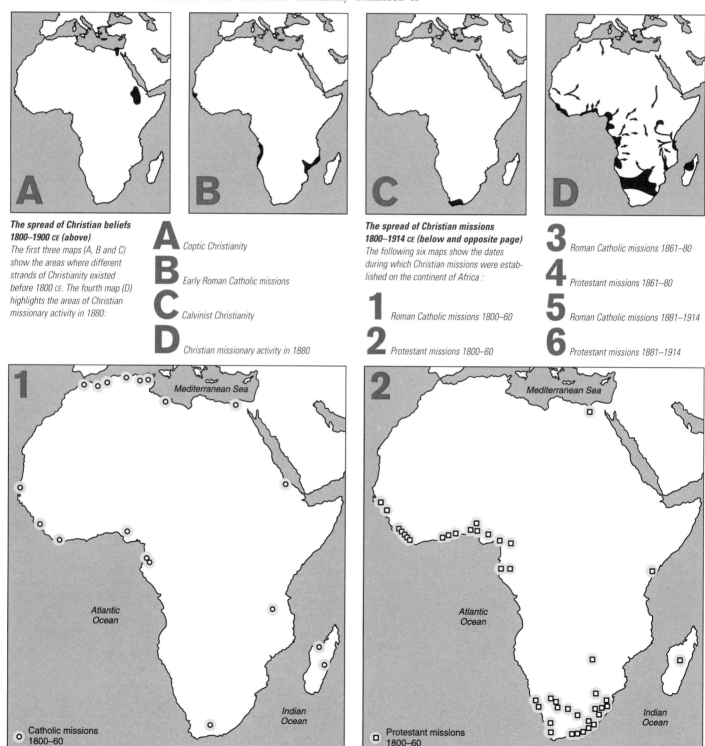

The spread of Christian beliefs 1800–1900 CE (above)
The first three maps (A, B and C) show the areas where different strands of Christianity existed before 1800 CE. The fourth map (D) highlights the areas of Christian missionary activity in 1880:

A Coptic Christianity

B Early Roman Catholic missions

C Calvinist Christianity

D Christian missionary activity in 1880

The spread of Christian missions 1800–1914 CE (below and opposite page)
The following six maps show the dates during which Christian missions were established on the continent of Africa :

1 Roman Catholic missions 1800–60

2 Protestant missions 1800–60

3 Roman Catholic missions 1861–80

4 Protestant missions 1861–80

5 Roman Catholic missions 1881–1914

6 Protestant missions 1881–1914

Catholic missions 1800–60

Protestant missions 1800–60

Spreading the word
One very important side-effect of colonialism was the fact that the powers also brought with them their own religions. The illustration (left) is of a nineteenth-century German missionary.

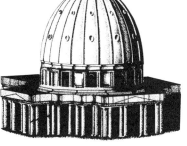

The largest church in the world
Constructed between 1987–1989 CE, this building—the Basilica of Our Lady of Peace—was commissioned by a former

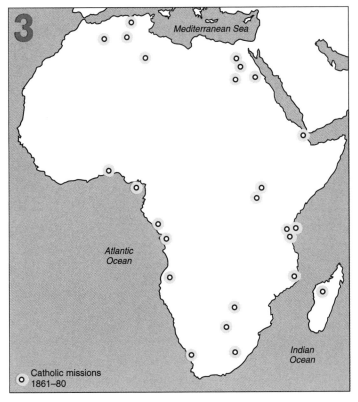

3

Mediterranean Sea

Atlantic Ocean

Indian Ocean

Catholic missions
1861–80

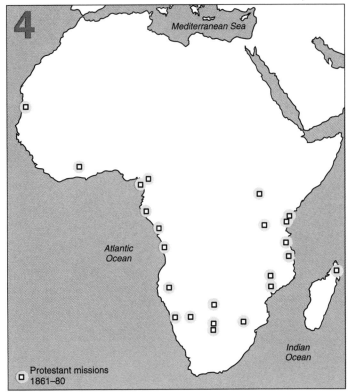

4

Mediterranean Sea

Atlantic Ocean

Indian Ocean

Protestant missions
1861–80

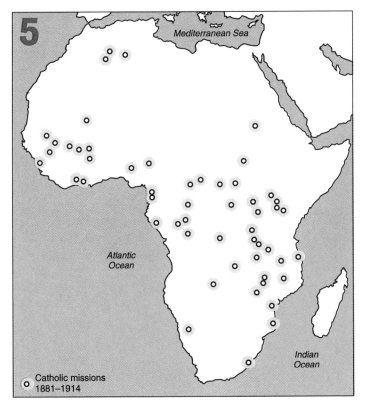

5

Mediterranean Sea

Atlantic Ocean

Indian Ocean

Catholic missions
1881–1914

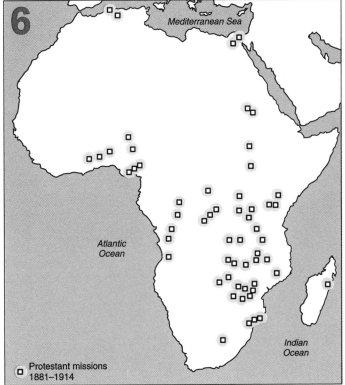

6

Mediterranean Sea

Atlantic Ocean

Indian Ocean

Protestant missions
1881–1914

Section Two **Development of the Continent**

70 Spread of Islam

Spread of Islam

Within four centuries of the Arab conquest of North Africa, which was completed by 711 CE, the great majority of the region's inhabitants had converted to Islam–the religion practiced by Muslims. Islam is also practiced widely throughout the rest of Africa.

Islam is a monotheistic religion (believing in one God) in which the universe, and all within it, are the creation of Allah who is considered all-powerful, just, and merciful. Islam is very much a communal and practical religion; more than just a moral code, it includes laws that affect all aspects of life. Most North Africans

Oldest mosque (above)
The mosque of Ibn Tulun was built in 876–79 CE and is the oldest surviving mosque in Egypt.

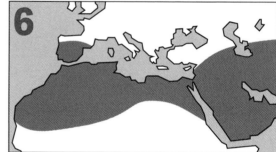

Caliphates (rulers) and emirates (Islamic states) in Africa
632–661 CE Four Righteous Caliphs
661–751 CE Omayyad caliphate
751–1258 CE 'Abbasid caliphate
756–929 CE Omayyad emirate of Cordova
789–926 CE Idrisid caliphate
800–909 CE Aghlabid emirate of Tunisia
909–1171 CE Fatimid caliphate
929–1031 CE Omayyad caliphate of Cordova

Muslim civilizations
After the death of the prophet Muhammad in 632 CE, Islam spread rapidly throughout the Middle East and North Africa. The Arabs began their conquest of North Africa in 640, and the year 642 saw Muslim rule in Egypt. The expansion westward to Tunisia had begun by 670 and, by 711, the whole of North Africa and Spain were under Islamic control. From then on the region spread slowly southward through trade, migration, and holy wars. As the Arab Empire grew larger, it became more difficult to control from Arabia and, as a result, independent emirates came into being. The spread of Islam is shown at the following dates:

1 642 CE **4** 750 **7** 1100 **10** 1600
2 670 **5** 900 **8** 1300 **11** 1800
3 711 **6** 1000 **9** 1400 **12** 1992

More than 50% Islam

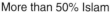
10–50% Islam

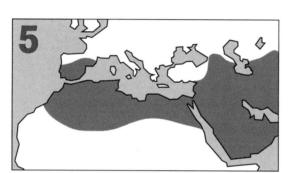

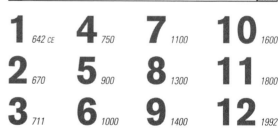

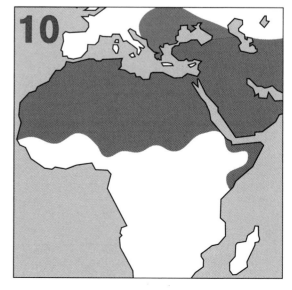

are Sunni Muslims, and Sunnis make up about 85–90 percent of all Muslims worldwide. Sunnis place less emphasis on the importance of a religious hierarchy led by imams (spiritual leaders) than do other Muslims.

Conflicts have existed for some time in North Africa between fundamental Muslims and believers in secular (non-religious) ideals of government. In recent years, these conflicts have combined with economic and social crises, most notably in Algeria and Egypt, to lead to violent outbursts by radical Islamic fundamentalists, seeking the creation of states governed by Sharia (Islamic holy) law, a code of conduct enforced in law. In Sudan, Sharia law was imposed in 1983 CE. Opposition to Sharia law was a major force in the civil war that has split Sudan into rival north and south factions.

Sufi lodge
During the seventeenth and eighteenth centuries the Islamic faith spread throughout North Africa, often by means of Sufi lodges, which would have housed students, guests and pilgrims.

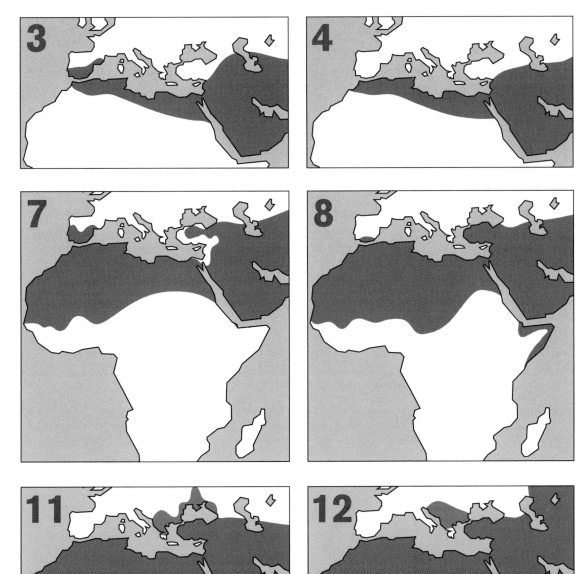

Sankoré Mosque
This was built in Timbuktu at the end of the fifteenth century, and became the center for Islamic scholarship in West Africa.

© DIAGRAM

European Exploration

From 700 CE to that of Henry the Navigator, prince of Portugal, in the fifteenth century, North Africa remained predominantly Islamic, a fortress maintained against the influences of the perceived 'infidels of Europe.' Slavery became the overriding, simple and recurring motive for the exploration of Africa by Europeans from the start of the fifteenth century. The Portuguese made a number of significant voyages to explore the continent from 1482 until the end of that century. European explorations of discovery again gained momentum towards the end of the eighteenth century with Britain, the Netherlands, France, Germany, and Sweden all showing strong interest in Africa. The nineteenth century saw perhaps what is now the best-known period of exploration with such men as Dr. David Livingstone, Sir Henry Morton Stanley, and John Hanning Speke reaching parts of the continent previously unknown to the colonial powers. Although slavery had been the original motive for exploration of the continent of Africa, much later attempts by explorers, such as Livingstone (who were intent on encouraging the spread of Christianity, and the expansion of trade with Europe) were intended to help to bring the inhuman slave trade to a long-awaited end.

Bartholomew Diaz
He was a Portuguese explorer who, in 1487 CE, sailed to the Congo, south as far as Walfish Bay and, without realizing, around the Cape of Good Hope. Upon his return to Portugal he was given the task of preparing a fleet to sail around Africa under Vasco da Gama.

A Portuguese carrack (above)
This was one type of ship used by the early European explorers of the West-African coast.

Voyages of discovery (right)
This map shows the most important voyages made by Portuguese explorers during the period 1482–1498 CE.

————	Diego Cão 1482–1484
————	Pedro da Covilhã 1487–1492 (approximate dates)
————	Bartolomeu Dias 1487–1488
————	Vasco da Gama (first voyage) 1497–1498

Angra Pequeña Portugese name

(Lüderitz Bay) Modern name

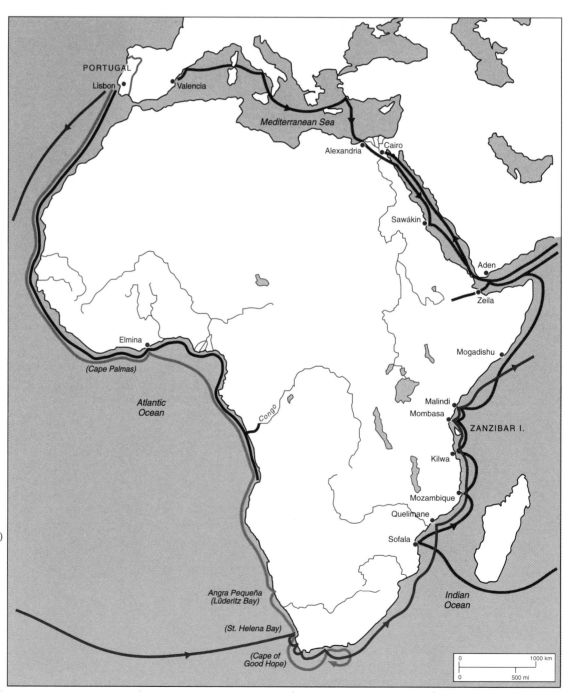

Mungo Park (1771–1806 CE)

A Scotsman by birth, he made two expeditions to Africa, on behalf of the African Association, in an attempt to open up the area around the Niger River for trade. This illustration shows Mungo Park surrounded by a group of African women, intrigued by his European clothes.

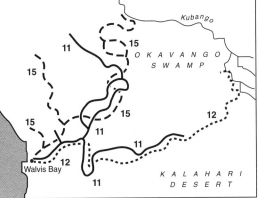

Major European explorations

The maps (left and below) show the locations of the major European explorations of Africa during the period 1769–1858 CE.

1 James Bruce (United Kingdom) 1769–1773

2 R.J. Gordon (Netherlands) 1777–1778

3 Mungo Park (United Kingdom) 1795–1797

4 Mungo Park (United Kingdom) 1805–1806

5 John Campbell (United Kingdom) 1813

6 Hugh Clapperton, Dixon Denham, and Walter Oudney (United Kingdom) 1822–1825

7 Hugh Clapperton and Richard Lander (United Kingdom) 1825–1827

8 René Caillié (France) 1827–1828

9 Richard and John Lander (United Kingdom) 1830

10 Heinrich Barth (Germany) 1850–1856

11 Sir Francis Galton and Karl Andersson (United Kingdom and Sweden) 1850–1852

12 Karl Andersson (Sweden) 1853–1854

13 William Baikie (United Kingdom) 1854

14 Sir Richard Burton (United Kingdom) 1854–1855

15 Karl Andersson (Sweden) 1857–1858

16 Sir Richard Burton and John Speke (United Kingdom) 1857–1858

17 John Speke (United Kingdom) 1858

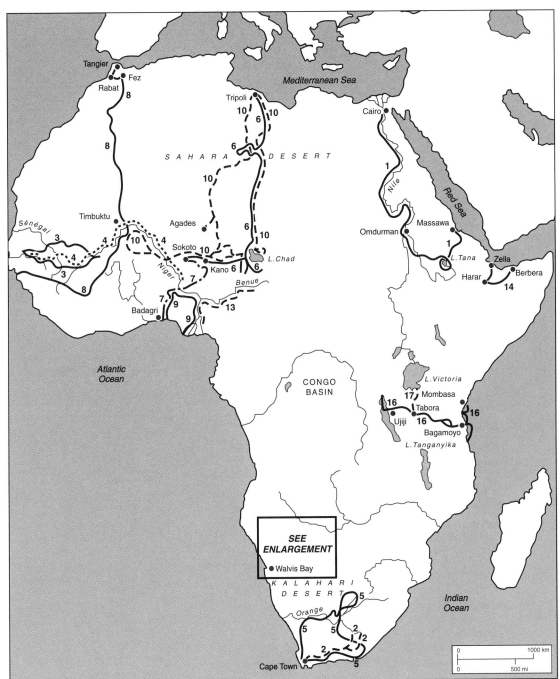

© DIAGRAM

Dr David Livingstone (1813–73 CE)
A Scottish missionary and explorer, Livingstone encouraged the spread of Christianity, and the expansion of trade with Europe, in East and Central Africa in the nineteenth century. He hoped that achieving these goals would help to bring an end to the slave trade.

Sir Henry Morton Stanley (1841–1904 CE)
Although famous as the man who found the missing David Livingstone in Africa in 1871, Stanley had had an eventful life prior to this discovery. After an unhappy childhood in Wales, he ran away to sea at the age of 15, fought in the American Civil War, and then became a newspaper reporter.

Livingstone's journeys (right)
This map shows the three major expeditions made by Livingstone during the period 1849–1873 CE.

Stanley meets Dr Livingstone (right)
The formal first meeting between the two men in 1871 CE. Stanley was an American journalist of Welsh birth who had been sent to Africa by the proprietor of the New York Herald, James Gordon Bennett, to prove that Livingstone, missing for three years, was still alive.

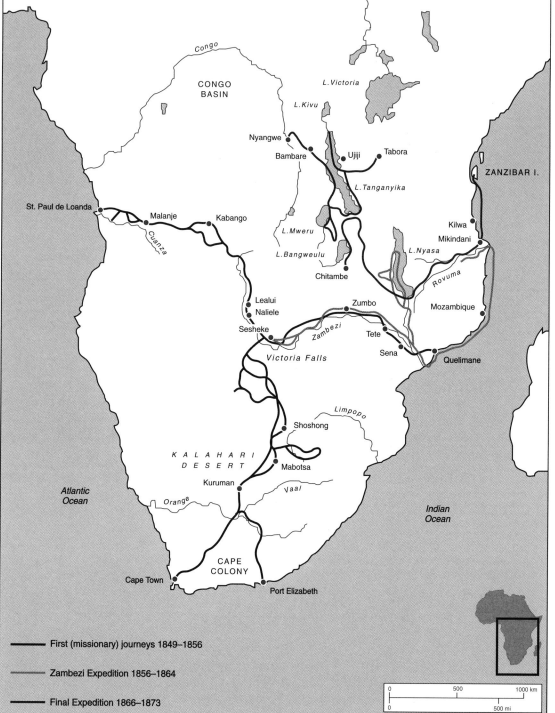

─────── First (missionary) journeys 1849–1856

─────── Zambezi Expedition 1856–1864

─────── Final Expedition 1866–1873

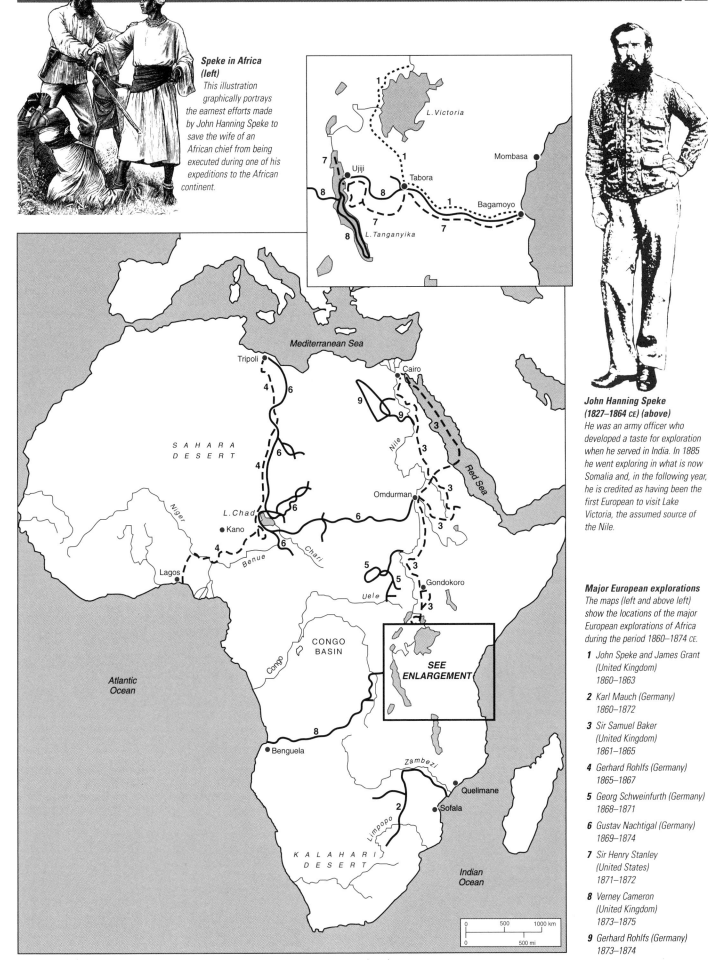

Speke in Africa (left)
This illustration graphically portrays the earnest efforts made by John Hanning Speke to save the wife of an African chief from being executed during one of his expeditions to the African continent.

John Hanning Speke (1827–1864 CE) (above)
He was an army officer who developed a taste for exploration when he served in India. In 1885 he went exploring in what is now Somalia and, in the following year, he is credited as having been the first European to visit Lake Victoria, the assumed source of the Nile.

Major European explorations
The maps (left and above left) show the locations of the major European explorations of Africa during the period 1860–1874 CE.

1 *John Speke and James Grant (United Kingdom) 1860–1863*

2 *Karl Mauch (Germany) 1860–1872*

3 *Sir Samuel Baker (United Kingdom) 1861–1865*

4 *Gerhard Rohlfs (Germany) 1865–1867*

5 *Georg Schweinfurth (Germany) 1868–1871*

6 *Gustav Nachtigal (Germany) 1869–1874*

7 *Sir Henry Stanley (United States) 1871–1872*

8 *Verney Cameron (United Kingdom) 1873–1875*

9 *Gerhard Rohlfs (Germany) 1873–1874*

© DIAGRAM

NORTH AMERICA

SOUTH AMERICA

Africa in the Americas
The tinted areas of the map (right) show where slaves were taken in the Americas. Today, African influences are unmistakable throughout the Americas. Rarely is it possible for individuals to trace their lineage to any particular African people, but contemporary diet, religion, music, language, and folktales often bear witness to a rich African heritage. In Brazil (the most important destination for slaves), African influences are clear, for example, in the rituals of the Candomblé religion, in which the gods are clearly Yoruba-derived.

Slavery in Africa

There were a few major instances of slavery before the the practice gained real momentum in the late sixteenth and early seventeenth centuries. During the Christian Reconquest of Spain (thirteenth to fifteenth centuries) many captured Muslims were enslaved. In continuing conflicts between North African Muslims and Christians of Spain and Portugal it remained common for those captured by either side to be sold into slavery. In Spain and Portugal many slaves were employed in domestic and agricultural roles.

From the thirteenth century, Europeans employed African slaves bought from Arab traders on sugar plantations in the Mediterranean. During the fifteenth century, the Portuguese established sugar and coffee plantations on islands off the West African coast and used slaves obtained through trade with African kingdoms.

In the early sixteenth century, European colonists in the Caribbean and Central and South America forced Native Americans and European convicts to work their mines and plantations. Most of these unwilling workers died of disease and cruel treatment, so the settlers turned to Africa to solve their labor needs, believing that Africans could best withstand the harsh working conditions and tropical climate. The Spanish and Portuguese were the first to enter the Atlantic slave trade, but by the late sixteenth and early seventeenth centuries many other European nations had established forts and trading posts along the coast of West Africa from present-day Senegal to Angola. By

the time the slave trade was finally halted in the late nineteenth century (over fifty years after it was banned by Britain in 1807, and the United States in 1808), over 15 million African men, women, and children had been transported across the Atlantic.

Slavery existed before the European arrival in Africa, with prisoners of war, debtors, or criminals being common victims of enslavement. Slavery and slave trading had never been practiced on such a large scale before, however, nor with such a scant disregard for human suffering. The introduction of material incentives–goods exchanged for slaves–resulted in the established rules governing enslavement breaking down, and "wars" were provoked to legitimize kidnapping. Most slaves originated from relatively short distances from the coast and few peoples were left unaffected by the trade. Local economies were distorted and social relationships undermined.

Factors, or resident agents, dealt with local rulers through a web of European and African traders who would skim off a proportion of the goods traded. Slave purchasers developed preferences for particular parts of Africa and crude, ethnic stereotypes evolved. For example, the Akan peoples of Ghana were regarded as being rebellious in nature; the Igbo of Nigeria were considered easy to control though prone to moodiness or even suicide; and the Manding peoples from Senegal were seen as excellent house servants. Such goods as iron bars, guns, beads, cloth, and alcohol were traded. In 1756 it was recorded that one man could be traded for 115 gal. (435 l) of rum, and a woman 95 gal. (360 l).

"The triangular trade"

Most slave ships sailed from European ports carrying goods to trade for African slaves. Slaves were delivered to trading posts and crammed into the ships' holds without delay. Ships' crews feared falling prey to the fever and dysentery that had reduced the life expectancy of European residents of West Africa to just two years. On board the ships, conditions were appalling: little ventilation, poor food, and no medical care. In general, up to one quarter of the Africans died (and sometimes more) during the three-

to six-week journey as a result of disease, suicide, or by being thrown overboard for acts of resistance or because of sickness. On arrival in the Americas, the Africans were sold and the ships were loaded with gold, silver, sugar, tobacco, cotton, and other goods. The ships then returned to Europe, unloaded, and resumed their triangular trading. This trade was also carried out by a smaller number of American slavers who crossed the Atlantic carrying rum, returning to America via the Caribbean.

1 Bristol, England
Trader loads cargo of firearms, alcoholic drinks (especially rum), cloth, and simple manufactured goods.

2 The Slave Coast
Cargo is exchanged for slaves at fortified trading posts along the coast. Sale value of slaves taken on is much greater than value of goods exchanged for them.

3 The Middle Passage
Packed into the cargo hold of the trader's ship and chained together to prevent rebellion, slaves receive little food or water. During the six-week voyage half may die.

4 Cuba
Slaves are unloaded, sold to dealers for a large profit, and sent to stockades until they can be auctioned to local plantation owners. The trader takes on a cargo of molasses and tobacco.

5 Nantes, France
Molasses and tobacco cargo is sold for a large profit to local merchants eager to meet massive European demand.

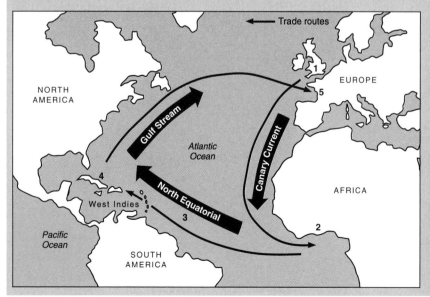

Trade routes

EUROPE

NORTH AMERICA

Gulf Stream

Atlantic Ocean

Canary Current

AFRICA

North Equatorial

West Indies

Pacific Ocean

SOUTH AMERICA

The African Slave Trade 1500–1900 CE

1500	**1517** Spain begins regular shipments of African slaves to the Americas
	1534 The first African slaves are landed in Brazil
	1542 Shipments of African slaves increase after Spain abolishes Native-American slavery in its colonies
	1575 The Portuguese found Luanda (Angola) as a base for slaving operations
	1592 English participation in the transatlantic slave trade begins
1600	**1605** Dutch begin carrying African slaves to the Caribbean
	1619 The first African slaves are sold to the colonists at Jamestown, Virginia
	1623–1626 Queen Nzinga of Ndongo is defeated in a war against Portuguese slave traders
	1640s The English import African slaves to work on sugar plantations in their Caribbean colonies
	1642 The English gain the right to buy slaves in Portuguese Africa
	c.1680–1730 The West African kingdoms of Oyo and Dahomey supply c. 20,000 captives a year for European slave traders
	1698 The "triangular trade" begins
1700–1749	**1713** British gain control of the slave trade to Spanish America
	1724 Dahomey prospers as a partner of European slave traders
1750–1799	**1777** The Vermont constitution is the first document in the USA to abolish slavery
	c. 1780 Transatlantic slave trade at its peak: up to 100,000 Africans are exported as slaves annually
	1783 English Quakers petition the British Parliament to abolish the international slave trade
	1787 The British settle 400 freed slaves in Sierra Leone
1800–1849	**1802** Denmark is the first European country to ban its citizens from engaging in the slave trade
	1807 Britain declares the slave trade illegal
	1808 The United States bans the import of slaves
	1810--1812 The slave trade becomes illegal in Mexico, Argentina, Chile, and Venezuela
	1815 France is forced to abolish the slave trade after its defeat in the Napoleonic Wars
	1820 Spain officially abolishes the slave trade in its colonies but does not enforce the ban effectively
	1821–1822 Liberia is founded for freed US slaves
	1833 Britain abolishes slavery throughout its empire
	1846 Slave trade between Portuguese Africa and Brazil at its peak
	1848 Slavery is abolished in French colonies
	1849 France founds Libreville in Gabon for freed slaves
1850–1888	**1850** Under British pressure Brazil agrees to equate the slave trade with piracy
	1860s The Spanish finally end the importation of slaves to Cuba
	1865 The Thirteenth Amendment abolishes slavery in the USA
	1873 The sultan of Zanzibar closes his slave market
	1880 Tippu Tip's central African empire flourishes, supplying slaves and ivory to Arab traders
	1880 Slave trade in Spain's colonies finally ends
	1882 Portugal bans the export of slaves from its African colonies finally ending the Atlantic slave trade: in all about 15 million Africans have been transported to the Americas since 1517
	1885–1898 Britain suppresses Arab slave traders in East Africa ending the Indian Ocean slave trade
	1888 Brazil becomes the last American country to ban slavery

Lives for sale!
This scene from a slave market is set in Zanzibar. The island attracted the attention of the British, who persuaded the ruling sultan to abolish the slave trade in 1873 CE.

Loading the ship
This old engraving depicts slaves being loaded onto a ship for transportation, probably to the Americas.

Estimated number of slaves imported (in thousands)

	1451–1600	1601–1700	1701–1810
Brazil (Portuguese and Dutch)	75	600	1,950
West Indies (French, British and other)	0	525	3450
America and Cuba (Spanish)	100	300	600
North America (British)	0	50	450

The importation of slaves.
The diagram (left) shows the estimated number of slaves imported by the Portuguese, Dutch, French, British and Spanish colonialists into North America, the Caribbean and Brazil over the period 1451–1810 CE.

© DIAGRAM

Slave sources and depots

These four maps show the peoples, kingdoms, and regions where slaves were found originally, and the places in Africa from which they were transported, during the height of the slave trade .

1 Sources 1450–1700 CE

2 Depots 1450–1700 CE

3 Sources 1700–1810 CE

4 Depots 1700–1810 CE

The Zanzibar slave market, 1872 CE
Although not new to the region, slavery reached an unprecedented level in the nineteenth century.

Collared

Slave traders leading a group of slaves chained at the neck to a single beam of wood. During the 350 years of the Atlantic slave trade, more than 15 million West Africans were enslaved.

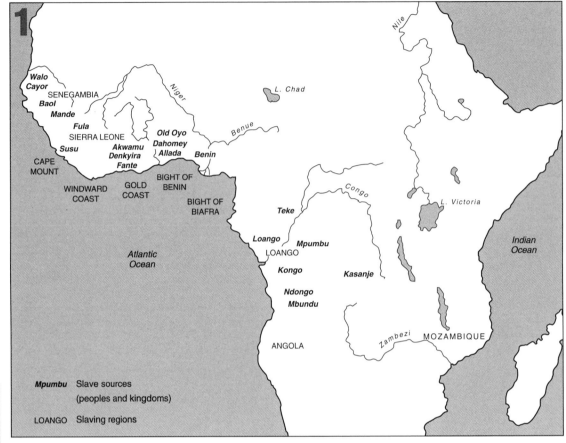

1

Walo
Cayor
SENEGAMBIA
Baol
Mande
Fula
SIERRA LEONE
Susu
CAPE MOUNT
WINDWARD COAST
GOLD COAST
Akwamu
Denkyira
Fante
Old Oyo
Dahomey
Allada
Benin
BIGHT OF BENIN
BIGHT OF BIAFRA
Niger
Benue
L. Chad
Nile
L. Victoria
Congo
Teke
Loango
LOANGO
Mpumbu
Kongo
Kasanje
Ndongo
Mbundu
ANGOLA
Zambezi
MOZAMBIQUE
Atlantic Ocean
Indian Ocean

Mpumbu Slave sources (peoples and kingdoms)

LOANGO Slaving regions

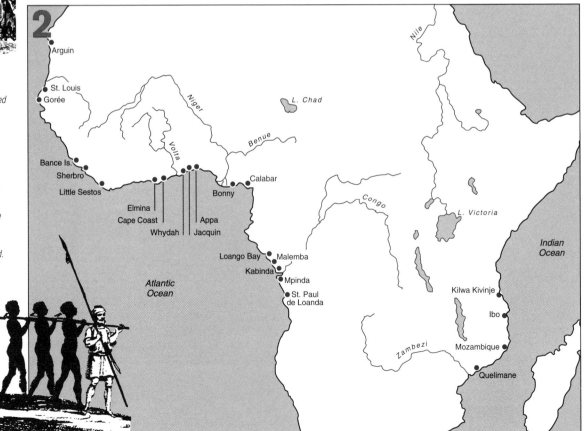

2

Arguin
St. Louis
Gorée
Bance Is.
Sherbro
Little Sestos
Elmina
Cape Coast
Whydah
Appa
Jacquin
Bonny
Calabar
Volta
Niger
Benue
L. Chad
Nile
Congo
L. Victoria
Loango Bay
Malemba
Kabinda
Mpinda
St. Paul de Loanda
Kilwa Kivinje
Ibo
Mozambique
Quelimane
Zambezi
Atlantic Ocean
Indian Ocean

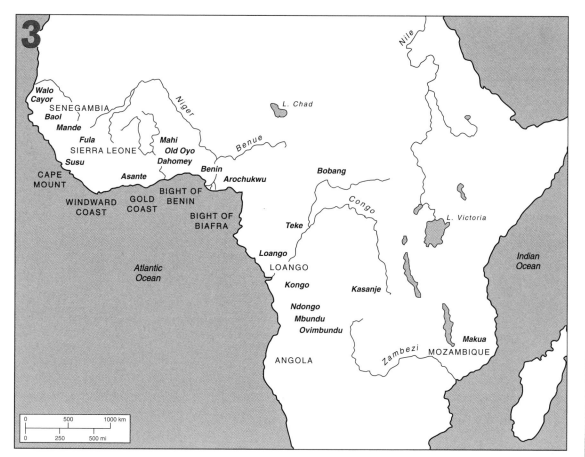

3

Walo
Cayor
SENEGAMBIA
Baol
Mande
Fula
SIERRA LEONE
Susu
CAPE
MOUNT
WINDWARD
COAST
GOLD
COAST
Asante
Mahi
Old Oyo
Dahomey
Benin
Arochukwu
BIGHT OF
BENIN
BIGHT OF
BIAFRA
Bobang
Teke
Loango
LOANGO
Kongo
Kasanje
Ndongo
Mbundu
Ovimbundu
ANGOLA
Makua
MOZAMBIQUE
Atlantic
Ocean
Indian
Ocean
Niger
Benue
L. Chad
Congo
L. Victoria
Zambezi
Nile

0   500   1000 km
0   250   500 mi

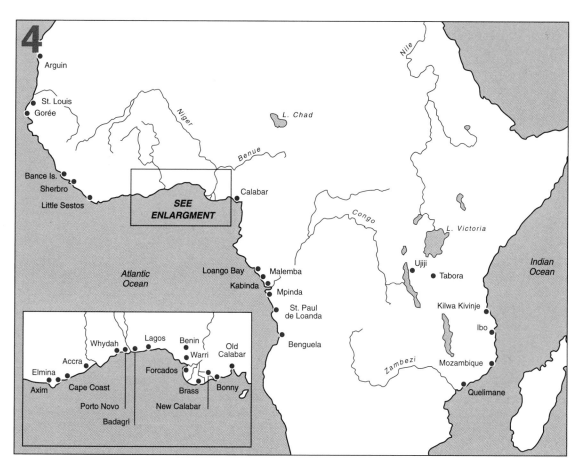

4

Arguin
St. Louis
Gorée
Bance Is.
Sherbro
Little Sestos
SEE
ENLARGMENT
Calabar
Loango Bay
Kabinda
Malemba
Mpinda
St. Paul
de Loanda
Benguela
Ujiji
Tabora
Kilwa Kivinje
Ibo
Mozambique
Quelimane
Atlantic
Ocean
Indian
Ocean
Niger
Benue
L. Chad
Congo
L. Victoria
Zambezi
Nile

Elmina
Axim
Accra
Cape Coast
Whydah
Porto Novo
Badagri
Lagos
Benin
Warri
Forcados
Brass
New Calabar
Bonny
Old
Calabar

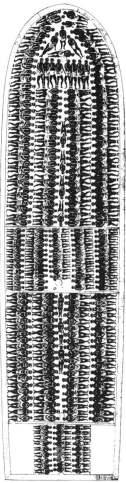

Casualties of the voyage
Many Africans did not survive the
difficult journey to the European
colonies of the New World. The
cramped conditions of a slave ship
are shown in this drawing of the
floor plan below deck in which,
not surprisingly, many people
perished before reaching their
destination.

Abolitionist engraving
An emblem created by a late
eighteenth century example of
"enlightened opinion" opposed to
the slave trade .

Olaudau Equiano
A former slave, he became a
prominent figure in the anti-
slavery movement in Britain.

ABOLITION OF SLAVERY AND THE SLAVE TRADE 1772–1873 CE

Pre 19th century

1772 Britain: Keeping of slaves in Great Britain banned following legal arguments that all persons residing in Britain should enjoy personal liberty. Slavery remains legal in British colonies.

1783 US: Britain recognizes American independence and loses control of plantations in America (until now the largest center of slave use in the British Empire).

1787 Britain: Society for the Abolition of the Slave Trade founded. Antislavery movement gains strength; Christian groups denounce slavery; some economists (including Adam Smith) argue that slavery is economically inefficient as well as immoral.

1788 France: *Société des Amis des Noirs* (Society of Friends of Black People) founded; dedicated to ending slave trade and slave ownership.

1792 Denmark: First country to ban slave trade in all its colonial possessions.

1794 France: Slavery abolished in all its colonies in accordance with the principles of the *Declaration of the Rights of Man* (1789). Former slaves win control of Caribbean island of Haiti (until now the center of slave use in the French Empire). Napoleon reestablishes slavery in French colonies but his military expedition to take back control of Haiti fails (1802).

19th century

1807 Britain: Slave trade made illegal throughout the British Empire, following campaign of William Wilberforce and others. Britain puts diplomatic pressure on other European countries to ban the trade. Virtual collapse of West African slave trade.

1814 Holland: Slave trade in its colonial possessions banned.

1815 France: Slave trade in its colonies banned during Napoleon's Hundred Days' administration.
Portugal: Slave trade in its colonies in northern hemisphere banned (ban extended to all colonies in 1830).

1820 Spain: Slave trade in all its colonies banned.

1822 Britain: Agreement concluded with sultan of Zanzibar (center of Arab trade in slaves), restricting East African slave trade. Second agreement (1846) further restricts the trade.

1823 Britain: Anti-Slavery Society established; dedicated to worldwide ban on slavery

1830 South America: Most states achieve independence from Spanish rule and abolish slavery or adopt programs of gradual emancipation.

1834 Britain: Slavery banned in all its colonies.

1848 France: Slavery banned in all its colonies by French provisional government following establishment of the 2nd French Republic.

1863 US: President Lincoln issues Emancipation Proclamation freeing all slaves in US (in practice, effective only in areas controlled by Union army).

1865 US: End of American Civil War. 13th Amendment to US constitution abolishes slavery.

1870 Spain: Policy of gradual slave emancipation adopted on Caribbean island of Cuba (the largest remaining center of slave use in Spanish colonial possessions).

1873 Britain: Now a dominant power in East Africa, Britain forces Sultan of Zanzibar to ban slave trade in his dominions, effectively ending East African slave trade from Zanzibar.

Suppression of the slave trade
These four maps show the extent to
which the slave trade was
suppressed in Africa during the
following periods CE:

1 Before 1870

2 1870–1880

3 1880–1890

4 1890 onwards

➤ Terminated European route

Loango European center of slave export

➤ Terminated Islamic route

Khartoum Islamic center of slave export/import

Darfur Islamic region of slave export

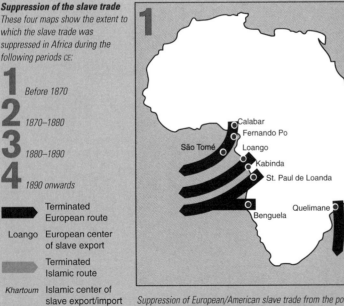

Calabar
Fernando Po
São Tomé
Loango
Kabinda
St. Paul de Loanda
Benguela
Quelimane

Suppression of European/American slave trade from the ports of Benguela,
St. Paul de Loanda, Loango, and Kabinda, Calabar, São Tomé, and
Quelimane.

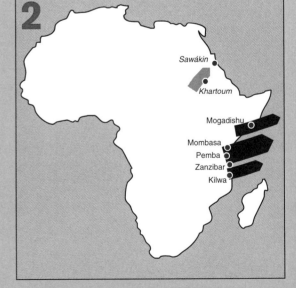

Sawákin
Khartoum
Mogadishu
Mombasa
Pemba
Zanzibar
Kilwa

Suppression of European slave trade from Mogadishu, Mombasa, Pemba,
Zanzibar, and Kilwa; and from Sawákin of Islamic trade.

Afro-American slavery 1600–1860 CE

1600–1699	**1619** First Africans sold to Jamestown colonists
	1690 Slaves in all English colonies
	1698 "Triangular trade" begins
1700–1749	**1712** Slave riots in New York City
	1725 Colonies have 75,000 slaves
	1739 Cato Conspiracy (Stono, SC)
1750–1799	**1776** Slave trade forbidden, or heavily taxed, in 11 states
	1776 Jefferson proposes plan for 'African colonization of the negroes'
	1777 Vermont ends slavery
	1784 Gradual emancipation adopted by Connecticut and Rhode Island
	1786 Underground "railroad" (escape network) exists
	1790 First petition to Congress for emancipation
	1793 Fereral fugitive slave laws
	1798 Georgia last state to abolish slave trade
1800–1849	**1801** Gabriel Plot in Virginia
	1808 Congress prohibits importation of slaves
	1815 1.3 million slaves in the US
	1817 American Colonization Society established
	1820 Missouri Compromise
	1820 Slave Importation Act
	1821 Monrovia, Liberia bought by American Colonization Society
	1822 Monrovia settled by black Americans
	1822 Vesey Slave Plot (Charleston, SC)
	1830 Underground "railroad" spreads through 14 northern states
	1831 Nat Turner Insurrection (Southampton Co, Va)
	1831 Mississippi Colonisation Society founded
	1831–32 Virginian Convention defeats emancipation proposals
	1833 American Antislavery Society founded
	1834 Proslavery riots in New York and Philadelphia
	1836 Adoption of the gag rule
	1839 Formation of antislavery Liberal Party
	1847 Independent Republic of Liberia, Africa
	1848 Antislavery 'Free Soil' convention and party
1850–1860	**1850** Compromise of 1850
	1854 Kansas-Nebraska Act
	1859 Southern Commercial Convention
	1859 John Brown's Raid on Harper's Ferry

A mix of cultures
The style of the American South was visible in Americo-Liberian architecture, such as the president's official residence

Declaration of Independence
Liberia's Declaration of Independence, written in 1847 CE when the Republic of Liberia was established, explains why Americans settled in Africa and expresses the aspirations that they had brought with them to their new homeland.

"We, the people of the Republic of Liberia, were originally inhabitants of the United States of North America.

In some parts of that country we were debarred from all rights and privileges of men–in other parts, public sentiment, more powerful than law, frowned us down...

We were made a separate and distinct class and against us every avenue of improvement was effectually closed. Strangers from other lands, of a color different from ours, were preferred before us...

...we looked with anxiety for some asylum from the deep degradation...

...In coming to the barbarous shores of Africa we indulged the pleasing hope that we would be permitted to exercise and improve those faculties which impart to man his dignity..."

Suppression of Islamic slave trade in Murzuk and other ports, causing inland trade to cease gradually from Kano, Kukawa, Khartoum, and Darfur.

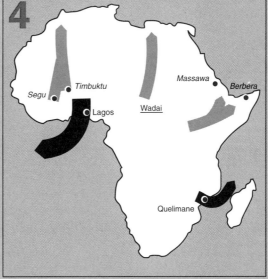

Suppression of European trade in Quelimane and Lagos; and Islamic trade from Wadai, Segu, and Timbuktu to the north coast and trade to Berbera on the east coast.

© DIAGRAM

Abd al-Qadir

Abd al-Qadir, the Emir (ruler) of Oran, led the struggle against French colonialism from 1832 CE. He opposed the arrival of French settlers who occupied large areas. Al-Qadir created an efficient state around Mascara, but he finally surrendered in 1847. He was then imprisoned in France.

Resistance to Colonialism (North Africa)

Soon after their territories had been occupied, many Africans, alerted to the implications of colonialism, took up arms against their new rulers. For example, in North Africa in the first half of the nineteenth century, the Algerians fiercely resisted French occupation between 1832–1847 CE. Their leader was Abd al-Qadir. To the west, Moroccan forces later clashed with French and Spanish troops in an attempt to hold back colonization; their resistance continued into the 1930s.

In northeastern Africa, many Egyptians strongly resisted British and French influence. However, following the Mahdist revolt in Sudan, an Anglo-Egyptian force was assembled to put down the rebellion and Sudan became an Anglo-Egyptian condominium.

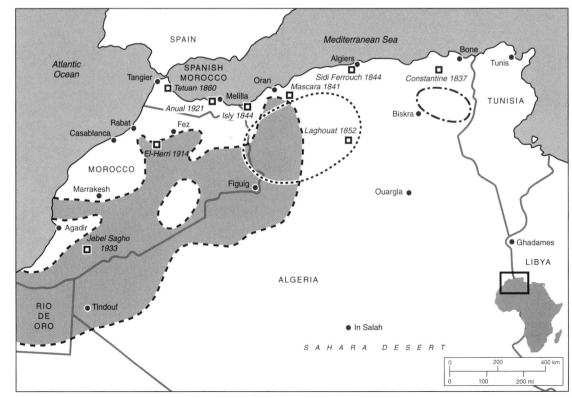

Rif resistance (left)

In 1909 CE the people in the Rif region attacked European settlers, who were farming land near Melilla, a tiny settlement on the Mediterranean coast which had been under Spanish control since 1497. Spain sent a 50,000-strong army to put down the rebellion and captives were held in the fortress at Melilla.

Abd al-Krim

In Morocco, the Berber leader Abd al-Krim is remembered as a major resistance leader. In 1921 CE, he became president of the rebel Republic of the Rif, but he was defeated by a French and Spanish force in 1926.

Northwest African resistance to European colonialism 1830–1933 CE		
19th Century		
	1832	Algerians led by Abd al-Qádir resist French (to 1847)
	1837	Algerians fight French at Constantine; Algerians defeated
	1841	Algerians fight French at Mascara; Algerians defeated
	1844	Algerians fight French at Isly and Sidi Ferrouch; Algerians defeated
	1852	Algerians fight French at Laghouat; Algerians defeated
	1857	Kabylie revolt against French; Moroccans defeated
	1860	Moroccans fight Spanish at Tetuan;
1900–33	**1912**	Berbers of Bled el-Siba resist French (to 1925)
	1914	Berbers of Bled el-Siba fight French at El-Herri; Berbers defeat French
	1921	Moroccans fight Spanish at Anual; Moroccans defeat Spanish
	1933	Berbers fight French at Jebel Sagho; Berbers defeated

——— Colonial borders 1933

 *Isly 1844* □ Site of major battle

- - - - - Boundary of area of resistance led by Abd al-Qadir 1834–1857

Bled el-Siba, an area that was only very loosely controlled by the Moroccan ruler

—·—·— Boundary of area of Kabylie revolts 1857

[Map showing North Africa with the following labels:]

SPAIN

Mediterranean Sea

Atlantic Ocean

Algiers

Bone

Tunis

Tangier

SPANISH MOROCCO

□ Tetuan 1860

Oran

Sidi Ferrouch 1844

Constantine 1837 □

Melilla

Mascara 1841

TUNISIA

Anual 1921

Isly 1844

Biskra

Rabat

Fez

Laghouat 1852 □

Casablanca

El-Herri 1914

MOROCCO

Figuig

Ouargla ●

Marrakesh

Agadir ●

Jebel Sagho
□ 1933

ALGERIA

Ghadames ●

LIBYA

RIO DE ORO

● Tindouf

● In Salah

SAHARA DESERT

0   200   400 km

0   100   200 mi

A French view (above)
In the nineteenth century, the French government wanted to persuade its citizens of the justness of its cause in the conquest and colonization of Algeria. To this end, it produced posters that represented the French as heroes who were fighting a dangerous and treacherous foe.

The Mahdi (left)
Muhammad Ahmad, who was known by his title of Mahdi (or Muslim Messiah), led a revolt against Anglo-Egyptian rule in Sudan in 1882 CE. Following early victories, he died in his capital, Omdurman, in 1885. His Mahdist state lasted until 1898, when the Mahdist forces were defeated at the Battle of Omdurman.

General Charles Gordon (above)
Gordon, a British soldier, served as governor of Sudan from 1877–1880 CE. He returned to the country four years later to help in the evacuation of Egyptian troops. In 1885, he held Khartoum for 317 days before he was killed–only two days before the arrival of a British relief column.

Northeast African resistance to European colonialism 1881–1932 CE

19th century

	1881	Egyptian nationalist revolt against British and French influence
	1882	Egyptian army fights British at Tel el-Kebir; Egyptians defeated
	1890	Rabih b. Fadl Allah begins to resist French in Lake Chad area (to 1900)
	1898	Mahdists fight British at Atbara and Omdurman; Mahdists defeated
	1899	Mahdists fight British at Umm Diwaykarat; Mahdist state destroyed
	1899	Rabih b. Fadl Allah fights French at Niellem and Kouno; Rabih defeats French
1900–32	**1900**	Rabih b. Fadl Allah fights French at Lakhta; Rabih killed
	1901	Rabih's son, Fadl Allah b. Rabih fights French at Gujba; Fadl Allah killed; resistance ends
	1912	Sanúsiyah, a militant Libyan Islamic movement, resists Italians (to 1932)
	1919	Egyptians rebel against British (to 1920)

Battle of Lakhta (1900)
Rabih b. Fadl Allah, a former slave trader from Darfur, the westernmost region of Sudan, served as a soldier under the Egyptians. In 1899, his army defeated the French. But he was defeated at the Battle of Lakhta, south of Lake Chad, in 1900. This illustration of his decapitated head appeared in a French magazine.

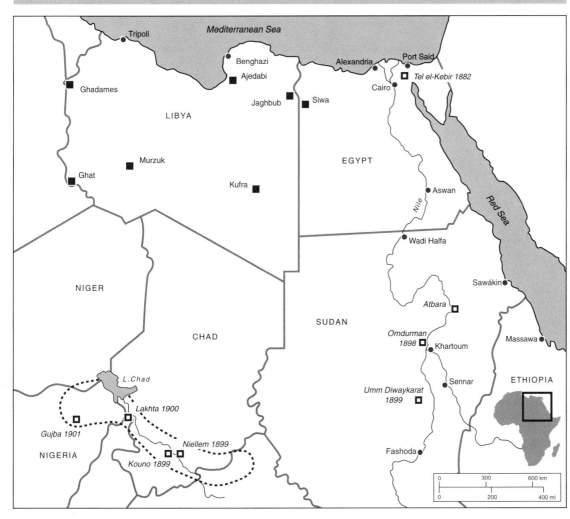

Present-day borders

Atbara 1898 ☐ Site of major battle

- - - - Boundary of area in which Rabih b. Fadl Allah resisted French expansion

■ Towns with major Sanúsiyah lodges

© DIAGRAM

Resistance to Colonialism (West Africa)

The main period of European colonization in Africa south of the Sahara occurred between the late 1870s and 1903 CE, with the British conquest of the Fulani-Hausa Sokoto Caliphate in what is now northern Nigeria. The conquest of the huge territory of French West Africa began in the long-established region around the Sénégal River. From this westerly location, French forces pushed inland, often meeting fierce resistance but finally conquering formerly independent African kingdoms. Among those who held up the French advance was

Samore Toure, who founded and led a massive Mandinka empire, which included much of present-day Guinea, Ivory Coast, and southern Mali. To the north, the French also had to overcome the Tukolor empire which resisted until 1894.

The British also met with fierce resistance from the Asante in the conquest of Ghana and by the Igbo, Hausa, and others in Nigeria. However, in Togo, the Germans generally maintained the pre-colonial economy and so violence in the territory was on a relatively small scale.

Sekou Ahmadu (left)
Sekou Ahmadu was the son of Al-Hajj Umar, a Muslim Fulani cleric who founded the Tukulor empire, which extended across what is now southern Mali, including part of northeastern Guinea. Sekou Ahmadu led the resistance to the French conquest of the area, which continued until 1894.

Colonel Borgnis-Desbordes
Colonel Borgnis-Desbordes was a French soldier who was instrumental in the conquest of French West Africa.

Samori Toure (c.1830–1904 CE)
Samori Toure led West African resistance to French colonialism. At first a trader, he served in the army of the Sise people for several years, then formed his own army and built up the Second Mandinka Empire, which by 1881 stretched from Guinea to Ivory Coast. He fought off French advances for seven years, but was captured and imprisoned in 1898, then exiled.

West-African resistance to European colonialism 1855–1894 CE

19th century

- **1855** Trarza resists French
- **1881** Mandinka Empire resists French (to 1894) and retreats eastward; Futa Bondu resists French (to 1887)
- **1883** Cayor resists French (to 1886)
- **1885** Sarrakole resist French (to 1887)
- **1890** Jolof resist French; Tukulor Empire resists French and retreats eastward (to 1893)
- **1893** Tukulor Empire resists French (to 1894); Tukulor Empire fights French at Kori-Kori; Tukulor Empire defeated

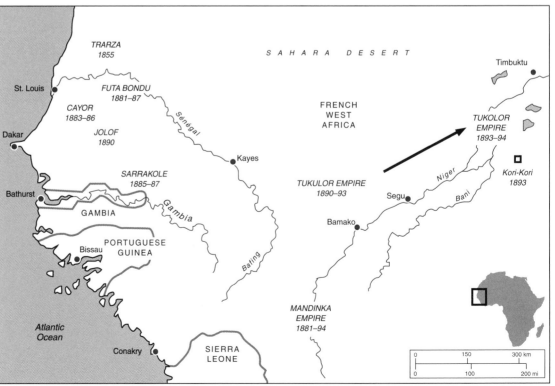

CAYOR 1883–86 People or state that resisted colonial expansion

→ Tukulor Empire's line of retreat 1890–1893 CE

— Colonial borders 1900 CE

Kori-Kori 1893 CE ☐ Site of major battle

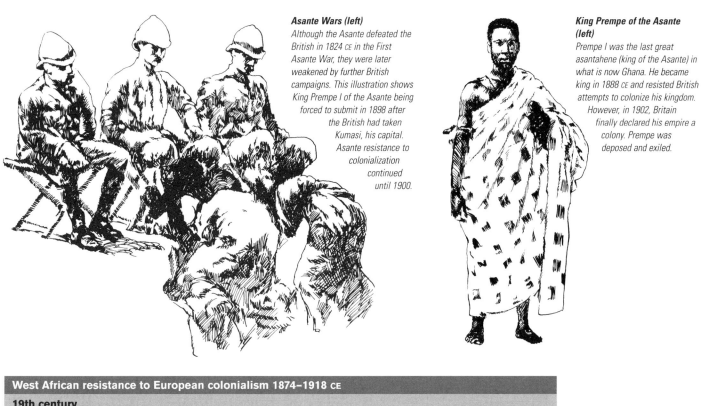

Asante Wars (left)

Although the Asante defeated the British in 1824 CE in the First Asante War, they were later weakened by further British campaigns. This illustration shows King Prempe I of the Asante being forced to submit in 1898 after the British had taken Kumasi, his capital. Asante resistance to colonialization continued until 1900.

King Prempe of the Asante (left)

Prempe I was the last great asantahene (king of the Asante) in what is now Ghana. He became king in 1888 CE and resisted British attempts to colonize his kingdom. However, in 1902, Britain finally declared his empire a colony. Prempe was deposed and exiled.

West African resistance to European colonialism 1874–1918 CE

19th century		
	1874	Asante War with British
	1881	Mandinka Empire resists French and retreats eastward (to 1894)
	1894	Mandinka Empire resists French (to 1898)
	1898	Temne-Mende resist French; French meet resistance at Sikasso
1900–18	**1900**	Asante rebel against British
	1901	Baoule rebel against French (to 1917)
	1910	Togo people migrate from harsh German laws
	1914	Kissi and Mossi migrate from French territory to avoid war recruitment (to 1918)

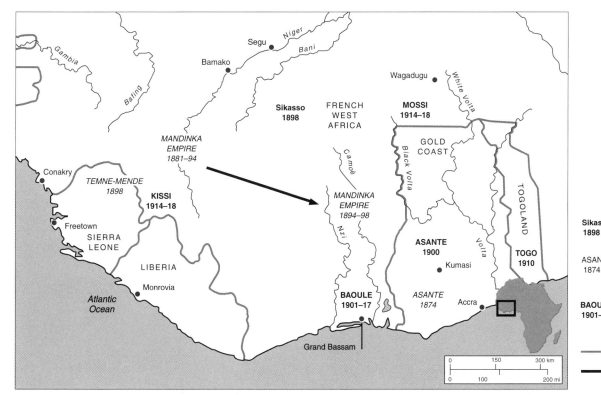

Sikasso 1898 CE — Center of resistance or rebellion

ASANTE 1874 CE — People or state that resisted colonial expansion

BAOULE 1901–17 — People that rebelled against an established colonial power

—— Colonial borders 1913

➜ Mandinka Empire's line of retreat 1894 CE

A Fulani cavalry charge (left)
The Fulani shown here were part of the cavalry engaged in a jihad; these Islamic holy wars were very common during the eighteenth and nineteenth centuries in West Africa.

A former king (above)
This is an illustration of Béjanzin, king of Dahomey, before he was deposed by the French in 1892 CE, and the kingdom became a French colony.

West-African resistance to European colonialism 1886–1918 CE

19th century

1886	Igbo resist British (sporadic to 1917)
1891	Kpe resist Germans (to 1894)
1892	British meet resistance at Ijebu; Dahomey resists French (to 1893)
1893	Mutiny at Douala against Germans
1894	Ebrohimi resists British
1895	Brass resists British
1897	Nupe and Ilorin resist British (first resistance by states of Sokoto Caliphate)

1900–18

1900	Bornu resists British
1901	Sokoto Caliphate fights British at Yola; British meet resistance at Arochukwu
1903	Sokoto Caliphate fights British at Kano, Burmi, Bima Hill, Gala, Bauchi, and Sokoto
1915	Rebellion against British at Bussa (to 1916)
1916	Rebellion against British at Iseyin; Borgu rebel against French (to 1917)
1917	Tuareg seize Agades from French
1918	Egba rebel against British

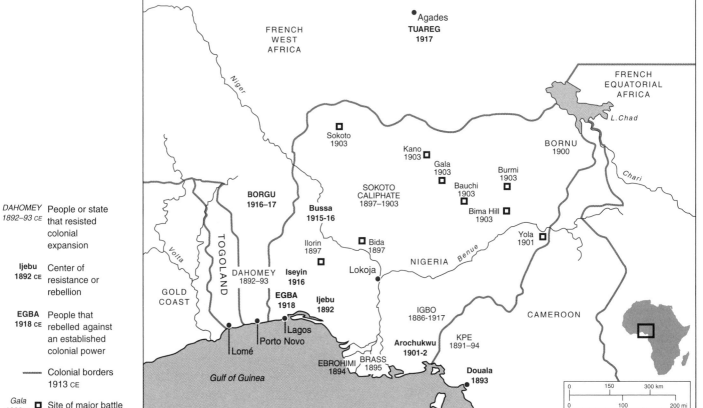

DAHOMEY
1892–93 CE   People or state that resisted colonial expansion

Ijebu
1892 CE   Center of resistance or rebellion

EGBA
1918 CE   People that rebelled against an established colonial power

——   Colonial borders 1913 CE

Gala
1903 CE □ Site of major battle

Resistance to Colonialism (Central Africa)

French colonization in Central Africa was less dynamic than in French West Africa. But it was accompanied by forced labor and other harsh measures, which provoked the anger of resistance of the local people. The agents appointed by King Léopold of Belgium in the Congo Free State, Léopold's "magnificent African cake", were similarly brutal in their methods.

Mwene Putu Kasonga (above)
Mwene Putu Kasonga was the king of the Yaka, the Suku kingdom in what is now the southwestern part of the Democratic Republic of Congo. The Belgian Congo authorities arrested the king in 1906 CE as a result of a misunderstanding by government officials. Everywhere in colonial Africa, the existing kingdoms and societies were being undermined and stripped of power.

Central African resistance to European colonialism 1890–1919 CE		
19th century		
	1891	Arab traders resist Belgians in Arab wars (to 1894)
	1892	Bassa resist Germans (to 1905); Zande resist Belgians (to 1912)
	1895	Yaka resist Belgians; Mutiny at Luluabourg against Belgians
1900–16	**1900**	Bashi resist Germans (to 1916); Mutiny at Boma against Belgians
	1901	Manja rebel against French (to 1905)
	1902	Yaka resist Belgians; Bailundo state resists Portuguese
	1903	Babua (to 1904) and Budja (to 1905) rebel against Belgians; peoples of southern Cameroon rebel against Germans ("Southern rebellion") (to 1910)
	1906	Fang rebel against French; Yaka rebel against Belgians
	1907	Dembos rebel against Portuguese (to 1910); Luba rebel against Belgians (to 1917)
	1910	Kota and Dar Kuti (to 1911) rebel against French; Babua rebel against Belgians
	1913	Ovimbundu and Kongo (to 1917) rebel against Portuguese
	1916	Banda (to 1918) and Zande (to 1917) rebel against French; peoples of western French Equatorial Africa rebel against French ("Western rebellion") (to 1919)

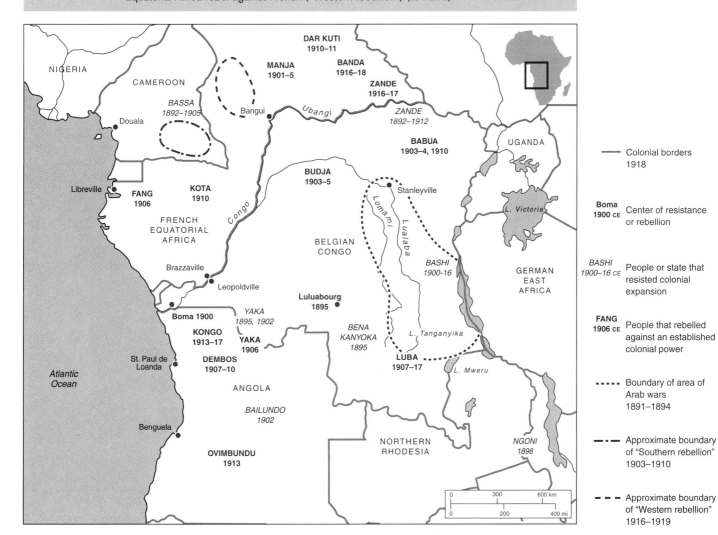

Legend	
——	Colonial borders 1918
Boma 1900 CE	Center of resistance or rebellion
BASHI 1900–16 CE	People or state that resisted colonial expansion
FANG 1906 CE	People that rebelled against an established colonial power
·····	Boundary of area of Arab wars 1891–1894
—·—·	Approximate boundary of "Southern rebellion" 1903–1910
– – –	Approximate boundary of "Western rebellion" 1916–1919

© DIAGRAM

Shaka (above)
Shaka was the founder of the Zulu kingdom. His brilliant military campaigns led to the Mfecane, a period of wars and migrations. The Zulu later fought brilliantly against the Afrikaners and British, but the Zulu kingdom was finally annexed in 1887 CE.

Merina resistance
The French deposed Queen Ranavalona in 1894 CE. They took Antananarivo in 1895 and the queen signed a treaty recognizing the establishment of a protectorate (colony).

BS Basutoland

SW Swaziland

——— Colonial borders
1900 CE

Ulundi ◻ Site of major battle
1879 CE

SOTHO People or state that
1880 CE resisted colonial expansion

SHONA People that rebelled
1896–97 CE against an established colonial power

Resistance to Colonialism (Eastern & Southern Africa)

Italy was active in the colonization of the Horn of Africa, but Christian Ethiopia was never colonized, although it was briefly conquered by Italy between 1935–1941 CE.

German and British colonizers were met with resistance in East Africa. For example, In Tanganyika (the mainland part of Tanzania), the Germans put down the Maji Maji rebellion of 1905 with great ferocity.

The Germans also acted harshly against uprisings in German Southwest Africa, while the Afrikaners and the British faced resistance from the Ndebele, Xhosa, Zulu and other peoples in southern Africa. The French in Madagascar also had to fight to subdue the Merina people who dominated the land prior to colonization.

Southern African resistance to European colonialism 1650–1917 CE	
Pre 19th century	
1650	Khoisan resist Dutch and British (to 1770)
1779	Xhosa resist Boers and British (to 1836)
19th century	
1837	Ndebele fight Boers at Marico; Ndebele defeated and retreat north
1838	Zulus fight Boers at Blood River; Zulus defeated
1879	Zulus fight British at Isandhlwana and Ulundi; Zulus defeat British at Islandhlwana but are defeated at Ulundi
1880	Sotho resist British in the "Gun War"; Sotho defeated
1883	Merina resists French
1893	Zulus (to 1896) and Ndebele resist British
1894	Shangane resist Portuguese (to 1895); Khoikhoi revolt against Germans
1895	Gaza resist Portuguese; Merina resist French (to 1897)
1896	Shona (to 1897) and Ndebele rebel against British
1898	Ngoni resist Portuguese
1900–17	**1900** Yao resist Portuguese (to 1912)
	1904 Herero, Nama (to 1907), and Khoikhoi (to 1906) rebel against Germans; Southern Malagasy resist French (to 1905)
	1906 Zulus rebel against British
	1917 Makombe revolt against Portuguese

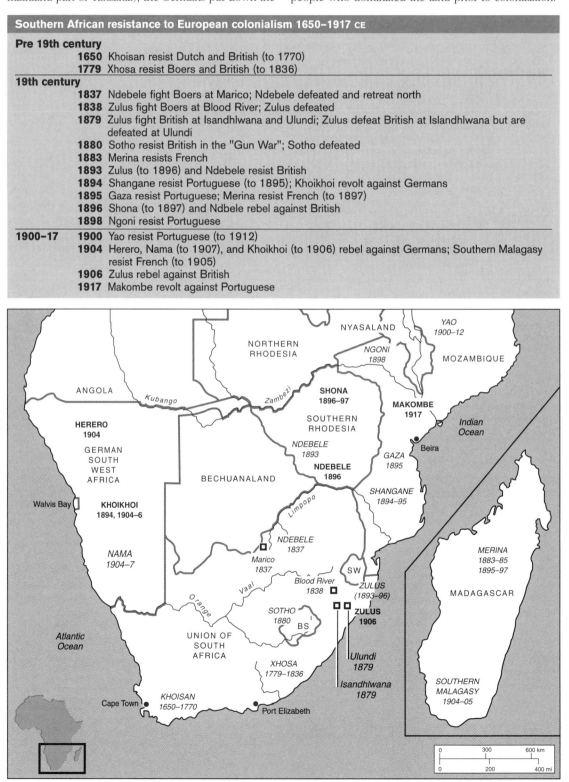

East African resistance to European colonialism 1887–1915 CE

19th century

1887 Karonga Arabs resist British traders (to 1895). Ethiopians fight Italians at Dogali; Ethiopians defeat Italians

1888 Swahili Arabs revolt against Germans (to 1889)

1890 Nyoro resist British (to 1899)

1891 Hehe (to1898) and Mbunga (to 1902) resist Germans

1892 Nyamwezi (to 1893) and Pogoro (to 1902) resist Germans

1895 Ethiopians fight Italians at Amba Alagi; Ethiopians defeat Italians

1896 Ethiopians fight Italians at Makale and Adowa; Ethiopians win, ending Italian attempts to colonize Ethiopia. Zanzibar uprising against British

1897 Ugandans mutiny against British

1900–15

1900 Nandi resist British (to 1905); Yao resist Portuguese (to 1912)

1901 Kikuyu resist British (to 1906)

1904 Embu resist British (to 1905)

1905 Maji Maji rebellion against Germans (to 1907); Gusii resist British

1915 The Rev. John Chilembwe leads uprising against British

Mutesa, king of Buganda
The British met with opposition in Uganda from the traditional rulers, including the Mutesas of Buganda, the kingdom that occupied the area lying north of the shores of Lake Victoria. Buganda became a British protectorate (colony) in 1894 CE.

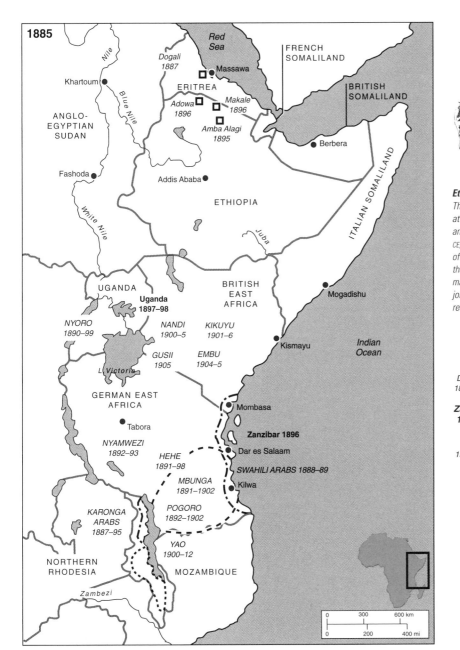

Ethiopian cavalrymen
The Ethiopian empire resisted attempts by Europeans to occupy and colonize it. However, in 1935 CE, Italian troops launched an offensive using modern weaponry that the Ethiopians could not match. In 1941, Ethiopian troops joined Allied forces in the reconquest of their country.

Menelik, Emperor of Ethiopia
He was the king of Shoa, the central province of Ethiopia and, in 1896 CE, defeated an Italian army at the Battle of Adowa, thus preserving Ethiopian independence.

© DIAGRAM

Colonial Occupation and Independence

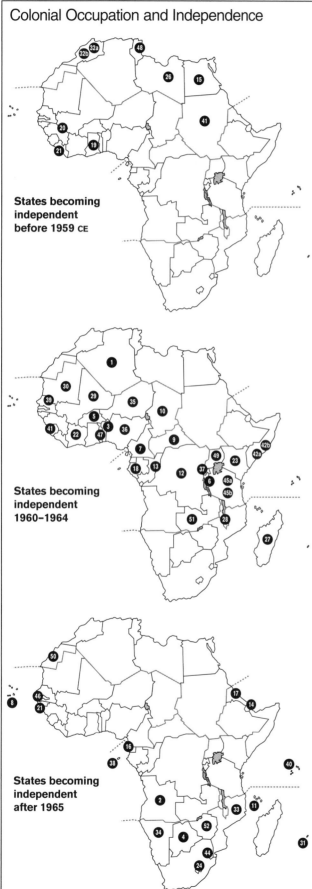

States becoming independent before 1959 CE

States becoming independent 1960–1964

States becoming independent after 1965

Country	
1	Algeria
2	Angola
3	Benin (as Dahomey)
4	Botswana (as Bechuanaland)
5	Burkina Faso (as Upper Volta)
6	Burundi (as part of Ruanda–Urundi)
7	Cameroon
8	Cape Verde
9	Central African Republic (as Oubangui–Chari, part of French Equatorial Africa)
10	Chad (as part of French Equatorial Africa)
11	Comoros
12	Congo [Dem. Rep] (as the Congo Free State and the Belgian Congo, formerly Zaire)
13	Congo [Rep of] (as Middle, or French, Congo, part of French Equatorial Africa)
14	Djibouti (as French Somaliland then French Territory of the Afars and the Issas)
15	Egypt
16	Equatorial Guinea including Bioko Island (as Fernando Póo)
17	Eritrea
18	Gabon (as part of French Equatorial Africa)
19	Ghana (as Gold Coast)
20	Guinea (as French Guinea)
21	Guinea-Bissau (as Portuguese Guinea)
22	Ivory Coast (as part of French West Africa)
23	Kenya
24	Lesotho (as Basutoland)
25	Liberia
26	Libya
27	Madagascar
28	Malawi (as Nyasaland)
29	Mali
30	Mauritania (as part of French West Africa)
31	Mauritius
32a	Morocco: (French)
32b	Morocco: (Spanish)
33	Mozambique
34	Namibia (as South West Africa)
35	Niger (as part of French West Africa)
36	Nigeria
37	Rwanda (as part of Ruanda-Urundi)
38	São Tomé and Príncipe
39	Senegal (as part of French West Africa)
40	Seychelles
41	Sierra Leone
42a	Somalia (As British Somaliland)
42b	Somalia (As Italian Somaliland)
43	Sudan
44	Swaziland
45a	Tanzania (as Tanganyika)
45b	Tanzania (Zanzibar)
46	The Gambia
47	Togo (as Togoland)
48	Tunisia
49	Uganda (as Uganda Protectorate)
50	Western Sahara (as Río de Oro)
51	Zambia (as Northern Rhodesia)
52	Zimbabwe (as Southern Rhodesia then Rhodesia)

Note: Ethiopia was never colonized, though it was invaded by Italy in 1936; Italy was driven out in 1941.
South Africa was not a single colony; it consisted of a group of rival Boer (Afrikaner) and British colonies which were united in 1910
to form the Union of South Africa. South Africa became an independent member of the Commonwealth in 1931.

Independence	Occupied*	Colonial powers
July 3, 1962	1842	France
November 11, 1975	1670	Portugal
August 1, 1960	1892	France
September 30, 1966	1885	Britain
August 5, 1960	1892	France
July 1, 1962	1890	Germany 1890–1919; Belgium 1919–1962
January 1, 1960	1884	Germany 1884–1919; France and Britain divided and took control of Cameroon after Germany's defeat in WWI
July 5, 1975	1587	Portugal
August 13, 1960	1894	France
August 11, 1960	1900	France
July 6, 1975	1843	France
June 30, 1960	1876	Belgium
August 15, 1960	1885	France
June 27, 1977	1884	France
February 28, 1922	1798–1801 1882	France Britain
October 12, 1968	1845 (mainland) 1493 1778	Spain Portugal Spain
May 24, 1993	1889	Italy 1889–1941; Britain 1941–1952; ruled by Ethiopia 1952–1993
August 17, 1960	1839	France
March 6, 1957	1896	Britain
October 2, 1958	1898	France
September 10, 1974	1880	Portugal
August 7, 1960	1914	France
December 12, 1963	1895	Britain
October 4, 1966	1868	Britain
		Liberia has been independent since its establishment in 1847
December 24, 1951	1911	Italy
June 26, 1960	1895	France
July 6, 1964	1891	Britain
June 20, 1960	1898	France
November 28, 1960	1903	France
March 12, 1968	1715	France 1715–1810; Britain 1810–1968
March 2, 1956 April 7, 1956	1912 1912	France Spain
June 25, 1975	1505	Portugal
March 21, 1990	1884	Germany 1884–1919; occupied by South
August 3, 1960	1908	France
October 1, 1960	1880	Britain
July 1, 1962	1890	Germany 1890–1919; Belgium 1919–1962
July 12, 1975	1493	Portugal
June 20, 1960	1890	France
June 29, 1976	1742	France 1742–1814; Britain 1814–1976
April 27, 1961	1787	Britain
June 26, 1960 July 1, 1960	1884 1886	Britain Italy 1886–1941; 1950–1960; Britain 1941–1950
January 1, 1956	1898	Under joint British and Egyptian rule
September 6, 1968	1894	Britain (administered by the Boer's South African Republic 1894–1902)
December 9, 1961 December 10, 1963	1885 1890	Germany 1885–1920; Britain 1920–1961 Britain
February 18, 1965	1816	Britain
April 27, 1960	1884	Germany 1884–1919; France 1919–1960
March 20, 1956	1881	France
October 9, 1962	1888	Britain
(ceded to Morocco and Mauritania in 1975)	1885	Spain
October 24, 1964	1890	Britain
18 April, 1980	1890	Britain

* The years given for the beginning of colonial occupation of the modern-day nation states are those by which a significant area of coastal and hinterland territory had been effectively occupied by a colonial power.

Coups d'Etat in Africa

The struggle for independence from colonial powers proved difficult to achieve for many African nations. Yet, once independence had been achieved, different problems beset the new states. As the maps (right and below) show, some nations were subject to instability and military *coups d'état* after independence.

1 *2* *3* *4*

1 *1957 Habib Bourguiba seized power and became Tunisia's first prime minister (1956–57) and its first president (1957–87). He was deposed by his prime minister.*
2 *1965 Houari Boumedienne gained power in Algeria after a bloodless coup against the first president Ben Bella.*

3 *1966 Dr. Kwame Nkrumah was overthrown by a military coup in Ghana (formerly Gold Coast).*
4 *1966 General Jean-Bédel Bokassa seized power in a military coup, and later renamed the Central African Republic as the 'Central African Empire.'*

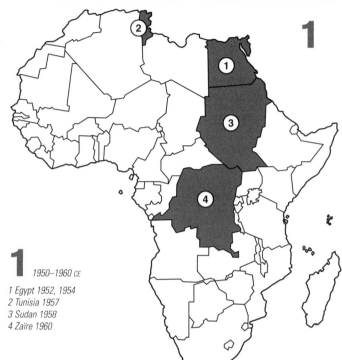

1 *1950–1960 CE*

1 Egypt 1952, 1954
2 Tunisia 1957
3 Sudan 1958
4 Zaïre 1960

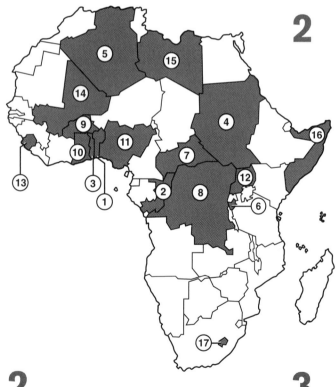

2 *1961–1970 CE*

1 Benin 1963, 1965, 1967, 1969
2 Congo 1963, 1968
3 Togo 1963, 1967
4 Sudan 1964, 1969
5 Algeria 1965
6 Burundi 1965, 1966
7 Central African Republic 1965
8 Zaïre 1965
9 Burkina Faso 1966
10 Ghana 1966
11 Nigeria 1966
12 Uganda 1966
13 Sierra Leone 1967, 1968
14 Mali 1968
15 Libya 1969
16 Somalia 1969
17 Lesotho 1970

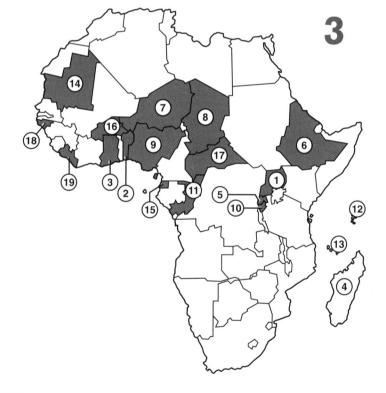

3 *1971–1980 CE*

1 Uganda 1971, 1979
2 Benin 1972
3 Ghana 1972, 1978, 1979
4 Madagascar 1972
5 Rwanda 1973
6 Ethiopia 1974
7 Niger 1974
8 Chad 1975
9 Nigeria 1975
10 Burundi 1976
11 Congo 1977
12 Seychelles 1977
13 Comoros 1978
14 Mauritania 1978, 1980
15 Equatorial Guinea1979
16 Burkina Faso 1980
17 Central African Republic 1980
18 Guinea-Bissau 1980
19 Liberia 1980

5

6

7

8

9

10

11

12

13

14

15

16

17

18

5 1966 Sir Abubakar Tafawa Balewa, the federal prime minister of Nigeria, was assassinated during a military coup.
6 1967 Gnassingbe Eyadéma became president of Togo after a bloodless coup.
7 1967 Siakia Probyn Stevens fled Sierra Leone when the army seized power, but returned in 1968 to become the head of govern-

8 1968 Modibo Keita was deposed by a military coup led by Moussa Traoré in Mali.
9 1969 Muhammad Gaafar Nimeri seized power in the Sudan in a coup; he was later deposed in 1985.
10 1971 Idi Amin Dada seized power in Uganda; he was deposed in 1979 and fled into exile in Saudi Arabia.

11 1974 Major Mengistu Haile-Meriam, and other members of the ruling committee, seized power in Ethiopia.
12 1974 Haile Selassie, Emperor of Ethiopia since 1930, was deposed by the army.
13 1979 Jerry Rawlings seized power, and again in 1981, before becoming elected as president of Ghana in 1992.

14 1980 Luiz Cabral, president of Guinea-Bissau, was overthrown in a coup.
15 1980 Samuel Doe took power after a military coup in Liberia; he was later assassinated in 1990.
16 1984 Lansana Conté took power in Guinea after leading a bloodless coup after the death of Sekou Touré.

17 1985 Apollo Milton Obote was deposed from the presidency of Uganda, a position he had held since 1980.
18 1993 General Sanni Abacha became head of Nigeria's military government and delayed his country's return to democratic government.

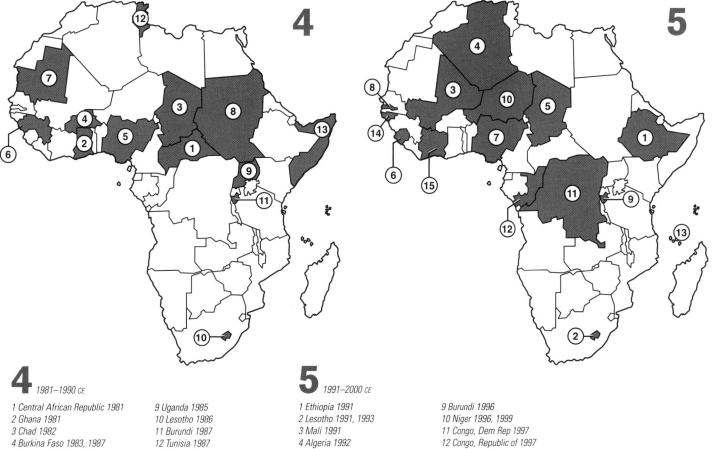

4 1981–1990 CE

1 Central African Republic 1981
2 Ghana 1981
3 Chad 1982
4 Burkina Faso 1983, 1987
5 Nigeria 1983
6 Guinea 1984
7 Mauritania 1984
8 Sudan 1985, 1989

9 Uganda 1985
10 Lesotho 1986
11 Burundi 1987
12 Tunisia 1987
13 Somalia 1990

5 1991–2000 CE

1 Ethiopia 1991
2 Lesotho 1991, 1993
3 Mali 1991
4 Algeria 1992
5 Chad 1992
6 Sierra Leone 1992, 1997
7 Nigeria 1993
8 Gambia 1994

9 Burundi 1996
10 Niger 1996, 1999
11 Congo, Dem Rep 1997
12 Congo, Republic of 1997
13 Comoros 1999
14 Guinea Bissau 1999
15 Ivory Coast 1999

SECTION

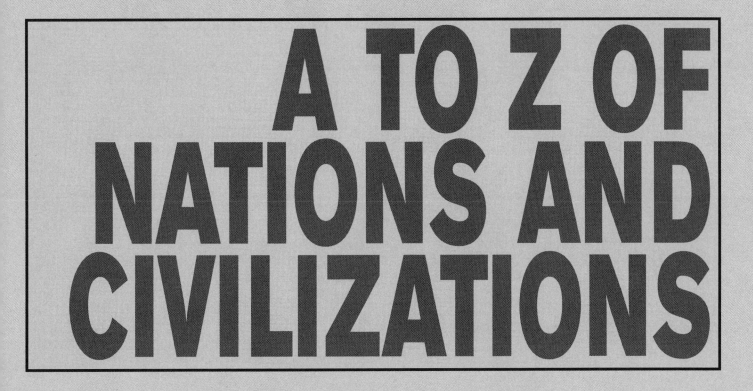

'Abbasids

The 'Abbasid dynasty ruled from Baghdad, replacing the Ommayads in 750 CE. The 'Abbasids controlled North Africa, or Ifriqiyah as it was then known, but from 789 CE on lost their African territories to independent Berber or Arab dynasties–the Idrisids, Aghlabids, and Tulunids. In 905 CE the 'Abbasids regained Egypt from the Tulunids and ruled there until 935 CE when they were overthrown by the Ikshidids. *See also* **Aghlabids**; **Ifriqiyah**; **Tulunids**.

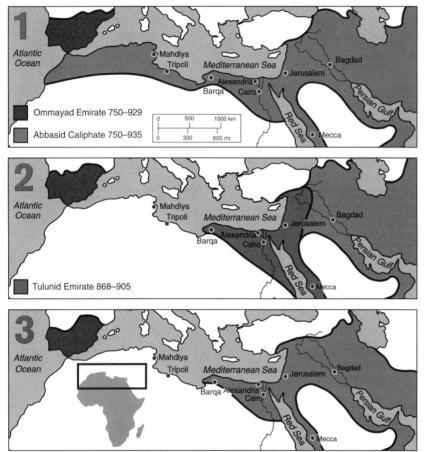

1. Ommayad Emirate 750–929
   Abbasid Caliphate 750–935

2. Tulunid Emirate 868–905

3.

'Abbasids and Ummayads

After overthrowing the Ommayads in 750 CE the Iranian 'Abbasid dynasty conquered all Omayyad territories, apart from their Spanish possessions, by 771 CE. After 789 CE the 'Abbasids began to lose territory to Berber and Arab peoples.

1 771 CE

2 904 CE

3 934 CE

Abyssinia

Abyssinia is a name that Europeans used for many years interchangeably with 'Ethiopia.' The origin of the term Abyssinia is not agreed. It may have come from the Arabic term *habishat*, meaning mixed, referring to Ethiopia's ethnic diversity, or it may have derived from one of the early peoples who lived in the region. *See also* **Ethiopia**.

Accra

See **Ga towns**.

Modern extent of the Afar people

Afars and Issas, French Territory of

The French Territory of the Afars and Issas was an earlier name for the Republic of Djibouti. The earlier name referred to the two main groups of people who lived in the territory, which was originally called French Somaliland. The French Territory of the Afars and Issas was the colony's official name from 1967–1977 CE, when it became independent as the Republic of Djibouti. *See also* **Djibouti**.

Aghlabids

The Muslim Aghlabid dynasty controlled Ifriqiyah (North Africa), supposedly on behalf of the 'Abbasids, from 800–909 CE. They were generally independent from any overlords, however, and through high taxes they maintained a splendid court. The Aghlabids were overthrown by the Fatimids in 909 CE. *See also* **Abbasids**; **Fatimids**; **Ifriqiyah**.

Aïr, Sultanate of

The Sultanate of Aïr emerged as a centralized Tuareg state in the early fifteenth century, with its capital at Agades (Niger). The sultanate's wealth was based on control of trans-Saharan trade routes, and the state was actually a confederation of Tuareg traders. To avoid conflict among themselves, they founded the sultanate so that someone could settle disputes and fix dues. Aïr was conquered by the Songhay empire at the start of the sixth century, then it fell to Borno. During the seventeenth and eighteenth centuries, Aïr regained some independence but was often in conflict with Borno and Kebbi, a Hausa state. *See also* **Niger**; **Kanem–Borno**.

Akan states

The Akan group includes such peoples as the Asante and Fante of Ghana and the Anyi and Baulé of Ivory Coast. For information about the history of these peoples, *see also* **Ghana (Peoples)**; **Ivory Coast (Peoples)**.

ALGERIA People's Democratic Republic of Algeria

Berbers settled in what is now called Algeria around 5,000 years ago. The coastal area became important in Mediterranean trade around 3,000 years ago, when the Phoenicians began to found colonies there. By the third century BCE, the area was divided into three Berber kingdoms. Following Rome's conquest of Carthage in 146 BCE, the eastern part of what is now northern Algeria became part of the Roman province of Africa Nova, while the west became part of the Berber kingdom of Mauretania. The Romans annexed Mauretania between 40–42 CE.

Following the collapse of the Roman empire, part of the region was conquered by the Vandals. But soon afterwards, northern Algeria became part of the Christian Byzantine (East Roman) empire. In the seventh century CE, Arabs invaded northern Africa, spreading their Islamic culture. The area was then governed by Muslim dynasties.

In the early sixteenth century, Spaniards captured some coastal settlements in the region, but a Turkish sea captain, Barbarossa, drove them out in 1518 CE. He eventually allied the areas under his control with the Turkish Ottoman empire. In the early nineteenth century, the Algerian coast became a haven for corsairs (pirates), giving France a pretext to invade in 1830 CE. From 1848 CE, Algeria was ruled as part of France.

During the colonial period, many French and other European *colons*, who were all granted French citizenship, settled in Algeria. By contrast, Muslim Algerians found it hard to obtain French citizenship. Resentment against French rule caused a major revolt, led by Abd al-Qadir, but the rebels were defeated in 1847 CE.

Recent history

In 1954 CE, Algerian Muslims formed the *Front de Libération Nationale* (National Liberation Front, or FLN), which launched a revolution on November 1, 1954 CE. The uprising was brutally suppressed. However, peace negotiations in 1961 CE finally led to independence on July 3, 1962 CE. Most *colons*, including nearly all the administrators, doctors, entrepreneurs, teachers, and technicians, left Algeria, totally disrupting the economy. In 1963 CE, Muhammad Ahmed Ben Bella, the country's prime minister and FLN leader, was elected president. He proclaimed Algeria a socialist state and urged workers to take over the abandoned businesses and farms. In 1963, Ben Bella increased his powers and made the FLN the sole political party.

Alarmed at Ben Bella's dictatorial rule, army officers, led by former minister of defence, Colonel Houari Boumedienne, deposed Ben Bella in June 1965 CE. The new government, the Council of the Revolution, was composed mainly of military figures, with Boumedienne as its president. The government's main objective was the creation of an 'authentic socialist society', with an economic policy based on government ownership. Revenue from oil and natural gas, Algeria's chief exports, was used to finance new industries such as fertilizer plants and steel mills. In 1976 CE, under a revised constitution, Boumedienne was elected president unopposed and, in 1977 CE, a National Assembly was elected, all candidates being members of the FLN.

Fateful blow (left)
When the Bey of Algiers struck the French Consul it gave the French a pretext to invade.

Propaganda
Illustrations such as that on the left helped to persuade the French people to see the situation in nineteenth-century Algeria as an heroic struggle by the French military against treacherous indigenous peoples.

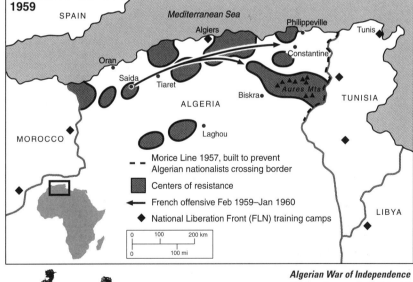

1959

SPAIN — *Mediterranean Sea*

Algiers — Philippeville — Tunis

Oran — Constantine

Saida — Tiaret — Biskra — Aures Mts — TUNISIA

ALGERIA

Laghou

MOROCCO

LIBYA

-- Morice Line 1957, built to prevent Algerian nationalists crossing border

■ Centers of resistance

← French offensive Feb 1959–Jan 1960

♦ National Liberation Front (FLN) training camps

0 100 200 km
0 100 mi

Occupiers
French armored troops guard against FLN attacks.

Algerian War of Independence
The French responded with brutal reprisals to attacks on French military and civilian targets by the FLN in November 1954 CE. An offensive by French forces begun in 1959 CE was ended after the French government acknowledged Algeria's right to self-determination. Renegade French soldiers and civilians continued the fight until 1962 CE.

Prehistoric Algeria (above)
Paintings on the rocks of Tassili-n-Ajjer, Algeria, depict life in the Sahara thousands of years ago, when the desert had rivers, lakes, and a wealth of plant and animal life.

Islamic fundamentalism (above)
Muslims at prayer in a North African town. Radical Islamic fundamentalism grew increasingly popular in the 1990s. Radical Muslim groups in Algeria and Egypt, in particular, are employing terrorist tactics and attacking foreigners to further their causes.

Muslim protests (above)
Fearing the popularity of radical Islamic fundamentalists, the Algerian government canceled the second round of multiparty elections in 1991 CE. Rioting followed and radical Muslim fundamentalists battled with pro-government death squads.

Algerian timeline

Pre 19th century
c. 3000 BCE	Berbers migrate to the Algeria region
c. 1000 BCE	Phoenicians found colonies on the Algerian coast
c. 200 BCE	Massinissa establishes the kingdom of Numidia in northern Algeria
105 BCE	The Romans defeat King Jugurtha of Numidia
44 CE	Numidia is formally annexed by the Roman Empire
432	The Vandals settle on the coast of Algeria
682–702	Muslim Arab conquest of Algeria
1518	The Turkish pirate Barbarossa captures Algiers for the Ottoman Empire

19th century CE
1815	US navy attacks bases of the Barbary Corsairs in Algiers
1827	France blockades Algiers
1830	The French capture Algiers
1834	The first French settlers (*colons*) arrive in Algeria
1847	Algerian resistance leader Abd al-Qadir defeated by France
1848	Algeria is declared an integral part of France
1871	French suppress the Kabylie uprising of Muhammad al-Moqrani

1900–49 CE
1902	Algeria's present boundaries established
1923	French deport the nationalist leader Emir Khaled
1943	Ferhat Abbas calls for Algerian independence
1944	French citizenship granted to many Algerians
1945	France deports the nationalist leader Messali Hadj
1947	Algerian Muslims are given limited voting rights

1950–59 CE
1954	National Liberation Front (FLN) begins war of independence against France
1956–1957	France defeats the FLN in the Battle of Algiers
1958	French army rebels and French settlers seize control of the colonial government in Algeria
1959	President de Gaulle of France decides to offer Algeria self-determination

1960–69 CE
1960	Rebellion of French settlers suppressed
1962	**July 3** Algeria becomes independent of France after a referendum
1963	Muhammad Ben Bella of the FLN becomes president
1963	Short border war with Morocco
1964	Ben Bella suppresses an attempted military coup
1965	Military coup overthrows Ben Bella; Boumedienne becomes president
1968	Boumedienne survives an assassination attempt

The Algerian constitution
A stamp, issued in 1963 CE, marking the proclamation of the Algerian constitution.

1970–79 CE
1970	The French withdraw from their last military base in Algeria
1971	French oil concessions nationalized
1976	Boumedienne introduces a new constitution
1978	Boumedienne dies of a rare blood disease
1979	Chadli Bendjedid of the FLN becomes president after an election in which he is the only candidate

1980–89 CE
1989	Algeria, Morocco and Tunisia form the Arab Maghrib Union

1990–99 CE
1990	Fundamentalist Islamic Salvation Front (FIS) enjoys unexpected success in local government elections
1991	After the FIS wins first round in general elections, the government declares a state of emergency
1992	President Bendjedid resigns, a military regime is established and Islamic fundamentalists begin a terrorist campaign
1995	Liamine Zeroual is appointed president
1996	Algerians approve a new constitution banning political parties based on religion, sex or language
1999	President Zeroual resigns and Abdulaziz Bouteflika is elected president

2000–09 CE
2000	Under an amnesty, large numbers of Islamic militants hand over their arms
2001	Riots occurred among Berbers in the Kabylie region, who feared a loss of their culture

The A-bomb
French tests of nuclear weapons in southern Algeria in 1960 CE met with protests and rioting by Algerians. Dummies wearing French military uniforms were set up in the test zone and equipped with instruments to measure the strength of the blast.

When Boumedienne died in 1978 CE, he was succeeded by Chadli Bendjedid, who slowed the rate of industrialization to give priority to agricultural and consumer goods. But in 1980 CE, Berbers rioted when Bendjedid announced a policy to make Arabic the sole official language. Further riots in 2001 CE showed that Berbers still feared a loss of their culture.

In 1989 CE, following a constitutional change introducing a multiparty system, a number of opposition parties were formed. In elections in 1991 CE, the *Institut Islamique du Salut* (Islamic Salvation Front, or FIS) won a majority but the FLN government prevented the Islamic fundamentalists from achieving power by nullifying the election result.

Tassili-n-Ajjer
This site lies at the heart of the Sahara Desert in the south of Algeria close to its border with Libya. It is a block of sandstone that has been carved by the erosive power of water and wind into a maze of weird, pillarlike columns of rock separated by deep, dry gullies.

The National Assembly was dissolved and Bendjedid resigned in 1992 CE. The new military regime banned the FIS and the army fought a civil war against the Islamic fundamentalists. About 100,000 died during the civil conflict in the 1990s. Elections were held in 1999 CE based on a constitutional change whereby political parties based on religion were banned. Abdelaziz Bouteflika, who was elected president after his six opponents withdrew, claiming that the army was rigging the election, later announced an amnesty to Islamic militants who handed in their arms. The government also finalized a deal with the military wing of the FIS, inviting units to disband in return for a full pardon. Bouteflika's policy moves greatly reduced the scale of killing in 2000, restoring peace to urban areas.

Peoples
ARABS
The Arabs, who originated in Arabia, conquered the Berbers of North Africa in the late seventh century, introducing their language, Arabic, and their religion, Islam. Today Arabs make up more than 80 percent of Algeria's population. They include the Bedouin nomads who are pastoralists.

BERBERS
Berbers are the earliest known inhabitants of Algeria. They were settled along the North African coast by 3000 BCE, but little is known about their history before the third century BCE. By about 250 BCE, the Berbers had set up three kingdoms, Mauretania in what is now northern Morocco, and Massaesylian Numidia and Massylian Numidia in Algeria and western Tunisia. (*See also* **Berber kingdoms**.)

The modern history of the Berbers begins with their conversion to Islam in the late seventh century CE. Over the years, Arab invasions forced many Berbers out of coastal regions and into the mountains and desert. But many others were absorbed into the Arab population. Following the Arab invasion of North Africa, Algeria came under the Ommayad dynasty, but, in 750 CE, the Ommayads were overthrown by the another dynasty, the Abbasids. From 789 CE, the 'Abbasids lost territory to independent dynasties, notably in Algeria, such as the Idrisids (789–926 CE) and the Aghlabids (801–909 CE). From 1054 CE, a confederation of Muslim Berber groups, the Almoravids, formed a new and powerful dynasty in northwest Africa. After its collapse in the mid-12th century, the Almohad dynasty took over most of Morocco and Algeria. The Almohad Empire finally collapsed, losing their last possessions in 1269 CE.

In the twenty-first century, Berbers make up less than 20 percent of Algeria's population. In 1990 CE, Arabic was made the sole official language in Algeria, much to the resentment of the Berbers. But the government reversed the decision in 1994 CE, when Berber became the second official language.

Coexistence
A French poster that promoted coexistence between French settlers and Algerians.

Modern extent of the Berber people

Houari Boumedienne
President of Algeria from 1965–1978 CE, he gained power after a bloodless coup against the first president Ben Bella.

© DIAGRAM

Abd al-Qadir
He led the resistence to European invasion in western Algeria.

Algeria's major political figures

Abbas, Ferhat (1899–1985 CE)
One of the leaders of Algeria's fight for independence, Ferhat Abbas was the first president of the Algerian provisional government in exile (1958–61). He also served as president of Algeria's National Assembly (1962–64), until differences with Muhammad Ahmed Ben Bella led to his resignation and house arrest (1964–65).

Abd al-Qadir (1807–1883 CE)
Abd al-Qadir, Emir (ruler) of Oran, led the resistance to the French conquest of Algeria. He fought the French from 1832, scoring several victories, but was eventually defeated and surrendered in 1847. Imprisoned in France, he was freed by Emperor Napoleon III in 1852 and died in Damascus, Syria.

Abdessalam, Belaid (1928 CE–)
Abdessalam served as prime minister of Algeria between 1992 and 1993. However, his failure to stop internal conflict and to stabilize the economy led to his dismissal. Abdessalam, a nationalist leader during the independence struggle and a supporter of the FLN's National Liberation Army, became known as the father of Algerian industrialization. He served as Minister of Industry and Energy between 1965 and 1977, and as Minister for Light Industry between 1977 and 1979.

Ben Bella, Muhammad Ahmad (1916 CE–)
One of the leaders of the struggle for Algerian independence, Ben Bella was twice imprisoned by the French (1950–2 and 1956–62). The first prime minister of Algeria (1962–3), Ahmad Ben Bella became the first elected president, in 1963. His dictatorial style of government aroused opposition, and he was deposed and arrested in a bloodless military coup in 1965, led by Houari Boumedienne. He was detained until 1979.

Bendjedid, Chadli (1929 CE–)
Bendjedid was a leader in the struggle for independence in Algeria. After the country became independent in 1962, he served in the army and later became Defense Minister. He was elected president of Algeria in 1979 and was reelected in 1984 and 1988. He resigned from the presidency in 1992 after the second round of the 1991 elections were cancelled following the victory in the first round by the fundamentalist Islamic Salvation Front.

Boumedienne, Houari (1925–1978 CE)
A former guerrilla fighter against the French, Boumedienne replaced Ben Bella as president of Algeria after a coup in 1965. He established an Islamic socialist government and served as president until 1978.

Bouteflika, Abdelaziz (1937 CE–)
Bouteflika, who was born in Morocco of Algerian parents, served in the FLN during the the Algerian struggle for independence. In 1999, he was elected president of Algeria, when the other six candidates withdrew, alleging electoral irregularities. The media suggested that Bouteflika was the army's preferred candidate. Bouteflika's priority as president was to end the civil conflict and restore peace.

Zéroual, Liamine (1941 CE–)
Zéroual fought against France in Algeria's war of independence and he rose to become land forces chief in 1989. He then resigned from the army and became defence minister in 1993. Zéroual was appointed president of Algeria in 1994 and elected in 1995. In 1999, he stepped down and was replaced as president by ABDELAZIZ BOUTEFLIKA. As president, Zéroual tried to resolve Algeria's domestic crisis and unsuccessfully attempted to negotiate peace with the Islamic Salvation Front.

Expansion and decline of the Almohad empire
This map and the four that follow trace the territorial gains and subsequent losses of the Almohads in Spain and North Africa during the following periods:

1 *1150 CE*

2 *1152 CE*

3 *1172 CE*

4 *1228 CE*

5 *1269 CE*

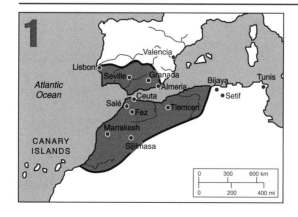

Almohad empire

A Berber dynasty, originating in Morocco, the Almohad dynasty secured Morocco (1147 CE) and Spain (1150–1172 CE) from the Almoravid dynasty. In 1212 CE, the Almohad dynasty received a crushing defeat at the hands of Spanish Christians and, by 1228 CE, they had been driven out of Spain. The empire then began to shrink. In 1269, the loss of Morocco to the Marinids marked the complete collapse of the Almohad empire. *See also* **Almoravid empire**; **Marinids**.

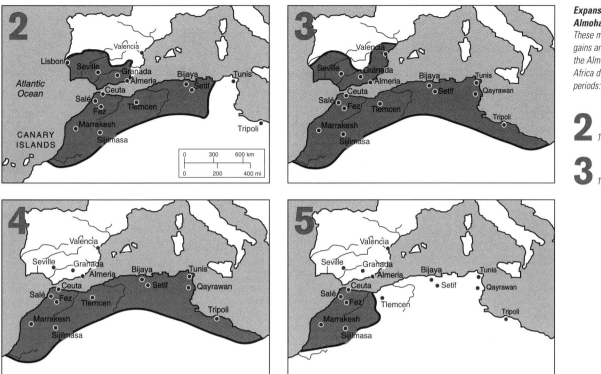

Expansion and decline of the Almohad empire (cont.)
These maps trace the territorial gains and subsequent losses of the Almohads in Spain and North Africa during the following periods:

2 *1152 CE* **4** *1228 CE*

3 *1172 CE* **5** *1269 CE*

Almoravid empire

The Almoravid dynasty emerged in 1054 CE, when the Almoravids–Muslim Berbers from the western part of the Sahara–began to take control of a huge area of northwest Africa. In 1055, they began to invade what is now Morocco and, between 1086–1106 CE, they conquered Ummayad Spain. The Almoravid empire was succeeded by the Almohad empire. *See also* **Almohad empire**.

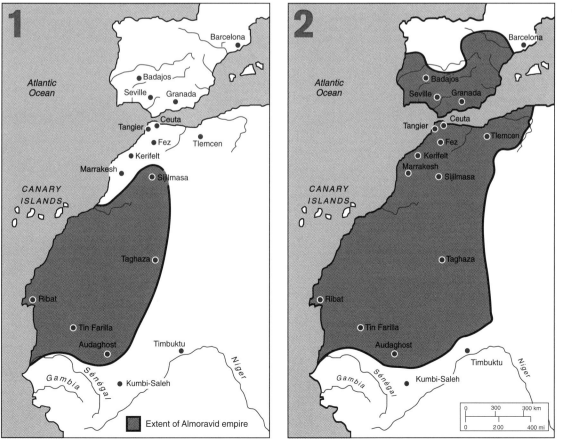

Almoravid expansion
Over the course of little more than a century the Almoravids made spectacular territorial gains until they controlled the western Sahara, modern day Morocco, and most of Spain.

1 *1055 CE*

2 *1146 CE*

Alodia, kingdom of *See* **Sudan (Peoples [Funj])**.

Anglo-Egyptian Sudan

Anglo-Egyptian Sudan was the name given to modern Sudan when it was jointly ruled as a condominium by Britain and Egypt from 1899 CE until independence in 1955 CE. *See also* **Sudan**.

Alwa

See **Nubia**.

ANGOLA Republic of Angola

The first people who probably lived in what is now Angola were Khoisan hunter-gatherers, but they were displaced by iron-using, Bantu-speaking farmers in the thirteenth century CE. Although many Bantu groups lived in small, isolated communities, some major kingdoms developed. The leading kingdom was that of the Kongo in the north. To the south was the Ndongo kingdom, founded by the Mbundu people.

Portuguese explorers looking for a route around Africa to Asia first reached the Angolan coast in 1483 CE. Seven years later, the Kongo's king, (Nzinga Mbemba, later Alfonso 1), was converted to Christianity, but soon the Portuguese began to exploit the area, exporting slaves to their colony, Brazil, from their main slave port, Luanda. Despite an uprising in the south (1623–1626 CE) and a short period of Dutch rule (1641–1648 CE), the Portuguese maintained control over the coast.

From the late nineteenth century, they extended their rule inland and, by 1921 CE, they were in control of the entire territory. The economy grew slowly and all development was directed towards Portugal's benefit, with the local population, who were subject to forced labour, having little stake in the country's fortunes. Armed opposition to Portuguese rule continued until 1930 CE. After the dictator António de Oliviera Salazar came to power in Portugal in the late 1920s, more Portuguese settlers arrived in Angola and the economic growth rate increased, especially after World War II. In 1951 CE, Angola became an Overseas Province of Portugal but, at the same time, nationalist opposition to Portuguese rule in Angola was mounting.

Recent history

Full-scale opposition to Portuguese rule began in several areas in 1961 CE. In February, the *Movimento Popular de Libertaçâo de Angola* (MPLA), which had been formed in 1956 CE, staged a revolt in Luanda. The MPLA owed much of its support to the Mbundu people, who had rebelled in central Angola the previous month against forced cotton production. In March 1961 CE, a wages dispute among the landless Kongo in the north also led to widespread violence.

However, the Angolan nationalists were split by cultural and political differences, which led to the establishment of several nationalist groups. In the north, the Kongo were led by Holden Roberto's *Frente Nacional de Libertaçâo de Angola* (FNLA), while in the south the Ovimbundu supported the *Uniâo Nacional para a Independência Total de Angola* (UNITA) led by Jonas Savimbi. The existence of these rival groups complicated the ensuing war of independence.

A coup in Portugal in April 1974 CE which overthrew the authoritarian government of Marcello Caetano led the new military regime to negotiate independence for Angola, which was achieved on November 11, 1975 CE. The MPLA formed the government and Dr Antoniu Agostinho became the first president. However, the civil war continued, and the Marxist MPLA received support from the Soviet Union and Cuba. The MPLA defeated its enemies in April 1976 CE, taking control of 12 of Angola's 15 provinces. However, UNITA rebels in the south conducted a guerrilla war, receiving aid from the West, notably South Africa and the United States. The western-backed FNLA also conducted guerrilla activities against the MPLA, but it became inactive in 1984 CE. In December 1988 CE, an agreement was signed under which South Africa and Cuba agreed to

Invaders
A soldier of 1807– part of the military presence that brought Angola under Portuguese control by 1921.

Foreigners
This nineteenth-century carving in wood from Angola gives a sharp insight into the way in which Africans viewed Europeans. It shows a trader holding a glass and a bottle of gin, with a barrel of alcohol balanced on his hat.

Brutality
An MPLA supporter is beaten by members of the Portuguese-appointed Angolan police force (left) and below, a stamp marking the MPLA's eventual victory.

ANGOLA

1.50

VIVA O MARXISMO-LENINISMO

Propaganda
Communist heroes Marx, Engels, and Lenin glorified by the MPLA on a street poster in the 1980s.

withdraw their troops and, finally, a peace accord was signed in May 1991 CE.

In multiparty elections held in September 1992 CE, the MPLA, which had renounced its Marxist-Leninist policies, won a majority, and José Eduardo dos Santos was reselected president. But UNITA's representatives refused to accept the result and the civil war resumed in 1994 CE. A coalition government was formed in 1997 CE, but Jonas Savimbi, who had been offered the vice-presidency, refused to collaborate.

Full-scale civil war resumed in 1999 CE. The government, which declared its unwillingness to take part in further talks with Savimbi, was funded by a boom in oil production from its recently discovered offshore wells, while UNITA's modern weaponry was purchased from the illegal sale of diamonds mined in areas under their control and smuggled through neighboring territories. Meanwhile, from 1998 CE, Angolan troops fought alongside Namibians and Zimbabweans in the Democratic Republic of Congo in support of President Laurent Kabila's army, which was struggling against rebel forces aided by Rwanda and Uganda.

Peoples
CHOKWE

One of the principal Angolan ethnic groups, the Chokwe live principally in the northeast of the country, although a minority live in the southern Congo. There are currently about one million Chokwe, three-quarters of whom live in Angola.

In the seventeenth century Mwata Yamvo, the son of a Lunda chief, emigrated with his followers from the Southern Congo into northeastern Angola. By setting up chiefs who were related to himself and to one another he gained control over the indiginous peoples. Lunda culture blended with that of the indiginous populations, and gave rise to a distinctive Chokwe culture combining hunting, agriculture and, in later years, trade. The Chokwe were governed by the Lunda kings until 1895 CE, when they invaded Lunda territories to the north, took the Lunda capital, and became rubber producers. By the mid-nineteenth century the Portuguese had expanded inland to dominate the economic, political, social and religious life of the Chokwe. By the beginning of the twentieth century this domination had turned into a systematic colonization, and led to the Angolan war of liberation which began in 1961 CE. Angola became independent in 1975 CE.

KONGO

Kongo is the name of a former kingdom, which covered northern Angola, and adjacent areas in the Democratic Republic of Congo and the Republic of Congo. It was founded in the fourteenth century, and its first known king was Nimi a Lukeni, the son of the chief of Bungu, north of the Congo River. He led a group of followers to conquer lands south of the river and married the daughter of Kabunga, a Kongo chief. Kabunga had the title of *mani* (king), which Nimi adopted as his own. From then on, the ruler was known as Mani-Kongo. The king was spiritual leader of his people, as well as their ruler and military leader. He had a council of ministers to help him.

When the Portuguese explorers and traders landed on the coast in 1482 CE, Kongo was a flourishing king-

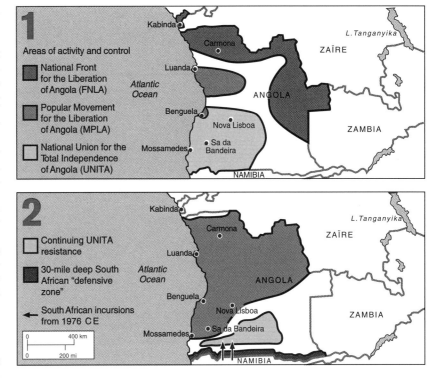

Angolan Civil War (above)
Even before independence from Portugal had been achieved, three opposing groups were struggling for power within Angola.

1 July 1975 CE **2** Feb. 1976 CE

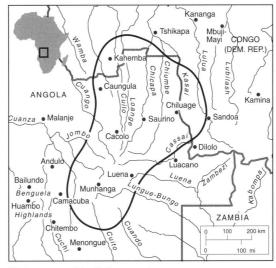

Modern extent of the Chokwe people

Ndumba Tembo (below)
This portrait of the Chokwe king Ndumba Tembo was drawn in 1878 CE. The lands governed by Ndumba Tembo in the nineteenth century covered much of present-day central Angola.

dom. For many years, the Kongo maintained diplomatic ties not only with Portugal, but also with the Vatican. The Portuguese gave advice and military help in exchange for trading rights, the main trade being in slaves for export to the new European settlements in the Americas. This alliance did not endure. The Portuguese fostered Kongo's internal rivalries in their pursuit of slaves and, following the 1568 CE invasion of the Kongo kingdom by the Jaga, a Lunda people from northeast Angola, the Portuguese gradually lost interest. After the Kongo king tried to break Portuguese influence by balancing it with that of

© DIAGRAM

Kongo tumba

Kongo tumba
This tomb sculpture probably dates from the nineteenth century. Tumba were produced at least as early as the sixteenth century, and mostly came from northern Angola. This may be the tumba of a chief as the figure appears to be chewing a plant stem, which he would then have spat out on others during certain rituals.

Wooden staff
The rise of powerful Angolan chieftainships in the sixteenth and seventeenth centuries inspired artists to produce prestige items, such as Ovimbundu staffs. Many men carried staffs as walking aids, but the quality of the carving here suggests it was owned by a wealthy or noble man, and its primary function was probably as a status symbol.

Angolan presidents

Nov 11 1975–Sep 10 1979 CE
Agostinho Neto

Sep 10 1979 CE–
José Eduardo dos Santos
(acting until Sep 21 1979)

José Eduardo dos Santos
MPLA leader José Eduardo dos Santos became Angola's president in 1979 CE.

the Dutch, the Portuguese decisively defeated his armies at the Battle of Ambuila in 1665 CE. After this battle, the kingdom fragmented and the Kongo eventually came under colonial rule.

LUNDA

The Lunda live in eastern Angola and also in parts of the Democratic Republic of Congo. For an account of their history, *see also* **Congo, Democratic Republic of**.

MBUNDU

The Mbundu live in north-central Angola, including Luanda. From the end of the fifteenth century, the Mbundu founded the Ndongo kingdom. The ruler of Ndongo was known as the Ngola. In the seventeenth century, the Ndongo kingdom was ruled by Nzinga Nbandi, or Anna Nzinga, who reigned from 1623 to 1663 CE. This famous African queen was a leader of anti-colonial resistance.

OVIMBUNDU

The Ovimbundu arose from a merging of two peoples: the indigenous people of what is now the Benguela Highlands in south-central Angola, and the Jaga, a Lunda people from northeast Angola, who invaded central and western Angola from northeast Angola. By the 1770s, the Ovimbundu were firmly established, with royal families providing both political and ritual leadership through the king and his counselors. Originally, they incorporated many of the warrior traditions of the Lunda, but these features were diluted as the Ovimbundu became a mainly trading people.

The economic history of the Ovimbundu is largely a record of violent contact with, and then commercial exploitation by, Portuguese colonists. This began around 1600 CE. The slave trade remained an important element of the Ovimbundu economy until the early twentieth century, by which time more than three million slaves had been exported, mainly to Brazil. In the nineteenth century, the location of the Ovimbundu kingdoms–between the coast and the peoples of the interior–helped to promote a rich trading economy, with the Ovimbundu acting as middlemen. Trading commodities included slaves, ivory, wax, and rubber. The economy of the Ovimbundu, who were among the greatest traders in Africa, reached its peak between about 1874–1900 CE, when high-grade rubber became almost the sole export from the port of Benguela. A huge fall in the price of rubber, together with continu-

Modern extent of the Kongo people (above)

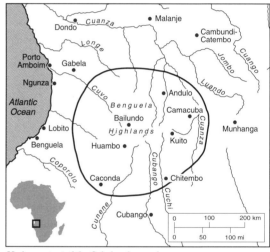

Modern extent of the Ovimbundu people

ing injustices and exploitation by the Portuguese led to decline, which resulted in the Bailundo War of 1902–1903 CE. The Portuguese occupation in subsequent years, together with the collapse in caravan trading (by companies of travelers) by 1911 CE resulted in widespread famine. The Ovimbundu region was where the Angola war of liberation began in 1961 CE.

Angola's major political figures

Chipenda, Daniel (1931–1996 CE)
From l962, Daniel Chipenda was a prominent guerrilla leader of the *Movimento Popular de Libertação de Angola* (MPLA) in the independence struggle against the Portuguese. In 1975, the MPLA split and Chipenda became allied with the rival *Frente Nacional de Libertação de Angola* (FNLA). Following the defeat of the FNLA by the MPLA, Chipenda went into exile in Portugal. He returned to Angola in 1992 and tried to negotiate peace in the ongoing civil war. He managed to make peace with rebel leader Jonas Savimbi, and attempted to mediate between him and Angolan president José Eduardo dos Santos.

dos Santos, José Eduardo (1942 CE–)
Dos Santos became president of Angola on the death of Antonio Agostinho Neto in 1979. He was reelected in 1985 and 1992, and in 1994–5 negotiated a ceasefire in the war with South African-backed rebels.

Angola timeline

Pre 19th century CE

1483	Portuguese explorers reach Angola
1490	Portuguese convert King Nzinga Nkuwu of Kongo (in northern Angola) to Christianity
1575	The Portuguese found Luanda as a base for slaving operations
1623–1626	Queen Nzinga of Ndongo in present-day Angola is defeated in a war against Portuguese slave traders
1641	The Dutch drive the Portuguese out of Angola
1648	The Portuguese regain control of Angola from the Dutch

19th Century CE

1884	The Portuguese begin to extend their control inland from the coast

1900–49 CE **1921** Portugal gains full control of all of modern Angola

1950–59 CE **1956** Pro-independence Popular Movement for the Liberation of Angola (MPLA) is formed

1960–69 CE **1961** An MPLA uprising in Luanda is defeated by the Portuguese
1962 Northern Angolan rebels organize the Front for the Liberation of Angola (FNLA)
1966 Southern Angolan rebels form the National Union for the Total Liberation of Angola (UNITA)

1970–79 CE **1974** Portugal announces its intention to withdraw from Angola. Civil war breaks out between MPLA, FNLA and UNITA. Cuban troops arrive to support MPLA, South Africans give aid to UNITA.
1975 Nov 11 Angola becomes independent of Portugal: MPLA unilaterally forms a government in Luanda
1976 The UN recognizes the MPLA as the legitimate government of Angola
1977 Attempted coup by dissidents within the MPLA

1980–89 CE **1981** South African forces advance 100 miles into Angola to support UNITA
1984 FNLA withdraws from military operations
1986 US begins to send aid to UNITA
1988 Cuba and South Africa agree to stop aiding the MPLA and UNITA
1989 MPLA and UNITA agree a cease-fire

1990–99 CE **1990** The MPLA renounces Marxism
1991 MPLA and UNITA agree a ceasefire
1992 The MPLA's José Eduardo dos Santos becomes president after multiparty elections. UNITA begins the civil war again
1993 Peace talks start at Lusaka, Zambia
1994 New peace agreement signed by the MPLA and UNITA
1995 UN peacekeeping force arrives to oversee the peace agreement
1996 Angola joins the Community of Portuguese-speaking Countries
1997 New government of national unity formed
1999 Civil war breaks out again between MPLA and UNITA

2000–09 CE **2000** UNITA launches new offensives, continuing the civil war

An MPLA soldier (above)
A young soldier of the Popular Movement for the Liberation of Angola, typical of the forces that faced foreign-backed incursions by UNITA and the FNLA during Angola's bitter civil war.

Neto, Dr Antoniu Agostinho (1922–1979 CE)
A poet and Marxist politician, Agostinho Neto became the first president of Angola (1974–79). He had led the *Movimento Popular de Libertação de Angola* (MPLA) forces in the guerrilla war against the Portuguese colonial regime from 1961 until 1974. Neto presided over the beginning, in 1975, of Angola's civil war between the government and rebel forces (principally those of Jonas Savimbi), which continued after his death.

Savimbi, Jonas (1934 CE–)
Jonas Savimbi led the forces of the *União Nacional para a Independência Total de Angola* (UNITA), formed in 1966 to fight in the Angolan war of independence from Portuguese rule (1961–74). After independence (in 1975), UNITA fought a twenty-year war against Agostinho Neto's government forces, which ended in 1994–5, although fighting resumed around the turn of the century.

Nzinga Nbandi, (Anna) (1582–1663 CE)
Nzinga was a queen of Ndongo and later queen of Matamba (both in what is now Angola). As queen of Ndongo, she tried to keep her country free from Portuguese control and fought the slave trade. In 1623, she went to the Portuguese colony of Angola to negotiate with the governor, and while there, she was baptized a Christian as Dona Aña de Souza. The negotiations failed, however, and the Portuguese drove her out of Ndongo in 1624. She then conquered the kingdom of Matamba, which allied itself with the Dutch and became prosperous by collaborating with the Portuguese slave trade.

Rebels (above)
Soldiers from the União Nacional para a Independência Total de Angola *(UNITA), a United States- and South African-backed rebel movement in Angola. In 1995 CE, Dr Jonas Savimbi, the leader of UNITA agreed to accept José Eduardo dos Santos – the leader of* Movimento Popular de Libertação de Angola *(MPLA) – as president of Angola, officially bringing a temporary end to the twenty-year civil war.*

© DIAGRAM

Anjouan

Anjouan is the second largest island in the Comoros. In 1997 CE, its people, together with those of nearby Mohéli, proclaimed their desire to secede from the country, partly because they resented domination by the people on the largest island, Grande Comore. In 1998 CE, 99.54 percent of the population of Anjouan voted for independence in a referendum. *See also* **Comoros**.

Ankole

Ankole, or the kingdom of Nkore, was established in what is now western Uganda by 1350 CE. Ankole was often in conflict with its larger neighbor Bunyoro, which lay to the north. Under Nkare IV, the Ankole extended their borders greatly and, by the time Nkare V came to power in 1875 CE, Ankole was at its height. Ankole was annexed by Britain in the 1890s. *See also* **Uganda Protectorate**; **Uganda**.

Asante empire

This West African empire was located in what is now Ghana. It arose in the late seventeenth century and, despite its singular victory over Britain in the first Anglo-Asante war of 1824 CE, it finally became a British possession in 1902 CE. *See also* **Ghana (Asante)**.

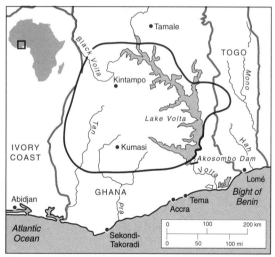

Modern extent of the Asante people

Gold pendant
Because they have been mining and trading gold for centuries, the Asante are masters of gold working. This gold pendant is exquisitely decorated and comes from the royal regalia of the Asantehene.

The Asante Wars
1824–1896 CE

Resistance fighter (right)
King Prempe of the Asante resisted British imperialism in West Africa.

Asante battle formation
Asante battle formation was a precision instrument that few enemies resisted successfully. In outline, it bore a striking resemblance to a modern airplane. At the "nose" is a party of scouts; the "fuselage" is made up of a column of warriors, followed by the commander-in-chief and his military staff; the "tail" section comprises a rearguard; and the "wings" consist of five columns of men each. At the rear of each wing is a group of medical personnel–rather like wing flaps. This awesome arrangement of men was the secret of the Asante Empire's military success.

The First Asante War
Despite victory over the British in the First Asante War (1824 CE), the Asante empire was pushed back and fragmented in subsequent British campaigns. By 1888 CE the Asante kingdom had revived on a smaller scale and continued to resist the British. As shown in this engraving, King Prempe of the Asante was forced to submit to the British in 1896 after they had taken and destroyed his capital, Kumasi. Asante resistance continued until 1900 CE when the empire was finally dismantled by the British and declared a possession (1902 CE).

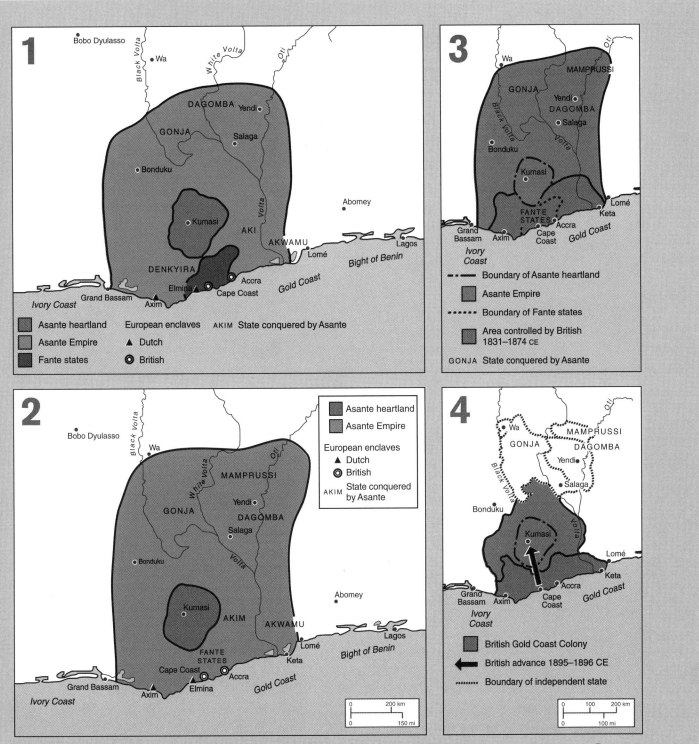

Map 1 legend:
- Asante heartland
- Asante Empire
- Fante states
- European enclaves
- ▲ Dutch
- ◎ British
- AKIM State conquered by Asante

Map 3 legend:
- ▬·▬·▬ Boundary of Asante heartland
- Asante Empire
- ▪▪▪▪ Boundary of Fante states
- Area controlled by British 1831–1874 CE
- GONJA State conquered by Asante

Map 2 legend:
- Asante heartland
- Asante Empire
- European enclaves
- ▲ Dutch
- ◎ British
- AKIM State conquered by Asante

Map 4 legend:
- British Gold Coast Colony
- ◀ British advance 1895–1896 CE
- ▪▪▪▪▪ Boundary of independent state

Anglo–Asante Wars

In 1800 CE the Asante heartland around Kumasi was surrounded by the conquered states of the Asante Empire. The rival Fante states competed with the Asante and were host to British and Dutch trading posts. By 1816 CE the Asante had crushed the Fante states and become the most powerful force in the region. Nervous of Asante power the British attacked the Asante Empire in 1824 CE under the pretext of liberating the Fante. In this the first Anglo-Asante War the British were defeated.

After their defeat in the first Anglo–Asante war the British launched a second campaign in 1826 CE in which Fante soldiers participated.

Victory led to the "liberated" Fante states becoming a British protectorate in 1831 CE. In the third Anglo–Asante war of 1863 CE the Asante were again defeated. Folowing the fourth and final Anglo–Asante war in 1874 CE lands including the Fante states were declared the British Gold Coast Colony. Under constant pressure from the British the Asante Empire began to fragment and between 1895 and 1896 CE the British invaded the Asante heartland and destroyed Kumasi. Asante was declared a British protectorate and, in 1902 CE, became a British possession.

1 1800 CE
2 1824 CE
3 1831 CE
4 1896 CE

© DIAGRAM

Ascension

Ascension is a small British island in the South Atlantic Ocean, which is geographically considered part of Africa. It is governed under the administration of St. Helena. *See also* **St. Helena**.

Axum, kingdom of

Also spelled Aksum, the Axumite kingdom was the earliest Ethiopian kingdom. It was centered on Axum and it was founded in the first century CE in the Tigre region. It flourished as a commercial maritime nation, trading via the port of Adulis on the Red Sea. It grew so wealthy that, in the fourth century, its rulers put gold coins into circulation. The people of Axum became Christians in the fourth century. From the seventh century, Axum came into conflict with its Muslim neighbors. But, although the kingdom declined, Axum remained Christian. *See also* **Ethiopia**.

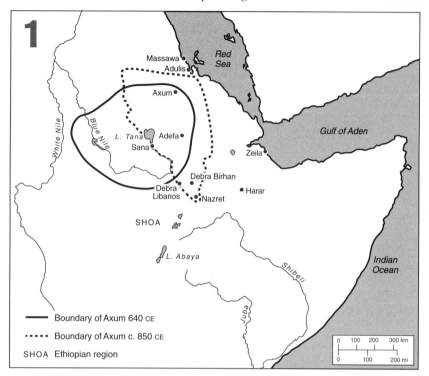

1

- —— Boundary of Axum 640 CE
- ----- Boundary of Axum c. 850 CE
- SHOA Ethiopian region

0 100 200 300 km
0 100 200 mi

2

■ Sites of Axumite culture
● Current towns and cities

0 100 200 300 km
0 100 200 mi

Axumite kingdom (left)
Founded in the first century CE by farming peoples from northeast Africa the Axumite kingdom grew steadily in wealth and power. By the fourth century CE Axum was a major maritime trading nation. The fourth century also saw the introduction of Christianity into the region by Syrian monks.

1 *c.850 CE*

Axumite carving (above)
Produced in the fifth century CE this limestone statue of a sitting woman probably had religious significance.

Decline (left)
After 600 CE the Axumite kingdom began to decline. Under pressure from Muslim peoples who gained control of Arabia, the Red Sea, and the coast of North Africa, Axum foreign trade began to dry up. Axum continued to be largely Christian and the region is still home to a substantial Christian community today.

2 *c.600 CE*

Royal burial monument (right)
Erected in the fifth century CE this royal burial monument has carved architectural features typical of Axumite timber and drystone buildings.

Bagirmi

Bagirmi was a historic state in southern Chad, founded in the early sixteenth century. At times it was part of the Borno empire. *See also* **Chad**.

Bamum kingdom

For information about the history of the Bamum kingdom, *see* **Cameroon (Peoples—Bamum)**.

Bapedi empire *See* **South Africa (Peoples—Sotho)**.

Barotseland

In the 1890s the British South Africa Company (BSAC) conquered the Lozi kingdom, which joined Northern Rhodesia as Barotseland. *See also* **Lozi kingdom**; **Northern Rhodesia**.

Basutoland

Basutoland was a landlocked British protectorate (colony) in southern Africa, which was renamed Lesotho when it became independent in 1966 CE. *See also* **Lesotho**.

Moshoeshoe I (right)
He united the Sotho people, created the kingdom of Basuto, fought off attacks from neighboring peoples, and also resisted the British and the Boers. In 1868 CE he invited the British to annex Basutoland to prevent the Boers from taking control of it.

Henry Sylvester Williams
A Caribbean-born advisor to King Lerotholi of Basutoland. He practiced as a lawyer in Cape Town in 1903 CE and was secretary of the Pan-African Association–a position that earned him death threats and forced him to leave the country in 1904 CE.

Royal visit
This stamp was issued to commemorate the visit of the British monarch, King George VI, to Basutoland in 1947 CE.

Baulé kingdoms

For information about the history of the Baulé kingdoms, *see* **Ivory Coast (Peoples—Baulé)**.

Bechuanaland Protectorate

Bechuanaland Protectorate was the original name for the landlocked British colony in southern Africa. It was renamed Botswana when the country became independent in 1966 CE. *See also* **Botswana**.

Begemder, kingdom of

For information about this Oromo kingdom, *see* **Ethiopia (Peoples—Oromo)**.

Belgian Congo

Belgian Congo was the name given to what is now the Democratic Republic of Congo between 1908 CE, when the Belgian government took over the administration of what was formerly called Congo Free State, and 1960 CE, when the country became independent. *See also* **Congo, Democratic Republic of**.

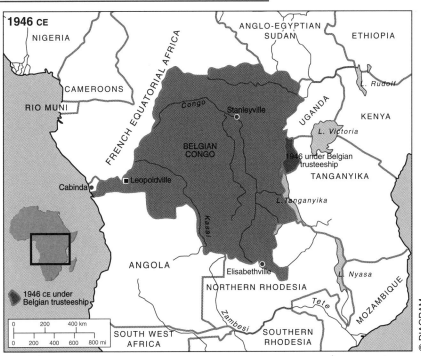

The Belgian Congo (below)
The vast, resource-rich area of the Belgian-ruled Congo in 1946 CE.

© DIAGRAM

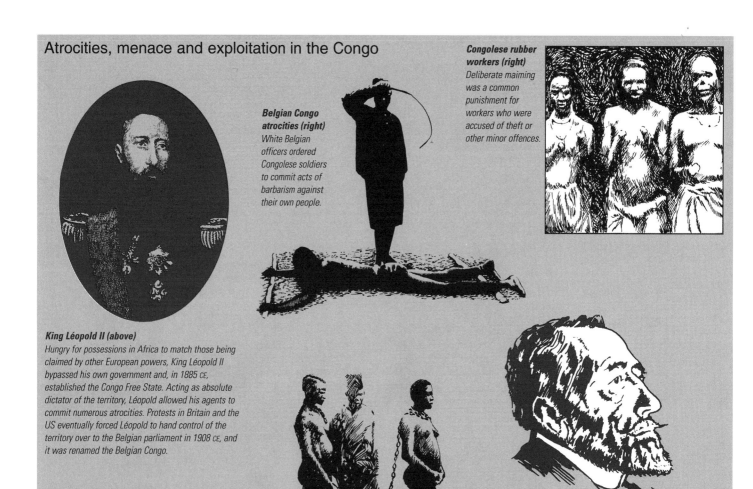

Atrocities, menace and exploitation in the Congo

King Léopold II (above)
Hungry for possessions in Africa to match those being claimed by other European powers, King Léopold II bypassed his own government and, in 1885 CE, established the Congo Free State. Acting as absolute dictator of the territory, Léopold allowed his agents to commit numerous atrocities. Protests in Britain and the US eventually forced Léopold to hand control of the territory over to the Belgian parliament in 1908 CE, and it was renamed the Belgian Congo.

Belgian Congo atrocities (right)
White Belgian officers ordered Congolese soldiers to commit acts of barbarism against their own people.

Congolese rubber workers (right)
Deliberate maiming was a common punishment for workers who were accused of theft or other minor offences.

Exploitation in the Congo (right)
African women in chains during the reign of Léopold II. The Belgians were ruthless in their exploitation of the Congo's vast human and natural resources.

Joseph Conrad (above)
The Polish-born novelist, famous for his tales of struggle and adventure set in far-flung locations. One of his most popular novellas, Heart of Darkness, is set in the Congo. Its themes of menace and madness misinformed many westerners' views of the African interior.

Belgian colonial soldiers
Many Africans fought in the armies of the European colonial powers during World War II. These men fought for the Belgian colonial army.

Bemba kingdom

The Bemba people of northern Zambia migrated from what is now the Democratic Republic of Congo more than 300 years ago. Gradually, they conquered or absorbed the original inhabitants of the region. One of the most important of the migrant groups was the Bena Yanda (Crocodile Clan), who settled on the banks of the Chambeshi River in the second half of the seventeenth century. They were led by a chief called Chiti. Bemba kings have adopted the name *Chitimukulu*, which means "Chiti the great," ever since. This small kingdom steadily expanded during the eighteenth and nineteenth centuries. It became one of central Africa's most important kingdoms, and the name Bemba was applied to all people who acknowledged the rule of the current Chitimukulu. In 1889 CE the Bemba kingdom was incorporated into Northern Rhodesia by the British South Africa Company. *See* also **Northern Rhodesia**; **Zambia**.

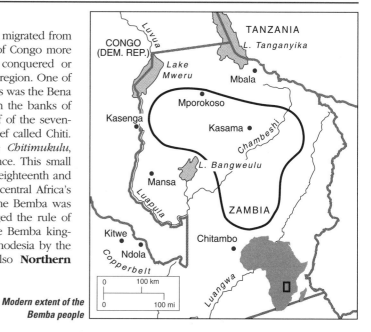

Modern extent of the Bemba people

BENIN Republic of Benin

Benin, which was called Dahomey until 1975 CE, was the site of several African kingdoms from the eleventh and twelvth centuries. After the Portuguese arrived in the second half of the fifteenth century, the region became a hub of the slave trade. Especially important was the kingdom of Abomey, which was founded by the Fon people in 1625 CE and had its capital at Abomey, in what is now south-central Benin. Its kings, who were absolute monarchs, supplied slaves to traders on the coast and the kingdom grew in power.

The Fon kingdom was one of the few African states to maintain an army for slavery and to acquire new territory. In the eighteenth century, the enlarged state was named Dahomey, and consisted of three provinces–Abomey, Allada and Whyda (now Ouidah).

The power of Dahomey was greatly diminished in the nineteenth century, after the British succeeded in abolishing the slave trade. Palm oil then replaced slaves as the main commodity of trade. In 1851 CE, France signed a trade agreement with Dahomey, but, in 1892 CE, following attacks on French coastal trading posts, France defeated the Dahomeans and deposed their ruler Behanzin. Finally, in 1904 CE, France annexed Dahomey and incorporated it into its massive territory of French West Africa. During World War I, French forces from Dahomey took part in the conquest of Togoland from Germany. After World War II, Dahomey became an overseas province of France in 1946 CE, but nationalist opposition to French rule increased.

Recent history

France granted Dahomey internal self-government in 1958, and the country finally became fully independent on August 1, 1960 in 1946 CE. A new constitution was adopted in November 1960. but, for the first decade of independence, Dahomey suffered from social unrest and political instability, caused mainly by political and regional rivalries. The first president, Hubert Maga, who led a coalition of three parties, was removed in 1963 CE by an army coup led by General Christophe Soglo. This was the first of a series of alternating civilian and military regimes.

A three-man presidential council was set up in May 1970 CE , with the former president Hubert Maga as the

first head of state in this rotational system. But this government was overthrown by a coup in 1972 CE, which brought to power Lt.-Col. Mathieu Kerekou, who, from 1980 CE , was known as Ahmed Kerekou. As president, Kérékou proved to be a remarkable survivor despite the many economic problems, factional conflict and frequent plots that occurred in this unstable country. In 1973 CE and 1974 CE, he consolidated his power and, in 1975 CE, his government announced that Dahomey would be renamed the People's Republic of Benin and that it would be a Marxist-Leninist state. The government took command of some sectors of the economy, though many private businesses still enjoyed official toleration. In 1977 CE, a new constitution was adopted, making Benin a one-party state, the one party being the *Parti de la Révolution Populaire du Bénin* (the Benin People's Revolutionary Party, or PRPB). The PRPB held power until 1989, when Kerekou announced that Benin would follow the example of eastern European countries and officially abandon Marxist-Leninism.

In 1990 CE, a civilian group, 'the National Conference of Vital Elements of the Nation', took over the government and introduced a new democratic constitution with a presidential system of government. Under this constitution, which was approved in a referendum, the president would be directly elected for renewable five-year terms while the 83-member National Assembly would be elected to four-year terms by proportional representation. The interim government legalized all parties and strictly limited Kerekou's powers by appointing a former World Bank executive, Nicéphore Soglo, as the prime minister of the provisional government, to serve until elections were held in 1991.

In 1991 CE, Soglo was elected president, defeating Kérékou by winning two-thirds of the votes in a run-off poll. However, in 1996 CE, Kerekou defeated Soglo in another election run-off, obtaining 52.5 percent of the vote, returning to power as president. He formed a government of national unity, which tried to revive the country's weak national economy. In 1999 CE, when 35 parties contested the elections to the National Assembly, Kerekou's opponents won a small majority of the seats.

Samori Toure
A 1978 CE stamp commemorating a hero of anti-colonial resistance.

Benin presidents

Aug 1 1960–Oct 27 1963 CE Hubert Maga (1st time) (Head of state until 31 Dec 1960)	**Nov 27 1965–Nov 29 1965 CE** Justin Ahomadegbé-Tomêtin (1st time) (acting)	**Dec 21 1967–Jul 17 1968 CE** Alphonse Alley (Head of state)	(Chairman of the presidential council)
Oct 27 1963–Oct 28 1963 CE Provisional Government - Hubert Maga - Sourou Migan Apithy - Justin Ahomadegbé-Tomêtin	**Nov 29 1965–Dec 22 1965 CE** Tahirou Congacou (acting)	**Jul 17 1968–Dec 10 1969 CE** Émile Zinsou	**May 7 1972–Oct 26 1972 CE** Justin Ahomadegbé-Tomêtin (2nd time) (chairman of the presidential council)
	Dec 22 1965–Dec 19 1967 CE Christophe Soglo (2nd time)	**Dec 10 1969–Dec 13 1969 CE** Maurice Kouandété (2nd time) (Chief-of-staff of the army)	
Oct 28 1963–Jan 25 1964 CE Christophe Soglo (1st time) (Head of provisional government)	**Dec 19 1967–Dec 20 1967 CE** Jean-Baptiste Hachème (Chairman of the revolutionary committee)	**Dec 13 1969–May 7 1970 CE** Paul-Émile de Souza (Chairman of the directory)	**Oct 26 1972–Apr 4 1991 CE** Mathieu Kerekou (1st time)
Jan 25 1964–Nov 27 1965 CE Sourou Migan Apithy			**Apr 4 1991–Apr 4 1996 CE** Nicéphore Soglo
	Dec 20 1967–Dec 21 1967 CE Maurice Kouandété (1st time) (Head of state)	**May 7 1970–May 7 1972 CE** Hubert Maga (2nd time)	**Apr 4 1996 CE–** Mathieu Kerekou (2nd time)

The Benin kingdom

The historic kingdom of Benin in southwestern Nigeria was founded by the Edo people some time before 1300 CE. Little is known of the kingdom's early history, but it reached its peak between the fourteenth and seventeenth centuries. It is now renowned for its superb court art, especially its magnificent bronze sculptures. Benin traded in palm oil, ivory, and pepper, both with its neighbors and with Europeans. Another commodity was slaves, though slave trading was kept to a minimum. Towards the end of the eighteenth century, Benin began to decline –the cities and states within its dominion grew strong through trade with Europeans and so broke away. During the nineteenth century, Benin continued to decline as an imperial power and was eventually incorporated into British Southern Nigeria in 1897 CE. **See also Nigeria (Edo)**.

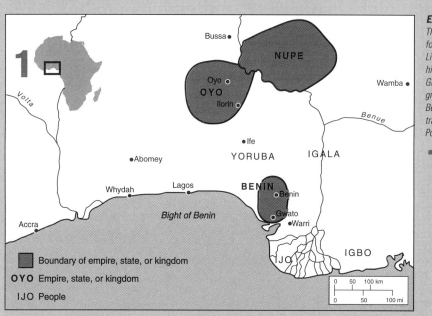

Expansion of Benin (left)
The city of Benin was probably founded between 900 and 1300 CE. Little is known about its early history but the reign of Ewuare the Great (c.1440–80 CE) was a time of great expansion. After 1480 CE Benin was involved in the slave trade, selling captives to Portugese traders.

1600 CE

Art of Benin (above)
During the period 1500 to 1800 CE– the "Era of Firearms and the Slave Trade" in West Africa–the Portuguese introduced firearms to the coastal states of West Africa. This Benin bronze depicts a Portuguese soldier with his gun.

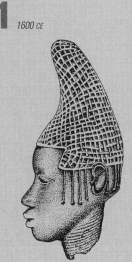

A queen mother (left)
This cast bronze head (right), from the Kingdom of Benin, was probably made in the sixteenth century. It represents a queen mother, who held an important position in this historic kingdom.

Decline of Benin (below)
During the 1700's Benin's power began to decline as its neighbors grew stronger through trade with Europeans.

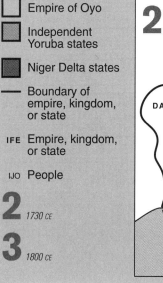

■ Empire of Oyo

■ Independent Yoruba states

■ Niger Delta states

— Boundary of empire, kingdom, or state

IFE Empire, kingdom, or state

IJO People

2 *1730 CE*

3 *1800 CE*

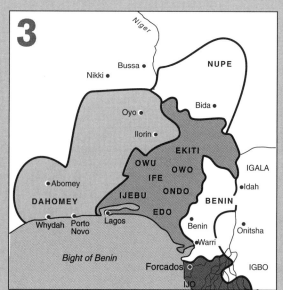

Peoples

FON

At its peak, the Fon kingdom of Dahomey had a population of about 250,000 people. But, with a highly centralized rule, a king and an efficient bureaucracy at the helm, it became one of West Africa's most powerful nations, successfully resisting European control until the end of the nineteenth century. The foundations of the Fon kingdom were laid in the early seventeenth century, when a group of warriors from Allada gradu-

Benin

By 1700 CE Benin's power over its conquests had begun to decline and its empire began to fall apart. States warred constantly to gain the upper hand in the lucrative slave trade with the Europeans. During the nineteenth century Benin's influence continued to decline until, in 1897 CE, it was taken by the British and incorporated into British Southern Nigeria.

4 1835 CE

5 1890 CE

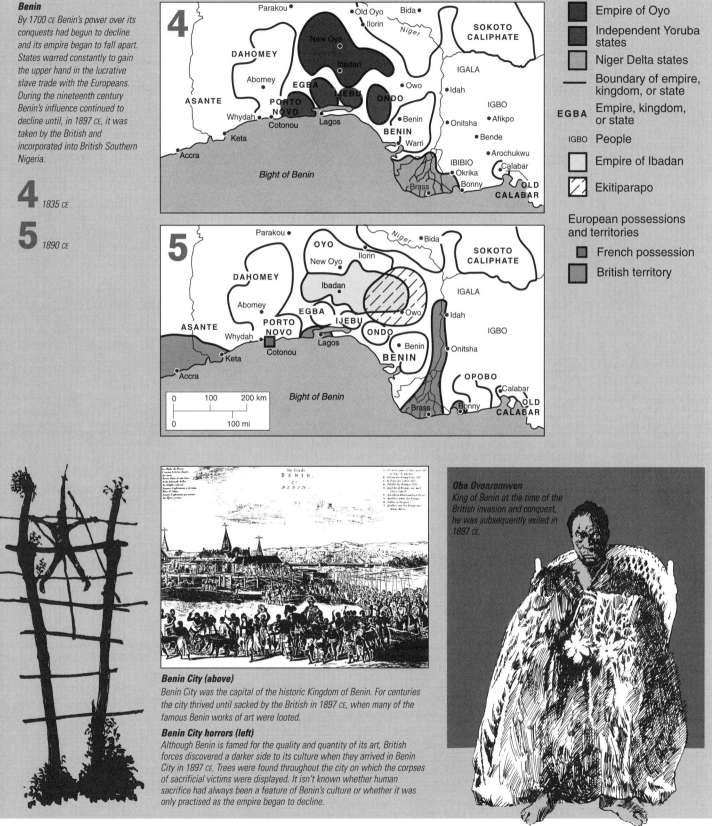

Empire of Oyo

Independent Yoruba states

Niger Delta states

— Boundary of empire, kingdom, or state

EGBA Empire, kingdom, or state

IGBO People

Empire of Ibadan

Ekitiparapo

European possessions and territories

French possession

British territory

Benin City (above)
Benin City was the capital of the historic Kingdom of Benin. For centuries the city thrived until sacked by the British in 1897 CE, when many of the famous Benin works of art were looted.

Benin City horrors (left)
Although Benin is famed for the quality and quantity of its art, British forces discovered a darker side to its culture when they arrived in Benin City in 1897 CE. Trees were found throughout the city on which the corpses of sacrificial victims were displayed. It isn't known whether human sacrifice had always been a feature of Benin's culture or whether it was only practised as the empire began to decline.

Oba Ovonramwen
King of Benin at the time of the British invasion and conquest, he was subsequently exiled in 1897 CE.

ally gained control of much of the interior, as far north as where present-day Abomey is located. At Abomey, the first ruler of the Fon kingdom built his palace on the grave of the local king he defeated, establishing a tradition followed by future kings. The charismatic King Agaja, who is remembered as a great statesman, reigned from 1708 to 1732 CE, when he greatly extended the kingdom.

The Kingdom of Dahomey was one of Africa's few states to maintain an army, which increased from about

Benin timeline

Pre 19th century CE		
	1625	King Dako of Abomey founds the kingdom of Dahomey in present-day Benin
19th century CE		
	1807	Britain outlaws the slave trade, causing an economic crisis in Dahomey
	1851	France signs a trade agreement with Dahomey
1900–49 CE	1904	France annexes the kingdom of Dahomey and incorporates it into French West Africa
	1946	Dahomey becomes an overseas territory of France
1950–59 CE	1958	Dahomey is granted self-government by France
1960–69 CE	1960	**Aug 1** Dahomey becomes a fully independent republic
	1960–1972	Frequent changes of government due to military coups
1970–79 CE	1972	Gen. Mathieu Kerekou becomes president after a military coup
	1975	Dahomey is renamed Benin. Marxist-Leninism introduced
1980–89 CE	1989	Marxist-Leninist ideology abandoned
1990–99 CE	1990	Kerekou's government is dissolved and political parties are legalized
	1991	Nicéphore Soglo becomes president after Benin's first multiparty elections
	1996	Kérékou returns to power as a democratically-elected president
	1997	Labor unions protest government's economic liberalization measures
2000–09	2000	Kerekou is reelected president

King Behanzin as a shark
This painted, wooden figure shows a fusion of man and shark, representing King Behanzin. Fierce animals, most commonly the leopard, are often used as symbols for depicting African rulers.

3,000 soldiers in the early eighteenth century to 12,000 in the mid-nineteenth century. It included up to 2,500 ferocious female warriors – women dedicated to the personal protection of the king. Arms obtained from European traders enable the Fon to extend their territories. Control of the coast allowed the Fon to have greater control over the profitable slave trade and to protect their own people from capture and sale. Fon ports along what was known as the "Slave Coast" became important points on the so-called triangular trading route that linked Europe with Africa and the Americas. For example, in the late eighteenth century, the port of Ouidah was recorded as receiving each year 40–50 Dutch, English, French, and Portuguese ships importing arms and other goods and exporting slaves.

Palm oil became the key export activity after the end of the slave trade. However, falling oil prices weakened Dahomey's economy and the French–who had greater military might–seized control of the coast in 1889 CE. In despair, the king, Glele, committed suicide and was succeeded by his son Behanzin. Despite the fierce resistance, King Behanzin and his armies, Dahomey was conquered in 1892 CE. The French then employed local chiefs to help administer the new territory.

YORUBA
The Yoruba founded important kingdoms, extending from central Benin, through parts of Togo into southwestern Nigeria. For an account of the history of the Yoruba kingdoms, *see also* **Nigeria (Peoples—Yoruba)**.

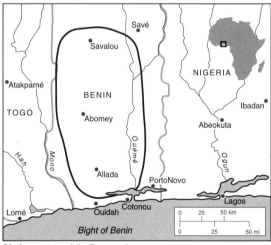

Modern extent of the Fon people

Benin's major political figures

Behanzin (1845–1906 CE)
Behanzin was the last king of Dahomey. He succeeded his father Glélé in 1889, but, in 1890, he unsuccessfully attacked Cotonou, a port which his father had lost to the French. He was subsequently defeated by the French in 1892-1894 and he was deported to Martinique and later Algeria, where he died.

Kérékou, Mathieu Ahmed (1933 CE–)
Mathieu Kérékou became president and head of the government of Dahomey (now Benin) in 1972, following a coup. He proclaimed the country a Marxist-Leninist (socialist) state, but the government abandoned Marxism-Leninism in 1989. Kérékou was defeated by Nicéphore Soglo in multiparty elections in l991, but regained power in l996. He was reelected in 2001.

Maga, Hubert Coutoucou (1916 CE–)
Maga was president of Dahomey (Benin) between 1960 and 1963 and again between 1970 and 1972. On both occasions, he was removed from office by coups and he was under house arrest between 1972 and 1981. A former teacher, born in northern Dahomey, he entered politics after World War II and served in the territorial assembly, as well as the National Assembly.

Obas
In the past, much ceremony surrounded obas (kings), who spent most of their time hidden from view. They appeared in public only at important events and, even then, surrounded by attendants and totally hidden by a crown and a robe which had been made of thousands of coral beads.

Benin (French)

Benin was the name given by the French to the colony they established in southern Dahomey before it was incorporated into the larger colony of Dahomey (now the Republic of Benin). The name Benin appears on stamps issued in southern Dahomey in the 1890s.

Berber kingdoms

The Berbers, a people of unknown origin, were probably the first inhabitants of North Africa. They had settled along the coast by around 5,000 years ago, but little is known of their early history. By the third century BCE, three Berber kingdoms had been established in northwestern Africa: Mauretania, Massaesylian Numidia, and Massylian Numidia. At times, the Berbers were in conflict with their neighbors, the city-state of Carthage which was located near the present-day city of Tunis, or the Romans who had colonized the coast. The Romans made an alliance with the Berber king, Masinissa, who ruled over Numidia, He forced many Berbers to settle on the land as farmers and built up a strong kingdom, which broke up at his death.

The two Numidias were united in 203 BCE. After the second Punic War, in 201 BCE, the Numidians encroached upon much of the Carthaginian hinterland. The introduction of Roman rule in Carthage in 146 led to Numidia's division again in 46 BCE. The western part was added to Mauritania, while the eastern part became the Roman province of Africa Nova. Mauretania was annexed by the Romans between 40–42 CE.

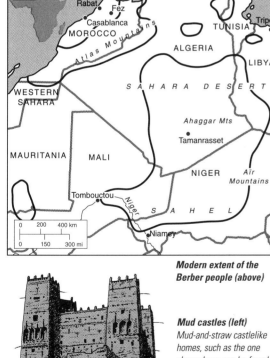

Modern extent of the Berber people (above)

Mud castles (left)
Mud-and-straw castlelike homes, such as the one shown here, can be found in Berber communities in the Atlas Mountains. They are not typical dwellings but homes of the wealthy, holy men, or landowners.

Berber kingdoms
Probably the original inhabitants of northern Africa, little is known about the Berbers or their states before the 3rd century CE.

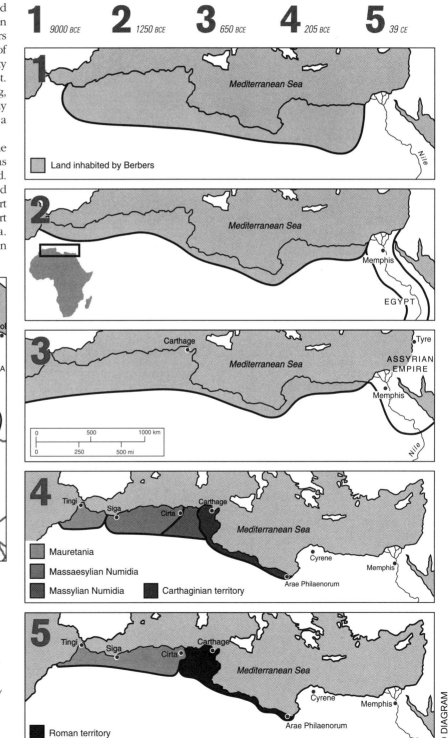

© DIAGRAM

Betsimisaraka kingdom *See* **Madagascar (Peoples—Betsimisaraka)**.

Biafra

The breakaway Republic of Biafra was proclaimed in the Eastern Region of Nigeria on May 30, 1967 CE. Among the reasons for this proclamation were fears by the Igbo (Ibo) of political domination by the Muslim

Biafra: the end (left)
This French magazine cover announces the end of the Biafran War, and the end of the hopes of the Igbo people for a nation of their own. The bitter and bloody fighting between Nigeria and the breakaway Republic of Biafra lasted two and a half years and ended with the Biafrans being starved into submission.

Breakaway republic (right)
Proclaimed on May 30th, 1967 CE the Republic of Biafra was formed by Igbo and other peoples of Nigeria who feared oppression by the Muslim northern region. Despite early military successes the Biafrans were steadily pushed back by Nigerian forces and were finally forced to surrender on January 13th, 1970 CE.

Northern Region, especially following the slaughter of thousands of Igbo that had taken place in northern and western Nigeria. Another reason was that oil had been discovered in the Eastern Region.

Civil war broke out on July 6, 1967 CE. The Nigerian government hoped for a quick ending to Biafra secession, but a bitter and bloody war continued for two and a half years. The Biafrans had early successes but, by December 1969 CE, Biafran-held territory had been reduced to a very small area. Without access to food and military equipment, the Biafrans were starved into submission and they surrendered at Amichi on January 13, 1970 CE. The president of Biafra, Chukwuemekwa Ojukwu, fled into exile. *See also* **Nigeria**.

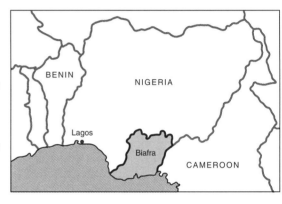

Boer republics

The Boers are the ancestors of southern Africa's Afrikaner population. Dutch settlers began settling the Cape of Good Hope in the seventeenth century, and they came to be called Boers ("farmers") after their primary occupation. In the nineteenth century, the British took control of the Cape, and the Boers began migrating inland to escape what they felt was oppressive rule. Most of the mass migrations occurred in the 1830s and are referred to as the Great Trek. Inland the Boers established several independent republics. *See also* **Lydenburg**; **Soutpansberg**; **Natal (Natalia)**; **Orange Free State**; **Potchefstroom**; **South African Republic (Transvaal)**.

THE GREAT TREK AND THE FIRST BOER REPUBLICS (1836–54 CE)

Large-scale treks begun in 1836 CE came to be called the Great Trek and its participants *Voortrekkers*. Afrikaner farmers wishing to be independent, especially from British rules and regulations, organized large family groups to travel inland away from the Cape. For the years that they were on the move, the trekkers led a nomadic existence, stopping for a few days wherever grass and water were found. Progress was slow and only a few miles were covered each day. Some groups ventured east over the Drakensberg Mountains where they encountered the Zulu. Despite their victory over the Zulu at Blood River in 1838 CE and the establishment of the Natalia republic in

1839 CE, the Afrikaners trekked back over the mountains after Natalia was annexed by the British in 1843 CE. West of the Drakensberg, on the highveld north of the Orange River, several independent Boer republics had been established. Annexed by the British in 1848 CE, they were recognized as independent from 1852 CE and came to form the Orange Free State and the South African Republic (which became Transvaal).

The Great Trek
A series of massive northeastward migrations of Boers (Afrikaners) from 1836–1848 CE came to be called The Great Trek, and its participants Voortrekkers.

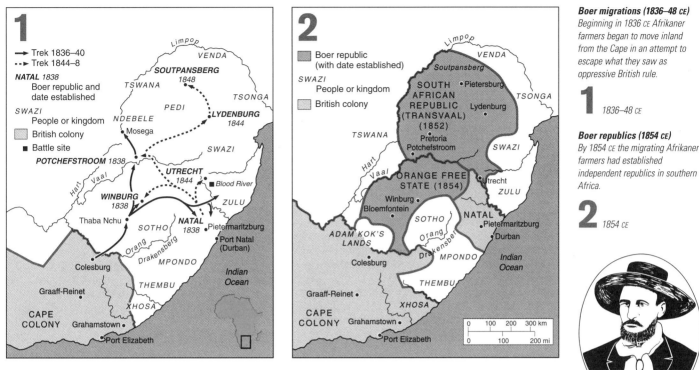

Boer migrations (1836–48 CE)
Beginning in 1836 CE Afrikaner farmers began to move inland from the Cape in an attempt to escape what they saw as oppressive British rule.

1 *1836–48 CE*

Boer republics (1854 CE)
By 1854 CE the migrating Afrikaner farmers had established independent republics in southern Africa.

2 *1854 CE*

Piet Retief
An Afrikaner of French Huguenot descent and the commander of a militia, Piet Retief published a manifesto in 1837 CE setting out the reasons behind the Great Trek (1836–48 CE). His complaints included:

We despair of saving the colony from the turbulent and dishonest conduct of vagrants...the severe losses which we have been forced to sustain by the emancipation of our slaves...the continual plunder which we have endured from the Caffres [the Xhosa] and other colored classes..

Bonny

Bonny town (formerly Ibani) on the Bonny River in southern Nigeria was once the base of a trading kingdom that flourished from the fifteenth to the nineteenth century. It was one of the largest slave-exporting depots of West Africa but switched to trading palm oil after slavery was banned in the 1830s. *See also* **Nigeria**.

Bophuthatswana

Bophuthatswana, a former "Bantu homeland" or "Bantustan" peopled mainly by Tswana people, consisted of seven separate areas in what were then western Transvaal, northern Cape, and Orange Free State. This state, which was highly dependent on South Africa was declared to be independent in 1977 CE, but it was abolished in 1994 CE, and its land reverted to South Africa.

Borgu

Borgu is a historic kingdom that still survives as an emirate in Niger state, western Nigeria. Bussa, the kingdom's capital, was destroyed during the creation of Kainji Lake in 1968 CE. France and Britain divided Borgu between their colonies in 1898 CE, and the Bussa chiefdom (founded 1730 CE) became an emirate. *See* also **Nigeria**.

Borno (Bornu)

See **Kanem–Borno**.

BOTSWANA Republic of Botswana

Around 20,000 years ago, nomadic Khoisan people occupied the area that is now Botswana. Around 2,300 years ago, some of these people, known as the Khoikhoi, developed a cattle-rearing culture in the north, while others, called the San, continued their mainly nomadic hunting and gathering culture.

During the first millennium CE, Bantu-speaking people, using iron tools and pursuing a farming culture, gradually began to move into the area, displacing the Khoisan. The main group from around 900 years ago were the Tswana, who are also called the Western Sotho (one of the three main divisions of the Sotho people). The Tswana, who today make up three-quarters of Botswana's population, took over the fertile savanna grasslands in the east, pushing the San westward into the semiarid Kalahari region.

The nineteenth century was a troubled time. The Tswana suffered from the civil wars that followed the period of Zulu expansion in southern Africa, together with conflict with Europeans. The first contacts with European explorers and missionaries, the most famous of whom was David Livingstone, were peaceful. However, Afrikaner (Boer) and British forces competed for Tswana territory until, in 1885 CE, the British divided the Tswana lands between South Africa and the British Protectorate (colony) of Bechuanaland (present-day Botswana) South Africa continued to press Britain for the transfer to South Africa of Bechuanaland, together with Basutoland and Swaziland, but Britain stated in 1935 CE that no takeover by South Africa would take place until the people in the territories approved it–something which never happened.

© DIAGRAM

Independence
A 1966 stamp celebrating independence and depicting the Botswana National Assembly Building.

AIDS in Botswana
Some estimates suggest that over a quarter of the adult population of Botswana may be infected with HIV or has AIDS. This could be reflected in a dramatically declining average life expectancy for Botswanans. Children born in the early years of the twenty-first century in Botswana may have an average life expectancy of about 40 years rather than the 70 years predicted for those in normal health.

Recent history

In 1950 CE, a crisis occurred when Chief Seretse Khama (later Sir Seretse Khama), grandson of Khama III (called the Good), who had played a major role in ensuring his nation's survival, married a white woman, Ruth Williams. Seretse was exiled in Britain, while South Africa's ruling Nationalist party brought pressure on Britain to bar him from the chieftainship. In 1956 CE, after he had been forced to return to Bechuanaland as an ordinary citizen, he became involved in politics.

Executive and legislative councils were established in 1961 CE and a constitution providing for internal self-government was introduced in 1965 CE. In the first general election, the Bechuanaland (now Botswana) Democratic Party (BDP), led by Seretse Khama, won 28 of the 31 seats in the Legislative Assembly. The country became independent as the Republic of Botswana on September 30. The prime minister (Seretse Khama) became president and the elected Legislative Assembly became the first National Assembly.

Although strongly influenced by South Africa to the south, and by settler-ruled Rhodesia (now Zimbabwe) to the north, Botswana became a stable multiparty democracy. Following Sir Seretse Khama's death in 1980, Dr Ketumile Masire became head of the BDP. Masire continued in office until 1998 CE when he retired, to be succeeded by Festus Mogae. In 1999 CE, the BDP won a majority in elections to the National Assembly, defeating the Botswana National Front which had been gaining popularity. This was the seventh free and fair election since independence.

At independence, Botswana was one of Africa's poorest nations, with an economy based on the export of meat and live animals. But mineral production has transformed the situation. The discovery of diamonds at Orapa was especially important and, by 1997 CE, Botswana had become the world's leading producer. Other mining enterprises, producing coal, cobalt, copper and nickel, helped Botswana to increase its per capita GNP (gross national product) had reached US $3,240 in 1999, one of the highest in Africa, though many people remain poor. The diversification and expansion of the economy has enabled the country to introduce wide-ranging social programmes and to set up large national parks and game reserves, which have led to an expansion in tourism aimed at wildlife enthusiasts who undertake safaris, notably to the game-rich Okavango delta.

However, Botswana also faces problems, including a high unemployment rate, overgrazing and the associated problem of desertification, and the spread of HIV/AIDS, which affects more than 25% of adults in Botswana. Deaths from AIDS is greatly reducing the average life expectancy. One forecast in 1999 CE predicted that children born in the early years of the 21st century would have an average life expectancy of 40. Without AIDS, it would have been nearly 70.

Peoples

KUNG

The Kung (or !Kung as it is often written) are a Khoisan people who live in the Dobe region of northwestern Botswana and in northeastern Namibia. Like other Khoisan groups, the Kung are not black Africans, but they are descended from southern Africa's first known human inhabitants.

SHONA

Some Shona live in Botswana, but for an account of their history, *see* **Zimbabwe (Peoples—Shona)**.

TSWANA

Tswana are one of the main groups of Bantu-speaking peoples in southern Africa. They live in eastern and northwestern Botswana and in South Africa. Their ancestors migrated southward from present-day eastern Nigeria, reaching the eastern part of their present territory in about 300 and 400 CE. From there, groups spread slowly westward over the following 200 years, setting up new territories and settlements. The Tswana originally emerged as a separate group within the Sotho group sometimes before the fifteenth century. Over many years, groups of Sotho clans (several families linked by a common ancestor or ancestors) came together to form the three main divisions of the Sotho people: the Northern Sotho, the Southern Sotho, and the Tswana (or Western Sotho). The Tswana are now generally viewed as a separate group.

The first half of the nineteenth century was a period of turmoil for the Tswana. They had to endure a series of civil wars followed by the Mfecane/Difaqane—a period of devastating invasions by neighboring people fleeing the Zulu expansion. The Tswana's first contact with Europeans came in 1801 CE, when a small group of explorers reached the southernmost Tswana settlements. These events were followed by occupation and

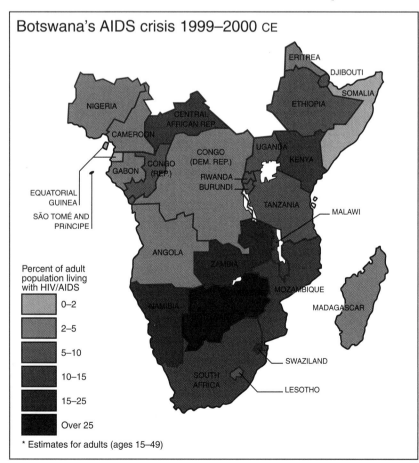

Botswana's AIDS crisis 1999–2000 CE

ERITREA
DJIBOUTI
SOMALIA
NIGERIA
CENTRAL AFRICAN REP.
ETHIOPIA
CAMEROON
CONGO (REP.)
CONGO (DEM. REP.)
UGANDA
KENYA
GABON
RWANDA
BURUNDI
EQUATORIAL GUINEA
SÃO TOMÉ AND PRÍNCIPE
TANZANIA
MALAWI
ANGOLA
ZAMBIA
MOZAMBIQUE
MADAGASCAR
NAMIBIA
SWAZILAND
SOUTH AFRICA
LESOTHO

Percent of adult population living with HIV/AIDS
0–2
2–5
5–10
10–15
15–25
Over 25

* Estimates for adults (ages 15–49)

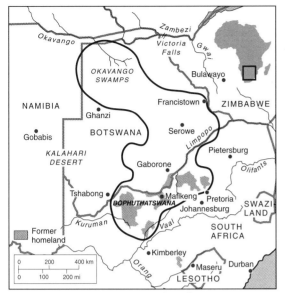

Modern extent of the Tswana peoples (above)

rule by the Afrikaners (or Boers) and the British under whom the Tswana lands were divided between South African and the British protectorate (colony) of Bechuanaland (now Botswana). *See also* **South Africa (Peoples—Tswana)**.

Tswana warriors
Pictured in the nineteenth century, which was a time of great turmoil for the Tswana, the Tswana warrior in front is carrying a distinctively-shaped shield.

Botswana presidents

Sep 30 1966–Jul 13 1980 CE
Sir Seretse Khama

Jul 13 1980–Mar 31 1998 CE
Quett Masire (from 1991, Sir Ketumile Masire)
(acting until 18 Jul 1980)

Apr 1 1998–
Festus Mogae

Botswana's major political figures

Khama, Sir Seretse (1921–1980 CE)

Seretse Khama became the first prime minister of Botswana (formerly Bechuanaland) in 1965, and the country's first president from its independence in 1966 to his death in 1980. He was exiled from Bechuanaland from 1950 to 1956 because of his marriage to a white British woman in 1948. As president, he helped to make his country one of Africa's most stable democracies.

Khama III (1837?–1923)

A paramount chief of the Ngwato, a Tswana people. Khama III became an ally of the British during the colonial period in southern Africa. By repulsing the attacks of the Ndebele chief Lobengula and, in 1885, by having Bechuanaland made a British protectorate, he ensured the survival of the Ngwato at a time of great disorder.

Masire, Sir (Quett) Ketumile Joni (1925 CE–)

A founder of the ruling Botswana Democratic Party (BDP), Ketumile Masire became Botswana's vice-president in 1966. He became president in 1980, following the death of Seretse Khama, and he was reelected in 1984, 1989, and 1994. He returned in 1998 and was succeeded by Vice-President Festus Mogae

Mogae, Festus (1939 CE–)

A former planning officer, financial administrator and Vice-President of Botswana, Mogae was sworn in as President of Botswana in April 1998. He succeeded Sir Ketumile Masire who had announced his impending retirement in 1997.

Sir Seretse Khama
He was the first prime minister of Botswana, and also the country's first president from its independence in 1965 CE until his death in 1980 CE. Born the grandson of Chief Khama III, he was forced to renounce his own status as chief after he married a white British woman, Ruth Williams, in 1950 CE. Returning from exile in Britain in 1956 CE, he entered politics as an ordinary citizen and secured the victory of his party, the Bechuanaland Democratic Party, in the 1965 CE elections to establish a government for self-rule.

© DIAGRAM

Botswana timeline

Pre 19th century

c. 420 CE Earliest dated evidence of farming and ironworking in Botswana
c. 1095 Tswana people migrate to the area of modern Botswana from the north
c. 1795 Ngakwetse chiefdom dominates central Botswana region

19th century CE

1801 British missionaries visit the Tswana people
1817 The London Missionary Society creates a permanent mission station at Kuruman
1830s Tswana attacked by migrating Kololo and Ndebele peoples
1840s David Livingstone active as a missionary in Botswana
1860s Tswana seek British protection against their enemies
1867–1869 An influx of white prospectors follows the discovery of gold in Botswana
1885 With the agreement of King Khama III and other chiefs, Britain declares the Bechuanaland Protectorate
1894 Tswana chiefs visit London
1895 Tswana chiefs cede land to the British South Africa Company for railroad construction

1900–49 CE **1935** Britain rejects a request for Bechuanaland to be transferred to South African control

1950–59 CE **1950** Chief Seretse Khama is refused permission to return to Botswana after he marries an Englishwoman while studying in Britain
1956 Seretse Khama given leave to return to Botswana

1960–69 CE **1960** Bechuanaland is granted a legislative assembly
1961 Seretse Khama forms the Bechuanaland (later Botswana) Democratic Party (BDP)
1964 A new administrative capital is built at Gaborone
1965 Britain grants Bechuanaland internal self-government
1966 Sept 30 Bechuanaland becomes independent as the republic of Botswana. Seretse Khama becomes the first president
1967 Diamonds discovered at Orapa
1969 The national assembly reelects Seretse Khama as president

1970–79 CE **1974** Program of agricultural improvements permits enclosure of grazing land
1977 The first all-weather road between Botswana and Zambia is completed

1980–89 CE **1980** Seretse Khama dies, Dr Ketumile Masire succeeds as head of the BDP
1982 Drought causes serious losses of livestock
1984 The BDP wins the first elections after Khama's death
1985 South Africa withdraws from a non-aggression treaty with Botswana
1986 South African army raid on Gaborone
1987 South Africa blockades the capital Gaborone
1989 South African covert operations against African National Congress refugees cause tension

1990–99 CE **1990s** Botswana becomes the second largest exporter of diamonds after Russia
1991 Opposition parties form a united front against the BDP
1994 BDP wins general elections but with a reduced majority
1998 Masire retires and Festus Mogae becomes president
1999 BDP retains power in general elections

A British Somaliland soldier
A soldier of the King's African Rifles. Recruited from the native peoples of Africa, such men saw active service against German troops during the East African campaigns of World War I.

British Bechuanaland

British Bechuanaland was a small territory south of the Bechuanaland Protectorate that became a British colony on September 30 1885 CE. It included such settlements as Mafeking (now Mafikeng) and Kuruman. In November 16, 1895 CE, Cape Colony annexed British Bechuanaland, which became part of South Africa.

British Cameroons

This territory was created after World War I, when the former German Kamerun was partitioned, creating two League of Nations mandated territories, one ruled by Britain and the other by France. After World War II, the mandated territories became United Nations trust territories. British Cameroons consisted of two separate areas along the Nigerian border: Northern and Southern Cameroons. In 1961 CE, the northern area joined Nigeria, while the southern part joined French Cameroon to become the Federal Republic of Cameroon. *See* also **Cameroon** (map).

British Central Africa

British Central Africa was a term used in the nineteenth century for the land north of the Zambezi River which had been colonized by Britain. It included what are now Malawi, Zambia and Zimbabwe.

British Central Africa Protectorate

This name was used for Nyasaland (now Malawi), where the British proclaimed a protectorate (colony) in December 1889 CE in order to forestall the Portuguese. Between 1890–1895 CE, as the British Central Africa Protectorate, the territory included northeast Rhodesia (now northeastern Zambia). In 1907 CE, it reverted to the name of Nyasaland. Between 1900–1910 CE, it again administered northeast Rhodesia. *See* also **Malawi**.

British East Africa

British East Africa was the term used from the late nine-teenth century for the British territories in East Africa, namely East Africa (which was later renamed Kenya), Uganda, and Zanzibar. Tanganyika (formerly German East Africa) became part of British East Africa after World War I.

British Kaffraria

British Kaffraria was a British colony in South Africa, created in December 1847 CE in areas west of the Kei River. Its capital was King William's Town and the offi-cial port was East London. British Kaffraria was pro-claimed a separate province in 1860 CE but, in 1866 CE, it was incorporated into Cape Colony and was divided into two districts: King William's Town and East London.

British Northern Cameroons *See* **British Cameroons**.

British Somaliland

This British protectorate (colony) in the Horn of Africa was established in the 1880s. It was occupied by Italy in 1940 CE, but it was reoccupied by British troops in 1941 CE. British Somaliland became independent on June 26, 1960 CE and, on July 1, 1960, it united with the former Italian Somaliland to form the Republic of Somalia. In 1991 CE, the area that once made up British Somaliland declared its independence from Somalia as the Somaliland Republic, but it did not gain any inter-national recognition.

A British East Africa soldier
A member of the Somaliland Camel Corps, a unit originally established by the British to combat internal conflict.

British Southern Cameroons *See* **British Cameroons**.

British Togoland

British Togoland was created after World War I, when British and French troops occupied German Togoland. The League of Nations mandated the western third to Britain, while the eastern two-thirds became French Togoland. In 1946 CE, both British and French Togoland became United Nations Trust Territories. In 1956 CE, British Togoland united with Gold Coast, which became independent as Ghana in 1957 CE, while French Togoland became independent as Togo in 1960 CE. *See also* **Togo**.

Buganda

The historic kingdoms of Buganda and Bunyoro are the basis of the modern-day Uganda state. Buganda was founded by the Ganda, or Baganda, people some-time before the fourteenth century.

There is plenty of information on Ganda history as each *clan* (extended families who share an ancestor or ancestors) kept its own oral history while court historians preserved royal accounts. The Ganda are descendants of Bantu-speaking people who migrated to East Africa from Central Africa around 1000 CE. Some settled on the northwest corner of Lake Victo-ria around the Kyadondo region. By the fourteenth century, this was the heart of the Buganda Kingdom.

The head of state was the kabaka whose role initially was one of arbiter rather than ruler. His power was lim-ited by that of the batakas, or clan heads. During the eighteenth century, however, successive kabakas skill-fully increased their powers at the expense of the batakas. Buganda eventually became a centralized monarchy with the kabaka acting as king.

Despite clashes with the dominant, northerly king-dom of Bunyoro, Buganda increased in size from the sixteenth century onward. By 1870, Buganda was a wealthy and influential nation state with a highly orga-nized system of government led by the kabaka with help from his Lukiko (council of ministers). A currency of cowrie shells, their value denoted by the holes

Somali Resistance (right)
Sayyid Muhammad Abdille Hassan led resistance to British and Italian expansion into Somaliland between 1900 and 1920 CE.

Kabaka Mutesa II (left)
The Ganda people, who lived on the northern shores of Lake Victo-ria, were one of the largest groups in what is now Uganda to estab-lish monarchies. Buganda was ruled by a kabaka (king). Kabaka Mutesa II ruled Buganda from 1939 until 1967 CE. He also served as president of Uganda from 1962 until 1966 when he was dismissed by the prime minister Milton Obote. In 1967 CE, Uganda became a republic. Obote became presi-dent and abolished the country's traditional kingdoms.

© DIAGRAM

Growth of the Buganda kingdom
The Baganda people first settled near Lake Victoria around 1000 CE. Steadily over the centuries they expanded their influence until they eclipsed the power of the neighboring Bonyoro kingdom that had previously dominated the area. When the Buganda kingdom became a British protectorate in 1900 CE it was a wealthy, trading nation with a highly organized and stable system of government.

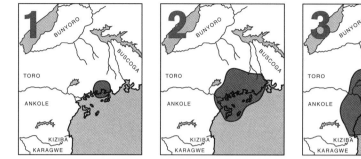

1 *Sixteenth century*

2 *Seventeenth century*

3 *Eighteenth century*

4 *Nineteenth century*

Bugandan hospitality
In the 1860s, the British explorers John Hanning Speke and James Augustus Grant visited Buganda in their search for the source of the Nile. This picture of the event shows them at the palace of Kabaka Mutesa I. Speke and his men were held as virtual prisoners for six months before Mutesa allowed them to leave.

Former leaders (above)
Mwanga, Kabaka of Buganda, and Kabaraega, Omukamu of Bunyora, two former leaders of the historic kingdoms which formed the basis of the modern state of Uganda.

drilled in the shells so that they could be suspended on strings, was in use. The Basese provided the *kabakas* with a useful naval capacity, and could sometimes muster fleets of as many as 100 vessels, each crewed by up to 30 men. This growing economic, political, and military strength had an effect on neighboring areas, particularly on Bunyoro. Buganda supplanted Bunyoro in importance and dominated the region throughout the nineteenth century, helped by several factors. Prime among these was the absence of a Ganda caste system, their military superiority, and their talent for administration.

In 1900 CE, the Buganda Agreement between the British and Bugandan regents (the reigning *kabaka* was still a boy at the time) made the kingdom a province of the Uganda Protectorate. Its territory was reorganized and numerous counties and parishes were created, each with its own head. In 1955 CE, a second Buganda Agreement made the *kabaka* a constitutional monarch and the Lukiko became an elected body. As the identity of the wider state of Uganda began to emerge, the solidarity of the Ganda became a block to national unity. Uganda finally became an independent republic in 1962 CE with Milton Obote as prime minister. *Kabaka* Mutesa II was made the first president the following year. He was arrested and dismissed in 1966 CE, however, by Obote–an act that led to widespread rioting in Buganda. In 1967 CE, traditional kingdoms

were abolished in Uganda. In 1993, however, the Bugandan monarchy, among others, was restored but with a purely ceremonial and cultural role. Although the monarchy has no real political power, the very fact that it has been restored is, in part, due to its political influence. *See also* **Bunyoro-Kitara**; **Uganda**.

Modern extent of the Baganda peoples

Mutesa I's tomb
The tall tomb of this Bugandan king is made from long, woven reeds. Mutesa I ruled over Buganda from 1852 until his death in 1884 CE. The kingdom reached its height during this period and, by then, the position of Kabaka was one of absolute monarch. Mutesa is renowned for having been a particularly cruel ruler. He was succeeded by his son who was young and inexperienced at a time when Buganda needed a decisive ruler.

Bunyoro–Kitara

The historic kingdoms of Bunyoro and Buganda are the basis of the modern-day Uganda state. Bunyoro was founded by the Nyoro, or Banyoro, people of the lakes region of northwestern Uganda.

Nyoro history is centered around the medieval empire of Bunyoro–Kitara and later the Bunyoro Kingdom. Oral history attributes the founding of the first Bunyoro-Kitara Empire to the mythical Abatembuzi (or Tembuzi) people. They were succeeded by the Bachwezi (or Chwezi) dynasty (c. 1350–c. 1500 CE) about whom little is certain except that they were a immigrant, cattle-herding people. The Bachwezi established a centralized monarchy over the local Bantu peoples. They had a hierarchy of officials and also maintained an army. After the death of the last Bachwezi *bakama* (king), Wamara, the Bunyoro-Kitara Empire broke up into several separate states, one of which was Bunyoro. The Babito dynasty took control of Bunyoro around the start of the sixteenth century. The Babito were originally Lwo-speaking River-Lake Nilotes–peoples who migrated from the Nile River in present-day southern Sudan to the lakes region of modern Uganda. Under their first *omukama* (ruler), Mpuga Rukidi, the Babito took over the country from the Bachwezi but kept many of the previous dynasty's rituals and customs. Raids against neighboring peoples expanded Bunyoro. By 1870 CE, it extended to the north and east of the Nile and to the west of Lake Victoria.

Bunyoro was governed as a loose federation of *saza* (provinces) each under a chief appointed by the *omukama*. These *saza* were semi-independent and some on the edges of Bunyoro territory broke away to form independent states. During the long reign of *Omukama* Kyebambe Nyamutukura III (1786–1835), for instance, four of his sons turned against him. One of them, Kaboyo Omuhanwa, took the *saza* of Toro and established his own kingdom. Toro then became one of the border regions in dispute between the various Nyoro factions.

Omukama Kabalega (reigned 1870–98) tried to unite Bunyoro once again and regain the ascendancy it had lost on the rise of Buganda, a kingdom to the southeast. Kabalega created the Abarusura, a standing army of 20,000 men in ten divisions, each with its own commander. One division went to the capital Masindi to maintain law and order, under Kabalega's greatest

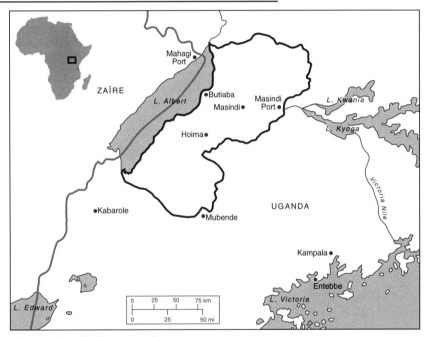

general, Rwabudongo. Omukama Kabalega defeated the British in 1872 CE at the battle of Baligota Isansa, when they tried to set up an Egyptian protectorate (colony) in the northern part of Bunyoro. Kabalega later led a guerrilla war against the British for seven years until he was deported by them to the Seychelles in 1897 CE. Toro and Bunyoro had already been made British protectorates in 1896 CE. In 1900 CE, they became part of the British Uganda Protectorate. *See also* **Buganda**; **Uganda**.

Modern extent of the Bunyoro peoples

Sir Tito Winyi Gafabusa
This picture, taken in 1936 CE, shows the (king) Bunyoro Omukama, Sir Tito Winyi Gafabusa. Seated on the royal stool, he is wearing ceremonial robes and a crown reserved for certain court appearances. The Bunyoro Kingdom was abolished in 1967 CE but was restored in 1993 CE. Sir Tito died before this in 1971 CE.

BURKINA FASO Democratic Peoples' Republic of Burkina Faso

Early inhabitants of what is now Burkina Faso (formerly Upper Volta) included the Bobo and Lobi. However, in the fourteenth century, horsemen from the south conquered much of the region. In the central part of the region, around the White Volta River, the invaders incorporated the farming people into a new society called the Mossi. The capital of the Mossi kingdom from the mid-fifteenth century was Ouagadougou. In the sixteenth century, the Mossi, who maintained their own military force, successfully resisted attacks by Songhay, but the fighting weakened the kingdom.

European explorers arrived in the Mossi kingdom in the 1880s. The French gradually extended their influence in the 1890s, placing the kingdom under their protection in 1897 CE. However, French influence was not strong because they did not regard the region as economically important. Although the French divided the country into administrative areas, they allowed the traditional rulers to maintain their authority.

Upper Volta (Haute-Volta) became a separate French colony in 1919 CE. In 1932 CE, France partitioned Upper Volta between Ivory Coast, Niger and French Sudan (now Mali), three of the territories that made up French West Africa. However, in 1947 CE, France recreated Upper Volta, and made it an overseas territory of the French Union, with its own national assembly. In 1958 CE, France made Upper Volta an autonomous republic within the French Union. The country became fully independent on August 5, 1960 CE, with a constitution that provided for an executive president and a Legislative Assembly, both elected to five-year terms.

Conservation
A 1993 CE stamp depicting the red-fronted gazelle.

Mogho naba (right)
A mogho naba (center) surrounded by his chiefs (naba). The mogho naba was the supreme ruler of the Mossi, and the role is still important today, though less powerful than in the past. He rules from the court of Ouagadougou, which is now the capital of Burkina Faso.

Recent history

The first president of Upper Volta (officially the République de Haute-Volta) was Maurice Yaméogo, a Mossi. His government became increasingly inefficient and corrupt, while the president's extravagant life style and autocratic rule caused much resentment. In 1966 CE, following a general strike, the army intervened to restore order and removed Yaméogo from office. The military under General Sangoulé Lamizana took power and suspended the constitution. Lamizana became the leader of the new military administration.

In 1970 CE, under a new constitution, the military surrendered some of their power. Lamizana remained president, though he turned over power to the prime minister. However, after three years, the military resumed power over a country, whose economy had been severely disrupted by inflation and a drought in the Sahel which caused starvation among the rural population. Lamizana continued to serve as president and, in 1977 CE, a new constitution was adopted and elections were held under a multiparty system. Lamizana was elected president in 1978 CE, but, in 1980 CE, he was overthrown in a military coup by Colonel Sayé Zerbo. Zerbo was, himself, overthrown in another coup in November 1982 CE, when the army installed Major Jean-Baptiste Ouédraogo as president of a new government.

But Ouédraogo's rule was shortlived, because he was removed from office in a coup in 1983 CE when Captain Thomas Sankara, leader of a group of radical young officers, seized power. Sankara and his allies formed a National Revolutionary Council, whose left-wing policies included the nationalization of arable land and the setting up of collectives. In 1984 CE, the government announced that the country would be renamed Burkina Faso, a term meaning 'the land of honest men'. Sankara established good relations with a similar administration in Ghana and also with Qaddafi's Libya, but it also maintained normal relations with France. Sankara worked to revive the spirit of nationalism, while, at the same time, striving to modernize it. He also appointed local committees, which undertook major projects, such as a massive vaccination cam-

Burkina Faso presidents	
Dec 11 1959–Jan 4 1966 CE Maurice Yaméogo	[provisional to Nov 11 1982] to Nov 26 1982, then head of state)
Jan 4 1966–Nov 25 1980 CE Sangoulé Lamizana	**Aug 4 1983–Oct 15 1987 CE** Thomas Sankara (chairman of the national revolutionary council and head of state)
Nov 25 1980–Nov 7 1982 CE Saye Zerbo (president of military committee of recovery for national progress)	
Nov 8 1982–Aug 4 1983 CE Jean-Baptiste Ouedraogo (chairman of the provisional committee of popular salvation	**Oct 15 1987 CE–** Blaise Compaoré (president of the popular front [from Oct 31 1987 also head of state] to Dec 24 1991)

paign, tree-planting to halt the encroachment of the Sahara into the Sahel, the doubling of the literacy rate, and the building of water storage tanks. He was also a champion of women's rights.

However, internal dissension led to a coup in 1987 CE, when Sankara and some of his aides were assassinated. Sankara was replaced by a former friend, Captain Blaise Compaoré. The son of a Mossi chief, Compaoré was elected president in 1991 CE and he worked to stabilize the economy. In 1997 CE, his party increased its majority in parliament (Assembly of People's Deputies), while in 1998 CE, Compaoré was reelected president, taking 88 percent of the votes against his two opponents.

Peoples

DYULA

The Dyula are a Mande people of mixed Bambara and Malinke origin, whose name literally means "trader" in the Dyula Manding language. The Dyula have long played a dominant role in long-distance trade between West and North Africa, and Dyula traders helped to make the medieval empire of Mali wealthy. Several large towns, such as Kong (now in northern Ivory Coast) and Bobo-Dioulasso in southwestern Burkina Faso, that grew up on major trade routes were largely inhabited by Dyula. Kong was at times an independent kingdom, reaching its height in the eighteenth century.

FULANI

The Fulani are one of West Africa's largest ethnic groups. For an account of their history, *see also* **Fulani states**.

MOSSI

Mossi as a term refers to a number of ethnic groups with similar cultures and lifestyles, but who maintain some ethnic identity. Mossi oral history states that Mossi society originated in the fifteenth century when a cavalry group from northern Ghana rode north in search of land. The invaders conquered various farming peoples who lived in the valley of the White Volta River and settled among them. Some people in the area fled to locations where the invaders' horses could not follow, such as Mali's isolated Bandiagara Cliffs, where the Dogon people sought refuge. However, other people remained behind in the newly created kingdoms, which included Ouagadougou, Ouahigouya (or Yatenga), Dagomba, and Namoba, and became part of

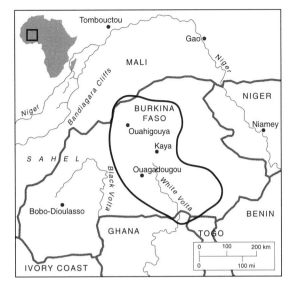

Modern extent of the Mossi peoples

President Quezzin Coulibaly
France made Upper Volta an autonomous republic within the French Union and president Quezzin Coulibaly died in 1958 CE.

a new society known as the Mossi.

The conquerors became a ruling class and were called the *nakomsé* ("the right and power to rule"). The defeated farmers became the commoners and were called the *nyonyosé*–"the ancient ones" or "children of the Earth," references to their origins as the original inhabitants of Mossi territory. The *nakomsé* generally respected the *nyonyosé*, maintaining preexisting clans (several extended families who share a common ancestor or ancestors) and assimilating many of their traditions into the new society. This reduced the likelihood of revolt and explains the cultural variations that are still found in Mossi society.

France gained control of the area in 1897 CE. Mossi myth explains that they were conquered not because they were weaker than the French, but because the ruler of Ouagadougou had ignored the warnings of the gods.

SONINKE

The Soninke are a large ethnic group who live in many West African countries. The Soninke people were citizens of the historic Ghana empire, which lay to the north of the Senegal and Niger rivers in what is now western Mali and southern Mauritania. The Soninke eventually overthrew the Maga, the people who had founded ancient Ghana. *See also* **Ghana**, **Ancient**.

Burkina Faso's major political figures

Compaoré, Captain Blaise (1951 CE–)
Blaise Compaoré became president of Burkina Faso after a coup in 1987 and was reelected in 1991. In 1983, he had helped to organize the coup that brought his predecessor, Thomas Sankara, to power. Sankara was killed in the 1987 coup, a fact that made Compaoré widely unpopular.

Lamizana, Sangoulé (1916 CE–)
Sangoulé Lamizana, who became army chief of staff of Upper Volta (now Burkina Faso) in 1961, led a military coup to overthrow Maurice Yaméogo and became head of state in 1966. He served as president until 1980, when he was ousted by a military coup led by Colonel Zerbo.

President Maurice Yaméogo
He was the first president of Upper Volta (now Burkina Faso) from 1958–1966 CE, after which he was deposed by a military coup and went into exile.

Sankara, Thomas (1949–1987 CE)

Sankara became prime minister of Burkina Faso in 1982, after a military coup led by Colonel Ouédraogo, who became president. Frustrated by Ouédraogo's failure to tackle the country's dire economic problems, Sankara staged another coup in 1983 and took over as president. A popular leader, he embarked on a series of ambitious development programs intended to restructure the economy and make the rural areas self-reliant. To do so, Sankara had to cut government spending in other areas. This brought him into conflict with the country's powerful trade unions, and the subsequent discontent led one of his closest advisors, Blaise Compaoré to mount a coup in 1987 in which he was killed.

Yaméogo, Maurice (1921–1993 CE)

Maurice Yaméogo was the first president of Upper Volta (now Burkina Faso) from 1958 until 1966, when he was deposed by a military coup led by Sangoulé Lamizana. He was imprisoned from 1966 until 1970, when he went into exile.

Burkina Faso timeline		
Pre 19th century CE		
	c. 1300	Mossi kingdom founded in the area of present-day Burkina Faso
	c. 1450	Mossi establish a capital at Ouagadougou
19th century CE		
	1896	France captures Ouagadougou
	1897	The Mossi kingdom formally becomes a French protectorate
1900–49 CE	**1919**	France creates the colony of Upper Volta within the borders of present-day Burkina Faso
1950–59 CE	**1958**	France grants Upper Volta internal self-government
1960–69 CE	**1960 Aug 5**	Upper Volta becomes independent: Maurice Yaméogo becomes president
	1966	Yameogo is overthrown by a military coup: Gen. Sangoulé Lamizana becomes president
1980–89 CE	**1980**	Lamizana is overthrown by a military coup
	1983	Capt. Thomas Sankara becomes president: he changes the name of the country to Burkina Faso
	1987	Sankara is assassinated during a military coup: Capt. Blaise Campaoré becomes president
1990–99 CE	**1997**	Drought severely affects agriculture 1998
	1998	Campaoré is reelected president

BURUNDI Republic of Burundi

The earliest inhabitants of Burundi (formerly Urundi) and Rwanda (Ruanda) were probably the Twa, a hunting and gathering people, who now make up about one percent of Burundi's population. At some time during the first millennium CE, Bantu-speaking people, the ancestors of the present-day Hutu, migrated into the area from the west, introducing an iron-using, farming culture. Around 600 years ago, a third group, the ancestors of the Tutsis, moved into the area from the north.

The Tutsi established kingdoms in both Burundi and Rwanda, each ruled by a king, or *mwami*. Although numerically a minority, the Tutsi aristocracy became feudal rulers, who treated the Hutu as slaves. In the reign of Mwami Rugamba, from the late eighteenth to the mid-nineteenth century, the kingdom expanded, but it broke up when the *mwami* made his sons, the ganwa, provincial rulers. When Europeans first arrived in the 1880s, the kingdom was divided.

The feudal social structure survived after European colonization, which began in 1897 CE when Germany made Ruanda–Urundi part of German East Africa. However, following the defeat of Germany in World War I, the League of Nations asked Belgium to rule Ruanda-Urundi as a mandated territory. In 1946 CE, the newly constituted United Nations made Rwanda a UN Trust Territory under the administration of Belgium. In 1961 CE, the people of Urundi voted to become an independent monarchy under the Tutsi Mwami, Mwambutsa IV, who had ruled since 1915, while Ruanda voted to become a republic. The two countries became independent, as Burundi and Ruanda, on July 1, 1962 CE.

Recent history

In 1965 CE, animosity between the Hutu and Tutsi came to a head in two incidents. First, assassins killed the Tutsi prime minister Pierre Ngendandumwe in January and, second, Hutu officers launched an unsuccessful coup in September. The uprising was harshly repressed and most of the Hutu leaders were executed. In July 1966 CE, when the *mwami* was in Switzerland, his son proclaimed himself head of state as Ntare V. But in November 1966, the Tutsi prime minister Michel Micombero deposed Ntare and declared Burundi a republic with himself as president.

Between 1966 and 1972 CE, purges removed most Hutu, and some Tutsis, from high office and the army. In 1972, the Hutu rebelled in an attempt to overthrow the Tutsi government and end Tutsi domination. The rebellion led to between 100,000 and 200,000 deaths, most of the victims being Hutu. In 1976 CE, a Tutsi, Colonel Jean-Baptiste Bagaza, seized power. Bagaza introduced some reforms, but became increasingly oppressive. Relations between the government and the Roman Catholic Church, which supported Hutus, deteriorated and this was one of the factors that led army officers to remove Bagaza from office in 1987.

Independence
A 1962 CE stamp showing King Mwambutsa IV that celebrated independence.

Bagaza was replaced by a Tutsi, Major Pierre Buyoya, who also introduced some conciliatory policies. But, in 1988 CE, another uprising occurred when 5,000 or more people, again mostly Hutu, were killed. In 1993 CE, Buyoya was defeated in presidential elections by a Hutu, Melchior Ndadaye, but Ndadaye and six ministers were killed in a military coup a few months later. This led to further civil conflict in Burundi. In 1994 CE, the new president, Cyprien Ntaryamira, another Hutu, was killed in a plane crash, along with Rwanda's president. This incident was thought to have been an assassination. Ntaryamira was succeeded by another Hutu, Sylvestre Ntibantunganya.

In 1996 CE, as the civil war continued, the army seized power and installed Buyoya as president for a second time. This caused several nations to impose sanctions on Burundi, including an arms embargo. In 1997 CE, Buyoya met with the heads of state of several African nations who were concerned about the coup and the ongoing civil war. In 1998 CE, the Organization of African Unity requested all parties to join talks which were mediated by Julius Nyerere, former president of Tanzania. Following Nyerere's death, the former South African President Nelson Mandela took over as mediator. In August 2000 CE, Buyoya, and most Hutu and Tutsi political parties signed an agreement to set up an ethnically balanced government and to end the seven-year civil war, though some extremist Tutsi parties refused to sign. After the talks, ethnic conflict continued between the army and Hutu rebels.

Peoples

HUTU AND TUTSI

The Hutu and the Tutsi are the two largest ethnic groups who live in Burundi and Rwanda and also in the neighboring Democratic Republic of Congo. In the past, the Bantu-speaking Hutu have formed as much as 90 percent of the population of both countries and the Tutsi around nine percent. Minority groups form the rest of the population.

The Hutu migrated into the area from the west a long time ago, displacing the original hunting and gathering peoples, who retreated into the forests. The Hutu developed a farming society based on clans, which were headed by *bahinza* (kings). The Tutsi moved into the area from Ethiopia around 600 years ago and they soon began to dominate the Hutu, creating a lord-vassal relationship, with the Hutu becoming virtual slaves producing crops for the Tutsi in exchange for protection.

The Tutsi founded two kingdoms, known as Ruanda and Urundi, each of which was ruled by a *mwami*, or king, and a small group of aristocrats called the *Ganwa*. Rwanda became especially powerful. The cultures of the two groups became increasingly integrated –both groups speak Bantu languages (Kirundi in Burundi and Kinyarwanda in Rwanda), which were originally used by the Hutu, and both follow the same religious beliefs. However, the Tutsi continued to dominate the region and form the aristocracy, even after Europeans established colonial rule. The conflict between the Hutu and Tutsi, which has marred the histories of Burundi and Rwanda since the two countries achieved independence, is a reflection of the region's complex history.

Paying his respects
In 1996 CE, Burundi's Hutu president, Sylvestre Ntibantunganyu, accompanied by Tutsi soldiers, attended the funeral of 320 victims massacred by suspected Hutu rebels at a refugee camp in Burundi. Soon after this Ntibantunganyu was deposed in a coup led by former president Pierre Buyoya.

TWA

The Twa were a nomadic hunting and gathering people who lived in the forests of Burundi and Rwanda. Their early history is obscure, but they were probably the first inhabitants of the region. However, today they make up only about one percent of the population. Their survival has depended largely on the close relationship they enjoyed with later immigrants. In return for forest products supplied by the Twa, the Hutu farmers supplied farm and metal products in exchange. This mutual relationship still survives, though many Twa now live in settled communities.

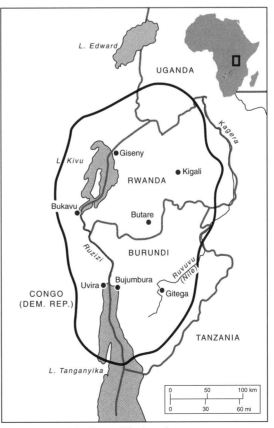

Modern extent of the Hutu and Tutsi peoples

A victim of war
This child has been orphaned by the recent conflicts between the Hutu and Tutsi in Rwanda and Burundi.

Burundi timeline

Pre 19th century

1st millennium CE	The Hutu people settle in the Burundi region
14th century	The Tutsi invade Burundi and conquer the Hutu

19th century CE

1897	Burundi becomes part of German East African territory of Ruanda-Urundi

1900–49 CE

1916	Belgian troops occupy Ruanda-Urundi
1920	The League of Nations awards Ruanda-Urundi to Belgium as a mandated territory

1960–69 CE

1961	Urundi votes to separate from Ruanda-Urundi and become the independent kingdom of Burundi
1962 July 1	Burundi becomes independent
1966	Burundi becomes a republic

1970–79 CE

1972	An unsuccessful Hutu revolt results in about 100,000 deaths

1990–99 CE

1994	Hutu-Tutsi massacres occur when a plane carrying newly elected president Ntaryamira of Burundi and president Habyarimana of Rwanda is shot down over Rwanda
1996	Burundi expels thousands of Rwandan Hutu refugees

2000–09 CE

2000	Attempts to negotiate a peace treaty in Tanzania are thwarted by extremist group
2010	An attempted coup is suppressed

Burundi's major political figures

Bagaza, Jean-Baptiste (1946 CE–)

Bagaza became president of Burundi after leading a coup in 1976, overthrowing President Michel Micombero. He served until 1987 when he was removed from power in a bloodless coup which occurred when he was in Canada. During his early years in office, Bagaza introduced reforms, including the abolition of the feudal land system, but, later his repressive measures led to a drop in support from his fellow Tutsis.

Buyoya, Pierre (1949 CE–)

A Tutsi army officer, Pierre Buyoya became president in Burundi in 1987, displacing JEAN-BAPTISTE BAGAZA. In 1993, Buyoya was defeated in multiparty elections, but his successor, a Hutu named Melchior Ndadaye, was assassinated later that year, sparking off widespread ethnic conflict. Buyoya again became president in 1996 displacing the Hutu president Sylvestre Ntibantunganyu.

Micombero, Michel (1940–1983 CE)

In 1966, while the *mwami* (king) of Burundi was abroad, Micombero, the prime minister, declared the country a republic and made himself president. Micombero, a Tutsi, consolidated Tutsi supremacy in Burundi and purged the army and government of Hutus. After an abortive coup attempt in 1972, between one hundred thousand and two hundred thousand Hutu were brutally massacred. He was deposed in 1976 by Colonel Jean-Baptiste Bagaza and he went into exile in Somalia.

Mwambutsa IV (1912-1977 CE)

Mwambutsa served as *mwami* (king) of Burundi from 1915 until 1966. This covered the period of Belgian rule and the first years of independence. He was not a strong leader, though some members of his family became involved in the nationalist movement which led the struggle for independence. In 1965, after he conspired with a group of Tutsi officers in an unsuccessful coup, he fled the country and later died in exile in Switzerland. His son Crown Prince Charles Ndizeye was proclaimed *mwami* in 1966, becoming Ntare V, but he was removed from office when Burundi became a republic. Ntare was executed in 1972.

Michel Micombero

A prime minister of Burundi who, in 1966 CE, declared the country a republic while the king was abroad and initiated a purge of Hutus from the army and government. Following an attempted coup in 1972 CE, his government carried out the massacre of between 100–200,000 Hutus.

Ntaryamira Cyprien (1955–1994 CE)

Ntaryamira, former Burundi minister of agriculture, was elected president of Burundi in January 1994, succeeding Melchior Ndadaye, who had been assassinated in 1993. However, Ntaryamira was killed in an airplane crash in April 1994, together with the Rwandan president Juvénal Habyarimana. The deaths of the two presidents provoked violence, especially in Rwanda.

Ntibantungana Sylvestre (1956 CE–)

Ntibantunganya, a Hutu and the Speaker in Burundi's parliament, became president of Burundi in 1994, when President Cyprien Ntaryamira was killed in an airplane crash along with President Juvénal Habyarimana of Rwanda. He was deposed in 1996 by a military group, who installed Pierre Buyoya as president. Ntibantunganya spent nearly a year in the US Embassy where he had sought sanctuary.

Burundi kings and presidents			
Kings	**Presidents**	(chairman of the military committee of national salvation until Sep 9 1987)	**Oct 27 1993–Feb 5 1994** CE Sylvie Kinigi (f) (acting) 5 Feb 1994- 6 Apr 1994 Cyprien Ntaryamira
Dec 16 1915–Jul 8 1966 CE Mwambutsa IV Bangilicenge	**Nov 28 1966–Nov 1 1976** CE Michel Micombero		
Jul 8 1966–Sep 1 1966 CE Prince Charles Ndizeye (head of state)	**Nov 1 1976–Sep 3 1987** CE Jean-Baptiste Bagaza (chairman of the supreme revolutionary council until 10 Nov 1976)	**Jul 10 1993–Oct 21 1993** CE Melchior Ndadaye	**Apr 6 1994–Jul 25 1996** CE Sylvestre Ntibantunganya (acting until 1 Oct 1994)
		Oct 211993–Oct 27 1993 CE François Ngeze (chairman of the committee of public salvation, in rebellion)	
Sep 1 1966–Nov 28 1966 CE Ntare V Ndizeye	**Sep 3 1987–Jul 10 1993** CE Pierre Buyoya (1st time)		**Jul 25 1996** CE– Pierre Buyoya (2nd time) (provisional until 11 Jun 1998)

Bussa

See **Borgu**.

Cabinda

This coastal province lies to the north of Angola, between the borders of the two Congos, and is separated from Angola by a strip of the Democratic Republic of Congo. Inhabited by Bantu-speaking Black Africans for more than 2,000 years, it is a major oil-producing district of Angola that is separate from the rest of the country. Once known as Kabinda, the main city was established by the Portuguese as a trading port in the 16th century and became a major portal for the slave trade. Portugal controlled Cabinda until 1975 CE, when it became independent as part of Angola. Rebels who wanted Cabinda to be an independent state were defeated by Angolan–Cuban forces in 1976 CE. *See also* **Angola**; **Portuguese Congo**.

Calabar, New

Founded by Ijo-speaking people, New Calabar (or Elem Kalabari) was a historic state in the Niger Delta region of present-day Nigeria that profited greatly from the slave trade. The main commodity traded switched to palm oil in the nineteenth century, and conflict over control of this trade led to civil war in the 1880s. New Calabar then broke up into three separate kingdoms. *See also* **Ijo states**; **Nigeria**.

Calabar, Old

Old Calabar was established by Efik-speakers on the Calabar river near the mouth of the Cross river, southeastern Nigeria. It probably existed before the arrival of Europeans. The state profited greatly from the slave trade, which it controlled on the Cross and Calabar rivers. Slaves were also kept to work the Calabar plantations, but they staged rebellions in 1851 and 1852 CE. Old Calabar was ruled by men of the Ekpe society, which was controlled by the town's merchant houses. After slavery was abolished in the nineteenth century, Old Calabar turned to trading in palm oil. In the 1880s, Old Calabar was conquered by the British, and in 1904 CE it was renamed Calabar, the name it bears today. *See also* **Nigeria**.

CAMEROON Republic of Cameroon

The earliest people to live in what is now Cameroon were probably hunter-gatherers. However, iron-using, farming people were established in the area and eastern Nigeria hundreds of years BCE. From this region, they eventually migrated eastwards and southwards throughout eastern, central and southern Africa.

Portuguese navigators reached the area in the second half of the fifteenth century. The Portuguese were followed by other Europeans, including the Dutch and the English. Slave traders bought Africans along the coast between the sixteenth and nineteenth centuries. However, following Britain's abolition of slavery in the early nineteenth century, the region's chief exports gradually changed from slaves to ivory and palm oil. British missionaries founded the first European settlement - Victoria, by Mount Cameroon.

Britain, France and Germany competed for control of the area, but, in 1884 CE, Germany made a treaty with two Douala chiefs and they declared the area a protectorate (colony) called Kamerun. The protectorate's borders were fixed in 1913 CE. Germany set up a system of indirect rule while also encouraging commercial companies to develop the economy. But German rule was ended when French, Belgian and British troops invaded Kamerun during World War I. The country was partitioned and, after the war ended, the League of Nations mandated Britain and France to rule the region.

France ruled four-fifths of Kamerun while Britain took the rest, which was made up two separated areas along the Nigerian border. British Cameroons was divided into Northern and Southern Cameroons. The French and British areas developed culturally contrasting societies. During the period of colonial rule, progress was made in the fields of health and education. However, demands for independence began to increase after 1946 CE, when both France and Britain stated that they would eventually grant both parts of Cameroon self-government, or independence.

Union

A stamp celebrating the creation of the Federal Republic of Cameroon in 1962 CE.

Partition

Kamerun was declared a German protectorate in 1884. Following the defeat of Germany in World War I, the League of Nations mandated that the territory should be administered by France and Britain. French Cameroun became independent in 1960 and, in 1961 CE, the people of the British Cameroons voted to become a part of the Federation of Nigeria.

1 *1913 CE*   **3** *1961 CE*

2 *1929 CE*

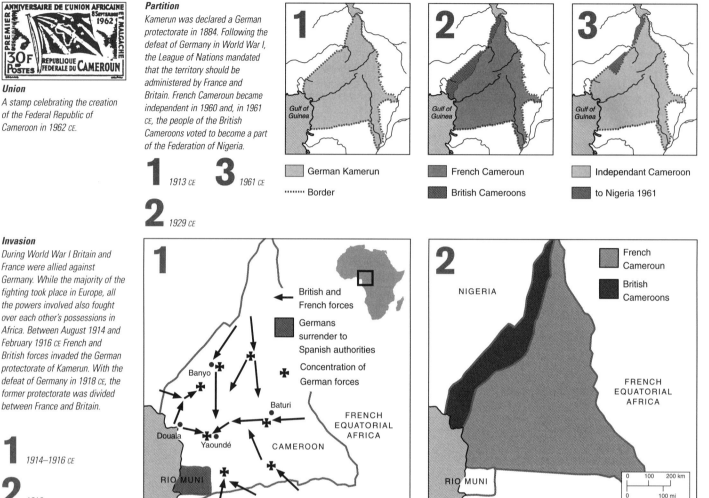

| German Kamerun | French Cameroun | Independant Cameroon |
| ······· Border | British Cameroons | to Nigeria 1961 |

1 — British and French forces; Germans surrender to Spanish authorities; Concentration of German forces — Banyo, Baturi, Douala, Yaoundé, CAMEROON, FRENCH EQUATORIAL AFRICA, RIO MUNI

2 — French Cameroun; British Cameroons — NIGERIA, FRENCH EQUATORIAL AFRICA, RIO MUNI

Invasion

During World War I Britain and France were allied against Germany. While the majority of the fighting took place in Europe, all the powers involved also fought over each other's possessions in Africa. Between August 1914 and February 1916 CE French and British forces invaded the German protectorate of Kamerun. With the defeat of Germany in 1918 CE, the former protectorate was divided between France and Britain.

1 *1914–1916 CE*

2 *1919 CE*

A German missionary

When Cameroon became a German protectorate in 1884, German occupiers such as this Christian missionary tried to impose their own beliefs upon the indigenous people.

Recent history

In 1946 CE, French Cameroun and the British Cameroons became UN trust territories. In 1948 CE, trade unionists organized the *Union des populations du Cameroun* (UPC), whose demands included the reunification of the country and independence from France. In 1955 CE, the UPC launched a revolt in French Cameroun, but the uprising failed. Its leaders fled the country, but a guerrilla war continued. Between 1957 and 1962 CE, between 10,000 and 20,000 people were killed. In the final years of the conflict, the UPC, claiming to be a liberation movement, received support from socialist and communist countries, but after 1962 CE the conflict became no more than bandit activity.

French Cameroun became independent as the Republic of Cameroon on January 1, 1960 CE and Ahmadou Ahidjo, a former prime minister, became the first president. In February 1961 CE, the people of British Cameroons voted on their future. Northern Cameroons opted to unite with the Federation of Nigeria and this was formally achieved on June 1, 1961 CE. Southern Cameroons voted to join the Republic of Cameroon and, four months later, they united as the Federal Republic of Cameroon, comprising two states–East and West Cameroon.

Ahidjo made both French and English the official languages, and he set about the integration of services and the establishment of a centralized administration, ruled, from 1966 CE, by a single party, the Cameroon National Union (CNU). In 1972 CE, a referendum approved a new constitution. The country was renamed the United Republic of Cameroon and a centralized form of government replaced the federal system. The country's official name was again changed to Republic of Cameroon in 1982 CE.

In 1981 CE, Cameroon and Nigeria were in dispute over offshore oilfields, but the Organization of African Unity resoved the problem. In 1982 CE, Ahidjo, concerned about his health, resigned as president. His successor was Paul Biya, who had served as prime minister. Ahidjo remained the leader of the CNU, but he clashed with Biya, who took control of the party. Ahidjo went into exile. A military coup in 1984 CE failed. Ahidjo was later convicted in absentia for conspiracy in attempted coups.

In 1985 CE, Biya renamed his party the People's Democratic Movement and, in 1992 CE, opposition parties were legalized. Elections in 1992 and 1997 CE resulted in victory for Paul Biya, who was returned as president, and his party. In the 1990s, Cameroon faced border disputes with Nigeria, especially over the oil-rich Bakassi peninsula and the maintenance of national unity remained a problem. The decision to make Cameroon the 52nd member of the Commonwealth in 1995 CE was seen partly as an attempt to placate the English-speaking community.

Peoples

BAMILEKE

The Bamileke in northwestern Cameroon are divided into about 90 or more small kingdoms, or chiefdoms. The largest kingdoms include Bafou, Bansoa, Foto, Banjoun, and Baham. The origins of the Bamileke are unclear. Some historians believe that they migrated into northwestern Cameroon after coming under pressure from the Fulani in the seventeenth century. The first Bamileke kingdoms emerged in the region at that time. Most recently, the Bamileke region suffered a devastating civil war (sometimes called the Bamileke rebellion) from 1958 to 1972 CE. *See also* **Fulani states.**

BAMUM.

The Bamum, Bamom, or Mom number somewhat less than 500,000 people living in the western region of Cameroon. The Bamum kingdom was established in the eighteenth century by Nchare, the first mfon (or king). The capital was at present-day Foumban, which is now a major Cameroonian town on the eastern edge of the southern end of the Adamawa plateau. The most famous Bamum *mfon* was Njoya, the seventeenth king, who wrote a book on the history of the Bamum that was translated into French. At the end of the nineteenth century, Njoya invented a written language that used 510 pictographic symbols. Pictographs are symbols that are used to represent words. Njoya's language was eventually condensed into an "alphabet" of 73

pictographs and 10 digits. Njoya converted to Islam in 1918 CE and he introduced the religion to the Bamum.

DYULA.

For information on the history of the Dyula, *see* **Burkina Faso (Peoples—Dyula)**.

FANG

For information on the history of the Fang, *see* **Equatorial Guinea (Peoples—Fang)**.

Njoya
The seventeenth king of the Bamum peoples of Cameroon. At the end of the nineteenth century he devised a written form of the Bamum language. In 1918 CE he converted to Islam and introduced the religion to his people.

Janus mask
This Bamileke court mask features the shapes of human heads in the hair and beard, and a woman's head on the rear.

Cameroon timeline

Pre 19th century		
	c. 200 CE	Bantu-speaking peoples, modern Africa's largest linguistic group, originate in Cameroon and eastern Nigeria
	1472 CE	Portuguese navigator Fernãndo Po becomes the first European to visit Cameroon
19th century CE		
	1884	Cameroon becomes a German protectorate
1900–49 CE	**1914**	French and British troops occupy Cameroon
	1922	Cameroon is divided between France (75 per cent) and Britain (25 per cent)
	1946	Britain and France agree to give their parts of Cameroon self-government or independence
	1948	Nationalists in French Cameroon found the People's Union of Cameroon (UPC)
1950–59 CE	**1959**	French Cameroon is granted internal self-government
1960–69 CE	**1960 Jan 1**	French Cameroon becomes the independent Republic of Cameroon. Alhaji Ahmadou Ahidjo of the UPC becomes president
	1961	The southern part of British Cameroons and the Republic of Cameroon combine to form the Federal Republic of Cameroon. Northern British Cameroon votes to join Nigeria
	1962	A UPC rebellion is put down by the Ahidjo regime
	1966	Ahidjo forms the Cameroon National Union (CNU): all other parties are banned
1970–79 CE	**1972**	Cameroon becomes a unitary (i.e. non-federal) state
	1977	Cameroon becomes an oil exporting country
1980–89 CE	**1982**	President Ahidjo resigns and is succeeded by Paul Biya
	1984	An attempted coup by ex-president Ahidjo is defeated
	1985	Biya renames the CNU the People's Democratic Movement
1990–99 CE	**1991**	Political parties legalized
	1992	Biya and the People's Democratic Movement retain power after Cameroon's first multiparty elections
	1995	Cameroon joins the Commonwealth of Nations
	1998	Cameroon and Nigeria take a fishing rights dispute to the International Court

Ahmadou Ahidjo
He led his country to independence, became its first president, and united the French- and English-speaking parts of the country before going into exile in France in 1983 CE.

© DIAGRAM

Cameroon presidents

Jan 1960–Nov 6 1982 CE
Ahmadou Ahidjo
(head of state until 5 May 1960)

Nov 6 1982 CE–
Paul Biya

André M'Bida
He became prime minister of French Cameroon in 1957 CE, was overthrown in 1958 CE, and returned from exile in 1960 CE to take up a position as opposition leader to the then current government.

Cameroon's major political figures

Ahidjo, Ahmadou (1924–1989 CE)

As prime minister of Cameroon (1958–60), Ahmadou Ahidjo led his country to independence and was its first president (1960–82). He achieved the complex task of uniting the French- and English-speaking parts of the country. In November 1982, he resigned the presidency and handed over his responsibilities to the prime minister, Paul Biya. In 1983, he went into exile in France.

Biya, Paul (1933 CE–)

Paul Biya, prime minister of Cameroon (1975–82), became the country's second president when Ahmadou Ahidjo resigned in 1982. He survived a coup attempt in 1984, which caused considerable loss of life, and after widespread protest, he legalized opposition parties in 1991. Biya was reelected president in an uncontested election in 1988 and in multiparty elections in 1992 and 1997.

M'Bida, André-Marie (1917 CE–)

Mbida, who had served as a Deputy in the French Assembly, became prime minister of what was then French Cameroon, in 1957. However, he was accused of being too pro-French and his government was overthrown in 1958. Following a period in exile, he returned in 1960 and became an opposition leader to the government of Ahmadou Ahidjo.

Cameroun

The French spelling of Cameroon. *See* **Cameroon**; **French Cameroun**.

Canary Islands

The Canary Islands form an arc in the Atlantic Ocean off the coast of northwest Africa. They are administered as two separate Spanish provinces. Lanzarote, Fuerteventura, Gran Canaria, Tenerife, and La Palma are the largest islands. Berbers were the original inhabitants of the seven islands and six islets that make up the Canary Islands. In 1404 CE the Spanish king named a French explorer king of the Canary Islands. Portugal attempted to take control of the islands, but by the turn of the century, they were completely under Spanish control. The Canary Islands were an important staging post for Spanish trading ships sailing to the Americas. *See also* **Algeria (Peoples—Berbers)**.

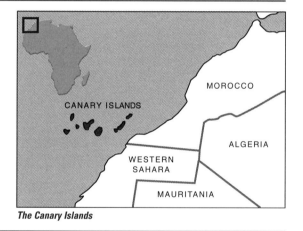

The Canary Islands

Sigcawu Mqikela (above)
The king of the eastern Mpondo (1887–1905 CE), he was arrested in 1895 CE for resisting the expansion of Cape Colony into Pondoland.

Cape Colony

British-controlled Cape Colony existed from 1806 CE in what is now South Africa. In 1795 CE the British wrested control of Cape of Good Hope from the Dutch; but gave it back eight years later (1803). In 1806 the British annexed the Cape Colony. In 1910 CE, Cape Colony became a province called the Cape of Good Hope in the Union of South Africa. In 1994 CE, the province was divided into three provinces: Eastern Cape, Northern Cape, and Western Cape. *See also* **Cape of Good Hope**; **South Africa**.

Cape Colony expansion (left)
Originally founded by the Dutch as a resupply station for European vessels making the long journey to India, China, and southeast Asia, Cape Colony slowly expanded during the seventeenth and eighteenth centuries.

1652–1750 CE

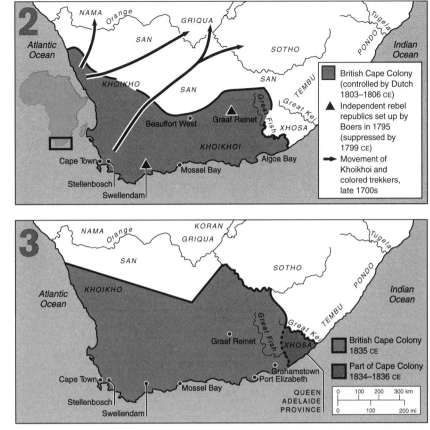

Cape Colony expansion (continued)

In 1795 CE the British occupied the Cape and, in 1814 CE, the Dutch formally ceded Cape Colony to Britain. Many of the Dutch farmers, known as Boers, who had settled in the colony were unhappy with British rule and began to migrate inland to seize land from the indigenous peoples and found new states of their own.

By 1835 CE the British had extended the area of Cape Colony. In the following year there were mass migrations of Boers—an event that came to be known as the Great Trek. The Boers established new states but, with the discovery of gold and diamonds, these too were seized by the British.

Further expansion in the Cape Colony is shown at the following dates:

2 *1795 CE*

3 *1835 CE*

Cape Juby

Cape Juby was a Spanish possession in North Africa. It was occupied by Spain in 1916 CE and made part of Spanish Sahara in 1950 CE. *See also* **Mauritania**; **Morocco**; **Spanish Sahara**.

Cape of Good Hope

Cape of Good Hope is the name Europeans gave the southernmost tip of Africa. In time, the name referred to large areas of what is now South Africa. In 1652 CE a Dutch garrison was established on the Cape that grew into Cape Town. The Portuguese extended the region under their control inland as far as the Orange and Great Fish rivers. The Cape was lost to the British in 1795 CE but regained in 1803 CE. The Dutch sold the Cape to the British in 1814 CE, although the British were already in control of the region by then. *See also* **Cape Colony**; **South Africa**.

CAPE VERDE Republic of Cape Verde

Portuguese navigators discovered in the fifteenth century the then uninhabited arid volcanic islands which make up modern Cape Verde. The first Portuguese settlers landed on the island of Sào Tiago, where they founded a city named Ribeira Grande. The islands eventually became important as provisioning stations and assembly points for slaves taken from the African mainland. The slave trade brought great prosperity to the islands, but the affluence of Ribeira Grande later made it a target for pirates and the city was finally abandoned in 1712 CE.

In the nineteenth century, the abolition of the slave trade, together with the persistent and lengthy droughts that affect the islands, brought to an end the prosperity which the islands had once enjoyed. Towards the end of the nineteenth century, the economy improved when Mindelo on Sào Vicente island developed as a coaling and submarine-cable laying station, but Mindelo declined after World War I when the number of ships using it decreased.

At first, Portugal governed the Cape Verde islands together with Portuguese Guinea (now Guinea-Bissau) but, in 1879, they were separated, becoming two Portuguese colonies. In 1951 CE, Cape Verde became an overseas province of Portugal and, in 1961 CE, all Cape Verdeans were granted Portuguese citizenship. However, opposition to Portuguese rule steadily increased and, from the 1950s, the African Party for the Independence of Guinea and Cape Verde (PAIGC) fought to overthrow Portuguese rule.

Recent history

In 1951 CE, Cape Verde became an overseas province of Portugal and, in 1961 CE, all Cape Verdeans were granted Portuguese citizenship. From 1956 CE, when the African Party for the Independence of Guinea and

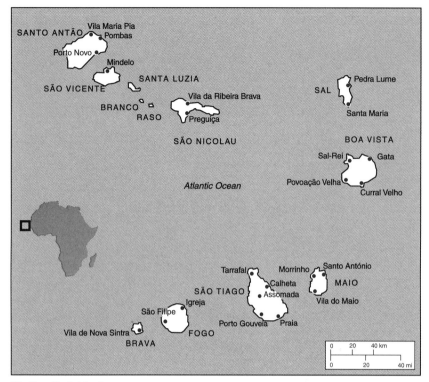

The Cape Verde Islands

Cape Verde (PAIGC) was formed, a long and ultimately successful guerrilla war was fought to overthrow Portuguese rule in both countries.

On April 25, 1974 CE, a military coup occurred in Portugal, overthrowing the dictatorship of Marcello Caetano. In Cape Verde, the government negotiated with the PAIGC, which it recognized had overwhelming support among the people on the nine inhabited islands. In pre-independence elections, more than 90 percent of the population voted for PAIGC candidates.

Cape Verde finally became independent on July 5,

1975 CE. Its first president was Aristides Pereira. who had become secretary general of the PAIGC following the assassination of Amilcar Cabral in 1973 CE. One of the chief objectives of the socialist PAIGC was to merge Cape Verde and Guinea-Bissau, which had become independent in September 1974 CE, into a federation. To this end, a joint commission on the question of federation was appointed in 1975 CE and, in 1977 CE, a Council of Unity was established under the chairmanship of the presidents of the two national assemblies.

In 1980 CE, a military coup in Guinea-Bissau put an end to any prospect of federation. The Cape Verde branch of the PAIGC was dissolved and, in 1981 CE, the African Party for the Independence of Cape Verde (PAICV) was formed, again under the leadership of Aristides Pereira. The PAICV was the only political party until 1990, when a new constitution permitted a multiparty system. In January 1991 CE, the PAICV was defeated in elections which were won by the opposition Movement for Democracy (MPD), which took 68 percent of the vote. In February 1991, the MPD candidate, Dr António Mascarenhas Monteiro, became president, receiving 74 per cent of the vote and defeating the President Pereira.

In December, 1995 CE, the MPD won 50 of the 72 seats in the National Assembly, while, in the following February, President Monteiro was reelected unopposed. In the 1990s, the government sought to liberalize the economy and a wide range of industries was privatized. However, the country remained dependent on overseas aid, together with assistance from the International Monetary Fund (IMF) and the World Bank. Relations with Guinea-Bissau improved and, in 1999 CE, Cape Verde helped to negotiate an agreement between the Guinea-Bissau government and rebels in that country. In 2001 CE the PAICV was reelected to power, defeating the MPD.

Independence
A 1976 CE stamp celebrating the first anniversary of Cape Verde's independence from Portugal.

Cape Verde's major political figures

Monteiro, António Mascarenhas (1944–)
Former president of Cape Verde's Supreme Court and opposition politician, Monteiro became president of Cape Verde in 1991. He defeated Aristides Pereira, who had been president since 1975.

Pereira, Aristides Maria (1924–)
An early independence leader, Pereira was one of the founders of the independence movement Partido Africano da Independencia do Guiné e Cabo Verde (PAIGC) in 1956. Pereira was elected president of Cape Verde in 1975 and served until 1991, when he was defeated by António Mascarenhas.

Cape Verde timeline

Pre 19th century CE

	1455	Cape Verde islands discovered by Portuguese navigators, Alvise de Cadamosta and Antonio Noli
	1492	Portuguese planters and their African slaves settle the Cape Verde Islands
1950–59 CE	**1956**	Pro-independence nationalists set up the *Partido Africano de la Independência do Guiné e Cabo Verde* (PAIGC)
1960–69 CE	**1961**	Guerrilla warfare breaks out
1970–79 CE	**1975**	Cape Verde Islands become independent of Portugal: Aristides Pereira of PAIGC becomes president
1980–89 CE	**1980**	Plans for a union with Guinea-Bissau are dropped
	1981	PAIGC changes its name to *Partido Africano de la Independência da Cabo Verde* (PAICV)
1990–99 CE	**1991**	Pereira and the PAICV lose power in Cape Verde's first multiparty elections
	1996	Cape Verde joins the Community of Portuguese-Speaking Countries

Carthage

Carthage was the name of a city-state and of the empire it came to control. According to tradition, Phoenician traders from city-states in the coastal regions of what are now Syria and Lebanon founded the city of Carthage in 814 BCE. The oldest ruins are at least 100 years later than this, however. Carthage was a port near modern-day Tunis, the capital of Tunisia in North Africa. By 600 BCE, Carthage was independent, and with its excellent harbors soon became wealthy through trade with Mediterranean and African nations. A century of wars with the Berber Numidian kingdoms and the Punic Wars with the Romans weakened Carthage, which was destroyed by the Romans in 146 BCE. A couple of decades later, the Romans built a new Carthage near the original site. The administration of Rome's African province was based at Carthago, as the Romans named it. Carthage was destroyed by Arab invaders at the start of the eighth century, then an era of Byzantine rule followed. The Byzantine Empire was the eastern half of the Roman Empire, which survived for 1,000 years after the western half no longer existed. The area fell to the Ottoman Turks, with the rest of the Byzantine Empire in the fifteenth century. After the Italo-Turkish War (1911–12 CE), the area came under Italian rule. Carthage today is a rural suburb of Tunis. *See also* **Tunisia**.

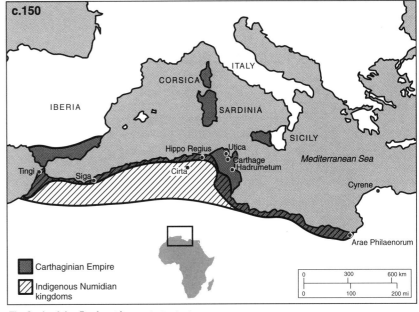

Key:
- Carthaginian Empire
- Indigenous Numidian kingdoms

The Carthaginian Empire at its greatest extent

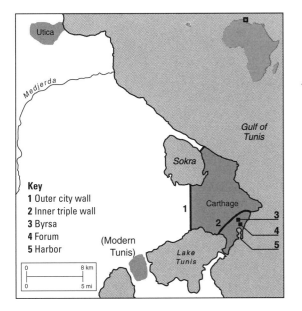

Key
1 Outer city wall
2 Inner triple wall
3 Byrsa
4 Forum
5 Harbor

A trading nation
Carthage had two excellent harbors and a large fleet of vessels. The oblong outer harbor was for merchant shipping. A narrow channel led to the circular inner harbor, which had berths for 220 warships. Trade with sub-Saharan Africa and across the Mediterranean Sea were the bases of Carthage's wealth and power. Dates and animal skins from the Sahara; ivory, slaves, and gold from West Africa; grain and copper from Sardinia; silver from Spain; tin from Britain; and grains, wine, glassware, and textiles from Carthage itself were traded.

Statues (right)
These terracotta heads show typical Carthaginian styles of dress. The man has a long beard yet no mustache, and the woman wears a long headdress. Both women and men often wore nose rings, as these two heads show.

Coinage (above)
An African elephant appears on this Carthaginian coin. Carthage did not have its own curreny until c. 400 BCE. The Carthaginians managed to tame elephants and Hannibal used them in the invasion of Italy during the Second Punic War (218–201 BCE).

Carthage's major political figures

Hamilcar (c. 270–228 BCE)

Hamilcar, father of Hannibal, was a Carthaginian general who resisted Roman attempts to capture the city-state of Carthage, in modern Tunisia. His full name, Hamilcar Barca, means "Hamilcar Lightning."

Hannibal (247–182 BCE)

Hannibal was Carthage's greatest general, and is best known today for taking an army, equipped with elephants, through Spain and France and across the Alps to attack the Romans. The son of Hamilcar he fought the Romans in Spain and Italy from 221 to 203 BCE, when he was recalled to defend Carthage. He was defeated by the invading Romans at the Battle of Zama. For a time, he ruled Carthage, but was driven into exile and later committed suicide.

Cazembe

See **Kazembe**

United Nations
A 1960 stamp celebrating the Central African Republic becoming part of the UN.

CENTRAL AFRICAN REPUBLIC Central African Republic

Little is known of the early history of what is now the Central African Republic, although hunting and gathering people probably lived in the area in early times. However, by the late seventeenth century, the region was in turmoil and its population was greatly reduced, largely as a result of the slave trade. Groups of people, such as the Baya, migrated from the north into the western part of the country, escaping from a *jihad* (religious war) launched by the Muslim ruler Usman dan Fodio. The Baya displaced the small Bantu-speaking groups who lived there. Other immigrants, including the Banda and Azande, migrated into the area from southwestern Sudan.

European explorers included a German, Georg August Schweinfurth, who reached the area occupied by the Azande in the northeast in 1870 CE, and Henry Morton Stanley, who reached the mouth of the Oubangui River in 1877 CE. The French established an outpost at Bangui in 1889 CE and in 1894 CE, they created a territory called Oubangui-Shari. In 1910 CE, this territory became part of French Equatorial Africa, which also included Chad, French Congo and Gabon. The French suppressed the slave trade in the north, but French concessionaires treated the people harshly. However, from the late 1920s, the French developed cotton cultivation and improved the infrastructure, although resistance to French rule continued until the 1930s. Oubangui-Shari became a French overseas territory in 1946 and, in 1958, the territory gained internal self-government as the Central African Republic. On August 13, 1960, it became a fully independent nation.

Recent history
Prior to independence, the dominant figure in nationalist politics was Barthelemy Boganda, leader of the *Mouvement d'Evolution Sociale en Afrique Noire* (MESAN), who had served as prime minister. However, when Boganda was killed in a plane crash in 1959, he was succeeded by his relatively inexperienced nephew David Dacko, who took over the leadership of MESAN and became the country's first president in 1960 CE.

The country became a one-party state in 1962 CE, but the economy stagnated and corruption was rife, especially, it was alleged, in the higher ranks of the civil service. In 1965 CE, an army coup brought General (later Marshal) Jean Bédel Bokassa into power. Bokassa proclaimed that he intended to revive the economy. However, the Central African Republic had enjoyed good relations with France, which had supplied much aid, but these relations deteriorated under Bokassa.

In 1972 CE, Bokassa declared himself president for life and, in 1976 CE, he changed the country's name to the Central African Empire. In December 1977 CE, amid scenes reminiscent of Napoleon's coronation, Bokassa crowned himself Emperor Bokassa I. In 1979 CE, student demonstrations were brutally suppressed. France suspended its military aid and, with French assistance,

"Emperor" of Central Africa
In 1976, president-for-life Jean-Bédel Bokassa declared himself "Emperor" and renamed the Central African Republic the "Central African Empire." A lavish coronation ceremony followed in 1977 CE, reputed to have cost more than US$20 million, which included substantial gifts from France and diamond-mining companies then operating in the country.

Bokassa was overthrown in September 1979 CE in a bloodless coup by his predecessor David Dacko. Dacko announced that the country would again become a republic and that he had assumed the office of president. Dacko's return to power provoked some opposition, especially from politicians who regarded him as a puppet of France. In 1981 CE, Dacko was overthrown in a coup and replaced by a military ruler, General André Kolingba. The new military regime banned all political parties, but Kolingba gradually introduced measures that would lead to the restoration of constitutional government.

Bokassa surprisingly returned to Central African Republic in 1986 CE and he was tried for committing murder and embezzlement. He was found guilty in 1987 CE and sentenced to death, though his sentence was later reduced to life imprisonment. In 1992 CE, Central African Republic adopted a multiparty constitution and, in 1993 CE, Kolingba was defeated in presidential elections by Ange-Félix Patassé, a former prime minister, who took 52 percent of the votes in the second round run-off. Reportedly angered by his defeat, Kolingba ordered the release of Bokassa from prison.

By 1996 CE, the economic situation had worsened to the extent that the country was facing bankruptcy. Payments to civil servants, teachers and soldiers were months in arrears. In April 1996, a group of soldiers staged an anti-government revolt, protesting that they had not received their wages. One month later, a second army insurrection led to rioting in Bangui and at least 40 people died in the conflict.

France sent in troops to restore order and Patassé agreed to form a government of national unity. In January 1997 CE, despite the ongoing truce between the government and the mutineers, French soldiers again clashed with the mutineers, killing at least ten of them. France agreed to withdraw its force, and, in 1998 CE, the French troops were replaced by a United Nations peacekeeping force. In November and December 1998 CE, Patassé's party won the most seats in parliament, while Patassé defeated Kolingba in the presidential elections in 1999 CE.

Peoples

BANDA

The Banda, one of the largest ethnic groups in the Central African Republic, probably came originally from Sudan's Darfur Mountains. They migrated from the Sudan in the nineteenth century after refusing to accept the rule of the sultans of Darfur and Wadai.

BAYA

The origins of the Baya (or Gbaya), the second largest ethnic group in the Central African Republic, are uncertain. In the tenth century, they lived on the savanna (grasslands) of northwestern Central Africa. They migrated southward and westward at the beginning of the nineteenth century in response to incursions by the Fulani ruler Usman dan Fodio into northern Central Africa (*see also* **Fulani states**). As the Baya moved south and west, they assimilated or displaced the peo-

ples they met. Once the Baya had consolidated themselves in their Central African territory, they were able to resist further incursions by slave traders from the north and west. This part of Central African became the French colony of Oubangui-Chari in 1894. The people suffered from the activities of the large companies that were granted exclusive rights over large areas, using brutality and forced labor to develop the territory. Armed resistance against colonial rule continued into the 1930s, with the Baya playing a major role.

SARA

For information on the history of the Sara, *see* **Chad (Peoples—Sara)**.

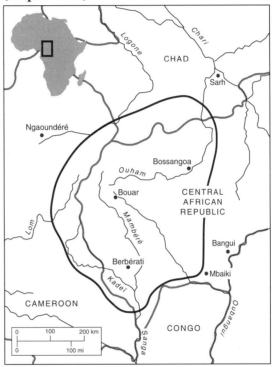

Modern extent of the Baya peoples

Central African Republic timeline	
19th century CE	
1805–1830	The Baya people settle in the CAR region
1889	The French establish an outpost at Bangui
1894	The French create the territory of Oubangoui-Shari in present-day CAR
1900–49 CE 1949	Independence movement founded by Barthelemy Boganda
1950–59 CE 1958	Oubangoui-Shari is granted internal self-government
1960–69 CE 1960	**Aug 13** Oubangoui-Shari becomes independent as CAR: David Dacko becomes the first president
1962	Dacko makes the country a one party state
1966	Gen. Jean-Bédel Bokassa seizes power in a military coup
1970–79 CE 1972	Bokassa becomes president for life
1976	Bokassa appoints himself emperor and renames CAR the Central African Empire
1979	Bokassa is overthrown by a French-supported coup
1980–89 CE 1987	Bokassa is imprisoned for murder and embezzlement
1990–99 CE 1992	A multiparty constitution is introduced
1993	Ange-Félix Patassé becomes president after multiparty elections
1996	France helps suppress a military rebellion
1997	President Patassé calls for the withdrawal of French troops amid growing anti-French hostility
1998	A UN force arrives in CAR to replace French troops
1999	Patassé is reelected president, defeating Kolingba

President Boganda
A 1959 CE stamp commemorating the first anniversary of the establishment of the Central African Republic (CAR), and showing President Boganda.

André Kolingba *(above)*
Head of state of the Central African Republic in 1981 CE, he was subsequently defeated in multi-party elections in 1993 CE.

Central African Republic's major political figures

Bokassa, Jean-Bédel (1921–96 CE)
As the Central African Republic's supreme military commander, Bokassa seized power from David Dacko in 1966 and served as president until 1976, when he made himself "Emperor" of the "Central African Empire." His rule was harsh and dictatorial and he was responsible for many deaths, including those of children. The republic was restored by a coup in 1979, led by David Dacko, and Bokassa went into exile. He returned in 1986 and served six years in prison for murder and fraud before dying from a heart attack in 1996.

Dacko, David (1930 CE–)
In 1960, David Dacko became the first president of the Central African Republic. He was deposed in a coup led by his nephew Jean-Bédel Bokassa in 1966 and placed under house arrest, but he returned to office when he overthrew Bokassa, with French assistance, in a popular bloodless coup in 1979. Although committed to political liberalization, Dacko attempted to curb opposition parties. After reports of ill-health, he was persuaded to hand over power to a military government, led by André Kolingba, in 1981.

Kolingba, André Dieudonné (1936 CE–)
André Kolingba became head of state of the Central African Republic in 1981, when he seized power from David Dacko in a peaceful coup, but he was defeated by Ange-Félix Patassé in multiparty elections in 1993. Kolingba had earlier served in the army, reaching the rank of general in 1973. During the years of JEAN-BÉDEL BOKASSA's dictatorship, Kolingba was abroad, in the diplomatic service.

Patassé, Ange-Félix (1937 CE–)
Former prime minister (1976-8), Patassé became president of the Central African Republic in 1993, when he defeated the military dictator Andre Kolingba. In 1996, the government and opposition parties agreed to set up a government of national unity.

Central African Republic presidents and emperors

Presidents	Presidents
Aug 14 1960–Dec 31 1965 CE David Dacko (1st time)	**Sep 20 1979– Sep 1 1981 CE** David Dacko (2nd time)
Jan 1 1966–Dec 4 1976 CE Jean-Bédel Bokassa (from Oct 18 1976, Salah Eddine Ahmed Bokassa)	**Sep 1 1981–Oct 22 1993 CE** André Kolingba (chairman of the military committee of national recovery until Sep 21 1985; head of state Sep 21 1985–Nov 29 1986)
Emperor **Dec 4 1976–Sep 20 1979 CE** Bokassa I	**Oct 22 1993 CE–** Ange-Félix Patassé

Ceuta

Ceuta is Spanish enclave in Morocco. The free port is a fortified city on the North African coast south of Gibraltar. The site was first settled by Phoenicians (Carthaginians), then Greeks and Romans before becoming independent under the Byzantine governor Count Julian. Europeans fought to gain control of the port's lucrative trade in gold, ivory, and slaves. Portugal took over the port in 1415 CE but lost it to Spain in 1580 CE. Ceuta has remained Spanish from that date, apart from a brief period of British occupation from 1810 to 1814 CE. *See also* **Morocco**.

CHAD Republic of Chad

Evidence of settlement in what is now Chad includes rock engravings and paintings dating back to about 5000 BCE. There is also evidence of Berber migrations into northern Chad in the early eighth century CE, when droughts were reducing grazing to the north. The Berbers were associated with the rise of several major kingdoms. The leading state in the area which now includes Chad was Kanem, which was founded in about 800 CE. Kanem grew prosperous because of its trade with Libya, Cairo, and Arab traders in East Africa. By the early thirteenth century, Kanem had expanded and it eventually became part of a larger state called Kanem-Bornu, which reached the height of its power in the sixteenth century.

In the sixteenth and seventeenth centuries, the smaller kingdoms of Baguirmi and Wadai developed near Kanem, and these two kingdoms, like Kanem–Bornu, enjoyed great prosperity by trading in various goods and slaves, such as the Sara who were abducted from areas to the south. Divided by wars and feuds, all these states were in decline in the nineteenth century and, between 1883–1893 CE, they fell to a Sudanese adventurer, Rabih bin Fadl Allah, whose name is also sometimes spelled Rabeh Zubair or Rabeh Zubayr.

The French reached the area in 1891 CE, when the colonization of Africa had reached its final stage. Rabih bin Fadi Allah was defeated in 1900 CE at the Battle of Lakhta, two years after the French had made the region a protectorate. The French restored the Kanembu dynasty, but the progress of the colony was slow.

In 1910 CE, Chad became part of French Equatorial Africa, which also included the Central African Republic, French Congo and Gabon. After World War II, Chad shared in the constitutional changes which affected all of French Equatorial Africa. First, it became a French overseas territory in 1946 CE, then it gained a large measure of autonomy in 1957 CE. Chad became an autonomous republic in 1958 CE, and independence was finally achieved on August 11, 1960 CE.

Recent history

Chad's first president was Ngarta Tombalbaye, a southerner. He faced severe problems, chiefly the country's poverty and also the tensions between the black, often Christian southerners and the conservative, Muslim people in the north. In 1962 CE, a rebel organization called the National Liberation Front (or FROLINAT after its French name, *Front de Libération National*) was formed by a group of mainly Muslim northerners. Civil war between FROLINAT and government forces broke out in the 1960s.

In 1963 CE, an alleged Muslim conspiracy led to the dissolution of the National Assembly and the declaration of a state of emergency. Elections in that year were contested only by government candidates and the country became a one-party state. In the 1960s, as the civil conflict against FROLINAT mounted, France sent aid to the government, while, from 1971, the northern rebels received aid from Libya. The Libyans were interested in the Aozou Strip, an area of land along Chad's northern border, which Libya claimed. The claim was based on a pact between France and Italy in the early twentieth century that would have transferred the Aozou Strip to Italian-ruled Libya. But the French National Assembly never ratified this pact.

President Tombalbaye was killed during a coup in 1975 CE. He was replaced by Félix Malloum, a southerner and army chief. Fighting continued and, following a military setback in 1978 CE, a new government was formed with an almost equal number of northerners and southerners. A former FROLINAT leader, Hissène Habré, became prime minister.

However, fighting continued, although it was mainly between northern factions, rather than a north-south conflict. Malloum fled the country in 1979 CE and two groups in the rebel forces, one led by Habré and the other by the new president, Goukouni Oueddei, competed for power. Oueddei's forces, aided by Libya, took control. Libyan troops remained in Chad until a peacekeeping force sent by the Organization of African Unity replaced them in 1981 CE.

In 1982, an army led by Habré overthrew Oueddei, who fled the country. Habré became president, but Oueddei, supported by Libya, returned to Chad in 1983 CE. Habré, supported by France, maintained control in N'Djamena, but Oueddei controlled the north. In 1986 CE, Oueddei's forces conflicted with Libyan troops and his army joined with Habré's forces to attack the Libyans. A truce was arranged in 1987 CE, though no agreement was reached on the Aozou Strip until the International Court of Justice ruled against Libya's claim in 1994 CE. Both nations had, at the outset of the case, agreed to accept the ruling of the International Court and the Strip was formally returned to Chad in May.

In 1990CE, a rebel group called the Patriotic Salvation Movement, consisting of Muslim northerners, overthrew Habré. A new government was formed with Idriss Déby, a former defense minister under Habré, as president. Déby cautiously began the process that would democratize Chad, including a law permitting political parties providing that they were not based on regionalism, tribalism, or intolerance. A new constitution, providing for multiparty elections, was adopted in 1996 CE. Presidential elections resulted in victory for

Déby, while Déby's party, the Patriotic Salvation Movement won the largest number of seats in the National Assembly in 1997 CE. In 1998 CE, the government signed a peace agreement with the main rebel group, the Armed Forces for a Federal Republic. In 2000 CE, Habré was charged in Senegal with torture and murder committed while he was Chad's head of state.

Peoples

BAGIRMI

The Bagirmi people, who now live in southern Chad along the Chari River, once comprised an historical state. The first Bagirmi king, Dala Birni, founded the Bagirmi kingdom in the early sixteenth century. By the start of the seventeenth century, Bagirmi had become an Islamic state and, for much of the following two centuries, jostled for power with the larger states of Borno (*see* Kanem–Bornu) to the northwest and Wadai to the northeast. At times, Bagirmi was part of the Bornu empire, but the Bagirmi rejected Borno's overlordship in the late eighteenth century. Today, the Bagirmi are a multiethnic society made up of Arabs, Barma, and Fulani peoples and their descendants.

BUDUMA

The Buduma (or Boudouma) live on islands in Lake Chad, mainly in Chad, but also in Niger and Nigeria. Until recently, they led a semi-independent existence out of the reach of central government. However, in the 1990s, the region around Lake Chad became involved in civil unrest, with rebel groups launching attacks in the region. Thousands of people in southern Chad fled the area, in fear of both government and rebel attacks..

SARA

The Sara, a group of non-Muslim peoples who live in southern Chad, are often called the Kirdi–a name used by Muslims, such as the Bagirmi, to refer to non-Muslims. The Bagirmi frequently raided the Sara in the nineteenth century for slaves. The colonial era transformed Sara society. As settled farmers in the fertile south of Chad, the Sara bore the brunt of colonial policies–the introduction of a cash economy and forced labor. They did, however, have greater opportunities for education. Many Sara people died in battles in World Wars I and II and thousands, who were sent to work on a railroad in what is now the Republic of Congo, never returned. To the Sara, independence meant not only freedom from the French, but also freedom from the northerners, who had once enslaved them. As a result, the Sara and other southerners now fill most government and other official posts. The religious, economic and social differences between the southerners and northerners have caused tension in post-independence Chad, and war has sometimes broken out between the two groups.

TEDA

Most Teda people live in the Tibesti Mountains in northwestern Chad, an arid region that is part of the Sahara. Like other northerners, the Teda are Muslims and religious, economic, and social differences have led to conflict between them and other northerners, and such people as the Sara, who live in the south.

Carrying water
A 1976 CE stamp depicting decorated gourds and a ladle.

Cave painting
Cave paintings made c. 5,000 BCE show scenes of hunting and herding in the region of the present-day Sahara desert. The climate then was very different from today.

Chad timeline

Pre 19th century

c. 5000 BCE	Rock paintings show scenes of hunting and herding in the Sahara desert
c. 500 BCE	Cattle-rearing peoples arrive in the region of Lake Chad
8th century CE	Berber peoples from the north migrate to Chad
11th century	Kingdom of Kanem begins to develop northeast of Lake Chad under Saifawas dynasty
c. 1100	Islam is introduced to the region by Arab merchants
13th century	Kanem merges with the neighbouring kingdom of Bornu
17th century	Frequent wars between Kanem–Bornu and its neighbours Baguirmi and Wadai

19th century CE

1808	The Hausa invade Kanem–Bornu
1822	English explorers Dixon Denham and Hugh Clapperton are the first Europeans to visit Chad
1846	The last king of the Saifawas dynasty is assassinated
1890	Kanem-Bornu, Baguirmi and Wadai are conquered by the Sudanese leader Rabeh
1898	France declares Chad a protectorate

1900–49 CE

1908	Chad becomes part of French Equatorial Africa
1912	Last resistance to French rule ended
1920	Chad becomes French colony with a separate administration
1930	Cotton farming begins in Chad
1935	France agrees to cede the Aouzou strip to the Italian colony of Libya but the agreement is never implemented
1940	Chad is the first colony to declare support for the Free French

1950–59 CE

1958	Chad is granted internal self-government

1960–69 CE

1960 Aug 11	Chad becomes independent of France: François Tombalbaye is the first president
1962	Chad becomes a one-party state
1965	Civil war breaks out after northern rebels form the *Front de Libération National du Tchad* (FROLINAT)

1970–79 CE

1971	Libya begins to support FROLINAT rebels
1972	FROLINAT forces advance to within a few miles of the capital N'Djamena
1973	Libya occupies the Aozou strip in northern Chad
1975	President Tombalbaye is killed during a military coup: Gen. Félix Malloum becomes president
1979	Efforts to establish a government of national unity end in failure

1980–89 CE

1980	Libya proposes a union between the two countries
1982	Hissène Habré becomes president
1984	Famine due to prolonged drought
1986	FROLINAT–Libyan alliance breaks down
1987	The government establishes its authority in the north, except for the Libyan occupied Aozou strip

1990–99 CE

1990	President Habré overthrown by a Libyan-supported coup: Gen. Idriss Déby becomes president and promises to introduce democracy
1992	Uprising by supporters of ex-president Habré is defeated with French aid
1993	New legislature appointed to oversee transition to democracy
1994	Libya agrees to withdraw from the Aozou strip after a ruling by the International Court
1996	Déby is re-elected president

2000–09 CE

2000	Habré is placed under house arrest in Senegal and charged with torture

Victims of war
The civil war in Chad began in 1979 CE. These casualties are awaiting evacuation.

Chad's major political figures

Déby, Idriss (1954 CE–)
In 1982, Déby led rebel forces that drove President Goukouni Oueddei from office and installed HISSÈNE HABRÉ as president of Chad. In 1990, he overthrew Habré and made himself president. After introducing a new democratic system, he was elected president in 1996.

Habré, Hissène (1936 CE–)
Habré was a leader of the rebel forces in northern Chad in the 1970s. After serving as prime minister, his forces seized power and he served as president from 1982 until 1990. He fled to Senegal, where, in 2000, he was charged with torture and killings committed while he was Chad's head of state.

Oueddei, Goukouni (1944 CE–)
Oueddei served under Hissène Habré in rebel forces in the 1970s. In 1979, he became Chad's president, but was overthrown in 1982. He returned to Chad in 1983, but after defeat by Habré's troops, he fled into exile in Libya.

Rabih b. (bin) Fadl Allah (c. 1840–1900 CE)

Rabih b. Fadl Allah was a Sudanese adventurer who carved out a huge empire in west-central Africa, south of Lake Chad. A former slave, he became an Egyptian soldier, then took to slave trading himself. He raised a large army, based himself in what is now Chad, and began twenty years of conquest. He was eventually killed by a French army at the Battle of Lakhta.

Tombalbaye, Ngarta (c. 1918–1975 CE)

Ngarta Tombalbaye (formerly François Tombalbaye) was the first president of Chad. He served in office from 1962 until he was assassinated during an army coup. led by Félix Malloum, in 1975. He had earlier served in the role of prime minister (1959–62).

Chad presidents			
Aug 11 1960–Apr 13 1975 CE François Tombalbaye (from Aug 30 1973, N'Garta Tombalbaye) (head of state until Apr 23 1962)	head of state May 12 1975–Aug 29 1978) **Mar 23 1979–Apr 29 1979 CE** Goukouni Oueddei (1st time) (chairman of the provisional council of state)	**Sep 3 1979–Jun 7 1982 CE** Goukouni Oueddei (2nd time) (chairman of the provisional administrative committee until Nov 10 1979, then president of the transitional government of national union)	until Jun 19 1982, chairman of the council of state Jun 19–Oct 21 1982) **Dec 1 1990–Dec 2 1990 CE** Jean Alingue Bawoyeu (acting)
Apr 13 1975–Apr 15 1975 CE Milarew Odingar (interim head of state)	**Apr 29 1979–Sep 3 1979 CE** Lol Mohamed Shawa (president of the transitional government of national union)	**Jun 7 1982–Dec 1 1990 CE** Hissen Habré (chairman of the command council of the armed forces of the north	**Dec 2 1990 CE–** Idriss Déby (president of the patriotic salvation movement Dec 2–4 1990, head of state Dec 4 1990–Mar 4 1991)
Apr 15 1975–Mar 23 1979 CE Félix Malloum (chairman of the higher military council until May 12 1975,			

General Malloum
General Felix Malloum Ngakoutou Bey-Ndi, leader of the Supreme Military Council in the 1970's.

Changamire dynasty

See **Rozvi empire**.

Ciskei

Ciskei was one of the ten 'homelands' established before and during South Africa's apartheid era. The white-controlled South African government forced black South Africans to live in these areas, which often bore no relation to their true homelands. The vast majority of Ciskei's inhabitants were Xhosa people.

Ciskei was declared "independent" in 1981 CE, but its independence was not genuine and never recognized internationally. After the first multiracial elections held in 1994 CE, Ciskei was officially reincorporated into South Africa. *See also* **South Africa**

COMOROS Federal Islamic Republic of the Comoros

The Comoros is a group of four islands located at the northern end of the Mozambique Channel. Three of the islands–Grande Comore (or Njazidja), Anjouan (or Nzwani) and Mohéli–together form the Federal Islamic Republic of the Comoros. The most easterly of the islands, Mayotte (also called Mahoré) is a French dependency. France took over Mayotte in 1843 CE and, in 1886 CE, the other three islands were placed under French protection. From 1914 CE, the islands were administered from Madagascar but, in 1947 CE, they became a French overseas territory. In 1958 CE, the people of the Comoros voted to retain their status as an overseas territory of France and, in 1960 CE, the islands became internally self-governing.

In the 1970s, the French government decided that each of the islands should vote separately on its future status. In 1974 CE, about 95 percent of the people of the three western islands voted for independence, while 65 percent of the people of Mayotte voted to remain under French rule. Independence for the three western islands was achieved on July 6, 1975 CE. In December 1976 CE, France granted Mayotte the status of a territorial collectivity, an intermediate state between an overseas territory and an overseas department of France.

Location of the Comoros Islands

Island nation
A 1977 CE stamp depicting a swordfish–a popular food source for the people of the Comoros.

Recent history

Because of ethnic differences and political rivalries, the Comoros have suffered great instability since 1975 CE. Only one month after independence, the country's first president, Abderrahman Ahmed Abdallah was overthrown in a coup by Ali Soilih, who was backed by mercenaries led by a Frenchman, Bob Denard. Four unsuccessful coups occurred during the three years when Soilih was president, but, in a fourth coup in 1978 CE, he was finally overthrown. The 1978 coup was again led by the mercenary leader Denard, who had been hired to overthrow the man he had brought to power. With French support, Abdallah again became president. He declared the country to be an Islamic republic and held elections. Denard remained in the Comoros, acting as head of the president's mercenary bodyguard. Unsuccessful coups occurred in 1983 CE, 1985 CE and 1987 CE, but, in 1989 CE, a fourth coup led to the death of Abdallah.

Said Mohammed Djohar, head of the Supreme Court, became the interim president during a period of total confusion when French troops prevented mercenaries under Denard from creating their own regime. How-ever, the country returned to democracy in March 1990 when elections were held. Amid allegations of electoral fraud, Djohar was returned as president in a second-round ballot. In 1996 CE, another coup was mounted by Denard while Djohar was having medical treatment in Réunion. The coup failed and the prime minister Caabi el Yachourtu Mohammed announced that he would act as the interim president. Presidential elections were held in March 1996 and Mohammed Taki was returned as president.

In 1997 CE, a crisis occurred when Anjouan and Mohéli announced their secession from the Comoros and affirmed their wish to reestablish contacts with France. In September, about 300 troops from Grande Comore attempted, but failed, to conquer Anjouan and in 1998 CE, Anjouan's secessionist government intro-duced a constitution affirming its independence. Attempts at restoring unity were made by the Comorian government, the Organization of African Unity, and the French government, which had ruled out any support for the separation of Anjouan, but negotiations proved fruitless.

In November 1998, Taki died suddenly of natural causes and Tadjiddine Ben Said Massounde became the acting president. At talks held by the OAU in Mada-gascar's capital, Antananarivo, an agreement was drawn up proposing greater autonomy for Anjouan and Mohéli, together with a rotating presidency between the three islands. Anjouan did not sign the agreement and opposition to the government's pro-posal to increase the powers of the two smaller islands mounted on Grande Comore. In April, 1999 CE, Colonel Azali Assoumani seized power in a bloodless coup, the nineteenth in 25 years. The new regime suspended the constitution, parliament and the supreme court.

People

Most of the people of the Comoros are of mixed ances-try. Early inhabitants probably include Malayo-Polyne-sians from what is now Indonesia but, by 1600 CE, other groups included Africans, Arabs, Indonesians, Mada-gascans, and Persians.

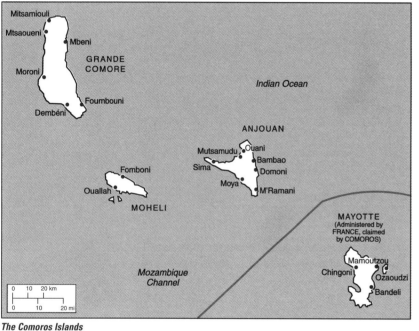

The Comoros Islands

Comoros's major political figures

Abdallah, Abderrahman Ahmed (1919-1989 CE)
Abderrahman Ahmad Abdallah became the first president of the Comoros, but he was deposed only one month after independence day. He returned to power after a coup in 1978. He made the Comoros an Islamic, one-party republic and was reelected in 1984. He was assassinated in 1989 and succeeded by Said Muhammad Djohar.

Cheikh, Said Muhammad
Dr. Cheikh was a leading figure during the struggle for independence in the Comoros. He was elected the first head of state in 1961. However, he failed to attract the support of militant young people.

Djohar, Said Muhammad (1918 CE–)
Said Djohar, head of the Comoros Supreme Court, became interim president of the country in 1989, following the assassination of Abderrahman Ahmad Abdallah. Elected in 1990, Djohar sought to balance the ethnic and politi-cal factions in his country. In 1995, he fled after a failed coup and returned in 1996 to be given a symbolic posi-tion, but only after he agreed not to contest the elections.

Soilih, Ali (1938-1978 CE)
Ali Soilih served as president of the Comoros from 1975, when he took office after a coup led by French merce-naries, until 1978, when he, too, was overthrown by mercenaries. Under Soilih, the Comoros invaded the French island of Mayotte, but his forces were repulsed by the local population. Soilih was shot two weeks after the 1978 coup. The reason given was that he was trying to escape.

Comoros presidents

Jul 6 1975–Aug 3 1975 CE
Ahmed Abdallah (1st time)
(president of the government to
Jul 7 1975, then head of state)

Aug 3 1975–Jan 3 1976 CE
Said Mohamed Jaffar
(chairman of the national council
of the revolution until Aug 10
1975, then chairman of the
national executive council)

Jan 3 1976–May 13 1978 CE
Ali Soilih
(head of state until Oct 28 1977)

May 13 1978–May 23 1978 CE
Said Atthoumani
(chairman of the politico-military
directorate)

May 23 1978–Oct 3 1978 CE
Ahmed Abdallah (2nd time) +
Mohamed Ahmed (co-chairmen [to
Jul 22 1978, politico-military]
directorate)

Oct 3 1978–Nov 26 1989 CE
Ahmed Abdallah (3rd time)
(chairman of the directorate until
Oct 25 1978)

Nov 27 1989–Sep 29 1995 CE
Said Mohamed Djohar (1st time)
(acting until Mar 20 1990)

Sep 29 1995–Oct 2 1995 CE
Ayouba Combo
(coordinator of the transitional
military committee)

Oct 2 1995–Oct 5 1995 CE
Mohamed Taki Abdoulkarim (1st
time) + Said Ali Kemal (acting
jointly)

Oct 5 1995–Jan 26 1996 CE
Caambi el-Yachourtu (interim)
Jan 26 1996–Mar 25 1996

Said Mohamed Djohar (2nd time)

Mar 25 1996–Nov 6 1998 CE
Mohamed Taki Abdoulkarim
(2nd time)

Nov 6 1998–Apr 30 1999 CE
Tadjidine Ben Said Massounde
(interim)

Apr 30 1999 CE–
Azali Assoumani
(chief of staff of the national
development army until May 6
1999, then head of state)

Comoros timeline

Pre 19th century CE
- **5th century CE** Indonesian settlers become the first inhabitants of the Comoros Islands
- **12th century** Muslim traders from East Africa settle on the islands

19th century CE
- **1843** France annexes Mayotte
- **1886** France takes control of the rest of the Comoros islands

1960–69 CE 1960 France grants the Comoros internal self-government

1970–79 CE 1974 Anjouan, Grande Comore and Mohéli vote for independence, Mayotte votes to remain a French colony
- **1975 Jul 6** The Comoros become independent under president Ahmad Abdallah who is soon over thrown in a coup
- **1978** President Abdallah is returned to power with the aid of foreign mercenaries

1980–89 CE 1989 President Abdallah is assassinated

1990–99 CE 1995 Attempted coup by mercenaries is defeated with French help
- **1997** Anjouan and Mohéli declare independence from the Comoros: their independence is not recognized internationally
- **1999** A military coup overthrows the government.

Congo (Brazzaville)

The two countries in Africa called Congo are sometimes identified by their capital cities. Brazzaville is the capital of the Republic of Congo. *See* **Congo**, **Republic of**.

Congo (Kinshasa)

The two countries in Africa called Congo are sometimes identified by their capital cities. Kinshasa is the capital of the Democratic Republic of Congo. *See* **Congo**, **Democratic Republic of**.

Congo Free State

The central African colony of the Belgian king, Léopold II (reigned 1865–1909 CE), was called the Congo Free State. In 1885 CE Léopold laid claim to a large area that now lies in the northern art of the Democratic Republic of Congo. Léopold was primarily interested in controlling central African trade routes and maximizing profits from the rubber trade. "Citizens" of the Congo Free State were forced to work as slaves, and punishments for resistance were severe. In 1908 CE, growing outrage in Belgium and abroad to Léopold's administration led to the country being annexed by the Belgian government. The Congo Free State was then known as the Belgian Congo until its independence in 1960 CE as part of the Democratic Republic of Congo. *See also* **Belgian Congo**; **Congo, Democratic Republic of**.

Belgian colonialism
One expansionist scheme supported by King Léopold II of Belgium was the monopoly of rubber production in the Congo Free State. This contemporary cartoon satirically portrays the dilemma of the African caught up in the the pressure to increase the output of rubber for his colonial master.

© DIAGRAM

CONGO Democratic Republic of Congo

The earliest known inhabitants of this vast country were probably hunter-gatherers, who lived in much the same way as the Mbuti who still live in the northeast of the country. Over the last 2,000 years, people from other parts of Africa, including Bantu-speaking people from the northwest, gradually moved into the area, and some of them eventually set up major civilizations. Important among these people were the Kong, Kuba, Luba, and Lunda. The kingdoms founded by these people grew prosperous by engaging in long-distance trade. The Portuguese reached the mouth of the Congo River in 1482 CE and established relations with the Kongo kingdom, which embraced the Roman Catholic faith. Soon, however, the slave trade became the leading activity in the region.

Europeans knew little about the interior until the second half of the nineteenth century. In 1876 CE, the British explorer Henry Morton Stanley explored the Congo River, traveling from east to west. In 1878 CE, the Belgian King Léopold II employed Stanley to set up Belgian posts in the area, which, as the Congo Free State, became his personal property. The local population suffered greatly as Belgian agents, employed by Léopold, used forced labor to develop the economy. In response to international criticism of Léopold's rule, the Belgian government took over the colony in 1908 CE, renaming it the Belgian Congo. The Belgian Congo proved to be rich in resources, including copper, diamonds, and gold, but the local population benefited little from Congo's wealth. After World War II, demands for independence mounted.

Kazembe *IV*

A Portuguese portrait of the Lunda ruler, Kibangu Keleka (reigned c. 1805 to c. 1850 CE) the fourth Kazembe. He rightly saw the Portuguese as a threat to his kingdom.

Patrice Lumumba

He was the first prime minister of the Congo Republic (now known as the Democratic Republic of the Congo). The victim of an army mutiny and regional secessions, he was forced from office, imprisoned, and finally murdered.

Recent history

On June 30, 1960 CE, the Belgian Congo became independent as the Republic of the Congo, though it was often called Congo (Léopoldville) to distinguish it from its neighbor, which was named Congo (Brazzaville). The country's first president was Joseph Kasavubu and the prime minister was Patrice Lumumba, two political opponents who had agreed to share power. However, army revolts, ethnic conflicts, and the secession of two mineral-rich provinces, Kasai and Katanga, almost immediately plunged the country into conflict. Kasavubu dismissed Lumumba who was assassinated in 1961 CE. The country was reunited in 1963 CE, when Katangan secession was ended. In 1964 CE, Moise Tshombe, who had led the secessionists in Katanga, became the prime minister of the reunited country and, in 1965, a loose coalition led by Tshombe won the national elections. But. after the army seized power in November 1965 CE, General Joseph Desire Mobutu became the president, making the country a one-party state in 1970 CE.

In 1971 CE, under a policy of *authenticité*, Mobutu renamed the country Zaire while its capital Léopoldville became Kinshasa. He also changed his own name to Mobutu Sese Seko. Mobutu's government used strong measures to hold the country together. He also, as emerged later, became rich at his country's expense. Mobutu banned Christian teaching and and closed Christian schools, encouraging people to regard him as a god. However, because Mobutu was useful in the struggle against world Communism, western powers largely ignored his corruption and his repressive policies. However, with the collapse of Communism in Russia and eastern Europe, Mobutu came under mounting pressure to restore democracy. In 1990 CE, he permitted the formation of political parties, though he repeatedly postponed elections.

In 1996 CE, after the ethnic conflicts in Burundi and Rwanda had spilled over into eastern Zaire, where more than a million Hutu refugees had taken refuge, an opponent of Mobutu, Laurent Kabila, led Tutsi rebels living in Zaire in a rebellion against Mobutu. Kabila was supported by Uganda and Rwanda, which both feared an attack by Hutu forces based in Zaire. Kabila's Alliance of Democratic Forces for the Liberation of Congo-Zaire advanced westward. In May 1997 CE, Mobutu fled the country and Kabila became president, renaming the country the Democratic Republic of Congo.

However, Kabila soon fell out with his former allies,

and Rwanda and Uganda, together with Burundi, supported a group of rebel factions to overthrow him. Civil war began in 1998 CE. Forces from Angola, Chad, Namibia, and Zimbabwe arrived to support Kabila's troops, creating a major conflict. In July 1999 CE, a peace accord signed by six African heads of state, including Kabila, and by representatives of several rebel factions, failed to halt the fighting. In 2001, Kabila was assassinated by a member of his bodyguard. He was succeeded by his son, Major-General Joseph Kabila. Hopes were raised of a peace settlement, but conflict continued.

Peoples

ALUR

For information on the history of the Alur, *see* **Sudan (Peoples—Alur)**.

AZANDE

The Azande live in northeastern Congo, together with neighboring Central African Republic and Sudan. They are of mixed origins. More than 200 years ago, a people known as the Ambomou lived on the banks of the Mbomou River, which forms part of the present-day border between the Central African Republic and the Democratic Republic of Congo. The Ambomou were dominated by the royal Avongara clan, who led them in a campaign of conquest against neighboring subgroups. The campaign led them into what is now Sudan. Some of the conquered subgroups retained their own languages, but most of them now regard themselves as Azande, no matter how much they differ from one another.

KONGO

For information on the history of the Kongo people, *see* **Angola (Peoples—Kongo)**.

LUBA

Luba is the name for several ethnic groups who live in the southwestern part of the Democratic Republic of Congo. They include the Luba of Katanga (formerly Shaba); the Luba Hemba (or Eastern Luba) in northern Katanga and southern Kivu provinces; and the Luba Bambo (or Western Luba) of Kasai province. Archeological investigations have revealed an uninterrupted culture in the Katanga region from the eighth century CE onward, though the area has undoubtedly been occupied for longer than that. Some authorities believe that the idea of government through chiefs originated in this area as early as the eighth century or before. By the fourteenth century, the region contained well-established chieftainships. Increasing population levels and land shortages set these chiefs against each other. As a result, larger and more military groups evolved. The most important of these was the Luba group, which emerged around the Lake Kisale area.

According to oral traditions, the original rulers of the Luba (then called the Kalundwe) were the Songye, who had come from the north. The Songye *kongolo* (ruler) married the Kalundwe queen and established a new state, which became the Luba kingdom, covering the lands between the Lualaba and Lubilash rivers. In the fifteenth century, the Songye rulers of the Luba were displaced by the Kunda from the north. Led by

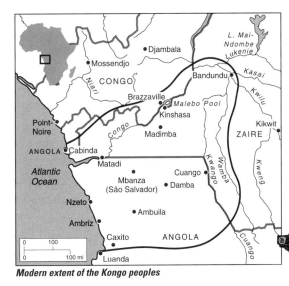

Modern extent of the Kongo peoples

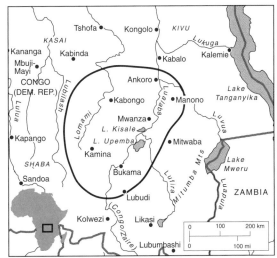

Modern extent of the Luba peoples

Kongo crucifix
At least 200 years old, this crucifix is made from bronze, metal, and wood. Kongolese crucifixes helped to spread Christianity in Kongo. Over the years, the Christian message of such crucifixes has been overlaid with interpretations based on the Kongo religion, in which the cross represents the junction between this world and the next.

Luba chief
This present-day Luba chief is holding his staff of office. The geometric patterns on the broad sections serve both to decorate the staff and to empower the owner. They are considered more important than the human figures.

Mbili Kiluhe, the Kunda were at first welcomed by the ruling *kongolo*, Mwana. Kiluhe married two of Mwana's sisters, one of whom gave birth to a son, Kala Ilunga. Kala Ilunga became a great warrior and he challenged the *kongolo* for the Luba throne, claiming he was the legitimate ruler through matrilineal descent (descent traced through the mother). The *kongolo* was eventually defeated and Kala Ilunga founded the Kunda dynasty to rule over the Luba and took the title of *mulopwe*.

By 1550, the Luba kingdom had a powerful central government. The *mulopwe* was the head of the government and also the religious leader, believed to have supernatural powers. He had a group of ministers, *balopwe*, to help him, each with special duties. The *sungu* was a sort of prime minister, who mediated between the people and the *mulopwe*. The *nsikala* acted as a temporary ruler when a king died or was unwell. The *inabanza* had charge of ritual matters, concerning the *mulopwe's* sacred role. This included taking care of the king's sacred spears. Finally, the *twite* was the army and police commander. All these ministers, and any other chiefs who ruled sections of the Luba, were themselves descendants of Kala Ilunga. In this way, the Luba kept power in the hands of a small aristocracy.

The Kunda dynasty lasted until the arrival, in the 1880s, of the Belgians, who turned what is now the Democratic Republic of Congo into a private colony called Congo Free State, owned and ruled by the Belgian King Léopold II. The king's rule was characterized by abuses, brutality, and atrocities aimed at developing the rubber trade. The Luba fought wars of resistance to colonial rule from 1907–1917 CE. *See also* **Katanga**.

LUGBARA

For information on the history of the Lugbara people, *see* **Uganda (Peoples—Lugbara)**.

LUNDA

The name 'Lunda' covers scores of groups who once lived within the precolonial Lunda empire Around half live in the southern part of the Democratic Republic of Congo, around third in eastern Angola, and the rest in Zambia.

The Lunda are descended from Bantu-speaking peoples who settled in Central Africa in the part of the first millennium CE. By the sixteenth century, the Lunda occupied separate territories in what is now the southern part of the Democratic Republic of Congo. Around 1600, Kibinda Ilunga (probably a relation of the sixteenth century Luba king Kala Ilunga) married the Lunda's senior chief–a woman called Lueji–and became paramount chief. Kibinda's son by another wife, Lusengi. introduced Luba methods of government. Lusengi's son, Naweji, began conquering new lands, thus laying the foundation of the Lunda Empire. By 1700 CE, the Lunda Empire had a capital, Mussumba; a king with the title Mwata Yamvo; and a tax-gathering system run by provincial administrators. These changes coincided with a local growth in trade. Central African commodities, such as copper, honey, ivory, and slaves, became increasingly sought after by European and Arab traders based on Africa's west and east coasts. Profiting from their strategic location, the Lunda

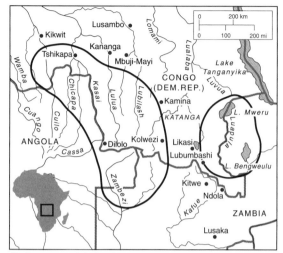
Modern extent of the Lunda peoples

charged passing merchants transit taxes, or bartered with them for guns and other manufactures.

Partly to extend their hold on trade and partly to avoid paying tribute to the Mwata Yamvo, some Lunda groups migrated west, south, and east in the seventeenth and eighteenth centuries. These Lunda migrants set up kingdoms in what are now Angola and Zambia. The most important of these was the Zazembe kingdom in present-day Zambia. This kingdom developed in the late seventeenth century, when the Mwata Yamvo, Muteba, rewarded the loyalty of one of his citizens by giving the man's son, Ngonda Bilonda, the title Mwata Kazembe and by putting him in charge of the eastward expansion. Bilonda's successor, Kanyembo (Kazembe II) became ruler of the lands east of the Lualaba River, and he and his successors completed the expansion into present-day Zambia. Kazembe prospered through trade and tribute and, by 1800 CE, its capital controlled many of the trade routes that crossed the continent.

However, disagreements weakened Lunda rule in the nineteenth century and, in the 1880s, the empire broke up under pressure from the Chokwe, a people it had once controlled. Then the European nations of Belgium, Britain, and Portugal colonized Lunda lands.

MANGBETU

The Mangbetu of the northeast part of the Democratic Republic of Congo are unique in having created one of the few centralized political systems in Central Africa. The Mangbetu kingdom was founded in the first half of the nineteenth century by a leader called Nabiembali, who extended Mangbetu control over non-Mangbetu speakers for the first time. By the second half of the nineteenth century, the court of the Mangbetu king, Mbunza, was famed as a center for the arts and performance. Mbunza was probably the most powerful of a number of Mangbetu kingdoms.

MONGO

The Mongo (or Lomongo) people inhabit the central Congo River basin in the Democratic Republic of Congo. Bantu-speaking peoples began to settle the Congo basin in the early part of the first millennium CE and they gradually displaced the local tropical forest

Wooden bowstand
Bowstands were never seen in public but were kept by Luba rulers as a symbol of their authority, and to commemorate the founder of the Luba dynasty, Mbili Kiluhe–a famous hunter. They often incorporated female figures that represented important women or the king himself who, it is believed, would return as a woman after he died.

foragers. These settlers and the indigenous peoples are the ancestors of the present-day Mongo people. Initially, they engaged in fishing, hunting, and yam farming, but, by 1000 CE, bananas had become the staple crop. Over the years, new areas of forest were cleared for settlement and agriculture. Populations increased and surplus labor was freed to engage in craft production, such as pottery-making, ironworking, and the construction of dugout canoes. Agriculture assumed greater importance and was integrated with trapping, hunting, gathering, and fishing.

In the mid-nineteenth century, the increased European demand for ivory stimulated Mongo traders to buy ivory from specialized elephant hunters, especially from Twa hunters. The Mongo traded crops, such as cassava, tobacco, and corn, and craft goods, such as knives, iron, salt, and dugout canoes with neighboring peoples and European traders. In exchange, they received other locally produced goods, such as pieces of copper and brass, and European manufactured goods. The village elders and the village chief exercised strong control over local trade and, together with the traders, they amassed power and fortune. However, following the Belgian King Léopold's establishment of the Congo Free State, the Mongo suffered during a period of harsh exploitation. Some communities waged war on the European rubber agents while others opted for migration. The leaders of rebellious communities were punished or humiliated if caught. International outcry led the Belgian government to take over the State in 1908. This resulted in a less oppressive, if nonetheless strongly colonial, period of government.

NDEMBU

The Ndembu are one of the peoples who make up the Lunda people. The precolonial Lunda Empire brought together a variety of Central African peoples, who, like the Ndembu, are often just referred to as the Lunda. While some live in the northwestern part of present-day Zambia, the Ndembu inhabit the southern regions of the historic Lunda Empire, which is now the southern part of the Democratic Republic of Congo.

The Ndembu separated from the Northern Lunda in the eighteenth century, leaving the lands of the Lunda Empire and migrating south. During the nineteenth century, the Ndembu were regularly raided, and many were enslaved by Chokwe and Ovimbundu slave traders. A small Ndembu community was established in Angola in the early twentieth century when some crossed the border to escape taxation.

PENDE

The Pende inhabit a region in the Democratic Republic of Congo between the Kasai and Lutshima rivers between the Kasai and Lutshima rivers in the southwestern part of the country. They are divided into two main subgroups: the eastern Pende and the western Pende. The two groups differ linguistically, culturally and economically from each other. The Pende probably originated in northern Angola, but fled to their present regions to escape slave raids by the Chokwe, who traded slaves, ivory and wax with the Ovimbundu in exchange for Portuguese goods.

SONGYE

The Songye are a subgroup of the Luba peoples of Central Africa, who live in the southeastern part of the Democratic Republic of Congo, mainly between the Lubufu and Lomami rivers. According to oral histories, the Songye were the founders of the powerful Luba kingdom, which covered the lands between the Lubilash and Lualaba rivers. The Luba kingdom reached its height under Songye rulers, but they were displaced by the Kunda some time in the fifteenth century.

SUKU

The Suku live in the southwestern part of the Democratic Republic of Congo in a region called Kwango. In the seventeenth century, the Lunda Empire was conquering lands in the southwest of present-day Congo, and refugees from the Lunda invasions established the Suku kingdom. The king was known as the Yaka of Minikongo, and, hence, the Suku were once known as the Yaka of Minikongo. In the nineteenth century, the Suku profited as intermediaries of the trade in oil, raffia, cloth, beads, and guns. The carving up of Africa by European colonialists brought an end to this trade and Sukuland became an economic backwater.

The King of the Yaka
Mwene Putu Kasonga was arrested by the Congo authorities in 1906 CE as a result of a misunderstanding by government officials.

Modern extent of the Mongo peoples

© DIAGRAM

Internationalism
A 1973 CE stamp marking Zaire's Third International Fair at Kinshasa.

Sir Henry Morton Stanley
Like the man wiith whom his name is always associated, David Livingstone, he was a man brought up in poverty who achieved great fame as an explorer of Africa.

The last expedition
Stanley arrived in 1887 CE at Lake Albert in East Africa with the intention of rescuing Emin Pasha and his troops who had been cut off by an uprising in the Sudan.

Congo, Democratic Republic of, timeline

Pre 19th century
- **c. 800 CE** Bantu-speaking ironworking peoples arrive in the Congo region
- **15th century** Kongo kingdom develops in northern Angola and western Congo region
- **1483** Portuguese navigator Diogo Cão discovers the mouth of the Congo River
- **16th century** Kongolo people found the Luba kingdom in southern Congo region
- **17th century** Lunda empire develops in southern Congo region
- **18th century** Kuba kingdoms develop in central Congo region

19th century CE
- **1868–1881** The Zanzibari merchant Tippu Tip maintains a private slave trading empire in the Congo River basin
- **1874–1877** Henry Morton Stanley follows the course of the Congo River from its upper reaches to the Atlantic
- **1878** King Léopold of Belgium employs Stanley to investigate the potential of the Congo region for colonization
- **1884** The Berlin Conference on Africa recognizes King Léopold as sovereign of the Congo Free State

1900–49 CE
- **1908** The Belgian government takes over administration of the Congo Free State
- **1957** Belgians permit the formation of African political parties

1950–59 CE
- **11959** Belgium announces its intention to make Congo independent

1960–69 CE
- **1960 Jun 30** Congo becomes an independent republic under Joseph Kasavubu
- **1960 July** Katanga province secedes
- **1960 Sept** Kasavubu dismisses and jails his prime minister Patrice Lumumba
- **1961** Lumumba is murdered in Katanga
- **1963** Katanga is forcibly reunited with the rest of the country
- **1964** White mercenaries used to suppress widespread rebellions
- **1965** Gen. Joseph-Désiré Mobutu becomes president after a military coup
- **1966** Mobutu abolishes the office of prime minister
- **1967** Mobutu nationalizes the copper mining industry

1970–79 CE
- **1970** Mobutu declares the country a one-party state
- **1971** Congo is renamed Zaire, the capital Léopoldville is renamed Kinshasa
- **1973** Over 2,000 foreign-owned businesses are seized by the government and handed over to Zairians
- **1974** Mobutu's Popular Revolutionary Movement is made the "sole institution of society"
- **1976** International Monetary Fund (IMF) backs an economic stabilization plan
- **1977** Rebellion in Shaba province (formerly Katanga) is put down with French assistance
- **1978** A second rebellion in Shaba province is put down with French assistance

1980–89 CE
- **1980** Zaire's national debt is rescheduled
- **1984** Mobutu is re-elected president in elections in which he is the only candidate
- **1986** CIA uses Zaire as a base for supplying arms to UNITA rebels in Angola
- **1989** Mobutu visits the US and obtains a loan of $20 million dollars from the World Bank

1990–99 CE
- **1990** Mobutu lifts the ban on political parties
- **1991** Economic problems lead to widespread rioting
- **1992** A constitutional conference replaces the government with a High Council of the Republic
- **1993** The president and the High Council appoint rival prime ministers
- **1994** One million Hutu refugees flee to Zaire from Rwanda
- **1995** Outbreak of the deadly Ebola virus in Kikwit
- **1996** Hutu-Tutsi conflict in Rwanda and Burundi spreads to the Tutsi of eastern Zaire
- **1997** Laurent Kabila overthrows the Mobutu government and becomes president with the support of Tutsi forces: name of the country is changed to Democratic Republic of Congo
- **1998** Civil war breaks out. Angola, Chad, Namibia and Zimbabwe send forces to support Kabila against rebels supported by Burundi, Rwanda and Uganda

2000–09 CE
- **2000** Kabila is assassinated and is succeeded by his son major-General Joseph.Kabila. The civil war continues.

Civil unrest
Protesters make their point during a demonstration against Lumumba that took place in July, 1960 CE.

Democratic Republic of Congo's major political figures

Kabila, Laurent Desire (1939–2001 CE)
In October 1996, Kabila became head of the Alliance of Democratic Forces for the Liberation of Congo-Zaire, a rebel force, consisting mainly of Tutsis from eastern Zaire. Following the flight of President Mobutu, Kabila proclaimed himself head of state in May 1997 and renamed the country the Democratic Republic of Congo. Kabila was a member of the Luba ethnic group. In the 1960s, when the country was in turmoil, Kabila was a Marxist politician and a known opponent of Mobutu. He was assassinated by one of his bodyguards in 2001 and was succeeded by his son, Major-General Joseph Kabila.

Kasavubu, Joseph Ileo (1913–69 CE)
In 1960, Joseph Kasavubu, who favored a federal system of government for the Congo Republic (now Democratic Republic of Congo), became the country's first president. Faced with an army mutiny and the secession of Katanga (now Shaba) province, Kasavubu dismissed his prime minister Patrice Lumumba, who favored the creation of a strong central government. Kasavubu was deposed in 1965 by General Mobutu Sese Seko.

Katangan leader
In 1960 CE, Moïse Tshombe declared mineral-rich Katanga (Shaba) independent from Congo (Dem. Rep.). The rebellion collapsed in 1963 CE when Tshombe fled the country, but was followed by another in 1964–65 CE.

Lumumba, Patrice Emergy (1925–1961 CE)
Patrice Lumumba was the first prime minister of the Congo Republic (now Democratic Republic of Congo) from June to September 1960, when he was dismissed by President Joseph Kasavubu. Lumumba was shot dead in 1961, allegedly by rebels from Katanga province. He was widely regarded as a hero throughout Africa.

Mobutu Sese Seko (1930–1977 CE)
Mobutu Sese Seko, originally named Joseph-Désiré Mobutu, was Zaire's head of state from 1965. He became an army commander in 1960, and briefly led a provisional government in Congo (Léopoldville), which is now Democratic Republic of Congo. In 1965, he again took power and became president, restoring the power of the central government and making Zaire a one-party state. He promised a multiparty system in 1990, but he set no election dates. Accused of corruption, he went into exile in 1997 and a new regime was set up under Laurent Kabila.

Tshombe, Moïse Kapenda (1919–1969 CE)
Moïse Tshombe led the mineral-rich "Republic of Katanga" (now the province of Katanga) that declared itself independent from the Congo Republic (now Democratic Republic of Congo) in 1960. Following the occupation of Katanga by United Nations troops in 1963, Tshombe went into exile. In 1964 he returned to become head of the central government of the Congo Republic, but he was dismissed in 1965. He again went into exile, in Spain, after Mobutu Sese Seko took power, and a Congolese court sentenced him to death in his absence. In 1967, he was kidnapped and taken to Algeria, where he remained under house arrest until his death.

Congo (Kinshasa) presidents	
Jul 1 1960–Nov 25 1965 CE Joseph Kasavubu (head of state until Aug 1 1964)	**Nov 25 1965–May 16 1997** CE Joseph-Désiré Mobutu (from Jan 10 1972, Mobutu Sese Seko)
Mar 31 1961–Aug 5 1961 CE Antoine Gizenga (head of state, in rebellion, at Stanleyville)	**May 17 1997** CE– Laurent Kabila (head of state until May 29 1997)

President Kasavubu
The first president of the Democratic Republic of Congo in 1960 CE, he was later deposed in 1965 CE by General Mobutu.

CONGO Republic of Congo

In the first millennium CE, Congo was populated by Bantu-speaking peoples, who practiced farming. These people gradually displaced the hunter-gatherers, who were probably the first inhabitants of the region. The Bantu-speaking groups included the ancestors of the Kongo people, who formed the Kingdom of Kongo, which stretched at its greatest extent from what are now the southern parts of the Republic of Congo and the western part of the Democratic Republic of Congo, into northern Angola. Other important people in the Congo were the Teke, traders who clashed with the Kingdom of Kongo in the fifteenth and sixteenth centuries. The Teke traded in slaves. However, in the late eighteenth century, the Teke villages were also raided for slaves by the Bobangi people who lived upriver.

Contact with Europeans began in 1483 CE, when Portuguese navigators reached the mouth of the Congo River. Between the fifteenth and eighteenth centuries,

Pierre de Savorgnan de Brazza
In 1880 CE this French explorer of the Congo region founded a trading post on the site of what is now known as Brazzaville, which was to become the capital of French Equatorial Africa in 1910 CE.

© DIAGRAM

At the court of the Teke king

In 1882 CE the French explorer Pierre de Savorgnan de Brazza signed a treaty with the Teke king, Ilo Makoko, which made the territory north of the Congo River a French protectorate called French Congo. Before signing the treaty Brazza was entertained at the court of the king.

Celebrating the revolution

A 1971 stamp commemorating the eighth anniversary of the 1963 revolution.

the Congo region was important in trade, the chief commodities being slaves and ivory. In 1875 CE a French explorer, Pierre de Savorgnan de Brazza explored the region and, in 1880 CE, he founded a trading post on the site of what is now Brazzaville. In 1882 CE, he signed a treaty with the Teke king, Ilo Makoko, making the territory north of the Congo River a French protectorate called French Congo.

The territory was renamed Middle Congo in 1903 CE and, in 1910 CE, it became part of French Equatorial Africa. This huge territory, which also included Chad, Gabon, and Ubangi–Shari (later called Central African Republic), had its capital at Brazzaville. In 1946 CE, Middle Congo became an overseas territory of France and, in 1956 CE, it was granted an elected legislature. Territorial elections followed in 1957 CE and, following a referendum, Congo became an internally self-governing territory within the French Union in 1958 CE. The two main parties were the UDDIA (*Union Démocratique de Défense des Intérets Africains*). led by Abbé Fulbert Youlou, and the MSA (*Mouvement Socialist Africain*), led by Jacques Opangault.

Recent history

The country became fully independent as the Republic of the Congo on August 15, 1960 CE. The first president, Abbé Fulbert Youlou, adopted authoritarian measures to consolidate his power. However, in 1963 CE, he was forced to resign following the arrest of trade union leaders, an action which was part of his government's attempts to curb the opposition. His successor, Alphonse Massamba-Débat, who established a one-party system in 1964 CE, pursued socialist policies, with the government taking control of many industries. But his measures were insufficiently radical for some of his opponents, who favored even more left-wing policies.

The army arrested Massamba-Débat in 1968 CE and Major Marien Ngouabi became head of state in 1969 CE. In 1970 CE, Ngouabi declared Congo to be a Marxist-Leninist (Communist) country, although the government maintained good relations with France. Ngouabi was assassinated in 1977 CE and a military council, which took control of the government, appointed Colonel Joachim Yhombi-Opango president. In 1979 CE, the military council was abolished, Yhombi-Opango resigned, and Colonel Denis Sassou-Nguesso became president. At first, Sassou-Nguesso ruled in a dictatorial manner, but his government became increasingly pragmatic. In 1990 CE, Congo abandoned its Communist policies and, in 1991 CE, opposition parties were legalized. Sassou-Nguesso remained president, but with greatly reduced powers. With the country moving towards a market economy, the Cuban troops, who had been in Congo for 14 years, withdrew.

Democracy was restored in 1992 CE, when free legislative and presidential elections were held. The Pan-African Union for Social Democracy (UPADS) won the largest number of seats in the National Assembly and Pascal Lissouba became president, defeating Bernard Kolelas, leader of the Congolese Movement for Democracy and Integral Development. Following a vote of no confidence in the National Assembly, further legislative elections were held in 1993 CE, in which UPADS increased its number of seats. However, ethnic and political rivalries continued, while the problem of disarming local militias, such as Sassou-Nguesso's 5,000-man militia called the Cobras, remained unsolved.

In 1997 CE, fighting broke out when the government sent troops to disarm the Cobras. In October 1997 CE, Sassou-Nguesso's forces, aided by 3,500 troops from Angola, seized Brazzaville and Pointe-Noire. Angola supported Sassou-Nguesso because Lissouba's government had aided UNITA forces in Angola's civil war. Lissouba fled into exile. The 1997 conflict caused the deaths of between 10,000 and 15,000 people and the economy was severely damaged. Sassou-Nguesso became president in October 1997 and his government restored some degree of order in 1998. However, conflict again erupted in January 1999 CE when rebel militias loyal to Lissouba attacked the southern parts of Brazzaville. A peace agreement was signed in November 1999, but despite this the causes of instability, including ethnic divisions and discrimination between north and south, remained unresolved.

Peoples

BAKOTA

For information on the history of the Bakota people, *see* **Gabon (Peoples—Bakota)**.

KONGO

For information on the history of the Kongo people, *see* **Angola (Peoples—Kongo)**.

TEKE

The Teke, or Bateke, live in the central part of the Republic of Congo and in neighboring parts of Gabon and the Democratic Republic of Congo. The descendants of the Bantu-speaking Teke settled in the Congo basin in the earliest centuries of the first millennium CE. By the fifteenth century, the Teke were long-established in the middle reaches of the Congo River in an area around its confluence with the Kasai River. They then became a powerful, river-trading people. In the fifteenth and sixteenth centuries, the Teke waged war with the Kongo to the southwest and, by the mid-fifteenth century, the Teke were trading in slaves and tobacco. By the early eighteenth century, the Teke kingdom had grown very large and powerful through trade and military conquest. It extended on both sides of the Congo River from Malebo (formerly Stanley) Pool northward to the area around Bolobo.

By the late eighteenth century, the Teke had lost some of this territory to neighboring groups. During the nineteenth century, many skirmishes took place upriver between the Teke and the Bobangi. The Bobangi set up villages closer and closer to Malebo Pool and began raiding Teke villages for slaves. Following a series of battles, the Teke agreed to let the Bobangi trade at the pool, but did not allow them to build villages. In 1890 CE, the French explorer, Pierre Savorgnan de Brazzaville, started a trading station, which later became the town of Brazzaville, near Malebo Pool. De Brazza met the great Teke king, Ilo Makoko, and negotiated with him for the region to become a French colony. In 1882 CE, the Teke kingdom was ceded to the Middle (Moyen) Congo colony, which became part of French Equatorial Africa. In the late nineteeenth and early twentieth centuries, the French operated a harsh, violent and oppressive regime. Ilo Makoko's successors tried unsuccessfully to revolt against the colonialists in 1898 CE. More than three-quarters of the Teke were killed in reprisals.

Teke chief
This Teke chief is wearing traditional attire. His arms, chest, and face are made-up with white clay and his headdress is made from parakeet and cock feathers. His multilayered necklace includes the teeth of meat-eating animals such as panthers and small blue, glass beads, which were once used as a form of currency.

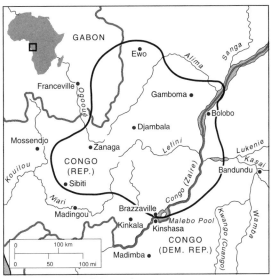

Modern extent of the Teke peoples

Congo, Republic of, presidents			
1Aug 5 1960–Aug 15 1963 Fulbert Youlou	**Sep 4 1968–Sep 5 1968** Marien Ngouabi (1st time) (chairman of the national council of the revolution)	**Mar 19 1977–Feb 5 1979** Joachim Yhombi-Opango (chairman of the military committee of the Congolese Labour Party to Apr 3 1977, then head of state)	**Feb 8 1979–Aug 31 1992** Denis Sassou-Nguesso (1st time) (head of state until Aug 14 1979)
Aug 15 1963–Aug 16 1963 David Moussaka + Félix Mouzabakani (officers in charge of the provisional government)			**Aug 31 1992–Oct 15 1997** Pascal Lissouba
	Sep 5 1968–Jan 1 1969 Alfred Raoul (acting head of state)	**Feb 5 1979–Feb 8 1979** Jean-Pierre Thystère Tchicaya (chairman of the presidium of the central committee of the Congolese Labour Party)	**Oct 25 1997–** Denis Sassou-Nguesso (2nd time)
Aug 16 1963–Sep 4 1968 Alphonse Massemba-Débat (chairman of the national council of the revolution to Dec 19 1963)	**Jan 1 1969–Mar 18 1977** Marien Ngouabi (2nd time) (head of state to Jan 3 1970)		

Congo's, Republic of, major political figures

Ngouabi, Marien (1938–1977 CE)
Marien Ngouabi seized power in Congo in 1968 in a coup that deposed Alphonse Massamba-Débat. He adopted Marxist-Leninist policies and became president in 1970. Power struggles and ethnic tensions during Ngouabi's presidency led to political instability in the country and he was assassinated in 1977.

Sassou-Nguesso, Denis (1943 CE–)
Sassou-Nguesso became president of Congo in 1979, promising to continue the government's Marxist policies, though his policies were, in practice, more liberal than those of his predecessors. In 1990, bowing to public pressure, the government renounced Marxist ideology, and in 1991, it legalized opposition parties and stripped Sassou-Nguesso of all his powers. In the 1992 multiparty elections, Sassou-Nguesso was defeated by Pascal Lissouba. He returned to power in 1997 after his militia forced Lissouba into exile.

Youlou, Abbé Fulbert (1917–1972 CE)
A Roman Catholic priest, Abbé Youlou became the first president of Congo in 1959. In 1963, he was forced to resign and went into exile after widespread unrest and a general strike. He was succeeded as president by Alphonse Massamba-Débat.

Congo, Republic of, timeline

Pre 19th century CE
1483 Portuguese navigator Diogo Cão discovers the mouth of the Congo River

19th century CE
1874–1877 Henry Morton Stanley follows the course of the Congo River from its upper reaches to the Atlantic
1875 French explorer Pierre Savorgnan de Brazza explores the region
1880 De Brazza and the Bateke king Makoko sign a treaty making the region north of the Congo River a French protectorate
1891 Colony of French Congo created

1900–49 CE **1903** French Congo becomes known as Middle Congo
1910 Middle Congo becomes part of the colony of French Equatorial Africa
1921–1935 Up to 20,000 African forced laborers die during construction of the Congo-Ocean railway
1925 The first roads are built in Middle Congo
1940 Middle Congo supports the Free French in World War II
1944 Brazzaville conference on the future of France's African colonies
1946 French end the practice of forced labor

1950–59 CE **1958** Middle Congo is granted internal self-government

1960–69 CE **1960 Aug 15** Congo becomes an independent republic: Fulbert Youlou becomes the first president
1963 Labor uprising overturns the Youlou government
1964 Congo becomes a one-party state
1965 US breaks off diplomatic relations after its consular staff are mistreated
1969 A group of army officers under Capt. Marien Ngouabi seizes power

1970–79 CE **1970** Congo declares itself a Marxist country and is renamed People's Republic of Congo
1972 President Ngouabi defeats an attempted coup
1977 Ngouabi is assassinated: Col. Jaochim Yhombi-Opango succeeds
1979 Yhombi-Opango resigns: Col. Denis Sassou-Nguesso becomes president

1980–89 CE **1988** Conference in Brazzaville paves the way for Namibia's independence

1990–99 CE **1990** Congo renounces Marxism
1991 Political parties are legalized
1992 A new multiparty constitution is approved by a referendum: the country resumes its old name, Republic of Congo
1993 President Sassou-Nguesso is defeated in elections by Pascal Lissouba
1994 Anti-government urban militias clash with government forces
1997 Sassou-Nguesso seizes power with the support of Angolan troops
1998 The Republic of Congo and the Democratic Republic of Congo begin negotiations for the demarcation of their common frontier
1999 Further fighting is concluded by a concord between the government and rebel forces.

Corisco

See **Elobey**, **Annobon**, and **Corisco**.

Côte d'Ivoire

The official name of the Ivory Coast since 1985 has been Côte d'Ivoire. *See* **Ivory Coast**.

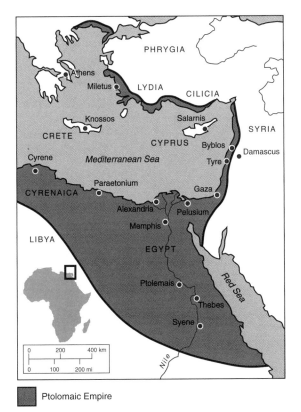

Cyrenaica

The northeast region of what is now Libya was settled by ancient Greeks in the seventh century BCE. It was known as Cyrenaica after one of the region's most important cities–Cyrene. For a while Cyrenaica was controlled by ancient Egypt, when it was ruled by the Ptolemies (330–323 BCE). In 74 CE Cyrenaica fell under Roman control and became a colony joined with Crete. In the seventh century, Arabs conquered the region, and years of Egyptian-based dynasties followed. In the fifteenth century Cyrenaica was made part of the Turkish Ottoman Empire. In 1912 CE, Italy fought Turkey over possessions in North Africa, and won. Libya became independent in 1951 CE, and Cyrenaica ceased to be an official political division after Libya's provinces were abolished in 1963 CE. *See also* **Libya**.

An Italian possession
In 1912 CE Italy fought Turkey over a number of territories based in North Africa, one of which– Cyrenaica–is commemorated on this stamp.

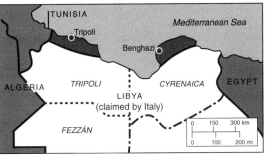

Cyrenaica during the Italian occupation 1914 CE.

Occupied by British

French possession

Italian possession

- - - - Provincial boundary

—·—·— Boundary of area claimed but not occupied by the British

FEZZAN Libyan province

Cyrenaica during the Ptolemaic Empire (320–330 BCE).

Ptolomaic Empire

Dagomba kingdom

According to Mossi tradition, the Dagomba kingdom was founded by northern invaders in the fourteenth century. The Mossi inhabit what are now the northernmost parts of Ghana and Burkina Faso. They established several kingdoms, including Dagomba. This kingdom stretched as far south as the Black Volta River, but it was reduced in size by the conquests of the Gonja in the mid-seventeenth century. At the end of that century, Dagomba was conquered by the Asante who were, in turn, conquered by the British. *See also* **Burkina Faso**; **Ghana**.

Dahomey

Dahomey was a West African kingdom that became a French colony of the same name. In 1625 CE the Fon people founded a kingdom at Abomey, in what is now central Benin. Under King Agaja (reigned 1708–1732 CE), the Kingdom of Dahomey, or Fon Kingdom, flourished. For a while Dahomey came under the influence of the Yoruba Oyo Kingdom but it was fully independent by the mid-1850s. Dahomey profited from the slave and palm oil trades but the French had taken control of the coastal regions by 1889 CE. By 1892 CE, despite fierce resistance of the king and his army, Dahomey was conquered and became a French colony. *See also* **Benin**.

Dahomey medal
A silver medal, with a rayed star above and an anchor and flags below, for those who took part in the French Dahomey campaign in 1892 CE.

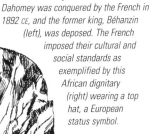

A French colony
Dahomey was conquered by the French in 1892 CE, and the former king, Béhanzin (left), was deposed. The French imposed their cultural and social standards as exemplified by this African dignitary (right) wearing a top hat, a European status symbol.

Darfur

Darfur is the westernmost region of Sudan but, in the past, was an independent sultanate. The earliest rulers of Darfur, the Daju or Daga, were around at the time of ancient Egypt, more than 4,000 years ago. The Daja rulers were followed by the Tunjur (Tungur). From 900 to 1200 CE, Darfur was a Christian state, but, as the empire of Kanem–Borno advanced eastward, Islam was introduced to Darfur. Darfur became a province of Kanem–Borno in the thirteenth century. Under the rule of the Keira clan, 1640–1916 CE, Darfur became wholly Islamic and regained its independence.

In 1870 CE Darfur was conquered by Egypt but lost shortly after to the forces of al-Mahdi. After the overthrow of al-Mahdi's successor, Darfur was incorporated into Anglo-Egyptian Sudan. At first, the sultan kept his position, but he was killed one year after launching an uprising in 1915 CE. Today, Darfur is divided into three provinces: Gharb Darfur, Janub Darfur, and Shamal Darfur. *See also* **Mahdists**; **Sudan**.

Muhammad Ahmad, the Mahdi
In 1882 CE, the Mahdi led a revolt against the the British and Egyptian conquerors of the Sudan and created a powerful Islamic state which covered much of present-day Sudan.

Darfurian expansion
Darfur's early years as an independent state were dominated by conflict with Wadai, its western neighbor, until about 1750 CE when Darfur began to expand in both southward and westward directions. It controlled the trade routes to both Egypt and the Red Sea coast, and traded mainly in slaves. The ruler's court was established at El Fasher before 1800 CE.

In 1874 CE Darfur was annexed by Egypt, but the territory came under the control of the Mahdi in 1883 CE, who held it until his defeat in 1898 CE,. Darfur briefly reasserted its independence until it was incorporated as a province of the Anglo-Egyptian Sudan in 1916 CE.

1 1600–1800 CE

2 1898 CE

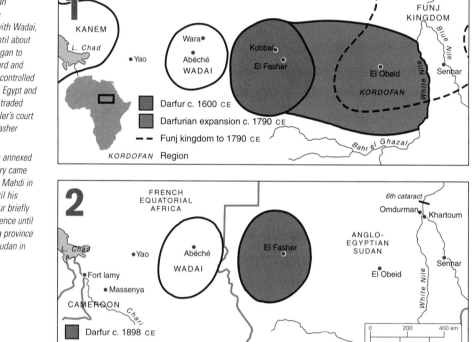

Postage stamp
This was issued by the French colonial authorities in the 1890s.

Daura

Daura was one of the historic Hausa states that once dominated the north of what is now northern Nigeria and southwestern Niger. *See also* **Hausa states**.

Diégo–Suarez

Diégo–Saurez is a port on the northernmost tip of Madagascar. In 1840 CE, the French declared it a separate protectorate (colony) from the rest of Madagascar. In 1896 CE, it reverted back to the main Madagascan colony. *See also* **Madagascar**.

DJIBOUTI Republic of Djibouti

From the third century BCE, people from Arabia moved into the area that is now the Republic of Djibouti. They were the ancestors of the Afar people. Later immigrants, the Issas (a Somali clan) moved into the south. Islam was introduced in the ninth century and Arabs controlled the region's coastal trade until the sixteenth century, when the Portuguese arrived. The Arabs later reasserted their dominance. From their settlement at Tadjoura, they sent trading caravans (companies of travelers) into the interior of Ethiopia.

In 1862 CE, France acquired the port of Obock on the northern shore of the Gulf of Tadjoura. In 1884 CE, the French signed treaties with the the sultans of Obock and nearby Tadjoura, while, in 1888 CE, they also claimed an uninhabited area which now contains the city of Djibouti, a new port built to rival British Aden in Yemen. The French united the areas they controlled into a single territory called French Somaliland (Côte Française de Somalis). In 1892 CE, Djibouti became capital of the new territory. Djibouti later grew in importance as the terminus of a railroad which reached Addis Ababa, capital of Ethiopia, in 1917 CE. After World War II, Djibouti lost some of its importance to the port of Assab, Eritrea, which began to handle much of Ethiopia's trade.

In the late 1940s and 1950s, the Issa and some other groups in the territory began to demand independence from France. However, in 1958 CE, against the opposition of the Issa who either abstained or voted against, the majority of the people voted to make French Somaliland an autonomous state in the French Union. The people who voted in favor included the Afar people, together with most of the local Europeans.

Recent history

In 1967 CE, another referendum was held on the territory's future status. The Issa again favored independence, but the Afar, encouraged by the French, campaigned for keeping ties with France. Following the referendum, in which 60 percent voted to remain French, the territory was renamed the French Territory of the Afars and Issas. However, in the 1970s, the influence of the Issa gradually increased, partly because of Somali immigration and partly because the French revised its citizenship law which had discriminated against the Somali majority. Finally, France agreed to another referendum, which resulted in a large majority favoring independence. As a result, the fully independent Republic of Djibouti was born on June 27, 1977 CE.

The country's first president was Hassan Gouled Aptidon. He faced many problems caused by instability, arising from the tensions that had been created between the Afar and the Issa peoples. After independence, the Afar complained of discrimination and they, in turn, were accused of violent, anti-government incidents. This conflict involved Djibouti's neighbors, with Eritrea and Ethiopia favoring the Afars, while Somalia supported the Issas. However, Djibouti remained independent in the Ogaden conflict of 1977 CE and 1978 CE, although the refugees who flocked into Djibouti caused severe economic problems, increasing the country's dependence on foreign aid, especially from France, Saudi Arabia and the United States. In 1981 CE, Djibouti adopted a one party system, the sole party being the *Rassemblement Populaire pour le Progrès* (RPP).

Afar fears of Issa domination caused ethnic conflict in 1989 CE and, in 1991 CE, an unsuccessful Afar-led coup resulted in a series of arrests. In November 1991, Afar rebels who belonged to the Front for the Restoration of Unity and Democracy (FRUD) began a guerrilla war against government forces. But FRUD declared a ceasefire in 1992 CE. Later in 1992, Djibouti adopted a new constitution allowing for multiparty politics, but maintaining strong executive power for the president. Fighting resumed between FRUD and government forces in December 1992 and January 1993 CE but, in May 1993, Gouled was reelected president.

In December 1994 CE, FRUD signed a "Peace and National Reconciliation Agreement" with the government. This agreement envisaged the formation of a national coalition government, the revision of the electoral roll, and the integration of FRUD militants into the army and civil service. Further elections were held in 1997, when a coalition formed by the RPP and FRUD

won all the seats in the Chamber of Deputies (parliament). In 1999 CE, Gouled, who had served as Djibouti's president since independence, announced that he would not seek reelection. The RPP nominated Gouled's nephew, Ismail Omar Guelleh, as its presidential candidate. He was elected in April 1999, with 74 percent of the vote, defeating Moussa Ahmed, the candidate of a coalition of opposition parties. The election was regarded as fair, although international criticism was directed at the new government for human rights violations and the harassment of journalists. Later in 1999, Moussa Ahmed was arrested and charged with publishing seditious articles.

Peoples

AFAR

The Afar (or Danakil) live in Djibouti, Ethiopia and Eritrea. The ancestors of the Afar were settled livestock raisers in the highlands of Ethiopia, but, before 1000 CE, they gradually shifted to a nomadic (unsettled) way of life and moved to the lowlying area they occupy today. Their history has been filled with violence, marked by fighting with invading armies and, later, imperial and national governments. Disputes with neighboring peoples continued into the twentieth century.

ISSA

The Issa are a Somali people, who live in Djibouti and also in Ethiopia, Eritrea, and Somalia. In recent years, they have clashed with the Afars in Djibouti. Historically, the two peoples were not especially divided, but, from the nineteenth century, competing European interests in the region created tensions between the two groups. After the French established the colony of French Somaliland, they tended to favor the minority Afar community. In 1967 CE, the colony was renamed the French Territory of the Afars and Issas, some say to emphasize the division. Since the colony became independent in 1977 CE, clashes have occurred between the Issa, who have dominated the government, and the Afar. See **Somalia (People—Issa)**.

Afar man
Rural Afar men often wore the traditional sanafil, *which is wrapped around the waist and tied on the right hip. Some also wear a top called a* harayto. *In the past, men would wear a* jile, *a 15-in. (38-cm.) long dagger, the blades of which were curved and extremely sharp.*

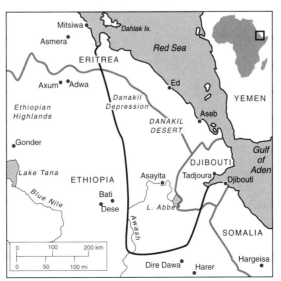

Modern extent of the Afar peoples

Postage stamp
A 1978 CE stamp from Djibouti depicting a seashell.

Djibouti stamps
The landscape of Dlibouti (top) and a French gunboat (above) as depicted on two postage stamps.

Djibouti's major political figures

Gouled Aptidon, Hassan (1916 CE–)
Hassan Gouled, who was born into a nomadic Somali family, became the first president of Djibouti when it gained independence in 1977. He was reelected in 1981, 1987, and 1993.

Djibouti presidents

Jun 27 1977–May 8 1999 CE
Hassan Gouled Aptidon

May 8 1999 CE–
Ismail Omar Guelleh

Djibouti timeline

Pre 19th century

3rd century BCE Ancestors of the Afar people migrate to the Djibouti area from Arabia
825 CE The Afars are converted to Islam
14th century Kingdom of Adal dominates the Djibouti region
1415 Christian Ethiopians kill the Muslim ruler of Saylac (near modern-day Djibouti city)
1527 Ahmed Gran of Adal invades Ethiopia
1543 Ahmed Gran killed in battle with an Ethiopian-Portuguese army
18th century Somali Issa people migrate into the southern Djibouti region

19th century CE

1862 France purchases the Afar port of Obock
1881 France establishes a coaling station for ships at Obock
1884 France signs protectorate agreements with the sultans of Obock and Tadjoura
1888 France establishes the colony of French Somaliland
1896 Newly developed port of Djibouti city becomes the capital of French Somaliland
1897 Djibouti becomes the official port of trade for Ethiopia

1900–49 CE 1917 A railway is completed from Djibouti to the Ethiopian capital, Addis Ababa
1924-1934 Road building program opens up the interior of Djibouti
1946 Djibouti is granted a representative council and a deputy in the French national assembly
1947 Issa nationalists begin a campaign for independence

1950–59 CE 1958 French Somaliland is granted internal self-government

1960–69 CE 1967 French Somaliland votes to remain a French territory and is renamed the French Territory of the Afars and Issas

1970–79 CE 1977 Jun 27 Afars and Issas become the independent republic of Djibouti after a referendum: Hassan Gouled Aptidon becomes the first president
1979 The Afar Popular Liberation Movement is banned

1980–89 CE 1981 Djibouti becomes a one party state
1988 Ethiopia and Somalia recognize Djibouti's borders
1989 Fighting breaks out between Afars and Issas in Djibouti city and Tadjourah

1990–99 CE 1991 Guerrilla warfare breaks out between the Afars and Issa dominated government forces
1992 President Gouled Aptidon introduces a multiparty constitution
1993 Gouled Aptidon re-elected in multiparty elections
1994 Afars and Issas reach a peace agreement
1996 Exiled opponents of the Gouled Aptidon regime are abducted from Addis Ababa

2000–09 CE 2001 Work is completed on Djibouti's port, increasing its capacity by 50%

Dongola

After the fall of the kingdom of Meroe in 324 CE, Nubia broke up into three kingdoms: Nobatia; Makuria; and Alodia. Between 575 and 599 CE, Makuria absorbed Nobatia and formed the larger kingdom of Dongola (or Dunqulah). This kingdom disappeared after Arabs invaded the region in the fifteenth century. *See also* **Nubia; Sudan**.

Dunqulah

See **Dongola**.

East Africa Protectorate

To secure access to their Uganda colony, Britain claimed Kenya as the East Africa Protectorate (colony) in 1895 CE. Imperial British East Africa (IBEA), a commercial company, was granted the administration of East Africa, which it occupied on behalf of the British government. In 1920 CE British East Africa was renamed Kenya. *See also* **British East Africa; Kenya; Uganda Protectorate**.

East Africa

In the nineteenth century Britain established colonies in eastern Africa, namely Kenya (initially British East Africa), the Uganda Protectorate and Zanzibar. Together, the separate colonies were known as East Africa. *See also* **British East Africa**; **Uganda Protectorate**; **and Zanzibar**.

East African Community

In the 1960s Kenya, Tanzania ad Uganda established the East African Community, but it collapsed as a result of political differences. However, the three countries initiated a New East African community in 1999 CE, which aimed at creating a customs union. a common market, a monetary union and, ultimately, a political union.

Colonialisation
A stamp issued in 1910 CE bearing the head of then current British monarch.

EGYPT Arab Republic of Egypt

For an account of the history of Ancient Egypt, *see* **Egypt**, **Ancient**. Ancient Egypt began to decline from 1070 BCE, when it fell to a series of invaders, including Nubians, Assyrians, and Persians. In 332 BCE, Egypt became part of the empire of Alexander the Great, who founded the city of Alexandria. In 30 BCE, Egypt became part of the Roman empire, but Roman power weakened after 395 CE when the Roman empire split into eastern and western parts.

Arab armies conquered Egypt between 639 and 642 CE, introducing the Arabic language, and Islam, which gradually replaced Coptic Christianity as Egypt's main religion. Egypt was then ruled by Muslim dynasties–the Ummayads, the 'Abbasids. and the Shiite Fatimids. However, in 1171 CE, Saladin, the great Muslim general, overthrew the Fatimids and restored the Sunni form of Islam. Saladin's descendants formed the Ayyubid dynasty, which was replaced by the Mamluks in 1250 CE. Mamluk rule continued until 1517 CE, when Egypt became part of the Ottoman (Turkish) empire.

Napoleon invaded Egypt in 1798 CE, but British and Ottoman troops defeated the French in 1801. France became involved in Egypt in the mid-nineteenth century when it built the Suez Canal, which opened in 1869 CE. However, Britain bought Egypt's shares in the canal in 1876 CE and, in 1882 CE, it annexed Egypt. In 1914 CE, as Egypt was still officially part of the Ottoman empire, which was allied to Germany, Britain made Egypt a protectorate (colony). In 1922 CE, Britain granted Egypt nominal independence, but it retained the right to keep troops in the country. In 1923 CE, Egypt was made a constitutional monarchy.

Turkish rule of Egypt

Muhammad Ali *(left)*
The pasha (military leader) of Egypt from 1805–48 CE acted as an independent ruler, and retained only nominal allegiance to the Ottoman Sultan.

Arabi Pasha *(left)*
He led a rebellion to overthrow the ruler Ismail Pasha in 1871 CE. The British invasion of Egypt in 1882 CE, which was intended to maintain control of the Suez Canal, resulted in his defeat and subsequent exile.

Khedive Ismail Pasha *(right)*
The Egyptian ruler who was overthrown during a popular revolution in 1879 CE.

Abbas II Hilmi *(left)*
The last Turkish Khedive of Egypt who ruled from 1892–1914 CE, after which a British protectorate was established.

Saad Zaghlul *(right)*
Along with other nationalists, Saad Zaghlul demanded the abolition of Egypt's status as a British protectorate. In 1923 CE Egypt became a constitutional monarchy and he became prime minister of the new government in 1925 CE.

Zangid Empire and Ayyubid Sultanate (right)

The Zangid Empire was founded by the Atabeg (ruler) of Mosul, who swept in a southeast direction and took Fatimid Egypt in 1169 CE. The governorship was given to Saladin, a Kurd, who seized power in 1173 CE and founded the Ayyubid dynasty, a champion of Islam.

1 1172 CE

2 1249 CE

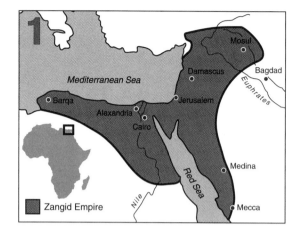

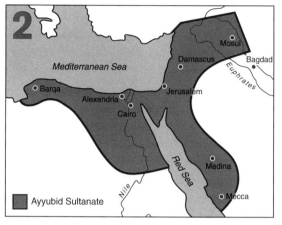

The Mamluks (rught and below right)

The Mamluks seized power from the Ayyubids in 1250 CE, and ruled the sultanate for a total of 267 years. During the 1300s they pushed in a southerly direction into Christian Nubia spreading the Islamic faith. During the 1400s they gained control of the Red Sea trading routes, especially those to Mecca and Medina. Their rule ended in 1517 CE when the Ottomans seized control of Egypt.

1 1300 CE

2 1317 CE

3 1400 CE

4 1450 CE

5 1475 CE

6 1516 CE

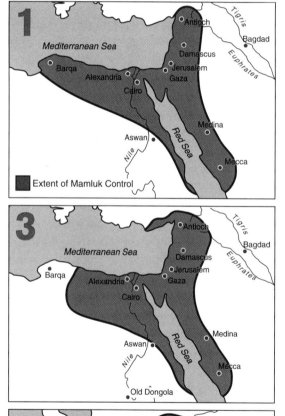

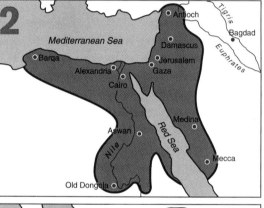

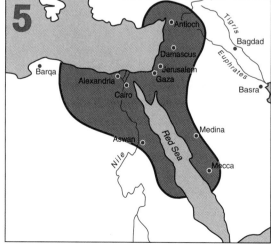

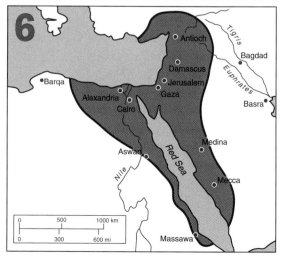

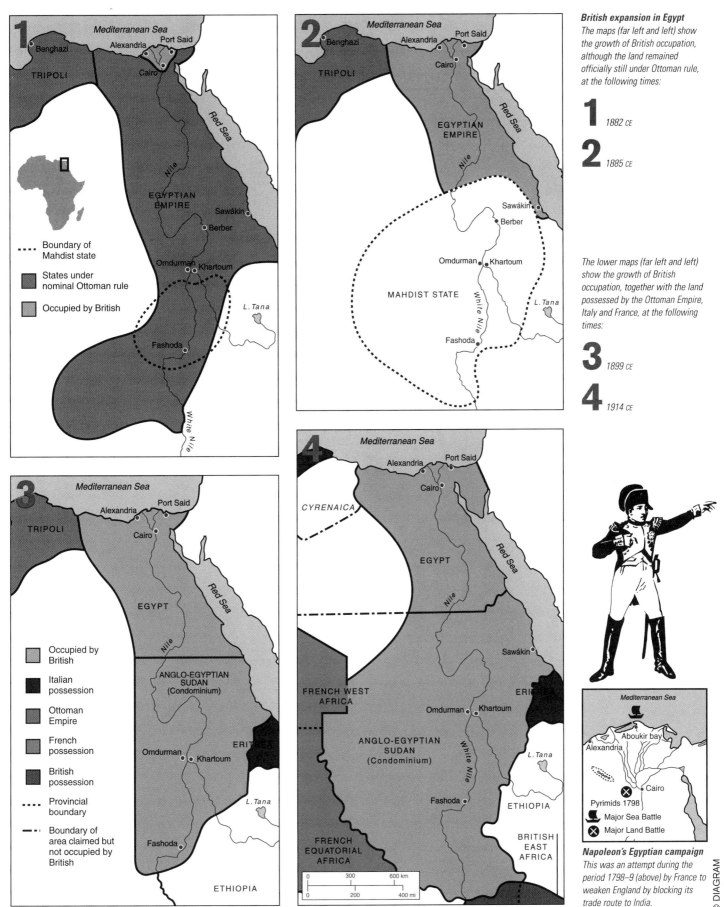

1
Mediterranean Sea
Benghazi
Alexandria
Port Said
Cairo
TRIPOLI
Nile
Red Sea
EGYPTIAN EMPIRE
Sawákin
Berber
Omdurman   Khartoum
L. Tana
Fashoda
White Nile

- - - - Boundary of Mahdist state
▨ States under nominal Ottoman rule
▨ Occupied by British

2
Mediterranean Sea
Benghazi
Alexandria
Port Said
Cairo
TRIPOLI
EGYPTIAN EMPIRE
Nile
Red Sea
Sawákin
Berber
Omdurman   Khartoum
MAHDIST STATE
White Nile
L. Tana
Fashoda

3
Mediterranean Sea
Alexandria   Port Said
Cairo
TRIPOLI
EGYPT
Nile
Red Sea
ANGLO-EGYPTIAN SUDAN (Condominium)
Omdurman   Khartoum
ERITREA
L. Tana
Fashoda
ETHIOPIA

▨ Occupied by British
■ Italian possession
▨ Ottoman Empire
▨ French possession
▨ British possession
···· Provincial boundary
–·–· Boundary of area claimed but not occupied by British

4
Mediterranean Sea
Alexandria   Port Said
Cairo
CYRENAICA
EGYPT
Nile
Red Sea
Sawákin
FRENCH WEST AFRICA
ERITREA
Omdurman   Khartoum
ANGLO-EGYPTIAN SUDAN (Condominium)
White Nile
L. Tana
Fashoda
ETHIOPIA
FRENCH EQUATORIAL AFRICA
BRITISH EAST AFRICA

| 0 | 300 | 600 km |
| 0 | 200 | 400 mi |

British expansion in Egypt
The maps (far left and left) show the growth of British occupation, although the land remained officially still under Ottoman rule, at the following times:

1 *1882 CE*

2 *1885 CE*

The lower maps (far left and left) show the growth of British occupation, together with the land possessed by the Ottoman Empire, Italy and France, at the following times:

3 *1899 CE*

4 *1914 CE*

Napoleon's Egyptian campaign
Mediterranean Sea
Aboukir bay
Alexandria
Cairo
Pyrimids 1798
⛵ Major Sea Battle
⊗ Major Land Battle

This was an attempt during the period 1798–9 (above) by France to weaken England by blocking its trade route to India.

© DIAGRAM

The Egyptian Camel Corps
During World War II British army units based in North Africa joined together with Egyptian soldiers to combat the threat posed by the Axis forces of Germany and Italy.

The Suez Crisis
A newspaper cartoon takes a humorous view of the war which took place in 1956 CE.

Superior military strength
The Egyptian army was heavily defeated in the Yom Kippur War against Israel in 1973 CE.

Recent history

During World War II, German and Italian armies invaded northwestern Egypt in an attempt to seize the strategic Suez Canal, but Allied armies drove them out. After the war, Egyptian nationalists called for the withdrawal of British troops from their country. In 1948 CE, Egyptian and other Arab armies fought alongside the Palestinians against the new State of Israel, but Israel survived and a truce was signed in 1949 CE. In 1952 CE, a military rebellion in Egypt overthrew King Farouk I and Egypt became a republic in 1953 CE. The first president, General Muhammad Neguib, was replaced in 1954 CE by much younger Colonel Gamal Abd an-Nasser. In the same year, Britain agreed to the gradual withdrawal of its troops from the Suez Canal zone.

Nasser set about developing education and other services and the economy. Central to his strategy was the building of the Aswan High Dam to provide hydro-electricity and water for irrigation.When Britain and the United States withdrew their offers of assistance to construct the dam, Nasser seized the Canal in 1956 CE. In retaliation, Britain, France and Israel, whose relations with Egypt had greatly worsened, invaded the Sinai peninsula and the Canal region. But soon, under international pressure from the United States, the Soviet Union and other powers, the invasion force withdrew. The defiant Nasser emerged as a major figure throughout the Arab world, although, when Egypt lost further territory to Israel in 1967 CE in the Six-Day War, Nasser offered his resignation. His resignation was rejected and he continued to serve as president until his death in 1970 CE.

Egypt's vice-president, Muhammad Anwar al Sadat, succeeded Nasser. In 1973 CE, Egyptian and Syrian forces launched a surprise attack on the Sinai peninsula, but its troops were finally pushed back to the Suez Canal. After the October War, Sadat made a peace agreement with Israel in 1979 CE. Under the agreement, Egypt regained the Sinai peninsula.

Extremists assassinated Sadat in 1981 CE and he was succeeded by the vice-president, Muhammad Hosni Mubarak. Mubarak continued to play an important part in Middle Eastern affairs, including active support for the Arab-Israeli peace process. In 1990 CE, Egypt condemned Iraq's invasion of Kuwait and Egyptian troops took part in the Persian Gulf War of 1991 CE.

At home, Mubarak faced opposition from Islamic fundamentalists, who were disturbed at what they saw as the increasing westernization of their country. In the 1990s, attacks by fundamentalists on foreign visitors damaged the tourist industry and led to many arrests. In September 1999 CE, Mubarak was himself attacked while campaigning in a presidential referendum, but he survived with a minor wound. Mubarak, the only candidate who had earlier been chosen by the Egyptian parliament, was reelected to a fourth six-year term. Parliamentary elections in 2000 CE resulted in victory for Mubarak's National Democratic Party, who won about 87 percent of the parliamentary seats. Attempts to suppress poitical dissent prior to the elections were strongly criticized by international human rights groups.

Peoples

ARABS

Arabs, whose ancestors came from Arabia, live throughout North Africa. An Arab general, Amr ibn al As, led an army, 4,000 strong, into Egypt in 640 CE, beginning the Arab invasion of North Africa At that time, Egypt was part of the Byzantine, or East Roman, Empire. In 642 CE, the Byzantines surrendered Egypt to the Arabs. The country came under the rule of governors appointed by the caliphs, the rulers of the Arab world. By 711 CE, when the Arabs began their occupation of Spain, the Arabs had conquered all of North Africa. Many intermarried with local peoples and, as a result, the people of present-day Egypt are a mixture of Arabs and the descendants of the Ancient Egyptians.

BEDOUIN

The Bedouin, a nomadic Arab people, arrived in North Africa from Arabia soon after the eighth-century Arab conquest of that region. Most Bedouin today speak Arabic and are Muslims.

NUBIANS

Nearly 3,000 years ago, in what is now southern Egypt and southern Sudan, the Kingdom of Nubia became independent from ancient Egypt from which it lay upriver along the Nile. For a while, the Nubians even controled ancient Egypt. Until recently, descendants of the Nubians still lived in this region. However, the building of the Aswan High Dam on the Nile River flooded much of Nubia and more than 100,000 Nubians were relocated elsewhere in Egypt and Sudan. The region is now covered by Lake Nasser. UNESCO launched a campaign to save Nubia's historical treasures, including such temples as Abu Simbel, statues, pottery, and tombs full of gold, silver, jewelry, and other treasures. While greatly influenced by ancient Egypt, the origin and expression of Nubian culture was distinctly black African.

Control of the Suez Canal
In 1956 ships were sunk to blockade the Canal and, despite French, British, and Israeli military intervention, Egypt maintained control. The canal later closed from 1967 until 1975,

Egyptian–Israeli conflict 1956–1973 CE

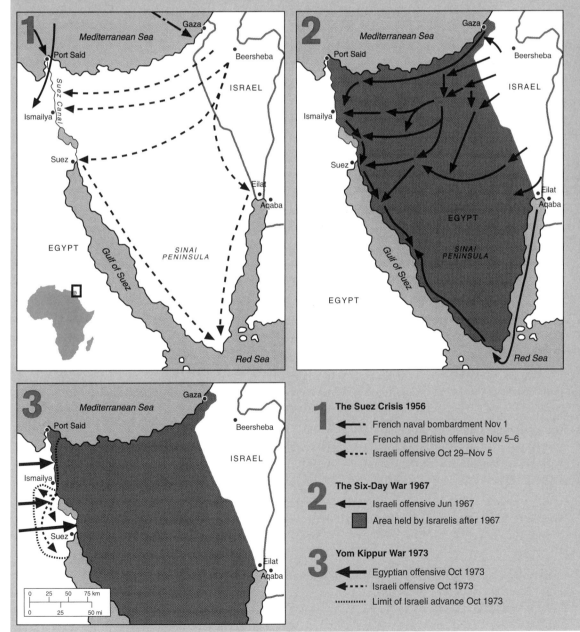

1 **1956** CE
Tension between Egypt and Israel became critical when, in July 1956 CE, Egypt decided to nationalize the Suez Canal and close it to Israel. Britain and France were worried by the potential effect of this act on world commerce. Between October 29 and November 6, Israel invaded the Sinai peninsula, and Britain and France bombed Egyptian air bases and invaded the Suez Canal Zone. A cease-fire was agreed on November 6. United Nations (UN) troops replaced Israeli ones, and Britain and France withdrew from the Canal Zone.

2 **1967** CE
In 1967 CE, the Israelis began the Six-Day War with Egypt and Syria because they feared attack, especially after Egypt had requested the withdrawal of UN troops from Sinai. On June 5, Israel launched air attacks on Egypt and invaded Sinai up to the Suez Canal. June 10 saw a cease-fire but Sinai remained in Israeli hands.

3 **1973** CE
The Yom Kippur War started on October 6, 1973 CE when Egypt and Syria attacked Israel, hoping to regain the 1967 CE borders. The Egyptians crossed the Suez Canal and overwhelmed the Israeli forces. By October 18, however, the Egyptians faced defeat. There was a cease-fire on October 24.

1 **The Suez Crisis 1956**
◄--- French naval bombardment Nov 1
◄— French and British offensive Nov 5–6
◄···· Israeli offensive Oct 29–Nov 5

2 **The Six-Day War 1967**
◄— Israeli offensive Jun 1967
▨ Area held by Israrelis after 1967

3 **Yom Kippur War 1973**
◄— Egyptian offensive Oct 1973
◄--- Israeli offensive Oct 1973
······· Limit of Israeli advance Oct 1973

© DIAGRAM

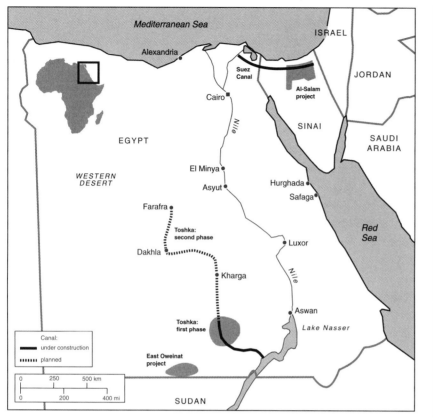

Irrigating the desert (above)
The construction of a canal to carry water from Lake Nasser to the Western Desert of Egypt in 1999 CE was intended to transform formerly barren areas into food-producing ones.

Redirecting the water (right)
More constructive use of the River Nile's constant water supply was intended drastically to reduce the threat of drought in areas within its watershed.

Egypt's major political figures

Anthony of Egypt (or Thebes or Memphis), Saint (c. 250–356 CE)
Saint Anthony was an Egyptian Copt who founded the first Christian monastery. From the age of 20, he lived as a hermit near the Red Sea, and in 305, he organized his fellow hermits into a monastery. At the age of 100 he preached against false beliefs in Alexandria.

Arabi, Ahmad (Arabi Pasha) (1839–1911 CE)
Ahmad Arabi, an Egyptian soldier and revolutionary popularly known as Arabi Pasha, led a rebellion to overthrow the Egyptian rulers Ismail Pasha in 1879 and Tewfik Pasha in 1881. Britain invaded Egypt in 1882 to maintain control of the Suez Canal, and defeated him at the Battle of Tell al Kebir. The British captured him and tried him for sedition, exiling him to Ceylon (now Sri Lanka) until 1901.

Boutros-Ghali, Boutros (1922 CE–)
In 1992 CE, Boutros-Ghali, an Egyptian, became the first African Secretary-General of the United Nations. Egypt regarded his appointment as recognition of its moderating influence in the region. He had earlier served in the Egyptian government as deputy prime minister and, as foreign minister, he helped to win Arab support for the 1991 Gulf War. He was succeeded as Secretary-General by Kofi Atta Annan on January 1, 1997.

Farouk I (1920–1965 CE)
Farouk I, a descendent of Mehemet Ali, was the last king of Egypt. He reigned from 1937 until 1952, when he was deposed by army officers led by General Muhammad Neguib. He was known for his extravagance, which, together with the defeat of Egyptian forces by Israel in 1948–49 and his failure to end the British military occupation of Egypt, made him unpopular. In 1959, he became a citizen of Monaco.

Boutros Boutros-Ghali
He became the first African Secretary-General of the United Nations in 1992, and remained in office until the end of 1996.

Egypt timeline

Pre 19th Century
639–642 CE	Muslim Arabs conquer Egypt
640	Cairo founded as a military base
969–1171	The Shiite Fatimid dynasty rules Egypt
1171	Saladin becomes ruler of Egypt
1250–1517	The Mamluk dynasty rules Egypt
1260	The Mamluks defeat the Mongols at Ain Jalut in Palestine
1517	The Ottoman Turks conquer Egypt
1798	Napoleon invades Egypt

19th century CE
1801	French troops in Egypt surrender to a British and Ottoman army
1805	Muhammad Ali (Ali Pasha) seizes power in Egypt
1859–1869	Construction of the Suez Canal
1875	Egypt sells its share in the Suez Canal to Britain
1882	Britain annexes Egypt

1900–49 CE
1914	Britain makes Egypt a protectorate
1922	Britain grants Egypt nominal independence
1922	Howard Carter discovers the tomb of Tutankhamun
1923	Egypt becomes a constitutional monarchy
1940–1941	The British defeat an Italian invasion of Egypt
1942	British defeat the Italians and Germans at the battle of El Alamein
1945	Egypt is a founder member of the Arab League
1948	Egypt and other Arab countries invade Israel
1949	Egypt accepts an armistice with Israel

1950–59 CE
1952	King Farouk is deposed by a military coup
1953	Egypt becomes a republic
1954	Gamal Abd an-Nasser becomes president of Egypt
1954	Britain agrees to withdraw its troops from the Suez Canal zone
1956	Suez Crisis: Israel, Britain and France invade after Nasser announces the nationalization of the Suez Canal
1958	Egypt and Syria form the United Arab Republic (UAR)

1960–69 CE
1960	Construction begins on the Aswan High Dam
1961	Syria withdraws from the UAR
1967	Egypt, Syria and Jordan defeated by Israel in the Six Day War
1968	Aswan High Dam completed

1970–79 CE
1970	Death of Nasser: Anwar al-Sadat succeeds him as president
1973	Egypt and Syria are defeated by Israel in the Yom Kippur War
1977	Sadat visits Jerusalem to begin Egyptian-Israeli rapprochement
1978	Camp David accords between Egypt and Israel
1979	Egypt and Israel sign a peace treaty

1980–89 CE
1981	President Sadat is assassinated: Hosni Mubarak succeeds him as president

1990–99 CE
1990–1991	Egypt joins the US-led coalition against Iraq in the Gulf War
1993	15 Islamic fundamentalist terrorists executed.
1997	Islamic fundamentalist terrorists kill 60 western tourists
1999	Hosni Mubarak is re-elected as president

2000–09 CE
2000	The ruling National Democratic Party wins a large majority of the seats in the National Assembly, although opposition groups made gains.

A royal wedding
A 1951 CE stamp celebrating the wedding of King Farouk I and Queen Narriman

Gamal Abd an-Nasser
He came to power in Egypt in 1954 CE, and his nationalization of the Suez Canal in 1956 CE led to French, British, and Israeli forces invading the country.

Sadat assasinated
On October 6th, 1981 CE President Sadat of Egypt was murdered by Islamic fundamentalist gunmen in Cairo during a military parade to commemorate the beginning of the Egyptian offensive in the 1973 CE Arab–Israeli War.

Egyptian heads of state

Kings

28 Apr 1936–26 Jul 1952 CE
Faruq I (Faruq ibn Ahmad Fu'ad)

26 Jul 1952–18 Jun 1953 CE
Fu'ad II (Ahmad Fu'ad ibn Faruq)

President

18 Jun 1953–25 Feb 1954 CE
Muhammad Nagib (Naguib)

Chairman of the Revolutionary Command Council

25 Feb 1954–27 Feb 1954 CE
Abu Khalid Gamal `Abd an-Nasir (Nasser)

President

27 Feb 1954–14 Nov 1954 CE
Muhammad Nagib (Naguib) (2nd time)

Chairman of the Revolutionary Command Council

14 Nov 1954–25 Jun 1956 CE
Abu Khalid Gamal `Abd an-Nasir (Nasser) (2nd time)

Presidents

25 Jun 1956–28 Sep 1970 CE
Abu Khalid Gamal `Abd an-Nasir (Nasser)

**28 Sep 1970–6 Oct 1981 CE
(acting to 17 Oct 1970 CE)**
Muhammad Ahmad Anwar as-Sadat

**6 Oct 1981–14 Oct 1981 CE
(acting)**
Sufi Abu Talib Sadat

14 Oct 1981CE–
Muhammad Hosni Mubarak

(1) Fu'ad II reigned under a Council of Regency and the ruling Revolutionary Command Council.

(2) From 22 Feb 1958 CE to 28 Sep 1961 CE Nasser ruled as vice president of the United Arab Republic, comprising Egypt and Syria.

© DIAGRAM

Hosni Mubarak
He became president of Egypt in 1981 CE following the assasination of Anwar al Sadat and, in 1995 CE, he himself survived an assasination attempt during a visit to Ethiopia.

Anwar al Sadat
He made peace with Israel at the Camp David talks in 1979 CE in the United States; and was later then assassinated in 1981 CE by Islamic fundamentalists.

Greatest extent
The kingdom of Egypt was at its greatest geographical extent under Tuthmosis 1 c.1500 BCE.

Mehemet Ali (1769–1849 CE)

Mehemet Ali, also known as Muhammad Ali, was an Albanian-born Ottoman (Turkish) soldier who became viceroy (ruler) of Egypt in 1805, ruling on behalf of the Ottoman Empire. He massacred his main enemies, the Mamluks, who were the remnants of a Turkish dynasty that had been defeated by the Ottomans in 1517. He also reformed the Egyptian administration, army, and navy, and conquered large parts of Sudan, and when he fell out with his Turkish masters, his army defeated them. As a result, the Ottomans made him hereditary ruler of Egypt, and his descendants ruled until a republic was declared in 1953. The last of them to rule was Farouk I, deposed in 1952 CE.

Mubarak, Muhammad Hosni (1928 CE–)

A former air force officer, Hosni Mubarak became president of Egypt in 1981 following the assassination of Anwar Sadat, having served as vice-president from 1975. Mubarak has pledged to deal firmly with Muslim extremists in Egypt and to continue the peace process with Israel. In 1990, he sent Egyptian troops to help defend Saudi Arabia after Iraq's invasion of Kuwait, and in 1995, he survived an assassination attempt during a visit to Ethiopia.

Nasser, Gamal Abd an- (1918–1970 CE)

Nasser was prime minister of Egypt (1954–6 CE) and president from l956 until 1970. He was one of the leaders of a military coup that overthrew King Farouk I in 1952, and took power after ousting General Muhammad Neguib in 1954. Nasser pursued socialist policies aimed at raising living standards and was widely respected by the Arab world. To finance the building of the Aswan High Dam, he nationalized the Suez Canal, provoking an invasion by British, French, and Israeli troop–a conflict that was ended by the United Nations. Nasser offered to resign after military failures in the 1967 Six-Day War with Israel, but the Egyptian people refused to accept his offer.

Neguib, Muhammad (1901–1984 CE)

An Egyptian general, Muhammad Neguib became prime minister and president of Egypt after the overthrow of King Farouk I in l952. Popular for his condemnation of British policies in Egypt, Neguib was a conservative Muslim. He was removed from office in 1954 and replaced by the more radical Gamal Abd an-Nasser.

Sadat, Muhammad Anwar al (1918–1981 CE)

Anwar Sadat, vice-president of Egypt, became president on the death of Gamal Abd an-Nasser in 1970. He is remembered for his dramatic peace initiative that led to the Camp David peace treaty, signed in 1979, ending the conflict between Egypt and Israel. He shared the 1978 Nobel Peace Prize with Israel's Menachem Begin. Sadat was assassinated in 1981 by Muslim extremists.

Egypt, Ancient

Egypt has one of the world's oldest civilizations and has been in existence since c. 4500 BCE. The dynastic Egypt of the pharaohs (kings) emerged in c. 3100 BCE. At its greatest extent (in the 1400s BCE), the Kingdom of Egypt reached as far as present-day Syria. For one hundred years from c. 1670 BCE, Egypt was ruled by "Hyksos" – literally "foreigners." After the end of the Twentieth Dynasty in c. 1070 BCE, a period of decline set in. Various nations invaded Egypt, which then fell under their control: Nubians (Sudanese) from the 700s; Assyrians from 671 CE; Persians from 525 CE; and Macedonians (Greeks) under Alexander the Great from 332 CE. After the death of Alexander, one of his generals, Ptolemy, claimed Egypt. His successors were known as the Ptolemies. They ruled Egypt until 30 BCE when it became part of the Roman Empire. Arabs from southwest Asia conquered Egypt in 642 CE and converted most of its people to Islam. Since this time, Egypt has been dominated by the language and culture of the Arabs.

Egyptian civilization arose in, and continues to be based around, the Nile Valley. Every year, beginning around July, the river flooded. When the floods retreated, around September, they left a deposit of rich, black, fertile soil along each bank about 6 miles (10 km) wide. Here, the Ancient Egyptians grew their crops. In an otherwise arid environment, the Nile provided water for irrigation as well as fertile soil. In ancient times, the river was the main transport route and most of Ancient Egypt's population lived in the Nile Valley. For these reasons, Ancient Egypt has been described as "the gift of the Nile."

Egyptian society had three main classes: upper, middle, and lower. The upper class comprised the royal family, religious and government officials, army officers, doctors, and wealthy landowners. Merchants, artisans, and manufacturers made up the middle class. There were many skilled workers such as architects, engineers, teachers, accountants, stonemasons, and carpenters. The majority of people, however, were of the lower class – laborers who mostly worked on farms owned by the upper classes. The main crops grown were wheat and barley, which were often given as wages to the workers. Other crops included vegetables and fruit. Bread made from wheat was the staple food and beer made from barley the main drink. Flax was grown to make linen. Farmlands were irrigated with water taken from canals. Antelopes, cattle, goats, sheep, donkeys, and pigs were raised. Egyptians also kept dogs and cats, and at one time hyenas.

The Ancient Egyptians made many long-lasting contributions to worldwide civilization. They established the first national government, built many great cities, and devised a 365-day calendar.

Ancient Egyptians believed in an afterlife and many gods and goddesses who ruled over different aspects of the world. The most important of these was the Sun god Re, who could grant good harvests, and the creator-god Ptah. The fertility goddess Isis, wife and sister of Osiris (judge of the dead), was the mother of Horus, the lord of Heaven. The pharaohs were believed to be incarnations of Horus. Every city and town also had its own particular god or goddess. The people of Thebes, for instance, worshiped a Sun god called Amon. Over time, Amon became identified with Re and was known as Amon-Re.

Ancient Egyptians used picture symbols called hieroglyphs to represent ideas and sounds. They were used from c. 3000 BCE until after 300 CE when a new alphabet was introduced. Over 700 symbols were used. Hieroglyphs were most often used for religious and royal inscriptions in stone. Usually, trained scribes carved or wrote using hieroglyphs. As the demand for written records and communications grew, there was a need to simplify the process. The invention of paper made from papyrus (reedlike plants), pens made from sharpened reeds, and ink made by mixing soot and water, enabled writing to become more commonplace. Simplified forms of hieroglyphs developed called hieratic and demotic, which were suitable for writing quickly on papyrus.

The Egyptian pyramids are tombs that were built for royals and nobles. They are the oldest and largest stone structures in the world. Imhotep, a great architect, built the first–the Step Pyramid–for King Zoser in c. 2650 BCE. The following 500 years are known as the "Age of Pyramids" because many of the most magnificent pyramids were built during this time. Royalty and nobles spent fortunes building these elaborate tombs, which were stocked with everything a person could wish for in the afterlife. Many skilled craftsmen were employed to decorate and furnish the tombs. As thieves robbed many of the pyramids in ancient times, tombs were increasingly built in secret underground locations, such as the Valley of the Kings near Thebes, and without a pyramid to attract looters.

Amon-Re Re Ptah Osiris Isis Horus

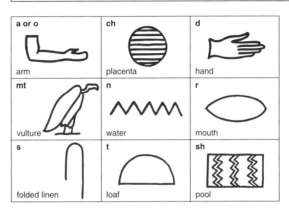

a or o	ch	d
arm	placenta	hand
mt	n	r
vulture	water	mouth
s	t	sh
folded linen	loaf	pool

Egyptian deities (above)
These pictures of Ancient Egyptian deities have been executed in a typically stylized fashion. Some are portrayed as having human bodies with animal heads, reflecting the different natures of the deities.

Hieroglyphic writing (left)
Ancient Egyptians used picture symbols that we call hieroglyphs to represent ideas and sounds. Over 700 symbols were used until after 300 CE when a new alphabet was introduced.

Nefertiti
She helped put forward plans to change the religion of Ancient Egypt from the worship of many gods to the worship of one god– Aton, the Sun.

Mummies (above)
The Ancient Egyptians preserved dead bodies so that people could use them in the afterlife. This involved removing and preserving the internal organs; filling the empty cavities; embalming the body and, finally, wrapping it in linen bandages. The mummified body (above left) would be placed in a wooden or stone coffin (above right) which would have been ornately decorated if the deceased were either wealthy or royal.

© DIAGRAM

Egypt, Hyksos and Thebes
These maps show the geographical extent of the three kingdoms in Egypt (Egypt, Hyksos and Thebes) at the following times:

1 *4500 BCE*

2 *2750 BCE*

3 *2250 BCE*

4 *1850 BCE*

5 *1670 BCE*

6 *1300 BCE*

Kingdoms

■ Egypt

■ Hyksos

■ Thebes

Hatshepsut
She was one of the few women to become ruler of Egypt in her own right, and became queen about 1505 BCE, probably jointly with Tuthmosis III, who was her nephew and stepson.

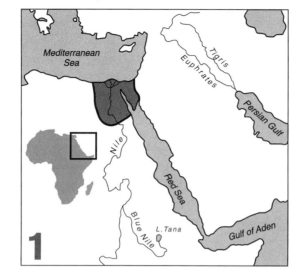

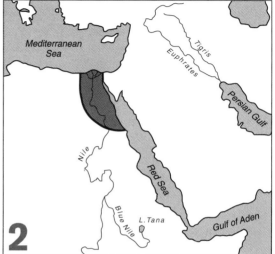

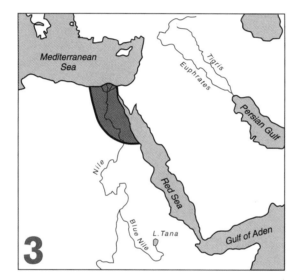

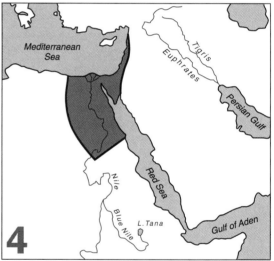

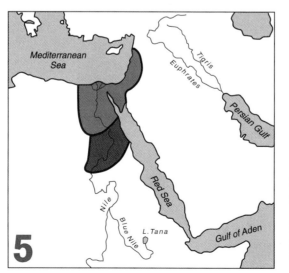

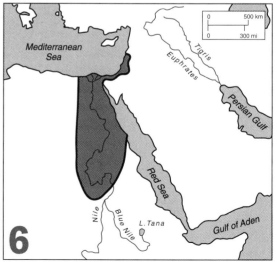

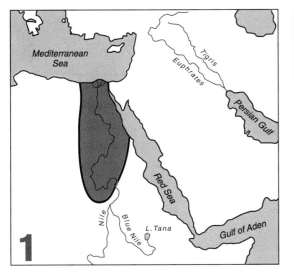

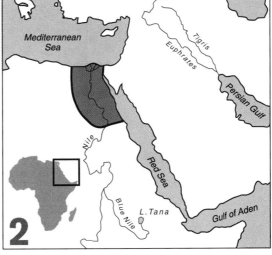

Egypt, and the Assyrian Empire

These maps show the geographical extent of the two kingdoms in Egypt (Egypt and Assyrian Empire) at the following times:

1 *1200 BCE*

2 *1000 BCE*

3 *825 BCE*

4 *670 BCE*

5 *580 BCE*

6 *375 BCE*

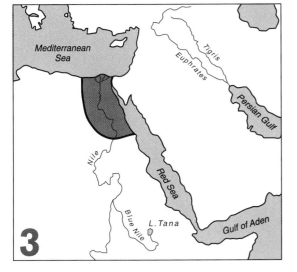

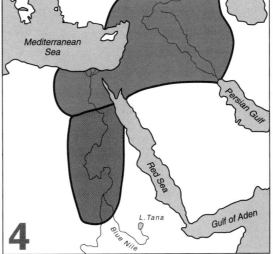

Kingdoms

| Egypt |
| Assyrian Empire |

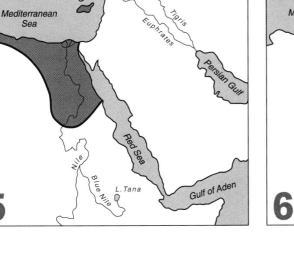

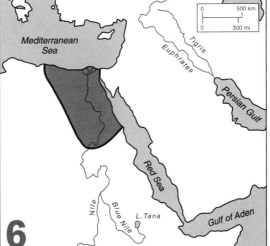

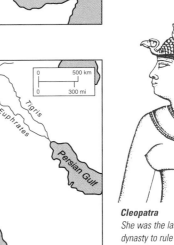

Cleopatra

She was the last of the Ptolemy dynasty to rule Egypt, and became queen in 51 BCE. Deposed by supporters of her husband, she was restored to the throne by Julius Caesar in 47 BCE and later became the lover of another Roman general, Mark Antony.

© DIAGRAM

Minerals and gemstones (right)
This map shows the mineral and gemstone resources in Egypt during the period c.3000–1570 BCE.

Ancient sites (far right)
This map shows the major sites of Ancient Egypt from c.3100 to 332 BCE.

Tutankhamen (below)
Few Ancient Egyptian tombs survived untouched until the twentieth century. One that did was that of the boy-king Tutankhamen, who died more than 3,300 years ago at the age of eighteen. The tomb, situated in the Valley of the Kings, had four rooms that contained more than 5,000 objects. Many objects were made of gold, such as this beautifully engraved mask, which covered the face of the dead king's mummy.

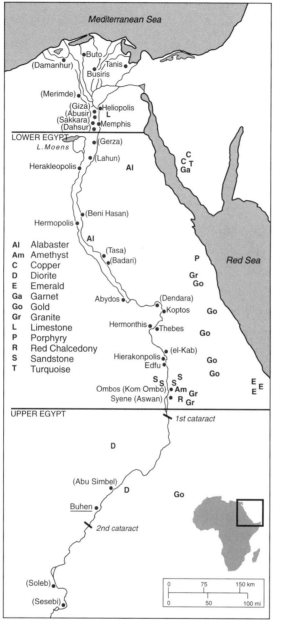

Mediterranean Sea

(Damanhur) • Buto
• Tanis
Busiris

(Merimde)

(Giza) • Heliopolis
(Abusir) **L**
(Sakkara)
(Dahsur) • Memphis

LOWER EGYPT

L. Moeris • (Gerza)

• (Lahun)

Herakleopolis

C
C
T
Ga

Al

• (Beni Hasan)
Hermopolis

Al

• (Tasa)
(Badari)

P

Red Sea

Gr
Go

Abydos • (Dendara)
• Koptos

Go

Hermonthis • Thebes

Go

(el-Kab)

Hierakonpolis
Edfu

Go

Go

Al	Alabaster	
Am	Amethyst	
C	Copper	
D	Diorite	
E	Emerald	
Ga	Garnet	
Go	Gold	
Gr	Granite	
L	Limestone	
P	Porphyry	
R	Red Chalcedony	
S	Sandstone	
T	Turquoise	

Ombos (Kom Ombo) **S** **S** **S**
Syene (Aswan) **R** **Am** **Gr**
Gr

E **E**
E

UPPER EGYPT

1st cataract

D

(Abu Simbel)
D

Buhen

Go

2nd cataract

(Soleb)

(Sesebi)

| 0 | 75 | 150 km |
| 0 | 50 | 100 mi |

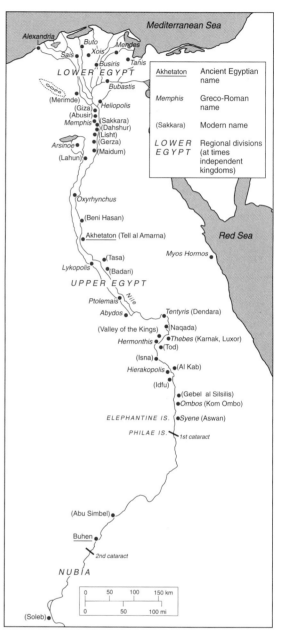

Mediterranean Sea

Alexandria • Buto • Mendes
Sais • Xois • Tanis
Busiris
LOWER EGYPT • Bubastis

(Merimde)
(Giza) • Heliopolis
(Abusir)
Memphis (Sakkara)
(Dahshur)
(Lisht)
Arsinoe (Gerza)
(Maidum)
(Lahun)

• Oxyrhynchus

(Beni Hasan)

Akhetaton (Tell al Amarna)

Red Sea

(Tasa)
Lykopolis (Badari)

Myos Hormos

UPPER EGYPT

Ptolemais
Abydos Tentyris (Dendara)
(Valley of the Kings) • Naqada
Hermonthis Thebes (Karnak, Luxor)
(Tod)
(Isna)
Hierakonpolis • (Al Kab)
(Idfu)
(Gebel al Silsilis)
Ombos (Kom Ombo)
ELEPHANTINE IS. • Syene (Aswan)
PHILAE IS. 1st cataract

(Abu Simbel)

Buhen
2nd cataract

NUBIA

Akhetaton	Ancient Egyptian name
Memphis	Greco-Roman name
(Sakkara)	Modern name
LOWER EGYPT	Regional divisions (at times independent kingdoms)

| 0 | 50 | 100 | 150 km |
| 0 | 50 | 100 mi |

(Soleb)

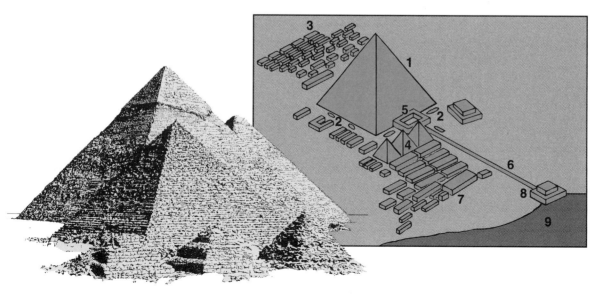

Great Pyramid of Khufu (left)
Called by the Egyptians the 'Pyramid that is the Sunset,' the Great Pyramid of Khufu is only one of many at the site of Giza. It was begun c. 2600 BCE and is 460 ft (140 m) high.

Key
1 Pyramid
2 Boat pits
3 Cemetery fields
4 Queen's pyramid
5 Mortuary temple
6 Causeway
7 Nobles' and courtiers' tombs
8 Valley temple
9 River Nile

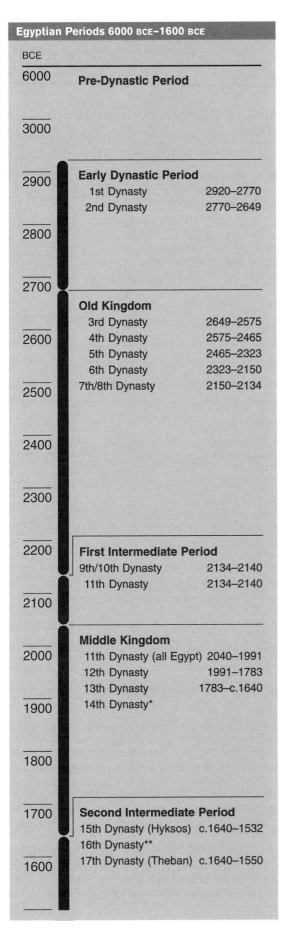

Egyptian Periods 6000 BCE–1600 BCE

BCE

6000 — **Pre-Dynastic Period**

3000

Early Dynastic Period	
1st Dynasty	2920–2770
2nd Dynasty	2770–2649

2900

2800

2700

Old Kingdom	
3rd Dynasty	2649–2575
4th Dynasty	2575–2465
5th Dynasty	2465–2323
6th Dynasty	2323–2150
7th/8th Dynasty	2150–2134

2600

2500

2400

2300

First Intermediate Period	
9th/10th Dynasty	2134–2140
11th Dynasty	2134–2140

2200

2100

Middle Kingdom	
11th Dynasty (all Egypt)	2040–1991
12th Dynasty	1991–1783
13th Dynasty	1783–c.1640
14th Dynasty*	

2000

1900

1800

Second Intermediate Period	
15th Dynasty (Hyksos)	c.1640–1532
16th Dynasty**	
17th Dynasty (Theban)	c.1640–1550

1700

1600

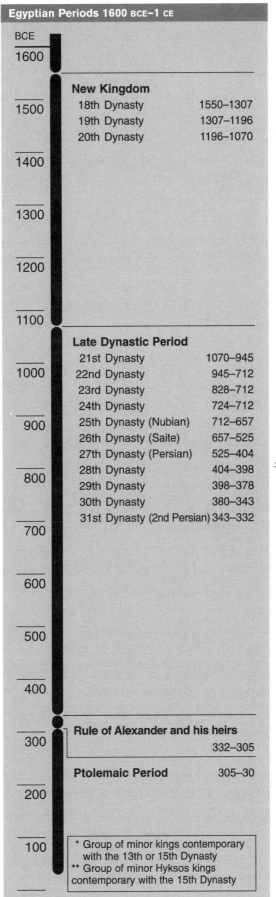

Egyptian Periods 1600 BCE–1 CE

BCE

1600

New Kingdom	
18th Dynasty	1550–1307
19th Dynasty	1307–1196
20th Dynasty	1196–1070

1500

1400

1300

1200

1100

Late Dynastic Period	
21st Dynasty	1070–945
22nd Dynasty	945–712
23rd Dynasty	828–712
24th Dynasty	724–712
25th Dynasty (Nubian)	712–657
26th Dynasty (Saite)	657–525
27th Dynasty (Persian)	525–404
28th Dynasty	404–398
29th Dynasty	398–378
30th Dynasty	380–343
31st Dynasty (2nd Persian)	343–332

1000

900

800

700

600

500

400

Rule of Alexander and his heirs	
	332–305

300

Ptolemaic Period	305–30

200

100

* Group of minor kings contemporary
  with the 13th or 15th Dynasty
** Group of minor Hyksos kings
  contemporary with the 15th Dynasty

Temple of Mentuhetep
Constructed in 2065 BCE at Der el-Bahari in Thebes, this temple is an example of Middle Kingdom architecture.

Temple, Island of Elephantine
This is one of the so-called Mammisi temples, or Birth Houses, which stood within the enclosures of larger temples. Located near present-day Aswan, it was constructed in 1408 BCE.

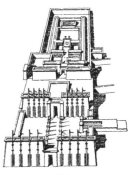

Great temple of Ammon
Often considered the grandest of all Egyptian temples, this great building owes its stature to the work of many kings. It was constructed between 1530–323 BCE.

© DIAGRAM

Major sites (right)
These maps shows major sites in
Egypt at the following times:

1 *The Greco–Roman period
c.332 BCE–350 CE*

2 *The Early Christian period
c.350 BCE*

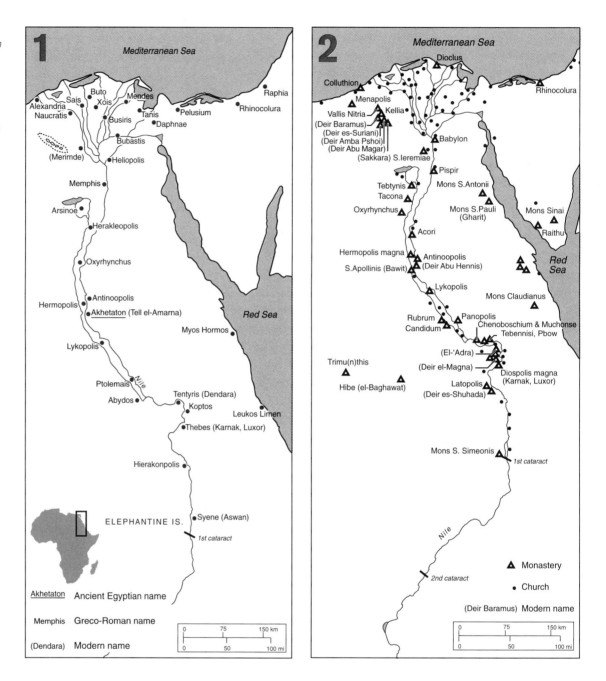

MAP 1 labels:

Mediterranean Sea

Buto
Sais — Mendes — Raphia
Alexandria — Xois — Rhinocolura
Naucratis — Busiris — Tanis — Pelusium
— Daphnae
Bubastis
(Merimde) — Heliopolis

Memphis

Arsinoe
Herakleopolis

Oxyrhynchus

Antinoopolis
Hermopolis — Akhetaton (Tell el-Amarna)

Myos Hormos

Red Sea

Lykopolis

Nile
Ptolemais
Abydos — Tentyris (Dendara)
Koptos
Leukos Limen
Thebes (Karnak, Luxor)

Hierakonpolis

ELEPHANTINE IS.
Syene (Aswan)
1st cataract

Akhetaton — Ancient Egyptian name

Memphis — Greco-Roman name

(Dendara) — Modern name

0 75 150 km
0 50 100 mi

MAP 2 labels:

Mediterranean Sea
Dioclus
Colluthion — Rhinocolura
Menapolis
Vallis Nitria — Kellia
(Deir Baramus)
(Deir es-Suriani) — Babylon
(Deir Amba Pshoi)
(Deir Abu Magar)
(Sakkara) S.Ieremiae
Pispir
Mons S.Antonii
Tebtynis
Tacona
Oxyrhynchus — Mons S.Pauli — Mons Sinai
(Gharit)
Acori — Raithu
Hermopolis magna
Antinoopolis
S.Apollinis (Bawit) — (Deir Abu Hennis)
Red Sea
Lykopolis
Mons Claudianus
Rubrum — Panopolis
Candidum — Chenoboschium & Muchonse
Tebennisi, Pbow
Trimu(n)this — (El-'Adra)
(Deir el-Magna) — Diospolis magna
Hibe (el-Baghawat) — (Karnak, Luxor)
Latopolis
(Deir es-Shuhada)

Mons S. Simeonis
1st cataract

Nile

2nd cataract

▲ Monastery

● Church

(Deir Baramus) Modern name

0 75 150 km
0 50 100 mi

Egypt, Ancient's major political figures

Cleopatra VII (69–30 BCE)
Cleopatra VII was the last of the Ptolemy dynasty (who were of Macedonian [Greek] origin) to rule Egypt. She took a great interest in her subjects' welfare and won their affection. Cleopatra became queen in 51 BCE but was deposed by supporters of her husband (and younger brother), Ptolemy XIII. She was restored to the throne in 47 BCE by Julius Caesar, a Roman general. Later, she became the lover of another Roman general, Mark Antony. They set up an empire based on Egypt, but were defeated by the Romans at the naval Battle of Actium (31 BCE). In 30 BCE, Antony committed suicide after hearing a false report that Cleopatra had died. Later that year, Cleopatra – unable to save her dynasty – also committed suicide, supposedly by causing a poisonous snake to bite her breast.

Hatshepsut (c. 1540–c.1481 BCE)
Hatshepsut was one of the few women to rule Ancient Egypt in her own right. She became queen in about 1505 BCE, probably jointly with Tuthmosis III, who was her nephew and stepson. She was devoted to religion, and built a magnificent temple at Deir al Bahri and two obelisks at the Karnak temple complex. She also sent an expedition to the Land of Punt (probably in modern Somalia), an exploit depicted in the Punt Hall at Deir al Bahri.

Imhotep (2900s BCE)

Imhotep was an Ancient Egyptian sage and architect. He was adviser to Pharaoh Zoser, for whom he designed the Step Pyramid at Saqqara–the first true (smooth-sided) pyramid ever built. He was also the only physician to have been venerated as a god after he died. In around 500 BCE, he was worshiped as the son of Ptah, the god of Memphis (once the capital of Egypt), and the Greeks identified him with Asclepius, their god of medicine.

Khufu (Cheops) (2500s BCE)

Khufu–also known as Cheops, the Greek name for him–was ruler of the kingdom of Memphis in Ancient Egypt. He ordered the building of the Great Pyramid at Giza, which is the largest of the Egyptian pyramids, plus smaller pyramids for three of his wives. One of his successors was his son Khafre (Chephren), who built the second-largest of the Giza pyramids.

Nefertiti (c.1385–c.1350 BCE)

Nefertiti helped her husband, the pharaoh (king) Amenhotep IV (Akhenaton), in his attempt to change the religion of Ancient Egypt from worship of its numerous traditional gods to worship of just one – Aton, the Sun. Nefertiti, who was famed for her beauty, had six daughters, one of whom married Tutankhamen.

Ramses II (reigned 1304–1237 BCE)

It has been suggested, but never proved, that Ramses II was the Egyptian pharaoh (king) who oppressed and enslaved the Israelites, as described in the Bible. Known as Ramses the Great, he was one of the most successful pharaohs and left many fine buildings, including the huge temple at Abu Simbel. His mummified body was discovered at Queen Hatshepsut's temple at Deir al Bahri in 1881 CE.

Tutankhamen (reigned 1361–1352 BCE)

He is known principally as a result of the discovery of his tomb in an intact condition in 1922 CE. Two mementos recovered from his tomb confirm that he was the son of Amenhotep III, who was the king of an earlier eighteenth century dynasty, and Tiy, who was possibly his chief queen. Tutankhamen was probably made king after the death of his brother, Smenkhkare, and his co-regent, and married Akhenaton's third daughter to solidify his claim to the throne. He moved his residence to Memphis, near modern Cairo, and restored the temples and privileges of the old gods. During his ninth year the Egyptians marched into Syria to aid the Mitanni kingdom in its struggle against the Hittites, at which point Tutamkhamen unexpectedly died. None of his children survived, and he was succeeded by Ay who married his widow.

Treasures of the past
The coffin of Tutankhamen being examined by Howard Carter in 1922 CE.

Elem Kalabari

See **Calabar**, **New**

Elobey, Annobón, and Corisca

Elobey, Annobón, and Corisca are the names of islands that are now part of Equatorial Guinea. Annobón, which means "good year," was probably sighted and named by Portuguese sailors on a New Year's Day between 1472 and 1475 CE. In 1778 CE, the Portuguese gave Annobón to the Spanish. From 1960 to 1968 CE, Annobón and Fernando Po formed an overseas province of Spain, but they are now part of Equatorial Guinea. *See also* **Equatorial Guinea**; **Fernando Po**.

EQUATORIAL GUINEA Republic of Equatorial Guinea

The earliest inhabitants of Mbini (or Rio Muni), the mainland part of what is now Equatorial Guinea, were probably hunter-gatherers, but they were displaced by Bantu-speaking peoples, such as the Bubi and the Fang, who gradually moved into the area. The first known inhabitants of the island of Bioko (formerly called Fernando Póo) were the Bubis, who settled there around 800 years ago. The Portuguese reached Bioko in 1472 CE and the island became a staging post for slaves taken from Central and West Africa. The island and the coast of Mbini became Spanish in the 1770s as part of a deal permitting Portugal to extend the western frontiers of Brazil beyond 50° West longitude.

The Spaniards who settled on Bioko suffered from yellow fever and they withdrew in 1781 CE. Spain leased Bioko to Britain in 1827 CE, and Britain landed freed slaves there. The descendants of these people, together with workers from Central and West Africa introduced later by Spanish plantation owners, are the Fernandinos, who form a small but significant community in modern Equatorial Guinea. In 1844 CE, Spaniards returned to Bioko and began to explore the mainland, but economic development did not begin until the end of the nineteenth century.

In 1959 CE, Spanish Guinea, as the territory was then known, was reorganized into two Spanish provinces and the people were granted the same rights as Spanish citizens. In 1963, the two provinces. renamed Equatorial Guinea, were granted a degree of autonomy.

Independence
A stamp celebrating the second anniversary of Equatorial Guinea's independence.

Recent history

Equatorial Guinea became an independent republic on October 12, 1968 CE. The first president, Francisco Macías Nguema, made the country a one-party state in 1970 CE and in 1971 CE he introduced a new constitution, making him president for life. His rule was tyrannical. He feared opposition and had many people assassinated. Around a third of the population, including many of the most skilled and educated, emigrated. Among those who departed were 20,000 Nigerians who worked on the cocoa plantations on Bioko. Their departure led Macías Nguema to introduce forced labor, but cocoa production declined and the economy was devastated. In 1977 CE, Spain broke off diplomatic relations with Equatorial Guinea and, in 1978 CE, the European Economic Community (now the European Union) suspended payments to the country because of the government's appalling record on human rights.

In 1979 CE, Macías Nguema was overthrown, tried for terrorism, and executed. He was succeeded by his nephew, Lt.-Col. Teodoro Obiang Nguema Mbsango, who ruled through a Supreme Military Council. Among his early measures were the release of 5,000 political prisoners and the restoration of links with Spain and the United States. He also broke the country's ties with the Communist bloc. A new constitution adopted in 1982 CE restored some institutions, including an 11-member Council of State, headed by the president, and a 41-member House of Representatives for the People, but the Supreme Military Council remained the sole political body. In 1983 CE, elections were held held for a new parliament. Among the economic reforms was the decision in 1985 CE to join the franc zone, giving a stable currency tied to the French monetary system.

Despite the reforms, Obiang Nguema continued to exercise supreme political control. Several attempted coups were harshly suppressed and the government was accused of many human rights abuses. In 1987 CE, a single new political party—the Democratic Party of Equatorial Guinea (PDGE)—was formed. In 1992 CE, a new constitution introduced a multiparty democratic system, with an elected 80-member National Assembly. Parliamentary elections in 1993 CE were won easily by the ruling PDGE, though only about 20 percent of the electorate registered their votes–most opposition parties having called for a boycott.

Presidential elections were held in 1996 CE, but nearly all the opposition candidates dropped out, complaining of government harassment. Obiang Nguema was reelected, claiming more than 99 percent of the votes in what observers called a "farcical" poll. Parliamentary elections held in 1999 CE resulted in another victory for the PDGE, but again the opposition parties protested that the election was unfair. The economy improved after 1992 CE, when oil was first produced. By 2001 CE the country had become sub-Saharan Africa's third largest oil producer, holding out hopes for the future.

Peoples

BUBIS

The Bubis are the original inhabitants of Bioko island (formerly Fernando Poó), which is now part of Equatorial Guinea. They are descended from Bantu-speaking peoples who probably migrated to the island from nearby Cameroon several centuries ago. Bioko was an important staging post in the slave trade from West and Central Africa to the Americas. The Portuguese reached the island in the fifteenth century and, in 1778 CE, the island became a Spanish colony. The Bubis resisted attempts to provide forced labor on the Spanish plantations and Spain began bringing coastal West Africans to the island–the ancestors of the modern Fernandino population, who came to dominate Equatorial Guinea's economy and politics after independence. Like others, the Bubis suffered greatly during the rule of the brutal dictator Francisco Macías Nguema, a mainlander, in the 1970s.

FANG

The Fang live in mainland Equatorial Guinea and in neighboring areas in southern Cameroon and northwest Gabon. In the early nineteenth CEntury, the Fang gradually migrated southward from the Sanaga River area of central Cameroon to the present location. The Fang were mostly farmers, hunters, and warriors before the arrival of the European colonial powers.

Trading posts and forts were first established on the Gabonese coast by the French in the early nineteenth century and Gabon became part of French Equatorial Africa in 1910 CE. The Fang in what is now Equatorial Guinea came under the control of Spanish colonizers in the late eighteenth century. In Cameroon, the Germans established the protectorate (colony) of Kamerun (now Cameroon). Although the Germans built bridges, hospitals, railroads, and roads. their rule was characterized by harshness, forced labor, and military excesses. During World War I, the British and French divided

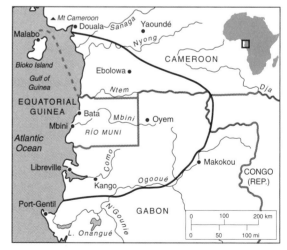

Modern extent of the Lunda peoples

Fang warrior
An illustration of an early twentieth-century Fang warrior.

Cameroon between them. The French increased the cultivation of cash crops, such as cocoa, palm oil, and lumber. This was often achieved at the expense of the Fang, who had to seek work on European plantations in order to pay high taxes, or they were forced to work as conscripts. The first president of independent Equatorial Guinea was Francisco Macías Nguema, a Fang, as also was his nephew, Obiang Nguema, who seized power in 1979 CE. He was elected as president in 1996 CE amid allegations of electoral irregularities.

Equatorial Guinea timeline

Pre 19th Century
c. **1200 CE** Bubi people from the mainland settle Bioko island
1472 Fernão do Po sights Bioko and claims it for Portugal
1777–1778 Portugal cedes its claim to the area to Spain by the treaties of San Ildefonso and Pardo

19th century CE
1843–1858 Spain conquers the area and establishes the colony of Spanish Guinea

1900–49 CE 1900 The borders of Spanish Guinea are fixed by the Treaty of Paris
1936 The colony supports Franco in the Spanish Civil war

1960–69 **1968 Oct 12** The country becomes independent as Equatorial Guinea: Macias Nguema becomes the first president

1970–79 **1970** A one-party dictatorship is declared
1979 Lt.-Col. Teodoro Obiang Nguema Mbsango seizes power in a military coup: Macias Nguema is executed

1990–99 **1992** A multiparty constitution is introduced
1993 The Democratic Party wins 68 of 80 seats in elections
1996 Obiang Nguema is re-elected as president amid allegations of vote rigging
1998 Mass arrests of Bubi separatists on the island of Bioko

Equatorial Guinea presidents

Oct 12 1968–Aug 3 1979 CE
Francisco Macías Nguema (from Jul 14 1972, Francisco Macías Nguema Biyogo; from Sep 26 1975, Macías Nguema Biyogo Ñegue Ndong; from 1976, Masie Nguema Biyogo Ñegue Ndong)

Aug 3 1979 CE–
Teodoro Obiang Nguema Mbsango (chairman of the revolutionary military council until Aug 25 1979, chairman of the supreme military council Aug 25 1979–Oct 12 1982)

Equatorial Guinea's major political figures

Macías Nguema, Francisco (1922–1979 CE)
The first president of Equatorial Guinea (1968–79), Francisco Macías Nguema was a brutal dictator whose reign of terror led to the flight of up to two-thirds of the population. He was deposed in a military coup in 1979, led by his nephew Obiang Nguema Mbasogo, and was executed.

Obiang Nguema Mbsango, Teodoro (1942 CE–)
Obiang Nguema became president of Equatorial Guinea in 1979 after leading a coup against his uncle, President Macías Nguema. Under Obiang, power remained highly centralized and, despite the introduction of a multiparty system, Obiang was re-elected in 1996 with more than 99 percent of the vote. His opponents had withdrawn, objecting to voting irregularities.

ERITREA State of Eritrea

Around 4,000 years ago, immigrants from the interior of Africa settled in what is now Eritrea. Around 3,000 years ago, other migrants arrived from the Arabian peninsula. From the first century CE, Eritrea formed part of the Kingdom of Axum, though the kingdom's capital, also called Axum, now lies in northern Ethiopia. Facing the Red Sea, Axum became prosperous through trading, reaching the height of its power between the fourth and seventh centuries. Its rulers were converted to Coptic Christianity in the fourth century and, from the seventh century, the Christian people clashed with their Muslim neighbours. However, Axum maintained much of its independence until the Ottoman Turks took over in the sixteenth century.

Between the seventeenth and nineteenth centuries, the status of Eritrea was disputed by the Ottoman Turks, Ethiopia, Egypt, and Italy. Italy took the port of Assab in 1882 CE and, by 1899 CE, it had conquered most of the area that is now Eritrea. In 1889 CE, the Treaty of Uccialli between Italy and Emperor Menelik II recognized Italy's possessions on the Red Sea and Eritrea became an Italian colony. Its name came from the Latin name for the Red Sea–*Mare Erythraeum*.

The Italians used the port of Massawa and the territory of Eritrea as a launching pad for its invasion of Ethiopia in 1896 CE and again in 1935–1936 CE. Eritrea then became one of the provinces of a region known as Italian East Africa. Under Italian rule, some plantations and industries were established, but, in 1941 CE, during World War II, British and Ethiopian troops drove out the Italians. Eritrea then came under British military administration. In 1950 CE, the United Nations General Assembly voted to federate Eritrea with Ethiopia as a self-governing unit. This resolution was put into effect in 1952 CE, providing Ethiopia with much-needed ports on the Red Sea, through which it could trade with the outside world. But many Eritreans opposed the incorporation of their territory into their large neighbor.

Independence
One of the first stamps to be issued by newly-independent Eritrea in 1995 CE.

Liberation
This is the insignia of the Eritrean Popular (or People's) Liberation Front (EPLF). The EPLF launched a rebel movement fighting for Eritrean independence from Ethiopia in the 1960s. In 1991 CE, they achieved their goal when Eritrea was liberated from Ethiopia.

Recent history

To maintain its control over Eritrea, Ethiopia banned political parties and trade unions. This provoked the formation of the Ethiopian Liberation Front (ELF) which began a guerrilla struggle for independence in 1961 CE. In 1962 CE, Ethiopia changed the status of Eritrea to that of a province, making Ethiopia a unitary state instead of a federal one. Later, other nationalist groups were formed with different ideologies from the ELF, such as the Eritrean People's Liberation front (EPLF) which, from 1970 CE, split away from the Muslim-dominated ELF and gradually replaced it as the chief guerrilla group.

Following a major famine in Ethiopia, Emperor Haile Selassie I was overthrown by a military coup and the military established a government led by Lt.-Col. Mengistu Haile-Mariam. The EPLF attempted to negotiate independence for Eritrea, but the Soviet-backed government turned down Eritrean demands and continued the civil war. In spite of having inferior weaponry, the EPLF continued its struggle, with women playing an important part on the front lines. Gradually, the EPLF took over large areas of territory and its disciplined personnel set up its own social services and schools.

EPLF victories in 1987 CE and 1988 CE, combined with famine in the mid-1980s and fighting on another front against Somali secessionists in Ogaden, weakened the central government. In 1991 CE, Eritrean, Tigrean and other forces defeated the Mengistu regime. Rebels from Tigre province set up a national government in Ethiopia, while the Eritreans established their own government in Asmara. Following a referendum, Eritrea was declared an independent country on May 24, 1993 CE, with Issaias Afewerki, secretary-general of the EPLF, as its first elected president, leading a transitional government. In 1994 CE, the EPLF converted itself into a political party called the People's Front for Democracy and Justice. A new constitution was ratified in 1977 CE and Afewerki was reelected in presidential elections.

In December 1995 CE, Eritrea had a brief military conflict with Yemen over the Hanish islands in the Red Sea, but, in 1998 CE, the World Court ruled that the islands belonged to Yemen. However, Eritrea's relations with Ethiopia remained cordial until 1998 CE, when fighting broke around the town of Badme on Eritrea's southwestern border. The border conflict widened with the bombing of targets in both countries, including Asmara airport in Eritrea and Mekele in Ethiopia.

Attempts at conciliation failed and the conflict continued into 2000 CE, when Ethiopia launched a major offensive against Eritrea. This led to the signing of a peace plan drawn up by the Organization of African Unity (OAU). Later that year, UN observers arrived and began to carry out the terms of the peace plan, including the creation of a buffer zone along the disputed border. However, the peace agreement confirmed that the boundary would remain the same except for minor adjustments.

Peoples

AFAR

For information on the history of the Afar, *see* **Djibouti (Peoples—Afar)**.

ISSA

For information on the history of the Issa, *see* **Djibouti (Peoples—Issa)**.

TIGRE

The Tigre, or Tigrinya, are one of the largest ethnic groups in Eritrea, while in Ethiopia they form the largest group in the province of Tigre. This Ethiopian province, which lies in the northernmost part of the country, once contained the capital of the Axumite Kingdom (*see also* **Axum, kingdom of**).

The Tigre share an imperial heritage with the Amhara, whose history is described in Ethiopia (Peoples). Members of both groups provided emperors for the throne of the Ethiopian empire. The last Tigre emperor was Yohannes IV, who reigned in the second half of the twentieth century. In more recent times, the Tigre were active in Eritrea's struggle for independence and Ethiopia's fight to establish democracy during the reign of the dictator Haile Mariam Mengistu. The Tigre People's Liberation Front became the most prominent of the groups fighting for the independence of Eritrea.

Eritrean presidents
24 May 1993 CE– Issaias Afewerki

Eritrea timeline		
Pre 19th Century		
	c 1–975 CE	The kingdom of Axum dominates the region of present-day Eritrea
19th century CE		
	1882–1889	Italy conquers Eritrea
1900–49 CE	**1935**	Italians use Eritrea as a base for their conquest of Ethiopia
	1941	The British expel the Italians from Eritrea
1950–59 CE	**1952**	Under a UN agreement, Eritrea is federated with Ethiopia
1960–69 CE	**1961**	Civil war breaks out between the Eritrean Liberation Front (ELF) and the Ethiopian government
1970–79 CE	**1970**	Eritrean People's Liberation Front (EPLF) replaces the ELF as the main Eritrean resistan movement
1980–89 CE	**1987–1988**	EPLF victories end Ethiopian control in Eritrea
1990–99 CE	**1991**	Eritrean and Tigrean rebels overthrow the Ethiopian government
	1993 May 24	Eritrea becomes independent: Issaias Afewerki of the EPLF becomes president
	1998–1999	Armed clashes along the Ethiopian border
2000-09 CE	**2000**	Eritrea and Ethiopia sign a peace treaty to end the border conflict

Border conflict between Eritrea and Ethiopia 1998–2000
There were three significant stages to the conflict.

1 Eritrea gained independence from Ethiopia in 1993 CE. After five years of border disputes Eritrean forces invaded Ethiopia in 1998 CE and captured large tracts of land along the border in the Badine (Yarga) and Shararo districts.

2 The Ethiopian military launched a counter attack in 1999 CE that ended in stalemate along the new border. From mid-1999 to May 2000 CE the border was the scene of World War I-style trench and artillery warfare with huge casualties on both sides. A major Ethiopian offensive launched in May 2000 recaptured most of the lost territories and pushed into Eritrea. Eritrea feared an attempt to reach the coast to capture a seaport.

3 As of 2000, there are five major areas along the border between Ethiopia and Eritrea which both nations claim as their own.

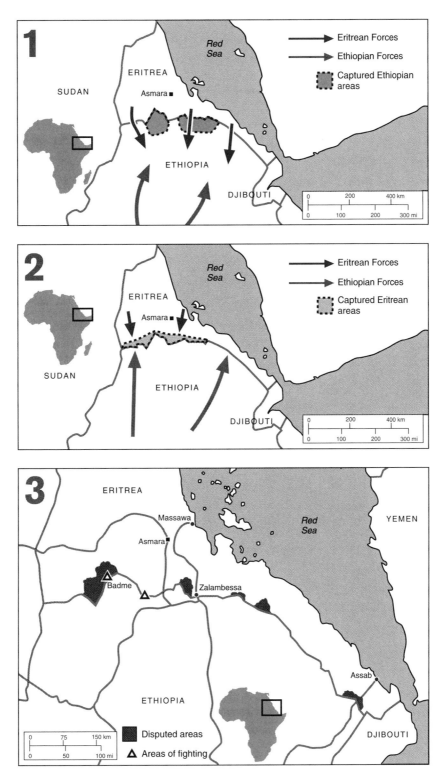

Eritrea's major political figures

Afewerki, Issias (1945 CE–)
Afewerki was a former guerrilla leader in the struggle against the Ethiopian government of HAILE MENGISTU MARIAM. Secretary-general of the Eritrean People's Liberation Front, he was elected president of Eritrea in May, 1993 CE, when the country became independent. He was reelected in 1997 CE.

ETHIOPIA Ityo (Ethiopia)

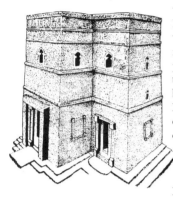

A Christian heritage (above)
Many centuries-old churches were cut out of the rock at Lalibela, Ethiopia. Ethiopia has a long history of Christianity dating back more than 1,700 years.

Ethiopia was known to Ancient Egypt around 4,000 years ago. By around 200 BCE, the region that is now Ethiopia was populated by two main groups of people, Cushites, whose descendants include the Amhara and the Oromo, and Semitic traders from southern Arabia. From the first century CE, northern Ethiopia was part of the Kingdom of Axum. Axum became prosperous through trading, reaching the height of its power between the fourth and seventh centuries. In the fourth century, its king, Ezana, was converted to Coptic Christianity, which became the kingdom's official religion. From the seventh century, Muslims gained control of the Red Sea coastal plains, weakening Axum, and reducing the area occupied by the Christian Amhara people, who gradually became the dominant group in the Ethiopian highlands. In 1137 CE, the Zagwé dynasty began to rule in Ethiopia. Their capital was Roha (now Lalibela) where they built superb churches carved out of the rock. After the fall of the Zagwé dynasty in 1270 CE, the Ethiopian empire was ruled by the Solomonid dynasty, which claimed descent from the Biblical King Solomon and the Queen of Sheba.

Ethiopia's Christian culture interested people in Europe and, in the sixteenth century, the Portuguese helped Ethiopia to expel the Muslim sultan of the Somalis. The unification of Ethiopia began under Emperor Tewodros (Theodore) in the mid-nineteenth century and completed by Emperor Menelik II. In 1896 CE, Menelik's army defeated an Italian force at the Battle of Adowa and, as a result, Ethiopia did not become a European colony.

Recent history

Ras Tafari, who adopted the title of Haile Selassie I in 1930 CE, was Ethiopia's last emperor. His reign was interrupted in 1935 CE when Italy invaded the country. Haile Selassie went into exile in 1936 CE, pleading his country's cause at the League of Nations. In 1941 CE, during World War II, he returned at the head of a British-Ethiopian force, which defeated the Italians. He then resumed his program to modernize the country. In 1952 CE, Eritrea (once Italian Somaliland) was federated with Ethiopia, giving the landlocked country access to Red Sea ports. In 1962 CE, Ethiopia made Eritrea a province, but Eritrean nationalists started a 30-year war for independence.

Haile Selassie's reforms were slow and, after a severe drought had caused famine, a group of military leaders overthrew the emperor and declared the country to be a socialist republic. Lt.-Col. Mengistu Haile-Mariam, who became head of state, broke up the estates of large landowners and redistributed the land among peasant farmers. But the new government faced many problems arising from Ethiopia's ethnic diversity. In addition to the secessionist war in Eritrea, the government also had to contain the Tigre People's Liberation Front and combat the ethnic Somalis in the southern region of Ogaden. The Somali government supported the secessionist Ethiopian Somalis and the Ogaden war continued until 1988 CE.

Eritrean and Tigrean forces finally defeated the Mengistu regime in 1991 CE and the Tigrean-dominated

British invaders
A member of a gun-train in the Ethiopian mountains after the defeat and death of King Theodore II at Magdala in 1868 CE.

Ethiopia and its neighbours 1855–1936 CE

From 1855 CE onward, Ethiopian rulers determined to reclaim their empire and prevent foreign colonization. The first to attempt this was Emperor Tewodros II (reigned 1855–1868 CE) in northern Ethiopia. Yohannes IV (reigned 1872–1889 CE) successfully stopped Egyptian and Mahdist expansion into Ethiopia. Menelik II (the Shoan king from 1864 to 1913 CE) became emperor in 1889 CE. Ethiopia expanded greatly from this time and remained independent of the European powers. In 1884 CE, the Italians made the first of several invasions. In 1896 CE, they were decisively defeated by Ethiopia at the battle of Adowa. After the battle, Menelik signed a treaty to define his empire's borders with the other colonial powers, which by then surrounded his empire. The Italians did not succeed in occupying Ethiopia until 1936 CE.

The Battle of Adowa
Under the command of King Menelik II, Ethiopian forces defeated the Italian army at the Battle of Adowa in 1896 CE and thus preserved the independence of their country. The battle was commemorated in a number of ways, including the illustration (right) and the drawing (below) which is housed in Addis Ababa University. The maps (far right) define the situation in 1860, 1889 and 1896 CE in respect of the colonial powers which then surrounded the Ethiopian empire.

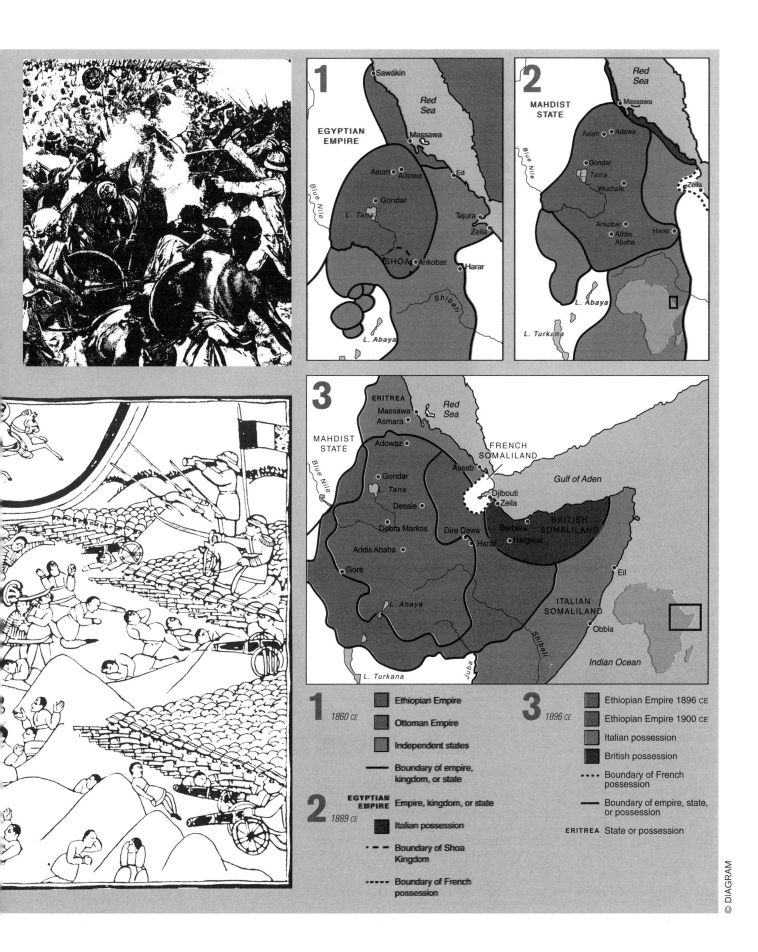

1
Sawákin
Red Sea
EGYPTIAN EMPIRE
Massawa
Axum
Adowa
Ed
Gondar
L. Tana
Tajura
Zeila
Blue Nile
SHOA
Ankobar
Harar
Shibeli
L. Abaya

2
MAHDIST STATE
Red Sea
Massawa
Axum
Adowa
Gondar
Tana
Wuchale
Zeila
Blue Nile
Ankobar
Addis Ababa
Harar
L. Abaya
L. Turkana

3
ERITREA
Massawa
Asmara
Red Sea
MAHDIST STATE
Adowaz
FRENCH SOMALILAND
Assab
Gulf of Aden
Gondar
Blue Nile
L. Tana
Djibouti
Zeila
Dessie
Debra Markos
Dire Dawa
Berbera
BRITISH SOMALILAND
Addis Ababa
Harar
Hargeisa
Gore
Eil
L. Abaya
ITALIAN SOMALILAND
Obbia
Shibeli
L. Turkana
Juba
Indian Ocean

1 *1860 CE*
- Ethiopian Empire
- Ottoman Empire
- Independent states
- —— Boundary of empire, kingdom, or state

2 EGYPTIAN EMPIRE *1889 CE*
- Empire, kingdom, or state
- Italian possession
- – – Boundary of Shoa Kingdom
- ----- Boundary of French possession

3 *1896 CE*
- Ethiopian Empire 1896 CE
- Ethiopian Empire 1900 CE
- Italian possession
- British possession
- ---- Boundary of French possession
- —— Boundary of empire, state, or possession
- ERITREA State or possession

© DIAGRAM

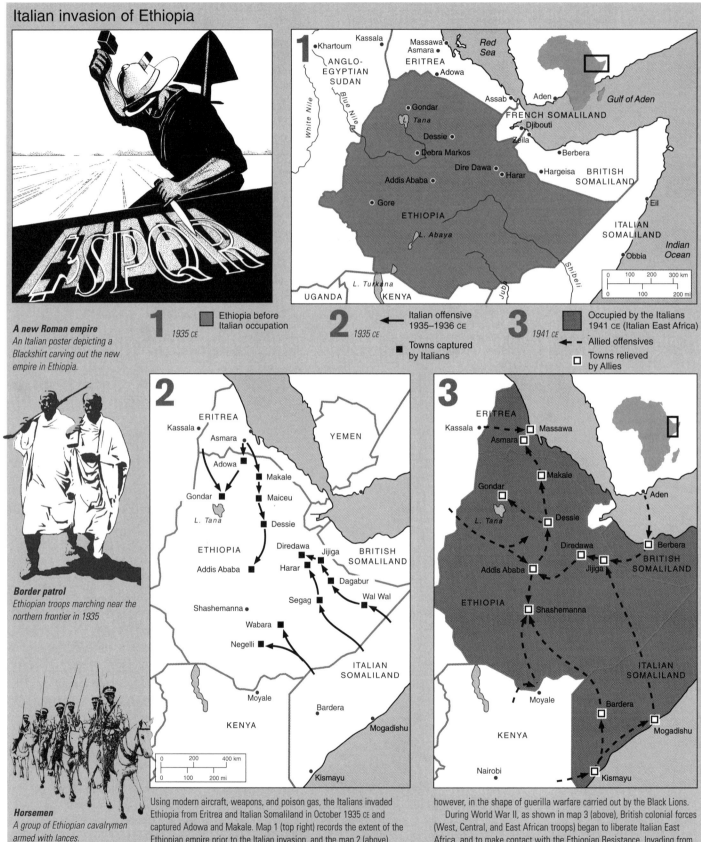

Italian invasion of Ethiopia

A new Roman empire
An Italian poster depicting a Blackshirt carving out the new empire in Ethiopia.

1 *1935 CE* — Ethiopia before Italian occupation

2 *1935 CE* — Italian offensive 1935–1936 CE

■ Towns captured by Italians

3 *1941 CE* — Occupied by the Italians 1941 CE (Italian East Africa)

◄-- Allied offensives

□ Towns relieved by Allies

Border patrol
Ethiopian troops marching near the northern frontier in 1935

Horsemen
A group of Ethiopian cavalrymen armed with lances.

Using modern aircraft, weapons, and poison gas, the Italians invaded Ethiopia from Eritrea and Italian Somaliland in October 1935 CE and captured Adowa and Makale. Map 1 (top right) records the extent of the Ethiopian empire prior to the Italian invasion, and the map 2 (above) defines the main direction of the Italian offensive, and the towns which were captured. The Ethiopian Army was defeated at Maiceu in March 1936 CE. In May, Haile Selassie, the Emperor of Ethiopia, went into exile, and the Italians took the capital, Addis Ababa. Ethiopian resistance continued,

however, in the shape of guerilla warfare carried out by the Black Lions.
During World War II, as shown in map 3 (above), British colonial forces (West, Central, and East African troops) began to liberate Italian East Africa, and to make contact with the Ethiopian Resistance. Invading from Anglo-Egyptian Sudan, Kenya, and British and Italian Somaliland, the Allies relieved Asmara, Jijiga, Diredawa, and Addis Ababa in April 1941 CE, allowing the emperor to return.

Ethiopian People's Revolutionary Democratic Front set up a transitional government in Addis Ababa. It was headed by Meles Zenawi, former guerrilla leader, who became prime minister. Meanwhile, the Eritrean People's Liberation Front established its own regime in Asmara. Eritrea became independent of Ethiopia in 1993 CE, while in 1994 CE Ethiopia adopted a new federal constitution. The constitution divided the country into nine regions, which were based, except for the capital and southern region, on the predominant ethnic group in each region. The regions had their own assemblies and were granted the right to secede, following a referendum.

Relations with Eritrea remained cordial until 1998 CE, when Eritrean forces fought with Ethiopians along a stretch of disputed border around the northwestern frontier town of Badme. The conflict increased in scale, when the Ethiopians bombed Asmara's airport, while the Eritreans bombed Mekele, a town in northern Ethiopia. The war continued until 2000 CE. Following a major Ethiopian offensive, both Ethiopia and Eritrea agreed a ceasefire and peace plan sponsored by the Organization of African Unity. In September 2000, United Nations observers arrived to carry out the terms of the peace plan. This involved setting up a buffer zone between the warring armies and policing it until the border could be demarcated on an internationally agreed basis. However, the agreement confirmed that the border would remain essentially the same except for some very minor adjustments.

Military control (left)
In September 1974 CE Major Mengistu Haile-Mariam (far left) and other members of the ruling committee seized power. He became president and subsequently adopted Marxist policies.

The spoils of war (below)
A Soviet-made Somali tank captured by Ethiopian troops in 1977 CE during the invasion of the Ogaden region.

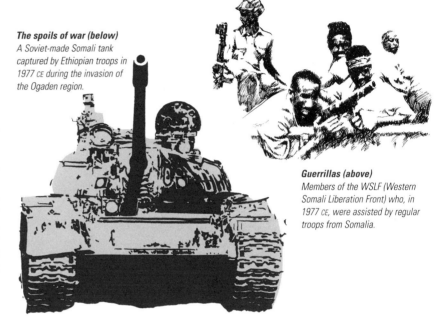

Guerrillas (above)
Members of the WSLF (Western Somali Liberation Front) who, in 1977 CE, were assisted by regular troops from Somalia.

Internal conflict (right)
Government forces and the militant Maitatsine religious movement clashed in 1980 CE, resulting in the deaths of hundreds of people, including its leader. An artist reconstructed the scene in this stylized painting.

Propaganda (left)
A poster issued by the Worker's Party in Ethiopia in 1984 CE.

Ethiopian offensive, May 2000 (right)
A major military offensive was launched by Ethiopia in which it recaptured most of the territories lost to Eritrea in 1998 CE.

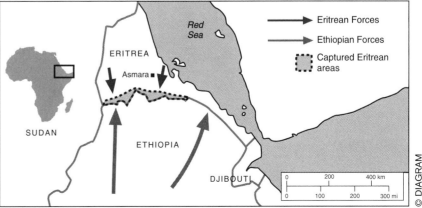

→ Eritrean Forces
→ Ethiopian Forces
▢ Captured Eritrean areas

Red Sea
ERITREA
Asmara ■
SUDAN
ETHIOPIA
DJIBOUTI

| 0 | 200 | 400 km |
| 0 | 100 | 200 | 300 mi |

© DIAGRAM

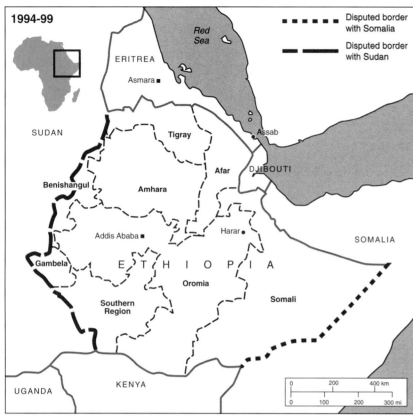

1994-99

Red
Sea

ERITREA

Asmara ■

SUDAN

Tigray

Assab

Afar

DJIBOUTI

Benishangul

Amhara

Addis Ababa ■

Harar ●

SOMALIA

Gambela

E T H I O P I A

Oromia

Southern
Region

Somali

UGANDA

KENYA

------ ■ ■ ■ ■ ■ Disputed border
with Somalia

------ Disputed border
with Sudan

0		200		400 km
0	100	200		300 mi

Disputed borders
*In addition to Eritrea, Ethiopia also
disputed its borders with both
Somalia and the Sudan in the
1990s.*

Ancient kingdom
*A pillar which is over 98 ft (30 m)
high marks the tomb of an Axum
king. The Axumite kingdom
flourished over 2,000 years ago in
Ethiopia.*

Peoples

AFAR

For information on the history of the Afar, *see* **Djibouti
(Peoples—Afar)**.

AMHARA

The Amhara are a Cushitic people whose ancestors
lived in Ethiopia more than 2,000 years ago. The
Cushites were the first food producers in Africa. The
facts that, for thousands of years, the region has been
the site of international trade routes, and that the
Amhara have been influenced by the Semitic cultures
of Arabia, suggest that Arabs and Greeks were probably among the Amhara's ancestors as well as Africans.
The earliest Ethiopian kingdom was centred on Axum
(*see also* **Axum, kingdom of**). According to tradition,
the Queen of Sheba (now part of Yemen) visited King
Solomon in Jerusalem and, together, they produced a
son, Menelik. Solomon allowed Menelik to make a
copy of the Ark of the Covenant, one of the most
sacred Jewish objects. Menelik secretly exchanged the
copy for the real Ark and took it to Axum, where he
founded a kingdom, reigning between about 975 CE
and 950 BCE. However, historical records place the
emergence of this kingdom in the first century CE.

The Kingdom of Axum grew to dominate much of
what is now Ethiopia and southern Sudan, and it also
had great influence over southern Arabia. When the
kingdom's power declined from about 400 CE, the
Amhara from the south of the kingdom gradually
gained political dominance over the Ethiopian Highlands. After Syrians converted Ezana, king of Axum
(320-355 CE) to Christianity, the Amhara gradually
adopted the religion too. The spread of Islam in surrounding areas from the seventh century resulted in the

isolation of the Amhara until the arrival of the Portuguese in the sixteenth century.

For centuries, emperors ruled Ethiopia. Many of
them claimed to be descended from King Solomon and
the Queen of Sheba, the dynasty having been restored
in 1270 CE by King Yekuno Amlak. This Solomonic
dynasty survived both Muslim encroachment and European colonization (apart from the Italian occupation
from 1935–1941 CE) until 1974 CE, when Emperor Haile
Selassie I was overthrown by the military.

ANUAK

The Anuak occupy an area that straddles western
Ethiopia and southern Sudan, though the civil war in
Sudan in recent years has led many Anuak to seek
refuge in Ethiopia. The Anuak are Nilotes, who originated in the cradleland of the so-called River-Lake
Nilotes– southern Sudan. Some time after 1000 CE, the
ancestors of the Anuak migrated south from their
cradleland, reaching present-day Juba in southern
Sudan. From Juba, the Anuak returned north to occupy
their present lands.

ISSA

For information on the history of the Issa, *see* **Djibouti
(Peoples—Issa)**.

KONSO

Konso is the name given to three related ethnic groups
living in southern Ethiopia–the Garati, the Takadi, and
the Turo. They speak similar dialects of the Konso language and live on a region south of Lake Shamo, in the
northern tip of the Great Rift Valley of East Africa. The
Konso are descended from Cushitic ancestors, who
originated in the Ethiopian highlands. They spread out
from their original dispersal site to occupy much of
northeastern Africa, reaching the Kenyan highlands by
1000 BCE. The Konso probably emerged as a separate
ethnic group during the last 1,000 years. The Konso are
concentrated in more than 30 walled towns, designed
to deter surprise attacks. To cultivate sloping land, they
have built huge terraces (steps) into hillsides.

OROMO

The Oromo, who live in southern Ethiopia and part of
northern Kenya, are also called Galla, a name which
they dislike. The Oromo are a Cushitic people, who
originated in the Ethiopian highlands and were the first
food producers in East Africa. Historians think that the
ancestors of the Oromo lived in Ethiopia at least 5,000
years ago. From the highlands of Ethiopia, the Cushites
gradually expanded to occupy most of northeast Africa,
slowly migrating south and east to their present homelands. They began expanding northward in the sixteenth century and, by 1563 CE, they controlled about a
third of Ethiopia. Sometime after 1600 CE, they began
raiding southward and, by 1699 CE, they had reached
Malindi, Kenya. In 1788 CE, one of their chiefs, Ali,
founded the Kingdom of Begemder in central and
northwest Ethiopia. Other Oromo chiefs founded kingdoms in the early nineteenth century. Oromo chiefs
also served as ministers in the Ethiopian government,
which they dominated.

In 1853 CE, Kassa, a former bandit, overthrew Ras Ali
of Begemder and married the successor to the
Begemder throne. In 1855 CE, he made himself
emperor of Ethiopia with the title of Tewodros (or

Theodore) II. He was later overthrown by a British military expeditionary force. In the 1880s, the forces of Menelik II, the Amhara ruler of the Ethiopian province of Shoa, began to overrun Oromia. Menelik made the Oromo into slaves and he and Queen Taitu personally owned 70,000 of them. The unfortunate Oromo people fared little better under the last Ethiopian emperor, Haile Selassie I, or under the Italians who occupied the country from 1935–1941 CE. Thousands of Oromo died in the civil war that racked Ethiopia from the 1960s until 1991 CE.

TIGRE

For information about the history of the Tigre people, *see* **Eritrea (Peoples—Tigre)**.

Modern extent of the Oromo peoples

Holy tomb
The Oromo make frequent pilgrimages to the shrines or tombs of saints and holy figures. This is the tomb of an ancient miracle-worker called Sheikh Hussein, and it is visited by people hoping to benefit from its healing powers. It has been covered with cloths to mark a celebration.

Haile Selassie
Emperor of Ethiopia 1930–1974 CE.

Ethiopia's major political figures

Haile Selassie I (1892–1975 CE)
Originally Ras (Prince) Tafari, Haile Selassie was Emperor of Ethiopia from 1930 until the army deposed him in 1974. He was exiled to Britain during the Italian occupation of Ethiopia (1936–41), and after his return he sought to introduce reforms, but his critics considered that the rate of change was too slow. He was a prominent figure in African affairs, especially in the Organization of African Unity (OAU). He also came to be revered as a divine being by the Rastafarian religious group, which is named after him.

Menelik II (1844–1913 CE)
Menelik II was the king of Shoa, the central province of Ethiopia, and he became Emperor of Ethiopia in 1889. He modernized Ethiopia and kept it from Italian invasion, defeating an Italian army at the Battle of Adowa (modern Adwa) in 1896 and thus preserving Ethiopian independence.

Mengistu, Haile-Maryam (1937 CE–)
Haile-Maryam Mengistu seized power in Ethiopia in 1974 after a revolution that removed the emperor, HAILE SELASSIE I. In 1977, he became Ethiopia's first president. Mengistu pursued socialist policies and received aid from the former Soviet Union, but his period in office was marked by famine and civil war. He was overthrown by rebel forces in 1991 and took refuge in Zimbabwe.

Menelik II
Emperor of Ethiopia 1889–1913 CE.

© DIAGRAM

Sidama Stone
So-called by present inhabitants of the Rift Valley in Ethiopia, these monoliths were believed to have been erected by their predecessors, the Sidama. They probably commemorate deceased warriors or leaders.

International conference
Stamp marking the first session of the Economic Conference for Africa, in 1958 CE.

On the brink of death
Victims of the prolonged drought during the 1980s, and displaced from their homelands by civil wars and invasions from neighboring countries.

Ethiopia timeline

Pre 19th Century

4.4 million years ago Date of the oldest known human fossils, discovered in the Awash region of Ethiopia
c. 1–975 CE The kingdom of Axum dominates northern Ethiopia
c. 350 King Ezana of Axum becomes the first African ruler to be converted to Christianity
639–642 Arab conquest of Egypt cuts Ethiopia off from the rest of the Christian world
1137–1270 The Zagwe dynasty rules Ethiopia
1270 Yekuno Amlak overthrows the Zagwe and founds the Solomonid dynasty
1415 Ethiopians kill the Muslim ruler of Saylac (in modern-day Djibouti)
1492 The Portuguese make contact with the Emperor of Ethiopia
1527 Ahmed Gran of Adal invades Ethiopia
1543 Ahmed Gran killed in battle with an Ethiopian-Portuguese army
1557 A Jesuit mission is sent to Ethiopia
16th century Ethiopia fragments into small semi-independent kingdoms
1632 Jesuits expelled for undermining the Ethiopian Orthodox church

19th century CE

1855 Emperor Tewodros II reunifies Ethiopia
1867 Tewodros imprisons the British consul
1868 Tewodros commits suicide after a British punitive expedition captures his fortress at Magdala
1889 Emperor John killed fighting the Mahdists of the Sudan: he is succeeded by Menelik II
1896 Menelik defeats an Italian invasion at Adowa

1900–49 CE

1916 Emperor Lij Yasu is overthrown after he converts to Islam
1923 Ethiopia becomes a member of the League of Nations
1930 Ras Tafari becomes emperor, adopting the name Haile Selassie
1931 Haile Selassie gives Ethiopia a written constitution
1935 Italy invades Ethiopia
1936 The Italians capture the capital Addis Ababa
1941 The British drive the Italians out of Ethiopia
1948 Ethiopia regains full independence

1950–59 CE

1952 Eritrea is federated with Ethiopia by the UN

1960–69 CE

1961 Eritrean rebels begin a war of independence
1962 Ethiopia formally annexes Eritrea

1970–79 CE

1972–1974 Prolonged drought leads to devastating famine
1974 Emperor Haile Selassie overthrown by a military coup: Lt.-Col. Mengistu Haile-Maryam becomes president and adopts Marxist policies
1974 An insurrection breaks out in Tigre province
1975 Haile Selassie dies in prison
1977 Somalia invades the disputed Ogaden region of Ethiopia

1980–89 CE

1984-1987 Prolonged drought causes famine on a massive scale
1988 Ethiopia and Somalia sign a peace treaty
1989 Mengistu agrees to hold peace talks with the Eritrean and Tigrean rebels but refuses their demands

1990–99 CE

1990 USSR cuts off economic aid to Ethiopia
1991 Mengistu regime overthrown by Eritrean and Tigrean rebels
1992 The Tigrean dominated Ethiopian People's Revolutionary Democratic Front (EPRDF) forms a transitional government
1993 Ethiopia recognizes Eritrea's independence
1994 A new constitution is introduced giving provinces the right to secede
1995 The EPRDF wins the first elections under the new constitution
1998–2000 Armed clashes along the Eritrean border

2000–09 CE

2000 Ethiopia and Eritrea sign a peace treaty
2001 A buffer zone was created along disputed borders

Military service
This is compulsory for all Ethiopian men.

Ethiopian emperors, heads of state and presidents

Solomonic dynasty	Apr 3 1930–Sep 12 1974 CE	Heads of state and chairmen of the provisional military administrative council	Presidents
Mar 1889–Dec 12 1913 CE Menelik II	Haile Selassie (= Ras Tafari Makonnen) (May 2 1936–May 5 1941 in exile)	**Sep 12 1974–Nov 23 1974 CE** Aman Mikael Andom	**Sep 10 1987–May 21 1991 CE** Mengistu Haile-Maryam
Dec 12 1913–Sep 27 1916 CE Iyasu V	**May 1 1936–Dec 17 1936 CE** Ras Imru (regent)	**Nov 28 1974–Feb 3 1977 CE** Tafari Benti	**May 21 1991–May 28 1991 CE** Tesfaye Gebre Kidan (acting)
Sep 27 1916–Apr 2 1930 CE Zauditu (f)		**Feb 11 1977–Sep 10 1987 CE** Mengistu Haile-Maryam	**May 28 1991–Aug 22 1995 CE** Meles Zenawi (interim)
Sep 27 1916–Apr 2 1930 CE Ras Tafari Makonnen (regent)			**Aug 22 1995 CE–** Negasso Gidada

Tewodros (or Theodore) II (c. 1816–1868 CE)

Tewodros II, born Theodore Kassai, reunified Ethiopia, then called Abyssinia, by conquering rival chiefs who had split the country between them. He was crowned king in 1855 as Tewodros II. After failing to form alliances with Britain and France against Ethiopia's Muslim neighbors, he developed a hatred of Europeans and imprisoned a number of them at the fort of Magdala. A British army sent to free them defeated him, and he then shot himself.

Zenawi, Meles (1955 CE–)

Meles Zenawi, an opponent of the military regime of Haile Mariam Mengistu, became head of state of Ethiopia in 1991, at the end of the civil war. He was elected by the Council of Representatives set up by the ruling coalition, the Ethiopian People's Revolutionary Democratic Front. He was reelected in 1994.

Fang

For information on the history of the Fang, *see* **Equatorial Guinea (Peoples—Fang)**.

Fatimids

The Fatimids were Syrian Arabs who conquered and unified the emirates of North Africa over a 60-year period. They overthrew the Aghlabids in the eastern Maghrib in 909 CE, the Idrisids in Morocco in 926 CE, and the Ikshidids in Egypt in 969 CE. The Fatimid dynasty held sway in North Africa until c. 1000 CE, when it started to lose control over some of its territory as it increasingly focused on affairs in the Middle East. Their loss of interest allowed the Omayyads to expand from Spain; the Omayyads took what is now Morocco. Algeria fell to the Hammadids in 1015 CE, and what is now Tunisia to the Zirids in 1041 CE. By 1100 CE, the Fatimid caliphate consisted only of Egypt, although it did exercise loose control over the eastern Maghrib until the mid-1100s. The Fatimids were finally overthrown by the Zangids in 1169 CE. *See also* **Aghlabids**; **Egypt**.

Expansion and contraction
The six maps below and below left show the extent of the Fatimid dynasty at the following times:

1 *909 CE*   **4** *1015 CE*
2 *926 CE*   **5** *1041 CE*
3 *969 CE*   **6** *1100 CE*

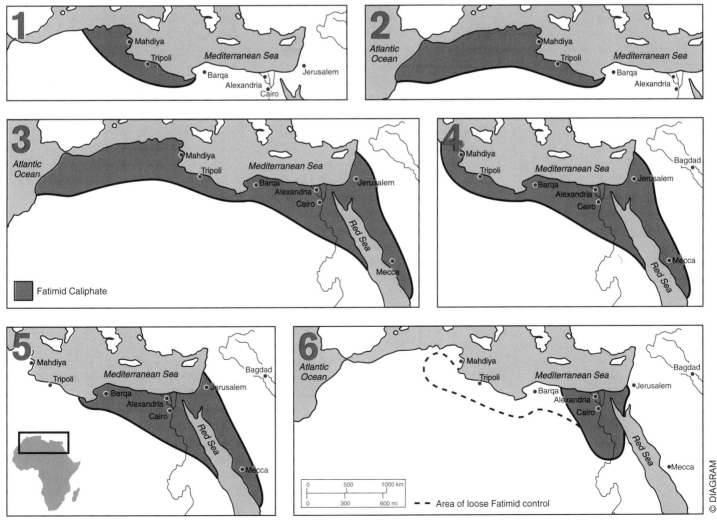

© DIAGRAM

Governor Chacon
A former Spanish colony, the island of Fernando Po gained independence as part of Equatorial Guinea in 1968 CE.

Fort of Sebha
A former Italian colony, Fezzan became independent in 1951 CE and, until 1963 CE , it was a federal republic of the Kingdom of Libya.

Fernando Po

Fernando Po (or Fernando Póo) is the former name of Bioko, the island that, along with mainland Rio Muni, makes up Equatorial Guinea. Around 1469–1472 CE the Portuguese navigator Fernão do Po became the first European to land on the island, which had long been inhabited by Bantu speakers from mainland Africa. He named the island Formosa ("beautiful"). Fernando Po was a Portuguese possession from the late fifteenth century to 1778 CE, when it was ceded to Spain in return for lands in what is now Brazil. The West African island was colonized as part of Spanish Guinea, along with Rio Muni, Annobón, and other islands. From 1960 CE, together with Annobón, it formed an overseas of province of Spain and was made self-governing in 1964 CE. In 1968 CE, the island gained independence as part of Equatorial Guinea. While Macías Nguema was president (1973–1979), Fernando Po was known as Macías Nguema Biyogo. After the overthrow of this brutal dictator, the island was renamed Bioko. *See also* **Annobón**; **Equatorial Guinea**.

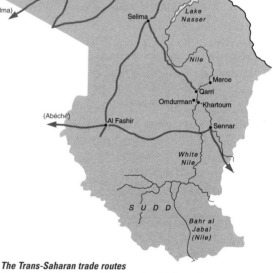

The Trans-Saharan trade routes
The unique position occupied by Fezzan in what is now known as southwest Libya made it both an important point on the Trans-Saharan trade routes, and an obvious target for conquest by colonial powers over the centuries including the Romans, Arabs, and the Turks.

Fezzan

Now a region in southwestern Libya, in ancient times Fezzan—then known as Phazania—was an important station on the trans-Saharan trade routes. This group of lush oases in the Sahara included strategic Ghadames. Fezzan was part of the Roman Empire for the initial centuries of the first millennium. A period of independence was followed by Arab conquest and rule from 666 CE on. This pattern of interchanging local and Arab rulers continued until Fezzan was annexed by the Turkish Ottoman Empire in 1842 CE. In 1911–1912 CE, Italy fought Turkey over possessions in North Africa, and won. Italy occupied the Fezzan and ruled it as one colony (Libya) with Cyrenaica and Tripolitana. This colony became independent in 1951 CE, and until 1963 CE Fezzan was a federal province of the Kingdom of Libya. When the country became a unitary state, all the provinces were abolished. *See also* **Cyrenaica**; **Libya**; **Tripolitana**.

Fipa states *See* **Tanzania (Peoples—Fipa)**.

Fon Kingdom

The kingdom established by the Fon people of West Africa about 400 years ago is better known as the Kingdom of Dahomey. *See* **Dahomey, Kingdom of**; **Benin**.

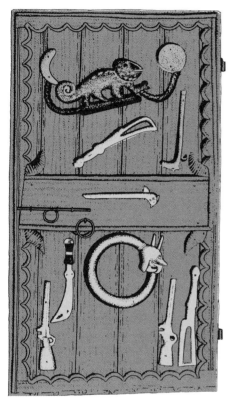

Reliefs
A collage of animals and weapons decorate this wooden door from a royal palace in Abomey, the former capital of the Kingdom of Dahomey. The snake and the chameleon shown feature in many West African legends.

French Cameroun

Most of present-day Cameroon was a French colony–called French Cameroun–from 1919 to 1960 CE (the southern half of the British Cameroons joined with independent Cameroon one year later). *See also* **British Cameroons**; **Cameroon**; **German Cameroons**.

French Congo

From 1897 to 1910 CE the name French Congo referred to all the French colonies in equatorial Africa, namely Gabon, Middle Congo, and Ubangi-Shari (Oubangui-Chari), which then comprised modern Central African Republic. In 1910 CE, these colonies were made into one federal territory called French Equatorial Africa. After 1910, the term French Congo was used only to refer to Middle Congo, now the independent Republic of Congo. *See also* **Central African Republic**; **Congo, Republic of**; **French Equatorial Africa**; **Gabon**.

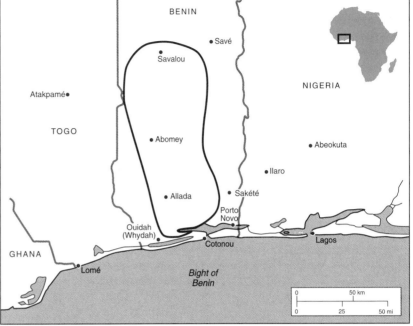

Modern extent of the Fon people

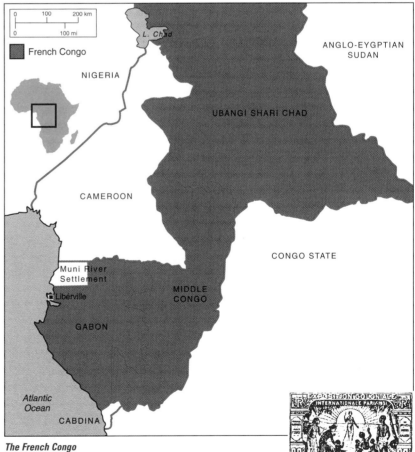

The French Congo
In 1906 it was estimated that the region had a population of six to eight million, of which 1 million were whites.

"France the civilizer"
A stamp issued in 1931 CE which portrayed France as a civilizing influence on indigenous peoples.

© DIAGRAM

The empire awaits you!
A recruitment poster for the French colonial forces issued in 1940–41 CE.

De Brazza and landscape
A stamp issued in 1951 CE celebrating the birth of the French explorer who gave his name to Brazzaville in what is now known as the Republic of Congo.

French colonies (right and far right)
These maps show the areas in Africa which were occupied by France at the following times:

1 1885 CE

2 1895 CE

Marshal Lyautey Statue, Casablanca
A stamp issued in 1946 CE when Morocco was still occupied by the French.

French Equatorial Africa

In 1910 CE all the French colonies in equatorial Africa, namely Gabon, Middle Congo, and Ubangi-Shari (what is now the Central African Republic) were made into one federal territory called French Equatorial Africa. In 1920 CE, Ubangi-Shari-Chad was formed by the addition of what is now the Republic of Chad. In 1960 CE, Ubangi-Shari-Chad became independent as Chad and the Central African Republic; the Middle (or Moyen) Congo as the Republic of Congo; and Gabon as the Republic of Gabon. *See also* **Central African Republic**; **Chad**; **Congo, Republic of**; **Gabon**.

French Guinea

The French protectorate of Rivières du Sud was separated from Senegal as a separate colony in 1890 CE. As French Guinea it became part of French West Africa in 1895 CE. *See also* **French West Africa**; **Guinea**.

Albert Schweitzer
A philosopher, theologian, musician, pastor and winner of the Nobel Peace Prize, Schweitzer studied medicine in 1905 CE to enable him to work as a missionary doctor. His wife trained as a nurse, and they then both moved to Lambaréné on the banks of the Ogowe River in French Equatorial Africa. They were forced to finance a hospital from their own funds as local missionary societies disagreed with Schweitzer's theological views. He had scarcely started his work at the hospital when World War I broke out and, as German subjects living in French territory, they were interned and repatriated to a prison camp in Provence. Unfortunately his wife became ill, and was unable to accompany him upon his return to Africa in 1923 CE. He rebuilt the hospital after the devastation of the war and, while continuing his general medical work, concentrated primarily on the treatment of leprosy until his death, at the age of 90, in 1965 CE.

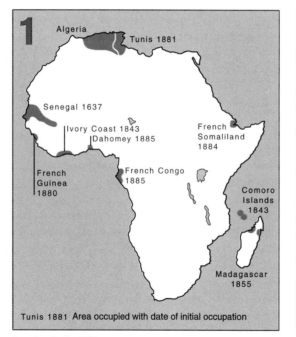

French colonies 1885 CE

Tunis 1881 Area occupied with date of initial occupation

French colonies 1895 CE

Undefined or vague boundary

French Morocco

The French first occupied parts of the Kingdom of Morocco in 1907 CE. They controlled the ports and coastal regions in the bulk of the country, leaving the northern tenth to Spain. The Moroccan sultan's brother led a rebellion and took the throne but was unable to bring the rebellion to a halt. He sought the aid of the French, who demanded that he sign a treaty, in 1912 CE, declaring his kingdom a French protectorate (colony). In 1956 CE French and Spanish Morocco joined with the independent zone of Tangier to constitute the Kingdom of Morocco. *See also* **Morocco**; **Spanish Morocco**; **Tangier**.

French Somaliland

French Somaliland (*Côte Française des Somalis*) was established in 1888 CE. Djibouti became the official capital of French Somaliland in 1892 CE. This French colony acquired the status of an overseas territory in 1948. From 1967 it was called the French Territory of the Afars and Issas, which became independent as the Republic of Djibouti in 1977 CE. *See also* **Djibouti**; **French Territory of the Afars and Issas**.

French Sudan

In the mid-1850s, the French conquered what is now Mali, and it became part of French West Africa. Then called the French Sudan, the area became an overseas territory of the French Union in 1946 CE. In 1958 CE French Sudan was proclaimed the Sudanese Republic, which a year later united with Senegal to form the Mali Federation. Owing to political differences, Senegal left the federation, and in 1960 CE, the remaining territory was proclaimed the independent Republic of Mali. *See also* **French West Africa**; **Mali**; **Senegal**.

French Territory of the Afars and Issas

French Territory of the Afars and Issas is a former name for the Republic of Djibouti. In 1967 CE the name of the colony French Somaliland was changed to the French Territory of the Afars and Issas. The colony became independent as the Republic of Djibouti in 1977 CE. *See also* **Djibouti**.

French Togoland

At the start of World War I, French and British troops occupied German Togoland. The western half became British Togoland, and the eastern half French Togoland. In 1946 CE, British and French territories were placed under the trusteeship of the United Nations. French Togoland became independent as Togo in 1960 CE. *See also* **Togo**.

French West Africa

From 1895–1958 CE the French territories of West Africa were grouped as French West Africa. The colonies of French West Africa were Dahomey (now Benin), French Guinea (now Guinea), French Sudan (now Mali), Ivory Coast, Mauritania, Niger, Senegal, and Upper Volta (Burkina Faso). French West Africa was dissolved in 1958 CE; by 1960 CE all of the former territories were independent nations. *See also* **Benin**; **French Guinea**; **Ivory Coast**; **Mali**; **Mauritania**; **Niger**; **Senegal**; and **Upper Volta (Burkina Faso)**.

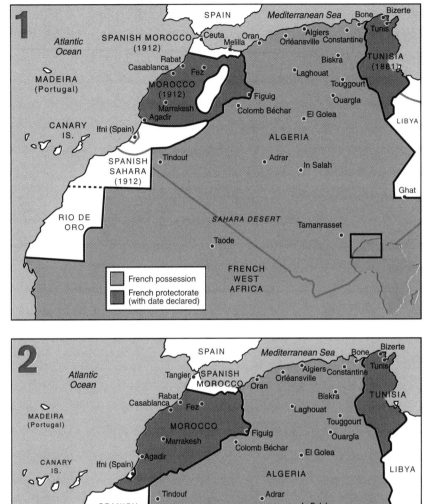

Colonial expansion (above)
These two maps show the extent of French colonial rule in the north-western part of Africa at the following dates:

1 1918 CE

2 1933 CE

Ambush in North Africa
A French army detachment ambushed by Moors in which two officers and two NCOs were killed.

French West African soldiers
A 10c stamp issued at the end of World War II.

© DIAGRAM

Fulani Empire

The Fulani are a West African people with a history of nation building. From the eighth century, they were migrating south into West Africa from what is now Mauritania. They settled in Futa Toro in northern Senegal and Futa Djallon in Guinea, but other Fulanis continued to spread throughout West Africa. By the sixteenth century, they had established themselves at Macina on the Niger River in what is now southern Mali. By the fourteenth century, many Fulani had converted to Islam, and in the 1670s, they launched a series of *jihads* (wars to conquer non-Muslims). Futa Toro, Futa Djallon, Macina, Wali, and Bundu were among the *jihad* states established by the start of the nineteenth century.

The most important of the nineteenth century jihad states was the Sokoto Caliphate, or Fulani Empire, founded by the Muslim scholar, Usman dan Fodio, in the early nineteenth century. A citizen of the Hausa state of Gobir (northern Nigeria), Usman dan Fodio accused the Hausa leaders of being pagans and led a rebellion against them. He claimed the Islam that the Hausas practiced was not pure and criticized them for bad government practices. The Hausa rulers were already unpopular for the high taxes they imposed on their people, and Usman dan Fodio's public speeches on such matters attracted many followers. Muslims from elsewhere in northern Nigeria visited Gobir to meet Usman dan Fodio, who presented them with a flag to carry into battle against their rulers. *Jihads* swept across northern Nigeria, the leaders looking towards Usman dan Fodio for direction. His caliphate had both Fulani and Hausa supporters and spread over large areas of modern northern Nigeria, Benin, and Cameroon. Sokoto was the capital city and today houses Usman dan Fodio's shrine.

After dan Fodio's death in 1817 CE, the empire passed to his son Muhammad Bello, under whom it reached its peak. In 1903 CE, however, the British conquered northern Nigeria and the Fulani Empire. *See also* **Futa Djallon**; **Futa Toro**; **Guinea**; **Macina**; **Nigeria**; **Senegal**; **Tukolor Empire**.

Fulani's major political figures

Usman dan Fodio (1754–1817 CE)

In 1804, Usman dan Fodio, a Fulani ruler and Islamic scholar, proclaimed a *jihad* (Islamic holy war) that led to the creation of a Fulani-Hausa empire–the Sokoto Caliphate–in present-day Benin, Cameroon, Niger, and northern Nigeria. He later handed over power to his son Muhammad Bello, and retired to teach and write.

Fulani warriors
Although guns were available in West Africa during the eighteenth- to nineteenth-century period of jihads (Islamic holy wars), the Fulani jihadists disdained to use them, considering them fit only for slaves. The Fulani shown here were part of the cavalry.

Fulani timeline

Pre 19th Century

700s–1400s CE	Fulani migrate southward and eastward from present-day Morocco and Mauritania
1650	Muslims migrate into Futa Toro and Futa Djallon
1673	Unsuccessful Fulani *jihad* (Islamic holy war) in Futa Toro
1725	First successful Fulani *jihad* launched in Futa Djallon
1775	Second, successful, Fulani *jihad* launched in Futa Toro

19th century CE

1800	Fulani Islamic *jihad* states of Futa Toro, Futa Djallon, Wuli, and Bundu in existence
1804–1809	Fulani *jihad* in Hausaland led by Usman dan Fodio; Sokoto Caliphate established
1827	Independent Islamic state of Macina established
1830	Sokoto Caliphate reaches greatest extent
1852	Al Hajj Umar declares jihad in Futa Toro; Tukolor (Fulani) Empire established
1862	Macina conquered by Tukolor Empire
1893	French defeat Tukolor Empire

1900–49 CE	**1903**	British defeat conquer the Sokoto Caliphate
1950–59 CE	**1950–1970s**	West African states become independent
1960–69 CE	**1960s–1980s**	Recurring drought (period of inadequate rainfall) causes famine in Sahelian countries
1990–99 CE	**1994**	Widespread unrest and economic hardship in African Franc Zone after CFA franc is devalued by 50 percent
	1999	Nigeria returns to civilian rule

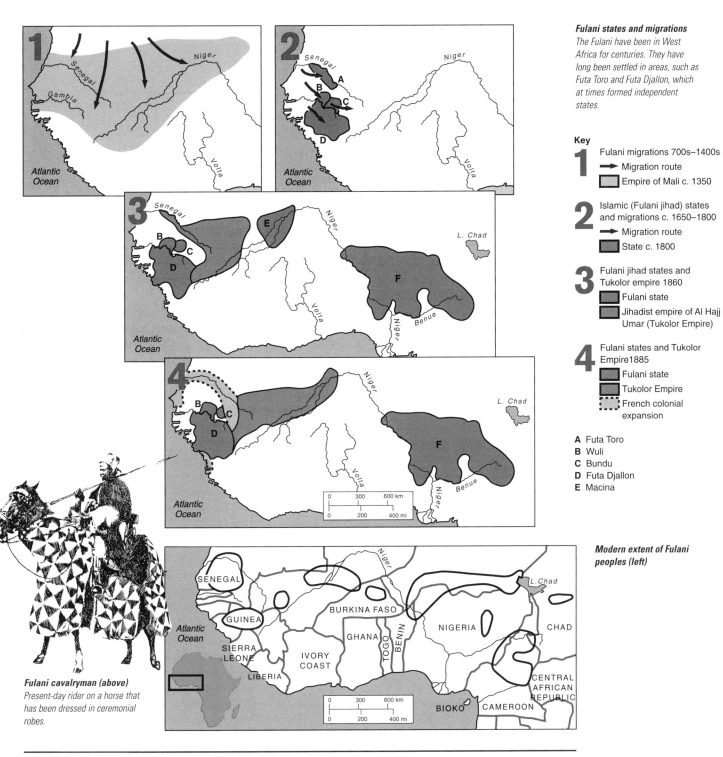

Fulani states and migrations
The Fulani have been in West Africa for centuries. They have long been settled in areas, such as Futa Toro and Futa Djallon, which at times formed independent states.

Key

1 Fulani migrations 700s–1400s
→ Migration route
Empire of Mali c. 1350

2 Islamic (Fulani jihad) states and migrations c. 1650–1800
→ Migration route
State c. 1800

3 Fulani jihad states and Tukolor empire 1860
Fulani state
Jihadist empire of Al Hajj Umar (Tukolor Empire)

4 Fulani states and Tukolor Empire1885
Fulani state
Tukolor Empire
French colonial expansion

A Futa Toro
B Wuli
C Bundu
D Futa Djallon
E Macina

Modern extent of Fulani peoples (left)

Fulani cavalryman (above)
Present-day rider on a horse that has been dressed in ceremonial robes.

Fung sultanate *See* **Sudan (Peoples—Fung)**.

Funj kingdom

During the 1400s, Funj herders migrated north from the Blue Nile and occupied the Christian kingdom of Alodia. Between 1504–1505 CE, the kingdom expanded, and, by the end of the century, the Funj had converted to Islam. Through the seventeenth century, with Arab help, the Funj expanded westward across the White Nile to Kordofan. Funj expansion eastward, however, was prevented by Ethiopia. The Funj reached their greatest extent in the eighteenth century, but it was weakened by increasingly powerful warrior and merchant classes. In 1790 CE, they lost Kordofan to Darfur, and in 1821 CE Funj was invaded and destroyed by Egypt. *See also* **Sudan**.

Fur state *See* **Sudan (Peoples—Fur)**.

© DIAGRAM

Futa Djallon

Futa Djallon is a mountainous region of west-central Guinea that was once the site of an independent Islamic state. The region was first organized by Fulani and Mandingka *jihadists* (Muslim warriors) led by Karamoko Alfa and his successor Ibrahima Sori from the mid-1720s. The Muslim state of Futa Djallon dominated both central and coastal Guinea, until it became part of the colony French Guinea at the end of the nineteenth century. *See also* **Fulani Empire**; **Guinea**.

Futa Toro

The Futa Toro region on the upper reaches of the Séné-gal river was once an independent Islamic state and then the base of an Islamic empire in West Africa. The Torobe Fulani people, led by Suleiman Bal, rose up against their non-Muslim overlords and overthrew their king in 1776 CE in a *jihad* (Muslim holy war). In the mid-nineteenth century Futa Toro was the base of the Tukolor Empire of Al Hajj Umar. *See also* **Senegal**; **Tukolor Empire**.

Ga towns

The Ga (or Gan) people have long been organized into six independent towns: Accra, Osu, Labadi, Teshi, Nungua, and Tema. Each town had a stool as a symbol of religious and political authority; Accra, now the capital of Ghana, was the most important Ga town. *See also* **Ghana**.

GABON Gabonese Republic

Independence
A 1965 stamp depicting President M'Ba, and marking the fifth anniversary of independence.

The earliest people to live in the region that is now Gabon were probably hunter-gatherers. But they were displaced at some unknown time in the Christian era by Bantu-speaking peoples, including the Mpongwe and the Fang. Portuguese mariners first reached the Gabon coast in 1472 CE. They were followed by French, British, and Dutch traders who soon developed the slave trade which dominated the region's economy until the nineteenth century.

The French founded a settlement on the site of Libreville in 1839 CE. Ten years later, the settlement was named Libreville (meaning "free town"), when freed slaves were landed there. Between 1843 and 1886 CE, French naval officers administered the area in conjunction with the administrators of French West Africa. Towards the end of this period, the French began to explore the interior. One important journey was the exploration of the Ogooué (or Ogowe) River by the explorer Pierre Savorgnan de Brazza, who, in 1880, founded the town of Franceville in southeastern Gabon. In 1889 CE, Gabon became part of Middle Congo (now the Republic of Congo), although the local people mounted resistance against colonial rule between 1905 and 1911 CE.

In 1910 CE, Gabon became a separate territory in French Equatorial Africa, which also included what are now Central African Republic, Chad, and the Republic of Congo. In the early twentieth century, French concessionary companies, who used ruthless methods to exploit the region's people and its natural resources, controlled Gabon. Despite many protests, these companies continued to operate until the 1930s.

Recent history

In 1946 CE, Gabon became an overseas territory of France, with its own elected assembly, but, after World War II, nationalists in Gabon began increasingly to call for independence. In 1958 CE, Gabon became an autonomous republic in the French Union and full independence was achieved on August 17, 1960 CE.

Independent Gabon's first president was Léon M'Ba, leader of the Bloc Démocratique Gabonais (BDG). M'Ba had led the struggle for independence and served as president since 1958 CE, although his critics regarded him as too pro-French and conservative. In 1964 CE, M'Ba was overthrown in a coup led by his main rival, Jean-Hilaire Aubame, But when M'Ba appealed to France for help under defense agreements made in 1960 CE, French troops restored him to power. After this failed coup, M'Ba's rule became increasingly authoritarian, but he died in office in 1967 CE.

M'Ba's successor was the vice-president, Albert Bernard Bongo, who adopted Islam in 1973 CE and changed his name to El Hadj Omar Bongo. In 1968 CE, Bongo made the country a one-party state and reconstituted the BDG as the *Parti Démocratique Gabonais* (Gabonese Democratic Party, or PDG), the sole party. Bongo's long period in office, which extended into the twenty-first century, was marked initially by authoritarian rule and conservative policies. However, despite some discontent, the country's political stability, combined with economic policies based on free trade and private enterprise, helped Gabon achieve considerable economic success. By attracting considerable foreign investment, the country developed its abundant mineral resources, including its oil and natural gas reserves, manganese, and uranium. But the high costs of development, combined with the 1974 CE international oil crisis which led to falls in oil revenues, created an economic crisis. Bongo managed to stabilize the country's finances, but the economic setbacks provoked mounting political opposition. Bongo was also criticized by some radical African leaders for his 'moderate' foreign policies. In 1977 CE, Gabon was accused of supporting an unsuccessful coup in Benin, a charge which Bongo strenuously denied.

In 1989 CE, following the discovery of an attempted coup in Gabon, Bongo decided to open up the political system. In 1990, amid considerable political unrest, the government legalized opposition parties. Later that year, despite allegations of voting irregularities, the PDG won a majority of the seats in the 120-member National Assembly. In 1993 CE, Bongo was reelected president, but the opposition parties refused to accept the result and announced plans to set up a rival government. To resolve the crisis, a coalition government was formed in 1994 CE. However, in 1996 CE, the PDG restored its position as the governing party, by winning a large parliamentary majority and, in 1998 CE, Bongo was returned comfortably in presidential elections.

Peoples

BAKOTA

The Bakota (or Koto, or Kota) live mainly in the north and east of Gabon and across the border in neighboring parts of the Republic of Congo. They were probably driven into their current region from the north and west during the nineteenth century by the people who were being pushed onto Bakota lands by Fang expansions. The Bakota are famed for their sculptures, which can be found in museums around the world. The Kota *mbulu-ngulu* sculptures are especially admired. These metal-covered wooden sculptures are reliquary figures–that is, they were used to guard the relics, such as bones, of dead ancestors.

FANG

For information about the history of the Fang, *see* **Equatorial Guinea (Peoples—Fang)**.

Gabon presidents	
Aug 17 1960–Feb 17 1964 CE Léon M'ba (1st time) (acting until Feb 17 1961)	**Feb 18 1964–Feb 19 1964 CE** Jean-Hilaire Aubame (head of provisional government)
Feb 17 1964–Feb 18 1964 CE Revolutionary Committee –Daniel Mbene –Valère Essone –Jacques Mombo –Daniel Mbo Edou	**Feb 19 1964–Nov 28 1967 CE** Léon M'ba (2nd time) **Nov 28 1967 CE–** Albert-Bernard Bongo (from Sep 29 1973, Omar Bongo)

A popular leader
A 1985 CE bank note depicting President Omar Bongo, who was reelected four times to this office.

Gabon timeline	
Pre 19th Century	
13th century CE	The Mpongwe people settle in Gabon
c 1800	The Fang begin to settle in Gabon
1472	Portuguese explore the coast of Gabon
19th century CE	
1839	France establishes a naval and trading post on the present site of Libreville
1849	A group of freed slaves is settled at the station which is named Libreville (free town)
1875	The Fang have become the dominant ethnic group in Gabon
1883	Libreville becomes the capital of the French colony of Gabon
1885	The Berlin conference recognizes French control of Gabon
1889	Gabon becomes part of the French colony of Middle Congo (now Republic of Congo)
1900–49 CE 1910	Gabon becomes a territory of French Equatorial Africa
1940	Gabon supports the Free French in World War II
1946	Gabon is given an elected legislature
1950–59 CE 1957	Gabon is given internal self-government
1960–69 CE 1960	**Aug 17** Gabon becomes independent: Léon Mba is the first president
1964	An attempt to overthrow Mba is crushed by French troops
1967	Mba dies in office: he is succeeded by Bernard-Albert Bongo
1968	Bongo declares Gabon a one-party state
1970–79 CE 1973	Bongo is re-elected president and changes his name to El Hadj Omar Bongo
1974	Construction of the Trans-Gabon railroad begins
1975	Gabon becomes a member of OPEC
1977	Gabon supports an unsuccessful military coup in Benin
1979	Bongo is re-elected president in elections in which he is the only candidate
1980–89 CE 1982	The opposition National Reorientation Movement is suppressed
1984	Bongo gives France permission to build a nuclear plant in Gabon
1986	Bongo is again re-elected president in elections in which he is the only candidate
1989	Riots follow the murder of Joseph Redjambe, the leader of the Gabonese Progressive Party, in Libreville
1990	Opposition parties are legalized: the ruling Gabonese Democratic party wins the assembly elections
1990–99 CE 1993	Bongo retains the presidency after he wins Gabon's first multiparty elections
1996	Gabon withdraws from OPEC
1998	Bongo wins presidential elections with 66 percent of the vote

Gabon's major political figures

Bongo, Omar (1935 CE–)

Omar (formerly Albert-Bernard) Bongo has been president of Gabon since 1967. He also served as prime minister from 1968 until 1976. He made Gabon a one-party state in 1968, and despite some discontent, the country retained its political stability until the late 1980s, when increasing unrest forced a switch to multiparty politics in 1990. Bongo was reelected president in 1993 and 1998.

M'Ba, Léon (1902–1967 CE)

Léon M'Ba became president of Gabon in 1960 when the country became independent. He had earlier served as head of the government from 1957 until 1960. In 1964, with the help of French troops, he survived an attempted coup. He was reelected in 1967, but died later that year and was succeeded by Omar Bongo.

GAMBIA The Republic of The Gambia

A British colony
A stamp issued in 1869 CE when Gambia was governed as part of the colony of Sierra Leone.

Independence
A 1975 CE stamp celebrating the tenth anniversary of Gambia's independence.

Gambia, the smallest country on the African mainland, is a narrow strip of land, occupying both banks of the Gambia River. Between the thirteenth and fifteenth centuries, it formed part of the Mali empire which extended eastward from the Atlantic coast, through what is now Senegal, into the eastern part of present-day Mali.

Portuguese navigators reached the mouth of the Gambia River in 1455 CE and the Atlantic coast eventually became an important center in the Portuguese and English slave trades. The Portuguese sold the trading rights in the area to the English in 1588 CE and, in 1618 CE, the English King James I granted a charter to a company formed for trading in Gambia and what is now Ghana. A settlement was established on James Island in the Gambia River in 1661 CE, but the English had to compete with the French, who were also trying to control the area.

In 1765 CE, Britain set up a colony called Senegambia, which included parts of modern Senegal and Gambia, but Britain ceded Senegal to France in 1783 CE. The abolition of the slave trade by Britain in 1807 CE initially reduced Gambia's importance, though Britain founded the settlement of Bathurst (now Banjul) in 1816 CE. Gambia became a British colony in 1843 CE and, between 1866–1888 CE, it was governed as part of the colony of Sierra Leone. The colony's borders were fixed in 1889 CE and, in 1893 CE, Britain declared a protectorate over the interior. Finally, in 1902 CE, Britain controlled the entire area which now forms Gambia.

Recent history

Before World War II, British rule made little impact on Gambia which was governed largely through nominated local chiefs. After World War II, in which Gambian troops served in the British army, economic development accelerated as Britain improved the infrastructure and tried to diversify production. One ambitious project supported by the British government in the late 1940s was an attempt to produce eggs on a large scale around the town of Yundum in western Gambia. The Yundum project proved to be a disaster in financial terms, because of unforeseen problems. Large numbers of birds died of fowl typhoid, while suitable poultry feed was not available in the country.

Political development was also slow and the first modern political parties did not emerge until the 1950s and they were confined mainly to the Wolof people in Bathurst (now Banjul). Sir Dawda Jawara's Protectorate People's Party (later renamed the People's Progressive Party), founded in 1960 CE, was the first to draw support from people in the interior, including the Manding. Gambia achieved internal self-government in 1963 CE and it became fully independent on February 18, 1965 CE. In 1970 CE, the country became a republic, with Jawara, the former prime minister, becoming the first president. The main concerns of the government were the development of the economy and relations with Senegal. Tourism increased quickly, especially after the publicity given to Gambia by Alex Haley's book *Roots* (1976), and the subsequent television series.

In 1967 CE, Gambia and Senegal concluded a treaty of association and, six years later, talks were held on the proposed unification of the two countries. In 1978 CE, relations with Senegal grew closer with the creation of the Gambian River Development Organization, which was intended to develop the river for the benefit of both countries. After an attempted coup in Gambia in 1981 CE, when Senegalese troops helped to put down the rebels, the Confederation of Senegambia was established in 1982 CE. Under the agreement establishing the confederation, both countries maintained their independence, but integrated their military and monetary resources. However, Gambia drew back in 1989 CE when the confederation was dissolved.

In 1994 CE, after soldiers had rampaged through Banjul demanding back pay, Captain Yahya Jammeh deposed Jawara in a bloodless coup. Jammeh became head of the new military government and all political activity was suspended. In 1996 CE, under a new constitution which restored civilian rule, members of the Military Council resigned in order to join a new party, the Alliance for Patriotic Reorientation and Construction (APRC). Presidential elections in 1996 CE resulted in a victory for Jammeh over three opponents, while the APRC won 33 out of the 45 seats in the National Assembly in 1997 CE. Political parties active during the years of Jawara rule were barred from participation in the elections and, in the late 1990s, Jammeh was criticized for his authoritarian rule and abuses of human rights.

Peoples

DYULA

For information about the history of the Dyula, *see* **Burkina Faso (Peoples—Dyula)**.

FULANI

For information about the history of the Fulani, *see* **Fulani states**.

MANDING

For information about the history of the Manding, *see* **Mali (Peoples—Manding)**; **Mandinko empire**.

SONINKE

For information about the history of the Soninke, *see* **Burkina Faso (Peoples—Soninke)**.

WOLOF

The Wolof (or Jolof, Djollof, or Yolof) live in both Gambia and Senegal. Positioned with the Sahara to the north and the Atlantic in the west, the Wolof became powerful from involvement in both the Atlantic and Saharan trades. By the end of the fifteenth century, the Wolof Kingdom had become an empire, with much of modern-day Senegal under its control. The empire was divided into separate kingdoms: Djollof, which lay inland, and Baol, Caylor, Sine, Saloum, and Walo on the coast. Each *burba*, or king, was elected, and sixteenth-century Portuguese travelers recorded that the Burba Djollof had an army that was more than 100,000-strong.

Gambian presidents
Apr 24 1970–Jul 22 1994 CE Sir Dawda Jawara
Jul 22 1994 CE– Yahya Jammeh (chairman of the armed forces provisional ruling council until Sep 28 1996; head of state until Oct 18 1996)

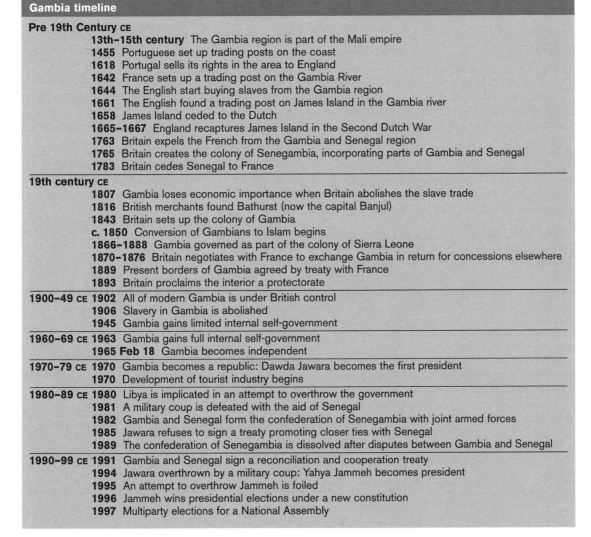

Gambia timeline

Pre 19th Century CE

13th–15th century	The Gambia region is part of the Mali empire
1455	Portuguese set up trading posts on the coast
1618	Portugal sells its rights in the area to England
1642	France sets up a trading post on the Gambia River
1644	The English start buying slaves from the Gambia region
1661	The English found a trading post on James Island in the Gambia river
1658	James Island ceded to the Dutch
1665–1667	England recaptures James Island in the Second Dutch War
1763	Britain expels the French from the Gambia and Senegal region
1765	Britain creates the colony of Senegambia, incorporating parts of Gambia and Senegal
1783	Britain cedes Senegal to France

19th century CE

1807	Gambia loses economic importance when Britain abolishes the slave trade
1816	British merchants found Bathurst (now the capital Banjul)
1843	Britain sets up the colony of Gambia
c. 1850	Conversion of Gambians to Islam begins
1866–1888	Gambia governed as part of the colony of Sierra Leone
1870–1876	Britain negotiates with France to exchange Gambia in return for concessions elsewhere
1889	Present borders of Gambia agreed by treaty with France
1893	Britain proclaims the interior a protectorate

1900–49 CE

1902	All of modern Gambia is under British control
1906	Slavery in Gambia is abolished
1945	Gambia gains limited internal self-government

1960–69 CE

1963	Gambia gains full internal self-government
1965 Feb 18	Gambia becomes independent

1970–79 CE

1970	Gambia becomes a republic: Dawda Jawara becomes the first president
1970	Development of tourist industry begins

1980–89 CE

1980	Libya is implicated in an attempt to overthrow the government
1981	A military coup is defeated with the aid of Senegal
1982	Gambia and Senegal form the confederation of Senegambia with joint armed forces
1985	Jawara refuses to sign a treaty promoting closer ties with Senegal
1989	The confederation of Senegambia is dissolved after disputes between Gambia and Senegal

1990–99 CE

1991	Gambia and Senegal sign a reconciliation and cooperation treaty
1994	Jawara overthrown by a military coup: Yahya Jammeh becomes president
1995	An attempt to overthrow Jammeh is foiled
1996	Jammeh wins presidential elections under a new constitution
1997	Multiparty elections for a National Assembly

Sir Dawda Jawara
Gambia's longest-serving head of state, he served as prime minister from 1963–1970 CE*, and president from 1970–1994* CE*.*

Gambia's major political figures

Jammeh, Captain Yahya (1965 CE–)

Jammeh seized power during a military coup in Gambia in 1994, when he became Chairman of the Armed Forces Provisional Ruling Council. He was elected president in 1997 when civilian rule was restored. He joined the army in 1984 and was commissioned in 1989, becoming a captain in 1994.

Jawara, Alhaji Sir Dawda Kairaba (1924 CE–)

Sir Dawda Jawara was the longest-serving Gambian head of state. He was prime minister from 1963 to 1970, and president from 1970 until 1994. He survived several attempted coups, but was finally deposed by a military junta in 1994. A group of junior officers then took over the government.

Gaza

In the first half of the nineteenth century, the Zulu king Shaka was establishing his kingdom in what is now South Africa. One of the kingdoms he defeated in the process was the Ndwandwe kingdom of King Zwide. During and after Shaka's Zulus merciless attack on the Ndwandwe capital at the end of the 1818–1819 CE war, refugees fled from their homelands. Two Ndwandwe generals, Soshangane and Zwangendaba, led the remnants of their army north into what is now southern Mozambique. Soshangane reorganized his people and established a powerful military state that he named Gaza, after his grandfather. Gaza stretched from Delgoa Bay to the Zambezi valley. The state grew rich by raiding and extracting tribute, including some from European settlements on the coast, and from trading in ivory. War captives were sold as slaves to the Portuguese. The citizens of Gaza were known as the Shangaan, while the ruling and military elite were known as Ngoni. Four years of civil war followed Soshangane's death in 1858 CE, but the state remained powerful enough to be a major obstacle to the Portuguese takeover of Mozambique in the 1890s. Gaza was finally defeated by the Portuguese, in 1898 CE. *See* **Mozambique (Peoples—Ngoni); Ndwandwe; Zulu.**

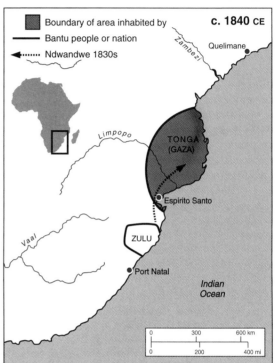

Area occupied by the Bantu people c.1840 CE

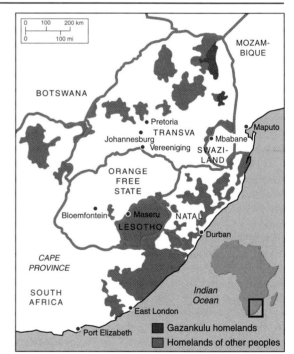

Shangane warrior
An early twentieth-century photograph of an old warrior in traditional costume.

Gazankulu

Gazankulu was a nonindependent black homeland in northeastern Transvaal, South Africa, made up of four separate pieces of land. During South Africa's era of white-minority rule and, later, apartheid ("separate development"), black South Africans were forced to live in so-called homelands that were designated according to their ethnic group. Gazankulu was created for Shangaan and Tsonga people. The Tsonga people, the inhabitants of the area, were joined by Shangaan migrants from Gaza in what is now Mozambique. A final wave of Shangaan refugees arrived after the Gaza kingdom was conquered by the Portuguese in 1898 CE. Gazankulu was officially made self-governing in 1973 CE but had no real power or resources. After South Africa's first multiracial elections and the end of the apartheid era, Gazankulu became part of the new Northern province in 1994 CE. *See also* **South Africa**.

The Gazankulu, and other homelands, in 1985 CE.

German Cameroons

British missionaries determined to help stamp out the slave trade were active in what is now southern Cameroon in the early nineteenth century and it was the British who founded the region's first permanent European settlement, Victoria, in 1858 CE. However, during the "scramble for Africa," Germany, not Britain, took over the area. Germany proclaimed a protectorate (colony) over the region on July 12, 1884 CE and extended its control inland. The new territory was called Kamerun, or German Cameroons. At the start of World War I, the territory was occupied by both British and French troops and partitioned between the two countries.

German East Africa

Between the 1890s and World War I, present-day Rwanda and Burundi, the continental portion of Tanzania, and a small part of Mozambique comprised German East Africa. Rwanda and Burundi formed Ruanda-Urundi, and mainland Tanzania was known as Tanganyika. In 1891 CE, the German imperial government took over administration of the area from the commercial German East Africa Company. The colony was not completely under German control until 1907 CE. During the war, German East Africa was occupied by the British. The Versailles Treaty (1919 CE) gave most of Germany's colonies to Britain, except for Ruanda–Urundi, which passed to Belgium. *See also* **Burundi**; **Mozambique**; **Rwanda**; **Tanzania**.

German possessions in Africa
Germany's colonial influence in Africa in 1895 CE was centered in four main areas: Togoland, Cameroon, German East Africa, and German South West Africa.

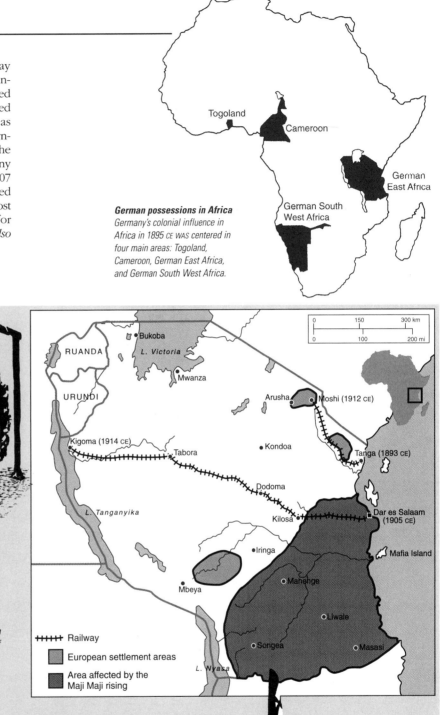

Railway

European settlement areas

Area affected by the Maji Maji rising

German East Africa

Execution (above)
German soldiers hanging Africans durring the Maji Maji rebellion in East Africa in 1905 CE.

Maji Maji uprising, 1905 CE (right)
Economic changes designed to stabilize German rule in German East Africa resulted in a form of inter-tribal solidarity to resist German rule that was given expression in the Maji Maji rebellion.

After the battle (right)
Wounded soldiers resting after the battle of Massiwa in October 1917 CE, one of the last conflicts in the German East Africa Campaign.

'Askari 'soldiers (right)
During World War I in German East Africa, many Africans fought in the colonial armies. The photograph (right) shows a typically-dressed soldier carrying a flag, while the Swahili sculpture (far right) portrays a soldier in a more stylized way.

© DIAGRAM

German Southwest Africa

In 1884 CE Germany declared Southwest Africa (present day Namibia) a protectorate (colony). German rule in Southwest Africa has been described as the most brutal regime in the whole of Africa. In the following decades, rebellions were so harshly suppressed that the Herero peoples were almost exterminated, concentration camps were set up, and settlers treated African workers with great brutality. In 1915 CE, South Africa occupied Southwest Africa, and remained there illegally until 1990 CE. *See also* **Namibia**; **South West Africa**.

Hendrik Witbooi
A former collaborator with the Germans against the Herero, he then led the Nama people against German rule. After a long and bitter struggle he was killed in battle in 1905 CE.

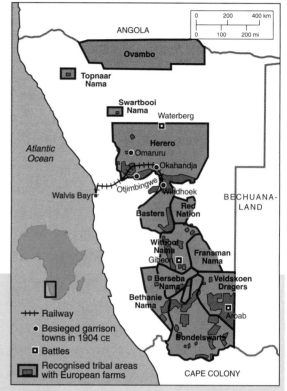

+++ Railway
● Besieged garrison towns in 1904 CE
▣ Battles
▣ Recognised tribal areas with European farms

The Herero and Nama rebellions 1904–5 CE

German East Africa

Maherero
Orlam-Afrikaner bandits, who had settled at Windhoek around 1840 CE, subjected local people to their rule. One of the Herero chiefs even sent his son, Maherero, to Windhoek to lead Herero mercenaries fighting for the Afrikaners

Victims of the massacres
Following a revolt in 1904 CE, the German colonial authorities massacred the Herero people. More than three-quarters died as a result of the massacres; they were either killed outright, or died from starvation.

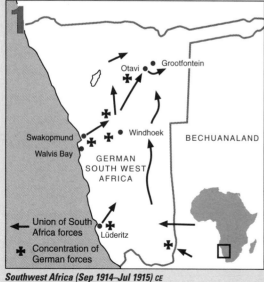

Union of South Africa forces
✚ Concentration of German forces

Southwest Africa (Sep 1914–Jul 1915) CE

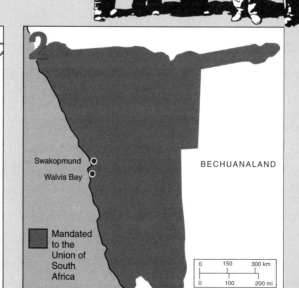

▣ Mandated to the Union of South Africa

Southwest Africa 1920 CE

A chain gang
African prisoners in German Southwest Africa were chained together by their necks when they were marched to work.

Territorial losses (left and far left)
These maps show the situation in German Southwest Africa as follows:

1 *German territories fell within 12 months of the Allied invasions in 1914 CE.*

2 *After the war, the territories were mandated by the League of Nations to neighboring colonial powers.*

German Togoland

See **Togoland**.

Ghadames

Ghadames (or Ghudamis) is an oasis in northwestern Libya, near the Tunisian and Algerian borders. Situated at the junction of ancient Saharan caravan routes, the town was an important trade depot. It was also the site of the ancient Roman stronghold Cydamus before the Christian era and then an episcopal *see* under the Byzantines. The Arabs conquered the oasis in the seventh century, but relinquished it to Tunisian rulers. In the sixteenth century, it fell to the Turkish Ottoman Empire as part of Tripoli. In 1911–1912 CE, Italy took Tripolitana and Cyrenaica from Turkey. *See also* **Libya**.

GHANA Republic of Ghana

Modern Ghana was named after the ancient Ghana empire which lay to the northwest. Although no part of modern Ghana lay within the boundaries of ancient Ghana, many historians believe that the ancestors of the Akan people came from the north and settled in the forests and coastlands of modern Ghana from the fourteenth century. There, they founded kingdoms, the most powerful of which was that of the Asante. Between the fourteenth and sixteenth centuries, northern Ghana probably came under the influence of Mande traders and Hausa merchants, while, in the southeast, the Ewe founded an important society.

In 1471 CE, Portuguese mariners reached the area, which was called the Gold Coast. In the seventeenth century, the Dutch captured Portuguese forts and the coast became a major area for slave trading. Danish and English traders competed with the Dutch and, by 1872 CE, Britain was in control of the coast. In 1874 CE, Britain won the Second Asante War and made the Gold Coast a British colony. In 1901 CE, Britain made the north a protectorate (colony). After World War I, the western part of the former German Togoland was mandated to Britain and Britain ruled it as part of the Gold Coast. British Togoland became part of the Gold Coast in 1956 CE. After World War II, nationalist opposition to British rule mounted and the country achieved internal self-government in 1952 CE. Kwame Nkrumah became prime minister in 1952 and he led his country to independence on March 6, 1957 CE, when Gold Coast was renamed Ghana.

Recent history

Ghana was the first black African colony to win independence and African nationalists throughout the continent regarded Ghana as the spearhead of the liberation of the rest of Africa. Nkrumah, the apostle of pan-Africanism, who believed in the creation of a socialist United States of Africa, became president when Ghana became a republic in 1960 CE. However, his reputation suffered in 1964 CE, when Ghana became a single-party nation, looking increasingly to the Communist bloc for its political inspiration, trade, and aid. Nkrumah encouraged a personality cult, while his rule became increasingly authoritarian. The economy weakened as cocoa prices fell and Ghana was plunged into debt by vast expenditure on development projects, corruption, and mismanagement.

In 1966 CE, Nkrumah, who had survived earlier assassination attempts, was overthrown by a military coup. The new military council suspended the constitution,

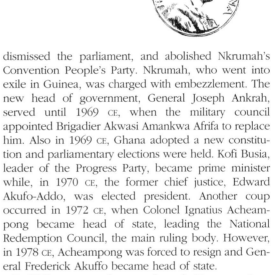

Republic Day honor
A medal awarded to all those who were serving on July 1, 1960 CE.

dismissed the parliament, and abolished Nkrumah's Convention People's Party. Nkrumah, who went into exile in Guinea, was charged with embezzlement. The new head of government, General Joseph Ankrah, served until 1969 CE, when the military council appointed Brigadier Akwasi Amankwa Afrifa to replace him. Also in 1969 CE, Ghana adopted a new constitution and parliamentary elections were held. Kofi Busia, leader of the Progress Party, became prime minister while, in 1970 CE, the former chief justice, Edward Akufo-Addo, was elected president. Another coup occurred in 1972 CE, when Colonel Ignatius Acheampong became head of state, leading the National Redemption Council, the main ruling body. However, in 1978 CE, Acheampong was forced to resign and General Frederick Akuffo became head of state.

In 1979 CE, yet another coup brought Lieutenant Jerry Rawlings to power and Afrifa, Acheampong, and Akuffo were executed. A civilian government was elected in 1979, but the new president, Hilla Limann,

Opoku Ware II
The Asantehene, or King, of the Ashantis in Ghana from 1970 CE.

Nkrumah's downfall
Nkrumah was overthrown by a military coup in 1966 CE, a fall from power reflected by this broken statue of the former president.

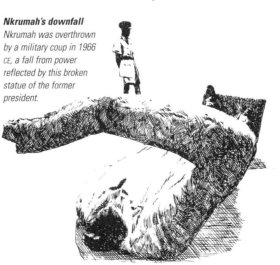

Freedom Day
A 1959 CE stamp marking Africa Freedom Day.

Soldiers
Two typically-dressed, and extremely well-armed, members of the Ghanaian army. Note the knives attached to their shoulders as well as the firearms.

Independence celebrations
This strip is one of a collection which was woven to celebrate the independence of the Gold Coast in 1957 CE, when the country was renamed Ghana. The inlay picture depicts the actual inkpot and pen which were used to sign the Instrument of Independence.

faced appalling economic problems. In 1981 CE, Rawlings, who had become a leading critic of Limann, staged a second coup and became chairman of the Provisional National Defense Council, in which supreme power was vested. He abolished political parties, dissolved parliament, and suspended the constitution. At first, Rawlings tried to restore the economy with socialist measures, but he was soon forced to adopt austerity programs to prevent economic collapse.

In 1988 CE, Rawlings began political liberalization and, in 1991 CE, he announced a return to multiparty democracy. A new constitution, with a presidential system based on that of the United States, was approved in 1992 CE. Under this constitution, Rawlings, candidate of the National Democratic Congress (NDC), was elected president and, because the opposition boycotted the elections, the NDC won nearly all the seats in the legislature. Despite continuing problems and ethnic conflict, Rawlings was reelected as president in 1996 CE. He was defeated in December 2000 CE, however, by the opposition candidate John Kufuor.

Peoples
AKAN
The Akan form a large family of related ethnic groups who live in southern Ghana and the southeastern Ivory Coast. The Asante and Fante of Ghana are Akan peoples, as also are the Anyi of the Ivory Coast. For information about the history of the Anyi people, *see also* **Ivory Coast (Peoples—Anyi)**.

Between the thirteenth and fifteenth centuries, a number of small groups of Akan-speaking peoples, including the Asante and Fante, settled in the forested regions of what is now Ghana. Several important Akan states developed in the area in response to the profitable gold trade and the region came to be known as the Gold Coast. The Asante was the greatest of these states, reaching the height of its powers in the nineteenth century. While Asante's wealth was based on its trade with Europeans, the gold mining industry in the Akan forest region was well developed before contact with Europeans by Dyula traders from the north, *see also* **Burkina Faso (Peoples—Dyula)**. The Dyula sold the gold to Arab traders traveling across the Sahara.

ASANTE
The Asante (or Ashanti), Ghana's largest ethnic group, live mostly in the forest regions of south-central part of the country. They are one of the Akan-speaking groups in West Africa and are descended from people who settled in what is now Ghana between the eleventh and thirteenth centuries,

The Asante chiefdoms were united by Osei Tutu in the 1670s, when he took the title of *asantehene* (king) and founded the Asante Empire. Osei Tutu fell in battle in 1717 CE and was succeeded by Opuku Ware, who continued the Asante expansion. By the time of his death in 1750 CE, the Asante Empire was the largest and most powerful state in the region. Much of the Asante success lay in the strength and flexibility of its fighting units and battle formations. Its prosperity was based on mining and trading in gold and also in slaves, with both the Europeans, who visited the coast (which came to be known as the Gold Coast), and with other African kingdoms to the north.

At its height under Osei Bonsu, who ruled from 1801 to 1824 CE, the Asante Empire covered all of modern Ghana, as well as parts of Burkina Faso, Ivory Coast, and Togo. The Fante people on the Gold Coast were conquered in 1816 CE. This brought the Asante increasingly into conflict with the British, who wanted to control the gold trade. The result was a series of Anglo-Asante wars. In the first, in 1824 CE, the Asante defeated the British. In the second, in 1826 CE, the Asante were defeated, but the British did not pursue their victory. In 1863 CE, the Asante twice defeated joint Anglo-Fante troops. When Asante troops crossed the Pra River in 1874 CE–to reconquer the Fante–they were driven back by the British, who invaded the Asante capital, Kumasi, and blew up the royal palace, leaving the empire in disarray. Agyeman Prempe I became *asantehene* in 1888 CE and began reuniting the Asante. Nervous of his success, the British forced him into exile in 1896 CE and declared the Asante Kingdom (Prempe never recovered the full empire) a protectorate (colony). A further war followed in 1900 CE, led by the *ohemmaa* (most senior woman). Despite great resistance, the Asante were defeated and the British annexed their lands in 1902 CE.

Modern extent of the Ewe peoples

EWE
The Ewe live mostly in the area around the southern end of the border between Ghana and Togo. They are closely related to the Fon, *see also* **Benin (Peoples—Ewe)**. According to Ewe oral history, the Ewe migrated to their present lands from what are now Benin and Nigeria in the mid-seventeenth century. For many years, the coastal Ewe traded with Europeans, at first selling war captives as slaves and–when the slave trade ended– selling raw materials, such as copra (the dried "meat" of coconuts) and palm oil. In the late nineteenth century, the western Ewe came under British colonial rule in what was then known as the Gold Coast, while the Germans ruled the eastern Ewe in German Togoland. After World War I, Togoland became a joint British and French protectorate (colony). When the Gold Coast was about to become independent as

Ghana in the 1950s, some Ewe in Togoland voted to join Ghana. The rest are now in independent Togo.

FANTE

The Fante are an Akan people who live in a small region of south-central Ghana, the southern border of which is formed by the coastline. The coast was once part of the famed "Gold Coast"–a region that grew rich from trading in gold, and later in slaves. Gold was traded long before contact was made with the Europeans, but several Fante states, based as they were near the coast, grew especially wealthy from trading with Europeans before they were eclipsed by the much larger Asante Empire. The Asante conquered the Fante in 1816 CE. By the late nineteenth century, however, Asante power was weakening and the Fante launched a joint, but unsuccessful, offensive against the Asante, with the British, in 1863 CE.

MAMPRUSI

The Mamprusi, one of the ethnic groups which make up the Mossi people, live in a region of northern Ghana bounded on the north by the White Volta River. They probably emerged as a distinct group in the fifteenth century, when a cavalry group from northern Ghana rode north in search of land. These people established the seven main Mossi kingdoms, one of which was Mamprusi. Historically, the king had an important religious as well as political role., but this role diminished in the late twentieth century as more and more Mamprusi converted to Islam.

MOSSI

For information about the history of the Mossi people, *see also* **Burkina Faso (Peoples—Mossi)**.

Ghanaian Presidents

Jul 1 1960–Feb 24 1966 CE Kwame Nkrumah	**Aug 7 1970–Aug 31 1970 CE** Nii Amaa Ollennu (acting)	**Jul 5 1978–Jun 4 1979 CE** Fred W.K. Akuffo (chairman of the supreme military council)	**Dec 31 1981 CE–** Jerry John Rawlings (2nd time) (chairman of the provisional national defense council until Jan 7 1993)
Feb 24 1966–Apr 2 1969 CE Joseph Arthur Ankrah (chairman of the national liberation council)	**Aug 31 1970–Jan 13 1972 CE** Edward Akufo-Addo		
	Jan 13 1972–Jul 5 1978 CE Ignatius Kutu Acheampong (chairman of the national redemption council until Oct 9 1975, then chairman of the supreme military council)	**Jun 4 1979–Sep 24 1979 CE** Jerry John Rawlings (1st time) (chairman of the armed forces revolutionary council)	
Apr 2 1969–Aug 7 1970 CE Akwasi Afrifa (chairman of the national liberation council until Apr 3 1969, then chairman of the presidential commission)		**Sep 24 1979–Dec 31 1981 CE** Hilla Limann	

Ghana's major political figures

Acheampong, Ignatius Kutu (1931–1979 CE)
Acheampong became the military ruler of Ghana in 1972, when his forces removed the government of Kofi Busia. He sought to restore Ghana's depressed economy, but poor harvests in 1976 and 1977, combined with inflation and charges of government corruption, forced his resignation in 1978. He was convicted of corruption in 1979 and subsequently executed.

Aggrey, James Emman Kwegyir (1875–1927 CE)
Aggrey was a major scholar and advocate of racial equality. He studied in Ghana and in the United States, where he was influenced by the ideas of the African-American Booker T. Washington. Upon his return to Africa, he encouraged Ghanaians to seek advanced education and influenced a younger generation of African nationalists.

Akuffo, Frederick (1937–1979 CE)
Akuffo replaced Ignatius Acheampong as the military ruler of Ghana in 1978, but he served only one year before he was removed by Lieutenant Jerry Rawlings. He reduced the corruption that marked Acheampong's rule, but could not halt inflation. He was overthrown in 1979 and executed.

Ankrah, Joseph Arthur (1915 CE–)
Ankrah became the military head of state of Ghana in 1966, following the coup that deposed Kwame Nkrumah. He served as a soldier in World War II and also in the Congo conflict in 1960 and 1961. Ankrah took no part in the coup that toppled Nkrumah, but he was appointed head of state by the National Liberation Council. Under Ankrah, Ghana's economy declined and, following accusations of petty corruption, he was forced to resign in 1969.

Annan, Kofi Atta (1938 CE–)
On January 1, 1997, Annan became Secretary-General of the United Nations, the first to have come from Africa south of the Sahara. Born in Kumasi, Ghana (then the Gold Coast), he worked for the UN from 1962, except for two years when he was head of the Ghana Tourist Development Company. From March 1, 1993, he was under-secretary-general of peace-keeping operations and worked in Somalia and Bosnia-Herzegovina.

Summit conference
The Organization of African Unity (OAU) was founded in 1963 CE. This stamp marks the OAU summit conference which was held in Ghana in 1965 CE.

Nkrumah
A former prime minister of the Gold Coast in 1951 CE, then the first president of the renamed Ghana in 1960 CE, Nkrumah was eventually overthrown in a military coup in 1966 CE.

Lady Victoria Opoku Ware
Married to Opoke Ware II, she was both an influential figure at her husband's court, and a powerful ambassador for her country in her official trips abroad.

Ghana Timeline

Pre 19th Century CE

14th century CE Akan people migrate to the Ghana region from the north and establish kingdoms
15th century Kingdoms develop among the Asante people in southern Ghana
1471 Portuguese navigators explore the region which they name the Gold Coast
1482 The Portuguese build a fortress at Elmina ("the mine")
17th century The Akans defeat invasions by the Doma people
1637–1642 The Dutch capture Portuguese bases on the Gold Coast
c.1650–1730 Akwamu empire monopolizes slave-trade routes to the coast
1651 Danes establish trading posts on the Gold Coast
1664 English merchants establish headquarters at Cape Coast Castle

19th century CE

1824–1826 First British Asante War: Britain occupies the Asante capital, Kumasi
1830–1844 British merchants establish an informal protectorate over the Gold Coast
1850 Britain buys out Danish commercial interests on the Gold Coast
1872 The Dutch withdraw from their trading posts on the Gold Coast
1874 The Second British Asante War: British forces sack Kumasi and the Gold Coast is declared a British colony
1893–1894 Defeated in the Third Asante War, the Asante accept a British protectorate
1895–1896 The Fourth Asante War: the British put down an Asante uprising

1900–49 CE **1900** The last Asante resistance to the British is extinguished
1901 British protectorate established over northern Ghana
1922 The western part of German Togoland is mandated to Britain by the League of Nations: it is administered as part of Ghana
1925 The first Africans are elected to the colonial legislative council
1947 Kwame Nkrumah organizes a Ghanaian nationalist party
1948 Nationalists riot in Accra

1950–59 CE **1951** Ghana gains full internal self-government
1952 Kwame Nkrumah becomes prime minister of Gold Coast
1956 In a UN-sponsored referendum, British Togoland votes for full union with Gold Coast
1957 Mar 6 Gold Coast becomes independent as Ghana

1960–69 CE **1960** Ghana becomes a republic: Kwame Nkrumah becomes the first president
1965 The Akosombo dam begins production of hydroelectric power
1966 Nkrumah is ousted by a military coup: Gen. Joseph Ankrah becomes head of government
1969 Ankrah resigns and is replaced by Brigadier Akwasi Amankwa Afrifa who restores civilian rule

1970–79 CE **1972** Col. I. K. Acheampong becomes head of government after a military coup
1978 Acheampong resigns and is replaced by Gen. Frederick Kwasi Akuffo
1979 Akuffo is overthrown by coup led by Lieut. Jerry Rawlings. Afrifa, Acheampong and Akuffo are executed and a civilian government is elected

1980–89 CE **1981** Rawlings seizes control of the government in another coup: political parties are outlawed
1983 A housing crisis follows the expulsion of one million Ghanaian migrant workers from Nigeria

1990–99 CE **1992** Rawlings is elected president under a new multiparty constitution
1994 A state of emergency is declared following the outbreak of inter-ethnic violence in northern Ghana
1996 Rawlings reelected president

2000–09 CE **2000** John Kufuor is elected president, defeating Rawlings

Busia, Kofi Abrefa (1914–1978 CE)
Dr Busia, an opponent of Kwame Nkrumah, served on the National Liberation Council of General Joseph Ankrah and helped to prepare Ghana for a return to civilian rule. He became prime minister in 1969, but his repressive measures and his failure to solve the country's economic problems led to his overthrow in 1972 by General Ignatius Acheampong.

Nkrumah, Dr Kwame (1909–1972 CE)
Kwame Nkrumah became prime minister of Gold Coast (later Ghana) in 1951, and then the first president of Ghana, in 1960. He was overthrown in a military coup in 1966. A campaigner against white domination, Nkrumah was widely respected throughout Africa. He became increasingly autocratic, however, and economic crises dogged his final years in office.

Opoku Ware II (1919–1999 CE)
A Ghanaian lawyer, Opoku Ware succeeded his uncle Sir Osei Agyeman-Prempe II as *asantehene* (king) of the Asante people in 1970. He was succeeded by Nana Kwako Dua.

Opoku Ware, Lady Victoria (1929–1996 CE)
The senior wife of Opoku Ware II, Lady Victoria was an influential figure at court and accompanied the king on foreign trips. In 1981, she helped to arrange the Asante exhibitions that were staged in London and New York City. A powerful personality, she used her influence to defend the Asante kingdom's interests while maintaining an allegiance to the Ghanaian state.

Osei Bonsu (1779–1824 CE)
Osei Bonsu expanded the Asante Empire to its greatest size, covering modern-day Ghana and parts of Togo, Burkina Faso, and Ivory Coast. The seventh Asante king, his name means "Osei the Whale." He encouraged Asante arts and crafts and made the nation rich from their goldmines.

Osei Tutu (died 1717 CE)
Osei Tutu united the separate Asante chiefdoms in the 1670s to create the Asante Empire, now part of Ghana as the Asante Kingdom. To join the empire, the chiefdoms had to acknowledge the authority of the Golden Stool. This was a wooden stool, covered in gold and said to have been conjured from the sky, that symbolized the spirit of the Asante. Osei Tutu embarked on a series of wars of expansion in 1701, and was killed in battle in 1717.

Prempeh I (1871–1931 CE)
Prempeh I was the last great *asantehene* (king) of the Asante in Ghana. He became king in 1888 and resisted attempts by the British to make his kingdom a protectorate (colony). He was deposed and sent into exile before the British annexed Asante to the Gold Coast colony in 1901. He returned to his country as a private citizen, although his people still regarded him as their king.

Prempeh II (1892–1970 CE)
Prempeh II succeeded Prempeh I as *asantehene* (king) of Asante in 1931. In 1933, when Britain decided to create the Asante Confederacy, he was recognized officially. He opposed many nationalist policies in the 1940s, but he supported Kwame Nkrumah before independence. His authority was weakened when Nkrumah abolished the chiefs' councils in 1957.

Rawlings, Jerry John (J. J.) (1947 CE–)
Son of a Scottish father and a Ghanaian mother, Jerry John Rawlings seized power in Ghana in a peaceful coup in 1979, but ruled for only 112 days before restoring civilian government. Rawlings, an air force officer, was immensely popular for his anticorruption policies. He again seized power in 1981, but his reluctance to return power to a civilian government after this second coup lost him some support. In 1992, however, he was elected president, but he was defeated in 2000 by John Kufuor.

King Prempeh I
He became king of the Asante in 1888 CE and resisted attempts by Britain to make his kingdom a protectorate.

Jerry Rawlings
He seized power in both 1979 CE and 1981 CE, before being elected president in democratic elections in 1992 CE. He was defeated in elections in 2000 CE.

Ghana, Ancient

Ancient Ghana lay to the north of the Senegal and Niger rivers in what is now western Mali and southern Mauritania. The capital city was Kumbi Saleh, which lay southwest of Timbuktu (Tombouctou). The modern nation of Ghana bears no relation to this historic empire. Tradition holds that the empire, called Wagadu by its Soninke citizens, was founded in the fourth century CE. The Soninke overthrew their Berber ruler, whose title was *ghana* or war chief. The empire came to be known for the title of its rulers, and by the ninth century had emerged as a powerful empire.

Trade in gold and salt was the source of Ghana's wealth, and the empire controlled the West African ends of the trans-Saharan trade routes. Although the people followed their own religion, Kumbi Saleh became a center for Islamic learning. Muslim Almoravids took the important Saharan market town Audaghost from Ghana in 1054 CE, and in 1076 CE they conquered Ghana, but only for a decade. Ghana remained powerful until rebellions and invasions by the Susu people in the thirteenth century weakened the state. In 1240 CE, the capital city was destroyed by the troops of the Mali emperor, and what remained of the empire became part of Mali. *See also* **Almoravid empire; Mali; Mauritania.**

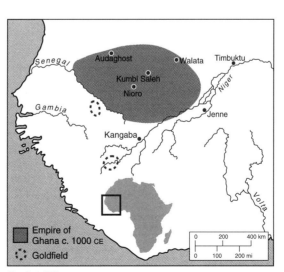

Empire of Ghana
This map of the Empire of Ghana shows its territories c. 1000 CE, toward the end of its era of power. Kumbi Saleh was the capital and Walata, Timbuktu, and Audaghost were major trading centers.

© DIAGRAM

Ghudamis

See **Ghadames**.

Gobir

Gobir was one of the historic Hausa states, which once dominated the north of what is now northern Nigeria and southwestern Niger. *See also* **Hausa states**.

Gonja

Gonja is the name of a trading nation founded in the sixteenth century and now a chiefdom in modern Ghana. It was established in what is now northern Ghana by Mandingka cavalrymen of the Songhay empire. Gonja was incorporated into the Asante Empire during the eighteenth century. *See also* **Asante**; **Ghana**; **Songhay**.

Gold Coast

The Gold Coast is a section of the coast of the Gulf of Guinea, West Africa, that includes much of the coast of modern Ghana. Profitable trade in gold, and later slaves, gave the area its name.

In the seventeenth century, Europeans fought for control of the coastline, which became a British possession in the nineteenth century. During the colonial era, Gold Coast also referred to the territory that is now Ghana. Together with the Ashanti protectorate and the Northern Territories, the Gold Coast became independent as Ghana in 1957 CE. *See also* **Ghana**.

Gold Coast
The illustration (left) graphically portrays the first day of the Yam Festival which took place at Kumasi, Asante, in 1817 CE. Note that the British flag is flying over the proceedings, a situation which survived until the Gold Coast became independent, and was renamed Ghana, in 1957 CE. The illustration (right), which appeared in a collection of cigarette cartds, shows a soldier of the Gold Coast Regiment when it was still under British rule. This regiment played a major part on behalf of Britain, in the Ashanti Wars of 1873–74 CE.

Grande Comore

Grande Comore is the largest of the Comoro Islands. They became a French protectorate (colony) in 1886 CE and independant in 1974 CE. However, in 1997 CE, the two smaller islands, Anjouan and Mohéli seceded and troops from Grande Comore failed to conquer Anjouan. In the early twenty-first century CE, the status of the islands remained unresolved. *See also* **Comoros**.

Great Zimbabwe

From around the late twelfth century, the Shona people constructed dry-wall enclosures which served as palaces and became known as *zimbabwes*. This building system was perfected at the site of Great Zimbabwe from the fourteenth century onward. By the end of the fifteenth century the Shona abandoned this site and moved north to found a new dynasty, the Mwene Mutapas. In 1480 CE the kingdom split. The southern part was dominated by the Rozvi peoples, a Shona subgroup. When the Rozvi Empire collapsed in the early nineteenth century. more than 100 more Shona states took its place. After 1850 CE most of the area was colonized by the British, and renamed Southern Rhodesia. In 1965 CE the white population declared independence from British rule as Rhodesia. After a prolonged civil war, full independence and majority rule were granted in 1980 CE. *See also* **Zimbabwe**.

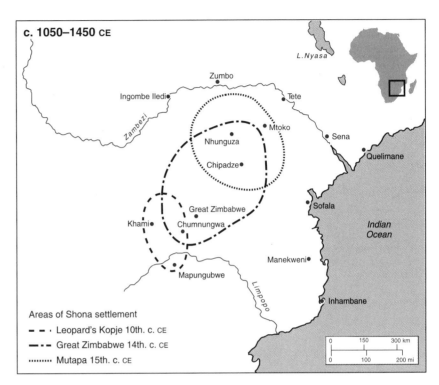

Ingot (left)

The currency of Great Zimbabwe consisted of copper ingots (metal bars). Soapstone molds for making these ingots have been found at Great Zimbabwe, and the ingots themselves have turned up as far away as China.

The Shona Empire and Great Zimbabwe (right)

First occupied around the fourth century by by Iron-Age farmers, the Zimbabwe plateau was reoccupied in the tenth century by the Shona people. They developed a sophisticated civilization, and rebuilt the original site from the mid-fourteenth century. It was abandoned from c.1450 CE, and the people then moved north to create the new kingdom of Maputa.

c. 1050–1450 CE

Areas of Shona settlement
- – · Leopard's Kopje 10th. c. CE
- – · Great Zimbabwe 14th. c. CE
········· Mutapa 15th. c. CE

Griqualand East and West

The Griqua people of South Africa had both Afrikaner and African, generally Khoikhoi, ancestors. They wore European clothes, were Christians, and spoke Dutch but were not accepted by Afrikaner (Boer) society. In the late eighteenth century, many Griquas began trekking northwards. They established Griqualand north of the junction of the Vaal and Orange rivers. From the 1820s on, Boer farmers increasingly began to buy and settle on Griqualand. Adam Kok III, the Griqua leader, was concerned that he would become the leader of a landless state so, in 1860 CE, he led about 2,000 Griqua, together with most of their cattle, on a two-year trek eastward. Their migration took them through what is now Lesotho and they finally settled on the slopes of the Drakensberg, an empty but fertile region, where they established a new state: Griqualand East. The capital of the new state, which was founded in 1862 CE, was Kokstad. The original Griqualand, became known as Griqualand West.

Griqualand West was formally annexed by the British in 1871 CE and became part of the Cape Colony nine years later. In 1879 CE Griqualand East was annexed to the Cape Colony. In 1903 CE Griqualand East was established as a black African council and was admitted into the Transkeian territories. Today, the eastern and western regions of Griqualand East are part of Eastern province. The central portion is now part of KwaZulu/Natal. *See also* **Cape Colony**; **South Africa**.

1872

Griqualand West (1871)
Griqualand East (1866)
- - - Boundary of annexed territory
- · - Boundary between indigenous kingdoms

Nicholas Waterboer

When diamonds were found in the lower Vaal area during 1867–68 CE, the area was claimed by both Boer republics, by Nicholas Waterboer, the Gringua chief, and by the Tlhaping chiefs. Territorial disputes over the diamond fields continued until the British assumed control of the fields for themselves in 1871 CE, by annexing all the land claimed by Nicholas Waterboer as the new British colony of Griqualand-West.

Independence
A 1959 CE stamp celebrating Guinea's independence and depicting its first president Sékou Touré.

New currency
One of the first coins issued by the newly-independent Republic of Guinea–a 10 franc bronze coin portraying Sékou Touré.

A working-class hero
The son of a peasant farmer, Sékou Touré became active in trade union organization before helping to found what became the leading party in nationalist politics.

GUINEA Republic of Guinea

From the eleventh century CE, the area that is now eastern, or Upper Guinea, formed part of the ancient Ghana and then Mali empires. The powerful Mali empire, founded by the Malinke (Manding) people, declined in the sixteenth century. From the fourteenth century to the early eighteenth century, the Muslim Fulani invaded the region from the north, fighting a series of *jihads* (holy wars) with the Malinke. They finally won control of much of Guinea, including the Futa Djallon plateau.

The first Europeans to reach the area were the Portuguese in the mid-fifteenth century and the area soon became linked with the slave trade. Traders from other European countries were active on the coast by the seventeenth century, but it was the French who first explored the interior. During the nineteenth century, France established settlements on the coast and, in 1881, the ruler of Futa Djallon placed his state under French protection. This protectorate (colony) was called Rivières du Sud until 1890 CE, when it was separated from Senegal and later was called French Guinea and incorporated into French West Africa. Resistance to French rule came from Samouri Touré, a Malinke leader, but he was defeated in 1898.

In 1946 CE, after World War II, Guinea became an overseas territory of France and its people became French citizens. But demands for independence increased and, in 1958 CE, Guinea was the only French territory to vote against joining the French Community. Instead, it opted for full independence which was achieved on October 2, 1958 CE.

Recent history

Guinea's first president was Ahmad Sekou Toure, leader of the *Parti Démocratique de Guinée* (PDG), which had been formed in 1947 CE. Following independence, the PDG was made the only political party in order to provide the stability needed after France's sudden withdrawal, and cancellation of all technical assistance and financial aid. Toure was a radical leader, much admired among black nationalist politicians throughout Africa, and an ally of Ghana's Kwame Nkrumah. Like Nkrumah, Toure favored socialist policies, adapted to African conditions. He was also a Pan-Africanist, and supported the concept of a United States of Africa.

Because of its bad relations with western countries, Guinea turned to the Communist world for trade and aid, and it adopted a policy of "positive neutralism" in the Cold War. But in 1961 CE, Guinea's government expelled the Soviet ambassador on the grounds of "interfering with the internal affairs of the country". From that point, the United States became the main supplier of aid and investment. Relations with France were also restored in 1963, but the economy was in a poor state. Toure's rule became increasingly oppressive in the 1960s and early 1970s, when all opposition was suppressed. International criticism of Guinea's poor record in human rights led to an improvement in the situation in the late 1970s, when large numbers of political prisoners were released and a degree of economic liberalization was introduced.

A few days after Touré died in March 1984 CE, military leaders seized control of the country. They suspended the constitution and abolished the PDG. Their leader was Colonel Lansana Conté, who headed a military council and became head of state. Conté introduced free market policies, strengthened economic ties with France, and removed the most repressive of Touré's security measures. In 1985 CE, a failed coup increased Conté's popularity, but he gradually became more authoritarian, ignoring his cabinet. In the late 1980s and early 1990s, the economy began to improve, although many people protested against the austerity measures imposed on Guinea by the World Bank and the International Monetary Fund. In 1991 CE, the government legalized political parties and began a transition to democracy. Conté was elected president in 1993 CE, despite opposition allegations of voting fraud, and, in 1994 CE, Conté's Party for Unity and Progress won 71 out of the 114 seats in the National Assembly. Despite internal disturbances, Conté was reelected president in 1998 CE.

In the late 1990s, Guinea was troubled by tensions with its neighbors. In 1998 CE, refugees from Sierra Leone flooded into UN-run camps in Guinea, while, in 1999 CE, Guinea's forces clashed with Sierra Leone rebels. Liberia also accused Guinea of harboring and arming Liberian rebels, while, in 2001 CE, Guinea accused Liberia of suporting rebels in Guinea.

Peoples

FULANI
For information about the history of the Fulani, *see* **Fulani states**.

MANDING
For information about the history of the Manding, *see* **Mali (Peoples—Manding)**; **Mandinko empire**.

SUSU
The Susu, or Soso, are a Manding people, the vast majority of whom live in Guinea. All Manding peoples originated in a mountainous region of the same name that sits astride the border of Mali and Guinea. Before the thirteenth century, the area was ruled by a Susu leader called Sumunguru. However, in 1235 CE, Sumunguru was defeated by Sundiata–the famous Malinke leader who founded the vast medieval Empire of Mali. After Mali began to disintegrate in the fifteenth century, the Susu left their homeland, migrating west to the Futa Djallon plateau of Guinea. From there, they continued to spread westward.

TUKULOR
For information about the history of the Tukulor people, *see* **Senegal (Peoples—Tululor)**.

Guinea premiers
Apr 26 1972–Apr 3 1984 CE Louis Lansana Beavogui
Apr 5 1984–Dec 18 1984 CE Diara Traoré
Jul 9 1996–Mar 8 1999 CE Sidia Touré
Mar 8 1999 CE– Lamine Sidimé

Guinea timeline

Pre 19th Century CE

11th century	Guinea region forms part of the Ghana empire
16th century	Guinea region forms part of the Mali empire
18th century	Kingdom of Futa Jalon develops in western Guinea

19th century CE

1849	France establishes control of the coast of Guinea
1865	Eastern Guinea forms part of Samouri Touré's Mandinke empire
1881	Futa Jalon becomes a French protectorate
1886-1892	France conquers the Mandinke empire
1895	The area of Guinea is incorporated into French West Africa
1898	Samouri Touré is captured by French forces and exiled

1900–49 CE **1947** Democratic Party of Guinea (PDG) founded to campaign for independence

1950–59 CE **1952** Sekou Toure becomes leader of the PDG

1958 Oct 2 Guinea rejects French offer of internal self-government and votes for independence: Toure becomes president.

1980–89 CE **1984** On the death of Toure, the army under Col. Lansana Conté seizes power

1990–99 CE **1990** Conté appoints a transitional government to oversee a return to civilian rule

1993 Conté narrowly retains the presidency in multiparty elections

1998 Conté is reelected president

2000–09 CE **2001** Guinea becomes involved in a refugee crisis caused by civil wars in Liberia and Sierra Leone

Guinea's major political figures

Conté, Lansana (1945 CE–)

Lansana Conté took power in Guinea in 1984, when he led a bloodless coup a few days after the death of the first president, Sekou Toure. At first, he introduced liberal policies, but after a failed coup in 1985, he adopted a more repressive approach. After the introduction of a multiparty system in 1991, he was elected president in 1993. In 1996, he survived a crisis when the army mutinied over pay.

Touré, Ahmad Sékou (1922–1984 CE)

A major figure in the struggle for independence from colonial rule, Sekou Touré became president of Guinea in 1958. From 1971, following an unsuccessful invasion by opposition forces based in Guinea-Bissau, Touré imposed restrictions on the opposition, but improved his human rights record before his death in 1984. He was succeeded as president by Lansana Conté.

Lansana Conté
He seized power in Guinea in 1984 CE after a bloodless coup. After the introduction of a multiparty system in 1991 CE, he was elected president in 1993 CE.

GUINEA-BISSAU Republic of Guinea-Bissau

From the thirteenth century CE, the area that is now Guinea-Bissau lay on the western margins of the Mali empire. Following the collapse of Mali in the fifteenth century, waves of Mande people spread across western Africa, but, by the nineteenth century, the interior was dominated by Fulani states.

The first Europeans to arrive in the area were the Portuguese who reached the coast in the 1440s. There, they developed the slave trade. In the sixteenth century, wars caused by the expansion of the Mande peoples led to an increase in the number of slaves available from the area and traders from England, France, and Holland also operated in the area. The Portuguese also used what is now Guinea-Bissau as a base to colonize Cape Verde, which became an assembly point for slaves from the mainland. Slaves were also used to develop plantations on the islands, establishing links between the islands and mainland Guinea which persisted throughout the period of colonial rule.

At first, Portugal appointed a governor to administer the two territories, but, in 1879 CE, the Portuguese separated the administration of the mainland territory which was named Portuguese Guinea, from that of Cape Verde. The interior proved difficult to conquer and the Portuguese did not have complete control until 1915 CE, while some occasional resistance continued into the mid-1930s. Economic progress was slow, because Portuguese settlers preferred to migrate to the country's healthier territories of Angola and Mozambique. In 1951 CE, both Cape Verde and Portuguese Guinea became overseas provinces of Portugal.

Recent history

Opposition to Portuguese rule gradually increased and, in 1956, the formation of the African Party for the Independence of Guinea and Cape Verde (PAIGC) marked the start of a long guerrilla war. In 1973 CE, the people of Portuguese Guinea declared their territory independent, though official independence came later on September 10, 1974 CE. Guinea-Bissau's first president was Luiz de Almeida Cabral, one of the six founders of the PAIGC and the brother of Amílcar Cabral, who had led the PAIGC rebel army until his assassination in 1973 CE. Luiz Cabral maintained good relations with Portugal, but he was unable to solve the many economic problems caused largely by the long civil war. The lack of educated people to run the country, combined with corruption, also damaged the regime, which became increasingly authoritarian. Cabral also lost popularity among people who resented what they saw as

ESTADO DA GUINE-BISSAU

Amilcar Cabral
A 1976 CE stamp commemorating a leader in the struggle for independence against Portuguese rule assassinated in 1973 CE.

© DIAGRAM

the privileged status of people from Cape Verde in their government.

In 1981 CE, the prime minister, João Bernardo Vieira overthrew Cabral. The National Assembly was abolished and a military Revolutionary Council, which excluded people from Cape Verde, was set up to govern the country. Cape Verde broke off relations with Guinea-Bissau and the Cape Verde branch of the PAIGC, which had favored unification of the islands with Guinea-Bissau, was dissolved. Unsuccessful coups in the 1980s led Vieira to become more authoritarian, but a new constitution was introduced in 1984 CE, with a Council of State replacing the Revolutionary Council. A National Assembly was elected in 1984 and, in turn, it elected Vieira president. However, Guinea-Bissau remained a single-party state until 1991 CE, when the formation of opposition parties was legalized. From 1986, the government's Marxist policies were dropped, the economy was liberalized, and foreign investment was encouraged as Vieira moved closer to the West.

After several postponements, elections were held in 1994 CE. Vieira was elected president, defeating Kumba Iala, leader of the Party for Social Renewal (PRS), while the PAIGC won a majority in the National Assembly. However, despite various economic measures, including the adoption of the CFA franc as Guinea-Bissau's official unit of currency–replacing the *peso*–the econ-omy remained weak. In 1998, Vieira dismissed Ansumane Mane, army chief of staff, for allegedly helping rebels in Casamance, a Senegalese province bordering Guinea-Bissau to the north

Mane's dismissal led to an army mutiny and a civil war lasting 11 months, causing much destruction. Vieira was criticized for bringing in troops from Guinea and Senegal to help him oppose the rebels, and, in May 1999, a military coup led by Mane overthrew Vieira. The Speaker of the National Assembly, Malam Bacai Sanhá, became interim president and Veira left the country.

Following elections in 1999 and 2000, the PRS won the greatest number of seats in the National Assembly and its leader, Kumba Iala, was elected president in a second round of voting, winning 72 percent of the vote. In November 2000, during an unsuccessful coup attempt, Mane was shot dead.

Peoples
FULANI
For information about the history of the Fulani, *see* **Fulani states**.

MANDING
For information about the history of the Manding, *see* **Mali (Peoples—Manding); Mandinko empire**.

Amilcar Cabral
The founder of the African Party for the Independence of Guinea and Cape Verde (PAIGC) in 1956 CE.

Guinea-Bissau presidents

Sep 24 1973–Nov 14 1980 CE
Luís de Almeida Cabral
(chairman Council of State)

Nov 14 1980–May 14 1984 CE
João Bernardo Vieira (1st time)
(chairman Council of the Revolution)

May 14 1984–May 16 1984 CE
Carmen Pereira
(president of the National People's Assembly)

May 16 1984 –May 7 1999 CE
João Bernardo Vieira (2nd time)
(chairman Council of State to Sep 29 1994)

May 7 1999–May 14 1999 CE
Ansumane Mané
(commander of the Military Junta)

May 14 1999–Feb 17 2000 CE
Malam Bacai Sanhá (acting)

Feb 17 2000 CE–
Kumba Ialá

Guinea-Bissau

Pre 19th century CE		
	1480	Portugal founds trading posts on the Guinea coast
	1687	Portuguese found Bissau city as a fortified center for the slave trade
19th century CE		
	1879	The region becomes the Portuguese colony of Portuguese Guinea
1950–59 CE	1951	Portuguese Guinea becomes an overseas province of Portugal
	1956	Nationalists form the *Partido Africano da Independência do Guiné e Cabo Verde* (PAIGC)
1960–69 CE	1963	PAIGC begins a war of independence
1970–79 CE	1974 Sept 10	Portuguese Guinea becomes independent as Guinea- Bissau: Luiz Cabral is the first president
1980–89 CE	1980	Cabral overthrown by a military coup: Maj. João Bernardo Vieira becomes president
	1984	A new constitution creates a National People's Assembly and Council of State
1990–99 CE	1991	The law making the PAIGC the sole political party is abolished
	1994	PAIGC wins Guinea-Bissau's first multiparty elections: Vieira retains the presidency
	1998–1999	An army revolt causes widespread disturbance in Bissau
2000–09 CE	2000	Kumba Iala is elected president

Guinea-Bissau's major political figures

Cabral, Amílcar (1931–1973 CE)
Leader of the independence struggle against Portuguese rule in Guinea-Bissau, Amílcar Cabral was assassinated in 1973. He was the founder of the independence movement *Partido Africano da Independência do Guiné e Cabo Verde* (PAIGC) in 1956.

Cabral, Luiz (1929 CE–)
Brother of Amílcar Cabral and a prominent leader in the independence struggle, Luiz Cabral became the first president of Guinea-Bissau in 1974. Cabral promoted the interests of Cape Verdeans in Guinea-Bissau while allowing the economy to decline. He was overthrown in a coup led by the prime minister, João Vieira, in 1980.

Vieira, João Bernardo (1939 CE–)
In 1980, João Vieira, prime minister of Guinea-Bissau, led a military coup against Luiz Cabral and became head of state. He was made executive president in 1984, then reelected in 1989 and again in 1994 in the country's first multiparty elections.

Luiz Cabral
He was the brother of Amilcar Cabral, and the first president of Guinea-Bissau from 1974 CE until his overthrow in 1980 CE.

Gwari

Gwari was one of the historic Hausa states that dominated what are now northwestern Nigeria and southwestern Niger. *See also* **Hausa states**.

Hausa Bakwai

The Hausa people of what are now northwestern Nigeria and southwestern Niger established several independent states, which were collectively called Hausa Bakwai. *See also* **Hausa states**.

Hausa states

What are now northwestern Nigeria and southwestern Niger were once dominated for several hundred years by independent states established by the Hausa people. According to tradition, the were seven "true" Hausa states, or Hausa Bakwai: Biram, Daura, Gobir, Kano, Katsina, Rano, and Zaria (Zazzau or Zegzeg). Other powerful Hausa towns included Zamfara, Kebbi, Yauri, Gwari, Nupe, and Kororofa (Jukun). The Hausa based their riches and power on the lucrative trade routes that passed through their cities, which were located at the southern end of many trans-Saharan routes.

Many Hausa communities had been established in the region by the end of the first millennium, and by 1350 CE, several states had emerged. Based around walled towns called *birane*, each Hausa state had its own royal family headed by a *habe* (king). By the fifteenth century, Katsina, Kano, and Zaria were the most important Hausa states. Islam became the state religion of the Hausa states in the same century, although many citizens stayed faithful to their own religions. The vast Songhai empire exacted tribute from the Hausa emirs and occupied their states during the sixteenth century. Kebbi was the only Hausa state that was able to assert its independence, and it remained independent until 1804 CE, when conquered by *jihads* (holy wars) that established the Fulani empire. Zamfara and then Katsina were the most prominent city-states in the seventeenth and nineteenth centuries. When the nineteenth century ended, Gobir had become the most important Hausa state. The ruthless taxation of the citizens of Gobir was a major trigger of the Fulani–Hausa *jihads*, however, and Gobir was incorporated into the Fulani empire. The Hausa states were then all incorporated into the Fulani empire, and they were reorganized into Muslim emirates. At the beginning of the twentieth century, the British took control of the former emirates, to which they attached Bornu to form the northern provinces (later, the Northern Region) of the Protectorate of Nigeria. *See also* **Fulani empire**, **Kano**, **Katsina**, **Nigeria**, **Zaria**.

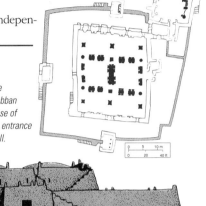

Masallaci Jumaa (right and below)
The Masallaci Jumaa (Friday Mosque) in Zaria was built in the nineteenth century. It was designed by the Hausa architect Babban Gwani Mikaila for Emir Abdulkarim. This mosque (Muslim house of worship) is a complex of buildings including a hall of worship, entrance lobbies, and washing chambers surrounded by an external wall.

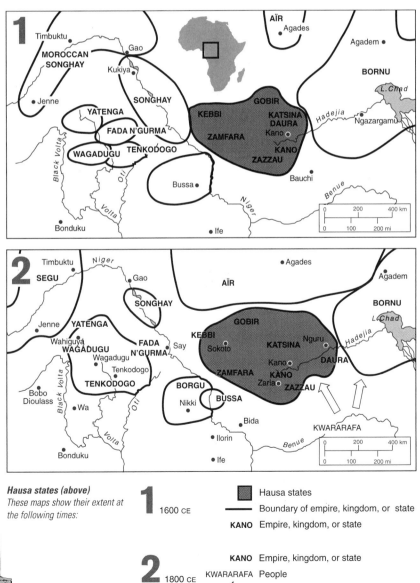

Hausa states (above)
These maps show their extent at the following times:

1 1600 CE

2 1800 CE

	Hausa states
——	Boundary of empire, kingdom, or state
KANO	Empire, kingdom, or state

KANO	Empire, kingdom, or state
KWARARAFA	People
⇐	Kwararafa raids 1600s

A decorated wall (right)
The external wall of a house in Zaria decorated with the modern motif of a car and a bicycle.

© DIAGRAM

Haya kingdoms *See also* **Tanzania (Peoples—Haya)**.

High Commission Territories

The collective name for the British-ruled states of Basutoland, Bechuanaland, and Swaziland was the High Commission Territories. The administrative head of these lands was the British High Commissioner based in South Africa. *See also* **Basutoland, Bechuanaland, Botswana, Lesotho, Swaziland**.

Ibadan

Today, Ibadan is the capital city of Oyo state, southern Nigeria, and it is that country's second largest city after Lagos. In the past, Ibadan was a kingdom founded by the Yoruba people that came to control an empire.

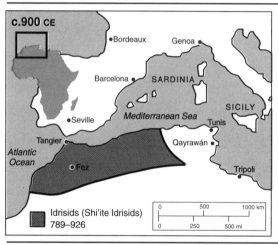

The Empire of Ibadan (above)
After fights for supremacy in the region, Ibadan established an empire in 1862 CE. Between 1877–1886 CE, the Kirijj War was fought between Ibadan and an alliance of various states in the east. Rebellion against Ibadan continued until it was absorbed by British Southern Nigeria in 1897 CE.

The Idrisid dynasty (right)
This Arabic Muslim dynasty ruled the Berber parts of what is now known as Morocco, and also parts of Algeria for a period of more than 100 years. It was eventually conquered by the Umayyad caliphs and the Fatimids of Cairo.

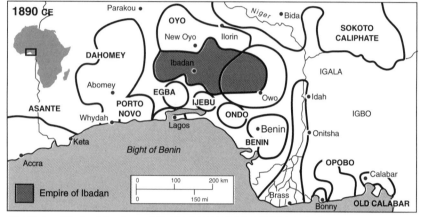

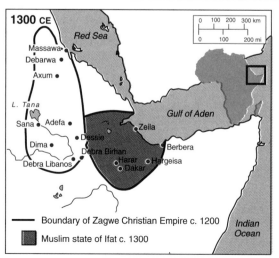

The state of Ifat (right)
Established toward the end of the thirteenth century, Ifat emerged as an independent state in central Ethiopia. After a period of continual rebellion it was annexed to Ethiopia in 1415 CE.

Exactly how Ibadan came into existence is not known, but it emerged as an independent kingdom from the ruins of the Oyo empire in the early nineteenth century. It was probably founded by refugees (military and civilian) from the demise of Oyo. After the fall of Oyo in the 1830s, Ilorin and Abeokuta became the most powerful Yoruba towns. Ibadan was governed at that time by a council of military leaders headed by the most able chief. The rulers of Ibadan and Ijaye took control of the Oyo empire. In c.1840 CE, the Ibadan army defeated invaders from Ilorin, who were attempting to take over Oyo and turn it into a Muslim state. By 1860 CE, Ibadan controlled much of what is now central Nigeria, including Ijaye. The king of Oyo retained his traditional position as leader of Oyo but real power was held by Ibadan. Conflicts with various Yoruba states in the late nineteenth century were brought to a halt after the British conquered the city in 1893 CE. *See also* **Ijaye, Ijebu, Ilorin, Nigeria, Oyo**.

Idrisid state

The Idrisids were an Arabic Muslim dynasty that ruled the Berber areas of what is now Morocco and parts of Algeria for more than 100 years. Idris I, the founder of the dynasty, reigned from 789–791 CE. Muslim Arabs had conquered much of North Africa in that century, and Idris was said to be a descendant of the founder of Islam, the prophet Muhammad. Idris II (reigned 803–828 CE), the son and successor of Idris I, founded the city of Fez in 808 CE, but the kingdom declined after his death. Eventually, the Idrisids were crushed by the Umayyad caliphs–a Muslim dynasty founded in Spain by Arabs–and the Fatimids of Cairo. The Fatimids deposed the Idrisid rulers of Fez in 921 CE, and the last Idrisid king was killed while a prisoner of the Umayyads in 985 CE. *See also* **Algeria, Morocco**.

Ifat

Ifat was a Muslim state that flourished in central Ethiopia from the late thirteenth century to 1415 CE. Established in the fertile uplands of eastern Shoa, Ifat emerged as an independent state and grew dominant in the region. In 1328 CE it was made tributary to the Ethiopian Empire and, after continual rebellion, was annexed in 1415 CE. *See also* **Ethiopia; Shoa**.

Ife

Ife in southern Nigeria, northwest of the Niger Delta, is perhaps the oldest Yoruba town and was once an independent kingdom. Little is known of Ife's early history, but it was the capital of a kingdom by the early eleventh century, though the city itself probably existed several centuries earlier. Ife was named for the Yoruba god of divination, Ifa, and Yoruba mythology holds that it is the birthplace of humankind. The fourteenth cen-

tury was a period of prosperity for Ife, which produced the great works of art for which it is famous during this period. It had great influence over the kingdom of Benin and resisted the *jihads* (holy wars) of the nineteenth century Fulani empire but was weakened by struggles for control of the region's slave trade in the 1820s. In 1914 CE the Protectorate of Nigeria was formed, which included the Yoruba kingdoms of Ife, Ilorin, and Oyo. Modern Ife is still the spiritual home of the Yoruba people and home to the palace of the present *oni* (king), who has no political power but great symbolic importance. *See also* **Ilorin, Nigeria, Oyo.**

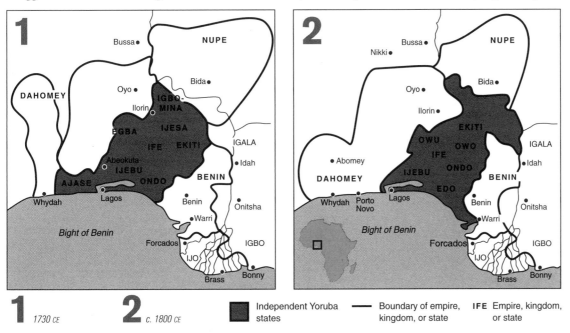

1 *1730 CE*

2 *c. 1800 CE*

■ Independent Yoruba states	— Boundary of empire, kingdom, or state	**IFE** Empire, kingdom, or state

Seated figure (above)
Made from copper, this seated figure, in a style typical of Ife, originated from the Nupe village of Tada in Nigeria.

A fight for commercial supremacy (left and far left)
Benin traded with Europe and its neighbors during the seventeenth century but, toward the end of the eighteenth century it began to decline as an imperial power. The cities and states within its dominion grew strong through profitable trade with Europeans, and broke away to become independent states.

Ifni

Ifni, now a part of southwest Morocco, was formerly an enclave of Spain. Situated on the Atlantic coast, Ifni was first settled in 1476 by Diego García de Herrera, Lord of the Canaries. Spanish Ifni was a fortified trading depot. In 1524 the settlement was abandoned after several outbreaks of disease and Berber attacks. Spain reoccupied Ifni in 1934, though a treaty was signed in 1860 with Morocco recognizing the enclave as a Spanish territory. In 1946 Ifni became part of Spanish West Africa. During the colonial era, in 1958, Ifni became a province but was returned to independent Morocco in 1969. *See also* **Morocco**; **Spanish West Africa**.

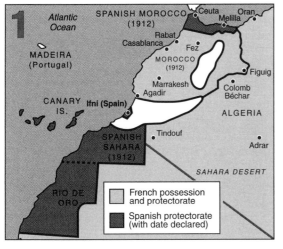

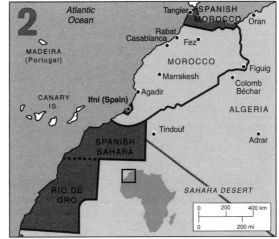

☐ French possession and protectorate	■ Spanish protectorate (with date declared)

Obas
In the past, much ceremony surrounded obas (kings), who spent most of their time hidden from view. They appeared in public only at important events and, even then, they were surrounded by attendants and totally veiled by a crown and robe made of thousands of coral beads.

A Spanish enclave (left and far left)
A part of independent Morocco since 1969 CE, Ifni was first settled by the Spanish in 1476 CE, subsequently abandoned in 1524 CE, then reoccupied in 1934 CE.

1 *1918 CE*

2 *1933 CE*

Ifriqiyah

Tunisia and, at times eastern parts of Algeria, were once called Ifriqiyah. This name was introduced by the Romans after they conquered Carthage more than 2,000 years ago. Ifriqiyah, or Africa Minor, was conquered by Arabs in the seventh century but lost to the Umayyads—a Muslim dynasty founded in Spain by Arabs. At first joined to the Egyptian lands of the Umayyads, Ifriqiyah became a separate province of the Umayyad Caliphate in 705 CE. From the mid-eigth century on, however, Ifriqiyah was ruled by a succession of Berber and Arab dynasties. *See also* **Abbasids**; **Aghlabids**; **Algeria**; **Tunisia**.

© DIAGRAM

Igbo

Many African peoples did not develop centralized states with a king, emir, or other distinct head of state. The Igbo in particular among these "acephalous" ("headless") states were remarkable for the size of their territory and the density of population. Igbo communities were organized in self-contained villages or feder-ations of village communities, with societies of elders and age-grade associations sharing the functions held by leaders elsewhere. However, Nri, a highly ritualistic monarchy, still survives today in northern Igbo territory. It is thought that the ancient Igbo Ukwu culture was a forerunner of Nri. *See also* **Nigeria**.

Igbo Ukwu

The Igbo Ukwu culture flourished in what is now southeast Nigeria more than 1,000 years ago. It was probably in existence by the ninth century, and the beautiful bronze and terracotta pots found on archeological digs are evidence of how highly developed the culture was. The bronzes–the first of which was accidentally uncovered by a man digging his land–were probably the burial items of a person of some standing, probably a priest-king.

Ijo states

The Ijo people of the Niger delta established several states in the last half of the first millennium: Nembe, Elem Kalabari, Bonny, and Okrika. Some historians believe the Ijo states emerged in response to the demand for slaves along the coast (seventeenth to nineteenth centuries). Other historians believe these states, like Benin, existed before the advent of the slave trade with the Europeans and that they developed in response to internal trade along the Niger River. The Ijo people patroled the Niger Delta in 30-man war canoes owned by houses. The leaders of these houses sat on the council of state. The king ruled with the aid of this council. Anyone who could afford to buy and crew such a canoe could found their own house. *See also* **Elem Kalabari**; **Bonny**.

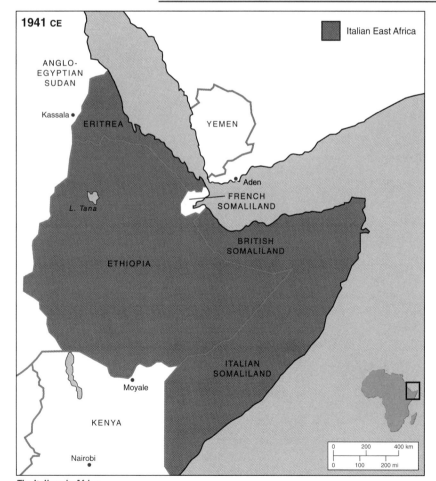

The Italians in Africa
Under the leadership of Mussolini, the Italian Fascist dictator, the Italians invaded Ethiopia from Eritrea and Italian Somaliland in 1935 CE, and the Imperial Ethiopian army was defeated in March 1936 CE. In April 1941 CE British colonial forces began to liberate Italian East Africa, allowing the Ethiopian emperor, Haile Selassie, to return to power.

Ilorin

Ilorin is now the capital of Kwara State, western Nigeria, but it was once an independent kingdom established by the Yoruba people and later a Muslim emirate. Founded in the late eighteenth century, Ilorin was initially part of the Oyo empire. In 1817 CE, however, the leader of Oyo's army, Afonja, declared Ilorin independent and successfully resisted attempts to quell the uprising he led. Afonja's successful rebellion was the main cause of the downfall of the Oyo empire. A few short years later, however, Afonja was assassinated, in c.1824 CE, by Muslim leaders of the city. After this Ilorin soon fell to the Fulani empire. Ilorin was reorganized into a Muslim emirate and remained an important trading center throughout the nineteenth century. As an emirate, Ilorin conquered several Yoruba towns and destroyed Old Oyo, the capital of the Oyo empire. Despite strong resistance, Ilorin was defeated by the British in 1897 CE, and became part of the Northern Nigerian Protectorate of Nigeria in 1900 CE, and part of the Prottectorate of Nigeria in 1914 CE. *See also* **Fulani empire**; **Ibadan**; **Ife**; **Nigeria**; **Oyo**.

Italian East Africa

In 1899 CE, Italy colonized Eritrea on the Red Sea and, in 1905 CE, it took over the southern part of what is now Somalia. In 1936 CE, Italian forces invaded and annexed Ethiopia. From 1936–1941 CE, when Allied forces defeated the Italians in East Africa during World War II, these territories were collectively known as Italian East Africa. The Italian King Victor Emmanuel I was named as the emperor of Italian East Africa. *See also* **Eritrea**; **Ethiopia**; **Italian Somaliland**; **Somalia**.

Italian Somaliland

In 1905 CE Italy took over the southern half of what is now Somalia. From 1936–1941 CE it was part of Italy's short-lived empire, Italian East Africa. In 1941 CE Italian Somaliland was lost to British troops. *See also* **Somalia**.

IVORY COAST République de la Côte d'Ivoire

The area that is now Ivory Coast (or Côte d'Ivoire as the country is officially known) lay south of what were the medieval empires of Ghana, Mali, and Songhay. It included many small kingdoms, such as those of the Baulé and Dyula, which remained comparatively undisturbed until the French penetration of the interior in the late nineteenth century.

The Portuguese were the first Europeans to reach the coast and, from their arrival in the second half of the fifteenth century, a flourishing trade in ivory and slaves developed. French missionaries arrived in 1637 CE. By the early nineteenth century French trading posts had been established on the southeast coast and treaties with local chiefs gradually extended the area under French influence. In 1893 CE, the French made Ivory Coast a colony, although the northern border was not settled until 1898 CE. In 1904 CE it became part of French West Africa, a vast administrative area that also included what are now Benin, Burkina Faso, Guinea, Mali, Mauritania, Niger, and Senegal, although the interior was not pacified until 1918 CE.

To develop the country, the French introduced a system of forced labor and this was one factor behind the formation of nationalist groups at the end of World War II. In 1946 CE, the French abolished compulsory labor, repealed some discriminatory laws, and made Ivory Coast an autonomous territory in the French Union. The port of the capital Abidjan was completed in the early 1950s and it became one of the leading financial centers of French West Africa.

Recent history

Ivory Coast achieved internal self-government in 1958 CE and it became fully independent on August 7, 1960 CE. The country's first president was Félix Houphouët-Boigny, who, in 1944 CE, had set up the African Agricultural Union (AAU) which represented African landowners. The AAU, which was one of the first anticolonial organizations in Ivory Coast, was transformed into the country's first political party in 1945 CE. As president, Houphouët-Boigny's rule was paternalistic and pro-Western, though it was also effective. For most of his period in office, the country enjoyed sustained economic growth, partly because his close contacts with France helped Ivory Coast find markets for its exports. The country's increasing prosperity led Abidjan to become known as "the Paris of Africa". Houphouët-Boigny's rule was based on a single-party system–the one party being the *Parti Démocratique de la Côte d'Ivoire* (Ivory Coast Democratic Party, or PDCI). However, some of its policies led to resentment among local educated people. In the 1970s, Houphouët-Boigny sought to correct this imbalance.

In 1983, the president's birthplace, Yamoussoukro, was designated as the country's new capital, though many of the functions of the capital remained in Abidjan. To enhance Yamoussoukro's status, one of the world's largest Christian churches, costing an estimated US $800 million, was built there in the 1980s. This massive expenditure came at a time when Ivory Coast was facing mounting economic problems, arising partly from the country's huge international debts, and partly

Pan-African conference (above)
A stamp marking the 1963 CE Conference of African Heads of State which took place at Addis Ababa, Ethiopia.

A king at rest (left)
Adjommani, king of the Bonboukou, pictured with his two sons.

The Basilica of Our Lady of Peace (below)
Former president of the Ivory Coast, Félix Houphouët-Boigny, commissioned this building, which was constructed from 1987–1989 CE. It is the largest church in the world.

Baulé pendant (above)
This unusual piece of decorative jewelry features a pair of crossed crocodiles and is fashioned out of gold.

from the falling international prices for several major exports, especially cocoa and coffee. However, after the legalization of opposition parties in 1990 CE, Houphouët-Boigny demonstrated his popularity when he was reelected president and the PDCI took most of the seats in the National Assembly. Following the death of Houphouët-Boigny in December 1993 CE, the president of the National Assembly, Henri Konan Bédié, took over as the country's head of state. In elections in 1995 CE, Bédié was elected president and the PDCI again won a large majority in the National Assembly.

Félix Houphouët-Boigny
A strong post-war nationalist leader in former French West Africa, he became president of the Ivory Coast when it gained its independence in 1960 CE.

© DIAGRAM

The new government continued to liberalize the economy, and was praised by the IMF (International Monetary Fund). However, it also faced various problems, including the presence in Ivory Coast of 300,000 refugees from Liberia. In December 1999 ce, an army mutiny occurred, with soldiers demanding back pay and better conditions. To restore order, retired Brigadier-General Robert Guei, who had served as the country's military chief between 1990 –1995 ce, mounted a bloodless coup and removed Bédié, who fled to Togo. General Guei, who led the ruling National Public Salvation Committee, promised a rapid return to democracy. When the presidential elections were held in October 2000 ce, the two main candidates were Guei and the veteran Laurent Gbagbo, who had contested the presidential elections in 1990. When it became clear that he was losing, Guei cancelled the poll. However, following protests, Gbagbo declared that he would form a government of national unity and Guei fled the country.

Massacre at Abidjan
On October 29 2000 ce the dead bodies at least 55 young men were found in a forest on the edge of Abidjan in the Ivory Coast. Violence erupted after a disputed election result; the young men were followers of the Muslim opposition leader Alassane Outtara, who lost the election to President Laurent Gbagbo after the military ruler, General Robert Guei, had been violently forced from power.

Ivory Coast

Pre 19th century CE
1637	French missionaries visit the Ivory Coast	
1730	Queen Aura Poka of the Asante founds the kingdom of Baule in present-day northern Ivory Coast	

19th century CE
1830s	French trading posts established along the Ivory coast	
1843	Coastal kingdoms of Aigini and Atokpora ask for French protection against the Asante	
1870	France withdraws from the Ivory Coast	
1887–1889	France reaches protectorate agreements with many local rulers	
1893	France claims Ivory Coast as a colony	
1895	Ivory Coast becomes part of the French West Africa colony	
1897	Northern kingdom of Kong destroyed by Samouri Toure	
1898	Present borders of Ivory Coast fixed after the capture of Samouri Touré	

1900–49 CE
1908	Military occupation of Ivory Coast completed	
1914–1918	Frequent rebellions as France tries to conscript Africans to fight in World War I	
1932	Most of the colony of Upper Volta (now Burkina Faso) is added to Ivory Coast	
1944	Félix Houphouët-Boigny and Auguste Denise form the African Farmers Union (SAA),	
1946	The African Democratic Union (RDA) is founded to campaign for independence for France's African colonies	
1947	Ivory Coast and Upper Volta are separated	

1950–59 CE
1950	Under the leadership of Houphouët-Boigny, the RDA begins a policy of cooperation with France	
1958	Ivory Coast gains internal self-government	

1960–69 CE
1960	**Aug 7** Ivory Coast becomes independent: Houphouët-Boigny becomes the first president	
1963	An attempted military coup is defeated	

1970–79 CE
1973	Another attempted military coup is defeated	

1980–89 CE
1980	An attempted military coup is defeated	
1981–1985	An agricultural recession causes rapid growth of the national debt	
1983	Work starts on a new capital at Yamoussoukro (Houphouët-Boigny's birthplace)	
1987	Economy badly hit by 50 percent fall in the price of cocoa	
1989	The largest Christian church in Africa is completed at Yamoussoukro	

1990–99 CE
1990	**Mar** After tax rises cause rioting, a new multiparty constitution is introduced	
1990	**Oct** Houphouët-Boigny wins the first presidential elections held under the new constitution	
1993	Houphouët-Boigny dies and is succeeded by Henri Konan Bédié	
1995	Bédié wins presidential elections held under rules that barred his main opponents	
1998	CIA announces that Ivory Coast is now a major center for growing and smuggling marijuana	
1999	Bédié is overthrown and a military regime is established under General Robert Guei	

2000–09 CE
2000	**Mar** Laurent Gbago is elected president, defeating Guei	

Peoples

AKAN

For information about the history of the Akan people, *see* **Ghana (Peoples)**.

ANYI

The Anyi are an Akan people, who are closely related to the Baulé people of Ivory Coast. The Anyi are concentrated in southeast Ivory Coast. In the mid-eighteenth century, sections of the Asante Empire, in what is now Ghana, broke away in search of fresh lands to the west. Some groups, led by a woman called Awura Poku, settled on lands to the east of the Bandama River. These and later migrations from the Akan homelands formed the present-day Akan and Baulé populations.

BAULÉ

The Baulé are an Akan people, closely related to the Anyi, who are concentrated in a central southeastern region of Ivory Coast, between the Bandama and Komoé rivers. In the mid-eighteenth century, people from the Asante Empire moved west in search of fresh lands. Some groups, led by a woman called Awura Poku, settled on the lands to the east of the Bandama River. These and later migrations from the Akan homelands formed the present-day Anyi and Baulé populations. Under Queen Akwa, the Baulé took over the gold-bearing land to the west of the Bandama region, but Baulé influence declined after her death.

DYULA

For information about the history of the Dyula people, *see* **Burkina Faso (Peoples—Dyula)**.

SONINKE

For information about the history of the Soninke people, *see* **Burkina Faso (Peoples—Soninke)**.

Ivory Coast presidents
Aug 7 1960–Dec 7 1993 CE Félix Houphouët-Boigny (head of state until Nov 3 1960)
Dec 7 1993–Dec 24 1999 CE Henri Konan Bédié
Dec 25 1999 CE– Robert Guéi (president of the national public salvation committee until Jan 4 2000)

Ivory Coast's major political figures

Bédié, Henri Konan (1934 CE–)

Bédié succeeded Félix Houphouët-Boigny as president of Côte d'Ivoire in December 1993. The formerly speaker of the country's National Assembly, he was reelected president of Cote d'Ivoire in 1996. Before entering politics, Bédié served in the diplomatic service and was Ambassador in the United States and Canada in the 1960s.

Houphouët-Boigny, Félix (1905–1993 CE)

Félix Houphouët-Boigny became the first president of Ivory Coast, in 1960, and he continued in this office, exercising a paternal style of government, until his death in 1993. He was born in Yamoussoukro, which in 1983 became the new political and administrative capital of Ivory Coast; Abidjan, the former capital, remains the economic and financial capital. During a visit in 1990, Pope John Paul II consecrated a basilica in Yamoussoukro; it is the largest Christian church in the world, and cost over US$800 million to build.

Félix Houphouët-Boigny
A silver 10 franc coin issued in 1966 bearing the image of the first president of the Ivory Coast.

Jubaland

Jubaland was a nineteenth-century British colony held at first by the British East Africa Company. In 1985 CE Jubaland became part of Britain's East Africa protectorate, later Kenya. In 1925 CE Britain ceded Jubaland to Italian Somaliland. *See* **British East Africa**; **Italian Somaliland**; **Kenya**; **Somalia**.

Jukun

Jukun is another name for Kororofa, one of the historic Hausa states, which once dominated what is now northern Nigeria. *See* **Hausa states**.

Kaarta

The Bambara are a Manding-speaking people who live chiefly in the grasslands in the upper Niger region of southern Mali. They established two Bambara states, Kaarta, along the middle Niger River in present-day Mali, and Segu, between the Sénégal and Niger rivers. Historians often credit the Bambara survivors of a battle with the king of Segu in the 1750s with the founding the city Kaarta, which was located to the west of Segu, near Kumbi, the site of the last capital of ancient Ghana. While the citizens of Kaarta were largely Bambara, the rulers were Massasi, who were descendants of Bambara, Berber, and Fulani ancestors.

Along with its more powerful neighbor, Segu, which reached its peak between about 1740–1800 CE, Kaarta was politically influential in West Africa until the mid-nineteenth century. In 1854 CE, Muslim troops, commanded by Al-Hajj Umar, conquered Kaarta. Kaarta was the first target of a series of *jihads* (holy wars of conquest) conducted against non-Muslim states. *See* **Mali (Peoples—Bambara** and **Malinke)**; **Segu**.

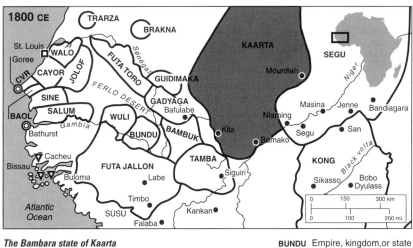

The Bambara state of Kaarta
The Bambara people established the state of Segu c.1600 CE, and the state of Kaarta in 1754 CE. Of the two Segu was the more powerful, especially after 1787 CE when it began to expand further down the River Niger.

BUNDU	Empire, kingdom, or state
SUSU	People
——	Boundary of state
▓	Bambara states

© DIAGRAM

A different role
The cavalry of the sultans of Kanem–Borno helped them control the important trade routes linking North and West Africa. The horses, not themselves indigenous to the area, had to be imported across the Sahara Desert.

Empire of Kanem
Kanem was founded in the ninth or tenth century BCE. By 1150 CE Kanem was a settled kingdom. During the thirteenth century it expanded northward and westward until, by 1230 CE, it was at its greatest extent. A move westward established the state of Bornu in 1386 CE which developed alongside Kanem. By 1526 CE the empire of Kanem–Bornu was founded, and it became the most powerful empire in sub-Saharan Africa. From 1671 CE the empire declined and, in 1846 CE, the original dynasty was replaced.

The four maps (right) show the empire at these critical dates:

1 ◼ c. 1150 CE
Kanem

2 ◼ c. 1230 CE
Empire of Kanem

3 ◼ c. 1500 CE
Kanem-Bornu

4 ◼ c. 1850 CE
Bornu

– – – Boundary of
Kanem-Bornu's
sphere of influence

Kabinda

See **Cabinda**.

Kalabar

See **Calabar, New**; **Calabar, Old**.

Kalabari Ijaw

See **Calabar, New**.

Kamerun

See **German Cameroons**.

Kanem

See **Kanem–Borno**.

A royal procession
A nineteenth-century engraving depicting the processsion of a sultan of Borno through one of the regional capitals.

Kanem–Borno

Kanem was founded in the ninth or tenth century BCE to the northeast of Lake Chad, West Africa. The founder of Kanem–Borno (or Kanem–Bornu) was a great Arab hero named Sayf bin Dhu Yazan, and the dynasty he established, the Sefawa, lasted for around 1,000 years. At its height, Kanem–Borno controlled what are now southern Chad, northern Cameroon, northeastern Nigeria, eastern Niger, and southern Libya.

The subjects of early Kanem–Borno were African nomads, and the state had no fixed towns at first. It was positioned to control some of the trade routes to and from Tunis, north of the Sahara. By the eleventh century, Kanem was an Islamic state though its kings were considered to be divine. The different nomadic peoples of Kanem gradually merged into a distinct group speaking one language, Kanuri. The Kanem state expanded, conquering several non-Kanuri people until the fourteenth century. This period was characterized by internal disputes over succession to the throne and battles with the Bulala. The Kanuri were eventually defeated by the Bulala and driven out of Kanem. They settled to the southeast of Kanem, in the southernmost province, Borno, west of Lake Chad. From there, the Kanuri finally managed reestablish their empire under *Mai* (King) Ali Gaji (died 1503). Kanem was retaken in

the early sixteenth century, at a time of great expansion, but Borno remained the heart of the new empire. The empire was often called simply Bornu during this second period. Its most famous king was Mai Idris Alooma (reigned c.1569–1603 CE), who, on his death, left Borno the most powerful state in the Sudan and a center of Islamic learning and scholarship. In 1808 CE the *mais* were driven from their capital by Fulani *jihadists*. The Kanuri retook their seat (but not all their territory) with the aid of a Kanem scholar named El-Kanemi (died 1837 CE). El-Kanemi, whose title was *shehu* (sheikh or sultan) of Borno, became the true power in Borno, while the *mai* became a ceremonial figure. In 1846 CE the *mai* and his son were executed by El-Kanemi's heir after the king tried to reassert the authority of the Sefawa dynasty. From that date, much-reduced Borno was ruled by the *shehu*.

The Sudanese warrior Rabah Zubayr defeated Borno in 1893 CE, but the French restored the *shehu* seven years later. Borno was then divided between France, Britain, and Germany. The current shehu was recognized only in British Borno, which retained its status as an emirate within the colony of Northern Nigeria. Today, the *shehu* is one of Nigeria's most important traditional leaders. *See also* **Nigeria**.

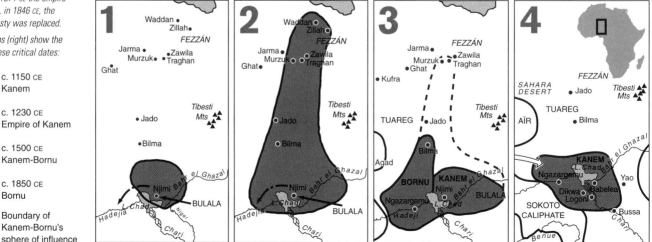

Kangaba, Kingdom of

Kangaba was a small, West-African kingdom that was the base of the huge medieval empire of Mali. *See also* **Mali, empire of**.

KaNgwane

KaNgwane, or Swazi, was one of the smallest of the ten homelands established during South Africa's apartheid era. The white-controlled South African government forced black South Africans to live in these areas, which often bore no relation to their true homelands. KaNgwane was created in 1977 CE in eastern Transvaal to house ethnic Swazis living in South Africa, not Swaziland. Black people were forced to live in these so-called "homelands." Apartheid came to an end in 1991 CE, and in 1994 CE homelands were abolished. KaNgwane is now part of Mpumalanga province. *See also* **South Africa**; **Swaziland**.

Kano

Kano was one of the most important of the Hausa *Bakwai*, or states, that once dominated what are now northwestern Nigeria and southwestern Niger. According to tradition, the Kano state was founded as one of the *Hausa Bakwai* ("Seven True Hausa States") in 999 CE by Bagauda, a grandson of the father of all Hausa people. During the reign of King Gajemasu (1095–1134 CE), the city of Kano was chosen for state capital, and a wall was built around the city. Scholars from the empire of Mali introduced Islam into Kano state in the 1340s.

Kano was tributary to Kanem–Borno for a while in the early fifteenth century and again in the eighteenth century, and was captured by Songhai in 1513 CE. Songhai's rule ended after the empire was destroyed by

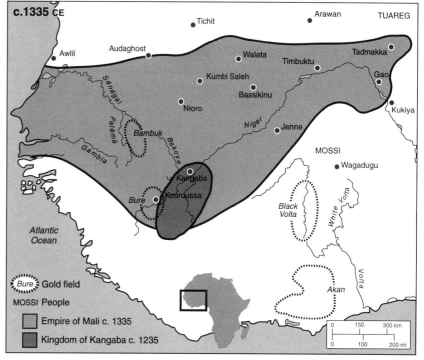

Bure Gold field
MOSSI People
Empire of Mali c. 1335
Kingdom of Kangaba c. 1235

Jewel in the crown
The map shows the extents of the Kingdom of Kangaba c.1235 CE, and the Empire of Mali c.1335 CE, after which the empire began to decline.

Moroccan invaders at the end of the sixteenth century. War with the *jihad* warriors of the Fulani empire (1804–07 CE) resulted in Kano state becoming an emirate. It also again became a major trading center, where cowries were used as currency. Goods from West and North Africa and Europe were traded there. The city was captured by the British in 1903 CE and joined to their colony of Northern Nigeria as part of Kano province. *See also* **Hausa states**; **Nigeria**; **Songhay**.

Katanga

Katanga is an important historical region of what is now southern Congo (formerly Zaire). Lake Tanganyika lies to the east, Zambia to the south, and Angola to the west. Some scholars think northern Katanga is where Bantu-speaking people first emerged as a distinct linguistic group many centuries ago, placing the region at the heart of African history. In more recent centuries, Katanga was the heartland of the Luba kingdom. By the fourteenth century, well-established chieftanships existed in the Katanga region. From these, the Luba kingdom emerged and dominated the region until Lunda rulers became more powerful.

Katanga was made part of the Congo Free State in 1885 CE. The Congo Free State was the personal colony of the Belgian king, Leopold II. He contracted a commercial company–*Compaigne du Katanga*–to run the province. In return, the company was given nearly a third of the province's land. At that time, the Yeke kingdom of Msiri was in charge of much of Katanga, and they resisted foreign control for many years. The Belgian government took control of the Congo Free State in 1908 CE after a great deal of international uproar over the treatment of the colonized Africans, many of whom were forced to work as slaves and were brutally mistreated.

Copper mining
In the 1920s and 1930s, copper mining boomed in the north of Northern Rhodesia (present-day Zambia). Largely worked by African miners but owned by white settlers, most of the profits of this lucrative industry went overseas. With its employees forced to live in inadequate "native reserves," mining was one of the few ways to make a living not denied to Africans. As a result, the copper industry drained labor away from rural areas leading to food shortages, and the disruption of whole communities.

Independence
In 1960 CE, Moïse Tshombe declared mineral-rich Katanga (Shaba) independent from the Congo (Dem. Rep.). The rebellion collapsed in 1963 CE when Tshombe fled the country, but was followed by another in 1964–65 CE.

© DIAGRAM

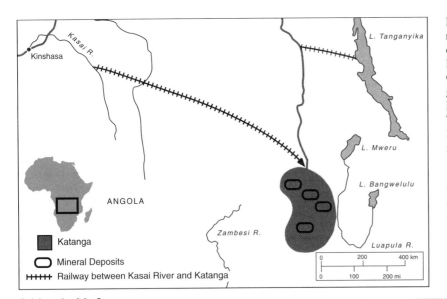

Before the arrival of Europeans, Katangans had been mining the region's rich copper deposits. Since the colonial era, this exploitation has continued, and Katanga has become the most industrialized part of Congo outside of the capital Kinshasa. In 1960 CE Belgian Congo became independent as the Congo Republic. In the same year, a Katangan politician, Moise Tshombe, declared Katanga an independent republic. He was supported by foreign mining interests, and much bloodshed followed as Congolese, Belgian, and UN forces intervened.

From 1963 CE, when Katanga was occupied by UN troops, the breakaway republic was reincorporated into Congo as a province. Further conflict occurred in 1977 CE when rebel Katangans unsuccessfully attempted to invade Zaire from their bases in Angola. Between 1971 CE and 1997 CE, Katanga was known as Shaba. *See also* **Congo, Democratic Republic of**; **Luba kingdom**; **Lunda Empire**; **Yeke kingdom**.

Belgian rule of the Congo
Katanga became part of the Congo Free State in 1885 CE; it was then controlled by the Belgian king, Leopold II. In 1891 CE, he contracted a commercial company, the Compagnie du Katanga, to occupy and develop the Katanga area, in return for which the company would be granted ownership of one third of the province. Msiri and his Yeke people opposed this situation from 1891–94 CE.

Katsina

Katsina was one of the most important of the Hausa Bakwai, or states, that once dominated what are now northwestern Nigeria and southwestern Niger. According to tradition, the kingdom was founded in the tenth or eleventh century. By the late fifteenth century, Katsina was a Muslim state. Along with Kano, Katsina was ruled by Songhai for much of the sixteenth century. The state was tributary to Borno until the late eighteenth century. During that century, Katsina was the most important Hausa state and center for Islamic learning in west Africa.

In 1806 ce Katsina was captured by Fulani warriors on a jihad (holy Muslim war) inspired by Usman dan Fodio. Their leader, Umaru Dallaji, was named the first Katsina emir. The Katsina emirate was part of the Fulani empire (or Sokoto Caliphate). In 1903 CE the emirate was joined to the British-ruled Northern Nigeria Protectorate. The following year, Katsina was reduced in size when Britain and France agreed the borders between Niger and Nigeria. During the colonial era, the emirate was part of Kano province. Today, its former territory lies mostly within what is now Katsina state. *See also* **Hausa states**; **Kano**; **Nigeria**; **Songhai**.

Kazembe kingdom

In the eighteenth and nineteenth centuries, the Kazembe kingdom was one of Central Africa's largest and most powerful states. Kazembe was an offshoot of the Lunda empire and was based in what is now southern Congo (formerly Zaire) and northern Zambia, southwest of Lake Tanganyika. At the beginning of the eighteenth century, the Lunda emperor, or Mwata Yamvo, sent one of his generals, Yembe Yembe, to conquer lands to the east of the empire. A man named Chinyanta told Mwata Yamvo that Yembe Yembe was disloyal. Chinyanta was killed by Yembe Yembe, who was, in turn, killed by the Mwata Yamvo's troops. In honor of Chinyanta, the Lunda emperor named the dead man's son Mwata Kazembe (Lord of the Kazembe) and sent him to continue the empire's eastward expansion. By the reign of the third Kazembe, the kingdom stretched from the Katanga region of southern Congo to northern Zambia. By 1800 CE, the Kazembe's capital was the hub of trade routes that crossed Africa. Particularly important links were with Swahili and Yao traders to the east and the Mwata Yamvo's lands to the west. The late nineteenth century was a period of political instability in Kazembe, however, as four rulers died violently; wars of succession weakened the kingdom. The power of Swahili traders in the region grew at the expense of Kazembe, and greatly increased slave raiding helped to further fragment the kingdom. In 1899 CE a British force marched on the Kazembe capital, where they met no resistance: the king had fled north, from where he negotiated his surrender. By 1900 CE, independent Kazembe no longer existed. *See also* **Congo, Democratic Republic of**; **Lunda empire**; **Zambia**.

At the crossroads
Following a period of expansion stretching back to the start of the eighteenth century, the Kazembe kingdom grew until, by 1800 CE, it had become the hub of trade routes that crossed Africa.

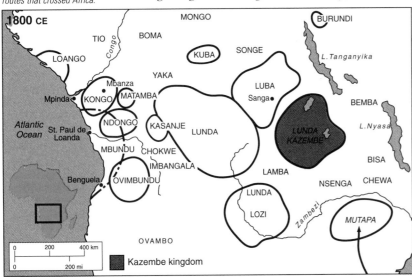

Kebbi

Kebbi was one of the *Hausa Bakwai*, or "Seven True States" that once dominated what is now northwestern Nigeria and southwestern Niger. It was founded by Muhammad Kanta in the fourteenth or fifteenth century. Like the other Hausa states, Kebbi was tributary to Songhai for a while. In 1516 CE, Kebbi declared independence from Songhai, and so began its rise to prominence. For a period in the sixteenth century, Kebbi wrested control of the other Hausa states from Songhay. Kebbi declined from the seventeenth century on, experiencing almost constant attacks from Air, Gobir, and Zamfara. In the early nineteenth century, Kebbi fell to the Fulani empire. In 1991 CE, Nigeria created the new federal state of Kebbi, incorporating the lands of historic Kebbi. *See also* **Fulani empire**; **Hausa states**; **Nigeria**; **Songhai**.

KENYA Republic of Kenya

The coast of what is now Kenya was a major trading center, with links to southern Arabia and beyond, from at least 2,000 years ago. In 1498 CE, Portuguese mariners led by Vasco da Gama reached the area, pioneering a route from Europe to Asia around the tip of southern Africa. Portugal took over the coast in the early sixteenth century, but Arabs drove them out. Little is known of the history of the interior until the nineteenth century when Arabs and Swahili-speaking peoples made caravan trips (groups of travelers journeying together) in search of ivory, slaves, and other goods. Because the caravans met with opposition from the Maasai people, many took routes to the south through what is now Tanzania.

Although some individual European explorers traveled inland in the mid-nineteenth century, the interior remained comparatively undisturbed until the European "scramble" for African territory in the late nineteenth century. Britain controlled the coast by 1895 CE and it extended its rule inland by building a railroad from Mombasa, on the coast, through Kenya, to the fertile lands around Lake Victoria in Uganda. This railroad was completed by 1903 CE. Known first as British East Africa, Kenya became a British colony in 1920 CE. In 1948 CE, the East African High Commission was formed to handle common services in Kenya, Tanganyika (now Tanzania), and Uganda. However, nationalist demands for independence increased after the end of World War II. In 1952 CE, the Mau Mau rebellion broke out among the Kikuyu people–the largest single group in Kenya.

Recent history

Kenya's senior nationalist politician, Jomo Kenyatta, was imprisoned in 1953 CE after having been convicted of leading the Mau Mau movement, a charge he denied. However, a new generation of young politicians, led by Tom Mboya, continued the political struggle for independence. In 1961 CE, elections were held for a new parliament. The Kenya African National Union (KANU) won a majority, but it refused to take office until Kenyatta was released from prison. The opposition party, the Kenya African Democratic Union (KADU), then formed a government. In August 1961 CE, Kenyatta was freed and a KANU–KADU coalition was set up. Kenya became independent on December 12, 1963 CE, with Jomo Kenyatta as its first prime minister. In 1964 CE, Kenya became a republic and Kenyatta became president. KANU and KADU merged, effectively making Kenya a single-party state.

The new government rapidly modified British colonial institutions and practices. Many formerly European-owned farms were sold or rented to black Africans, though non-Africans who became Kenyan citizens were allowed to keep their property. Kenyatta also sought to reduce the differences between the country's ethnic groups and, instead, promoted a national Kenyan identity. An opposition party, the Kenya People's Union, was formed in 1966 CE, but Kenyatta dissolved it in 1969 CE and the country reverted to being a *de facto* one-party state.

Relations with other countries were not always easy. In 1967 CE, the East African High Commission was transformed into the East African Community, but relations between Kenya and its partners, Tanzania and Uganda, gradually deteriorated and the Community was dissolved in 1977 CE. It was not until November 1999 CE that the East African Community was revived, with its aims of a customs union, a common market, a monetary union, and, ultimately, a political union.

Kenyatta's leadership brought many benefits, including a thriving economy and an expansion of tourism, which became a major source of foreign revenue. After his death in 1978 CE, he was succeeded by the vice-president, Daniel arap Moi. In 1982 CE, the government made KANU the only legal political party. It was accused of permitting widespread corruption and using repressive methods. Many Kenyans and international institutions, including the International Monetary Fund (IMF), called for radical reforms, including the restoration of civil rights and a return to democracy.

Moi was reelected in 1983, 1988 and 1992 CE, when multiparty elections

Jomo Kenyatta
The first prime minister of a newly-independent Kenya in 1963 CE, he then became president from 1964–1978 CE. During this time he encouraged ethnic and racial harmony, and presided over a thriving economy and an expansion of tourism.

© DIAGRAM

The Mau Mau rebellion

1952–1960 CE

UGANDA

KENYA

• Lodwar
L. Rudolf
• Baragoi
• Kapenguria
• Kitale
• Maralal
L. Baringo
• Eldoret
Kisumu
Thomsons Falls
Nakuru
Gilgil
Nanyuki
Nyeri
• Isiolo
• Meru
• Chuka
• Embu
Fort hall
Kiambu
Kikuyu
Ngong
Thika
Nairobi
Machakos
• Kitui
L. Victoria
TANGANYIKA
L. Natron
• Voi

0   100 km
0   50   100 mi

• Detention Camps
Principal area of conflict

Camps and conflicts (above)
This map shows the location of the detention camps, and the principal areas of conflict, during the Mau Mau rebellion.

Camp prisoners (below)
Alleged supporters of the Mau Mau rebellion were kept in detention camps. Around 80,000 Kikuyu were imprisoned by British security forces in an attempt to crush the Mau Mau rebellion in the early 1950s. Jomo Kenyatta was one of those imprisoned; he served eight-and-a-half years in prison before being released after Kenya won independence in 1963 CE.

Detention camp (above)
This detention camp was set up at Nyeri, Kenya, by the British in the 1950s and held people suspected of involvement in the anti-colonial Mau Mau uprising.

Protestors (right)
Supporters of the Mau Mau rebellion often assumed elaborate and striking costumes in order to draw attention to their cause.

were permitted following demonstrations and violence. The 1992 elections were marred by accusations of fraud but, in 1997 CE, the first genuinely democratic presidential and parliamentary elections since independence was gained were held. However, owing to the disunity of the opposition along ethnic lines, Moi defeated his 13 opponents and regained the presidency. KANU also won comfortably in the National Assembly elections.

Peoples

ACHOLI
For information about the history of the Acholi people, *see* **Sudan (Peoples—Acholi)**.

EAST AFRICAN ASIANS
Asians form a small but economically important East

African minority. Nairobi and Mombasa in Kenya have the largest East African Asian communities, but there are also significant concentrations in Dar es Salaam and Zanzibar in Tanzania, and a growing number are returning to Uganda after an absence of 20 years.

Asians have been in East Africa for many hundreds of years. The region has long attracted traders, and dhows (cargo-carrying sailboats) plied between India, the Arabian peninsula, and East Africa, supplying Indian-made textiles and iron goods in exchange for ivory, gold, slaves, and spices. However, the majority of the present-day Asian community dates back to the colonial era and the construction of the East Africa Railway (1896–1902 CE), linking Mombasa with Uganda. Local African labor was either unavailable or was considered unreliable or hostile, and so 32,000 laborers

The 'lunatic line'

Indian labour
These workers, brought over from India because Africans were either not available for such work, or else openly hostile, are taking a rest from building "the lunatic line" which traversed hazardous and difficult terrain such as desert, the Great Rift Valley, and tsetse-fly-infested land. More than 6,000 people were injured and 2,500 lives were lost in the process.

The Uganda Railway
Following the declaration of a Protectorate over Uganda in 1893 CE and for economic and strategic reasons, it became necessary to construct a railroad from the coast. The first line was laid at Mombasa on May 30, 1896 CE, and the railhead reached Nairobi in June 1899 CE; construction of the remainder of the railway was not completed until 1901 CE.

were recruited in India. Many of these workers died of tropical diseases, while others returned to India on completion of their contracts. However, about 7,000 Indians chose to settle in East Africa, while retaining close links with their home country. Although some Indians continued to work on the railroads, most established themselves as merchants, initially catering to the needs of fellow Indians, but soon expanding their businesses to cater for the African population as well. Hearing of the business opportunities to be found in East Africa, Indian immigrants continued to arrive into the 1920s, by which time Asians, through their trading activities, had done much to integrate even remote areas into the cash economy.

The East African Indian National Congress was formed in 1914 CE to represent the interests of the Asian community, especially in demanding equal representation on the Legislative Councils, equal economic opportunities (especially in relation to land ownership in the highlands of Kenya), and in opposing segregation between Europeans and Asians. Their complaints were principally aimed at the European settler community, whom they far outnumbered. In marked contrast to the Indian community of South Africa, and despite the urging of political leaders in India itself, East African Asians rarely took up common cause with the

Hindu temple
This Hindu temple in Mombasa was built by volunteers 1957–1960 CE.

Sikh temple
This Sikh temple at Makindu offered free food and lodging to travelers, although visitors were restricted to one night's stay per person.

© DIAGRAM

Kenyan tourism

National parks and game reserves

The map below shows the major national parks and game reserves of Uganda, Kenya, and Tanzania. The establishment of these protected areas curtailed many people's rights of access to vital resources, and some were even evicted from their land. Today, governments are beginning to realize the value of indigenous lifestyles that help to maintain the environment, and are allowing greater access to national parks and game reserves.

(Names in brackets indicate peoples affected by the establishment of that park or reserve)

1 Siboli
2 Marsabit (Boran)
3 South Turkana (Turkana)
4 Mount Elgon (Maasai)
5 Laikipia (Maasai, Laikipiak)
6 Losai
7 Samburu (Samburu)
8 Buffalo Springs (Samburu)
9 Shaba
10 Aberdares (Kikuyu)
11 Mount Kenya
12 Meru
13 Masai Mara (Maasai)
14 Amboseli (Maasai)
15 Chyulu
16 Tsavo (West)
17 Tsavo (East) (Taita)
18 Shimba Hills

Treetops (left)
In the Aberdares National Park, Kenya–once a Mau Mau stronghold–is Treetops Lodge, a world-famous hotel. It was first built in 1934 CE and has been visited by many members of European royal families.

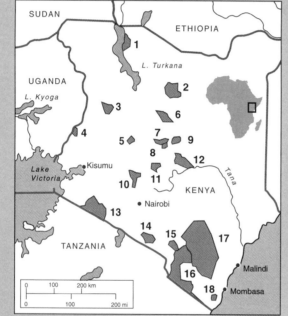

Kilaguni (above)
Tourists get the chance to see wildlife close-up at Kilaguni Lodge in Tsavo, Kenya's largest national park. Recently expanded to include a conference center, Kilaguni attracts many tourists.

African population, toward whom they tended to feel culturally superior.

At independence, Asians were given a choice. They could become citizens of the country in which they lived or they could retain British nationality, but without a right of residency in Britain. It was not an easy choice. Adopting local citizenship implied loyalty to a new nation, but many Asians felt that their security in Africa was limited and believed that British nationality offered some measure of protection in the event of anti-Asian hostilities. "Africanization" policies of the newly independent states resulted in Asians having to stop doing business in rural areas, but, in the cities, their skills and economic strength meant that they were not so easily replaced, Nevertheless, many found their shops nationalized or were pressured out of jobs, especially in government. In Kenya, the change happened slowly, thus avoiding disruption. But, in Uganda, the changes were sudden and brutal. In 1972, Uganda's dictator Idi Amin Dada expelled the entire Asian community of 80,000 from the country, distributing their businesses to his supporters. Although the expulsions were initially widely supported, they had a devastating

effect on Uganda's economy, from which the country is still recovering. In the 1990s, Uganda's government under Yoweri Museveni attempted to encourage the return of Ugandan Asians.

GUSII

The Gusii live in the western corner of Kenya, centered around the town of Kisii. The Kisii highlands were largely uninhabited before 1800 CE, when the ancestors of the Luo and Kipsigis began settling the surrounding savanna (grassland) in large numbers. The inhabitants of the savanna were dislodged, and the Gusii came to settle in the Kisii highlands, which, at that time, were largely covered by forest. Between 1901 and 1908 CE, military expeditions were sent by British forces to quell the resistance of the Gusii and their neighbors to foreign rule. In the 1960s, the Gusii were in conflict with the Maasai over land.

ITESO

For information about the history of the Iteso people, *See* **Uganda (Peoples—Iteso)**.

KALENJIN

The Kalenjin group is made up of several related peoples, the most numerous of which are the Kipsigis, the Nandi, the Okieks, and the Pokot. The Kalenjin language is an Eastern Sudanic language, and the ancestors of the Kalenjin were Highland Nilotes. The Highland Nilotes began dispersing from their original cradleland at the northernmost tip of Lake Turkana in present-day Ethiopia during the last millennium BCE. Many of the Highland Nilotes were absorbed by Bantu-speaking societies, but the Kalenjin were the largest group to remain distinct.

The Kipsigis did not emerge as a distinct group until sometime after 1000 CE, separating from the Nandi as late as 1600–1800. Okieks, unlike most Kalenjin groups, were originally hunter-gatherers in forest regions and they were regarded as inferior by their cattle-herding neighbors. The Pokot developed a culture that was influenced by the Karamojong and Iteso, who today are found mainly in Uganda.

KIKUYU

The Kikuyu, sometimes called the Gikuyu, are Kenya's largest ethnic group. The history of the Kikuyu is obscure. Ethnologists believe that they came to Kenya from the north and west and began to settle Kikuyuland in the sixteenth century. Their expansion into Kenya continued into the nineteenth century. However, their settled existence was disturbed after 1895 CE when the British government took over British East Africa, which was later renamed Kenya. British settlers took over Kikuyu land and many Kikuyu were forced to abandon farming and work for the settlers or in the factories that sprang up in Nairobi. The Kikuyu became third-class citizens (Asians formed the middle class). However, during World War II, many Kikuyu men joined the British army and fought against the Germans. After World War II, such men were bitter about their treatment. When progress to independence seemed to be too slow, some Kikuyu organized the Mau Mau society which began to commit acts of anticolonial terrorism. Fighting continued until 1956 CE, during which time 13,000 Africans, mostly Kikuyu, were killed.

LUO

The Luo live in the western corner of Kenya, mainly in the Nyanza region, and also in northwestern Tanzania. The Luo claim descent from a mythical ancestor called Ramogi. The Luo are actually Nilotes, belonging to the so-called River-Lake Nilotes, who originated in a region in what is now southern Sudan. The ancestors of the Luo, a Lwo-speaking people, migrated south probably between the fifteenth and eighteenth centuries, traveling along the Nile River to the lakes region of Kenya and Tanzania. The Luo arrived in Nyanza in four separate clan groups. The Jok group arrived in the sixteenth century, while the Jokowiny and the Jokomolo arrived in the early seventeenth century. Finally, the non-Lwo Abasuba arrived in the eighteenth and nineteenth centuries.

MAASAI

The Maasai (or Masai) live mostly in the grasslands of the Great Rift Valley that straddle the border of Kenya and Tanzania. They are Plains Nilotes—that is, their

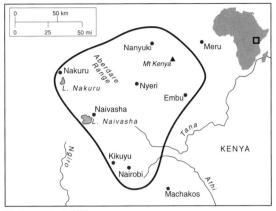

Modern extent of Kikuyu

ancestors were people from the southwestern fringe of the Ethiopian Highlands who migrated to the plains of East Africa. The Maasai initially settled to the east of the Great Rift Valley between Mounts Kenya and Kilimanjaro. But the Maasai "proper" migrated southward, while the Samburu turned east and settled in the mountains.

The eighteenth century was a period of increasing power and geographical expansion for the Maasai. By the early eighteenth century, despite their relatively small numbers, they dominated the region between Mount Elgon and Mount Kenya in the north, and Dodoma, now the capital of Tanzania, to the south. As a rule, they were not conquerors, but conflict with their neighbors or other Maasai groups began when they raided cattle or defended their own herds.

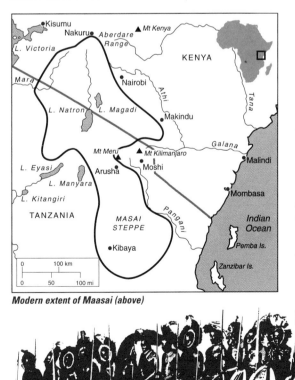

Modern extent of Maasai (above)

Battle dress (below)
This line-up of moran (the youngest age set) shows them in full battle dress. The feathered headdresses made it difficult for enemies to count their numbers. The Maasai frequently won their battles as they were well prepared both physically and psychologically. Their reputation for belligerence and ferocity, however, was largely fostered by Arab slave traders to scare competitors off inland trade routes.

© DIAGRAM

Kenya

Pre 19th century

1st century CE Greek merchants sail to East Africa from Egypt to buy ivory

c. 800 Trading towns develop on the East African coast

c. 1000 Arab merchants introduce Islam to the East African coast

1498 Portuguese navigator Vasco da Gama reaches Kenya via the Cape of Good Hope

1593 The Portuguese build a fortress at Mombasa

18th century Masai cattle herders migrate into the Kenya region from the north

1729 The Omanis oust the Portuguese from the Kenyan coast

19th century CE

19th century Kikuyu farmers migrate into the Kenya region from the south

1849 Johann Ludwig Krapf discovers Mt Kenya

1858 John Hanning Speke reaches Lake Victoria

1861 Control of the Kenyan coast passes to the sultanate of Zanzibar

1886 Britain and Germany reach agreement on their respective spheres of influence in East Africa

1887 A British business group leases the Kenyan coast from the sultan of Zanzibar

1888 The Imperial British East Africa Company is formed

1890 An Anglo-German treaty fixes the southern border of the Imperial British East Africa Company's territory

1895 The British government dissolves the Imperial British East Africa Company and establishes the East Africa Protectorate

1900–49 CE **1901** The British build a railroad from Mombasa to Lake Victoria, opening up the Kenyan highlands for white settlers

1920 The interior becomes the British Crown Colony of Kenya: the coast remains a protectorate, nominally ruled by the sultan of Zanzibar

1944 The Kikuyu and other Kenyan peoples form the Kenya African Union (KAU) to oppose British rule

1947 Jomo Kenyatta becomes leader of the KAU

1950–59 CE **1952** The Mau Mau terrorists begin attacks on white settlers and African supporters of British rule

1953 Kenyatta is jailed after he is wrongly convicted of being a Mau Mau leader

1956 Mau Mau movement is suppressed by the British

1957 The first Africans are elected to the colonial legislature

1960–69 CE **1961** Kenya African National Union (KANU) wins elections to a new parliament but it refuses to take office unless its leader Kenyatta is released from jail. Kenya African Democratic Union (KADU) takes office instead

1963 **Dec 12** Kenya becomes independent with Kenyatta as prime minister

1964 Kenya becomes a republic with Kenyatta as president. KADU merges with KANU to make Kenya a one-party state

1966 A new opposition party, the Kenya People's Union (KPU) is formed

1967 Kenya, Tanzania and Uganda form the East African Community

1969 Kenyatta dissolves the KPU

1970–79 CE **1975** Josiah Mwangi Kariuki, a leading critic of the Kenyatta government, is assassinated

1977 The East Africa Community is dissolved

1978 Kenyatta dies and is succeeded as president by Daniel arap Moi

1980–89 CE **1982** A new constitution makes KANU the only legal party

1982 A failed military coup is accompanied by widespread rioting and looting

1987 Islamic fundamentalists demonstrate in Mombasa

1990–99 CE **1990** Pro-democracy demonstrations break out in Nairobi and other cities

1991 Under pressure from aid donors, a multiparty constitution is introduced

1992 Moi and KANU win presidential and parliamentary elections held under the new constitution amid allegations of fraud

1995 The anthropologist Richard Leakey founds a new opposition party, Safina

1997 Moi is reelected president with 40 percent of the vote

1998 A car-bomb explosion outside the US embassy in Nairobi kills 250 people

1998 Kenya, Tanzania and Uganda sign a framework agreement establishing a new East-African Community, aimed at creating a common market in East Africa

Kenya's hidden past

More than 100 years ago Charles Darwin, the famous naturalist and author of *The Origin of Species*, suggested that human beings probably first evolved in Africa. A number of scientific discoveries, made in the 1950s, narrowed the habitat of our ancestors down to East Africa and, in particular, Ethiopia, Tanzania and Kenya. These forerunners of present-day human beings are known collectively as «hominids». Scientists group humans, apes, monkeys, and several other animals together as primates, and believe that the primates all had a common ancestor which lived in East Africa more than five million years ago.

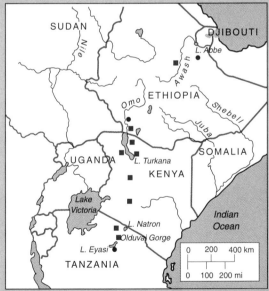

Australopithecus afarensis *fossil sites in East Africa*

Homo erectus *and* Homo habilis *fossil sites in East Africa*

Australopithecus *finds (right)*
These illustrations depict two fossil finds, perhaps from very early australopiths.

A Elbow joint, 4 million years old, from Kanapoi in Kenya.

B Jawbone, 5,5 million years old, which was discovered in Lothagam in Kenya.

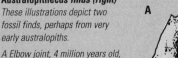

A

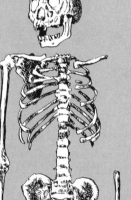

B

Homo erectus *finds (right)*
The illustration (below) depicts a cranium with heavy brow ridges, which is among the most complete and earliest erectus *skulls discovered. It is perhaps 1.6 million years old, and was found at Koobi Fora, east of lake Turkana, Kenya.*

The illustration (right) depicts the 1.6 million-year-old skeleton which belonged to a Homo erectus boy. Aged under 13, he was already 5ft 4 in (1.6 m) tall, so might have grown to 6 ft (1.8 m), which would have been taller than most modern men. Kenyan fossil hunter Kamoya Kimeu found these bones in 1984 CE, west of Lake Turkana.

A family of anthropologists
Much of the research into the existence of early humans in East Africa was carried out by Anglo-Kenyan anthropologists of the Leakey familt–Louis and Mary, and their sons Richard and Jonathan–and their Kenyan co-workers, including Bernard Ngeneo and Kamoya Kimeu. In fact, one of Kimeu's most important discoveries was a Homo erectus skeleton, which was more than 1.5 million years old, found in 1984 CE near Lake Turkana in northern Kenya.

Louis Leakey was a Kenyan, the son of British missionaries. With his wife, Mary, and later with their son, Richard, he found important fossil remains in East Africa, especially in Olduvai Gorge, Tanzania. These fossils included the 2-million-year-old remains of an early hominid (humanlike) species, Homo habilis ('Handy Man').

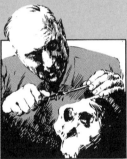

Leakey, Louis Seymour Bazett

Mary Leakey was an English-born archaeologist who moved to Kenya after marrying Louis Leakey in 1936 CE. In 1948 CE she discovered the fossil remains of a primitive ape thought to have lived 25–40 million years ago. Together with her husband she made many other important discoveries.

Leakey, Mary Douglas

Kenyan presidents
Dec 12 1964–Aug 22 1978 CE Jomo Kenyatta
Aug 22 1978 CE– Daniel arap Moi (acting until Oct 14 1978)

The nineteenth century was a period of increasingly frequent civil wars among the Maasai. In particular, the Maasai "proper"–united for the first time under one leader, the *laibon* (prophet) Mbatiany–were in conflict with the Laikipiak, an agricultural Maasai group. This conflict was followed by rinderpest (a cattle disease), smallpox, and cholera epidemics, and famine during the 1880s and 1890s. These disasters impoverished or killed thousands of Maasai and they also sparked further civil wars. This troubled period of Maasai history coincided with the British and German partition of East Africa. Europeans took over Maasai lands in British East Africa and the Maasai were restricted to reserves.

MIJIKENDA
The Mijikenda inhabit the coast of Kenya. They are a Bantu-speaking people who probably migrated into East Africa from the Katanga region in what is now the Democratic Republic of Congo. They are also sometimes called the Nyika–a name for the dry region they had to cross to reach the coast. In the early seventeenth century, oral history relates how several Mijikenda groups, including a subgroup called the Giriama, migrated south from the northern Kenyan coast around Lamu as a result of pressure from the Somalis and the Oromo. The Giriama built a fortress on top of a hill near Kilifi, roughly a hundred miles to the south.

TURKANA
The Turkana inhabit the semidesert regions of northwestern Kenya. They are sometimes regarded as part of the Karamojong cluster of peoples (*see also* **Uganda**). The Turkana and Karamojong share a common ancestry, descending from Nilotes who originated several millennia ago on the southwestern fringes of the Ethiopian Highlands. The Turkana are Plains Nilotes, who emerged as a new and powerful force in East Africa during the second millennium CE.

Kenya's major political figures

Delamere, Lord (Hugh Cholmondely) (1870–1931 CE)
During the colonial period, Lord Delamere became known as the leading champion of the rights of white settlers in Kenya. He believed in the creation of an East African Dominion, much like South Africa, where the white population would occupy a dominant position.

Tribute to a national hero
A stamp celebrating Kenyatta Day, 1978 CE.

Kenyatta, Jomo (c. 1889–1978 CE)
Jomo Kenyatta was prime minister of Kenya (1963–64) and president from 1964 until 1978. He studied anthropology at London University, England, in the 1930s, and wrote a major study of Kikuyu life, *Facing Mount Kenya* (1938). In 1952, he was arrested and imprisoned for his alleged role in managing the Mau Mau rebellion against British rule. Released from prison in 1959, he spent a further two years under house arrest. When he was eventually freed, in 1961, he assumed leadership of the Kenya African National Union (KANU), which won the preindependence elections in 1963..

Kenyatta, Margaret Wambui (1928 CE–)
The daughter of the Kenyan leader Jomo Kenyatta and his first wife, Margaret Kenyatta became an active campaigner on behalf of third-world women. During her father's jail term, she helped him to keep in touch with his supporters. In 1960, she entered local politics and became mayor (1970–6) of Nairobi, the capital.

Kimathi, Dedan (1931–1957 CE)
Dedan Kimathi was the leader of the Mau Mau rebellion that opposed British rule in Kenya in the 1950s. He was captured in 1956 and executed.

Mboya, Thomas Joseph (1930–1969 CE)
Tom Mboya, a Luo, was general secretary of the Kenya Federation of Labour from 1953 until 1962. He was prominent in opposing British colonial rule in the late 1950s when Jomo Kenyatta and other older leaders were in prison. He helped to found the Kenya African National Union (KANU) in 1960 and became its general secretary, and was later a member of the Kenyan government. He was assassinated in 1969.

Moi, Daniel arap (1924 CE–)
Daniel arap Moi was Kenya's vice-president from 1967 until 1978, when he succeeded Jomo Kenyatta as president. His party, the Kenya African National Union (KANU) was the sole legal party from 1982 until 1991 – when opposition parties were legalized. In elections in 1992 and 1997, Moi, who has been criticized for human rights abuses, was reelected president.

Khumalo chieftaincy *See* **Ndebele kingdom**.

Kikuyuland *See* **Kenya (Peoples—Kikuyu)**.

Kilwa

Kilwa was an important Islamic city-state of coastal East Africa centered around an island, sheltered by an inlet, on the coast of what is now southern Tanzania. By the tenth century CE, it was a thriving trade depot, with a mixed Arab, Persian, and African population. It was in places such as Kilwa that the coastal Swahili people emerged as a distinct group from such ancestors. For many years, Mogadishu was the most powerful city on the east coast of Africa, and in the twelfth century Shirazi people from Mogadishu founded a dynasty in Kilwa. The Shirazi claimed to originate from Persia, but by that time they were definitely African. Kilwa rose to prominence in the thirteenth century, led by the Shirazis. The Shirazis were supplanted by the Ahadali family, who were responsible for the construction of the great palace, Husuni Kubwa (thirteenth to fourteenth centuries), then the largest building in sub-Saharan Africa. Second only to Mogadishu, Kilwa became a wealthy and powerful state that monopolized trade, especially gold and ivory from the interior, with China. India, and Arabia. Kilwa declined in the fifteenth century as profits from the gold trade diminished .

In the sixteenth century the Portuguese started to take an interest in East-African city-states such as Kilwa. They wanted to establish supply bases and forts along the coast to secure the trade routes and prevent competition. In 1502 CE, Vasco da Gama led the first bombardment of Kilwa. Although Portugal held Kilwa briefly—until 1512 CE—the state's fortunes declined as European power dominated trade on the coast for much of that century. The power of Portugal waned in the seventeenth century, and Arabs from Oman began to control the coast. In the mid to late eighteenth century, the ruler of Kilwa asked the Portuguese to help rid him of the town's Omani governor. Kilwa once again became an important trade depot, this time providing slaves to the French from 1776 CE through much of the nineteenth century. *See* **Tanzania**; **Zanzibar**.

The Kilwa Plate (above)
The gereza (fortress) on Kilwa was built by the Portuguese in the sixteenth century. The Portuguese arrival on East Africa's Indian Ocean coast brought to an end the Swahili and Arab dominance of trade in that area.

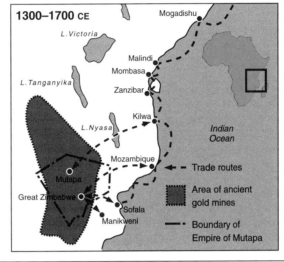

1300–1700 CE

Trade routes

Area of ancient gold mines

Boundary of Empire of Mutapa

Trade routes (left and below)
The map (below) shows the trade routes in the Indian Ocean c.1300–1700 CE. The map (left) shows the area of East Africa in much greater detail.

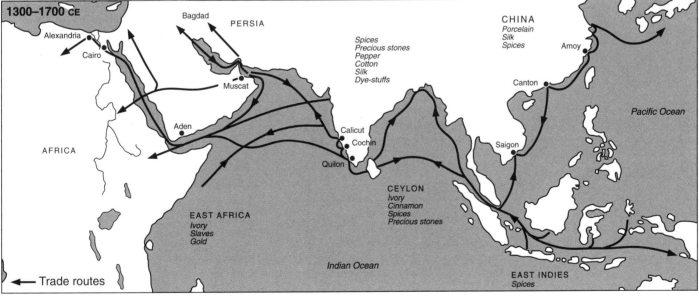

Trade routes

Kionga

Province of German East Africa, incorporated into Mozambique after World War I.

Kitara

See **Bunyoro-Kitara empire**.

Kong, kingdom of

The Dyula people, historically important Manding-speaking people of West Africa, established kingdoms on the northern trade routes in what is now Burkina Faso, including Kong, Bobo-Dioulasso, and Wa. The Kong kingdom emerged sometime after 1500 CE. *See also* **Bobo-Dioulasso**; **Burkina Faso**; **Wa**.

Kingdom of Kongo

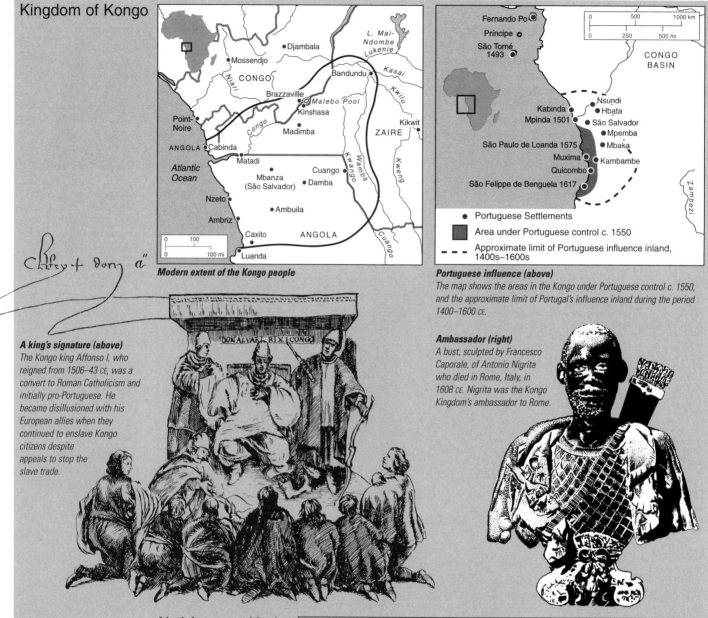

Modern extent of the Kongo people

Portuguese influence (above)
The map shows the areas in the Kongo under Portuguese control c. 1550, and the approximate limit of Portugal's influence inland during the period 1400–1600 CE.

A king's signature (above)
The Kongo king Affonso I, who reigned from 1506–43 CE, was a convert to Roman Catholicism and initially pro-Portuguese. He became disillusioned with his European allies when they continued to enslave Kongo citizens despite appeals to stop the slave trade.

Ambassador (right)
A bust, sculpted by Francesco Caporale, of Antonio Nigrita who died in Rome, Italy, in 1608 CE. Nigrita was the Kongo Kingdom's ambassador to Rome.

A battle for supremacy (above)
The Dutch and Portuguese colonial powers were rivals for control of the kingdoms situated near the mouth of the Congo River. In this illustration King Alvaro II of Kongo is shown welcoming Dutch ambassadors to his court.

Former glory (right)
This sixteenth-century engraving shows Mbanza, the capital of the Kongo Kingdom from the fourteenth century. Following the invasions of the Jaga people in the sixteenth century the city was destroyed, but a small village remains today.

Kongo, Kingdom of

The Kongo, or BaKongo, people are Bantu-speakers who live in southern Congo (formerly Zaire) and northern Angola around the mouth of the Congo River. The Kongo Kingdom was founded in the fourteenth century. The first known king of Kongo was Nimi a Lukeni, the son of the chief of Bungu, north of the Congo River. He led a group of followers to conquer lands south of the river and married the daughter of Kabunga, a Kongo chief. Kabunga had the title of *mani* (king), which Nimi adopted as his own. From then on the Kongo ruler was known as the Mani-Kongo. The king was the spiritual leader of his people, as well as their ruler and military leader. He had a council of ministers to advise him.

Kongo was already flourishing when Portuguese explorers and traders landed on the coast in 1482 CE. For many years, the Kongo maintained diplomatic ties not only with Portugal but also with the Vatican. The Portuguese gave advice and military help in exchange for exclusive trading rights. The main trade was in slaves for export to the new European settlements in the Americas.

This alliance did not endure, however. The Portuguese fostered Kongo's internal rivalries in their single-minded pursuit of slaves, and following the 1568 CE invasion of Kongo by the Jaga, from the interior, the Portuguese gradually lost interest. After the Kongo king tried to break Portuguese influence by balancing it with that of the Dutch, the Portuguese decisively defeated his armies at the Battle of Ambuila in 1665 CE. After this date, the kingdom fragmented and the Kongo eventually came under colonial rule. The Portuguese ruled Angola, the French ruled Congo (Rep.), and present-day Congo (Dem. Rep,) was under Belgian domination. Before becoming a Belgian colony, much of Congo (Dem. Rep.) formed the private colony of the Belgian king Leopold II, as the Congo Free State (1885–1908 CE). His rule was characterized by abuse, brutality, and the committing of atrocities in order to protect and maintain the lucrative rubber trade. The two Congos became independent in 1960 CE and Angola gained independence in 1975 CE. *See also* **Angola; Congo, Democratic Republic of**.

Kororofa

Kororofa, or Jukun, was one of the historic Hausa states that once dominated the north of what is now Nigeria. *See also* **Hausa states**.

Kuba kingdom

The Kuba people of south-central Congo (formerly Zaire) established a powerful central African state ruled by kings. Bantu-speaking peoples had begun settling in the varied habitats of the Congo (Dem. Rep.) Basin in about the third century CE. In the sixteenth century, one of these groups, the Kuba, moved from the lower part of the Basin to the Kasai region. This move was partly to escape the continuing attacks of the Jaga people and partly to avoid Portuguese influence from the Atlantic coast.

In the seventeenth century, a powerful Kuba state developed under the leadership of the Bushongo group–a name meaning "People of the Throwing Knife." The Bushongo probably gained their initial wealth from fishing, but in the seventeenth century they successfully grew corn and tobacco, adding to their wealth. By the early eighteenth century, a stable Bushongo government had allowed people to increase their production of agricultural surplus. This burgeoning economy supported a growing number of artisans and aristocrats. Economic growth furthered the development of trade and the Kuba began to export luxury cloth and ivory, and to import slaves, copper, beads, and salt. The Kuba came to control significant trade routes through parts of Central Africa, which remained important until well into colonial times. The kingdom reached its height in the eighteenth century, and remained stable until the late nineteenth century when invasions and upheavals destabilized the area.

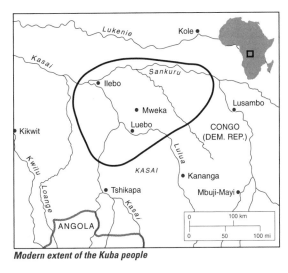

Modern extent of the Kuba people

Ndop sculpture (above)
Ndop was the name given to a series of sculptures made to commemorate dead Kuba kings, and to initiate new ones. The identity of the king was revealed by an emblem on the plinth. In this instance a royal drum is used to signify that the statue was of Kata Mbula (reigned 1800–1810 CE).

***Ikula** knife (above)*
In the early seventeenth century, the peace-loving king Shamba-Bolongongo forbade the use of the shongo knife. He introduced instead the wooden peace knife, which was called ikula.

Royal backrest
Dating from the early nineteenth century, this wooden backrest came from the Kuba capital of Nsheng.

The Kuba were incorporated into the private colony of King Leopold II of Belgium in 1885 CE. Like other ethnic groups in the region, the Kuba suffered during Leopold's oppressive Congo Free State regime. International outcry at Leopold's exploitative and brutal regime led to the Belgian government taking over in 1908 CE, resulting in a less oppressive period of government. The Belgian Congo, as it was then called, gained independence in 1960 CE as the Republic of Congo (called Zaire between 1971 CE and 1997 CE). *See also* **Congo, Democratic Republic of**.

Kush, Kingdom of

The independent Kingdom of Kush was one of Africa's earliest states; it was founded by Nubians–black Africans who then lived in what is now southern Egypt and northern Sudan. Kush began to emerge more than 5,000 years ago, around 3200 BCE. It was located on the Nile River, farther south than ancient Egypt, and its capital was Napata. Around 2400 BCE the kingdom entered an era of expansion but 900 years later it was conquered by ancient Egypt. Kush reached its territorial limit in 1750–1500 BCE. When it was overthrown by Egypt at the end of this era, Kush controlled the area from Syene (modern Aswan) to the fourth cataract of the Nile. In 900 BCE, a new Nubian kingdom emerged based around Napata. This kingdom, and its successor the Meroitic kingdom, are sometimes considered separate periods that continue the history of the kingdom of Kush. *See also* **Egypt**; **Egypt, Ancient**; **Meroitic kingdom**; **Nubia, Kingdom of**; **Sudan**.

Kot aPe
A picture of the Kuba king, Kot aPe, which was painted by a visiting European. Kot aPe was king at the beginning of the twentieth century.

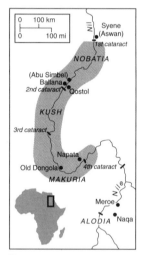

Key
NOBATIA Kingdom
(Abu Simbel) Modern city or town
• Historical site
▨ Kush (1750 –1500 BCE)

Ancient sites (above left)
Nubian kingdoms flourished along the Nile River from 3200 BCE to 1500 CE. The Kingdom of Kush is the oldest kingdom known of these kingdoms and the oldest in sub-Saharan Africa.

Lion Temple (right)
This is the northern gateway of the Lion Temple at Naqa, showing Queen Amanitore smiting her foes. Built 2,000 years ago, this Meroitic temple was dedicated to the god Apedemak.

KwaNdebele

KwaNdebele was one of the ten homelands established during South Africa's apartheid era. The white-controlled South African government forced black South Africans to live in these areas, which often bore no relation to their true homelands. The vast majority of KwaNdebele's inhabitants were Ndebele people. The homeland was established in 1979 CE and thousands of Ndebele were relocated there from elsewhere in South Africa. KwaNdebele was declared a self-governing national state in 1981 CE, but its autonomy was not genuine because the region was dependent economically and politically on South Africa. After the first multiracial elections held in 1994 CE, KwaNdebele was officially reincorporated into South Africa as part of Eastern Transvaal province, which has since been renamed Mpumalanga. *See also* **South Africa**.

KwaZulu

KwaZulu was one of the ten homelands established during South Africa's apartheid era. The vast majority of KwaZulu's inhabitants were Zulu people. Prime Minister Chief Buthelezi–the leader of the self-governing homeland–was a staunch opponent of apartheid. After South Africa's first multiracial elections were held in 1994 CE, KwaZulu was officially reincorporated into South Africa as part of Natal province, which was renamed KwaZulu/Natal. *See also* **South Africa**.

Labadi

One of the independent towns established by the Ga people of southeast Ghana. *See also* **Ga states**.

Lagos

Lagos, the former capital of Nigeria, was established several centuries ago as the terminus of trade routes from upriver. Originally part of the Yoruba kingdom of Benin, the small island port became an important depot in the slave trade with Europeans. In 1851 CE the British–who were trying to suppress the recently banned trade– destroyed the city for being a center of the slave trade. They installed as ruler of Lagos a man who was sympathetic to them, but ten years later Britain occupied the city and made it a colony. This colony included Lagos Island and a small part of the mainland. In 1906 CE, the Lagos Colony and Protectorate was joined with the Southern Nigeria protectorate, which was united with the Protectorate of Northern Nigeria in 1914 CE. Today, Lagos forms a separate federal state within independent Nigeria and consists of the island and its hinterland on the mainland. *See also* **Nigeria**.

Lamu

Lamu was one of the independent Swahili city-states that emerged on the east coast of Africa in the first millennium. Based on a coastal island off the coast of what is now Kenya, Lamu was established by African, Arabian, and Persian traders. Lamu was often allied to nearby Pate, part of the Lamu archipelago, and during the sixteenth century was, like the rest of the East-African coast, dominated by the Portuguese, who wanted to control the lucrative trade routes. In the seventeenth century Omani Arabs helped the Africans oust the Portuguese from their cities, but they, too, soon became unpopular as they tried to assert their control. From the mid-eighteenth century until the early nineteenth century, Lamu and Pate were nominally ruled by Mazrui dynasty based in Zanzibar. The Mazrui's forces were defeated in battle by troops from Lamu and Pate in 1812 CE, but one year later Lamu, in need of protection, submitted to the Arab ruler of Oman. The base of the empire that this ruler, Seyyid Said, established was transferred to Zanzibar, and for much of the nineteenth century Lamu was part of the Zanzibar Sultanate. *See also* **Kenya; Pate; Zanzibar**.

Lebowa

Lebowa was one of the ten homelands established during South Africa's apartheid era. The vast majority of Lebowa's inhabitants were Sotho people, such as the Pedi and Lovedu. The homeland was established in northern Transvaal and made self-governing in 1972 CE. After South Africa's first multiracial elections were held in 1994 CE, Lebowa was officially reincorporated into South Africa as part of Northern province. *See also* **South Africa**.

c. 1500 CE

L. Victoria
Kageyi
Mombasa
Tanga
Bagamoyo
Karonga
L. Nyasa
Kota Kota
Tete
Quelimane
Sofala

Shungway
Mogadishu
Barava
Kismayu
Pate Manda Lamu
Malindi
Kelifi
Zanzibar
Kilwa
Lindi
Mozambique
Angoche

Indian Ocean

MADAGASCAR

| 0 | 500 | 1000 km |
| 0 | 250 | 500 mi |

East African coastal trade
Lamu was established by African, Arabian and Persian traders on an island off the coast of what is now known as Kenya. It was often allied to nearby Pate, which was part of the Lamu archipelago. This map shows the situation c.1500 CE when, like the rest of the African coast, Lamu was dominated by the Portuguese who wanted to control the lucrative trade routes.

LESOTHO Kingdom of Lesotho

The first inhabitants of what is now Lesotho were probably the San, hunter-gatherers who left evidence of their existence in rock and cave paintings. The San were slowly absorbed and replaced by Bantu-speaking peoples, including the ancestors of the Southern Sotho people. In the seventeenth century, the area was peaceful, but it was disrupted in 1820 CE by the Mfecane, the mass migrations and wars caused by the rise of the Zulu kingdom. Refugees from various groups sought refuge in the highlands of Lesotho, where a chief, Moshoeshoe, offered them protection. By 1824, Moshoeshoe had about 21,000 followers who were united into the Basotho nation.

From 1856 CE, the Basotho had to fight off attacks by Boers (Afrikaners) and, in 1868 CE, Moshoeshoe asked Britain for protection. The territory, known as Basutoland, then became a British protectorate (colony). In 1871 CE, Basutoland was placed under the rule of Cape Colony (now part of South Africa). However, following an unsuccessful attempt by the Cape Colony govern-

© DIAGRAM

Independence
A 1966 CE stamp celebrating the independence of the Kingdom of Lesotho.

ment to disarm the Basotho during the Gun War (1880–1881 CE), Basutoland again became a British colony in 1884 CE. Whites were forbidden to own land and Britain assured Basutoland that it would remain independent of South Africa. In 1910 CE, the Basutoland Council, consisting of chiefs and elected members, was set up. It served as the national legislative council until independence. Also in 1910, at the request of the Basotho, Basutoland was excluded from the Union of South Africa, although South Africa continued to believe that it would eventually incorporate this land-locked country.

Recent history

In 1960 CE, Basutoland, which had been under the direct control of Britain through the High Commissioner for South Africa, adopted its first constitution and it became a constitutional monarchy in 1964 CE. In 1965 CE, the Basutoland National Party (BNP) won a narrow majority in the National Assembly. Chief Leabua Jonathan became prime minister, while Paramount Chief Motlotlehi Moshoeshoe II, direct descendant of Moshoeshoe I, became the king. Basutoland became independent as Lesotho on October 4, 1966 CE.

Problems soon arose when Moshoeshoe II demanded extra powers. Jonathan placed the king under house arrest, though he was later released when he agreed to accept a ceremonial role. In 1970 CE following elections in which the BNP appeared to have lost to the Basutoland Congress Party (BCP), Jonathan suspended the constitution and again placed the king under house arrest. Moshoeshoe left the country but was permitted to return in December 1970, though severe restrictions were placed on his political activities. Jonathan then began to rule in a repressive manner. Relations with South Africa also became strained and, in the 1980s, he became increasingly critical of South Africa's racial policies.

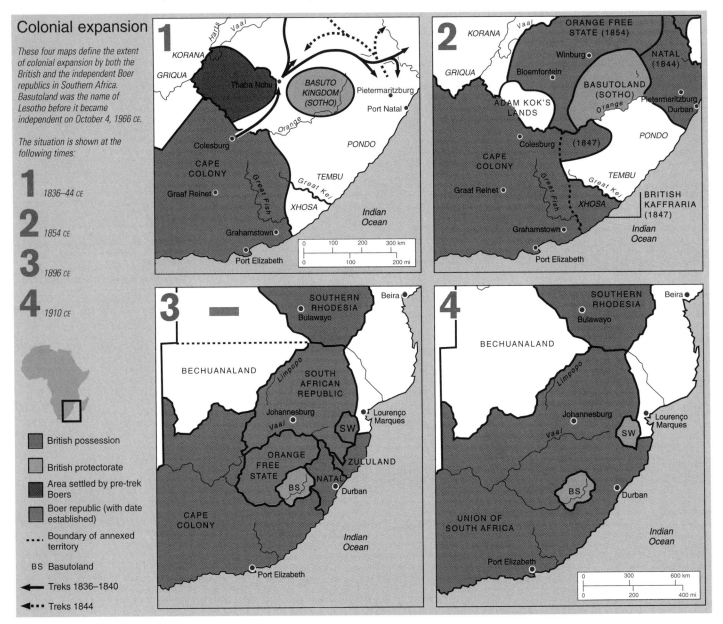

Colonial expansion

These four maps define the extent of colonial expansion by both the British and the independent Boer republics in Southern Africa. Basutoland was the name of Lesotho before it became independent on October 4, 1966 CE.

The situation is shown at the following times:

1 1836–44 CE

2 1854 CE

3 1896 CE

4 1910 CE

■ British possession

□ British protectorate

■ Area settled by pre-trek Boers

■ Boer republic (with date established)

···· Boundary of annexed territory

BS Basutoland

⟵ Treks 1836–1840

◀··· Treks 1844

In 1985 CE, Jonathan refused to turn over African National Congress (ANC) members who were active in Lesotho and South Africa imposed an economic blockade. In 1986 CE, the army overthrew Jonathan and military leaders, led by Major General Lekhanya, took control of the government and turned over executive authority to the king. In 1990 CE, Lekhanya removed several of the king's supporters from the military council in response to actions by the king which threatened to undermine his position. Lekhanya stripped the king of his powers and installed Moshoeshoe's son, Letsie III, in his place. However, in 1991 CE, Lekhanya was forced out of office and replaced by Colonel Elias Rameama. A new constitution was drafted and the ban on political parties was repealed. Moshoeshoe returned to Lesotho, but not as monarch.

In 1993 CE, elections were held in which the BCP won a landslide victory. The veteran nationalist Ntsu Mokhehle became prime minister. In 1995 CE, Moshoeshoe II was restored to the throne, but after he died accidentally in January 1996, Letsie III returned as monarch. In 1997, attempts to remove Mokhehle from the leadership of the BCP led him to form a new party, the Lesotho Congress for Democracy, which won nearly all the seats in the National Assembly in 1998 CE. Charges of electoral fraud led to an army mutiny and the prime minister, Pakalitha Mosisili, who had taken over from the ailing Mokhehle, requested South African and later Botswanan troops to restore order. The troops withdrew in 1999 CE, but the situation in Lesotho remained uneasy.

Peoples
Sotho
The Bantu-speaking ancestors of the Sotho (or Basotho) spread southward from present-day eastern Nigeria, reaching the Highveld–the high, arid plains to the west of the Drakensberg Mountains–and in the valleys of the Orange, Vaal, and Tugela rivers by about 1000 CE. They slowly absorbed the existing Khoisan population, adopting many aspects of their culture, including elements of their languages and many of their musical instruments. By about 1400 CE, the Sotho had established their main clans (several families who share the same ancestor or ancestors). Each clan adopted an animal, such as a wildcat, porcupine, or a crocodile as its symbol, or totem. Groups of these clans eventually came together to form three main divisions

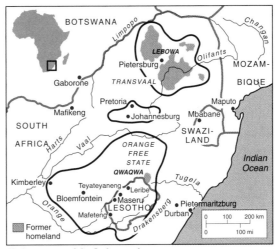

Modern extent of the Sotho people

of the Sotho people: the Northern Sotho, the Southern Sotho, and the Tswana (or Western Sotho). *See* **Botswana (Peoples—Tswana)**.

Between the seventeenth and the early nineteenth centuries, the Pedi group of clans among the Northern Sotho established what became known as the Bapedi Empire. *See* **South Africa (Peoples—Pedi)**. At the same time, the Southern Sotho were living in an age of relative peace and prosperity. However, in the 1820s, the lives of all the Sotho peoples were disrupted by the Mfecane/Difaqane–two decades of invasion, warfare, and famine triggered by the Zulu upheavals east of the Drakensberg Mountains. In the south, the only people to resist the Mfecane were some members of the Kwena (Crocodile) clan, led by their chief Moshoeshoe, who was able to unify the Southern Sotho clans and establish the Basotho Kingdom. After losing about two-thirds of his country's arable land to the Afrikaners, or Boers, to the Afrikaners' newly-formed Orange Free State, Moshoeshoe requested British protection in 1868 CE. The country became the British protectorate of Basutoland and it remained a British colony until 1966 CE when it became independent as Lesotho.

Zulu
For an account of the history of the Zulu peoples, *see* **Zulu, kingdom of**.

Lesotho's major political figures

Jonathan, Chief (Joseph) Leabua (1914–1987 CE)
Chief Leabua Jonathan was the first prime minister of Lesotho when it became independent in 1966, and he ruled the country for the next 20 years. A great-grandson of Lesotho's founder, Moshoeshoe I, Jonathan was a leading nationalist politician before independence. After independence, he forced King Moshoeshoe II to become mainly a figurehead and, in 1970, suspended the constitution and ruled by decree. He was overthrown by a military coup in 1986.

Lekhanya, Justin Matsing (1938 CE–)
Major-General Lekhanya overthrew the government of Lesotho in 1986 and governed for five years, when he was removed by Colonel Elias Ramaema. Lekhanya, who had supported Chief Leabua Jonathan's suspension of the constitution in 1970, gave executive power to Moshoeshoe II in 1986, but he later forced the king into exile and restored a constitutional monarchy.

Lesotho kings
Oct 4 1966–Feb 10 1970 CE Moshoeshoe II (1st time)
Feb 10 1970–Jun 5 1970 CE Leabua Jonathan (Tona-Kholo)
Jun 5 1970–Dec 5 1970 CE Queen 'MaMohato (f) (1st time) (regent)
Dec 5 1970–Nov 12 1990 CE Moshoeshoe II (2nd time)
Mar 10 1990–Nov 12 1990 CE Queen 'MaMohato (2nd time) (regent for exiled Moshoeshoe)
Nov 12 1990–Jan 25 1995 Letsie III (1st time)
Jan 25 1995–Jan 15 1996 CE Moshoeshoe II (3rd time)
Jan 15 1996–Feb 7 1996 CE Queen 'MaMohato (3rd time) (regent)
Feb 7 1996 CE– Letsie III (2nd time)

Lesotho timeline

19th century CE

c. 1818 Chief Moshoeshoe of the Moketeli leads a coalition of peoples into present-day Lesotho to escape the Zulu conqueror Shaka

c. 1824 Moshoeshoe unites his followers into the Basotho nation

c. 1833 Moshoeshoe invites missionaries to his fortress at Thaba Bosigo near modern-day Maseru

1856–1868 Boers attempt to conquer the Basotho

1868 Basotho appeal to Britain for protection against the Boers

1869 Britain establishes the protectorate of Basutoland

1870 Death of Moshoeshoe

1871 Basutoland comes under the administration of the British Cape Colony (now in South Africa)

1880 The Basotho rebel against British efforts to disarm them

1884 Britain reestablishes control of Basutoland

1900–49 CE **1910** The Basutoland Council of chiefs and elected representatives is formed

1943 Nine district councils are established as advisory bodies

1944 Britain declares that the Basutoland Council and the paramount chief will be consulted before any legislation is enacted

1946 The traditional courts are reorganized and a national treasury is established

1950–59 CE **1955** The Basutoland Council asks Britain for powers to legislate on internal matters

1956 Basutoland is granted full internal self-government

1960–69 CE **1960** Basutoland is given its first constitution

1964 The constitution is revised to provide for a constitutional monarchy

1965 In general elections under the new constitution, Chief Leabua Jonathan of the Basutoland National Party (BNP) becomes prime minister. Paramount chief Motlotlehi Moshoeshoe II becomes king

1966 Oct 4 Basutoland becomes the independent kingdom of Lesotho

1970–79 CE **1970** Chief Jonathan suspends the constitution after early election returns show the BNP is about to lose power

1980–89 CE **1983** South African saboteurs attempt to destroy the country's main power plant

1986 Chief Jonathan is overthrown by a South African-backed military coup. Maj. Gen. Justin Lekhanya becomes head of government

1990–99 CE **1990** The military government forces king Moshoeshoe II to abdicate in favor of his son Letsie III

1991 Lekhanya is forced to resign and is replaced by Col. Elias P. Ramaema

1993 Multiparty constitution introduced. Basotho Congress Party (BCP) under Ntsu Mohehle wins power

1995 King Letsie III abdicates in favor of his father Moshoeshoe II

1996 King Moshoeshoe II is killed in an automobile accident: Letsie III returns to the throne

1997 A dam project is suspended after protests by displaced local inhabitants

1998 Rioting follows a disputed election result and South African troops restore order

2000–09 CE **2000** Letsie III marries in a Roman-Catholic wedding, breaking his family's tradition of polygamy

Moshoeshoe I

In the 1820s, Moshoeshoe I, the son of a Sotho chief, founded a wealthy mountain kingdom–the Basuto (Bosotho) Kingdom–that was protected from the Zulu Mfecane/ Difaqane.

Letsie III (1964 CE–)

The son of King Moshoeshoe II of Lesotho, Crown Prince David Mohato Bereng Seeisa was made king, with the title Letsie III, by the country's military government in 1990. In 1995, he voluntarily abdicated to let his father, who had been deposed by the military, return. When his father was killed in a car crash in 1996, however, Letsie III once again became king.

Mokhehle, Ntsu (1919–1999 CE)

A nationalist leader, Ntsu Mokhehle won Lesotho's 1970 elections but the results were declared void and Mokhehle was imprisoned until 1972. After a failed coup attempt in 1974–allegedly by Mokhehle's supporters–he was forced to flee the country. Following the introduction of a democratic constitution, Mokhehle's Basotho Congress Party (BCP) won elections in 1993 and he became prime minister. He survived two attempted coups in 1994.

Moshoeshoe I (1786–1870 CE)

Moshoeshoe I, sometimes known as Moshesh, was a Sotho chief who created the kingdom of Basuto (now Lesotho). He united the various clans of the Sotho people, fought off numerous attacks by neighboring peoples, and fought the British and the Boers. In 1868, at his request, the British annexed his land (as the Basutoland protectorate) to prevent it being taken over by the Boers.

Moshoeshoe II (1938–1996 CE)

Born Constantine Bereng Seeiso, Moshoeshoe II was the grandson of Moshoeshoe I. He became king of Lesotho in 1960, but went into exile for eight months in 1970 after a clash with the country's first prime minister, Chief

Leabua Jonathan. He continued as king, with reduced powers, until 1990, when he was deposed and exiled after refusing to sanction changes proposed by the then military government. He was restored to the throne in January 1995, but was killed in a car accident the following year and succeeded by his son, Letsie III.

Ramaema, Elias Phisoana (1933 CE–)

Colonel Ramaema took power in Lesotho in 1991. He had earlier served as deputy to General Justin Lekhanya, whom he deposed when dissent over low pay in the army and the civil surface threatened the country's stability. Rameama negotiated a new constitution which was approved by Letsie III and he restored the multiparty electoral system. He withdrew from office after elections were held in 1993.

LIBERIA Republic of Liberia

Little is known of the early history of what is now Liberia. Portuguese mariners reached the coast in 1461 and the area soon became important for trading in ivory, slaves, and spices. The most prized spice–grains of malagueta pepper–was valued as highly as gold and accounts for the early name for the region–the Grain Coast. Interest in the coast mounted in the late eighteenth and early nineteenth centuries, when more and more people favored the abolition of slavery and many white people in the United States wanted to find a home for freed slaves. In 1816 CE, a philanthropic group called the American Colonization Society bought land along the Grain Coast, founding a settlement called Monrovia, which was named after the American President James Monroe.

The first freed slaves arrived in Monrovia in 1822 CE and they were soon joined by others who had been rescued from slave trading ships that the US Navy had intercepted. These people, who later became known as Americo-Liberians, faced many problems, including conflict with the indigenous ethnic groups in the interior. The people of Monrovia joined other settlements which the American Colonization Society had established along the coast to form the Commonwealth of Liberia in 1838 CE. Liberia declared its independence on July 26, 1847 CE and most countries recognized this act in 1848 CE and 1849 CE. However, the United States did not recognize the new country until 1862 CE. Joseph Jenkins Roberts, an Americo-Liberian born free in Virginia, became the first president of Liberia.

Recent history

Liberia's economy remained precarious until 1926 CE, when the government leased land to the American Firestone Tire and Rubber Company and loans were arranged through the Finance Corporation of America. The company's rubber plantations provided many jobs and much-needed revenue for the government. Rubber production was especially important during World War II, when, for the first time, the country's finances were fixed on a relatively stable basis.

In 1943 CE, William V S Tubman became president and he took Liberia into the war on the side of the Allies in 1944 CE. Although Tubman did not tolerate opposition, he worked to integrate the indigenous population, by improving social services, including education, and communications in the interior. His government increased the country's exports and he attracted foreign investment through his "open door policy" of tax and tariff exemptions, and repatriation of profits. Despite assassination attempts, he was repeatedly

A refuge for freed slaves
The illustration (above) shows J.J. Roberts, the first president of Liberia, arriving at Monrovia in January 1849 CE following a visit to England. It was the first settlement bought along the Grain Coast to house freed slaves from the United States. Liberia's coat of arms echoes this goal of freedom from oppression (right).

reelected president until his death in 1971 CE.

Tubman's successor was another Americo-Liberian, Vice-President William R Tolbert. He faced economic problems arising from falls in the international prices of iron ore and rubber, the chief exports. Prices for food, including rice, increased and riots occurred in 1979 CE. In 1980 CE, a military group from the non-Americo-Liberian population killed Tolbert and seized control of the government. Their leader, Master Sergeant Samuel K Doe, belonged to the Krahn ethnic group. Doe became head of state and chairman of the People's Redemption Council. A new multiparty constitution was adopted in 1984 and elections were held in 1985 CE. Despite accusations of fraud, Doe won the presidential elections and his party, the National Democratic Party of Liberia, won a majority in the legislature. Under Doe, many opponents of the government were killed or imprisoned, while members of the government were accused of corruption.

A rebellion that broke out in late 1989 CE developed into civil war, largely along ethnic lines. The two main rebel groups were the National Patriotic Front of Liberia, led by Charles Taylor, and the Independent National Patriotic Front, led by Prince Johnson. A peace-keeping force sent by the Economic Community of West African States (ECOWAS) attempted to restore

Joseph Jenkins Roberts
Although born in America Roberts emigrated to Liberia with his family in 1829 CE. He first became lieutenant governor in 1839 CE, then governor, and finally president from 1847–1856 CE when he retired from public office.

© DIAGRAM

Samuel Doe
He took power after a military coup in Liberia in 1980 CE. His assassination in 1990 CE led to the escalation of Liberia's civil war.

order, but in September 1990 CE, Doe was captured by rebel forces and killed. ECOWAS installed a provisional government led by Amos Sawyer, which sought to restore peace. However, a series of ceasefires were agreed and broken. In 1995 CE, the government invited Charles Taylor to join the government and, in elections in 1997 CE, he was elected president by a large majority. In the late 1990s, Taylor sought to restore stability and revive the shattered economy. But some rebel activity continued in Liberia and Britain acused Taylor of helping rebels in neighboring Sierra Leone.

Peoples

AMERICO-LIBERIANS
Until recently, the Americo-Liberians formed the dominant political and social elite in Liberia even though they accounted for less than three percent of the country's population. The origins of the Americo-Liberians lie in the founding of Monrovia in 1847 CE by a white philanthropic group, called the American Colonization Society. The society settled more than 16,000 African Americans in Liberia, although settlers had been arriving in the region since the 1820s. These freed slaves, or Congoes as they were then called, declared Liberia's independence in 1847 CE, though this was not recognized by the US government until 1862 CE, Many of the Congoes took African husbands or wives and this led to the emergence of the Americo-Liberian community. In recent decades, intermingling between ethnic groups

has led to the more widespread use of the term Kwi for people of part Americo-Liberian descent.

The settlers treated the non-Americo-Liberian population harshly, maintaining that they were "civilizing" the "barbarous shores of Africa". Until 1954 CE, only Americo-Liberians were allowed to vote in Liberian elections. After the 1980 CE coup, which sparked a long-running civil war, many Americo-Liberians (along with other Liberians) fled from Liberia. However, the pattern of Liberia's dominance by Americo-Liberians proved hard to break, because the less privileged groups had fewer members able to fill posts once held by Americo-Liberians, due to lack of education and skills.

KRU
The Kru occupy a region that covers more than half of Liberia–extending from Monrovia on the northern coast to Cape Palmas on the southern coast, and reaching roughly 60 miles (nearly 100 km) inland. The Kru have long been associated with seafaring and, in the past, Kru men spent much of each year sailing with trading ships around the coast of Africa or farther afield. In recent decades, investment in such ports as Buchanan have detracted from the activities on the Kru coast, which is now one of the most isolated parts of Liberia. Like other Liberians, the Kru have also been adversely affected by the Liberian civil war.

Liberia's major political figures

Blyden, Edward Wilmot (1832–1912 CE)
Edward Blyden was born in the Virgin Islands, but became a professor and major political leader in Liberia, where he settled in 1853. He served as secretary of state there (1864–6), but had to flee to Sierra Leone when his enemies tried to lynch him. He campaigned for African unity and opposed the idea of white superiority.

Carey, Lott (1780-1829 CE)
Carey was the first black governor of Liberia. In 1819, Carey, a former Virginia slave, bought his freedom and that of his two children, and joined the original group that sailed for Liberia. After Liberia was founded in 1822, Carey worked with Jehudi Ashmun, the white agent of the American Colonization Society. Carey became vice-agent in 1826, and succeeded Ashmun in 1828.

Doe, Samuel Kenyon (1951–1990 CE)
A former army sergeant, Samuel Doe became president of Liberia in 1980, following a military coup in which President William Tolbert was killed. Doe was elected president in 1985, despite allegations of vote rigging, and he was accused of human rights abuses. A civil war broke out in 1989. In 1990, Doe, a member of the Krahn people, was captured, tortured, and killed by a rival group. His death led to the escalation of Liberia's civil war.

Roberts, Joseph Jenkins (1809–1876 CE)
Roberts was born an American freed man in Virginia. In 1829, sponsored by the American Colonization Society, he and his family emigrated to Liberia. In 1839, he became lieutenant-governor of the colony, and later the governor. When Liberia was proclaimed independent in 1847, Roberts became its president. He was reelected until 1856, when he retired.

Sawyer, Amos (1945 CE–)
Sawyer became interim president of Liberia in September 1990, following the outbreak of civil war. Supported by the forces sent by the Economic Community of West African States, he sought to restore order. In 1994, he handed over his authority to an all-party transitional government, and then retired from politics.

Taylor, Charles Ghankay (1948–)
Formerly director of the General Services Administration, he fled Liberia after having been accused of embezzling federal funds. In 1989, he formed a militia, the National Patriotic Front of Liberia, one of the factions in the civil war which raged in the early 1990s. He joined the government in 1995 and in 1997, he was elected president.

Liberian presidents

Jan 3 1944–Jul 23 1971 CE
William V.S. Tubman

Jul 23 1971–Apr 12 1980 CE
William R. Tolbert, Jr.

Apr 12 1980–Sep 9 1990 CE
Samuel K. Doe
(chairman of the people's redemption council until Jul 25 1984)

Sep 9 1990–Nov 22 1990 CE
Conflicting claims
–Prince Yormie Johnson
–Charles Taylor
–David Nimley
–Amos Sawyer

Nov 22 1990–Mar 7 1994 CE
Amos Sawyer
(president of the interim government of national unity)

Liberia timeline

Pre 19th century CE

1461 Portuguese merchants arrive and establish a trade monopoly on what they call the Grain Coast (from the grains of local pepper they bought)

19th century CE

1816 The American Colonization Society (ACS) buys land along the Grain Coast and founds Monrovia

1822 The ACS settles the first group of freed slaves at Monrovia

1824 The ACS adopts the name Liberia for their settlement

1838 Monrovia joins other settlements on the Grain Coast to form the Commonwealth of Liberia

1841 The US approves a constitution for Liberia: a free-born black Virginian Joseph J. Roberts becomes governor

1847 Jul 26 Liberia becomes an independent state: Roberts becomes its first president

1849 Great Britain becomes the first country to recognize Liberia as an independent state after Roberts visits London

1856 Roberts resigns from the presidency

1862 The US recognizes Liberian independence

1871 Roberts returns to power after President Roye is imprisoned for corruption

1876 Death of President Roberts

1885-1892 Liberia's borders demarcated by treaties with Britain and France

1900–49 CE

1904 President Barclay promotes a policy of cooperation between the Americo-Liberians and the indigenous tribes

1915 Uprising by the indigenous tribes against the Americo-Liberians

1919 Liberia transfers 2,000 square miles of territory to French control

1926 Liberia leases land to the American Firestone Company for rubber plantations

1930s League of Nations investigates domestic slavery in Liberia

1942 Liberia signs a defense agreement with the US

1943 William V. S. Tubman becomes President

1944 Liberia declares war on Germany

1960–69 CE

1960 Liberia offers a "flag of convenience" to cost cutting ship owners

1964 The US transfers ownership of the port of Monrovia to the Liberian government

1970–79 CE

1971 Tubman dies: he is succeeded as president by William R. Tolbert

1979 Increase in the price of rice causes rioting against Americo-Liberian political domination

1980–89 CE

1980 Tolbert is killed during a military coup: master sergeant Samuel K. Doe of the Khran tribe becomes president

1984 Under US pressure Doe announces a multiparty constitution

1985 Doe and his National Democratic Party win multiparty elections amid allegations of vote rigging

1986 Doe survives an assassination attempt

1988 Doe gives US financial experts co-authority over the national budget

1989 A former Doe supporter, Charles Taylor invades from Ivory Coast

1990–99 CE

1990 Full scale civil war breaks out between Doe's Armed Forces of Liberia (AFL) and two rebel groups, the Independent National Patriotic Front of Liberia (INPFL) and Taylor's National Patriotic Front of Liberia (NPFL)

1990 Sept Doe is killed by the INPFL

1990 Nov West African peacekeeping troops arrive to police a cease-fire

1992 Renewed civil war after the NPFL attack Monrovia

1993 A seven-month cease-fire is agreed

1994 A transitional government fails to end the violence

1995 Charles Taylor is brought into the transitional government

1996 The warring parties sign a peace agreement but fighting breaks out again in Monrovia

1997 Presidential and legislative elections are held: Charles Taylor becomes president

1998 Nearly 480,000 Liberian refugees begin to return home

2000–09 CE

2000 The European Union suspended aid to Liberia following charges that Liberia had helped the rebels in Sierra Leone

United Nations
A stamp, issued in 1952 CE, which honored the United Nations.

Independence
A group of Liberians celebrate National Day amid a triumphant display of flags.

Tolbert, William Richard Jr. (1913–1980 CE)
William Tolbert was vice-president of Liberia from 1951–1971, and succeeded William Tubman as president in 1971. During his time in office, Liberia's economy suffered because the prices of iron ore and rubber fell and rice prices rose in 1979 leading to rioting. He was assassinated during an a coup, led by Samuel Doe, in 1980.

© DIAGRAM

Tubman, William V. S. (Vacanarat Shadrach) (1895–1971 CE)
William Tubman was president of Liberia from 1944 until his death in 1971, when he was succeeded by William Tolbert. Through his "open-door" policies, he attracted foreign investment and reduced the country's dependence on the United States.

LIBYA Great Socialist People's Libyan Arab Jamahiriya

Augusto Aubry

He was in command of the Italian navy when Italy invaded Libya in 1911 CE. The country remained under Italian rule until 1942 CE.

The Berbers are the earliest known people in what is now Libya. The coast became important in Mediterranean trade around 3,000 years ago when the Phoenicians began to found trading centers. In the sixth century BCE, Greek colonies were set up in the northeastern area called Cyrenaica. By the fourth century, the northwest, which had formed part of the Berber kingdoms, was part of the Carthaginian empire. This area became known as Tripolitania. Following the Roman defeat of Carthage in 146 BCE, Tripolitania became part of the Roman province of Nova Africa, while Cyrenaica became Roman 50 years later. The Vandals invaded the area in 431 CE, but the Christian Byzantines took over in the sixth century.

Arabs conquered northern Libya between 643–647 CE, introducing their language, Arabic, and their religion, Islam. Northern Libya was then ruled by a succession of Muslim dynasties, including the Umayyads, Abbasids, Aghlabids, Tulunids, and Fatimids. Ottoman Turks conquered Libya in 1551 CE and added an area called Fezzan in the south to the northern provinces of Cyrenaica and Tripolitania. In the early nineteenth century, the coast was a haven for pirates, who were attacked by the US Navy.

Italy invaded Libya in 1911 CE and began to modernize its infrastructure in the 1920s and 1930s, although the reformist Muslim Sanusi brotherhood bitterly opposed Italian rule. In 1942 CE, during World War II, British forces, aided by the Sanusi brotherhood, drove out the Italian forces. Britain took over the north, while the French controlled Fezzan in the south.

Recent history

Libya became independent as a monarchy on December 24, 1951 CE. Its king, who had been chosen by the national assembly in 1950 CE, was Muhammad Idris al-Mahdi, Emir of Cyrenaica, and leader of the Sanusi resistance to Italian rule. Political parties were forbidden. The country was then divided into the three partly autonomous provinces of Cyrenaica, Fezzan, and Tripolitania, but these provinces were abolished in 1963 CE in an effort to create a greater sense of national unity. In 1959 CE, the discovery of oil within easy reach of the coast transformed the economy. However, most people remained poor, deriving little benefit from the oil bonanza.

Discontent with the government led a group of officers called the Revolutionary Command Council to overthrow the monarchy and declare the country a republic–officially the Libyan Arab Republic. The new regime, led by Colonel Muammar al-Qaddafi, was strictly Muslim and pro-Arab. It broke Libya's close ties with Britain and the United States and sought to create unions with other Arab countries, including Egypt, Sudan, and Tunisia, But such unions were short-lived because of differences between the governments. Qaddafi used oil revenues to develop the economy

Italian colonialism

A stamp issued in July 1921 CE to celebrate Italian dominance of Libya.

and, in 1973 CE, he set up a series of local, regional, and national congresses through which the people could express their views. However, despite this apparently democratic structure, the government did not tolerate political opposition. In 1977 CE, Qaddafi declared Libya a one-party socialist *jamahiriya* ("state of the masses").

Qaddafi supported radical movements around the world, including the Palestine Liberation Organization (PLO). In the 1980s, the United States accused Libya of supporting international terrorism and, in 1986, the US broke all ties with Libya. The differences between the countries culminated in the US bombing of military installations in Tripoli and Benghazi. In 1992 CE, the UN imposed sanctions on Libya for refusing to hand over people suspected of planting bombs on a Panam airliner in 1988 CE and a French airliner in 1989 CE.

In the late 1990s, Qaddafi sought to improve Libya's relations with the West. He surrendered two Libyans suspected of planting the bomb on the Pan Am airliner which exploded over the Scottish town of Lockerbie. These Libyans stood trial in a court set up in The Hague, Netherlands, which was accepted as a neutral territory by Libya, the United Kingdom, and the United States. The trial ended in 2001 CE, when one of the defendants was acquitted. However, the other defendant was found guilty and sentenced to life imprisonment. The UN lifted many of its sanctions, including flights in and out of Libya. Qaddafi also accepted Libyan responsibility for the killing of a British policewoman in London, a gesture which led to the restoration of British-Libyan diplomatic links and, in 1999 CE, the lifting of all European Union sanctions, except for arms sales. Problems arising from the French disaster in 1989 CE appeared to be over following a trial in in 1999 in Paris but, in 2000 CE, a French magistrate issued a warrant for Qaddafi for his alleged role in the disaster.

Qaddafi's actions in the late 1990s certainly helped to restore his standing in Arab and African affairs. However, in 2000, clashes occurred between young Libyan Arabs and black African immigrants, mainly in the towns in the northwest. About 130 black Africans were reportedly killed and many houses were destroyed. Immigration began on a large scale in the mid-1990s and, by 2000, experts estimated that black Africans numbered around one million, out of a total population of six million. Many young Libyan Arabs believed the presence of the black Africans was the cause of the high unemployment rate; and the government began to deport thousands of black Africans in late 2000.

Peoples

ARABS

The Arabs conquered the Berbers of North Africa in the late seventh century CE, introducing their language, Arabic, and their religion, Islam. Arabs and Berbers now form more than 80 percent of Libya's population.

BERBERS

Berbers are the earliest known inhabitants of Libya. They were settled along the North African coast by 3000 BCE, but little is known about their history before the third century BCE.

The modern history of the Berbers begins with their conversion to Islam in the late seventh century CE. Over the years, Arab invasions forced many Berbers out of coastal regions and into the mountains and desert. But many others were absorbed into the Arab population and today, while most people are of Berber-Arab descent, few people speak the Berber language.

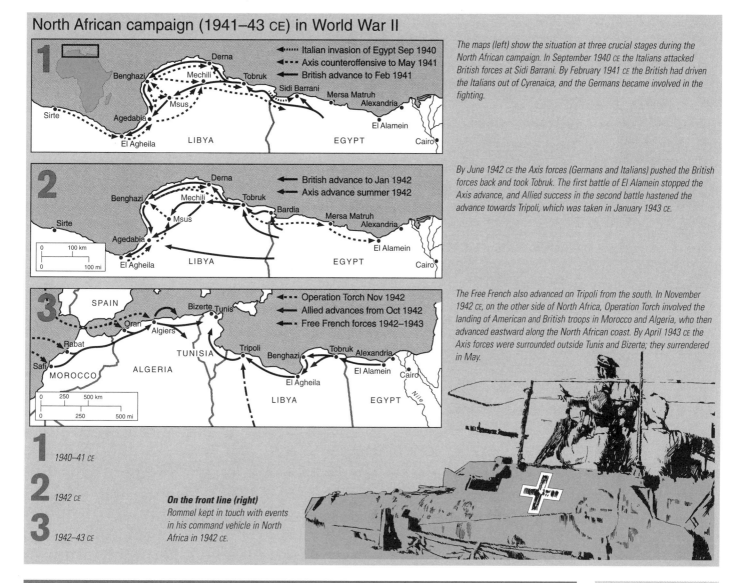

North African campaign (1941–43 CE) in World War II

The maps (left) show the situation at three crucial stages during the North African campaign. In September 1940 CE the Italians attacked British forces at Sidi Barrani. By February 1941 CE the British had driven the Italians out of Cyrenaica, and the Germans became involved in the fighting.

By June 1942 CE the Axis forces (Germans and Italians) pushed the British forces back and took Tobruk. The first battle of El Alamein stopped the Axis advance, and Allied success in the second battle hastened the advance towards Tripoli, which was taken in January 1943 CE.

The Free French also advanced on Tripoli from the south. In November 1942 CE, on the other side of North Africa, Operation Torch involved the landing of American and British troops in Morocco and Algeria, who then advanced eastward along the North African coast. By April 1943 CE the Axis forces were surrounded outside Tunis and Bizerte; they surrendered in May.

1 1940–41 CE
2 1942 CE
3 1942–43 CE

On the front line (right)
Rommel kept in touch with events in his command vehicle in North Africa in 1942 CE.

Libya's major political figures

Idris I (1890–1983 CE)
Idris I was king of Libya from 1951, when the country became independent, until 1969, when he was deposed in a coup led by Muammar al-Qaddafi and the monarchy was abolished. He had earlier led Libyan resistance to Italian rule.

Qaddafi, Muammar al- (1942 CE–)
Muammar al-Qaddafi became leader of Libya and commander-in-chief of the armed forces in 1969 after the overthrow of King Idris I. At home, Qaddafi sought to reorganize Libyan society along socialist, nationalist lines. Abroad, his support for radical movements, such as the Black Panthers in the United States and the Irish Republican Army (IRA) in Northern Ireland, made him a controversial figure. In 1986, US planes bombed several sites in Libya, missing Qaddafi but killing 37 people, many of them civilians.

King Idris 1
The first leader of an independent Libya in 1951 CE, he was deposed in a military coup in 1969 CE and the monarchy was abolished.

© DIAGRAM

A force for change
A stamp issued in 1978 CE marking International Anti-apartheid Year.

Muammar al-Qaddafi
The Libyan leader since 1969 CE, he has proved to be a controversial figure in international politics, not least in his relations with the United States in the 1980s, and the UN in the 1990s.

Libya timeline

Pre 19th century

9th century BCE Phoenician settlements founded on the Libyan coast
6th century BCE Tripolitania is part of the Carthaginian empire: Cyrenaica comes under Greek control
146 BCE Tripolitania becomes part of the Roman empire
96 BCE Cyrenaica becomes part of the Roman empire
643–647 CE Libya is conquered by the Islamic Arabs
868–972 Libya is independent under the Tulunid dynasty
990–1171 Libya is part of the Fatimid caliphate of Cairo
1551 Libya is conquered by the Ottoman Turks
1711 Libya becomes autonomous under the Qaramanli dynasty

19th century CE

1804 US navy attacks a base of the Barbary Corsairs at Tripoli
1835 Direct Ottoman rule is restored
1843 The puritanical Islamic Sanusiyah movement spreads to Libya

1900–49 CE

1911 The Turkish-Italian war breaks out
1912 The Ottomans cede Libya to Italy
1922 The Italians recognize the Sanusi leader Sayyid Idris as the autonomous emir of Cyrenaica
1923 The Italians gain full control over Tripolitania
1931 The Italians gain full control over Cyrenaica after they capture and execute the Sanusi leader Umar al Mukhtar
1940 The Italians invade Egypt from Libya
1941 German troops are sent to support the Italians in Libya after the British capture Benghazi
1943 The British drive the Italians and Germans out of Libya, and set up an Allied military government
1947 Italy abandons its claims to Libya
1949 The UN approves a proposal that Libya should become an independent state

1950–59 CE

1951 Dec 24 Libya becomes an independent kingdom of three federated provinces under emir Sayyid Idris al-Sanusi
1954 Idris grants the US military and naval bases in Libya
1959 Oil is discovered in Cyrenaica

1960–69 CE

1963 The provinces are abolished as Libya becomes a unitary state
1969 Emir Idris is overthrown by a military coup: Col. Muammar al-Qaddafi becomes head of state

1970–79 CE

1973 Qaddafi sets up a system of local, regional and national popularly elected congresses
1973 Libya occupies the Aouzou strip in northern Chad
1977 Qaddafi declares Libya a one-party socialist *jamahiriya* ("state of the masses")

1980–89

1980 Qaddafi proposes a union between Libya and Chad
1981 US downs two Libyan jets over the Gulf of Sirte
1986 US aircraft bomb Tripoli and Benghazi in response to Libyan support for international terrorism
1989 Libya joins the Arab Maghreb Union

1990–99 CE

1992 UN sanctions imposed on Libya after it refuses to hand over two agents suspected of the 1988 Pan Am Flight 103 bombing over Lockerbie, Scotland
1993 UN tightens sanctions against Libya
1994 The International Court awards the Aouzou strip to Chad
1996 An aqueduct to supply water to desert settlements is completed
1999 Qaddafi surrenders suspects for the 1988 bombing for trial
1989 Libya joins the Arab Maghreb Union

2000–09 CE

2000 Clashes occur between young Libyan Arabs and black African immigrants
2001 One of the two defendants in the 1988 bombing is found guilty at the trial in the Hague

Libyan kings, chairmen and general secretaries

King

Dec 24 1951–Sep 1 1969 CE
Idris I
(= Sayyid Muhammad Idris as-Sanusi)

Chairman of the revolutionary command council

Sep 8 1969–Mar 1 1979 CE
Muammar al-Qaddafi

General secretaries of the general people's congress (nominal chiefs of state)

Mar 2 1977–Mar 2 1979 CE
Muammar al-Qaddafi

Mar 2 1979–Jan 7 1981 CE
Abdul Ati al-Obeidi

Jan 7 1981–Feb 15 1984 CE
Muhammad az-Zaruq Rajab

Feb 15 1984–Oct 7 1990 CE
Mifta al-Usta Umar

Oct 7 1990–Nov 18 1992 CE
Abdul Razzaq as-Sawsa

Nov 18 1992 CE–
Zentani Muhammad az-Zentani

A victory salute
Italian troops hold up the flag of the defeated Turkish army during the Turkish-Italian war in 1911 CE.

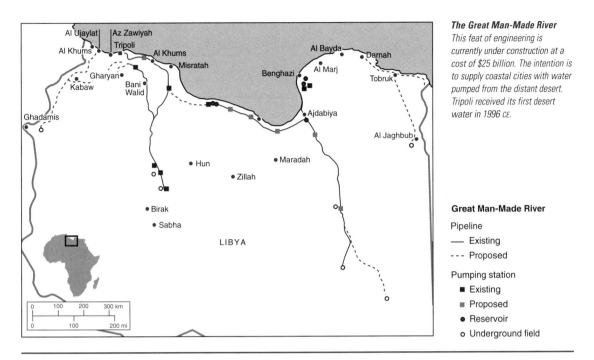

The Great Man-Made River
This feat of engineering is currently under construction at a cost of $25 billion. The intention is to supply coastal cities with water pumped from the distant desert. Tripoli received its first desert water in 1996 CE.

Great Man-Made River

Pipeline
— Existing
--- Proposed

Pumping station
■ Existing
■ Proposed
● Reservoir
○ Underground field

Lourenço Marques

Until 1976 CE the city of Maputo, Mozambique, was named Lourenço Marques after the Portuguese trader who was the first European to explore around Delgoa Bay in 1544 CE. By the end of the eigheenth century, it was a fortified trading base ruled by a Portuguese governor. In 1907, it was made the capital of Portuguese East Africa. *See also* **Mozambique**.

Lozi kingdom

The Lozi people of western Zambia established a prosperous kingdom several centuries ago. The Lozi are descended from the Luyi, a people who migrated from the north to the Zambezi floodplains around the seventeenth century or earlier. These Luyi migrants were led by a woman, Mwambwa, who was succeeded first by her daughter, Mbuywamwambwa, and then by Mbuywamwambwa's son, Mboo, the first *litunga* (king) of the Lozi. During Mboo's reign, the Lozi kingdom expanded by conquering and absorbing neighboring peoples. At that time, the kingdom was not so much a centralized state as a collection of semi-independent chiefdoms ruled by Mboo and his relatives. The unification of these chiefdoms into a single kingdom began in the rule of the fourth *litunga*, Ngalama, in the early eighteenth century, and was completed by Mulambwa, who ruled from about 1780–1830. Mulambwa was able to establish direct rule over the peoples conquered by the Lozi and over the numerous immigrant groups arriving in the kingdom from the north and west.

The most important of these immigrant groups was the Mbunda, who had been driven from their homes in Angola. Mulambwa allowed them to settle in border areas where they could help to defend the kingdom from raids by neighboring peoples such as the Luvale and the Nkoya. As well as helping the Lozi in this way, the Mbunda played a big part in the military and economic development of the kingdom. They brought with them military innovations–such as the bow and arrow–and new crops including cassava, millet, and yam, as well as medical and artistic skills.

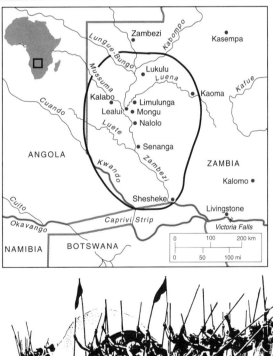

Modern extent of the Lozi people (left)

A festive time (below)
A scene from the Kuomboka Festival that marks the move of the Lozi king between capitals, caused by the annual flooding of the Zambezi River. Still celebrated today, the festival dates back to the founding of the Lozi kingdom in the eighteenth century.

© DIAGRAM

Francis Peregrino
Ghanaian by birth, he was a representative of the Pan-African Association, which was formed at the Pan-African Conference in London in 1900 CE. A publisher by profession, he acted as an advisor to the Lozi king Lewanika.

Negotiations at Lealui
Lochner, of the British South Africa Company (BSA), shown in Lealui , the Lozi capital, negotiating over trading concessions with the Lozi king Lewanika.

The Lozi prospered under Mulambwa's rule, but after his death the country was torn apart by a civil war between the army of his eldest son, Silumelume, and the supporters of a younger son, Mubukwanu. This war was won by Mubukwanu, supported by the Mbunda, but before he could reunite the kingdom it was attacked and conquered by the Kololo, a Sotho people from Southern Africa. The Kololo ruled the country (and introduced their language) from about 1840–1864 CE, when they were defeated by the armies of an exiled Lozi leader, Sipopa. For the next 40 years or so, the kingdom continued to prosper despite a series of leadership disputes, but its power began to wane when treaties agreed with the British in 1890–1900 CE placed it under the control of the Cecil Rhodes' British South Africa Company (BSA).

The British ruled the Lozi until the 1960s, incorporating the kingdom (as Barotseland) into the colony of Northern Rhodesia in 1924 CE. In 1958 CE, Northern Rhodesia became part of the white-minority ruled Central African Federation (CAF) along with Nyasaland (Malawi) and Southern Rhodesia (Zimbabwe). The CAF was dissolved in 1963 CE and Zambia won independence in 1964 CE. *See also* **Rhodesia**; **Zambia (Peoples—Lozi)**.

Luba kingdom

Luba chief
This present-day Luba chief is holding his staff of office. The geometric patterns on the broad section serve both to decorate the staff, and to empower the owner, They are considered more important than the human figures.

The Luba comprise several related groups living in southeastern Congo (formerly Zaire). The Luba kingdom was one of central Africa's most powerful states. Archeological excavations have shown that there has been an uninterrupted culture in the Katanga region from the eighth century CE onward, though the area has undoubtedly been occupied for longer than that. Some authorities think that the idea of government through chiefs originated in this area as early as the eighth century or before. By the fourteenth century, there were definitely well-established chieftainships in the region. Increasing population levels land shortages set these chieftaincies in conflict with one another and larger, more military groupings evolved as a result. The most important of these was the Luba group, which emerged around the Lake Kisale area.

According to oral traditions, the original rulers of the Luba (then called Kalundwe) were the Songye, who had come from the north. The Songye *kongolo* (ruler) married the Kalundwe queen and established a new state, which became the Luba kingdom and covered the lands between the Lualaba and Lubilash rivers.

In the fifteenth century, the Songye rulers of the Luba were displaced by the Kunda from the north. Led by Mbili Kiluhe, the Kunda were at first welcomed by the reigning *kongolo*, Mwana. Kiluhe married two of Mwana's sisters, one of whom gave birth to a son, Kala Ilunga. Kala Ilunga grew up to be a great warrior and he challenged the *kongolo* for the Luba throne, claiming he was the legitimate ruler through matrilineal descent (descent traced through the mother). The *kongolo* was eventually defeated and Kala Ilunga founded the Kunda dynasty to rule over Luba and took the title of *mulopwe*.

By 1550 CE, the Luba kingdom was powerful, with a strong central government. The mulopwe was the head

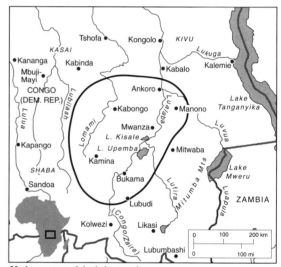

Modern extent of the Luba people

of the government and also the religious leader, believed to have supernatural powers. He had a group of ministers, the *balopwe*, to help him, each with special duties. The *sungu* was a sort of prime minister who mediated between the people and the *mulopwe*. The *nsikala* acted as a temporary ruler when a king died or was unwell. The *inabanza* had charge of ritual matters concerning the *mulopwe's* sacred role. This included taking care of the king's sacred spears. Finally, the *twite* was the army and police commander. All these ministers, and any other chiefs who ruled sections of the Luba, were themselves descendants of Kala Ilunga. In this way, the Luba kept power in the hands of a small aristocracy.

The Kunda dynasty lasted until the arrival, in the 1880s, of the Belgians, who turned what is now Congo

(Dem. Rep.) into a private colony called the Congo Free State, owned and ruled by the Belgian king, Leopold II. His rule was characterized by abuses, brutality, and atrocities in order to protect the lucrative rubber trade. The Luba were engaged in a war of resistance against colonial rule that lasted from 1907–1917 CE. The Belgian government took over the country in 1908 CE, as the Belgian Congo, which became independent in 1960 CE as the Republic of Congo (renamed Zaire in 1971 CE). *See also* **Congo, Democratic Republic of (Peoples—Luba)**; **Lunda empire**.

The great hunter
This nineteenth-century sculpture shows Kibinda Ilunga, who was revered by many Central African peoples. Originally a minor Luba prince, he took new hunting techniques to the Lunda at the start of the seventeenth century, united their chiefdoms, and founded the Lunda nation, which later became an empire.

Lunda Empire

The Lunda people of central Africa were forged by the mighty Lunda Empire that once ruled over what are now southern Zaire, northern Angola, and Zambia. The Lunda are descended from Bantu-speaking peoples who settled in Central Africa in the early centuries of the Common Era. By the sixteenth century, the Lunda occupied small separate territories in what is now southern Congo (Dem. Rep.). Around seventeenth century, Kibinda Ilunga (probably a relation of a sixteenth-century Luba king) married the Lunda's senior chief–a woman called Lueji–and became paramount chief. Kibinda's son (by another wife), Lusengi, introduced Luba methods of government. Lusengi's son Naweji, began conquering new lands, thus laying the foundation of the Lunda Empire. By 1700 CE, the Lunda Empire had a capital, Mussumba; a king bearing the title Mwata Yamvo; and a tax-gathering system run by provincial administrators. These changes coincided with a local growth in trade. Central African commodities such as copper, honey, ivory, and slaves became increasingly sought after by European and Arab traders based on Africa's west and east coasts. Profiting from their own strategic location, the Lunda charged passing merchants transit taxes or bartered food and goods with them for guns and other manufactured goods.

Partly to extend their hold on trade and partly to avoid paying tribute to the Mwata Yamvo, some Lunda groups migrated west, south, and east in the seventeenth and eighteenth centuries. These Lunda migrants set up kingdoms in what are now Angola and Zambia. The most important of these was the Kazembe kingdom in present-day Zambia. The building of this kingdom began in the late seventeenth century when the Mwata Yamvo, Muteba, rewarded the loyalty of one of his citizens by giving the man's son, Ngonda Bilonda, the title Mwata Kazembe and by putting him in charge of the eastward expansion. Bilonda's successor, Kanyembo (Kazembe II), became ruler of the lands east of the Lualaba River, and he and his successors completed the expansion into present-day Zambia.

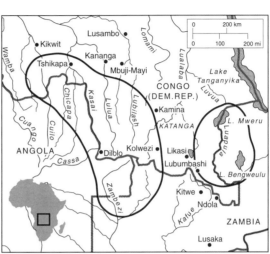

Modern extent of the Lunda people

Kazembe prospered through trade and tribute and by 1800 CE its capital controlled many of the trade routes that crossed the continent.

In the nineteenth century, however, disagreements weakened Lunda rule and in the 1880s the empire broke up under pressure from the Chokwe, a people it had once controlled. Then the European nations of Belgium, Britain, and Portugal colonized Lunda lands. The Portuguese ruled Angola, the British ruled Zambia as Northern Rhodesia (annexing Kazembe in 1899 CE), and Congo came under Belgian domination. Before becoming a Belgian colony, much of present-day Congo (Dem. Rep.) formed the private colony of the Belgian king, Leopold II as the Congo Free State (1885–1908 CE). His rule was characterized by abuses, brutality, and the committing of atrocities in order to protect and maintain the lucrative rubber trade. Congo became independent in 1960 CE, Zambia in 1964 CE, and Angola gained independence in 1975 CE. *See* also **Angola**; **Congo, Democratic Republic of (Peoples—Lunda)**; **Zambia**.

King Kazembe
A drawing made in 1831 CE portraying the ruler of a large Luba–Lunda state in the Katanga region of the Lunda Empire.

Lydenburg

Lydenburg was an independent republic established by Boers in the mid-nineteenth century. It lay at the northwestern edge of the Drakensberg Mountains, in what is now South Africa. Dutch settlers had first arrived in southernmost Africa several centuries ago but, until the nineteenth century, they were largely restricted to coastal regions of the Cape. These settlers came to be known as *boers* (the Dutch word for farmer). In the 1830s the Boers went on large-scale treks inland from the Cape region, to escape the rules and regulations being imposed by the British.

Lydenburg was founded in the late 1840s. Initially, the Boers based their republic at Ohrigstad on the northeastern side of the Drakensberg. The settlement was often attacked by Pedi, Tsonga, and Swazi people, though, and it was located in a region infested with tsetse flies and malaria. Half of Ohrigstad's citizens moved to Soutpansberg, and those left behind transferred to Lydenburg. The Boer republics eventually became part of the Transvaal Republic (1860 CE) and then the Union of South Africa (1910 CE). *See also* **South Africa**; **Transvaal**.

Machanganaland

See **Gazankulu**.

Macias Nguema Biyogo

While Macias Nguema was president (1973–1979) of Equatorial Guinea, the island of Fernando Po was known as Macias Nguema Biyogo. After the overthrow of this brutal leader, the island was renamed Bioko. *See also* **Equatorial Guinea**; **Fernando Po**.

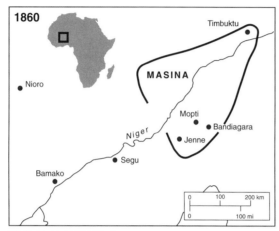

Modern extent of the Macina

Macina

Macina (or Masina) is the name of a state that grew up on the fertile inland delta of the Niger River between Segou and Tombouctou (Timbuktu) in modern-day Mali. At times during its history Macina was tributary to the empires of Mali and, later, Songhai. At the start of the nineteenth century, Fulani Muslims led or inspired by Usman dan Fodio, who founded the Fulani Empire, were organizing *jihads* (holy wars) in many West-African states. Led by Seku Ahmadu, the Fulani of Macina launched their own *jihad* against their overlords and created an independent Muslim state. Ahmadu ruled Macina with a 40-member council, of which he was an ordinary member. Ahmadu's state was governed strictly according to the laws of sharia, but it was taken, in turn, by another Islamic state 50 years later–the Tukolor empire of Al Hajj Umar. *See also* **Mali, empire of**; **Mali**; **Songhai**; **Tukolor empire**.

MADAGASCAR Democratic Republic of Madagascar

The first people in what is now Madagascar were probably Malayo-Polynesians who settled there in the first millennium CE. They were later joined by people from Africa and Arabia. Islam was introduced in the north from the fourteenth century by traders from eastern Africa. Several powerful kingdoms developed on the island from the fifteenth century. The three leading kingdoms were the Sakalava kingdom, which first developed on the west coast in the late sixteenth century; the Tsitambala conference, an alliance of chiefdoms which sprang up on the east coast in the seventeenth century; and the Merina kingdom, which devel-

Madagascan leaders

Andrianampoinimerina, the Merina king, created a unified state in Madagascar by 1797 CE (top left); his son and successor, King Radama 1, extended Merina control over most of the island (top middle); Rainilaiarivony, was Prime Minister of Madagascar from 1864–96 CE (top right); and Binao (bottom right), a former queen of the island.

Madagascan civilizations

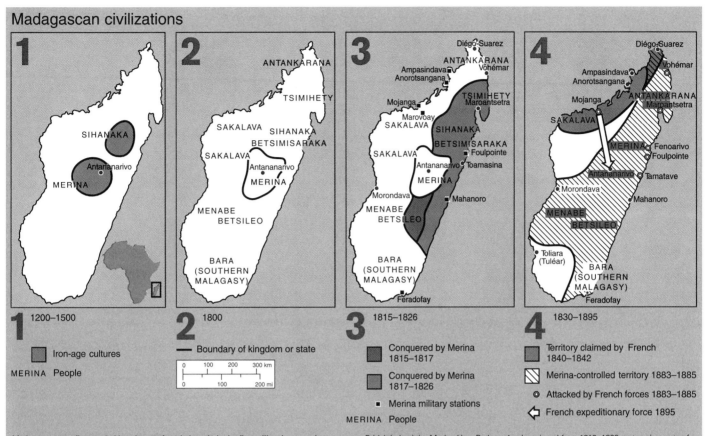

1 1200–1500

Iron-age cultures

MERINA People

2 1800

— Boundary of kingdom or state

0 100 200 300 km
0 100 200 mi

3 1815–1826

Conquered by Merina 1815–1817

Conquered by Merina 1817–1826

■ Merina military stations

MERINA People

4 1830–1895

Territory claimed by French 1840–1842

Merina-controlled territory 1883–1885

◎ Attacked by French forces 1883–1885

⇦ French expeditionary force 1895

Madagascar was first settled by migrants from Indonesia in the first millennium CE, who were probably joined by Bantu-speaking people in the eleventh century. By 1500 CE the Merina and Sihanka peoples had established themselves in the interior. By the end of the eighteenth century, the Merina had become the most powerful group. European influence on Madagascar only became important when the

British helped the Merina king, Radama 1, who reigned from 1810–1828 CE, to seize parts of the island. Merina power continued to increase until the French, allied with the Sakalava, made claims to the north. The Franco-Merina war of 1883–1885 CE ensued and, by 1896 CE, the island was a French protectorate.

oped in the central highlands from the fifteenth century. By the early nineteenth century, the Merina had gained control of most of the island.

The first European to reach the island was a Portuguese navigator, Diogo Dias, in 1500 CE. He was followed by other Portuguese ships which raided the Muslim settlements. Other Europeans, including the British and French, arrived later, and, in the late seventeenth and early eighteenth centuries, the island became a haunt of pirates. In the early nineteenth century, the Merina King Radama I welcomed British and French missionaries and, in 1861 CE, Radama II gave great powers to a French trading company. Britain recognized French control over Madagascar in 1890 CE. However, the Merina refused to submit, In January 1895 CE, French troops landed on the northwest coast and, in September of that year. they occupied Antananarivo. The queen was forced to recognize the French protectorate while, in return, she remained on the throne, ruling as a figurehead.

Opposition to Fench rule mounted after the end of World War I and, in 1946 CE, the country became a self-governing state in the French Union.

The Second Franco-Merino War
In 1894 CE Queen Ranavalo was deposed from the throne and replaced by General Galieni, an event graphically captured in this journal illustration (above). A second illustration chronicles the war in 1895 CE in which the Merina were eventually defeated by the French (right).

© DIAGRAM

Parti Social Démocrate
An election poster for Philibert Tsiranana's party (the PSD) displaying the party symbol of a wildcat.

Recent history

Madagascar became independent as the Malagasy Republic on June 26, 1960 CE. The first president, Philibert Tsiranana, leader of the *Parti Social Démocratique* (Social Democratic Party), followed pro-Western and especially pro-French policies, and his country's cordial relations with South Africa became a matter of controversy. He was reelected in 1965 CE and again in 1972 CE. But allegations of vote-rigging caused unrest, leading to Tsiranana's resignation. A military group, led by Major General Gabriel Ramanantsoa, then took control of the government. Ramanantsoa, who was confirmed as head of the government by a plebiscite in October 1972, distanced the new government from France. The government called for the removal of all French military personnel between 1972–1975 CE, and replaced French civil servants with Malagasy citizens. Ramanantsoa also broke off relations with South Africa and established contacts with the Communist bloc.

Unrest and an attempted coup in 1975 led Ramanantsoa to hand over power to Colonel Richard Ratsimandrava, who took the offices of president and prime minister. But six days later, Ratsimandrava was assassinated and Admiral Didier Ratsiraka became president and head of the ruling Revolutionary Council. A new constitution was approved in a referendum, confirming Ratsiraka as president and renaming the country the Democratic Republic of Madagascar. Under Ratsiraka, relations with France improved, though the country's close links with the Communist world were maintained. In Madagascar, the government pursued socialist policies, including the nationalization of mineral resources, including oil, banking, and insurance. Parliamentary elections held in 1977 CE were won by a party formed by Ratsiraka, the National Front for the Defense of the Revolution. This organization became the country's only legal political party.

Ratsiraka was reelected in 1982 CE. From 1983 CE, the government, faced with many economic problems, adopted more free-market economic policies, reducing the government's role in the economy. Ratsiraka was reelected in 1989 CE and, in 1990 CE, the government permitted the free formation of political parties. In 1991 CE, a group of opposition parties called for Ratsiraka's resignation. Although he remained in office, Ratsiraka formed a new transitional government, led by Albert Zafy. A new constitution adopted in 1992 CE restored a multiparty system. In 1993 CE, Zafy defeated Ratsiraka and became president. But, in 1996 CE, Zafy was faced with impeachment proceedings for alleged violations of the constitution. Although he denied the charges, Zafy resigned. In the elections that followed, he was defeated by Ratsiraka, who returned to office.

In 1998 CE, the voters approved constitutional changes, which included a shift from a unitary to a federal system of government, with increased power for the governments of the six provinces. The changes also reduced the power of the National Assembly and increased the powers of the president.

Peoples

MADAGASCAN PEOPLES

The Madagascan peoples can be divided into two main groups: those of Indonesian descent, who live mainly

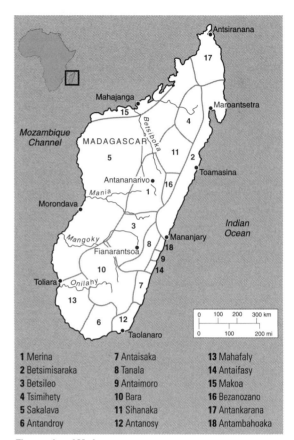

The peoples of Madagascar
This map shows the locations of the 18 principal ethnic groups of Madagascar, who are listed above in order of decreasing populations.

in the central and south-central highlands of the interior, and those of Black African descent, who inhabit the coastal regions and are sometimes collectively known as the *Côtiers* (coastal people). The most important of the highland people are the Merina, who make up nearly 27 percent of the country's total population, and the Betsileo, who make up 15 percent. The first people to settle on the island were of Malayo-Polynesian origin. They arrived on the island between 2,000 and 1,500 years ago, and they were later joined by waves of immigrants from Africa, Asia including Arabia, and Europe.

Madagascar's history is dominated by three large, powerful kingdoms, formed by the unification of smaller states. The first of these was the Sakalava kingdom—established along the west coast in the late sixteenth century. By the middle of the eighteenth century, it controlled nearly half of the island, but it began to fragment after the death of its last ruler, Queen Ravahiny, in 1808 CE. The second had its origin in the Tsitambala confederation, a seventeenth-century alliance of chiefdoms along the east coast. This confederation was taken over and expanded by Ratsimilaho, an English-educated son of an English pirate who created from it the Betsimisaraka kingdom. The third great kingdom emerged in the central highlands during the fifteenth century, when the Merina settled there and subjugated the original inhabitants, the Vazimba. The Merina kingdom grew and, after the fall of the Betsimisaraka kingdom in 1791 CE and the Sakalava kingdom in 1822 CE, it controlled most of the island.

European contact with the island began with the arrival of a Portuguese fleet in 1500 CE. For the next 300 years, the Portuguese, British, Dutch, and French tried to set up colonies, which were repeatedly destroyed by the islanders. However, the islanders tolerated small pirate bases set up in the late seventeenth century by pirates from Europe and the American colonies, who preyed on shipping in the Indian Ocean.

During the first half of the nineteenth century, the Merina ruler King Radama I opened up Madagascar to outside influences, particularly French and British. In 1817 CE, the British acknowledged him as king of all Madagascar, and British and other European advisors began helping him to establish schools, industries, a professional army, and to set up Christian churches. These policies were reversed when Radama died in 1828 CE, and was succeeded by his wife, Queen Ranavalona I. She evicted most of the Europeans, and closed the schools and churches, but the French and British began to return after her death in 1861 CE. Over the next 30 years, France, Britain and Merina argued over control of the island and war ensued between the

Merina and French from 1883–1885. In 1890 CE, Britain agreed to let France have Madagascar in return for control of Egypt and Zanzibar, and the country was declared a French protectorate in 1895 CE. Queen Ranavalona I and her people opposed this step and the French imposed their rule by force.

President Tsiranana
The first president of an independent Madagascar in 1959 CE, he was reelected in 1972 CE but poor health, allied with demonstrations against his regime, forced his resignation.

Madagascar's major political figures

Rabemananjara, Jean-Jacques (1913 CE–)
A Madagascan politician and poet, Jean-Jacques Rabemananjara played an important role in the liberation struggle against French colonial rule. As a deputy of the *Mouvement Démocratique pour la Rénovation Malagache* (MDRM), he was imprisoned and exiled to France from 1947 until 1950 after extremist MDRM members organized a violent revolt in which about 80,000 people were killed. From 1960, he served in the government of Philibert Tsiranana as foreign minister.

Ramanantsoa, Gabriel (1906–1979 CE)
Gabriel Ramanantsoa, Madagascar's armed forces commander, became president in 1972, when Philibert Tsiranana relinquished power to him in the face of widespread strikes and riots. He was initially popular for his maintenance of order and prosecution of corrupt officials, but in 1975, after several coup attempts, he handed over power to a military government and was succeeded by Didier Ratsiraka.

Ranavalona I, (1788–1861)
Ranavalona succeeded to the Malagasy throne in 1828, following the death of her husband, Radama I, who first united Madagascar into a single kingdom. She reversed Radama's pro-European policies, and expelled many Christian missionaries. By the time of her death, Madagascar was isolated from European influences.

Ratsiraka, Didier (1936 CE–)
Didier Ratsiraka, a former naval officer, became head of state in Madagascar in 1975, after the downfall of Gabriel Ramanantsoa. He was popular with both students and the bourgeoisie for his nationalist sentiments, and pledged to carry out administrative and rural reforms. He was elected president in 1976 and, despite several coup attempts, remained in office until he was defeated by Albert Zafy in the 1993 presidential elections.

Tsiranana, Philibert (1912 CE–)
Philibert Tsiranana became the first president of Madagascar in 1959. He was reelected in 1972, but poor health, and demonstrations against his regime, led him to appoint Gabriel Ramanantsoa in his place, and he resigned.

Madagascan presidents

May 1 1959–Oct 11 1972 CE
Philibert Tsiranana

Jan 1970–May 1970 CE
Triumvirate
(acting for Tsiranana)
–André Resampa
–Jacques-Félicien
–Rabemananjara
–Calvin Tsiebo

Oct 11 1972–Feb 5 1975 CE
Gabriel Ramanantsoa
(head of state)

Feb 5 1975–Feb11 1975 CE
Richard Ratsimandrava
(head of state)

Feb 12 1975–Jun 15 1975 CE
Gilles Andriamahazo
(chairman of the national military leadership committee)

Jun 15 1975–Mar 27 1993 CE
Didier Ratsiraka (1st time)
(chairman of the supreme revolutionary council until 4 Jan 1976)

Mar 27 1993–Sep 5 1996
Albert Zafy

Sep 5 1996–Feb 9 1997 CE
Norbert Ratsirahonana (acting)

9 Feb 1997 CE–
Didier Ratsiraka (2nd time)

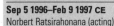
© DIAGRAM

International conference
A 1962 CE stamp marking the UNESCO Conference on higher education in Africa.

Madagascar timeline

Pre 19th century

1st–5th centuries CE Madagascar is settled by peoples from Indonesia
10th–13th centuries Muslims from east Africa settle the north of the island
1500 The Portuguese navigator Diogo Dias becomes the first European to visit Madagascar
1506–1507 Portuguese destroy Muslim trading towns in Madagascar
17th century Foundation of the kingdom of Merina
1643 The French found Fort Dauphin in southern Madagascar
1671 The French abandon Fort Dauphin
1680–1720 Madagascar is a important base for pirates
18th century The Sakalava kingdom dominates Madagascar
1787–1810 Merina wins control of most of Madagascar under King Nampoina

19th century CE

1810 King Radama I outlaws the slave trade
1817 Britain recognizes King Radama as king of all Madagascar
1845 Queen Ranavalona I defeats a British and French invasion and expels European missionaries and traders
1861 Death of Queen Ranavalona: King Radama II gives concessions to a French trading company
1869 The prime minister Rainilaiarivony imposes Protestant Christianity on the Malagasyl
1883–1885 The first Franco-Merina war: Merina cedes Diego Suarez to France
1890 France declares Madagascar a protectorate
1895 The second Franco-Merina War: France occupies the capital Antananarivo after Merina refuses to submit to French rule
1896 Madagascar is declared a French colony
1897 France deposes Queen Ranavalona III, the last monarch of Madagascar

1900–49 CE
1915 A nationalist secret society, the *Vy Vato Sakelika* (VVS), is outlawed
1920 A moderate nationalist movement calling for citizenship rights for the Malagasy is suppressed by France
1940 Madagascar supports the collaborationist Vichy French government
1942 British and South African forces occupy Madagascar
1943 The British hand Madagascar over to the Free French
1945 France gives Madagascar the right to elect an assembly
1947 A pro-independence rebellion breaks out
1948 France crushes the rebellion with the loss of 80,000 lives

1950–59 CE
1958 Madagascar gains internal self-government

1960–69 CE
1960 Jun 26 Madagascar becomes independent as the Malagasy Republic: Philibert Tsiranana is the first president
1965 Tsiranana is re-elected president

1970–79 CE
1971 An opposition party rebellion in southern Madagascar is crushed
1972 Mass demonstrations force Tsiranana to resign: the army takes power under Gen. Gabriel Ramanantsoa
1975 President Didier Ratsiraka nationalizes foreign-owned business and changes the country's name to Madagascar

1980–89 CE
1982 Ratsiraka is re-elected president
1983 Ratsiraka introduces measures to liberalize the economy

1990–99 CE
1991 President Ratsiraka places Albert Zafy in control of a transitional government
1992 A multiparty constitution is approved by voters at a referendum
1993 Zafy is elected president
1996 Zafy resigns from the presidency after he is impeached by the National Assembly
1997 Ratsiraka returns to power after presidential elections
1998 A new constitution provides for a federal system and increased presidential powers

2000–09 CE
2000 Tropical storms and floods cause great damage

Mahdist state

Al-Mahdi (1844–1885 CE) was a Sudanese Muslim from the Nubia region who created a vast Islamic empire that extended from the Red Sea to central Africa at its height. Al-Mahdi was a very religious man, who declared himself al-Mahdi, meaning "The Right-guided One," in 1881 CE: according to Islam, the al-Mahdi is one who will restore Islam. At that time, Sudan was ruled by Egypt, which itself was a province of the Turk-

ish Ottoman Empire. The Sudanese were discontented with their non-Muslim overlords and their harsh rules. Al-Mahdi led a successful rebellion, culminating in the capture of Khartoum in 1885 CE, and established a Muslim state in Sudan. In one battle (1883 CE), Mahdist troops defeated a 10,000-strong force of British soldiers. Britain had recently annexed Egypt. Al-Mahdi died suddenly in 1885 and was succeeded by his deputy, the

Khalifah. The Khalifah led campaigns that greatly enlarged the Mahdi nation, but these ultimately weakened the state. But his forces were almost destroyed in the Battle of Omdurman in September 1898 CE, and the Khalifa was killed later that year by the British, who had much superior weaponry. The Madhist leadership then passed to the Mahdi's son, who died in 1959 CE. *See also* **Sudan**.

Makuria

See **Makurra**.

Makurra

After the 324 CE fall of the Meroitic kingdom, which ruled over parts of modern southern Egypt and northern Sudan south of ancient Egypt, the Kushite kingdom was divided into three kingdoms: Nobatia, Makurra (or Makuria), and Alodia (Alwa). Makurra absorbed Nobatia and formed the larger kingdom of Dunqulah (Dongolah). *See also* **Alodia**; **Meroitic kingdom**; **Nobaita**; **Dunqulah**; **Sudan**.

Malagasy Republic

A French possession since 1896 CE, the island of Madagascar was proclaimed the autonomous Malagasy Republic within the French Union in October 1958 CE. The country achieved full independence in 1960 CE. However, in late 1975 CE, under a new constitution, the country's official name was changed to the Republic of Madagascar. *See also* **Madagascar**.

The Mahdist state
This map shows the fextent of the Mahdist state before its destruction by Anglo-Egyptian forces in 1898 CE.

MALAWI Republic of Malawi

The earliest people in what is now Malawi (formerly Nyasaland) were probably hunter-gathers, but they were displaced in the first millennium CE by Bantu-speaking immigrants. In the last 500 years, several kingdoms developed in the area. The Maravi Confederacy was founded in about 1480 CE and it later dominated central and southern Malawi. Another kingdom founded by the Ngonde people grew up in the north. In the eighteenth and nineteenth centuries, the slave trade became important and some local people, including the powerful Yao kingdom in the south, became involved in the trade.

The slave trade caused wars and great suffering. These were witnessed by the explorer David Livingstone when he reached the area in 1859 CE. Livingstone introduced Christianity and the Free Church of Scotland set up missions in 1875 CE. In 1891 CE, Britain made the area a protectorate (colony) called Nyasaland. From the early 1890s, it was called British Central Africa Protectorate, but it reverted to Nyasaland in 1907 CE. Some economic development, including road and rail construction and the introduction of cash crops, occurred under British rule, but the local people remained poor.

In 1953 CE, Britain joined Nyasaland with Northern and Southern Rhodesia (now Zambia and Zimbabwe) in a new political unit, called the Federation of Rhodesia and Nyasaland. Black nationalists in all three territories opposed the setting up of the federation, because they feared political domination by the Southern Rhodesia's prosperous white minority. In Malawi, the opposition to the federation was led by the African nationalist Dr Hastings Kamuzu Banda.

Recent history

Malawi was the poorest country in the Federation of Rhodesia and Nyasaland and many British settlers believed that it would benefit from being federated with the richer Rhodesias. However, many ordinary black Africans who had experienced racial discrimination in the Rhodesias did not want such conditions in their country. In 1958 CE, a state of emergency was declared. The opposition leaders, including Banda, were arrested and their party, the Nyasaland Congress Party, was banned. However, following Banda's release in 1960 CE, elections in 1961 CE resulted in victory for the renamed Malawi Congress Party (MCP). The federation was abolished in 1963 CE and Malawi achieved self-governing status with Banda as prime minister. The country became fully independent as Malawi on July 6, 1964 CE.

Malawi became a republic in 1966 CE and Banda became the first president of the single-party nation. In 1971 CE, he was proclaimed "president for life". Under Banda, the government pursued a controversial policy, especially because of its maintenance of close contacts with the white-dominated countries, which then existed in southern Africa. For many years, Malawi was the only African country to exchange ambassadors with South Africa. As a result, Malawi benefited from South African aid. This policy, which was strongly criticized by most of the continent's nationalist leaders, was largely dictated by Malawi's geographical position, its dependence on trade with South Africa and Rhodesia, and the fact that its access to the sea was through the Portuguese territory of Mozambique.

New coinage
A stamp depicting Malawi's new coinage in 1964 CE.

© DIAGRAM

On domestic affairs, the economy thrived as Banda attracted foreign investment and aid, and encouraged the introduction of new crops, such as rice. But his rule became increasingly autocratic and his government was criticized for its abuses of human rights. Malawi held its first parliamentary elections since independence in 1978 CE, and other elections were held in 1983 CE, 1987 CE, and 1992 CE. However, all the elected seats were occupied by candidates of the MCP, the sole political party. In the early 1990s, economic and other problems, including drought, harvest failures, and the cost of providing for nearly a million refugees from war-torn Mozambique, made the government less popular.

In 1993 CE, the people voted in a referendum to restore a multiparty system and, in October, a presidential council took control of the government while Banda was recovering from a brain operation in South Africa. Banda was stripped of his title "president for life", and he was defeated in presidential elections in 1994 CE by Bakili Muluzi, leader of the United Democratic Front. Banda retired from politics. In 1995 CE, he stood trial on a charge of murdering four

Dr Hastings Banda
A typical portrayal of the life-president of Malawi, who carried a fly-whisk with him at all times so that he could berate petitioners on his tours around the country.

opposition politicians in 1983 CE but he was acquitted. Presidential elections in 1999 CE resulted in a narrow victory for Muluzi.

Peoples
NGONDE
The Ngonde live in northern Malawi and are closely related to the Nyakyusa in Tanzania. Their home on the side of Lake Malawi was an important crossroads of historical trade networks, allowing the Ngonde to profit from the lucrative ivory trade, but suffer from the raids of slave traders. A powerful Ngonde kingdom (or chiefdom) arose in the nineteenth century, stimulated by the trade in ivory and slaves. This coincided with one of the most violent periods in Ngonde history. A Swahili slaver set up business in Ngonde country, initially with Ngonde consent, but the Swahilis attacked Ngonde villages and captured or killed many people.

YAO
The Yao people of East and Central Africa are found in Malawi, Mozambique, and Tanzania. The Malawian Yao population dates from the 1850s, when groups of Yao people from the north of present-day Mozambique began migrating into the region. One group, the Amchinga, settled at the northeastern corner of Lake Malawi in the 1860s. During the 1870s, Makanjila founded a powerful Yao kingdom in the area. Other smaller kingdoms (or chiefdoms) were established by other Yao leaders. The Yao states were important in East African trade between the coast and the interior, dominating the trade in slaves and ivory around the Lake Malawi region. During this era, the Yao came under the cultural influence of the Swahili people, adopting the Muslim religion, learning Arabic, and wearing Arab clothes.

Malawi Presidents
Jul 6 1966–May 21 1994 CE Hastings Kamuzu Banda
May 21 1994 CE– Bakili Muluzi

Malawi timeline

Pre 19th century		
	15th century CE	The Maravi (Malawi) kingdom dominates the Malawi region
	17th century	The Portuguese are the first Europeans to explore the region
19th century CE		
	1830s	Ngoni and Yao peoples settle in the area of present-day Malawi
	1859	The British missionary David Livingstone visits the region and finds it torn by civil wars
	1875	The Free Church of Scotland sets up a mission station
	1889	The British make protection treaties with local chiefs
	1891	The British proclaim the Protectorate of Nyasaland
1900–49 CE	**1915**	John Chilembwe leads an unsuccessful rebellion against British rule in which he is killed
	1944	The Nyasaland African Congress, the first national political movement, holds its first assembly
1950–59 CE	**1958**	Hastings Kamuzu Banda becomes leader of the Nyasaland independence movement, the Malawi Congress Party (MCP)
1960–69 CE	**1964 Jul 6**	Nyasaland becomes independent as Malawi: Banda becomes prime minister
	1966	Malawi becomes a one-party state: Banda becomes president
1970–79 CE	**1970**	Banda becomes president for life
1990–99 CE	**1993**	Banda gives up the life presidency and prepares to hold elections
	1994	Bakili Muluzi of the United Democratic Front Party becomes president after defeating Banda in multiparty elections
	1995	Banda is acquitted on charges of conspiracy to murder four opposition politicians in 1983
	1997	Following his death, Banda is given a state funeral
2000–09 CE	**2000**	Muluzi dismisses his entire cabinet following charges of corruption

Malawi's major political figures

Banda, Dr Hastings Kamuzu (c.1902–1997 CE)
Hastings Banda was appointed prime minister of Malawi in 1963 and president in 1966. His policies contrasted strongly with the socialist aims of some of his neighbors, and he encouraged officials to follow his example in buying farms and investing in businesses. He was voted "president-for-life" in July 1971, but that title was withdrawn when multiparty government was restored in l993. He lost the 1994 elections and Bakili Muluzi became president. In 1995, he was cleared of murdering four former ministers.

Chilembwe, John (c.1860–1915 CE)
John Chilembwe, a Baptist minister, studied theology in the United States and founded the Providence Industrial Mission at Mbombwe, Nyasaland in 1900, which set up seven schools. In 1915, he led an attack against British rule in Nyasaland (now Malawi). This attack was provoked by the cruelty of white plantation owners. It failed, and Chilembwe was captured and shot.

Hastings Kamuzu Banda
A ten-shilling banknote issued in 1964 CE, one year after he had been elected prime minister of Malawi, and two years before he became president.

Muluzi, Bakili (1943 CE–)
Following the adoption of a multi-party constitution in Malawi in 1994, Bakili Muluzi, leader of the United Democratic Front since 1992, was elected president of Malawi, defeating former President Banda and two other candidates.

MALI Republic of Mali

Between the fourth and sixteenth centuries CE, the area that is now Mali formed part of three powerful African empires–ancient Ghana, ancient Mali, and Songhay. These states became prosperous through trans-Saharan trade with North Africa. The leading commodities carried by the caravans (groups of travelers journeying together) included gold, ivory, salt, and slaves. Around 1,000 years ago, the North Africans introduced Islam and, in the fourteenth century, the city of Timbuktu became a great center of Muslim scholarship. However, after 1591 CE, when the Moroccans conquered Songhay, the Niger River valley was split up into small kingdoms, including those of the Tuaregs, the Fulani, and the Bambara.

The French attempted to colonize the area in the mid-nineteenth century. But they met with much resistance, and it was not until 1895 CE that they won control. In 1904 CE, the colony, which was then known as French Sudan, became part of French West Africa, a vast colony which also included what are now Benin, Burkina Faso, Guinea, Ivory Coast, Mauritania, Niger, and Senegal.

Great Mosque of Djenné
This mosque in Djenné, built in the twentieth century, stands on the same site as the original mosque built when the city was part of medieval Mali in the thirteenth century.

However, in 1946 CE, French Sudan became an overseas territory of France, with its own elected assembly and, in 1958 CE, it became a self-governing nation within the French Union called the Sudanese Republic. In 1959 CE, the Sudanese Republic and Senegal joined together to establish a federation called Mali. However, political differences led to the break-up of the federation in 1960 CE. The Sudanese Republic separated itself from Senegal and became fully independent as the Republic of Mali on June 20, 1960 CE.

Recent history
Mali's first president, Modibo Keita, made his country a socialist, one-party state and all opposition parties were banned in 1964 CE. Mali rejected all ties with France and established close links with Communist countries around the world. As a result, Mali obtained little Western aid. In 1962 CE, Mali attempted to create its own currency and left the franc zone–a financial arrangement whereby France supported the currencies of its former African colonies. Rapid inflation then caused severe economic problems. In 1967 CE, Mali again entered the franc zone, though the government had to accept a 50 percent devaluation of its currency and accept economic conditions imposed by France. In 1967 CE, Keita also launched a "cultural revolution" to uncover corruption, but, in 1968 CE, the arrest of several army officers by the People's Militia led the army to intervene. On November 19, Keita was overthrown in a bloodless coup and a Military Committee of National Liberation took control.

The president of the Military Committee was Moussa Traoré. The new government's main priority was to restore the country's finances and it advocated a mixed economy, with both private enterprises and the government being involved. But droughts in the 1970s made progress difficult in this poor country. In 1974 CE, the government held a referendum on a constitution

Independence
A 1963 stamp celebrating the proclamation of independence in Mali.

which provided for a National Assembly and a president elected on a one-party basis. The move to civilian rule was delayed, but, in 1976 CE, the government announced the creation of a new party, the *Union Démocratique du Peuple Malien* (UDPM). In 1978 CE, a crisis occurred when several members of the government were arrested and tried for treason–an action taken to prevent a planned coup.

Finally, in 1979 CE, the first elections were held under the 1974 constitution. Traoré was elected president and the UDPM was the only party to contest the elections. The new government was civilian, but the military remained a powerful influence. In the 1980s, Traoré ruled largely by decree and defeated five attempted coups. Opposition to Traoré's despotism and accusations of corruption against members of the government led to clashes in 1990 CE. In 1991 CE, a military group deposed Traoré.

A new constitution permitting multiparty elections was quickly drafted and approved by a referendum in 1992 CE. In the ensuing elections, a former opposition leader, Alpha Oumar Konaré, became the country's first democratically elected president. His party, the Alliance for Democracy in Mali (ADEMA) won 76 out of the 116 seats in the National Assembly. Traoré was reelected in 1996 CE and ADEMA won 130 out of the 147 seats in the National Assembly. The 1996 CE elections were marred by opposition boycotts and allegations of electoral irregularities.

Peoples

BAMBARA AND MALINKE

The Bambara (or Bamana) and the Malinke are the two main subgroups of the Manding peoples (also called Mande, Mandinka or Mandingo). The Bambara people live chiefly in the grasslands around Bamako in the upper Niger River region of southern Mali. The Malinke have tended to settle more woodland areas, and now live largely in Mali, Guinea, and Ivory Coast. Many also live in Burkina Faso, Gambia, Guinea-Bissau, and Senegal.

All the Manding peoples originate from a mountainous region of the same name that sits astride the border of Guinea and Mali. This area was the base of the vast medieval Empire of Mali. In 1235 CE, Sundiata–the Muslim ruler of the Malinke kingdom of Kangaba–won a decisive battle against the leader of the Susu, Sumanguru, who ruled the region at that time. Malinke settlers and troops pushed west to the Atlantic, and the Empire of Mali became one of the largest-ever West African realms. Fertile soils, gold-mining, iron-working, and trade led Mali to prosperity that peaked under Mansa Musa's rule in the fourteenth century. After his death in 1337 CE, Mali began to disintegrate and, by the fifteenth century, it was no longer important. In about 1490 CE, Mali's power was eclipsed by the Songhay Empire and, by about 1550 CE, it had ceased to exist.

The Bambara founded the upper Niger state of Segu (based around modern Ségou) in 1600 CE, which reached its peak between 1740–1800 CE. In 1754 CE, the Bambara founded the state of Kaarta (based around modern Nioro du Sahel) to the west of Segu. These were the strongest states in the region by 1800 CE. In the mid-nineteenth century, a Dyula man (part Malinke, part Bambara in origin) called Samori Toure attempted to revive the medieval Empire of Mali. By 1881, Toure had established a huge empire in West Africa, covering much of the present-day nations of Guinea and Ivory Coast. as well as southern Mali. It took the French seven years to defeat Toure's empire, but, by 1898 CE, the Second Mandinka Empire (as it was called) had fallen. By 1900 CE, European colonial powers controlled the entire region.

DOGON

The Dogon people of central Mali live in remote, rocky ravines along a 120-mile (190-km) stretch of the Bandiagara Cliffs and on the tropical savanna (grassland with scattered trees) on the plateaus above and below. Dogon culture is significant for several reasons, in particular because they were isolated from neighboring peoples and relatively free of outside influences until quite recently.

Little is known of the early history of the Dogon before they settled settled in the Bandiagara region. The Dogon believe that ancient human bones and

The Mali people of today
There are three principal groups of people from which the current population of Mali are descended. The map (right) relates to the Bambara and Malinke, whereas the map (far right) focuses on the Dogon. The Bambara live chiefly in the grasslands around Bamako in the upper Niger River region of southern Mali. The Malinke settled more woodland areas, and now live largely in Mali, Guinea, Ivory Coast, and also in Burkina Faso, Gambia, Guinea-Bissau and Senegal. The Dogon people of central Mali live in ravines along a 120-mile (190-km) stretch of the Bandiagara Cliffs, and on the plateaus above and below.

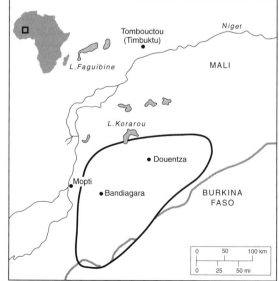

wooden sculptures found in caves suggest that, more than 2,000 years ago, the Bandiagara Cliffs were inhabited by a people called the Tellem. However, most of the wood carvings have been dated at no more than 200 years old and, stylistically, they resemble modern Dogon work. As a result, archeologists believe that the sculptures were made by Dogon artisans and that the oldest "Tellem" skeletons probably date from no earlier than the eleventh century.

The Dogon say their ancestors fled from the southwest to the Bandiagara Cliffs from the thirteenth century onward to escape conquest by the medieval empires of Ghana, Mali, and Songhay. The isolated and inhospitable terrain also proved to be excellent protection from attacks by the neighboring Mossi and Fulani peoples—in particular, during the eighteenth- and nineteenth-century period of jihads (Islamic holy wars) against non-Muslims. The cliffs made access difficult, while outsiders regarded the land to be of little value.

DYULA

For an account of the history of the Dyula people, *see* **Burkina Faso (Peoples—Dyula)**.

FULANI

For an account of the history of the Fulani people, *see* **Fulani, states of**.

MANDE

For information about the history of the Mande or Manding people, *see* **Manding** *below*.

MANDING

The Manding (or Mandinka or Mandingo) is a group of peoples found in West Africa, especially in Gambia, Guinea, Guinea-Bissau, Mali, Niger, and Senegal. This large family of related groups includes the **Bambara and Malinke** (*see above*). The group also includes the **Dyula**—*see* **Burkina Faso (Peoples—Dyula),** the **Mende**—*see* **Sierra Leone (Peoples—Mende),** the **Susu**—*see* **Guinea (Peoples—Susu)**, and also the **Soninke**—*see* **Burkina Faso Peoples—Soninke)**. The Mande homeland is centered on the border between present-day Mali and Guinea. Historically, the Manding people were founders of the Empire of Ghana and the Empire of Mali.

SENUFO

The Senufo are one of the larger ethic groups of West Africa, and they can be found living in regions bordered by the Bani River to the north, the Bagoe River to the northwest, and the Black Volta River to the east, thus placing them in the countries of Mali, Burkina Faso, and Ivory Coast. Various sub-groups exist, but the vast majority of Sefuno people are known as Southern Sefuno, nearly a quarter of whom are Muslim.

SONGHAY

The Songhay people, who live in eastern Mali and western Niger, emerged as a distinct ethnic group under the influence of the historic Songhay Empire, one of the most powerful of the West African precolonial states. The Songhay state was founded in about 750 CE on the Niger River, an important trade route. Its capital was Gao. From 1240–1340s, Songhay was part of the Empire of Mali. But under Sunni Ali (1464–1492 CE), Songhay became the most powerful empire in

Cliffside village (above)
This distinctively Dogon village clings to cliffs that can reach as high as 600 ft (180 m) above the plain below.

Mask art (left)
Masks are widely considered to be the most important Dogon art form. This kanaga ("Hand of God") mask is usually worn by boys newly initiated into men. It is made from wood and is painted red, white, and black. The mask is topped by a double cross, perhaps to represent a bird or a crocodile, or as a symbol of Heaven and Earth. The mask is surrounded by fiber dyed red and decorated with cowrie shells, and the wearer sports a red-stained skirt. Dancers move forwards and backwards allowing their masks to almost touch the ground.

Funeral drum (above)
Known as a pievo, *this drum originates from the Senufo people and was used at burials. Among the powerful symbols visible on its body, slave shackles can be seen.*

West Africa, absorbing much of Mali's land. Askia Muhammad (1493-1528 CE) extended Songhay's boundaries to their limit, and Songhay remained powerful until the Moroccans conquered it in 1591 CE.

SONINKE

For information about the history of the Soninke people, *see* **Burkina Faso (Peoples—Soninke)**.

Mali's major political figures

Mali presidents

Mar 1959–Nov 19 1968 CE
Modibo Keita
(chief of state to 1965)

Nov 19 1968–Mar 26 1991 CE
Moussa Traoré
(chairman of the military national liberation committee until Sep 19 1969; head of state from Sep 19 1969–Jun 19 1979)

Mar 26 1991–Jun 8 1992 CE
Amadou Toumani Touré
(chairman of the national reconciliation council until Mar 31 1991, then chairman of the transitional committee for the salvation of the people)

Jun 8 1992 CE–
Alpha Oumar Konaré

Keita, Modibo (1915–77CE)

In 1959, Modibo Keita became president of the Mali Federation, consisting of Senegal and French Soudan. This federation broke up in August 1960, and French Soudan became independent as Mali, with Keita as its first president. He was deposed by a military group led by Moussa Traoré in 1968.

Konaré, Alpha Oumar (1946 CE–)

A former teacher and writer, Konaré was elected president of Mali in 1992, following a period of military rule. He was reelected in 1997, taking 84 percent of the vote, the opposition groups having boycotted the election.

Mansa Musa, (c.1264–1337 CE)

Musa became *mansa* (king) of the medieval Empire of Mali in 1307 and set about reorganizing trade (especially the exporting of copper and gold) and spreading Islam. In 1324 he set off on a pilgrimage to Mecca with a large retinue and about twenty tons of gold. On the way he stopped off in Cairo, where his lavish spending caused severe inflation.

Traoré, Moussa (1936 CE–)

Moussa Traoré, an army officer, became head of state of Mali in 1968 after leading a military coup that deposed Modibo Keita. He was himself deposed by another coup in 1991, led by Amadou Toure. During his period in office, droughts in the semidesert Sahel region caused widespread famine in Mali.

Modibo Keita
Keita was a Pan-Africanist but his attempts to unite Mali with other African nations were unsuccessful. His left-wing politics alienated Western countries, while Communist ais was limited.

Mali timeline

Pre 19th century
- **c. 400 CE** The earliest city in sub-Saharan Africa develops at Jenne-jeno
- **c. 700-1205** Western Mali region dominated by the Ghana empire
- **c. 1000** Islam introduced into the Mali region by Arab and Berber merchants
- **c. 1240–1450** The empire of Mali is the dominant west African power
- **1312–1337** Timbuktu becomes a major center of Islamic culture under King Mansa Musa
- **c. 1450–1591** The Songhay empire dominates the Mali region
- **1493–1528** Songhay empire at its peak under Askia Muhammad
- **1591** Morocco destroys the Songhay empire

19th century CE
- **1850** Mali area conquered by the Islamic reformer al-Hajj Umar of the Tukolor caliphate
- **1866** The French begin the conquest of Mali
- **1895** France wins full control of Mali: it becomes the colony of French Sudan

1900–49 CE
- **1904** The French Sudan is incorporated into the French West Africa colony
- **1946** French Sudan is given a legislative council

1950–59 CE
- **1958** French Sudan gains full internal self-government
- **1959** French Sudan and Senegal merge to form the Federation of Mali

1960–69 CE
- **1960 Jun 20** The Federation of Mali becomes independent
- **1960 Aug 20** Senegal leaves the federation
- **1960 Sept 22** The independent republic of Mali is proclaimed: Modibo Keita is the first president
- **1968** Keita is overthrown by a military coup. Gen. Moussa Traoré becomes head of government

1970–79 CE
- **1974** Traoré makes Mali a one-party state

1990–99 CE
- **1991** Traoré is overthrown by a military coup: a transitional military-civilian government is created
- **1992** Alpha Oumar Konaré becomes president in elections under a new multiparty constitution
- **1993** An attempted coup to restore Traoré is defeated
- **1997** Konaré is re-elected president

2000–09 CE
- **2000** The World Bank and the International Monetary Fund (IMF) agree to reduce Mali's international debts

Mali, empire of

Medieval Mali was based on the smaller Kingdom of Kangaba, which was close to and dominated by historic Ghana. Kangaba was founded in around 750 CE on the upper Niger River by the Mandinka-speaking Malinke people. In 1224 CE, the Susu–a people now living in Guinea and Sierre Leone–overran Ghana, and six years later they invaded Kangaba The invaders put to death all the of the ruling family of Kangaba except for one crippled prince, Sundiata, who was not considered a threat. This was a mistake. Sundiata was a great hunter and a good soldier; he became known as the "Lion of Mali." Sundiata built up his forces, and in 1235 CE defeated the Susu. By 1240 CE, he had also conquered what was left of Ghana, and the Mali empire came into existence.

The empire gradually expanded and, by the 1330s, it extended to the Atlantic coast, covering present-day Senegal, Gambia, Guinea-Bissau, most of modern Mali, parts of Mauritania, and even southern Algeria. The major sources of Mali's wealth were control of both the gold-trade routes and the goldfields of Bambuk, Bure, and other sites on the Volta River and in the forests of what is now southern Ghana.

The last, and most powerful, ruler of this empire was Mansa Musa (1264–c.1337 CE). A devout Muslim, he went on pilgrimage to Mecca in 1324 CE, taking with him a huge quantity of gold. He stopped in Egypt en route, where he gave away and spent so much gold that its price fell drastically, with disastrous effects on Egypt's currency. After Mansa Musa died 13 years later, Mali began to disintegrate; some subject states rebelled while enemies of Mali captured others. By the 1490s, Mali was no longer politically important and by about 1550 CE it had been conquered by the Songhay empire. *See* **Ghana, empire of**; **Songhay**.

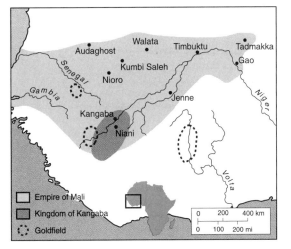

Empire of Mali
This is a map of Mali c.1335 CE, two years before the death of its most powerful ruler, Mansa Musa. By this time, Mali had reached its greatest extent.

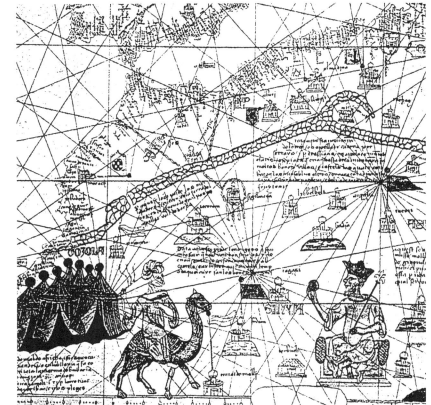

Malinke town (below)
Round houses with mud walls and thatched roofs form the Malinke town of Kirina, near Ségou in Mali. The barrel-like structures are grain stores. Hundreds of years old, Kirina is where the famous battle that led to the foundation of the Empire of Mali was fought between Sundiata and Sumanguru in 1235 CE.

Mansa Musa (right)
Mansa Musa, the Malian king, is depicted on this first European map of West Africa which was drawn in 1375 CE. He is shown in the bottom right-hand corner holding up a large gold nugget as part of a trade with the Arab merchant approaching him on a camel.

Mali Federation

The self-governing French West-African territories of the Sudanese Republic and Senegal united to form the Mali Federation in 1959 CE. The Federation was completely independent from French rule by April 1960 CE, though it remained within the French Community. In August of the same year, however, Senegal left the union to become an independent republic. The Sudanese Republic became the independent Republic of Mali. *See also* **French West Africa**; **Mali**; **Senegal**.

Malindi

Malindi was one of the many trading ports on the East-African coast that formed an independent city-state for much of its history. It was established on what is now the Kenyan coast some time after the tenth century CE by African, Persian, and Arab traders, who merged to form the coastal Swahili people. Malindi was a rival of Mombasa, and at times was either subject to, or in control of, this powerful sultanate. *See also* **Kenya**; **Mombasa**.

A gift to a Chinese emperor
This Chinese painting on silk shows the giraffe sent by the Swahili ruler of Malindi to the Ming Emperor of China, Ch'eng Tsu, in 1414 CE. The emperor received a second giraffe from Malindi three years later.

Mamprussi

Mamprussi was an important state in what is now northern Ghana. It was in existence by the fifteenth century CE, probably established by invaders from the Hausa region to the east. It was inhabited by Akan-speaking peoples. *See also* **Ghana (Peoples—Akan)**.

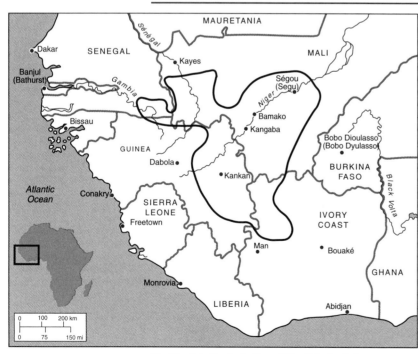

The Mandinka Empire (or Second Mandinka Empire)
Founded by Samori Toure in 1881 CE in an attempt to revive the medieval empire of Mali, this Empire lasted until defeat by the French in 1898 CE.

Manda

On the East-African coast, several historic trading ports emerged at the end of the first millennium CE. Ruled as independent city-states, they were established by African, Persian, Indian, and Arab traders, who merged to form the coastal Swahili people. Manda was perhaps the first of these settlements to emerge as a powerful entity. It was located on what is now the coast of Kenya, and took part in the Indian Ocean trade by the eighth century CE. It traded items such as mangrove trees, iron, and ivory in return for luxury goods such as fine pottery from China. After around 1050 CE, Manda was eclipsed in importance by other ports such as Kilwa. *See also* **Kenya**; **Kilwa**.

Mandinka Empire (or Second Mandinka Empire)

In the mid-nineteenth century a Dyula man named Samori Toure attempted to revive the medieval empire of Mali in West Africa. By 1881 CE, Toure had established a huge empire in west Africa, covering much of the present-day states of Guinea and the Ivory Coast as well as southern Mali. It took the French seven years to defeat Samori Toure's empire; but, by 1898 CE, his Mandinka Empire (or Second Mandinka Empire: Mali being the first) had fallen. By 1900 CE, European colonial powers controlled the whole region. *See also* **Guinea**; **Ivory Coast**; **Mali, empire of**.

Mangbetu kingdom *See* **Congo, Democratic Republic of (Peoples—Mangbetu)**.

Maputo

From the sixteenth to the eighteenth centuries CE three successive kingdoms formed by the Tsongo people of southern Africa–Nyaka, Tembe and Maputo–dominated the region around Maputo (formerly Delagoa) Bay in what is now southern Mozambique. These kingdoms grew powerful through agriculture—the introduction of corn by the Portuguese helped to expand both food production and the population—and trade in slaves, copper and ivory. However, the region came under Zulu influence in the nineteenth century, as Ngoni refugees arrived, escaping a turbulent era in southern Africa. As a result the Tsonga adopted cattle as the central aspect of their economy, as well as the Zulu language.

Mapungubwe

One of the most important Iron Age states of southern Africa, Mapungubwe was originally a trading settlement, It developed into a centralized state based on its control of gold mining and trade. Bambandyanalo just south of the LImpopo River was the center of the kingdom; it was first settled in the tenth century CE. Trade in ivory and cattle was more important at that time than trade in gold. As the state prospered, its rulers moved to nearby Mapungubwe hill. Mapungubwe was at its height between 1100–1300 CE, after which Great Zimbabwe became more dominant, and Mapungubwe was abandoned. *See also* **Great Zimbabwe**.

Marinids

The Marinids were a Berber dynasty that succeeded Almohad rule in Morocco. They were established in eastern Morocco by the mid twelfth century. In 1248 CE they captured Fez and then Marrakech in 1269 CE, making them the rulers of all Morocco. The Marinids tried, without success, to re-establish the Almohad empire but by the fifteenth century their kingdom was no longer completely under their control. In 1465 CE, they were overthrown by the Wattasids, who ruled for only a century. *See also* **Almohad**; **Morocco**.

Marrakech

Marrakech (or Marrakesh) was the first of Morocco's four imperial cities to be established. The city was founded by a military commander of the Almoravid dynasty, Ibn Tashufin, in the mid-eleventh century, on the fertile Haouz plain which is located south of the Tennsift River. The city gave its name to the Almoravid kingdom of which it was the capital. Marrakech fell to the Almohads in 1147 CE and, in 1297 CE, it came under the control of the Marinids whose capital was at Fès. In the sixteenth century it again served as the capital under the Sa'adians. Later Alawid rulers more often used Fès or Meknès. *See also* **Almoravid**; **Morocco**.

Mashonaland

Mashonaland was the British name for the historic heartland of the Shona people. In 1890 the British South Africa Company occupied Mashonaland, giving free land grants to white settlers. Mashonaland became part of self-governing Southern Rhodesia after 1923 CE, and then part of independent Zimbabwe after 1980. *See also* **Rhodesia**; **Shona**; **Zimbabwe**.

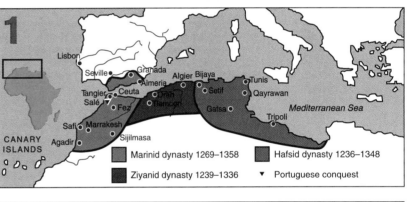

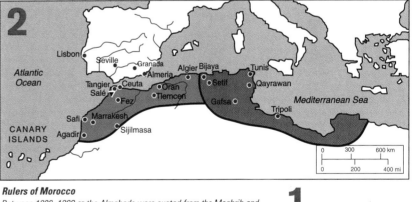

Rulers of Morocco
Between 1236–1269 CE the Almohads were ousted from the Maghrib and Tripolitania by the Hafsid, Ziyanid and Marinid dynasties. Of these three Berber dynasties, the Marinid emerged as the most dominant between 1336–1358 CE, after which it lost control to rival families, and the Hafsids and Ziyanids reappeared in a position of power. The map (top) illustrates the power-sharing between the Berber dynasties in North Africa in 1270 CE, and the map (bottom) the dominance of the Marinids in 1336 CE.

 1270 CE. / 1336 CE.

Masina *See* **Macina**.

Matapa *See* **Mwene Mutapa**.

A native Askari
The Matabele were one of the tribes who regularly provided disciplined and efficient recruits for the British South Africa Police.

Matabeleland

Matabeleland was the British name for the lands controlled by the Ndebele (or Matabele) of South Africa and Zimbabwe. The British defeated the Ndebele in 1893 CE, and Matabeleland was divided into two provinces–to the west, Matabeleland and Mashonaland in the east. *See also* **Rhodesia; Zimbabwe**.

Matamba kingdom *See* Ndongo.

Matshangana-Tsonga *See* Gazankulu.

Mauretania

Mauretania is the name for a historic, and at times independent, region of what now form northern Morocco and west-central Algeria north of the Atlas Mountains. Berbers were the first inhabitants of the region. More then 2,500 years ago, Phoenicians settled along the coast. About 42 CE Mauretania was annexed by the Roman Empire and divided into two provinces: Mauretania Tingitana and Mauretania Caesariensis. In the fifth century, Vandals arrived in Africa, and most of Mauretania became independent. *See also* **Algeria; Morocco**.

MAURITANIA Republic of Mauritania

The earliest known inhabitants of what is now Mauritania were Berbers in the north and black African groups in the south. From about 700 CE, the southern part of the area was dominated by ancient Ghana. The probable capital of this trading empire was Kumbi Saleh, which was located in southeastern Mauritania. Islam was introduced around 1,000 years ago and, in the eleventh century, it was the area where the Berber Almoravid dynasty originated before it attacked Morocco to the north. By the fifteenth century, Arabs had moved into Mauritania, dominating the Berbers.

Portuguese navigators reached the coast in the 1440s and began to trade in such commodities as gold, gum arabic, and slaves. The interior came under the domination of the Songhay empire, which was conquered by Morocco in 1591 CE. Between the seventeenth and nineteenth centuries, Britain, France, and the Netherlands competed for trade along the coast. France began its conquest of the interior in the mid-nineteenth century, but it was not until 1902 CE that the area was finally declared a French protectorate (colony). In 1920 CE, it became part of French West Africa, a vast territory that also included what are now Benin, Burkina Faso, Guinea, Ivory Coast, Mali, Niger, and Senegal, but it became a separate territory in the French Union in 1946 CE. In 1958 CE, Moktar Ould Daddah was elected prime minister and moved the capital to Nouakchott. Mauritania then became a self-governing country within the French Union. It became fully independent on November 28, 1960 CE.

Recent events

Morocco refused to recognize Mauritania, because it claimed that, historically, the new country was part of Morocco. This dispute continued until 1969 CE, when the Moroccan King Hassan II recognized Mauritania's independence. This was part of his plan to gain control of Spanish (now Western) Sahara.

Mauritania's first president, Moktar Ould Daddah, set up a one-party system in 1964 CE, with the *Parti du Peuple Mauritanien* (Mauritanian People's Party, or PPM) as the sole legal party. In 1968 CE, he made Arabic the official language, though his Islamic policies, especially the use of Arabic in schools, provoked opposition among many black African peoples in the south who feared Arab domination. In foreign affairs, Ould Daddah increasingly adopted an anti-Western stance, especially after the 1967 CE Arab-Israeli War. In 1973 CE, Mauritania withdrew from the franc zone, an anti-French gesture which created economic problems.

In 1974 CE, Morocco announced its intention to absorb Spanish (now Western) Sahara, which lay between Mauritania and Morocco. Mauritania also asserted its claim over the mostly barren territory. The International Court of Justice and the United Nations Decolonization Committee both favored self-determination for Spanish Sahara. But in 1975 CE, Spain negotiated an agreement with the two countries that the territory would be partitioned when Spain withdrew in 1976 CE. Mauritanian troops occupied the southern third of Western Sahara, but they were opposed by the guerrilla forces of Polisario (Popular Front for the Liberation of Saharan Territories). The war became a major drain on the economy and, in 1979 CE, Mauritania withdrew and Morocco occupied the entire territory.

In 1978 CE, Ould Daddah was overthrown in a bloodless military coup and a Military Committee for National Recovery began to govern the country. After a period of political uncertainty, Maaouiya Ould Sidi Ahmed Taya, an army colonel who had led the army against the Polisario guerrillas in Western Sahara, seized power in 1984 CE. He faced many problems, including the resentment of black Africans of what they saw as Arab domination in the government. In 1989 CE, Arabs turned on Senegalese workers in the capital Nouakchott. In response, Mauritanian shops in Senegal were looted. Mauritania then began expelling blacks, creating a major refugee problem. Another problem was the failure to eliminate slavery and semislavery (indentured labor), which was still common although it had been abolished in 1970 CE.

In 1991 CE, Mauritania adopted a new constitution which permitted multiparty democracy, with extensive powers for the president. In elections in 1992 CE, Taya was comfortably elected president and his Democratic and Socialist Republican Party (PRDS) took 67 out of the 79 seats in the National Assembly. The PRDS was again successful in legislative elections in 1996 CE, while Taya was reelected president in 1997 CE.

Peoples

MOORS

The meaning of the term Moor has varied over the years. It was once used to describe the people of Morocco and the Muslims who conquered Spain in the eighth century CE. Today, it refers generally to the people who form the majority in Mauritania and also to some of the people in Western Sahara. One group is formed by the Bidanis, or "White Moors", who are of Arab-Berber origin. The other group is made up of "Sudanis", or Black Moors. The Black Moors are largely of Black African origin and are related to the Fulani, Soninke, Wolof, Tukulor, and other peoples.

The ancestors of the Moors are said to have moved into what is now Mauritania in the eleventh century, with the spread of the Berber Almoravids led by Abu Bakr. Others followed in subsequent centuries. The Moors fall into several subgroups. Two of the most important are the Hassani and Zawiya, both Bidani. The Hassani are descended from a group of Arab people who settled in Mauritania from the fifteenth century onward. Moorish history holds that the division into Hassani and Zawiya occurred as a result of the Cherr Baba War between the Berbers and the Arabs between 1644–1674. Rivalries have long existed between the majority Moor population and the minority Black African population in Mauritania. Since the 1908s, this animosity has often turned into conflict. The government troops' support of the Moors has led to the deaths of hundreds of Black Africans.

SAHARAWIS

The people of Western Sahara, who are Moors of mixed Arab, Berber, and Black African descent, are often referred to as Saharawis. They were once nomadic peoples, but, since the 1950s, the majority of them have settled in towns and villages and become farmers or traders.

In 1976 CE, when Spain withdrew from Western (formerly Spanish Sahara) Mauritania occupied the southern third of the territory, while Morocco annexed the north. Many Saharawis supported the rebel Polisario (Popular Front for the Liberation of Saharan Territories) movement, which fought a guerrilla war for full independence. Exhausted by the war, Mauritania withdrew from the south in 1979 CE, and Morocco took over the whole territory. A large number of Saharawis left their homes in Western Sahara and, by the early twenty-first century, they were living in refugee camps in Algeria, which had offered support to Polisario and its government in exile. Attempts by the UN to organize a referendum on the future of Western Sahara were thwarted by the failure to produce an electoral register that was acceptable to both Polisario and the government of Morocco.

Modern extent of the Moorish peoples

Mauritanian presidents and heads of state	
President	**Jun 3 1979–Jan 4 1980 CE**
Nov 28 1960–Jul 10 1978 CE	Mohamed Mahmoud Ould Louly
Moktar Ould Daddah	**Jan 4 1980–Dec 12 1984 CE**
(acting to Aug 20 1961)	Mohamed Khouna Ould Haidalla
Heads of the military committee for national salvation (from Mar 20 1979 also heads of state)	**Dec 12 1984–Apr 18 1992 CE**
	Maaouya Ould Sidi Ahmed Taya
	President
	Apr 18 1992 CE–
Jul 10 1978–Jun 3 1979 CE	Maaouya Ould Sidi Ahmed Taya
Mustafa Ould Salek	

A former French colony
In 1958 CE Moktar Ould Daddah (shown below left with General Charles De Gaulle, below right) became prime minister, and Mauritania became a self-governing colony within the French Union. It became fully independent in 1960 CE.

Mauritania's major political figures

Ould Daddah, Moktar (1924 CE–)
The first president of Mauritania (1960–78), Moktar Ould Daddah worked to unify his ethnically divided people. Dissatisfaction with Mauritania's unsuccessful and costly attempt to take over the southern part of Spanish (now Western) Sahara, however, led to his overthrow.

Taya, Maaouiya Ould Sidi Ahmed (1943 CE–)
Colonel Taya became Mauritania's head of state when he seized power in 1984. Under a new constitution introduced in 1991, he was elected president of Mauritania in 1992 and reelected in 1997. Taya served in the war in Western Sahara between 1976 and 1978 and later served as prime minister and minister of defence.

Reunification
A 1976 CE stamp celebrating the reunification of Mauritania with southern Western Sahara.

Mauritania timeline

Pre 19th century

c. 700 CE–1205 Southern Mauritania region dominated by the Ghana empire
c. 1000 Islam introduced into the Mauritania region by Arab and Berber merchants
1448 The Portuguese establish a trading post on the coast of Mauritania
c. 1450–1591 The Songhay empire dominates much of Mauritania region
1591 Mauritania is conquered by Morocco

19th century CE

1858 France begins to extend military control over southern Mauritania
1898 Xavier Coppolani wins the Berber tribes of southern Mauritania over to French rule

1900–49 CE 1902 French authority is effective in most of Mauritania
1920 Mauritania becomes a French colony
1946 Mauritania becomes a territory of the French Union with a legislative council

1950–59 CE 1955 The Rigaibat are the last Mauritanian tribe to be pacified
1958 Mauritania is granted powers of internal self-government
1959 Mokhtar Ould Daddah becomes prime minister of Mauritania

1960–69 CE 1960 Nov 28 Mauritania becomes independent
1961 Ould Daddah is elected as the first president of Mauritania
1965 Mauritania becomes a one-party state

1970–79 CE 1976 Mauritania and Morocco take over administration of western Sahara (formerly Spanish Sahara)
1978 Ould Daddah is overthrown by a military coup
1979 Mauritania gives up its claim to western Sahara and withdraws

1980–89 CE 1980 After a long period of political uncertainty, Muhammad Ould Haidalla becomes head of government
1984 Col. Maawiya Ould Taya becomes president in a bloodless coup
1989 Inter-ethnic violence breaks out on the border with Senegal

1990–99 CE 1991 Taya introduces a multiparty constitution
1992 Maawiya Ould Taya is elected president in the first elections under the new constitution
1997 Taya is reelected president

MAURITIUS Republic of Mauritius

When Portuguese navigators reached what is now Mauritius in 1510, it was uninhabited. The Portuguese did not settle, and the Dutch took control from 1598–1710 CE. The Dutch named the island Mauritius for their head of state, Maurice of Nassau. The Dutch made two attempts to settle the island–between 1638–1658 CE and again between 1664–1710 CE. European contact proved fatal for the flightless dodo, which became extinct in 1680 CE, because of hunting and the destruction of its eggs by introduced animals. France took possession of the island in 1715 CE and named it the Île de France. French colonists from Réunion settled on the island in 1722 CE. The French slowly developed the economy, using slave labor to grow a variety of crops. They also built Port Louis and used it as a base for attacking the British in India. After the French Revolution, the French government tried to abolish slavery and this provoked the islanders to break away from France.

In 1810 CE, the British occupied the island and reinstated its original name of Mauritius. The British abolished slavery in 1833 CE and more than 75,000 slaves were freed. The British made sugar the main crop in their new colony and the planters imported more than 450,000 indentured laborers from India between 1835–1907 CE. Nearly three-quarters of the Indians were Hindus. The immigrants were often badly treated and immigration was finally ended in 1913 CE. Pressure for constitutional reform mounted and the island became internally self-governing in 1958.

Aviation
A 1971 stamp commemorating the twenty-fifth anniversary of Plaisance Airport

Recent history

Mauritius became independent on March 12, 1968 CE as a constitutional monarchy, with the British monarch, represented by a governor-general, as its head of state. From 1968–1982 CE, the Mauritius Labor Party (MLP) led by Sir Seewoosagur Ramgoolam, the prime minister, ruled the country. The MLP had been in the vanguard of constitutional reform since the 1930s and, in office, Ramgoolam worked to reconcile the conflicting interests of the diverse ethnic groups. In the 1970s, he had to deal with Muslim-Creole conflict, and unrest led him to impose a state of emergency between 1972–1978 CE.

Although generally pro-Western in foreign affairs, Ramgoolam opposed the transfer of the island of Diego Garcia, a nearby island in the Chagos Archipelago, from Mauritian authority in 1965 CE. The island was leased to the United States for 50 years and, between 1996 CE and the early 1970s, the people of Diego Garcia, called the Ilois, were resettled on Mauritius and Seychelles. Mauritius has claimed the Chagos Archipelago since 1982 CE. In 2000 CE, the Ilois won a victory when the British High Court ruled that the British government had acted illegally in expelling the Ilois, though it seemed unlikely that the US would agree to leave the base that they have built on the island.

When world sugar prices fell and Ramgoolam's program of free education and other social benefits became difficult to finance, the government's popularity decreased. In 1982 CE, the left-wing Mauritian Militant Movement (MMM) won control of the government and Aneerood Jugnauth became prime minister. However, the British appointed Ramgoolam to serve as governor of the island until his death in 1985 CE.

In 1983 CE, Jugnauth left the MMM and formed the Militant Socialist Movement (MSM). The MSM formed an alliance with two other parties and won further elections held in 1983. Following a landslide victory in elections in 1991 CE, Jugnauth pushed ahead with his long-term ambition of making Mauritius a republic. In 1992 CE, Mauritius severed its links with the British crown, and Sir Cassam Uteem became president, though the prime minister remained head of the government.

In 1995 CE, despite considerable economic progress based largely on free market policies, an opposition alliance swept Jugnauth's coalition from power in parliamentary elections. The elections were won by the MLP and the MMM and Sir Navinchandra Ramgoolam, the MLP leader, became prime minister. However, in power, the coalition proved to be an uneasy one. In 1997, the coalition split when Ramgoolam dismissed Paul Berenger, the MMM leader, from the cabinet.

Despite the country's economic success, tensions between the various ethnic groups have continued and, in 1999 CE, riots occurred after a popular singer, who had been arrested on drugs charges, died in police custody. The government threatened to declare a state of emergency, and its popularity was further dented when a drought led to water shortages and serious damage to the production of sugarcane, the country's chief commercial crop.

In 2000 CE, the ruling Mauritius Labor Party was defeated in legislative elections by the opposition MMM and its ally the MSM. The opposition alliance took 54 of the 62 legislative seats. Under an agreement between the two parties, Sir Anerood Jugnauth would serve as prime minister for three years and Paul Berenger, the MMM leader, for the remaining two year's of the government's term in office. Observers attributed the opposition victory to popular anger over allegations of corruption against Labor Party officials.

Peoples

CREOLES

About 30 percent of the people of Mauritius are of mixed European and African or European and Indian ancestry. These people are called Creoles. They speak a French dialect called Creole, which is now the lingua franca, although English is the official language.

ILOIS OF DIEGO GARCIA

Diego Garcia is an island in the British Indian Ocean Territory, which was under the control of Mauritius until 1965 CE. Its former population are a mixture of Polynesian, African, and Indian ancestors. The first settlers were Malayo-Polynesians, who reached the island several hundred years ago. After 1815 CE, the British brought African and Indian laborers to the island. These diverse groups developed a distinctive culture and a Creole language of their own.

In the 1960s, Britain leased the island to the United States for a period of at least 50 years. The Ilois were removed from the island, mostly without consent, to make way for a US defense base, the main US military base in the Indian Ocean. Some Ilois visiting Mauritius were not allowed to return to Diego Garcia, while others were forced to leave after crops were destroyed and food imports cut. Finally, in 1971, the remainder were deported, at first to smaller islands and finally to Mauritius. The UK authorities finally agreed to the Ilois demands for increased compensation in 1982, but payment was delayed and many Ilois suffered great hardships.In 2000, the Ilois appealed to the British High Court, which ruled that the British government had acted illegally in expelling the Ilois. The Ilois announced that they planned to sue the British and US governments for compensation, although it seemed unlikely that the US would agree to leave the military base which it has built on Diego Garcia.

Mauritius timeline		
Pre 19th century CE		
	1510	The Portuguese discover and explore Mauritius
	1598	The Dutch claim the uninhabited island and name it after Prince Maurice of Nassau
	1710	The Dutch abandon Mauritius
	1715	The French claim the island and name it Île de France
	1722	French colonists from Réunion settle and grow coffee, sugar, and spices using slave labor
19th century CE		
	1810	The British capture the island and rename it Mauritius
	1814	France formally cedes the island to Britain
	1833	Britain abolishes slavery in its empire: 75,000 slaves are freed on Mauritius
	1835	The first Indian laborers arrive to work on sugar plantations
1950–59 CE	1957	Mauritius gains internal self-government
1960–69 CE	1968 Mar 12	Mauritius becomes independent with Sir Seewoosagur Ramgoolam as prime minister
1980–89 CE	1982	The Militant Mauritian Movement wins elections and Aneerood Jugnauth becomes prime minister
	1983	Jugnauth forms the Socialist Party of Mauritius which wins new elections
1990–99 CE	1992	Mauritius becomes a republic: Cassam Uteem becomes president (a largely symbolic role)
	1995	Sir Navinchandra Ramgoolam replaces Jugnauth as prime minister
	1997	Uteem is reelected president
2000–09	2000	An opposition alliance wins legislative elections and Jugnauth returns as prime minister

Mauritius presidents
12 Mar 1992–30 Jun 1992 CE Sir Veerasamy Ringadoo
30 Jun 1992 CE– Cassam Uteem

Jugnauth, Sir Aneerood (1930 CE–)

Aneerood Jugnauth became prime minister of Mauritius in 1982 and introduced economic policies that increased the country's prosperity. However, in elections in December 1995, he was swept from power by an opposition alliance that favored a fairer distribution of the fruits of economic success. In 2000, Jugnauth was returned to power as prime minister following a sweeping victory by an opposition alliance formed by the Mauritian Militant Movement and the Mauritian Socialist Movement.

Ramgoolam, Sir Seewoosagur (1900–1985 CE)

Seewoosagur Ramgoolam served as chief minister of Mauritius from 1961 and became the country's first prime minister in 1964. He was prime minister when Mauritius became independent in 1968, but was defeated in the 1982 elections by Aneerood Jugnauth.

Mayotte

Mayotte is one of the islands located in the Comoros archipelago but is not part of the Federal Islamic Republic of the Comoros. Mayotte is a French "territorial collectivity," a state somewhere between a territory and a département of France. It is administered by France, and the head of state is the French president. The president appoints a prefect to administer Mayotte with the help of a General Council. Initially inhabited by people of Malay-Polynesian extraction at least 1,500 years ago, Africans and, later, Arabs settled on the island. The Arabs were the dominant influence until 1843 CE, when France took possession of Mayotte as part of Comoros. The Comoros became an overseas territory of France in 1947 CE, with representation in the French National Assembly. In 1961 CE Mayotte, with the other islands, was granted internal autonomy. In 1974 CE the inhabitants of Mayotte voted to continue French rule. *See also* **Comoros**.

Mazrui dynasty See Mombasa

Melilla

Melilla is a Spanish enclave on the northern coast of Morocco. The Berber town was colonized by Spain in 1497 CE and has remained Spanish ever since. The enclave was expanded to include the surrounding area in 1909 CE. It was the first Spanish town to rise against the Popular Front in July 1936 CE , partly triggering the Spanish Civil War. Ceuta, Melilla, and their environs constituted the Spanish Zone. In 1995 CE Melilla became an autonomous community within the Spanish nation.

Merina kingdom

The Merina are the largest ethnic group of the island nation of Madagascar. The Merina kingdom emerged in the central highlands during the fifteenth or sixteenth century, when the Merina settled there and conquered the original inhabitants, the Vazimba. The Merina kingdom grew and prospered, and after the fall of the Betsimisiraka kingdom (1791 CE) and Sakalava kingdoms (1822 CE), it controlled most of the island. King Radama I (reigned 1810–1828 CE) extended Merina control over most of the island, creating a united kingdom for the first time. Radama welcomed British and French missionaries and generally followed pro-European policies but, after his death in 1828 CE, his wife Ranavalona took power. She reversed her husband's strategies and, while she advocated modernization, she opposed Western influences. British and French forces, attempting to resist her policies, sent an expeditionary force, but Merina forces defeated it in 1845 CE. By the time of Ranavalona's death in 1861 CE, Western influence was slight. However, the Merina kingdom battled with France for control of the island from 1883–1885 CE. In 1895 CE the island was declared a French protectorate. The Merina continued to resist and French rule was imposed by force. *See also* **Betsimisiraka kingdom; Madagascar; Sakalava kingdom**.

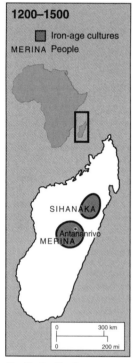

1200–1500

☐ Iron-age cultures
MERINA People

SIHANAKA
Antananrivo
MERINA

0   300 km
0   200 mi

The Merina kingdom
This kingdom emerged in the central highlands of Madagascar during the fifteenth or sixteenth century. It grew and prospered until, by the start of the nineteenth century, it controlled most of the island.

Meroitic kingdom

Several civilizations emerged in the historic region of Nubia, which covered parts of what are now southern Egypt and northern Sudan. The oldest, Kush, was replaced first by the Kingdom of Nubia and then by the Meroitic Kingdom. Nubia emerged as independent state separate from ancient Egypt in around 920 BCE. The capital of this kingdom was moved from Napata to Meroefarther south on the Nile, around 300 BCE. From there, the powerful Meroitic kingdom developed. Meroe became an important center of iron making. In 324 CE, the Meroitic kingdom collapsed after it was defeated by the Ethiopian Axumite kingdom. *See also* **Egypt; Egypt, Ancient; Kush, Kingdom of; Nubia, Kingdom of; Sudan**.

Middle Congo

Moyen-Congo, or Middle Congo, was the name of the French Colony that became independent as the People's Republic of Congo. See also **Congo, People's Republic of**.

A former French colony
A 5c stamp issued in 1928 CE by the Moyen Congo (Middle Congo).

Mogadishu

Mogadishu was probably founded by traders in the eleventh century CE and developed into a self-governing city-state. According to tradition, the people who founded Mogadishu came from what is now Bahrain. By controlling the trade in gold and ivory, Mogadishu grew rich and powerful, reaching its height in the thirteenth century. Mogadishu came under the Sultan of Zanzibar's control in 1871 CE; before that it had been dominated by Portuguese merchants and Omani Arabs. Mogadishu was leased (1892 CE) and then sold to the Italians (1905 CE), who made it the capital of Italian Somaliland. Since 1960 CE, Mogadishu has been the capital city and a major port of independent Somalia. *See also* **Kilwa**; **Mombasa**; **Somalia**.

Meroitic kingdom

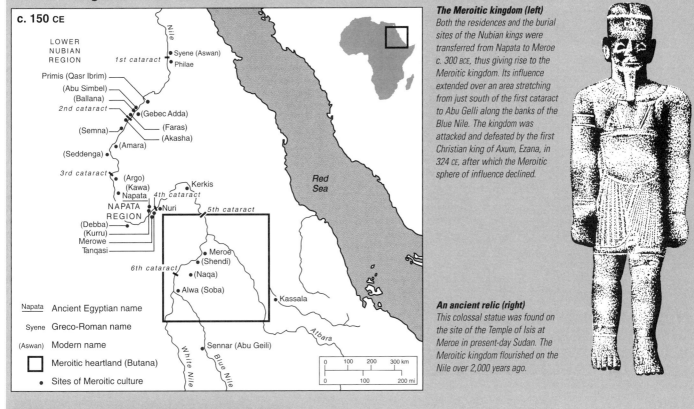

c. 150 CE

LOWER NUBIAN REGION

Syene (Aswan) — 1st cataract — Philae
Primis (Qasr Ibrim)
(Abu Simbel)
(Ballana)
2nd cataract
(Gebec Adda)
(Semna) — (Faras)
(Akasha)
(Amara)
(Seddenga)
3rd cataract
(Argo)
(Kawa) — Kerkis
Napata — 4th cataract
NAPATA REGION — Nuri — 5th cataract
(Debba)
(Kurru)
Merowe
Tanqasi
Meroe (Shendi)
6th cataract — (Naqa)
Alwa (Soba) — Kassala

Red Sea

Sennar (Abu Geili)
White Nile · Blue Nile · Atbara

Napata — Ancient Egyptian name
Syene — Greco-Roman name
(Aswan) — Modern name
☐ Meroitic heartland (Butana)
• Sites of Meroitic culture

| 0 | 100 | 200 | 300 km |
| 0 | 100 | | 200 mi |

The Meroitic kingdom (left)
Both the residences and the burial sites of the Nubian kings were transferred from Napata to Meroe c. 300 BCE, thus giving rise to the Meroitic kingdom. Its influence extended over an area stretching from just south of the first cataract to Abu Gelli along the banks of the Blue Nile. The kingdom was attacked and defeated by the first Christian king of Axum, Ezana, in 324 CE, after which the Meroitic sphere of influence declined.

An ancient relic (right)
This colossal statue was found on the site of the Temple of Isis at Meroe in present-day Sudan. The Meroitic kingdom flourished on the Nile over 2,000 years ago.

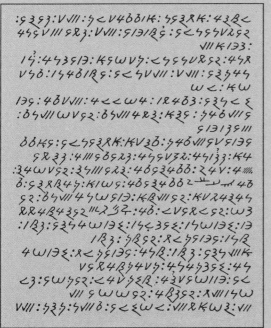

A	B	D	E	Ê	H (KH)	H (KH)	I	K	L	M	N

Ñ	P	Q	R	S	Š (SH)	T	TE	TÊ	W	Y	

Meroitic writing (above)
The people of Meroe developed a form of writing which used both characters and hieroglyphs (picture symbols). This form of writing was used for royal or religious inscriptions.

Meroitic script (left)
The Meroitic people invented their alphabetical script in about the third century BCE. This alphabet was used fpr general kinds of writing.

© DIAGRAM

Under Portuguese control
European colonial powers, such as Portugal, were keen to dominate profitable trade routes all along the east coast of Africa. Although their control of the coast was neither complete nor permanent from the fifteenth to the seventeenth centuries, they made trading unprofitable for other colonial powers by imposing heavy and restrictive duties on them.

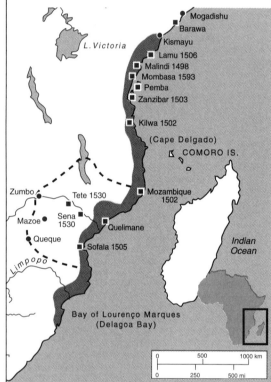

1400–1600 CE

■ Principal Portuguese settlements with approximate date of establishment, if known

● Other settlements where Portuguese had influence

▮ Area under Portuguese control c. 1550

– – – Approximate limit of Portuguese influence inland, 15th–17th centuries

L. Victoria

Mogadishu
Barawa
Kismayu
Lamu 1506
Malindi 1498
Mombasa 1593
Pemba
Zanzibar 1503
Kilwa 1502
(Cape Delgado)
COMORO IS.

Zumbo
Tete 1530
Mazoe
Sena 1530
Queque
Quelimane
Sofala 1505
Mozambique 1502

Limpopo

Indian Ocean

Bay of Lourenço Marques (Delagoa Bay)

| 0 | 500 | 1000 km |
| 0 | 250 | 500 mi |

Mombasa

In existence at least by 1000 CE, the historic city-state of Mombasa on the east coast of Africa grew rich through trade. It was established by African, Persian, and Arab traders, who merged to form the coastal Swahili people. In 1588 CE, despite strong resistance, the coastal island was conquered by the Portuguese. The Europeans were eager to dominate the profitable trade routes all along the East African coast, and Mombasa was one of the most influential trading posts. Their control of the coast was never complete or permanent, but by imposing heavy duties, they made trading unprofitable for many except themselves. The Portuguese made the port the headquarters of their activities in East Africa. In 1698 CE, Mombasa was wrested from Portuguese control by Omani Arab and Pate troops after a 33-month siege. Mombasa became the center of the Omani quest for control of the whole coast. In the late eighteenth century, the Mazrui rulers of Mombasa declared themselves independent of Oman. The Mazrui family grew powerful, extending their control over other coastal regions, including the island of Pemba to the south. The Omanis retook Mombasa in the first half of the nineteenth century but lost it to the British in 1895 CE. Mombasa then became part of British East Africa, later renamed Kenya. The port was the capital of their colony until 1907 CE, when it was replaced by Nairobi. *Ses also* **British East Africa; Kenya; Pate; Pemba**.

Moriuledegu, kingdom of

Inspired by the *jihads* (Muslim holy wars) of Macina and others, a Dyula marabout launched a *jihad* in Madina on the Senegal River in 1835 CE. He established the short-lived Muslim kingdom of Moriuledegu, which ended after its founder's death.

MOROCCO Kingdom of Morocco

Berbers had settled in what is now Morocco at least 3,000 years ago. The Mediterranean coast became important in the twelfth century BCE, when Phoenician colonies were founded. By the fifth century, the Carthaginians had settlements on the Atlantic coast.

Ambush at Tidj Kardje
Resistance to the French presence in Morocco was often fierce. For example, this French army detachment was ambushed by Moors resulting in the death of two officers and two NCOs.

After the fall of Carthage in 146 BCE, the Berber kingdom in Morocco became an ally of Rome but, in 46 BCE, it became part of the Roman province of Mauretania.

Arabs invaded northern Africa in the seventh century CE, spreading their Islamic culture. Morocco was governed by the Umayyad dynasty until 750 CE, when the Iranian Abbasids took over. The Abbasids lost control to the Idrisid dynasty, which began to rule Morocco in the 780s. In the eleventh century, the Almoravid dynasty was founded in southern Morocco. It was followed by the Almohad and Marinid dynasties. Following the expulsion of Muslims from Spain in the late fifteenth century, Spain and Portugal began to occupy areas in Morocco. Resistance came from families of sharifs (descendants of the prophet Muhammad). In the mid-sixteenth century, the Saadians, a sharifian family, took control of Morocco. They were followed in the mid-seventeenth century by the sharifian Alawis, who have provided Morocco's monarchs ever since.

By the early twentieth century, France and Spain were in control. In 1911 CE, a treaty ended Morocco's

Colonial occupation of Morocco

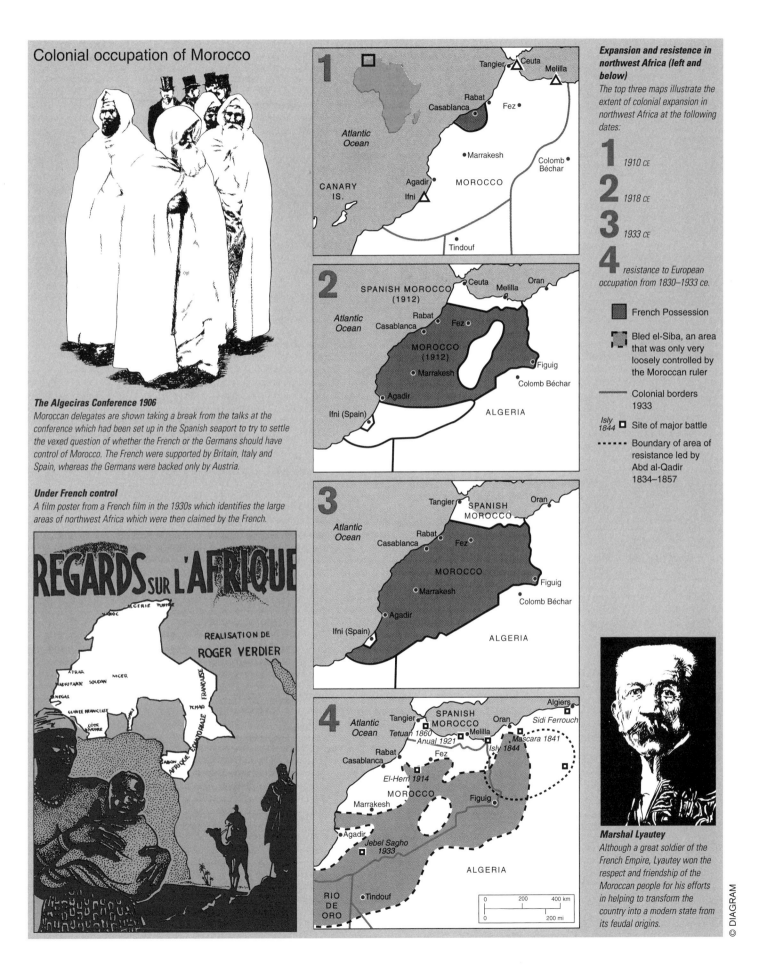

The Algeciras Conference 1906
Moroccan delegates are shown taking a break from the talks at the conference which had been set up in the Spanish seaport to try to settle the vexed question of whether the French or the Germans should have control of Morocco. The French were supported by Britain, Italy and Spain, whereas the Germans were backed only by Austria.

Under French control
A film poster from a French film in the 1930s which identifies the large areas of northwest Africa which were then claimed by the French.

Expansion and resistence in northwest Africa (left and below)
The top three maps illustrate the extent of colonial expansion in northwest Africa at the following dates:

1 *1910 CE*

2 *1918 CE*

3 *1933 CE*

4 *resistance to European occupation from 1830–1933 ce.*

■ French Possession

▢ Bled el-Siba, an area that was only very loosely controlled by the Moroccan ruler

— Colonial borders 1933

Isly 1844 □ Site of major battle

----- Boundary of area of resistance led by Abd al-Qadir 1834–1857

Marshal Lyautey
Although a great soldier of the French Empire, Lyautey won the respect and friendship of the Moroccan people for his efforts in helping to transform the country into a modern state from its feudal origins.

© DIAGRAM

The Rif War 1909 CE
The Rif, in Northern Morocco, proved to be one of the most difficult parts of Africa to subdue. In July 1909 CE the tribesmen killed numerous European laborers near the Spanish fortress of Melilla. The central government, under the control of the sultan, Mulai Hafid, proved to be ineffective in handling the crisis. So, in reply, Spain sent in an army of 50,000 men and, after four months' severe fighting, the Riffians were defeated. The illustration (right) shows some of the captured tribesmen being escorted into the Spanish fort at Melilla.

independence. France and Spain each administered parts of the country and, in 1923 CE, European powers made Tangier an international port. An uprising against foreign rule led by a rebel, Abd al Krim, was defeated in 1926 CE.

Recent history

Moroccan nationalism continued to increase in the 1930s and, during World War II, when Morocco was the scene of fighting between Allied and Axis forces, the Istiqlal (Independence) Party was formed. In 1947 CE, the sultan Muhammad V called for the reunification of Morocco and for self-government. In 1953 CE, the French exiled Muhammad and imprisoned Istiqlal leaders. Their actions provoked opposition to the French and a National Liberation Army was formed to fight for independence. In 1955 CE, the French brought back Muhammad and, on March 2, 1956 CE, Morocco became fully independent of France. Spain then gave up all of its claims except for two small enclaves in the north (Ceuta and Melilla), while Tangier became part of Morocco in October.

King Hassan II
King of Morocco from 1961 CE until his death in 1999 CE, he is shown in this illustration en route for the weekly prayer meeting wearing ethnic costume, and traveling in traditional style.

In 1957 CE, as part of Muhammad's plan to make Morocco a constitutional monarchy, Muhammad changed his title from sultan to king. However, instability led Muhammad to take over the office of prime minister in 1960 CE. In 1961 CE, Muhammad died and was succeeded by his son, who took the title of Hassan II. In 1962 CE, the country adopted a new constitution, though political unrest made him declare an emergency and dissolve parliament in 1965 CE. A new constitution restoring a limited parliamentary government was adopted in 1970 CE and, despite assassination attempts in the early 1970s, he carried out a series of reforms. In 1977 CE, a new Chamber of Representatives was elected and the country became a constitutional monarchy with a single chamber. In foreign affairs, Hassan was generally pro-Western and he played an important part in attempts to negotiate peace in southwestern Asia.

In 1974 CE, Morocco announced its intention to take over Spanish (now Western) Sahara, which lay to the south. Mauritania also had a claim to this mostly barren territory. The International Court of Justice and the UN Decolonization Committee both favored self-determination for Spanish Sahara. But, in 1975 CE, Spain negotiated an agreement with the two African countries, whereby the territory would be partitioned when Spain withdrew. In 1976 CE, Morocco occupied the northern two-thirds of Western Sahara, but the Moroccan and Mauritanian troops were opposed by the guerrilla forces of Polisario (Popular Front for the Liberation of Saharan Territories). In 1979 CE, Mauritania withdrew, exhausted by its massive expenditure on the struggle against Polisario. Morocco then occupied the entire territory. After the fighting ended, Polisario continued to agitate for independence. But United Nations attempts to hold a referendum were thwarted by the failure to draw up an electoral register acceptable to both Polisario and Morocco.

When Hassan died in 1999 CE, he was succeeded by his son who became Muhammad VI. While Muhammad was regarded as a modernizer, he was expected to follow the same cautious approach as his father to most of his country's many problems.

Peoples

ARABS

The Arabs, who originated in Arabia, conquered the Berbers of North Africa in the late seventh century, and, by 711 CE, they were in control of all of North Africa, including Morocco. They introduced the Arabic language and their religion, Islam, pushing out or absorbing the Berbers who lived there.

BERBERS

Berbers, who now make up about one third of Morocco's population, were the earliest known inhabitants of Morocco. They had settled along the North African coast by 3000 BCE, but little is known of their early history before the third century BCE. By about 250 BCE, the Berbers had set up three kingdoms, Mauretania in what is now northern Morocco, and Massaesylian Numidia and Massylian Numidia in Algeria and western Tunisia. *See also* **Berber kingdoms**.

The modern history of the Berbers began with their conversion to Islam in the late seventh century CE. Over the years, Arabs forced many Berbers out of coastal regions and into the mountains and desert. But many others were absorbed into the Arab population. Following the Arab invasion of North Africa, Algeria came under a series of dynasties, including the Ommayads (661–750 CE) and Abbasids (750–789 CE). From 789, the 'Abbasids lost territory to independent dynasties, notably the Idrisids (789–926 CE).

From 1054 CE, a confederation of Muslim Berber groups, the Almoravids, formed a new and powerful dynasty in northwest Africa. After the Almoravid dynasty collapsed in the mid-twelfth century, the Almohad dynasty took over most of Morocco. The Almohad dynasty finally collapsed, losing its last possessions in 1269 CE.

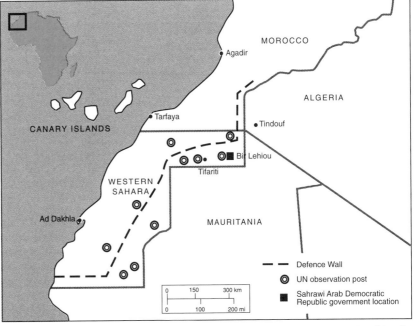

In memoriam (left)
The gravestone of an Arab sultan of Morocco dating from the thirteenth century. In 640 CE, Arabs first invaded North Africa from Arabia in southwest Asia; by 711 CE they had conquered the whole region. The Arabs brought with them their religion, Islam, and their language, Arabic, both of which now dominate North African culture.

Unwelcome intruders (above)
The Moroccan army constructed a sand and stone wall, which was 1500 miles long, in the 1980s to act as a defence against Polisario guerrillas who were based in Algeria.

King Mohammed V
He succeeded his father at the age of 16 in 1927 CE, a position he held until 1957 CE despite a two-year period in exile in Madagascar. He served as king from 1957 until his death in 1961 CE.

Morocco's major political figures

Abd al Krim (1882–1963 CE)

A Berber chief and a great Moroccan resistance fighter, Abd al Krim—"the Wolf of the Rif Mountains"—was founder and president of the Republic of the Rif (1921–26). He was defeated by a combined French and Spanish army of 250,000 troops in May 1926, and exiled to the island of Réunion in the Indian Ocean. He was freed in 1947 and went to Egypt.

Abd al Mumin (c. 1094–1163 CE)

Abd al Mumin was a Berber chief who founded the Almohad dynasty in North Africa. He succeeded Ibn Tumart, founder of the Almohad sect, and proclaimed himself caliph (ruler) of the dynasty. He overthrew the Almoravid dynasty, conquered Morocco, Tunis, and Tripoli, and paved the way for the Almohad conquest of Islamic Spain.

Hassan II (1929–1999 CE)

King of Morocco since 1961, Hassan II became commander of the armed forces in 1956 and prime minister in 1960. He became chairman of the Organization of African Unity (OAU) in 1972, but Morocco suspended its participation in the OAU in 1985 when representatives of the rebel Polisario group—the Sahrawi Arab Democratic Republic—were admitted. He died in July 1999 and was succeeded by his son, Sidi Mohamed.

Ibn Battuta (1304–1368 CE)

Ibn Battuta, born in Morocco, was probably the greatest Arab explorer and geographer. From 1325 to 1349, he traveled through East Africa and the basin of the Niger, as well as large parts of Asia including India and China. In the 1350s, he crossed the Sahara Desert and visited the medieval Songhay and Mali empires, of which he left graphic descriptions.

Abd al Krim
A celebrated resistance fighter, he was the founder, and then the president, of the Republic of the Rif from 1921 CE until his defeat by a combined Spanish and French army in 1926 CE. He was exiled for the next 27 years.

© DIAGRAM

Inauguration
A stamp issued in 1960 CE marking the inauguration of the Arab League Center.

Moroccan kings

A`lawi Filali Sharifi dynasty

Aug 14 1957–Feb 26 1961 CE
Muhammad V

Feb 26 1961–Jul 23 1999 CE
Hassan II

Jul 23 1999 CE–
Muhammad VI

Prince Hassan
He succeeded his father as king upon his unexpected death in 1961 CE, and subsequently became known as Hassan II.

Morocco timeline

Pre 19th century

475–450 BCE Carthaginians establish colonies on the Moroccan coast
40–44 CE Morocco becomes part of the Roman empire
682–683 Moslem Arabs from Tunisia raid Tangier and Agadir
702 The Berbers of Morocco submit to the Arabs and accept Islam
711 An Arab and Berber army invades and conquers Spain
788 Idris I Ibn Abdullah breaks away from the Arab caliphate and founds an independent Idrisid caliphate of Morocco
859 The world's oldest university founded at Fez
926 The Idrisid caliphate is conquered by the Umayyad emirate of Cordoba
1056 Yusuf Ibn Tashfin founds the Sanhaja Berber Almoravid emirate in southern Morocco
1076 The Almoravids conquer Ghana
1085 Yusuf invades and conquers Umayyad Spain
1147 The Almohad dynasty replaces the Almoravids
1269 Marinid dynasty overthrows the Almohads
1415 The Portuguese capture Ceuta
1465 Wattasid dynasty succeeds the Marinids in Morocco
1554 The Saadi dynasty replaces the Wattasids
1578 Moroccans defeat and kill king Sebastian I at Alcazarquivir
1591 Saadi sultan Ahmed al-Mansur captures Timbuktu and overthrows the Songhay empire
1666 Moulay al-Rashid is proclaimed sultan, founding the Alawi dynasty (still in power 1999)

19th century CE

1830 Armed clashes begin on the border of Morocco and French-ruled Algeria
1844 French defeat the Moroccans at Isly
1894 Tribal rebellion in the Rif provokes a Spanish invasion

1900–49 CE

1904 Britain recognizes Morocco as a French sphere of influence
1904 Franco-Spanish treaty grants Spain sphere of influence in northern Morocco
1911 German gunboat *Panther* causes an international crisis when it arrives at Agadir
1912 Mar Treaty of Fez; Morocco becomes a French protectorate
1912 Nov Spanish protectorate established over northern Morocco
1921–1926 Rebellion of Abd el-Krim in the Rif Atlas
1923 Tangier becomes an international city
1930s French settlement in good farming areas
1940 Jun Morocco comes under control of the collaborationist Vichy government following the fall of France in World War II
1942 Nov Operation Torch: Anglo-American landings in Morocco
1944 The Istiqlal (Independence) party is founded

1950–59 CE

1953 France deposes the nationalist sultan Muhammad V and replaces him with his uncle, Moulay Arafa
1955 Independence negotiations begin between France and Morocco
1956 Mar 2 Morocco becomes independent: Muhammad V is restored
1956 Apr Spanish zone (except Ceuta and Melilla) and Tangier are restored to Morocco
1957 Muhammad V exchanges the title of sultan for king

1960–69

1961 Death of Muhammad V: succeeded by his son, Hassan II
1963 Morocco repels Algerian cross-border raids
1965 Riots in Casablanca lead King Hassan to assume direct rule
1965 Hassan II orders the kidnapping from France and murder of opposition politician Ben Barka

1970–79 CE

1976 On Spanish withdrawal, Morocco and Mauritania partition Western Sahara (formerly Spanish Sahara)
1979 Mauritania cedes its claims in Western Sahara to the Polisario independence fighters
1979 Morocco claims sovereignty over all of Western Sahara and builds a fortified wall through it

1980–89 CE

1987 Hassan II calls on Spain to return Ceuta and Melilla
1989 Morocco joins other North African states in the Arab Maghrib Union

1990–99 CE

1991 Jan-Feb Morocco contributes troops for the liberation of Kuwait
1991 Sept Cease-fire between Morocco and Polisario in Western Sahara
1993 King Hassan opens the world's second largest mosque in Casablanca
1999 UN organizes a referendum on the future of Western Sahara to be held in 2000
1999 Jul 23 King Hassan II dies: succeeded by his son, Sidi Muhammad, who becomes Muhammad VI

Ibn Tumart, abu Abdullah Muhammad (c. 1078–1130 CE)

Ibn Tumart was a Berber religious leader who founded the Almohad religious sect in Morocco. He proclaimed himself Mahdi (one who is guided) and gathered a following of Berbers from the Atlas Mountains, paving the way for the Almohad dynasty that ruled North Africa and Spain from 1150 to 1269. He was succeeded by Abd al Mumin.

Muhammad V (1909–1961 CE)

Muhammad V, who was born Sidi Muhammad bin Yusuf, served as sultan of Morocco from 1927 until 1957, and as king from 1957 until his death. From 1943, he became involved in nationalist politics and the French exiled him between 1953 and 1955. Following Morocco's independence in 1956, he worked to make the country a constitutional monarchy, an objective which was finally achieved by his son Hassan II.

Muhammad VI (1963 CE–)

Muhammad VI, who was born Muhammad ibn al-Hassan, is the oldest son of Hassan II of Morocco. Born in Rabat, he was given the title Crown Prince Sidi Muhammad. He became King Muhammad VI on the death of his father in 1999. Educated mainly in Morocco and France, he was thought to favor modernization policies, including the extension of women's rights.

King Hassan II
The king of Morocco from 1961–99 CE, he was succeeded by his son Sidi Mohamad.

Mossi kingdom

The Mossi people of what is now Burkina Faso established a powerful kingdom based around, and named after, its seat at Wagadugu (modern Ouagadougou) in the fifteenth century. *See also* **Wagadu**.

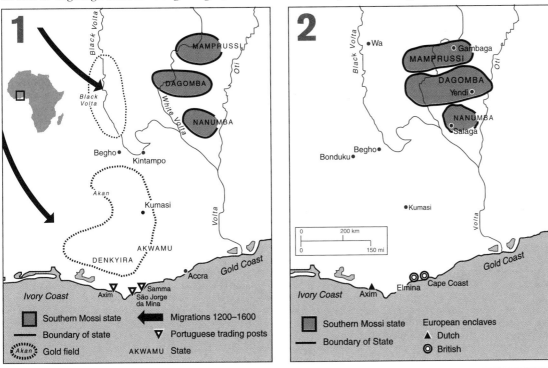

The Southern Mossi and Akan States (far left and left)
The Mossi people established three southern states–Mamprussi, Dagomba and Nanumba–which later came into conflict with other states that emerged in the Akan region, and in the area just to the north of it.

1 *c,1600 CE. The early seventeenth century saw a growth of trading activity in the Akan region. A series of states rose and fell, all of which sought to control the trade routes from the Akan gold field to the coast, and those to the north. Powerful trading states such as Denkyira and Akwamu emerged and, by 1640 CE, the Fante had settled on the coast.*

2 *1700 CE. These states all flourished until the eighteenth century and were eventually absorbed by the Asante Empire (see map left).*

Moyen-Congo

See **Middle Congo**.

MOZAMBIQUE Republic of Mozambique

The first inhabitants of what is now Mozambique were hunter-gatherers, who were probably similar to the San people of present-day Botswana. They were displaced from the third century CE by Bantu-speaking farmers. From around the tenth century, the ancestors of the Shona people founded a major empire in the interior and on the Zimbabwe plateau, ruled by a Shona dynasty called the Mwene Mutapas. These people erected stone buildings, such as Great Zimbabwe, and traded in gold and other commodities with the Arab and Swahili traders on the coast. After 1480 CE, the

empire split and a new empire was developed by a Shona subgroup called the Rovzi.

The Portuguese reached the coast in the 1490s. They attacked the Arab posts and established new settlements. Slaves captured by the Tsonga people, who founded several kingdoms in the southeast, soon became important in Portuguese trade. In the early nineteenth century, the Rovzi empire collapsed and the interior was dominated by powerful Ngoni kingdoms. The Ngoni, who were refugees from the Mfecane–the movements of peoples caused by the rise of the Zulu

© DIAGRAM

kingdom in southern Africa–did much to delay Portuguese subjugation of the interior.

The Portuguese first developed Mozambique through the *prazo* system of granting huge areas of land to *prazeros*, who were virtually autonomous estate holders, but this system was finally abolished because the *prazeros* became uncontrollable. In 1885 CE, Portugal's colonization of Mozambique (or Portuguese East Africa) was recognized by the European powers engaged in the "scramble for Africa".

Recent history

Mozambique became an overseas province of Portugal in 1950 CE, but nationalist opposition to Portuguese rule was rapidly increasing. In 1960 CE, a guerrilla movement was formed. Called the Front for the Liberation of Mozambique (or FRELIMO), it launched an armed campaign against the white government and, by 1964 CE, it controlled part of northern Mozambique. A coup in Portugal in April 1974 CE, which overthrew the authoritarian government of Marcello Caetano, led the new military regime to negotiate independence for Mozambique, which was achieved on June 25, 1975 CE.

Under FRELIMO, which was led by President Samora Machel, Mozambique became a one-party, Marxist state. The government took control of most services and industries, but it faced many problems. Following the UN imposition of sanctions against neighboring Rhodesia, it provided a base for guerrillas belonging to the Zimbabwe African National Union. This led to attacks on its territory by Rhodesian and South African forces. Problems did not end in 1980 CE when majority rule was established in Rhodesia, which was renamed Zimbabwe. Mozambique then faced problems with another powerful neighbor–South Africa. Because

Mozambique sheltered members of the African National Congress, South Africa gave support to a guerrilla force, called the National Resistance Movement, or RENAMO, who were opposed to the FRELIMO government. The civil war between government troops and RENAMO guerrillas shattered the economy. A non-aggression pact was signed by Mozambique and South Africa in 1984 CE, but the fighting continued. In 1986 CE, Machel was killed in a plane crash and he was succeeded as president by Joaquim Chissano.

During the 1980s, the government modified its Marxist policies and gradually permitted more and more private businesses. This led to the official ending of the government's Marxist policies in 1989 CE. In 1990 CE, Mozambique adopted a new constitution, legalizing opposition parties, providing for secret elections, and introducing a bill of rights. In 1992 CE, FRELIMO and RENAMO signed a peace agreement, ending 16 years of civil war. The country's first multiparty elections held in 1994 CE were won by FRELIMO, while Chissano defeated his RENAMO rival Afonso Dhlakama taking 53.3 percent of the vote. In 1999 CE, FRELIMO again won a majority in the National Assembly, winning 133 out of the 250 seats, while Chissano was reelected president, taking 52.3 percent of the vote. During the 1990s, Mozambique, whose government followed market policies advocated by the IMF (International Monetary Fund), rebuilt its economy. Development was so successful that, by 1999, Mozambique's economy was rated as the fastest growing in the world. But severe floods in 2000 CE caused a major disaster. The Limpopo and Zambesi rivers burst their banks and entire villages were swept away. Up to one million homes were destroyed, as also was one third of the corn crop. Further serious flooding occurred in 2001.

Independence

A stamp issued in 1980 CE marking the independence of neighboring Zimbabwe.

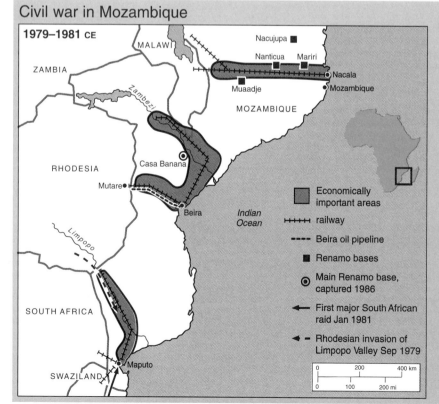

Civil war in Mozambique

1979–1981 CE

MALAWI
ZAMBIA
Nacujupa ■
Nanticua ■ Mariri ■
○ Nacala
Muaadje ■
○ Mozambique
MOZAMBIQUE
Zambezi
Casa Banana ◉
RHODESIA
Mutare ●
Beira
Indian Ocean
Limpopo
SOUTH AFRICA
Maputo
SWAZILAND

■ Economically important areas
╫╫╫╫ railway
---- Beira oil pipeline
■ Renamo bases
◉ Main Renamo base, captured 1986
◀— First major South African raid Jan 1981
◀- - Rhodesian invasion of Limpopo Valley Sep 1979

0   200   400 km
0   100   200 mi

A seventeen-year struggle

From 1975 CE (the year of independence) the ruling Marxist Mozambican Liberation Front (Frelimo) was opposed by the Mozambican National Resistance Movement (Renamo). The rebels were variously backed by Rhodesia (1976–1981 CE), South Africa (1981–1984 CE, and probably beyond), and Malawi (up to 1986 CE).

Renamo waged a campaign of terror against the local population and attacked economically important targets, such as railroads and the Beira oil pipeline. Rhodesia and South Africa constantly raided the country on the pretext that Frelimo was harboring their political enemies. The former invaded the fertile, rice-producing Limpopo Valley in September 1979 CE, for example; and the latter made its first major attack in January 1981 CE.

From December 1991 CE, Renamo and Frelimo began peace talks, which culminated in a conference in Rome in 1992 CE. This resulted in a number of ceasefires, and Frelimo began to move from Marxist to democratic government. In Rome, a declaration was signed in October 1992 CE to end the civil war.

The map (left) shows the situation inside Mozambique during the critical period of 1979–1981.

Mozambique timeline

Pre 19th century

3rd century CE Bantu-speaking herders and ironworkers move into the Mozambique region

12th century Manekweni develops as a center for the Indian Ocean gold trade

14th century Swahili merchants found trading cities at Sofala and Chibuene

1490 The Portuguese navigator Covilhã reaches Mozambique via Egypt and India

1505 The Portuguese sack the Muslim port of Sofala

1508 The Portuguese found the city of Moçambique

1531 The Portuguese begin to extend their control inland along the Zambesi River

1628 Portuguese missionaries convert the Monomatapa (the ruler of the Karanga) to Christianity

1693–1695 The Changamiras attack Portuguese settlements

19th century CE

1832 Portugal outlaws the much abused prazo system of land grants

1833 Shoshangane of the Nguni massacres the garrison of Lourenço Marques (now Maputo)

1836 Shoshangane burns Sofala

1851 Portugal begins to subdue the Bongas (half-caste chiefs) of the Zambesi valley

1859 Death of Shoshangane

1885 King Gungunhana of Gaza cedes mineral rights to the British South Africa Company

1890 Britain successfully claims inland territories claimed by Portugal for its central African colonies1891 Present borders agreed by international treaties

1891–1892 Antonio Enes reforms the administration of Portuguese East Africa

1894 Lourenço Marques is attacked by supporters of Gungunhana

1900–49 CE **1920** Mokombe of Tete, the last of the Bongas, is defeated

1921 Portugal introduces the assimilado system, which enables some Africans to attain Portuguese citizenship

1926 The "New State" regime introduces protectionist trade and investment policies

1930 Colonial Act encourages Portuguese emigration to Mozambique

1950–59 CE **1951** Mozambique becomes an overseas province of Portugal

1960–69 CE **1960** An independence demonstration in Muenda is crushed leaving 500 dead

1961 Front for the Liberation of Mozambique (FRELIMO) guerrilla movement founded to fight for independence

1964 FRELIMO gains control of northern Mozambique

1969 The moderate president Mondlane of FRELIMO is assassinated: he is replaced by the Marxist Samora Machel

1970–79 CE **1974** Portugal agrees to grant independence to Mozambique

1975 Jun 25 Mozambique becomes independent: Samora Machel becomes president

1976 Mozambique closes its border with Rhodesia (now Zimbabwe). Rhodesia forms the Mozambique National Resistance (RENAMO) to undermine the FRELIMO regime

1977 FRELIMO signs a friendship agreement with the Communist Party of the USSR

1980–89 CE **1980** South Africa begins supporting RENAMO after the white government of Rhodesia falls

1984 Mozambique and South Africa sign a non-aggression pact

1986 President Machel is killed in a plane crash, Joaquim Chissano becomes president

1989 Mozambique officially renounces Marxist policies

1990–99 CE **1990** Ban on opposition parties lifted

1992 FRELIMO and RENAMO sign a peace agreement

1994 FRELIMO leader Joaquim Chissano wins the first multiparty presidential elections

1995 Mozambique joins the Commonwealth of Nations

1996 Mozambique joins the Community of Portuguese-speaking Countries

1998 A cholera epidemic kills over 800 people

2000–09 CE **2000** Central and southern Mozambique devastated by floods caused by the worst rain in 40 years; one third of the country's corn crop is destroyed

2001 The Health Ministry announces that one in five pregnant women is infected with the HIV/AIDS virus

Mozambique presidents

Jun 25 1975–Oct 19 1986 CE
Samora Machel

Oct 19 1986–Nov 6 1986 CE
Political bureau of the central committee of FRELIMO (acting)
—Marcelino dos Santos
—Joaquim Chissano
—Alberto Joaquim Chipande
—Armando Emílio Guebuza
—Jorge Rebelo
—Mariano de Araújo Matsinhe
—Sebastião Marcos Mabote
—Jacinto Soares Veloso
—Mário da Graça Machungo
—José Óscar Monteiro

Nov 6 1986 CE—
Joaquim Chissano

Samra Machel (above)
The president of Frelimo since 1970 CE and president of Mozambique from 1975 CE until his death in a plane crash in 1986 CE.

A victory march (below)
A mural housed in the Maputo Museum in Mozambique captures the revolutionary mood.

© DIAGRAM

Peoples
NGONI

Many East Africans are descended from Nguni refugees who fled from the violence of the Mfecane, the population movement triggered by the rise of the Zulu kingdom under the brilliant general, Shaka (1819–1839 CE). They are known as Ngoni peoples. In Mozambique, the Ngoni refugees adopted Zulu battle tactics and raided the local Tsonga and Portuguese trading settle-

ments along the coast, dominating the region by the 1830s. Led by Shaka's former general, Soshangane, the Ngoni established a powerful military empire, called Gaza. Gaza was a major obstacle to the Europeans trying to colonize Mozambique in the 1890s. Ngoni refugees also formed other states in Central Africa, but they were eventually absorbed into local groups, forming centralized chieftainships.

SHONA

For information about the history of the Shona people, *see* **Zimbabwe (Peoples—Shona)**.

TSONGA

The Tsonga are one of the largest of Mozambique's ethnic groups, numbering about two million. At least another one million Tsonga also live in northern South Africa. The Tsonga have been living in this region for several hundred years, and were settled there before the sixteenth century. The Nguni peoples of southern Africa are probably descended from the Tsonga people of Mozambique.

The Tsonga established kingdoms in southern Mozambique, around the Bay of Maputo (formerly Delagoa Bay). The wealth of these kingdoms was based on agriculture and trade. After the Portuguese introduced corn into the fertile region south of Delagoa Bay in the sixteenth or seventeenth century, food production increased and, with increasing food supplies, the population also grew. Traders from various European countries visited the coast competing for influence and also providing increasing opportunities for trade in such commodities as copper and ivory, Other Africans captured by the Tsonga in battle were sold as slaves to the Europeans.

Such external trade played an important part in the emergence of three powerful Tsonga kingdoms: Nyaka, Tembe, and Maputo. These kingdoms successively dominated the region from the sixteenth to the eighteenth centuries. However, in the nineteenth century, refugees fleeing from the Mfecane, a turbulent era in southern Africa's history of mass migrations triggered by the rise of the Zulu kingdom, came to dominate what is now southern Mozambique. As a result, the Tsonga came under a Zulu cultural influence, adopting cattle as the central aspect of their economy, as well as the Zulu language.

YAO

For information about the Bantu-speaking Yao people who are found in Mozambique, Malawi, and Tanzania—not to be confused with the Yao people of Benin in West Africa—*see* also **Malawi (Peoples—Yao)**.

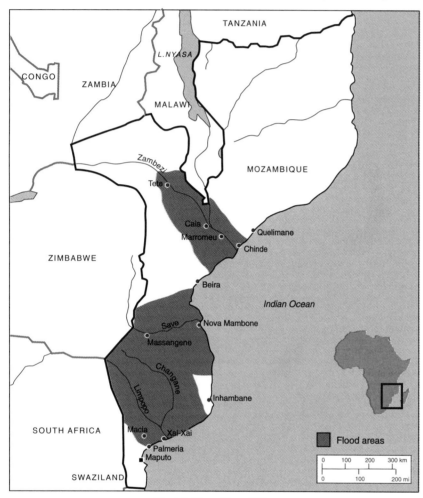

Floods in Mozambique, 2000 CE
Immense floods devastated much of southeast Africa, and Mozambique in particular, leaving hundreds of people dead in their wake, thousands facing an uncertain future of hunger and deprivation, and an economic revival in jeopardy. These were reputedly the worst floods in Mozambique in living memory. A combination of cyclonic winds and heavy rain swamped numerous villages, sweeping away buildings from their foundations, killing livestock, and ruining crops on which the people depended for their economic survival.

Mozambique's major political figures

Chissano, Joaquim Alberto (1939 CE–)

Joaquim Chissano became prime minister of Mozambique in 1974 and president in 1986. He took over as president after the death of Samora Machel, with whom he had worked closely in the *Frente de Libertação de Moçambique* (Frelimo) during its fight against Portuguese colonial rule. In 1992, he signed a peace treaty with Afonso Dhlakama, leader of the rebel *Resistência Nacional Moçambicana* (RENAMO). Chissano was reelected president in multiparty elections in 1994.

Dhlakama, Afonso (1953 CE–)
In 1982, Afonso Dhlakama became president of the *Resistência Nacional Moçambicana* (RENAMO), a guerrilla force founded in 1976, with Rhodesian and later South African support, to destabilize Mozambique. A former member of the *Frente de Libertação de Moçambique* (FRELIMO), which had fought for Mozambique's independence from Portuguese colonial rule, he joined Renamo shortly after it was formed.

Gungunyane, (1850-1906 CE)
Gungunyane was the last independent ruler of Gaza in southern Mozambique, and is now regarded as a national hero. He succeeded his father, Mzila, in 1884, seizing the throne with Portuguese assistance, but he later led the resistence to Portuguese rule. After a series of battles, he was captured in 1895 and exiled to the Azores where he eventually died.

Machel, Samora Moises (1933–1986 CE)
Samora Machel became the first president of Mozambique when the country gained its independence in 1975, and remained in office until he was killed in a plane crash in 1986. Machel had been active in the independence war against the Portuguese (1964–74) and was president of the ruling *Frente de Libertação de Moçambique* (FRELIMO) party, which followed Marxist-Leninist (socialist) policies.

Mondlane, Eduardo (1920–1969 CE)
A prominent Mozambican nationalist, Eduardo Mondlane became president of the liberation movement *Frente Nacional de Libertação de Angola* (FRELIMO) in 1962. He led a guerrilla war against the Portuguese rulers of Mozambique from 1964, and was assassinated in Tanzania in 1969.

Mthethwa

By the eighteenth century CE, the Mthethwa chieftancy of the Bantu-speaking Nguni people had emerged in the southeastern region of modern South Africa, on the eastern seaboard. By the early nineteenth century it was one of the most powerful kingdoms, along with Ndwandwe and Ngwane, in the region. The Mthethwa king at that time was Dingiswayo (c.1770–1818 CE). His kingdom controlled the coastal hunting forests and trade with Delagoa (modern Maputo) Bay. 1n 1818 CE the king of Ndwandwe attacked Dingiswayo's realm and succeeded in killing the king. From the ruins of the Mthethwa kingdom arose the mighty Zulu kingdom led by Shaka, one of Dingiswayo's most able military advisers and commanders. See also **South Africa**; **Zulu, kingdom of**; **South Africa**.

Mthethwa's major political figures

Dingiswayo (c. 1770–1818 CE)
Dingiswayo was ruler of Mthethwa, a kingdom that dominated present-day KwaZulu/Natal in the late eighteenth and early nineteenth centuries. He became overlord of 30 chiefdoms, including the Zulu chiefdom ruled by Shaka, one of his generals and military advisers. He was killed when his army was defeated by a neighboring kingdom, Ndwandwe, in 1818. This defeat led to the breakup of the Mthethwa kingdom and the expansion of Zulu power.

Mwene Mutapa state

Little is known of the early history of the Mwene Mutapa state—sometimes just called Matapa or Mutapa—which was founded by the Shona people of what is now Zimbabwe. According to some traditions, the founder was a man named Chikura (or Mbire), who controlled several chiefdoms in the Guruhuswa region north of the Limpopo River in the fourteenth century. The dynasty of kings were only known as the Mwene Mutapa since the reign of Mutota Nyatsimba (c.1420–c.1450 CE), the first holder of the title. Mutota and his son and successor Matope led a period of expansion until the Shona empire extended north to the Zambezi River and west to the Kalahari Desert. The Mwene Mutapa was a wealthy state because it controlled several important trade routes and the empire was well positioned on mostly fertile land. The successors of Matope were unable to remain in control of the empire, however, and it decreased drastically in size over following decades. When the Portuguese arrived in the sixteenth century, the state was much weakened, little more than a large chieftancy. They deposed the reigning king and forced his successor to grant them extensive trading and mining rights. The rise of the Rozvi empire had eclipsed the Mwene Mutapas almost completely by the end of the late seventeenth century.

The magnificent city of Great Zimbabwe lay within the boundaries of the Mwene Mutapa state. This city had been founded much earlier but the building of its huge stone walls, for which it is famous, flourished in the fourteenth and fifteenth centuries. Great Zimbabwe was the largest of about 200 similar *zimbabwes*–"stone houses"–scattered throughout Zimbabwe and neighboring parts of Mozambique and South Africa. These buildings were the palaces of Shona rulers. The dry-stone wall enclosures of Great Zimbabwe reached up to 30 ft (9 m) high, and the quality of the stonework is impressive. After the Mwene Mutapa state moved north to Mount Fura on the Zambezi River, Great Zimbabwe's decline began. The city was abandoned about 500 years ago. See also **Rozvi empire**; **Zimbabwe**.

Nyatsimba Mutota
Mutota was the founder of the Mwene Mutapa dynasty and ruled from c.1440 to c.1450 CE. During this period, he abandoned Great Zimbabwe and took the capital north to the Zambezi River, from where the expansion of Shona territory and influence continued.

© DIAGRAM

NAMIBIA Republic of Namibia

The first inhabitants of what is now Namibia were the hunter-gatherer San peoples. However, iron-using, Bantu-speaking farming people, the ancestors of the Herero and Ovambo, migrated into the area from the north in the fifteenth century CE. Portuguese navigators reached the area in 1485 CE, but the arid, uninhabited coast proved difficult to settle. Between the seventeenth and early nineteenth centuries, the Dutch and English explored the coast, while the offshore waters attracted whalers.

German influenece began in the mid-nineteenth century. In 1868 CE, German nationals settled on the coast and, in 1884 CE, they proclaimed the area a colony called German Southwest Africa, though the small enclave of Walvis Bay, annexed by Britain in 1876 CE, remained British. German rule was harsh. In the 1890s, the Germans forced the Khoikhoi (a San people) and the Herero out of the Windhoek area and this led to a Khoikhoi uprising in 1903 CE. A second uprising by the Herero between 1904–1907 CE resulted in about 65,000 Herero deaths.

South African troops occupied Southwest Africa in 1915 CE during World War I and, in 1920 CE, the League of Nations mandated South Africa to rule the territory. After World War II, the UN turned down South Africa's request to annex the territory. After the Nationalist Party came to power in South Africa in 1948 CE, discriminatory apartheid policies were introduced into Southwest Africa, which South Africa regarded as one of its provinces. This led to an international dispute about the status of the territory.

Recent history

In 1958 CE, political opposition within the territory mounted with the formation of the Ovamboland People's Party, which was renamed the South West Africa People's Organization (SWAPO) in 1960 CE. SWAPO attempted to negotiate with South Africa for independence, but, in 1966 CE, it launched a guerrilla war. In the same year, the UN General Assembly voted to end South Africa's mandate to rule Southwest Africa and, in 1971 CE, the International Court of Justice declared that South Africa's rule was illegal. In 1968 CE, the UN renamed the territory Namibia at the request of SWAPO.

The guerrilla war continued, especially after 1974 CE, when Angola became independent and SWAPO set up bases there. In 1973 CE, the United Nations recognized SWAPO as the legitimate representative of Namibia. In 1977 CE, South Africa announced a plan for independence under a white-dominated government, excluding many black groups. SWAPO boycotted the elections in 1978 CE. In the late 1980s, fierce fighting with SWAPO guerrillas based in Angola finally led South Africa to agree a ceasefire in 1989 CE. Later that year, elections were held. They were won by SWAPO, which gained a 41-seat majority in the Constituent (later the National) Assembly. In February 1990 CE, the Assembly voted for a new constitution, providing for elections of the president to two five-year terms and an elected bicameral legislature. The Assembly also selected Sam Nujoma, the SWAPO leader, as Namibia's first president. Nujoma set up a broad-based government, including whites, which declared its wish for 'national reconciliation". Namibia finally became independent on March 21, 1990 CE.

In 1994 CE, South Africa, which had ruled Walvis Bay since 1910 CE, handed this small, but economically important, enclave back to Namibia. Despite high unemployment and rising crime rates, Nujoma was reelected president in 1994 CE and SWAPO won more than 70 percent of the votes in the parliamentary elections. In 1998 CE, Nujoma was criticized for his autocratic style and also for sending troops to support the government in the civil war in the Democratic Republic of Congo (formerly Zaire). However, after the country's constitution was amended to allow the president a third term in office, Nujoma won a large majority in the 1999 CE presidential elections. SWAPO again won most seats in the parliamentary elections.

In 1999, a separatist group in the Caprivi Strip, a long finger of land which links northern Angola to Zambia and Zimbabwe, launched a rebellion. The rebels wanted independence for the Strip, which is populated mainly by Lozi people, who live mainly in Zambia, but government troops put down the forces of the Caprivi Liberation Front when they tried unsuccessfully to capture the regional capital, Kutima Mulilo.

Peoples
HERERO

In precolonial times, the Herero lived throughout the plateau area of central Namibia, but they are now widely dispersed, concentrated in small areas on the plateau they once dominated. The Herero and Ovambo share a common early history of migration, probably originating in the great lakes region of East and Central

Independence
A 1990 CE stamp depicting President Sam Nujoma, and marking Namibia's independence.

A Christian heritage
In the nineteenth century, Christian missionaries came to Namibia. Herero women adapted the clothing of the German missionaries' wives to produce the colorful variations that can still be seen today in Namibia.

Africa. Like the Ovambo, the Herero probably arrived in what is now Namibia in the fifteenth or sixteenth century from the area of modern Zambia. By the late seventeenth century, the Herero had reached the arid Kaokoveld plateau, bringing with them their herds of long-horned cattle. By the eighteenth century, they had moved on south to the superior grazing lands of central Namibia. Unlike the Ovambo, the Herero virtually abandoned agriculture and concentrated almost exclusively on cattle.

European traders, explorers, and missionaries entered Namibia in the nineteenth century. In 1884, Germany claimed Namibia (as South West Africa),

including the Herero's territory, as a colony. German settlers gradually seized Herero grazing land and property, even confiscating Herero cattle for "trespassing" on their newly acquired lands. In 1904, the Herero staged a revolt. Their leader, Samuel Maherero, decreed that only German soldiers and male settlers should be attacked – women, missionaries, English, and Afrikaners should be spared. However, the Herero warriors were no match for German weaponry, and Maherero and his followers fled into the Kalahari Desert. The German commander then ordered his forces to exterminate the Herero. In the six months before Germany ordered a halt to the genocide, the Herero were

Namibian president

Mar 21 1990 CE–
Sam Nujoma

Resistance fighters
The insignia of the South West Africa People's Organization (SWAPO). This organization led the resistance against South Africa's illegal occupation of Namibia.

Namibia timeline

Pre 19th century		
	15th century CE	Bantu-speaking peoples migrate into the Namibia region
	1485	Portuguese navigator Diogo Cão arrives at Cape Cross
	1773	The Dutch claim Angra Pequena (Lüderitz), Halifax island and Walvis Bay
19th century CE		
	1814	The Dutch cede their interests in southern Africa to the British
	1830s	Chief Jonker Afrikaner establishes Nama dominance over the Herero people
	1861	Death of Jonker Afrikaner
	1863–1892	Frequent Nama-Herero wars
	1868	German missionaries and farmers settle on the coast
	1870	Germans make peace agreements with local chiefs
	1876	Britain annexes Walvis Bay
	1884	Germany creates the German Southwest Africa colony
	1894	Chief Hendrik Witbooi is killed leading a joint Nama-Herero rebellion against the Germans
1900–49 CE	**1904**	The Herero rebel against German rule
	1907	The Germans crush the Herero rebellion in a genocidal campaign
	1910	Walvis Bay becomes part of South Africa
	1915	South African troops occupy German Southwest Africa in World War I
	1920	The League of Nations mandates Southwest Africa to South Africa
	1945	South Africa refuses a request to place Southwest Africa under UN trusteeship
	1946	The UN refuses to permit annexation of Southwest Africa by South Africa
	1948	South Africa's apartheid policies introduced into Southwest Africa
1950–59 CE	**1958**	The Ovamboland People's Organization is founded
1960–69 CE	**1960**	The Ovamboland People's Organization changes its name to South West Africa People's Organization (SWAPO)
	1966	The UN votes to end South Africa's mandate in Southwest Africa. SWAPO begins a guerrilla war for independence
	1967	The UN appoints a council to oversee Southwest Africa's transition to independence
	1968	At SWAPO's request, the UN changes the name of Southwest Africa to Namibia
	1969	South Africa ignores a UN ultimatum to withdraw from Namibia
1970–79 CE	**1971**	The International Court of Justice declares South Africa's occupation of Southwest Africa to be illegal
	1973	UN recognizes SWAPO as the legitimate representative of the Namibians
	1975	SWAPO sets up bases in Angola after it becomes independent from Portugal
	1977	South Africa announces a plan to make Namibia independent under a white dominated government
	1978	SWAPO boycotts South African organized elections
1980–89 CE	**1988**	After victories by Angolan-led SWAPO forces, South Africa agrees to make Namibia independent by 1990
	1989	South Africa and SWAPO agree a cease-fire
1990–99 CE	**1990 Mar 21**	Namibia becomes independent: Sam Nujoma, the leader of SWAPO, becomes the first president
	1992	Namibia and South Africa agree to joint administration of Walvis Bay
	1994	South Africa cedes Walvis Bay to Namibia
	1999	Nujoma is re-elected president. Fighting breaks out in the Caprivi Strip as separatist guerrillas clash with Namibian troops

Sam Nujoma
The founder of the resistance organization SWAPO, he fought against Namibia's occupation by South Africa. He became president of the independent state in 1990 CE, and was reelected in 1994 and 1999 CE.

© DIAGRAM

reduced by bullets, poison, thirst, and starvation from a population estimated at 75,000 to 90,000 to less than 20,000. The Herero survivors dispersed, many trekking north and east into the desert and semidesert regions of what is now Botswana. The Herero hoped that the defeat of Germany in World War I would lead to a positive change, but their position remained largely unaltered. Despite their relatively small numbers, the Herero played an extremely important part in Namibia's struggle for independence.

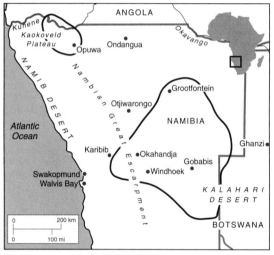

Modern extent of the Herero peoples

KUNG

For information about the Kung people, *see* **Botswana (Peoples—Kung)**.

NAMA

The Nama are a Khoisan people who lived originally in Namibia. Many fled into Botswana from Namibia in the early twentieth century, escaping the anti-German rebellion.

OVAMBO

The Ovambo live in the far north of Namibia and the far south of Angola. Historians believe that the Ovambo migrated to their present homeland from the northeast –in what is now Zambia–sometime around the fifteenth or sixteenth century. The Ovambo have a close cultural and historical relationship with the Herero who live in the central plateau. Legend states that these two peoples are descended from brothers who parted when they reached the present home of the Ovambo–Ovamboland.

In 1884 CE, Namibia became a colony of Germany. However, because of difficulties in controlling the smaller Herero and Nama population to the south, the Germans did not take much interest in the parts of Ovambo territory under their jurisdiction. In 1915 CE, Namibia, as South West Africa–and with it much of Ovamboland–came under South African administration. The South Africans took more interest in Ovamboland and they crushed Ovambo rebellions in the 1920s and 1930s. From 1948 CE, South Africa introduced

Namibia's major political figures

Kutako, Chief Hosea (1870–1970 CE)
Paramount chief of the Herero people of South West Africa (now Namibia), Chief Kutako opposed German colonization and the subsequent rule of the territory by South Africa. He was wounded in the Herero revolt in 1904–05, when around three-quarters of his people were either killed or driven from the country. From the 1950s, he regularly petitioned the UN for independence.

Nujoma, Sam Daniel (1929 CE –)
Sam Nujoma founded the South West African People's Organization (SWAPO) in 1958, and from 1966 led it in a guerrilla war against the illegal occupation of South West Africa (present-day Namibia) by South Africa. Nujoma became president of Namibia on its independence in 1990 and was reelected in 1994 and 1999.

A celebration of independence
This image appeared on a billboard in Windhoek, Namibia, in 1990 CE in recognition of its newly-acquired independent status.

its policy of apartheid in Namibia and, in 1973 CE, South Africa declared Ovamboland an "independent" homeland, a status which was rejected by the Ovambo people and by the international community. Under this policy, absences from Ovamboland were allowed only with a work permit–and then without any accompanying family members. Frustration with this system and the lack of opportunities in Ovamboland resulting from overpopulation and overgrazing, led to the development of an Ovambo workers' movement.

Opposition to South African rule led to the formation of the South West Africa People's Organization (SWAPO). After more than 20 years of armed struggle, SWAPO led Namibia to independence in 1990 CE. Although SWAPO has been accused of being dominated by the Ovambo, it upholds strong nontribal and nonracial principles. Many people object to being labeled Ovambo, preferring instead to be called Namibians.

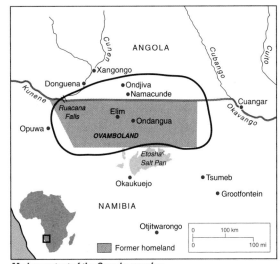

Modern extent of the Ovambo peoples

Natal

A former province of South Africa, Natal has been part of the KwaZulu/Natal province since 1994 CE. The Portuguese navigator Vasco de Gama sighted the coast on Christmas Day in 1497 CE and named the country "Terra Natalis," after the Portuguese word for Christmas, "Natal." At least 500 years ago, the Natal region was already occupied by Nguni people, including the Zulu, who set up a powerful kingdom there in the nineteenth century. The British established a trading post at Port Natal (now Durban) in 1824 CE but did not develop the interior, which had been ceded to them by the Zulus in a treaty. Natalia (or Natal) was the name the Boers gave to the republic they established in the region, with its capital at Pietermaritzburg. The Republic of Natalia (or Natal) was a short-lived nineteenth-century state founded in 1839 CE by Boers led by Andre Pretorius, who had been victorious at the infamous Battle of Blood River in 1838 CE. Armed with superior firepower, the Boers killed more than 3,000 Zulus while suffering no casualties themselves. The Boers made Durban on the coast (formerly Port Natal) part of their republic, but the British annexed the port in 1842 CE.

The Battle of Vegkop, 1836 CE
This battle was fought between Voortrekkers from the eastern Cape and the Ndebele in October 1836 CE. The Boers successfully defended themselves, and the Ndebele were expelled from the Transvaal highveld in 1837 CE. In this sketch, women are shown loading guns for the men in the background, while in the foreground a woman casts lead bullets (left), and the temporary 'hospital' is visible (right).

Colonial expansion
These four maps reflect the degree of expansion by the colonial powers evident in both southern Africa and the eastern Cape at the following times:

1 *1836–1844 CE*

2 *1854 CE*

3 *1872 CE*

4 *1894 CE*

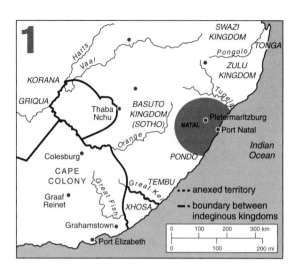

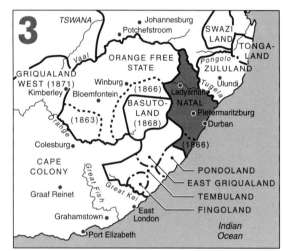

A regimental sergeant
Before the Union of South Africa was formed in 1910 CE, each of the four former self-governing colonies maintained its own militia. This illustration depicts a sergeant of the Kimberley Regiment against a background of Kimberley Town Hall

By 1843 CE the republic had been forced to accept British rule. The majority of Natalia's Boer citizens trekked northwest, where they joined other Boer communities and republics already settled on the highveld, such as Transvaal and Orange Free State. Under British rule, Natal was attached to the Cape Colony until 1856 CE, when it was made a crown colony. In 1910 CE Natal became a province of the Union of South Africa and in 1961 CE of the Republic of South Africa. *See also* **Cape Colony**; **KwaZulu**; **Orange Free State**; **South Africa**; **Transvaal**; **Zulu kingdom**.

John Langalibale Dube
Educated in America, Dube was the founder of the Ohlange Institute in Natal in 1889 CE, which followed the ideas on industrial education of the black American educationalist Booker T. Washington.

Natalia, Republic of

See **Natal**.

Ndebele (Matabele) kingdom

Lobengula
He was the king of the Ndebele whose kingdom was one of the most powerful, and prosperous, north of the Limpopo river.

Khumalo was a northern Nguni chieftaincy in existence by the eighteenth century. Nguni is the dominant Bantu language group between the Drakensberg mountains of southern Africa and the sea. Under their chief Mzilikazi, the Khumalo rebelled against their Zulu overlords in the early 1820s. After fierce Zulu retaliation, the Khumalo escaped to the north for safety, and by 1837 CE they had founded Bulawayo ("Great Place") in what is now southwestern Zimbabwe. They took over the remnants of the once-mighty Rozvi empire, already greatly declined by that time. Before reaching this site,

Mzilikazi had already established a powerful kingdom on the southern African highveld. In Bulawayo, they came to be known as the Ndebele or Matabele, and their kingdom as the Ndebele (or Matabele) kingdom. Mzilikazi's state was one of the most powerful north of the Limpopo River. The discovery of gold within his realm led to concerted efforts by Britain to conquer the kingdom. The British South Africa Company (BSAC)–a commercial venture set up by wealthy businessman Cecil Rhodes–instigated a war with the Ndebele kingdom in 1893 CE. The company had been granted a royal charter to colonize central Africa. The BSAC defeated the Ndebele in 1893 CE, and it came to be part of white-ruled Southern Rhodesia. *See also* **Matabeleland**; **Ndwandwe**; **Nguni chieftaincies**; **Southern Rhodesia**; **Zimbabwe**.

Ndongo kingdom

The Ndongo kingdom was founded by Mbundu farmers in the second half of the fifteenth century. (The Mbundu are Bantu-speakers who live in what is now Angola.) For many years, the ruler, or *ngola*, paid tribute to the more powerful Kongo kingdom to the north. Originally involved in the salt trade as well as farming, the Mbundu began to sell slaves to the Portuguese traders who had recently arrived in their lands in the mid-sixteenth century. By 1556 CE the Ndongo had broken away from the Kongo kingdom, and the *ngola* controlled a large area between the Lukala and Cuanza rivers. After being asked by the current *ngola* to help put down a rebellion, the Portuguese tried to colonize Ndongo. Settlers and troops arrived on the mainland in 1576 CE but they were fiercely resisted by the ngola's troops. The Portuguese did not completely conquer, and dismantle, the Kingdom of Benguela, as they called Ndongo, until 1619 CE. In that year, the capital Kabasa was overrun and the *ngola* fled to an island. The Pope put pressure on the Portuguese invaders to halt their brutal campaigns.

The *ngola's* sister, Anna Nzinga, negotiated a treaty with the Portuguese to allow her brother to return to Kabasa. The terms of the treaty were not kept to by the Portuguese, however, and war broke out. Anna Nzinga succeeded as *ngola*, and she led the fight against the Portuguese. Nzinga is still known today as the national heroine of anti-Portuguese campaigns. The Portuguese deposed Nzinga in 1626 CE, but she conquered the nearby Matamba kingdom and continued campaigning against the Portuguese. After years of resistance,

Nzinga's was one of the few unconquered Angolan states left when she finally signed a treaty with the Portuguese in 1656 CE–most of her lands were ceded to the ngola installed by the Portuguese. Though much-reduced, Nzinga's Matamba kingdom remained independent until her death 1663 CE.

In the 1660s the king of Ndongo rebelled against Portuguese control. He was defeated in 1671 CE, and all Ndongo territory was incorporated into Portuguese Angola. *See also* **Angola**; **Kongo Kingdom**.

Informal negotiation (above)
Nzinga Nbandi was both the queen of the Ndongo kingdom and the leader of the resistance to colonial domination. In the absence of an offer of a seat from the Portuguese governor, she is forced to use one of her attendants as a chair.

1550 CE

Atlantic Ocean

Nsundi
Kabinda
Hbata
Mpinda 1501
São Salvador
Mpemba
São Paulo de Loanda 1575
Mbaka
Muxima
Kambambe
Quicombo
São Felippe de Benguela 1617
Zambezi

■ Principal Portuguese settlements with date of establishment

Mossamedes

● Settlements where Portuguese had influence

▨ Area under Portuguese control c. 1550

- - - Approximate limit of Portuguese influence inland, 1400s–1600s

| 0 | 500 | 1000 km |
| 0 | 250 | 500 mi |

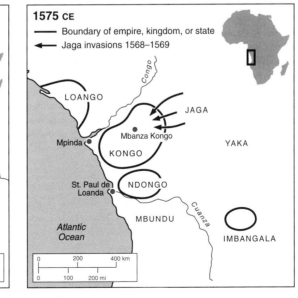

1575 CE

— Boundary of empire, kingdom, or state
← Jaga invasions 1568–1569

Congo
LOANGO
JAGA
Mpinda
Mbanza Kongo
YAKA
KONGO
St. Paul de Loanda
NDONGO
Cuanza
MBUNDU
Atlantic Ocean
IMBANGALA

| 0 | 200 | 400 km |
| 0 | 100 | 200 mi |

Emerging states and colonial influences (left)
Bantu-speaking people occupied all of central Africa by 1000 CE. A number of states emerged, one of which was the Ndongo Kingdom (left). Portuguese influence grew strong in the region, particularly from the fifteenth to the seventeenth centuries. The map (far left) reflects the overall situation in the region in 1550 CE.

Ndwandwe

Ndwandwe was a northern Nguni chieftaincy in existence by the eighteenth century. Nguni is the dominant Bantu language group between the Drakensberg mountains of southern Africa and the sea. During the

early nineteenth century, the Ndwandwe leader Zwide forged a powerful centralized kingdom. His expansionism might have been triggered by a severe drought. In 1816 CE the Ndwandwe forced the Ngwane people north of the Pongola River, triggering the Mfecane ("crushing"), a period of many wars and mass migrations among the peoples of southern Africa. Two years later the Ndwandwe defeated the Mthethwa kingdom, but they lost supremacy to the Zulu kingdom a few years later. The 1818–19 CE Ndwande–Zulu War destroyed Zwide's kingdom. Zwide retired, but his generals fled north and went on to establish the Ngoni states of East Africa, in what are now Zimbabwe, Malawi, Zambia, Mozambique, and Tanzania. One of the most powerful was the Gaza state established by the Ndwandwe general Soshangane in present-day Mozambique. *See also* **Gaza**; **Mthethwa**; **Nguni chieftainships**; **Ngwane**; **Zulu kingdom.**

Nembe

See **Ijo States**.

New Republic

The New Republic was a short-lived Boer republic of the late nineteenth century. In 1879 CE the warring Zulus and British made a peace settlement, and Britain divided the once-powerful Zulu kingdom into 13 chiefdoms. Internal conflicts, fostered by the British, led to civil war. The Boers, who had supported Chief Dinizulu in his struggle for supremacy, were ceded an area of about 4,700 sq. mi. (12,170 sq. km.). In August 1884 CE, this area was proclaimed the New Republic with its capital at Vryheid. At first, the New Republic proclaimed a protectorate over Zululand, but it later withdrew this claim under an agreement with the governor of Natal, who recognized their independence as a consequence of the withdrawal of their claim. But the New Republic was shortlived and, in 1888 CE, it was divided between the Boer Transvaal (or Southern African Republic) and Brirish Zululand. *See also* **South Africa**; **Transvaal**; **Zulu kingdom.**

New Oyo

See **Oyo empire**.

Ngoni states

Toward the end of the nineteenth century, well-established Ngoni chieftainships were in existence in what is now Zambia and a powerful Ngoni state—Gaza—had been established in the Mozambique region. The Ngoni were originally Nguni refugees from the period of wars and mass migrations (1819–1839 CE) in southern Africa termed the Mfecane. The Nguni are the main Bantu-speaking people between the Drakensberg mountains and the sea; those who fled the region and settled in east and central Africa came to be called Ngoni.

One of the most powerful Ngoni rulers in the Zambia region was Mpezeni, who settled with his followers north of Lake Bangweulu in the mid-1800s. Mpezeni was determined to resist British rule, but his troops were not armed with weapons that could match the British firepower, and his kingdom was finally destroyed in 1898 CE. *See also* **Gaza**; **Nguni chieftainships**.

Nguni chieftainships

Nguni is the dominant Bantu language group between the Drakensberg mountains of southern Africa and the sea. The Zulu, Swazi, and Xhosa are all Nguni peoples. Bantu-speakers were settled in the region by the third century CE. By the eighteenth century there were several Nguni chieftaincies in the region, including Thembu, Bomvana, Mpondo, Xesibe, and Hlubi. Of particular historical note were the northerly Mthethwa, Ndwandwe, Ngwane, Zulu, and Khumalo. The rise of the Zulu kingdom in the early nineteenth century led to a period of grea turmoil amog the Nguni. Known as the "Mfecane" (Nguni for "crushing"), this period of mass migrations and wars lasted from 1819–1839 CE. Nguni, particularly Ndwandwe, refugees who fled to the east and central Africa came to be know as Ngoni in their new homelands. The Khumalo left the region and went on to establish the Ndebele (or Matabele) kingdom. *See also* **Mthethwa**; **Ndebele kingdom**; **Ndwandwe**; **Ngoni states**; **Ngwane**; **South Aftrica**; **Zulu kingdom**.

Ngwane

Ngwane was a northern Nguni chieftaincy in existence by the eighteenth century. It was the forerunner of the great Swazi nation. Nguni is the dominant Bantu language in the region between the Drakensberg range of southern Africa and the sea and, during the nineteenth century, Ngwane emerged as one of the most powerful of the Nguni chieftaincies.

After a dispute with the Ndwandwe over land, the Ngwane fled north, led by their King Sobhuza I (c.1795–c.1836 CE); they settled north of their lands around the Pongola River in the region of present-day Swaziland. The migration of the Ngwane is regarded as the start of the "Mfecane" (Nguni for "crushing"), a period of many wars and mass migrations among the peoples of southern Africa. Under Sobhuza I, a contemporary of the Zulu kings Shaka and Zwide, the Ngwane began their northward migration in 1815 CE and were established in what is now Swaziland by 1818 CE. Under Sobhuza's leardership, the Ngwane and other people were forged into the Swazi nation.

However, it was not until the rule of Sobhuza's son and successor, Mswati (or Mswazi, c. 1820-1868 CE) whom many historians rate as the greatest of the Ngwane kings, that the Ngwane came to be known as the Swazi. *See also* **Nguni chieftaincies**; **Swaziland.**

The Nguni diaspora, or Mfecane

The Mfecane, or "Crushing," is the name given to the period of southern African history following the Zulu expansion of 1817 CE. The Zulu were a small branch of the Nguni nation. In 1816 CE, the ruthless military genius Shaka became the Zulu leader. Employing new tactics in 1817 CE, he launched a series of attacks on neighboring peoples. Such was the ferocity of these raids that mass migrations took place. The existing pattern of population and settlement was rearranged: many peoples fled north or south (for example, the Ndebele and Sotho), some forming new states (such as the Sotho Basuto Kingdom), others displacing existing ones (for example, the Kololo conquered the Kingdom of the Lozi and the Ndebele destroyed the Rozwi state).

With the murder of Shaka in 1828 CE, Zulu power waned, but such was the devastation and depopulation (the Mfecane left two million dead), that the Boers (Afrikaners) met relatively little resistance when occupying land during their "Great Trek" that began in 1836 CE.

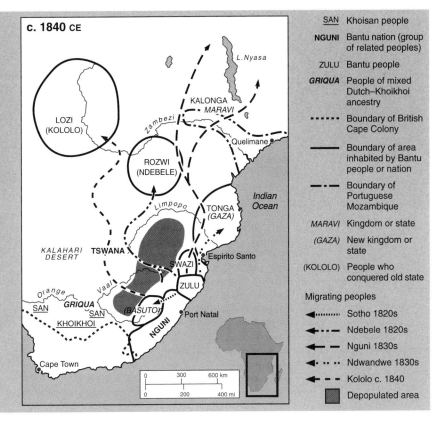

c. 1840 CE

SAN	Khoisan people
NGUNI	Bantu nation (group of related peoples)
ZULU	Bantu people
GRIQUA	People of mixed Dutch–Khoikhoi ancestry
------	Boundary of British Cape Colony
———	Boundary of area inhabited by Bantu people or nation
—·—·—	Boundary of Portuguese Mozambique
MARAVI	Kingdom or state
(GAZA)	New kingdom or state
(KOLOLO)	People who conquered old state

Migrating peoples

◄········ Sotho 1820s
◄—·—· Ndebele 1820s
◄— — Nguni 1830s
◄—··— Ndwandwe 1830s
◄— —· Kololo c. 1840
▪ Depopulated area

NIGER Republic of Niger

Tuaregs, a Berber people, migrated into the Aïr region of what is now northern Niger around 1,000 years ago. In the fifteenth century, they founded the powerful Sultanate of Aïr, which grew rich from trans-Saharan trade. At the same time, southwestern Niger was part of the Songhay empire and, in 1515 CE, Aïr was conquered by the Songhay leader, Askia Muhammad. But Aïr again became independent after Songhay was defeated by Morocco in 1591 CE. In the seventeenth and eighteenth centuries, Aïr expanded its boundaries, reaching its greatest extent in the nineteenth century, though it had declined by 1870 CE. In southern Niger and northern Nigeria, the Hausa built up powerful city-states. However, in 1804 CE, they were conquered by the Fulani people, led by a Muslim cleric, Usman dan Fodio. Fodio established the Fulani-Hausa Sokoto Caliphate, which reached its greatest extent in 1830 CE.

European explorers traveled through the area in the late nineteenth century. The French began the conquest of Niger in 1891 CE and were in control of most of the territory by 1900 CE, although they had to put down Tuareg resistance in the north in the early twentieth century. In 1922 CE, the French made Niger a colony within the federation of French West Africa, which also included what are now Benin, Burkina Faso, Guinea, Ivory Coast, Mali, Mauritania, and Senegal. In 1946 CE, Niger became an overseas territory of France, with its own territorial assembly. In 1958 CE, it became an autonomous territory in the French Community, while full independence was achieved on August 3, 1960 CE.

Rivalry in Niger
In the last two decades of the nineteenth century France's colonial drive embraced Niger. The illustrations show Sultan Ahmadu (above) and Colonel Borgnis-Desbordes (right) in 1883 CE.

© DIAGRAM

Samori Touré
Of Malinke origin, Touré became a symbol for resistance in the 1890s to European colonialism in the Niger region of Africa.

Niger presidents and chairmen
President
Nov 10 1960–Apr 15 1974 CE Hamani Diori
Presidents of the supreme military council
Apr 17 1974–Nov 10 1987 CE Seyni Kountché
Nov 10 1987–May 17 1989 CE Ali Saibou (interim to Nov 14 1987)
President of the supreme council of national orientation
May 17 1989–Dec 20 1989 CE Ali Saibou
Presidents
Dec 20 1989–Mar 27 1993 CE Ali Saibou
Mar 27 1993–Jan 27 1996 CE Mahamane Ousmane Chairman of the national salvation council
Jan 27 1996–Aug 7 1996 CE Ibrahim Baré Maïnassara
Aug 7 1996–Apr 9 1999 CE Ibrahim Baré Maïnassara
Chairman of the national reconciliation council
Apr 11 1999–Dec 22 1999 CE Daouda Malam Wanké
President
Dec 22 1999 CE – Tandja Mamadou

Recent history

Hamani Diori, prime minister of the autonomous republic of Niger, was elected as its first president in November 1960 CE. Diori soon established a reputation as a skilled negotiator in international and regional affairs, although he displeased France by his contacts with the Communist world and also because he favored the Nigerian government over the secessionist Biafra in the Nigerian civil war (1967–1970 CE). His command of domestic affairs was less sure and, in 1965 CE, he was nearly killed in a bomb attack. The economy deteriorated and charges of corruption were made concerning the cost of his many air trips. When a severe drought struck the country in the late 1960s and early 1970s, the distribution of foreign aid was mismanaged and much money was taken by corrupt officials. In 1974 CE, Diori was overthrown in a military coup that suspended the constitution. He was imprisoned for six years then placed under house arrest.

Diori's successor was Colonel Seyni Kountché, who became head of state and president of the ruling Supreme Military Council. Kountché punished those who had profited from the misappropriation of foreign aid and he began a program of agricultural development. He also formed a company, with 66 percent French capital, to exploit the country's valuable uranium deposits and uranium soon became Niger's leading export. In foreign affairs, he maintained good relations with France. He broke relations with Chad between 1981–1984 CE, but restored them when Chad was attacked by Libya.

Kountché died in 1987 CE and was succeeded by his cousin, Colonel Ali Saibou. Saibou founded a new party, the National Movement for the Developing Society (MNSD) which was intended to be the sole party under a new constitution. However, in 1991 CE, he convened a conference of political parties and mass organizations. This conference assumed sovereignty and Saibou's role became largely ceremonial, while a new constitution provided for multiparty elections. In 1992 CE, fighting broke out when Tuareg separatists launched a rebellion in the north. In 1993 CE, when presidential elections were held, Saibou was not allowed to stand and the victor was Mahamane Ousmane. The new government sought to make peace with the separatist Tuareg Liberation Front. A peace agreement was signed in 1995 CE, although one rebel group continued fighting until 1997 CE.

In 1996 CE, Niger's shortlived multiparty democracy was ended when Colonel Ibrahim Bare Mainassara overthrew Ousmane. Again, all political institutions were suspended, but elections were held later in the year and Mainassara was elected president. In 1999 CE, Mainassara was assassinated and Major Daouda Malam Wanké briefly became ruler. But parliamentary rule was restored when a new constitution was adopted in July 1999. In the following elections, a former colonel, Tandja Mamadou of the MNSD, became president.

Peoples

Hausa

For information about the history of the Hausa people, see **Hausa states**; **Nigeria (Peoples—Hausa)**.

Fulani

For information about the history of the Fulani people, *see* **Fulani states**.

Songhay

For information about the history of the Songhay people, *see* **Mali (Peoples—Songhay)**; **Songhay Empire**.

Tuareg

The Tuareg (or Kel Tamacheq or Kel Tagelmust) are Berber in origin. Most live in the Sahara from Niger and Mali in the south to Algeria and Libya in the north. About 5,000 years ago, the Berber ancestors of the Tuareg lived in North Africa along the Mediterranean coast, probably in present-day Libya. However, after the seventh-century Arab invasion of North Africa, the Tuareg moved south in a series of migrations. A proud and independent people, they fought with Arab, Turkish, and European invaders over the years.

In the fifteenth century, the Sultanate of Aïr emerged as a centralized Tuareg state with its capital at Agades (modern Agadez) in present-day Niger. Aïr's wealth was based on control of the trans-Saharan trade routes. Great Tuareg trading caravans (companies of travelers) crossed the Sahara bringing gold, ivory, ostrich feathers, and slaves from West Africa to the Mediterranean coast. Southbound caravans carried salt and Arab and European goods to West Africa. Agades was part of the Songhay empire from 1501–1532 CE and was tributary to the Kanem-Borno Empire from 1532 until the seventeenth century. After attacking Bornu, Aïr expanded its territory at the expense of neighboring states during the seventeenth and eighteenth centuries. Aïr reached its greatest extent in the nineteenth century, but, by 1870, Agades had lost its political importance. By 1900 Aïr had become part of the French West Africa colony.

Zerma

The Zerma (or Zarma or Djerma), Niger's largest ethnic group, are closely related to the Songhay people of Niger and Mali. The Zerma are thought to have originated in the swampy inland delta of the Niger River, near Lake Debo in present-day Mali. They were part of

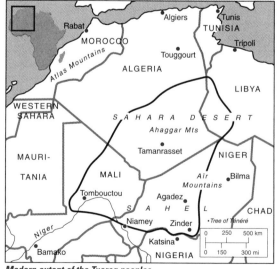

Modern extent of the Tuareg peoples

the western Songhay–the medieval empire founded by the Songhay people in about 750 CE on the Niger River, an important trade route. The Zerma began migrating southward in the fifteenth century, reaching their present lands in the seventeenth and eighteenth centuries.

UN anniversary
A 1961 CE stamp marking the first anniversary of Niger's admission into the United Nations.

Niger timeline

Pre 19th century

c. 1000 CE Tuareg nomads migrate to the Niger region from the central Sahara desert
14th century Eastern Niger becomes part of the Kanem-Bornu empire
15th century The Tuareg state of Air develops around Agadez. Western Niger becomes part of the Songhay empire
1515 Air is conquered by Askia Muhammad of the Songhay empire
1591 Air recovers its independence when Songhay is conquered by Morocco
18th century The Hausa expand into Niger from the south
1735–1756 The Great Drought aids Tuareg expansion at the expense of farmers

19th century CE

1804 Hausa refugees from the Fulani *jihad* flood into Niger
1891 The French begin the conquest of Niger
1898 An Anglo-French commission demarcates the border between Niger and Nigeria

1900–49 CE **1906** The French conquer Air. Niger's present borders are demarcated
1917 The French expel most of the Tuareg from Niger after a rebellion
1922 Niger is incorporated into the French West Africa colony
1946 The *Parti Progressiste Nigérien* (PPN) is formed by Hamani Diori

1950–59 CE **1957** A local legislature is set up under the left-wing trade unionist Djibo Bakary
1958 Despite Bakary's call for a "no" vote, Niger votes to retain links with France

1960–69 CE **1960 Aug 3** Niger becomes independent: Diori becomes the first president
1968–1973 A long drought devastates agriculture

1970–79 CE **1971** Uranium mining begins in Niger
1974 Military coup ousts Diori: Seyni Kountché becomes president

1980–89 CE **1983** An attempted military coup is defeated
1984 Nigeria closes its borders with Niger causing economic hardship
1986 Nigeria re-opens its borders
1987 On the death of Kountché, Col. Ali Saibou becomes president
1989 Saibou is elected president in elections in which he is the only candidate

1990–99 CE **1991** A national conference strips Saibou of his powers
1992 Niger adopts a multiparty constitution. A Tuareg rebellion breaks out in the north
1993 Mahamane Ousmane is elected president under the new constitution
1994 The government offers the Tuareg a degree of internal autonomy in return for a cease-fire
1996 Military coup ousts Ousmane: Gen. Ibrahim Bare Mainassara becomes president
1997 The government and the Tuareg sign a cease-fire in Algiers
1999 Mainassara is assassinated: Daouda Malem Wanke becomes president. In subsubsequent elections, Tandja Mamadou is elected president

Mungo Park
Scottish by birth, he is best remembered for his exploration of the upper and middle Niger in the last decade of the eighteenth century.

Niger's major political figures

Diori, Hamani (1916–1989 CE)
Hamani Diori became the first president of Niger when the country gained independence from France in 1960. After an assassination attempt in 1965, Diori harshly repressed criticism of his regime, but when Niger was badly hit by drought in 1973, some of his ministers were found with stocks of food and accused of hoarding food aid and selling it at inflated prices. In 1974, amid accusations of high-level corruption, Diori was overthrown by Seyni Kountché in a military coup and imprisoned (his wife died during the fighting). He was released from prison in 1980, but stayed under house arrest until 1984.

Kountché, Seyni (1931–1987 CE)
Major General Kountché overthrew Niger's President Hamani Diori and became the country's first military leader in a coup in 1974. He was a conservative in foreign affairs, while at home he worked to restore the economy, which had been shattered by drought and corruption. He included civilians in his government, but did nothing to restore democracy. After his death in 1987, he was succeeded by his cousin, Ali Saibou.

Mainassara, Ibrahim Bare (1949–1999 CE)

General Mainassara seized power during a bloodless coup in January 1996. In June 1966, he was elected president. However, he was assassinated in April 1999 by members of his presidential guard, one of whom, Daouda Malam Wanke, took over as head of state.

Saibou, Ali (1940 CE –)

Colonel Ali Saibou, former chief of staff of the armed forces, succeeded his cousin, Seyni Kountché, as leader of the military regime which ruled Niger in 1987. At first, he wanted to make Niger a constitutional one-party state, but he finally lifted the ban on political organizations, enabling elections to be held in 1993. He was succeeded by Ibrahim Bare Mainassara.

Niger Coast Protectorate

In 1893 CE the British-ruled Oil Rivers Protectorate was renamed the Niger Coast Protectorate. The colony had been set up in 1885 CE and comprised the delta of the Niger River. By that time, the British had established a protectorate over the hinterland of Lagos; this, and later the southern territories of the Royal Niger Company, were merged with the Niger Coast Protectorate in 1894. The Niger Coast Protectorate joined the British Nigerian territories as Southern Nigeria in 1900 CE. *See also* **Nigeria**; **Northern Nigeria**; **Southern Nigeria**.

NIGERIA Federal Republic of Nigeria

The oldest known sculptures found south of the Sahara were made by a civilization called Nok, named for a village in central Nigeria where sculptures were first discovered. Nok flourished between 500 BCE and 200 CE. Other Nigerian cultures distinguished by their superb sculpture are Ife, which emerged around 1000 CE, and Benin, whose greatest period was between the mid-fifteenth and mid-seventeenth centuries.

The early development of northern Nigeria was influenced by the empires which dominated the West African savanna belt. Northern Nigeria bordered the kingdom of Kanem but, in the fourteenth century, Bornu in northeastern Nigeria became Kanem's political center. After the collapse of Songhay in 1591 CE, Kanem-Bornu became powerful, but it began to decline in the late seventeenth century. From the fourteenth century, wealthy Hausa city states developed in northern Nigeria, but, in 1804 CE, they were conquered by the Fulani Muslim cleric, Usman dan Fodio, who founded the Sokoto Caliphate.

The Portuguese were the first Europeans to reach the Nigerian coast, which soon became important in the

Admission to union
A 1961 CE stamp marking Nigeria's admission into the Universal Postal Union.

A regimental lance-corporal
A member of the Nigeria Regiment with Government House, Lagos, in the background.

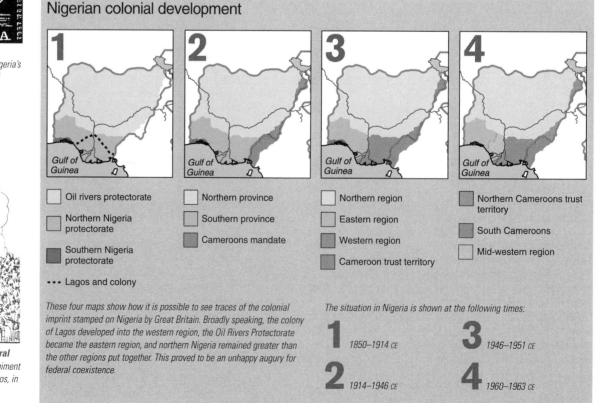

Nigerian colonial development

1 — Oil rivers protectorate
— Northern Nigeria protectorate
— Southern Nigeria protectorate
- - - Lagos and colony

2 — Northern province
— Southern province
— Cameroons mandate

3 — Northern region
— Eastern region
— Western region
— Cameroon trust territory

4 — Northern Cameroons trust territory
— South Cameroons
— Mid-western region

These four maps show how it is possible to see traces of the colonial imprint stamped on Nigeria by Great Britain. Broadly speaking, the colony of Lagos developed into the western region, the Oil Rivers Protectorate became the eastern region, and northern Nigeria remained greater than the other regions put together. This proved to be an unhappy augury for federal coexistence.

The situation in Nigeria is shown at the following times:

1 *1850–1914 CE*   **3** *1946–1951 CE*

2 *1914–1946 CE*   **4** *1960–1963 CE*

slave trade. Britain banned slavery in 1807 CE and, in 1851 CE, the British seized the port of Lagos, using it as a base for curbing the slave trade. Lagos became a British colony in 1861 CE and, in the 1880s and 1890s, it extended its influence in southern Nigeria through a series of treaties with local rulers. In 1903 CE, Britain conquered the Sokoto Caliphate in the north and, in 1914, all of Nigeria became a British colony.

Recent history

From the 1920s, Nigerians began to demand more representation in the government. However, differences between leaders of the country's rival ethnic groups caused disunity. When Nigeria became independent from Britain on October 1, 1960 CE, it was divided into three regions: the mainly Muslim North where the Hausa formed the leading group; the West, home of the Yoruba; and the East, where the Igbo (or Ibo) formed a majority. In 1963 CE, Nigeria became a federal republic and another region, the Midwest, was created, though this caused resentment among other groups who also wanted a region of their own.

In 1966 CE, the elected government was overthrown by a military coup and Nigeria's first prime minister, Sir Abubakar Tafawa Balewa, was killed. Balewa was a northerner, while the new military head of state, General Johnson Aguiyi-Ironsi, was an Igbo. He abolished the federal system of government and appointed many Igbos to high office. This led to rioting in the north. In July 1966 CE, Aguiyi-Ironsi was killed and General Yakubu Gowon, took power, but Colonel Odumegwu Ojukwu, military governor of the Eastern Region, opposed his appointment. In 1967 CE, in an attempt to give power to more ethnic groups, Gowon replaced the four regions with 12 states, but Ojukwu refused to accept the division of the Eastern Region. In May 1967 CE, he proclaimed the Eastern Region an independent republic called Biafra. Civil war followed until Biafra surrendered in January 1970 CE.

From the early 1970s, oil exports boosted the economy, but political problems continued. General Gowon was overthrown in 1975 CE. His successor, General Murtala Ramat Muhammed, was also killed in 1976 CE and was succeeded by General Olusegun Obasanjo, who increased the number of states in Nigeria to 19. Obasanjo ended military rule in 1979 CE. The elected President Shehu Shagari began the building of a new federal capital at Abuja in central Nigeria to replace Lagos. Shagari was overthrown in 1983 CE and Major General Muhammadu Buhari set up another military regime. He was replaced in 1985 CE by Major General Ibrahim Babangida, who promised a return to civilian rule. However, after presidential elections in 1993 CE were annulled, General Sanni Abacha took power and delayed the return to democracy.

When Abacha died in 1998 CE, he was replaced by General Abdulsalam Abubakar, who restored civilian rule. In elections in 1999 CE, Olusegun Obansanjo, the former army leader, was elected president, while his People's Democratic Party won a majority in parliament. By 1999, the Republic of Nigeria was divided into 36 states, plus the capital Abuja. However, Obasanjo faced many problems in maintaining national unity. In 2000 CE, Christian-Muslim clashes occurred when some northern states adopted *sharia* (Islamic law), while Hausa-Yoruba conflict broke out in the southwest.

Nnamdi Azikiwe
During the Biafran (Nigerian Civil) War, which lasted from 1967–70 CE, he acted initially as a spokesman for the Igbo people, but he later supported the federal government.

The Biafran (Nigerian Civil) War

1 *July 1967 In eastern Nigeria, the Republic of Biafra was proclaimed and it seceded on May 30, 1967 CE. The Igbos (and other peoples) of the eastern region of Nigeria feared political domination by the north. Many were educated professionals, and so were resented by other, less well-educated Nigerians. In fact, in the north and west between 10,000 and 30,000 Ibos had been murdered not long before the new republic was proclaimed. The material reason for secession was that oil had recently been discovered in the eastern part of the country.*

2 *1969–1970 In The civil war began on July 6, 1967 CE, when Nigeria hoped to stop Biafra seceding by using a quick "police action". It was not quick: the war lasted for two and a half years, and it was bloody and bitter. The Biafrans were successful at first, but counteroffensives by the Nigerian (federal) troops reduced Biafran-held territory to a small area by December 1969 CE. The Nigerians cut off all supply routes, so the Biafrans had little access to food or military equipment. They were starved into submission, and surrendered to the Nigerians at Amichi on January 13, 1970 CE.*

The staff college in Jaji
Officers from this college have been involved in many coups since Nigeria became independent in 1960 CE.

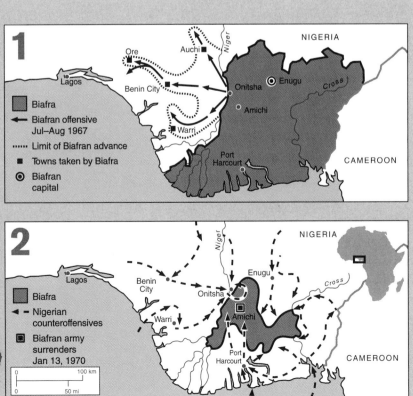

© DIAGRAM

Peoples

EDO

The Edo people of southern Nigeria are descendants of the Bini, who established the historic Kingdom of Benin–famed worldwide for its beautiful bronze sculptures. The capital of the kingdom was Benin City, which was founded by the Edo sometime before 1300 CE. The Kingdom of Benin reached its height between the fourteenth and seventeenth centuries, amassing wealth from the trade in ivory, pepper, palm oil, and slaves. The kingdom was ruled by an *oba*, and the Benin division of the modern Edo province still boasts a ceremonial *oba*. The British burnt Benin City to the ground in 1897 CE and removed more than 2,000 of its bronzes (which are actually brass). The Edo retain a strong tradition of metalworking and many still practice the art of lost-wax metal casting that was used to produce the famous Benin bronzes.

FULANI

For information about the history of the Fulani people, *see* **Fulani states**.

HAUSA

The Hausa live mostly in northern Nigeria, although Hausaland stretches northward to the Sahara in Niger, and to Lake Chad in the east. The first Hausa settlements were built during the eleventh and twelfth centuries. By about 1350 CE, many of the cities had developed into independent city states (*see also* **Hausa states**). The greatest upheaval in Hausa history came at the beginning of the nineteenth century. In 1804 CE, a Muslim cleric, Usman dan Fodio, declared a *jihad* (holy war) against the Hausa rulers. After a four-year struggle, all the Hausa states were conquered and Fodio established the Fulani-Hausa Sokoto Caliphate (*see also* **Fulani empire**).

Modern extent of the Hausa people

IBIBIO

The Ibibio, the largest ethnic group in southwestern Nigeria, live in the Niger delta region. Ibibio history, like that of the neighboring Igbo, is characterized by the marked avoidance of centralized states. Instead, the Ibibio lived in remarkably open and democratic societies based around dispersed villages with various means of regulating and controlling themselves, such as age sets, councils of elders, and men's and women's

societies. Wild palm oil trees grew in profusion in the northern part of Ibibio lands and trade in palm oil became the basis of the region's economy in the nineteenth century, after the slave trade had died out.

IGBO

The Igbo live in the forested southeast of Nigeria, north of the mangrove forests of the Niger delta. Their origins are unknown, but historians believe that they have lived in their present location since at least the ninth century, when the Igbo Ukwu culture flourished in what is now southeastern Nigeria. Portuguese traders visited the region in the mid-fifteenth century and, between the seventeenth and nineteenth centuries, tens of thousands of Igbo were captured or bought by Dutch and British traders and sent to the Caribbean or Brazil, where they were sold as slaves. Although Britain abolished the slave trade in 1807 CE, it continued profitably for another 50 years. However, as the nineteenth century progressed, British traders turned their atten-

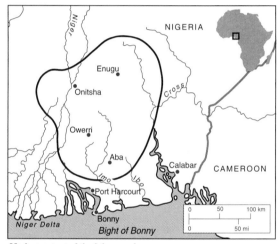

Modern extent of the Igbo people

Biafran soldier
This Igbo man is a Biafran soldier. Many thousands of Igbo suffered injury and loss when Biafra seceded from Nigeria in 1967 CE. The Biafran (Nigerian Civil) War ended unsuccessfully for the Biafrans in 1970 CE after Nigerian government troops harshly suppressed the rebellion.

tion to exploiting the region's raw materials, including ivory, palm oil, and lumber, relying on local intermediaries to deliver goods to them on the coast. Control of Igbo territory was difficult due to village self-rule, the fact that every adult man had a say in local affairs, and an absence of local chiefs with whom Europeans could make agreements. Resistance to British rule was fierce, and attacks on traders and soldiers were common.

In 1900 CE, Igbo territory became part of the British protectorate (colony) of Southern Nigeria, which, in 1960 CE, formed part of independent Nigeria.

After independence, regional rivalries mounted, with Nigeria' political parties representing various ethnic groups. In 1966 CE, an Igbo-led military coup was staged. Many people resented the large number of Igbo civil servants and army officers who were stationed across the country. In 1967 CE, following riots and the slaughter of thousands of Igbo in the north and west of Nigeria, an independent Igbo state, called Biafra, was declared, with its capital at Enugu. The Nigerian government sent the army to put down the rebels, who controlled the country's important oil reserves. Food supplies ran short, resulting in starvation and Biafran surrender in 1970 CE. *See also* **Biafra**.

KANURI

Also known as the Beri-beri, Borno, or Yerwa, the Kanuri are the dominant ethnic group in Borno province, northeastern Nigeria. Kanuri also live in Cameroon, Chad, and Niger. The Kanuri emerged as a distinct group in the time of the great Kanem-Borno empire (*see also* **Kanem–Borno**). By the thirteenth century, the Kanuri had emerged as a single ethnic group, speaking a distinct language. By that time, most Kanuri were Muslims. In what is probably an oversimplification of the truth, the Kanuri are supposed to be descended from the ruling Sefawa dynasty, while the people they ruled over were the Kanembu, the founders of Kanem-Borno. The Sefawa claimed descent from a semi-legendary Yemeni leader.

RUKUBA

The Rukuba, or Bache as they call themselves, are a small ethnic group who live around the town of Jos in central Nigeria. They reached their present location in the eighteenth century and set up several chiefdoms centered around separate villages. Rukuba society as a whole is now made up of a federation of such chiefdoms. Historically, the chief held a semi-religious position. If things were going badly, he would be held responsible and deposed.

TIV

The Tiv inhabit an area that stretches from the foothills of the Adamawa Mountains along the Cameroon-Nigerian border in the southeast to the Jos plateau in central Nigeria. Oral history states that the Tiv originally came from the highlands of northern Cameroon. Historically, like many other African societies, including the Ibibio and Igbo, the Tiv lived in noncentralized societies, with no acknowledged rulers. The basis of Tiv society was lineage (the greater, extended family to which a person belonged).

YAKURR

The Yakurr, or Yako, live in the Cross River region of southeastern Nigeria, northeast of the Niger delta. Their oral history states that they migrated north to their present lands perhaps as late as the early nineteenth century from the Oban hills to the southeast, just north of Calabar. They established five main towns in the region, although the majority of the Yakurr are nonurbanized, farming people.

YORUBA

The Yoruba live mainly in southwestern Nigeria. Through their myths, they believe that they have occupied their present homeland for thousands of years. The kingdom of Ife is accepted as the birthplace of the Yoruba as a separate people (*see also* **Ife**). The town of Ife is considered to be the Yoruba's spiritual capital, perhaps having emerged in the seventh or eighth centuries. The Yoruba's traditional ruling families can trace their ancestors back to the twelfth century.

From Ife, new Yoruba kingdoms were later established, the most powerful being the Oyo in the grasslands to the north. Oyo grew into a great empire, controlling the trade routes linking the sea with lands to the north. In the eighteenth century, the Oyo Empire was torn apart by civil war and it collapsed completely in the 1830s. After the demise of Oyo, Ibadan became the most powerful Yoruba town, eventually controlling a large empire (*see also* **Ibadan**). European slave traders benefited from Yoruba divisions, with rival kings capturing and selling large numbers of their enemies into slavery. Even today, clear elements of Yoruba culture survive in the Americas, especially in Brazil.

As the nineteenth century progressed, more and more British traders, missionaries, soldiers, and government officials entered Yoruba territory, making agreements with local kings, or forcefully stripping power from those who resisted, often destroying and looting their towns. By 1897 CE, the British had established control over the Yoruba and the region was incorporated into the protectorate (colony) of Southern Nigeria in 1900 CE.

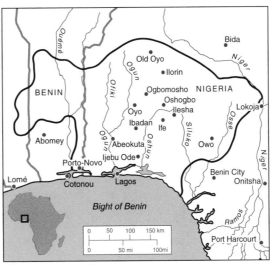

Modern extent of the Yoruba peoples

Nigeria timeline

19th century CE

1804	Usman dan Fodio begins a jihad (Islamic holy war) against the Hausa, creating the Sokoto caliphate
1808	British naval squadron arrives off Nigeria to enforce ban on the slave trade (1807)
1861	Britain annexes Lagos
1885	Britain declares the Oil Rivers protectorate over SE Nigeria
1886	The Royal Africa Company establishes a protectorate over much of western Nigeria
1892	Benin agrees to become a British protectorate and abolish human sacrifice
1893	The Yoruba agree to accept a British protectorate
1897	British consul-general Phillips killed by Benin forces

1900–49 CE

1900	The British government buys out the Royal Africa Company and assumes jurisdiction over its territory
1902	Britain conquers the Ibo
1903	Britain completes the conquest of the Sokoto caliphate
1914	Britain conquers Abeokuta, the last independent state in Nigeria
1914	Britain forms the colony and protectorate of Nigeria
1918	Abeokuta rebels against British rule
1929	Ibo and Ibibio women protest against British rule
1946	The Richards' Constitution gives Nigerians a role in government

1960–69 CE

1960 Oct 1	Nigeria becomes independent of Britain
1963	Nigeria declares itself a republic
1966	Military takes over the Nigerian government: Lt. Col. Gowon becomes leader of Nigeria
1967 May 30	Eastern Region under Ojukwu declares independence as Biafra: civil war breaks out

1970–79 CE

1970 Jan 12	Biafra surrenders ending the civil war
1975	Gowon is replaced by Gen. Murtala Muhammad in a bloodless coup
1976 Feb	Gen. Muhammad is killed in a failed coup attempt: Lt. Gen. Olesegun Obasanjo succeeds as leader
1978 May	Obasanjo approves a democratic presidential constitution to go into effect in 1979
1979 Aug	Alhaji Shehu Shagari's National Party of Nigeria wins federal elections
1979 Oct	Obasanjo resigns: Shagari takes office as president

1980–89 CE

1983 Dec	Shagari's government is overthrown by a military coup: Maj. Gen. Muhammad Buhari becomes president
1985 Mar	The military government expels 700,000 aliens
1985 Aug	Buhari overthrown by Maj. Gen. Ibrahim Babangida
1986 Jul	40 students killed in protests against the military government
1988 Mar–Apr	Elections for local and national government prepare for return of civilian government

1990–99 CE

1991	Nigerian government is transferred from Lagos to Abuja
1993 Jan	Interim government takes office under Babangida
1993 Jun	Social Democratic Party of Moshood Abiola wins federal elections
1993 Aug	Babangida annuls the election result and picks a non-elected civilian government
1993 Nov	Government overthrown by military coup of Gen. Sanni Abacha
1994 June	Abiola declares himself president and is arrested for treason
1995 Nov	Ken Saro-Wiwa and other members of the Movement for the Survival of the Ogoni People executed
1995 Nov	Nigeria expelled from the Commonwealth
1998 Jun	Death of Abacha: he is succeeded by Gen. Abdulsalam Abubakar
1998 Jul	Riots follow the sudden death of Moshood Abiola
1998 Oct	Hundreds of villagers killed after a leaking oil pipeline catches fire
1999 Feb	Former military dictator Olesegun Obasanjo is elected president
1999 Feb-Aug	Ethnic unrest interrupts oil production in SE Nigeria
1999 May	Military government hands over power to president Obasanjo

2000 CE–

2000	Muslim-Christian clashes occur in the north

Sanni Abacha

He was the head of Nigeria's military government from 1993 until his death in 1998.

Nigeria's major political figures

Abacha, General Sanni (1943–1998 CE)

Sanni Abacha became head of Nigeria's military government in November 1993. His postponement of the return to civilian rule, together with alleged abuses of human rights, provoked international criticism. In 1995, Nigeria's membership of the Commonwealth was suspended after the execution of nine political dissidents, including Ken Saro-Wiwa. His successor, General Abdulsalami Abubakar, pushed ahead with the restoration of civilian rule.

Abiola, Chief Moshood (1938–98 CE)
Chief Abiola, a Yoruba Muslim, led the Social Democratic Party to victory in elections in Nigeria in 1993, but the military government suspended the results and, in 1994, he was arrested and charged with treason. He was replaced by the dictator General Sanni Abacha. Abiola's wife Kudirat–a campaigner for the restoration of democracy in Nigeria–was murdered in 1996.

Aguiyi-Ironsi, Johnson (1924–66 CE)
Aguiyi-Ironsi served as Nigeria's head of state from January 15, 1966, when he rallied the army to put down the coup that had overthrown the elected government. But he was overthrown on July 29, 1966 and executed by rebel officers. An army officer, Aguiyi-Ironsi had commanded United Nations forces in Congo (Kinshasa), now the Democratic Republic of Congo, in the early 1960s.

Awolowo, Obafemi (1909–87 CE)
A major Yoruba leader, Nigerian statesman, and influential writer, Obafemi Awolowo was premier of Nigeria's Western Region (1954–9) and leader of the opposition in the federal parliament (1960–2) after independence. In 1962, Awolowo and other opposition leaders were arrested on charges of treasonable felony. Awolowo was eventually jailed between 1963 and 1966.

Azikiwe, Nnamdi (1904–96 CE)
Nnamdi Azikiwe was Nigeria's first president, from 1963 until 1966. In 1937, he took a leading part in the Nigerian nationalist movement, becoming president of the National Council of Nigeria and the Cameroons. He became prime minister of the eastern region (1954–9) and Governor-General of Nigeria (1960–3). During the Biafran (Nigerian Civil) War (1967–70), he first acted as spokesman for his fellow Igbo people, but he later supported the federal government.

Babangida, Ibrahim Badanosi (1941 CE –)
In 1985, as commander-in-chief of the army, Ibrahim Babangida led a coup against President Buhari and assumed the presidency himself. He held office until 1993, when, after declaring void the results of a general election won by Chief Moshood Abiola, he stood down in favor of a nonelected interim government.

Balewa, Sir Abubakar Tafawa (1912–66)
Abubakar Tafawa Balewa was elected first federal prime minister of Nigeria in 1959. A Muslim northerner, he was spokesman for the Northern People's Congress (NPC). The NPC was determined that a federal Nigeria would not be dominated by Western-educated southerners, and argued for official recognition of Islam and for at least half of federal representatives to be northerners. He was knighted when Nigeria became independent in 1960, and assassinated in January 1966 during a military coup.

Buhari, Muhammadu (1942 CE –)
Buhari served as Nigeria's military head of state between December 1983 and August 1985. He took power by overthrowing the elected President Shehu Shagari. He became chairman of the Supreme Military Council and commander-in-chief of the armed forces. Unable to solve the country's severe economic problems, he was removed by another military coup and detained until 1988.

Gowon, Yakubu (1934 CE –)
Yakubu Gowon became Nigeria's head of state and commander-in-chief of its armed forces in 1966, and led the country during the Biafran (Nigerian Civil) War (1967–70). He was deposed in 1975 and went into exile first in Britain and then in Togo.

Obasanjo, Olesegun (1937 CE –)
Lieutenant-General Obasanjo became Nigeria's military head of state in 1976, following the assassination of Brigadier Murtala Mohammed, but he returned the country to civilian rule in 1979. In 1999, as part of another process to return Nigeria to civilian rule, Obasanjo led his People's Democratic Party to victory and was himself elected president. A member of the Yoruba ethnic group, Obasanjo joined the army in 1958 and distinguished himself in the Biafran War. After 1979, when he retired from the army, he became a mediator in African affairs. In 1995 he was imprisoned for allegedly plotting a coup against General Sanni Abacha, but he was released in 1998.

Ojukwu, Chukwuemeka Odumegwu (1933 CE –)
Chukwuemeka Ojukwu was president of the breakaway state of Biafra during the Biafran (Nigerian Civil) War (1967–70). He went into exile after the rebellion collapsed.

Nnamdi Akikiwe
A former leader of the movement for Nigerian nationalism in the 1930s, he became its first president from 1963–1966 CE.

Sir Abubakar Balewa
The first federal prime minister of Nigeria in 1959 CE, he was assassinated in 1966 CE during a coup.

Lt. Colonel Gowon
He led Nigeria during the Biafran (Nigerian Civil) War, was deposed in 1975, and then exiled in Britain.

Chukwuemeka Ojukwu
He led Biafra during the (Nigerian Civil) War, and went into exile after the failure of the rebellion.

Shagari, Alhaji Shehu Usman Aliyu (1924 CE–)

Shagari was elected president of Nigeria in 1979 and was reelected in 1983, but, later that year, he was toppled by a military coup and held in detention until 1986. Shagari was a northerner, who had served in the cabinet of Sir Abubakar Tafawa Balewa following Nigeria's independence in 1960.

Nigerian presidents and heads of state			
President Oct 1 1963–Jan 16 1966 CE Benjamin Nnamdi Azikiwe	**Jul 29 1975–Feb 13 1976 CE** Murtala R. Muhammad	**President and chairman of the armed forces ruling council (from Jan 4 1993, president of the national defense and security council)** Aug 27 1985–Aug 26 1993 CE Ibrahim Babangida	**Chairmen of the provisional ruling council** Nov 17 1993–Jun 8 1998 CE Sani Abacha
Heads of the federal military government (from May 24–Aug 31 1966 CE, national military government) Jan 16 1966–Jul 29 1966 CE Johnson Aguiyi-Ironsi	**Feb 14 1976–Oct 1 1979 CE** Olusegun Obasanjo **President** Oct 1 1979–Dec 31 1983 CE Alhaji Shehu Shagari		Jun 9 1998–May 29 1999 CE Abdulsalami Abubakar
Aug 1 1966–Jul 29 1975 CE Yakubu Gowon	**Chairman of the supreme military council** Dec 31 1983–Aug 27 1985 CE Mohammed Buhari	**Interim president** Aug 26 1993–Nov 17 1993 CE Ernest Shonekan	**President** May 29 1999 CE– Olusegun Obasanjo

Nkore, kingdom of

Ruhinda was the ruler of a central African people called the Bahinda who established the kingdom of Nkore. The kingdom was situated between the lakes of east-central Africa, in the west of what is now Uganda. It was in existence by 1400 CE and had two classes: the ruling Babima, who were pastoralists (animal herders), and the Bairu, who were farmers. The eighteenth century was a period of expansion for the kingdom; by the end of the nineteenth century, Nkore had reached its height. Within a few years, though, serious outbreaks of human and animal diseases had weakened the kingdom. *See also* **Ankole**.

Nobatia

Several civilizations emerged in the historic region of Nubia, which covered parts of what are now southern Egypt and northern Sudan. After the fall of the Meroitic kingdom in 324 CE, Nubia broke up into three kingdoms: Nobatia, Makuria, and Alodia. Makurra eventually absorbed Nobatia and formed the larger kingdom of Dunqulah (Dongolah).

Most of the Nubian archeological finds–more than 100 ancient burial chambers have been discovered—date from the Nobatia Kingdom. Royal tombs were filled with treasures such as gold and silver jewelry, silverware and ironware, and many bronze articles; they were buried under large mounds. The sites have since been flooded by the building of the Aswan High Dam. *See also* **Alodia**; **Dunqulah**; **Kush**; **Meroitic kingdom**; **Nubia**; **Sudan**.

A terracotta figurine
A typical artistic achievement of the Nok culture, which existed from 500 BCE–200 CE, one of the earliest-known civilizations of west Africa.

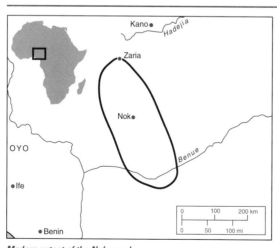

Kano
Hadejia
Zaria
Nok
OYO
Ife
Benue
Benin

| 0 | 100 | 200 km |
| 0 | 50 | 100 mi |

Modern extent of the Nok people

Nok culture

The Nok culture emerged in what is now Nigeria around 2,500 years ago. Nok is the earliest known civilization of West Africa. In the twentieth century, a tin miner working on Nigeria's central Jos Plateau accidentally unearthed the first of several fine terra-cotta figurines near the village of Nok, after which the ancient culture has been named. "Nok" figurines have since been found over a much wider area. Little is known of the culture, but it was in existence from about 500 BCE to 200 CE. Initially a Stone Age culture, the people of Nok made the transition to an Iron Age culture; iron-smelting furnaces dating from 300 BCE have been found in Nigeria. Some historians once thought that the Nok culture represented the earliest beginnings of iron-working. This is now known to be untrue, but Nok culture does represent the earliest know evidence of a developed sculptural tradition in Africa south of the Sahara. *See also* **Nigeria**.

Northeastern Rhodesia

See **Northern Rhodesia**.

Northern Nigeria

Northern Nigeria was the name given to the British-controlled territories that lie in what are now the northern provinces of Nigeria. Much of the region was first conquered by the Royal Niger Company–a commercial institution that was given a royal charter (in 1886 CE) to control trade on the Niger river and administer the immense territories of the Fulani empire and Borno. The British government canceled the charter in 1900 CE, and took over direct control of the company's lands. The southern parts were added to the Niger Coast Protectorate (later Southern Nigeria) and the northern parts became the Protectorate of Northern Nigeria. It took the first British governor of Northern Nigeria several years to completely conquer the Fulani empire and Hausa states. Southern and Northern Nigeria were joined as the Colony and Protectorate of Nigeria in 1914 CE. *See also* **Nigeria; Southern Nigeria**.

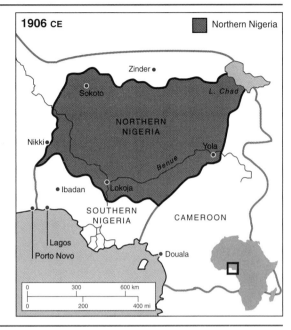

A former British protectorate
A stamp issued in 1912 CE, two years before Northern Nigeria became part of Nigeria.

Colonial expansion (left)
A map showing the extent of British colonial expansion in Northern Nigeria in 1906 CE.

Northern Rhodesia

The independent Republic of Zambia was formerly the British colony Northern Rhodesia. The region was occupied by well-established chieftaincies and kingdoms when the British arrived in the late nineteenth century. The most important and powerful of these states included the Lozi and Lunda (Kazembe) kingdoms, and Ngoni chieftainships. From the 1890s on, the British increasingly asserted their control over the region. While some treaties were made between rulers of states and the British South Africa Company (BSAC), many rulers were conquered by force. The BSAC was a commercial venture founded by the wealthy businessman Cecil Rhodes; the company was granted a royal charter in 1889 CE allowing it to colonize much of central-southern Africa, including what are now the states of Zambia, Zimbabwe, and Malawi. Until 1924 CE,

BSAC administered the region, which was then known as Northeastern Rhodesia. In that year it became a protectorate controlled by the British government, and in 1911 CE the territory's name was changed Northern Rhodesia. Despite strong opposition from the country's African citizens, Northern Rhodesia was joined with Nyasaland (Malawi) and Southern Rhodesia (Zimbabwe) to form the white-ruled Central African Federation of Rhodesia and Nyasaland in 1953 CE. Britain still controlled Northern Rhodesia and Nyasaland but some powers were handed to over to a federal government, which was based in Salisbury (modern Harare, Zimbabwe). The federation was dissolved in 1963 CE in the face of continued African opposition. Northern Rhodesia gained independence as the Republic of Zambia the following year. *See also* **Southern Rhodesia; Zambia**.

A British protectorate (above)
A stamp issued in 1938 CE before Northern Rhodesia became part of the Central African Federation.

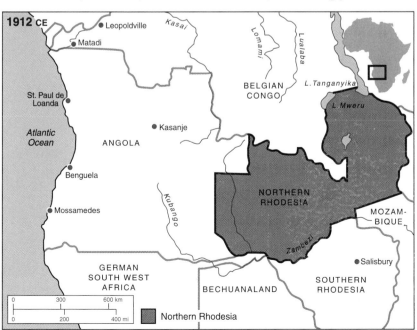

A regimental sergeant-major
A member of the Northern Rhodesia Regiment, with Government House, Lusaka, in the background. The regiment was formerly the military wing of the Northern Rhodesia police; it was subsequently separated from the police and became an independent regiment.

Colonial expansion (left)
A map showing the extent of British colonial expansion in Northern Rhodesia during the period 1895–1912 CE.

© DIAGRAM

Nossi-Bé

Nossi-Bé (or Nosy-Be), literally meaning "Big Island," lies about 5 miles (8 km) off the northwestern coast of Madagascar. The island has been part of Madagascar since 1896 CE, after a period of French rule beginning in 1840 CE. *See also* **Madagascar**.

Nosy-Be

See **Nossi-Bé**

Nubia

Nubia is a region of southern Egypt and northern Sudan that has one of the most ancient histories in Africa. Several civilizations have risen and fallen in the region, which should not be confused with the lands of the modern-day Nuba people, who live farther south in southern Sudan. The oldest civilization in sub-Saharan Africa, the Kingdom of Kush, emerged as early as 3200 BCE. Kush was conquered by ancient Egypt more than 1,500 years later. Around 920 BCE, a dynasty of Nubian kings in Napata began to govern, as the Kingdom of Nubia, independently from Egypt. Under King Piankhy (reigned 750–719 BCE), Egypt was conquered and Nubia reached its territorial zenith. These gains began to be lost to invading Assyrians during the seventh century BCE. In 671 BCE, the Nubians lost control of Egypt, including Memphis, the capital, and by 657 BCE they had lost it all to the Assyrians. The Nubian capital was moved from Napata to Meroe in c.300 BCE, from where the powerful Meroitic Kingdom emerged. Meroe was an important center for iron-making. In 324 BCE, the Meroitic Kingdom collapsed after being defeated by the Ethiopian's Axumite kingdom. After the fall of Meroe, Nubia broke up into three kingdoms: Nobatia, Makuria (or Makurra), and Alodia (or Alwa). *See also* **Egypt**; **Egypt, Ancient**; **Meroitic kingdom**; **Nubia, Kingdom of**; **Sudan**.

Numidia

Numidia is an historic region of North Africa that, at times, roughly correlated with the region covered by modern Algeria. The first people to inhabit Numidia were Berbers, but from the sixth century BCE Carthaginians began to occupy parts of the coast, eventually expanding inland as their power increased. A Numidian Berber king named Massinisa reversed this sequence of events, however, by allying with Rome in 206 BCE against Carthage during the Second Punic War. Massinisa was gained control over much of Carthage's former territory but on his death in 148 BCE, the Romans divided his kingdom into several vassal chieftainships.

A mausoleum
A Punic mausoleum dedicated to Ateban at Bougga, a powerful Numidian chief, and located in Tunisia c. 200 BCE.

A royal tomb
The Medracen, a second century BCE royal tomb of the Numidian kingdom located in eastern Algeria.

The Nubian kingdoms

An ancient Nubian oil lamp (above)
Nubian kingdoms flourished along the River Nile in what is now present-day Sudan over 2,000 years ago.

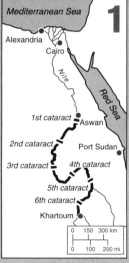

Nubian kingdoms
The maps (above and right) show the extent of the Nubian kingdoms, together with the main towns and cities, at the following dates:

1 c.4000 BCE   **4** c.1200 BCE

2 c.657 BCE   **5** c.1450 BCE

3 c.400 BCE

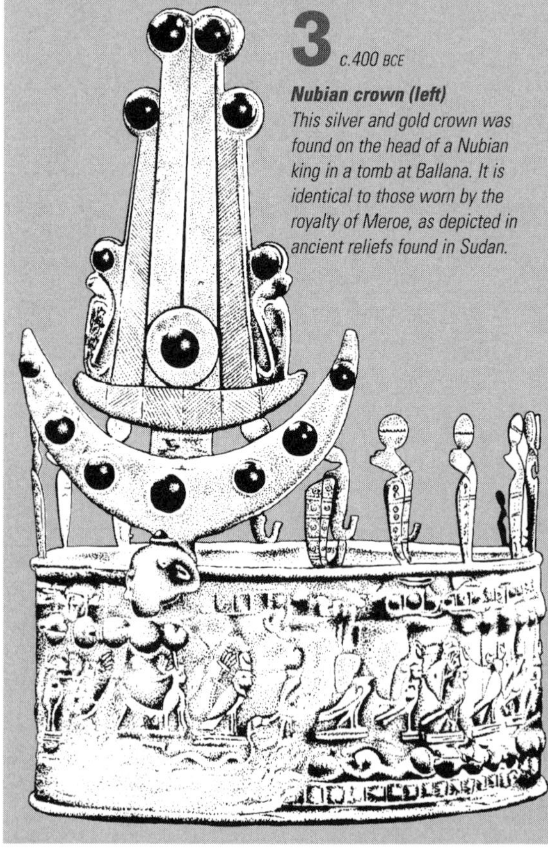

Nubian crown (left)
This silver and gold crown was found on the head of a Nubian king in a tomb at Ballana. It is identical to those worn by the royalty of Meroe, as depicted in ancient reliefs found in Sudan.

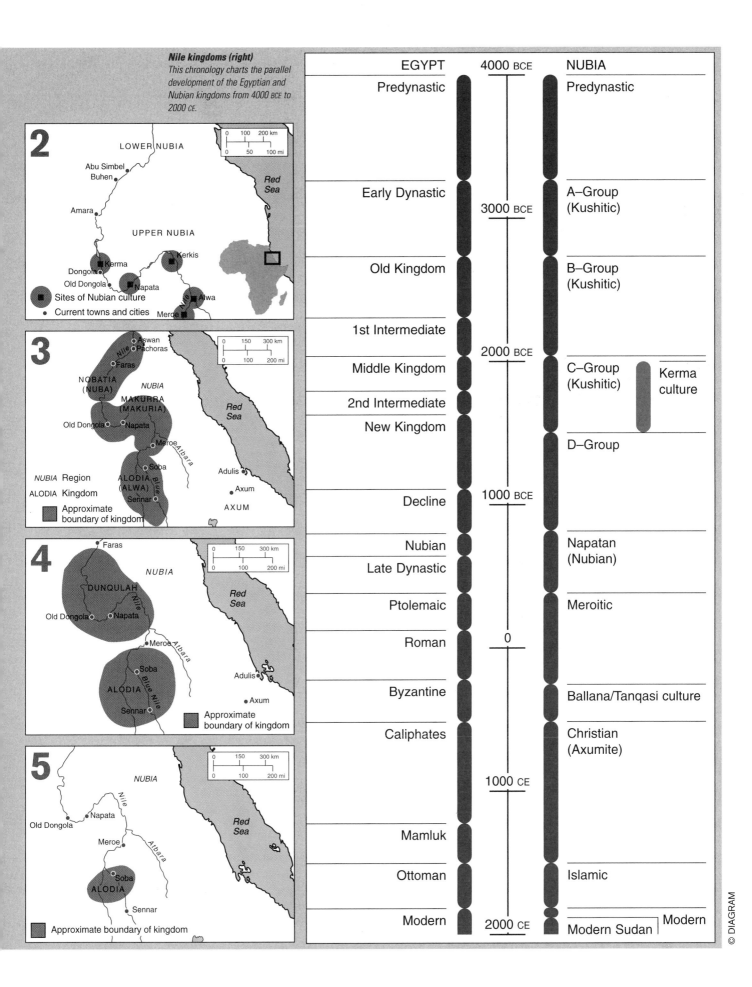

Nile kingdoms (right)
This chronology charts the parallel development of the Egyptian and Nubian kingdoms from 4000 BCE to 2000 CE.

2

LOWER NUBIA

Abu Simbel
Buhen

Amara

UPPER NUBIA

0 100 200 km
0 50 100 mi

Red Sea

Kerma
Dongola
Old Dongola
Napata
Kerkis
Alwa
Meroe

■ Sites of Nubian culture
• Current towns and cities

3

Aswan
Pachoras
Faras

NOBATIA (NUBA)
NUBIA
MAKURRA (MAKURIA)

Old Dongola
Napata

Meroe
Atbara

Soba
ALODIA (ALWA)
Sennar

Red Sea

Adulis

Axum

AXUM

0 150 300 km
0 100 200 mi

NUBIA Region
ALODIA Kingdom
■ Approximate boundary of kingdom

4

Faras

NUBIA

DUNQULAH

Old Dongola
Napata

Meroe
Atbara

Soba
Blue Nile
ALODIA
Sennar

Red Sea

Adulis

Axum

0 150 300 km
0 100 200 mi

■ Approximate boundary of kingdom

5

NUBIA

Old Dongola
Napata

Meroe
Atbara

Soba
ALODIA
Sennar

Red Sea

0 150 300 km
0 100 200 mi

■ Approximate boundary of kingdom

EGYPT		NUBIA
Predynastic	4000 BCE	Predynastic
Early Dynastic	3000 BCE	A–Group (Kushitic)
Old Kingdom		B–Group (Kushitic)
1st Intermediate	2000 BCE	
Middle Kingdom		C–Group (Kushitic) — Kerma culture
2nd Intermediate		
New Kingdom		D–Group
Decline	1000 BCE	
Nubian		Napatan (Nubian)
Late Dynastic		
Ptolemaic		Meroitic
Roman	0	
Byzantine		Ballana/Tanqasi culture
Caliphates		Christian (Axumite)
	1000 CE	
Mamluk		
Ottoman		Islamic
Modern	2000 CE	Modern Sudan — Modern

© DIAGRAM

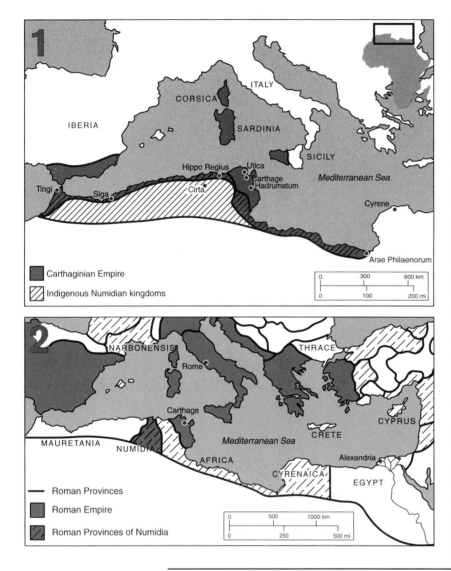

Carthaginian Empire

Indigenous Numidian kingdoms

Roman Provinces

Roman Empire

Roman Provinces of Numidia

The Nupe kingdom

The Nupe kingdom became a dominant force among the Niger Delta States during the sixteenth century, and is still in existence today. The map shows its extent in 1600 CE.

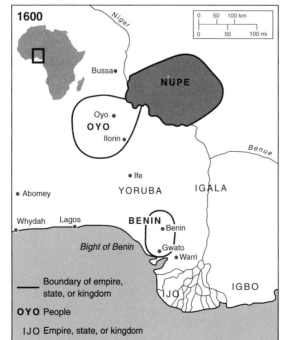

Boundary of empire, state, or kingdom

OYO People

IJO Empire, state, or kingdom

Jugurtha, the illegitimate grandson of Massinisa, reunited the Numidian kingdom in 118 BCE, but the Romans took control of it in 105 BCE. Subsequent Numidian kings were tributary to Rome, and Numidian lands were greatly reduced. Between 49–46 BCE, Juba I (c. 85–44 BCE) attempted to reestablish a powerful Numidian state. After being defeated by the Romans, he committed suicide and his son, Juba II (c.50–c.24 BCE) was installed as king by the Romans.

Numidia became the province of Africa Nova (or "New Africa") and it was later united with Africa Vetus ("Old Africa"), the Roman-ruled region around Carthage. However, a separate province of Numidia was established by the Roman Emperor Septimus Severus, who ruled from 193 to 211 CE. Under the Romans the region gained in security and grew in prosperity. Christianity was introduced in the third century, though Roman influence declined drastically after the Vandal invasion in the fifth century. Some local Berber traditions were revived and, having survived the Arab conquest of the seventh century, they still exist in the region today. *See also* **Algeria**; **Carthage**.

Numidian occupation
From the sixth century BCE Carthaginians occupied parts of the coastline of Numidia (top left). They expanded inland, but were defeated by an alliance between the Numidians and Roman forces. Numidia then fell under Roman control, and eventually became a separate province (left).

1 *c. 150 BCE*

2 *46*

Nungua

The Ga people of the southeast coast of Ghana were organized into six independent towns: Accra, Osu, Labadi, Teshi, Nungua, and Tema. Each town had a stool, which served as the central object of Ga ritual and war magic. *See also* **Ghana**.

Nupe

The Nupe are a people who live around the confluence of the Niger and Kaduna rivers in west-central Africa. The Nupe kingdom was established in the area by 1500 CE and still exists today. Nupe is ruled by a king, the etsu Nupe, and is divided into four zones for administration. The Beni and the Kede are both kingdoms within the greater Nupe kingdom.

By the sixteenth century, Nupe was a powerful state that dominated the weaker Oyo to the north. As Oyo's power grew, however, the situation reversed, and for some years, Nupe was part of the Oyo empire. But, in 1791 CE Nupe was powerful enough to defeat the mighty Oyo empire and re-assert its independence. Nupe became a Muslim state and was added to the Fulani empire (Sokoto Caliphate) after 1817 CE. *See also* **Nigeria**; **Oyo empire**.

Nyasaland

The British established colonial authority over what is now Malawi in 1891 CE, creating the Nyasaland Districts Protectorate. This colony became the British

Central Africa Protectorate in 1893 CE and Nyasaland in 1907 CE. Despite African opposition, Nyasaland was joined with Northern Rhodesia (Zambia) and Southern Rhodesia (Zimbabwe) to form the white-ruled Central African Federation of Rhodesia and Nyasaland in 1953 CE. Britain still controlled Nyasaland and Northern Rhodesia but some powers were handed over to a federal government based in Salisbury (modern Harare, Zimbabwe). The federation was dissolved in 1963 CE in the face of continued African opposition. Nyasaland gained independence as Malawi the following year. *See also* **Malawi.**

A former protectorate (left)
A stamp issued in 1897 CE when Nyasaland was still part of British Central Africa.

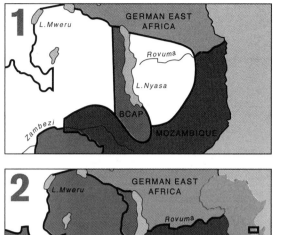

British Central Africa
In 1892 CE the British Central African Protectorate was surrounded by Portuguese and German possessions. By 1908 CE the British had also occupied Northern Rhodesia, and the Germans and Portuguese had extended their occupation north and south of the Rovuma River respectively.

1 *1892 CE*

2 *1908 CE*

■ British protectorate
■ British possession
■ Portuguese possession
■ German possession
BCAP British Central African Protectorate

Ohrigstad

See also **Lydenburg**.

Oil Rivers Protectorate

In 1885 CE the British established the Oil Rivers Protectorate over the Niger Delta region. The colony was renamed the Niger Coast Protectorate in 1893 CE. By that time, the British had established a protectorate over the hinterland of Lagos. This, and later the southern territories of the Royal Niger Company, were merged with the Niger Coast Protectorate in 1894 CE. The Niger Coast Protectorate joined the British Nigerian territories as Southern Nigeria in 1900 CE. *See also* **Nigeria**; **Northern Nigeria**; **Southern Nigeria**.

Okrika

See **Ijo states**.

Old Calabar

See **Calabar, Old**.

Omani Arabs

Because the East African coast profited from trade with Arabia, India, and other parts of Africa and Asia, Arab traders had been visiting and settling there for centuries before the Omani Arabs, after wresting control of the Persian Gulf from Portugal, rose to power in the seventeenth century. From the mid-seventeenth century, Omani Arabs began to displace the Portuguese from their positions on the East African coast.

In 1652 Omani Arabs sacked the Portuguese settlements in Zanzibar and Pate. After a three-year siege, Mombasa fell to Oman, with Zanzibar following a few years later. The city-states of the East African coast, such as Pate, Lamu, Kilwa, and Pemba, preferred to be independent, however: neither under the rule of Oman nor of Portugal. Resistance to Omani or Portuguese rule could be exercised without violent reprisals, and rulers often changed their allegiances from Portugal to Oman, or vice versa, whenever was convenient to

A tour of duty
A visit by the governor of the Oil Rivers Protectorate, together with his colleagues, to the King of Addo c.1896 CE.

them. If the Omani Arabs were acknowledged as rulers, their real authority was generally limited.

In the 1740s, the Mazrui rulers of Mombasa—themselves Omani Arabs—declared their city independent from Oman; others soon followed suit. Mombasa became the dominant power on the coast. In 1806 CE, however, Seyyid Said became ruler of Oman. By 1837 CE he controlled Pate, Pemba, Zanzibar, and Mombasa. In 1840 CE Seyyid Said moved the capital of Oman to Zanzibar, which became the center of the Sultanate of Oman and Zanzibar, or the Sultanate of Zanzibar. In 1856 CE, the Sultanate of Zanzibar became independent from Oman but was soon conquered by Britain and Germany. The sultanate was a focal point of international trade, including the slave trade that flourished until it was suppressed by the British in 1897 CE. *See also* **Zanzibar.**

Arabian dhows
Sailing boats, called dhows, enabled the Arabs to travel from Southwest Asia, using the monsoon winds, to trade in East Africa and elsewhere. Some of these traders settled in the region as early as the tenth century CE.

© DIAGRAM

Omayyads

The Omayyad (or Umayyad) dynasty lasted from 661–750 CE. The family were originally merchants based in Mecca (modern Saudi Arabia) at the time of the prophet Muhammad, who founded Islam in 622 CE. The Omayyads were the first great Muslim dynasty to rule the empire of the caliphate. Under the Omayyads, the empire was expanded, and by 710 CE the whole of North Africa was conquered, from modern-day Egypt west to Morocco. By 711 CE, Spain had been conquered by Omayyad troops from North Africa. In 750 CE Iranian 'Abbasids overthrew the Omayyads and controllled North Africa for the next few decades.

Omayyads and 'Abbasids
The Arab empire was ruled by the 'Four Rightly Guided Caliphs' after the death of Muhammad in 632 CE. They were Abu Bakr, 'Umar, 'Uthman, and 'Ali. The empire in Africa extended westward under 'Umar and 'Uthman. The Omayyad dynasty took control of the Arab empire in 661 CE and expanded into Spain in 711 CE. In 750 CE the Iranian 'Abbasids overthrew the Omayyads and, by 771 CE, they had completely conquered Omayyad territory except the Spanish possessions. From 789 CE onward the 'Abbasids lost North African territory to independent dynasties, including the Tulanids, and ruled there until 935 CE when they were overthrown by the Ikshidids.

Arab rule in the Mediterranean is shown at the following dates:

1 *711 CE* **2** *771 CE* **3** *904 CE* **4** *934 CE*

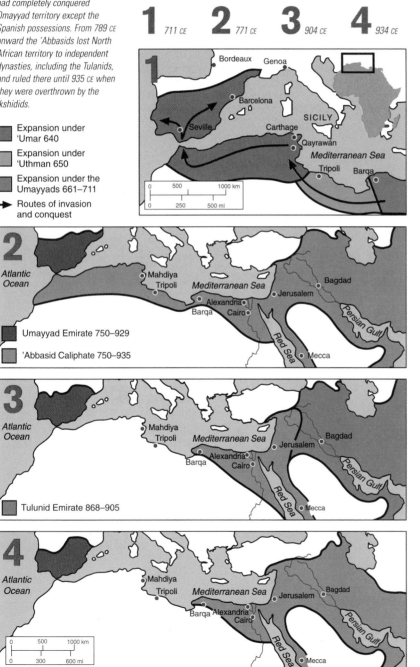

■ Expansion under 'Umar 640
■ Expansion under 'Uthman 650
■ Expansion under the Umayyads 661–711
➤ Routes of invasion and conquest

■ Umayyad Emirate 750–929
■ 'Abbasid Caliphate 750–935

■ Tulunid Emirate 868–905

An independent Omayyad caliphate survived in Spain. Known to history as the Omayyads of Cordoba, and its rulers had managed to exert control over what is now Morocco by the early decades of the first millennium. Omayyad rule was short-lived, however, because in 1031 CE the dynasty lost control to the Maghrawanids. A new threat then emerged–the Berber Almoravid dynasty. Between 1055–1069 CE the Almoravids took Morocco from the Maghrawanids. From there, they conquered Omayyad Spain between 1086–1106 CE. *See also* **Algeria**; **Egypt**; **Libya**; **Morocco**; **Tunisia**.

Opobo, kingdom of

The short-lived kingdom of Opobo arose in the Niger Delta region of what is now Nigeria. The kingdom was established in 1870 CE by Jaga, an Igbo ruler of one of the many "houses" that made up the largely Ijo state of Bonny (Ibani). His kingdom grew rich but fell to the British in 1887 CE. *See also* **Nigeria**.

Orange Free State

Before 1995 CE, the present-day South African province Free State was called the Orange Free State. The Orange Free State was founded as an independent Boer republic in 1854 CE. Before that, the land was home to Bantu-speaking peoples such as the Tswana. In the early nineteenth century, Tswana were dispersed by the emerging Zulu kingdom and the period of mass migrations and wars that accompanied it–the Mfecane. Other peoples such as the Sotho and Griqua moved into the region. Boer farmers (whites of Dutch descent) also began to migrate into the area, particularly during the Great Trek (1836–1848 CE), when large numbers of Boer farmers seeking freedom from British rule trekked north of the Orange River. In 1848 CE the British annexed the territory between the Orange and Vaal rivers, calling it the Orange River Sovereignty. The British withdrew in 1854 CE, however, after conflicts with the Sotho people. Sovereignty was handed over to local Boer settlers, who formed the independent Orange Free State. The Boers, too, battled with the Sotho people over the land, and two Free State/Sotho Wars were fought between 1858–1868 CE. Conflict increased with the discovery of valuable gold and diamond deposits in the region. Britain, again, started to show an interest in the area. The Boers of the Orange Free State and the South African Republic (Transvaal) declared war on Britain in 1899 CE. The South African, or Anglo–Boer, War lasted until 1902 CE, and it was the largest war the region had ever seen. Arpproximately 500,000 British troops were pitted against around 100,000 Boer troops.

In 1900 CE, the Orange Free State was annexed by Britain as the Orange River Colony. The Boers fought on for two more years, but a treaty in 1902 CE ended the war and imposed British rule over the Orange Free State and the South African Republic. Self-government was restored in 1907 CE, and, in 1910 CE, the colony became the Orange Free State Province within the Union of South Africa. *See also* **South Africa**; **South African Republic (Transvaal)**.

Growth and development of the Orange Free State

Boer farmers (white people of Dutch descent) began to migrate into the area which became known as the Orange Free State as part of The Great Trek (1836–44 CE). In 1854 CE the British withdrew and sovereignty was handed over to the local Boer settlers who formed the Orange Free State, which remained independent until 1902 when the British imposed their rule following victory in the Boer War. The relationship of the Orange Free State to neighboring territories controlled by various colonial powers is shown in four maps (below).

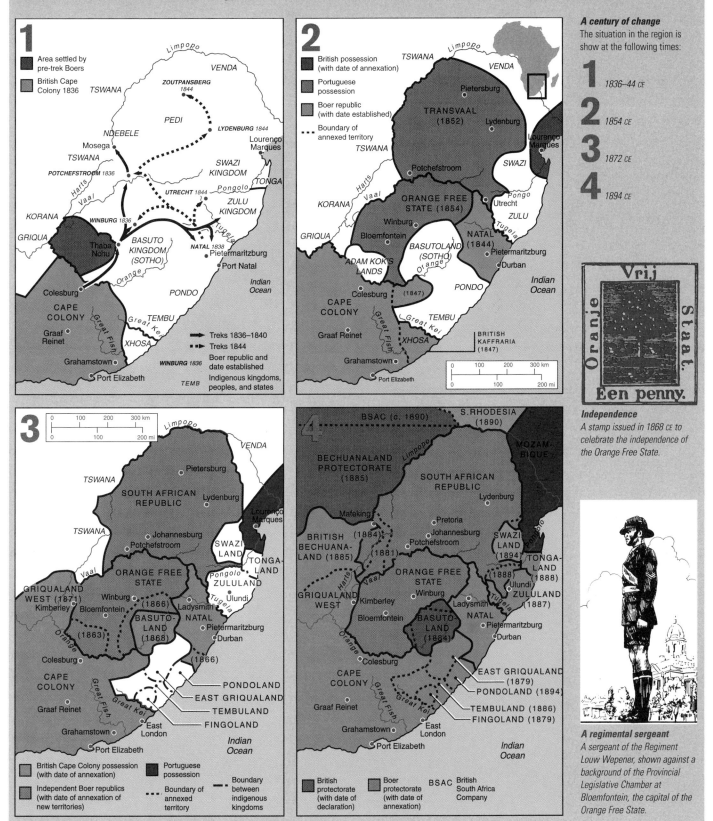

A century of change
The situation in the region is show at the following times:

1 1836–44 CE

2 1854 CE

3 1872 CE

4 1894 CE

Independence
A stamp issued in 1868 CE to celebrate the independence of the Orange Free State.

A regimental sergeant
A sergeant of the Regiment Louw Wepener, shown against a background of the Provincial Legislative Chamber at Bloemfontein, the capital of the Orange Free State.

Orange River Colony

Orange River Colony was the name given to the Orange Free State when it was colonized by Britain in 1900 CE. Orange Free State was previously an independent Boer republic. *See also* **Orange Free State**; **South Africa**.

Orange River Sovereignty

Orange River Sovereignty was a short-lived British colony established between the Vaal and Orange rivers in what is now South Africa in 1848 CE. The colony was relinquished to Boer settlers in 1854 CE, who turned it into an independent Boer republic–the Orange Free State. *See also* **Orange Free State**; **South Africa**.

Orange Free State and The Boer War (1899–1902 CE)

Conflict in the Eastern Cape increased with the discovery of gold and diamonds, particularly in the Transvaal, and Britain once again began to show an interest in the region. In an attempt to preserve their independence, the Boers of the Orange Free State and the South African Republic, or Transvaal, declared war on Britain in 1899 CE. Britain welcomed the conflict as Afrikaner nationalism posed a great threat to the powerful position of Britain in South Africa at the time. In 1900 CE the Orange Free State was annexed by Britain as the Orange River Colony. The war lasted a further two years; in 1902 CE a treaty ended the conflict and imposed British rule over the Orange Free State and the South African Republic. Self-government was later restored in 1907 CE.

J. H. Brand
A former president of the Orange Free State.

Sir Redvers Henry Buller
A general who served as commander-in-chief of the British forces in the Boer War, he was awarded the Victoria Cross in 1879 CE, and a knighthood in 1882 CE.

Boer guerrillas
Facing a much better equipped enemy during the Anglo-Boer War (1899–1902 CE), the Boers adopted guerrilla tactics. At first, they were successful in resisting the British. After the establishment of concentration camps by the British, and the destruction of their farms, the guerrillas found it hard to continue their successes.

British Maxim gunners
One major advantage the British forces possessed over their adversaries in the Boer War was superior weaponry, such as the Maxim gun shown here in action at Ladysmith, South Africa in 1900 CE.

Osu

The Ga people of the southeast coast of Ghana were organized into six independent towns: Accra, Osu, Labadi, Teshi, Nungua, and Tema. Each town possessed its own sacred stool that served as its central object in Ga ritual and war magic. See also **Ghana.**

A fortified town
A pre-nineteenth century illustration of the Danish fort at Christiansborg in Osu.

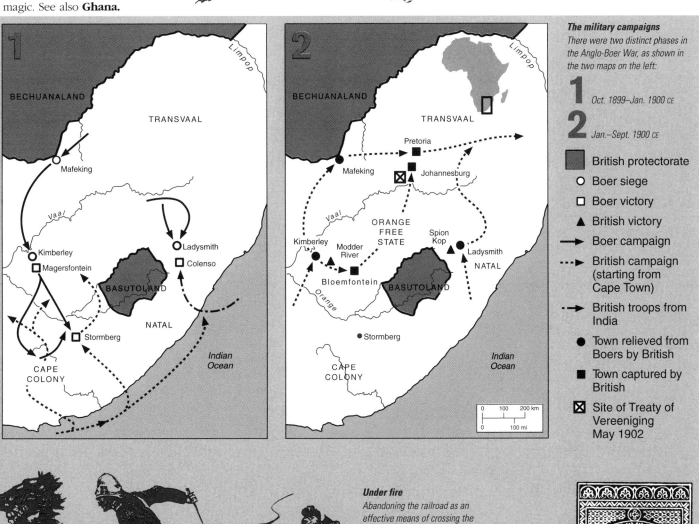

The military campaigns
There were two distinct phases in the Anglo-Boer War, as shown in the two maps on the left:

1 *Oct. 1899–Jan. 1900 CE*

2 *Jan.–Sept. 1900 CE*

■ British protectorate

○ Boer siege

□ Boer victory

▲ British victory

→ Boer campaign

┅► British campaign (starting from Cape Town)

┅► British troops from India

● Town relieved from Boers by British

■ Town captured by British

⊠ Site of Treaty of Vereeniging May 1902

Under fire
Abandoning the railroad as an effective means of crossing the country, British forces had to resort to other forms of transport, often at great risk of attack from the enemy.

An independent state
An example of a stamp issued during the period 1882–86 CE by the Orange Free State.

Ottoman Empire

The Ottoman Empire was established by Turks in Anatolia in the fourteenth century and survived for almost 600 years until 1922 CE, when modern Turkey was established. During that time, the Ottoman Empire grew vast, controlling lands in Europe, the modern Middle East and North Africa.

In 1510 CE, Ottoman Turks began to carry out raids, in the name of Islam, on Spanish possessions in North Africa. By 1519 CE, they had taken control of Algeria, and by 1521 CE they had also conquered eastern parts of North Africa as far as Barqa (northeast Libya). By 1574 CE, they controlled all of the lands from modern Tunis to Egypt in North Africa and parts of Nubia (southern Egypt and northern Sudan). They attempted to bring Fezzan in the interior under their control, but their hold on the area was never strong. Between 1705 –1714 CE the Ottomans lost control of their Maghrib lands but remained as the nominal rulers. In 1798 CE Napoleon of France took Egypt from the Ottoman Empire but the country was freed from French rule by British and Ottoman forces in 1801 CE. By 1805 CE Egypt had broken away from the Ottomans. *See also* **Algeria**; **Egypt**; **Libya**; **Nubia**.

The Ottoman Empire
This empire survived from the early fourteenth century until 1922 CE. Its extent is shown as follows:

1 *1510 CE*   **5** *1800 CE*

2 *1522 CE*   **6** *1845 CE*

3 *1574 CE*   **7** *1850 CE*

4 *1715 CE*   **8** *1881 CE*

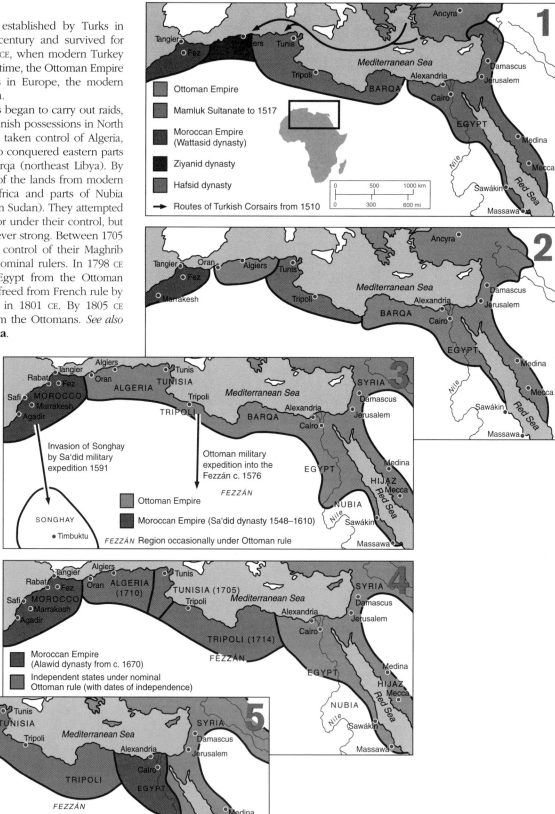

1

- Ottoman Empire
- Mamluk Sultanate to 1517
- Moroccan Empire (Wattasid dynasty)
- Ziyanid dynasty
- Hafsid dynasty
- → Routes of Turkish Corsairs from 1510

3

Invasion of Songhay by Sa'did military expedition 1591

Ottoman military expedition into the Fezzán c. 1576

- Ottoman Empire
- Moroccan Empire (Sa'did dynasty 1548–1610)

FEZZÁN Region occasionally under Ottoman rule

4

- Moroccan Empire (Alawid dynasty from c. 1670)
- Independent states under nominal Ottoman rule (with dates of independence)

5

- Ottoman Empire
- Independent states under nominal Ottoman rule
- French-occupied territory (under Napoleon) 1798–1801

FEZZÁN Region occasionally under Ottoman rule

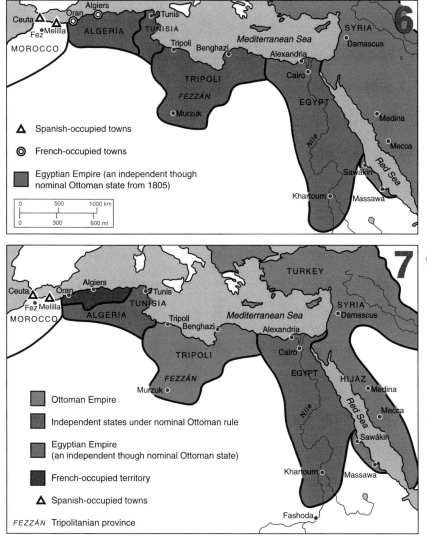

6

△ Spanish-occupied towns

◎ French-occupied towns

Egyptian Empire (an independent though nominal Ottoman state from 1805)

0 — 500 — 1000 km
0 — 300 — 600 mi

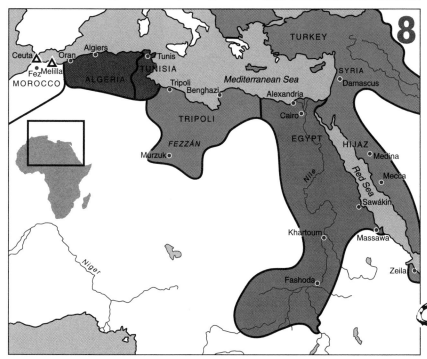

7

Ottoman Empire

Independent states under nominal Ottoman rule

Egyptian Empire (an independent though nominal Ottoman state)

French-occupied territory

△ Spanish-occupied towns

FEZZÁN Tripolitanian province

8

'The old Turk'
An early twentieth-century European view of a Turk presenting him as a bloodthirsty barbarian on a spiritual quest to massacre unbelievers in the name of Allah. The top section of the painting shows images of the rewards supposedly awaiting the faithful in the afterlife.

East meets West
Muhammad 'Ali Pasha of Egypt introduced many reforms to modernize Egypt, most of which could only be achieved with the aid of foreign experts. In this illustration, he is shown conferring with a French engineer.

© DIAGRAM

Oubangui–Chari

As a French colony, the Central African Republic was called Oubangui–Chari (or Ubangi–Shari). Its borders had been established by 1900 CE, although resistance to French rule was widespread and long-lasting. In 1910 CE, all the French colonies in equatorial Africa, namely Gabon, Middle Congo, and Oubangui–Chari, were made into one federal colony called French Equatorial Africa. Central African Republic was granted independence in 1960 CE. *See also* **Central African Republic**.

Oubangui–Chari–Tchad

In 1920 the two French colonies of Tchad and Oubangi–Chari (Ubangui–Shari) were joined to form Oubangi–Chari–Tchad (Ubangui–Shari–Tchad). In 1960 the two colonies gained independence as the Central African Republic and Chad respectively. *See also* **Central African Republic**; **Chad**.

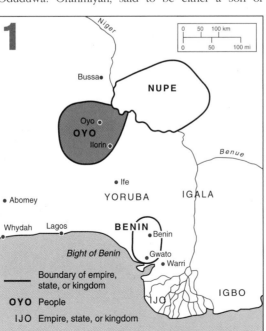

Ovimbundu

The Ovimbundu, the most populous people in Angola, emerged as a distinct group in the sixteenth and seventeenth centuries. The Ovimbundu were firmly established by the 1770s, with royal families providing both political and religious leadership through the king and his counselors. The Ovimbundu were divided into more than 20 small kingdoms, about half of which owed allegiance to a larger kingdom. Contact with the Portuguese began around the seventeenth century, and by the twentieth century they ruled the Ovimbundu. *See also* **Angola**.

——— Boundary of kingdom or state

L O Z I People

-■-■- Boundary of Portuguese influence 1800

Oyo empire

The Yoruba kingdom of Oyo existed in what is now southern Nigeria by the fourteenth century, although little is known of its early history. Oyo shares with Benin and Ife the myth in the Yoruba religion that it is the birthplace of humanity. Its kings, known as *alafins*, claim descent from the legendary founder of Ife, Oduduwa. Oranmiyan, said to be either a son or grandson of Oduduwa, left Ife to found Benin and then Oyo. Sango, the Yoruba god of thunder, was originally a king of Oyo; he was known for his skills as a warrior and magician and was said to be able to control thunder and lightning. Worship of Sango became the state religion in Oyo.

The Oyo empire

Oyo was a Niger Delta state which was in existence by the fourteenth century. During the sixteenth century Oyo's emergence as a power was threatened by the Nupe Kingdom. In the seventeenth century, Oyo expanded southward to take advantage of European trading activity on the coast. By 1700 CE Oyo was the most powerful of the Yoruba states, but was often in conflict with the slave-trading state of Dahomey. Oyo absorbed Dahomey in 1748 CE, and reached its greatest extent by 1789 CE. However, the 1790s witnessed the start of the empire's decline.

The maps (right) show the extent of the Oyo empire at the following times:

1 1600 CE **3** 1800 CE

2 1730 CE

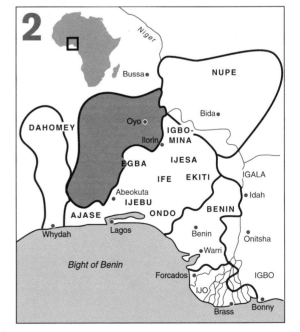

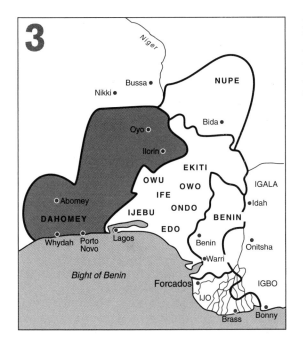

The seventeenth century was a period of expansion for Oyo, which grew southward to take advantage of European trading activity on the coast. Oyo grew powerful enough to break away from Nupe and, in turn, dominate its former overlords. By the start of the eighteenth century, several other Yoruba kingdoms came into in existence, but Oyo was the most powerful. By the early eighteenth century it was probably the most powerful state in West Africa. Oyo was often in conflict with Dahomey, to the south, and in 1748 CE Oyo absorbed Dahomey. By 1789 CE, Oyo had reached its greatest extent. The 1790s, however, saw the beginning of the empire's decline. In 1791 CE, for example, Nupe defeated Oyo in battle and asserted its independence. In the nineteenth century, a new threat emerged–the fast-expanding Muslim Fulani empire (Sokoto Caliphate) in the north. In 1817 CE, Oyo lost Ilorin to the Fulani *jihadists* (holy warriors). In 1818 CE, it lost Dahomey. The empire collapsed in 1836 CE, torn apart by civil wars, but nominally ruled by the *alafin* Oluewu. Oluewu's successor, Atiba, founded a new capital, New Oyo (present-day Oyo, Nigeria), from where he tried to re-establish an Oyo kingdom. The commander of Oyo's armies was in control of Ibadan, and Atabi made him his *basorun*, or head counselor. While this made Atiba the nominal overlord of Ibadan, real power lay with the army commander, Kurunmi. By 1914 CE, however, the Protectorate of Nigeria had been formed, and it included the Yoruba kingdoms of Ife, Ilorin, and Oyo. *See also* **Nigeria**.

Pate

Pate is a small island off the coast of what is now Kenya. The medieval Pate Chronicles relate how it was founded in the eighth century by Arabs, although African settlements were probably in existence before that date. The citizens of Pate, who came to include Africans, Arabs, and other Asians, profited from the Indian Ocean trade, as did other coastal towns such as Pemba, Mombasa, Kilwa, and Lamu. These towns were ruled as independent city-states, and their multicultural citizens formed the Swahili people. The Portuguese dominated the East African coast in the sixteenth century, conquering Pate at its beginning. Oman then displaced Portugal in the seventeenth century. In the eighteenth century, Pate and the other Swahili city-states were largely independent from foreign rule. The rulers of Pate allied with independent Mombasa under the Mazrui toward the end of the eighteenth century but reverted to Omani control in 1824 CE. Pate became part of Britain's Kenya colony after the Sultanate of Oman and Zanzibar was conquered at the end of the nineteenth century. *See also* **Kenya**; **Mazrui**; **Omani Arabs**; **Zanzibar**.

Pedi

The Pedi are a Sotho people of southern Africa. During the seventeenth century, the Pedi group of clans became dominant among the northern Sotho peoples. In the early nineteenth century, Sekwati united the various groups into a single kingdom. Sekwati was succeeded by his son Sekhukhuni in 1861 CE. Growing conflicts in the highvelds of southern Africa led to wars between the Pedi, Swazi, and Boers (or Afrikaners)–descendants of Dutch settlers who had trekked from the Cape to set up independent republics. Many refugees from the draconian and racist labor laws of the Boer's South African Republic (Transvaal), found shelter in the growing Pedi kingdom. The Pedi proved impossible to defeat for many years, until a joint Swazi–British force defeated them in 1879 CE. The Pedi kingdom was divided between two rulers. Much of its former land was set aside for the settlement of whites. *See also* **South Africa**; **South African Republic (Transvaal)**.

Pemba

Pemba is a small island that lies off the coast of what is now Tanzania, about 30 miles (48 km) northeast of Zanzibar. Pemba profited from the lucrative Indian Ocean trade routes, on which it was an important trade depot. Its citizens included people from mainland Africa, Arabia, India and Asia. Over the years, they formed the Swahili people. Along with other Swahili towns such as Pate, Mombasa, Kilwa, and Lamu, Pemba was ruled as an independent city-state. The Portuguese dominated the East African coast in the six-teenth century, conquering Pemba at its start. Oman then displaced Portugal in the seventeenth century. In the eighteenth century, Pemba and the other Swahili city-states were largely independent from foreign rule but fell to the Mazrui rulers of Mombasa towards the end of that century. Oman took back Pemba in the early nineteenth century, and the island remained attached to the Sultanate of Zanzibar, which became a British protectorate in 1890, including the island of Pemba. In 1963, the Sultanate regained its independence, with Pemba still a part of the state. The following year, the sultan was deposed and a republic declared. Zanzibar signed a treaty of union with the newly independent Tanganyika on the mainland. The two former colonies united to form a completely new country, Tanzania, of which Pemba is now a part. *See also* **Tanzania**; **Zanzibar**.

Portuguese Guinea

The Portuguese came to the coast of what is now Guinea-Bissau in the fifteenth century to trade in slaves. At first many slaves were sent to the islands of Cape Verde to work on plantations there, but at the height of the slave trade Africans were being shipped in huge numbers to the Americas. Although the Portuguese laid claim to the Guinea-Bissau area and administered it, they exercised little control over it. After the profitable slave trade ended during the late nineteenth century, the Portuguese did begin to assert their rule. By 1915 CE, the Portuguese had established complete control, often using violence, over their colony, which was called Portuguese Guinea. Cape Verde was separated from Portuguese Guinea by that time. The indigenous peoples resisted rule from Portugal throughout the colonial era, which lasted until 1973 CE, when the colony declared itself independent as the Republic of Guinea-Bissau. *See also* **Guinea-Bissau**.

Potchefstroom

Potchefstroom, now a town on the Mooi River in North-West province, South Africa, was established by nineteenth-century Boers. The Boers ("farmers"), or Afrikaners, were descended from Dutch settlers. In the first half of the nineteenth century they began migrating inland, away from the Cape region of southern Africa where they often came into conflict with the British. Several independent Boer states were established–Potchefstroom in 1838 CE. The Potchefstroom Boers established one of the strongest republics in the region. By the second half of the nineteenth century, the Potchefstroom Boers were calling their state the South African Republic. *See also* **South Africa**; **South African Republic**.

Prazos

Battle of Lakhta, 1900 CE
Following two decisive victories over the French forces and their allies in 1899 CE, Rabih bin Fadl Allah was defeated at the Battle of Lakhta on 22 April 1900 CE. This illustration is based on an engraving that appeared on the cover of a French magazine, and shows Rabih's decapitated head being paraded on a pole by a member of the victorious French forces.

The Portuguese invasion of Central Africa was a lengthy process. At the end of the sixteenth century, settlers from Portugal were granted lands either by the Portuguese government or from local rulers. Force and deceit were sometimes used to gain *prazos*. Some of these *prazos*, meaning "land grants," developed into wealthy and independent entities. They could raise large private armies and often exercised the same powers as African rulers in the region. The *prazeros*— *prazo*-holders—ruled with impunity, often punishing Africans in private prisons for minor offenses. They provided many slaves to the markets in Mozambique, and continued to do so after slavery was abolished. This embarrassed the Portuguese government, which abolished the *prazo* system in 1890 CE. Most *prazos* were concentrated in the lands of the Mwene Mutapa empire, including parts of Zimbabwe, Zambia, and Congo (formerly Zaire). *See also* **Zambia**; **Zimbabwe**.

Qwaqwa

Qwaqwa, or Basuto Qwaqwa, was a nonindependent black state established during South Africa's era of white-minority rule. Located in the Drakensberg Mountains of eastern South Africa, the territory was created from the merging of two "native reserves" in 1969 CE. Qwaqwa was granted self-government in 1974 CE, but the state was dominated by the repressive policies of apartheid South Africa.

In 1994 CE, South Africa abolished apartheid and Qwaqwa was reincorporated into Free State province (then called Orange Free State province). *See also* **South Africa**.

Rabih's Empire

Rabih bin Fadl Allah was a Darfurian slave trader who trained as a soldier under the Egyptians. Invading from the east in 1879 CE, he formed a "mobile" empire in the Dar Runga and Dar Kuti areas. In 1891 CE, he entered the valley of the Chari. By 1893 CE, he had claimed victory over the Bagirmi; he had also invaded and occupied Bornu.

Rabih effectively resisted French colonial invaders from 1899–1900 CE, when he was killed at the Battle of Lakhta. He was succeeded by his son, Fadl Allah bin Rabih. Fadl Allah was recognized as Sultan of Bornu by the British and continued to resist the French. He was killed by them, however, at Gubja, Norther Nigeria, in 1901 CE. His death spelt the end of the Rabih Empire.

The extent of Rabih's Empire
Rabib bin Fadl Allah effectively resisted French colonial invaders from 1899–1900 CE, when he was killed at the Battle of Lakhta. The map (right) shows the area in which he resisted French expansion over this period.

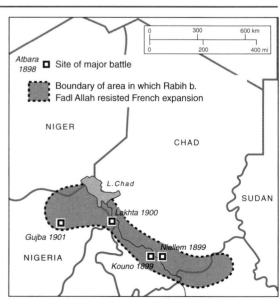

Rano

Rano was one of the historic Hausa states, which dominated what are now northwestern Nigeria and southwestern Niger. *See also* **Hausa states**.

Réunion

Officially named the Department of Réunion, this island southwest of Mauritius in the western Indian Ocean is a French overseas territory. Portuguese navigators first visited the, until then, uninhabited island in the early sixteenth century and had settled it by the mid-seventeenth century. The French established a staging post there for ships on their way to India. Slaves from mainland Africa were imported to work the coffee and sugar plantations until slavery was abolished in 1848 CE. Réunion was ruled by France as a colony until 1946 CE, when it became an overseas territory (*département*) of France.

Rhodesia

From 1964–65 to 1980 CE, modern Zimbabwe was the white-minority ruled state of Rhodesia. Formerly known as Southern Rhodesia, the land had been colonized by white settlers in the late nineteenth and early twentieth centuries, and it became part of the British Empire. The settlers were nominally ruled by the British government but they dominated the colony. The whites grew wealthy at the expense of Africans, who were exploited for their labor but denied basic human rights. In 1964 CE, Northern Rhodesia gained its independence as Zambia, and Southern Rhodesia was thereafter commonly known as Rhodesia. Its name was not officially changed, however, until the following year when the new government led by Ian Smith made a Unilateral Declaration of Independence (UDI) from Britain and renamed the country Rhodesia. Smith's administration practiced apartheid policies similar to those followed in South Africa, and Africans were denied the right to vote. After great international and internal pressure, Smith's government agreed to share

Sir Roy Welenski
He was the first minister of the Central African Federation, which comprised Northern and Southern Rhodesia and the Nyasaland Protectorate. A former train driver, he became a millionaire from copper mining, and was also a potent symbol of white supremacy.

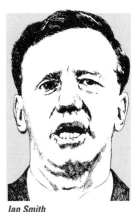

Ian Smith
He was the leader of the Southern Rhodesian government when it made its famous Unilateral Declaration of Independence (UDI) from Britain in 1965 CE. Smith subsequently shared power with the country's black leaders but it only became fully independent in 1980 CE, when it changed its name from Rhodesia to Zimbabwe.

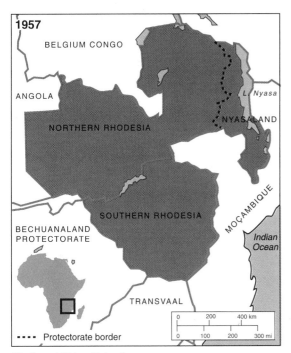

The Central African Federation
This federation was established in 1953 CE, and comprised the three British colonies of Southern Rhodesia, Northern Rhodesia and Nyasaland. Apart from the white settlers, the citizens were against the federation, and it was dissolved in 1963 CE in the face of continuous African opposition.

Three independent nations
Northern Rhodesia gained independence and became known as Zambia, and Nyasaland gained independence and became known as Malawi, in 1964 CE. Southern Rhodesia declared itself independent of British rule in 1965 CE and, on independence in 1980 CE, became known as Zimbabwe.

The Rhodesia Medal, 1980 CE
This medal was made to mark service in Rhodesia by the Commonwealth Monitoring Force that helped secure the formation of the new state of Zimbabwe.

© DIAGRAM

The Rhodesia Regiment
This regiment was formed from members of the Southern Rhodesia Volunteers and other citizens in the large towns. A sergeant is shown here, standing in front of the drill hall at Salisbury, Southern Rhodesia.

Queen Elizabeth II (above)
A stamp issued in 1954 CE in recognition of the Central African Federation of Northern and Southern Rhodesia and the Nyasaland Protectorate.

power with black Rhodesians in 1978 CE. Nearly a decade of internal warfare had led to the deaths of thousands and a million refugees. Rhodesia reverted to being the colony of Southern Rhodesia during the transition to independence in 1980 CE. On independence, Southern Rhodesia became Zimbabwe. *See also* **Northern Rhodesia**; **Southern Rhodesia**; **Zimbabwe**.

Learning to shoot (right)
These white women are being taught to shoot during the guerrilla war in Rhodesia. Ian Smith's illegal Unilateral Declaration of Independence (UDI) in 1965 CE set up a white-minority government, and was strongly opposed by the majority of the population, many of whom took up arms against the regime. These women, however, were prepared to fight to protect themselves and Smith's regime.

Rhodesia and Nyasaland, Federation of

Also called the Central African Federation, the Federation of Rhodesia and Nyasaland was a federal colony made up of Southern Rhodesia (Zimbabwe), Northern Rhodesia (Zambia), and Nyasaland (Malawi). It was established in 1953 CE when these three British colonies were merged. Most of the citizens of the colonies, apart from the white settlers, were against the federation. The citizens of Nyasaland and Northern Rhodesia feared that the powerful white community of Southern Rhodesia would simply take advantage of the federation for themselves, using the people as a vast labor pool and enforcing their racist laws and policies on the other two federal colonies. The federation was dissolved in 1963 CE in response to continued African opposition. In the following year, Northern Rhodesia gained independence as the Republic of Zambia and Nyasaland gained independence as Malawi. The white settlers of Southern Rhodesia declared themselves independent from British rule in 1965 CE, forming Rhodesia. *See also* **Malawi**; **Southern Rhodesia**; **Zambia**; **Zimbabwe**.

Cecil Rhodes (right)
Cecil Rhodes did much to impose British rule throughout Southern Africa, and the Rhodesian colonies were named after him. His methods included trickery, conquest, and diplomacy. He is shown (right) in a political cartoon from the beginning of the twentieth century that satirizes his failed ambition to conquer all of Africa "from the Cape to Cairo."

Río de Oro

The southern two-thirds of the Western Sahara (a disputed territory occupied by Morocco) once formed the Spanish-ruled territory of Río de Oro ("River of Gold"). The main town, Dakhla (formerly Villa Cisneros), lies on a narrow inlet of the Atlantic Ocean and was given its name by the Portuguese because the local inhabitants traded gold dust found in western Africa. In the 1880s the Spanish government claimed a protectorate over the adjoining coastal zone, and eventually controlled a large region called Río de Oro. In 1958 CE Spain united Río de Oro and its northerly neighbor Saguia el Hamra into a Spanish province called Spanish Sahara. The Spanish withdrew in 1976 CE, and the region was under nominal Mauretanian administration in the south and Moroccan occupation in the north. In the 1970s nationalist guerillas established the Popular Front for the Liberation of Saguia el Hamra and Río de Oro (Polisario Front) to fight the presence of both Mauretania and Morocco. In 1979 CE the Mauretanian government abandoned any claim and the entire area was occupied by Morocco. *See also* **Western Sahara**.

Rivières du Sud

See **French Guinea**.

Rio Muni

Modern Equatorial Guinea is made up of the island of Bioko (formerly Fernando Po) and Rio Muni on the mainland. Portugal ceded the lands to Spain in 1778 CE. Along with Fernando Po, Annobon, and other islands, Rio Muni became part of Spanish Guinea. In 1959 CE the mainland and islands were separated into two provinces. In 1963 CE the two provinces were merged again, and this is how, in 1968 CE, they gained independence as Equatorial Guinea. *See also* **Equatorial Guinea**; **Fernando Po**.

Rozvi empire

The Shona people of the Rozvi empire cntered their state upon one of the southern provinces of the Mwene Mutapa empire, in what is now southwestern Zimbabwe. The mighty Mwene Mutapa kings were responsible for building Great Zimbabwe, but by the late fifteenth century they were in decline. Changa, the ruler of Guruhuswa province, rebeled against the Mwene Mutapa in 1490 CE. Changa founded the Changamire dynasty and declared himself emperor; the rulers were known as *mambos*. Changa was killed in 1494 CE, but the empire he founded swallowed up much of the Mwene mutapa's lands as well as those of Mbire–the other former southern province, which had also rebelled against the Mutapas in 1490 CE. Ruled by wise leaders and based on a healthy pastoral (animal herding) and farming economy, the Rozvi empire grew powerful. The rise of the Rozvi empire had eclipsed the Mwene Mutapas almost completely by the end of the late seventeenth century. Celebrated campaigns in the 1680s and 1690s expelled the Portuguese, who had been settling on the Zimbabwe highveld. By the start of the nineteenth century, however, the Rozvi empire was in tatters, divided between warring factions and small chieftancies. Around the same time, large groups of refugees were fleeing a time of turmoil in southern Africa, and their raids also weakened the Rozvis. Ndebele people from Southern Africa took over the lands of the Rozvi. *See also* **Mwene Mutapa state**; **Ndebele kingdom**; **Zimbabwe**.

Ruanda–Urundi

The modern-day states of Burundi and Rwanda are based on two historic kingdoms: Urundi (or Rundi) and Ruanda (Rwanda) respectively. Hutu, Tutsi, and Twa people were settled in the region long before the Ruanda kingdom emerged in the sixteenth century. The rulers of the nearby Bunyoro kingdom launched a series of attacks in that century, causing the people to unite against them. The Tutsi rulers (known as Nyiginya) claimed descent from the supreme being Imana. The origins of the Urundi kingdom are less certain but it emerged with similar institutions and practices as Ruanda. The sixteenth to eighteenth centuries were a time of expansion for both kingdoms. They established centralized and stable realms, governed by officials. Each kingdom was ruled by a Tutsi king, the *mwami*. The cattle-owning Tutsi formed the aristocracy in both Ruanda and Urundi, with the Hutu making up the oft-exploited majority. In the nineteenth century Ruanda emerged as one of the most powerful states in the region, challenged only by Bunyoro.

In 1891 CE Germany made Ruanda–Urundi a joint territory as part of German East Africa, along with the continental portion of Tanzania and a small part of Mozambique. The imperial government took the territory over from the commercial German East Africa Company. The colony was not completely under German control until 1907 CE; the first German official did not visit until 1894 CE. During the war, German East Africa was occupied by the British. The Versailles Treaty (1919 CE) gave

Colonial policing
Ruanda–Urundi was administered by Belgium from 1922–1962 CE as part of the Belgian Congo. Urundi then became a monarchy under the name of Burundi, and Rwanda became an independent republic.

most of Germany's colonies to Britain, except for Ruanda-Urundi, which passed to Belgium. Ruanda-Urundi was administered by Belgium from 1922 CE to 1962 CE as part of the Belgian Congo. In 1962, the two countries became independent. Urundi, now called Burundi, remained a monarchy under its Tutsi *mwami*. Rwanda became an independent republic with a largely Hutu government. *See also* **Burundi**; **Rwanda**.

Pre-independence
A stamp issued before Ruanda and Urundi gained independence in 1962 CE.

Rundi kingdom

See **Ruanda–Urundi**.

Rwanda, kingdom of

See **Ruanda–Urundi**.

RWANDA Republic of Rwanda

Independence
A stamp issued in 1962 CE to celebrate the independence of Rwanda.

The earliest people known to have lived in Rwanda (formerly Ruanda) and Burundi (Urundi) were probably the ancestors of the hunter-gatherers, the Twa, who now make up less than one percent of Rwanda's population. At some time during the first millennium CE, Bantu-speaking people, the ancestors of the present-day Hutu, migrated into the area from the west, introducing an iron-using, farming culture. Around 600 years ago, a third group, the ancestors of the Tutsi, also moved into the area from the north.

The Tutsi established kingdoms in both Rwanda and Burundi, each ruled by a king, or *mwami*. Although numerically a minority, the Tutsi aristocracy became feudal rulers, who treated the Hutu as slaves. This feudal social structure survived after European colonization, which began in 1897 CE when Germany made Ruanda–Urundi part of German East Africa. However, following the defeat of Germany in World War I, the League of Nations asked Belgium to rule Ruanda-Urundi as a mandated territory. In 1946 CE, the newly constituted United Nations made Rwanda a UN Trust Territory under the administration of Belgium.

In 1959 CE, following the death of the king Mwami Mutara III, the Hutu launched an uprising against the Tutsi. About 150,000 people died in the conflict and about 150,000 Tutsis fled to Urundi and other neighboring countries. In 1961 CE, the people of Ruanda decided in a referendum to make their country a republic, while the people of Burundi opted in favor of a monarchy. Both countries finally became independent on July 1, 1962 CE.

Recent history

Rwanda's first president was Grégoire Kayibanda, leader of PARMEHUTU (*Parti de l'Émancipation du Peuple Hutu*), who had served as prime minister from 1960 CE. Kayibanda became as executive president from 1961 CE, following the departure of Mwami Kigeri V, who fled into exile following the referendum which made Rwanda a republic. Following independence, Kayibanda attempted to unite the country, but, in 1963 CE, a Tutsi force tried to seize power. This uprising provoked the Hutu into violent reprisals. More than 10,000 people were killed and 150,000 people fled into neighboring countries. Kayibanda was reelected in 1965 CE and 1969 CE, but his government failed to solve Rwanda's many economic problems, caused partly by overpopulation and a lack of natural resources. In 1973 CE, following renewed conflict between the Hutu and Tutsi, a military coup brought Major General Juvénal Habyarimana to power. Habyarimana dissolved the national legislature and declared himself president, appointing other military leaders to cabinet posts. However, Habyarimana gradually replaced them with civilians. In 1978 CE, Rwanda adopted a new constitution, becoming a one-party regime. The government pledged to end ethnic hostilities and Habyarimana tried to improve relations with Burundi and Uganda, which had taken in large numbers of Tutsi refugees.

In 1990 CE, a large Tutsi rebel force, the Rwandan Patriotic Front (RPF), formed from among the refugees in Uganda, invaded Rwanda from the north. They were

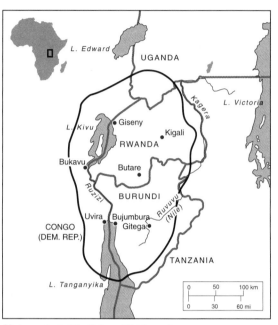

Modern extent of the Hutu and Tutsi peoples

defeated with French support and at great cost of life. In 1991 CE, Rwanda adopted a new constitution, restoring a multiparty system, but ethnic conflict continued. In April 1994 CE, Habyarimana and President Cyprien Ntaryamira of Burundi were both killed when the plane on which they were traveling was apparently shot down by Hutu extremists. Many Hutu extremists then began a campaign of genocide against Rwanda's Tutsi minority, but in the ensuing civil war, the RPF defeated the Hutu forces and set up a government of national unity, including moderate Hutu as president and prime minister. During the carnage in 1994 CE, an estimated million Rwandans and more than two million people were forced to flee into exile, mainly into Zaire (now the Democratic Republic of Congo). In the later 1990s, attempts were made to try those accused of crimes against humanity in 1994 CE. Meanwhile, the Hutu-Tutsi conflict spilled over into Zaire, when Tutsi forces, supported by Rwanda and Uganda who both feared a Hutu attack, supported Laurent Kabila, who overthrew the Zairean government in 1997 CE.

In 2000 CE, the resignation of Rwanda's President Pasteur Bizimungu led to conjecture that his position as a Hutu had become untenable. He was succeeded by the Tutsi General and former Vice-President Paul Kagame, who had been Rwanda's effective ruler since he ended the genocide in 1994 CE.

Peoples

HUTU AND TUTSI

For information about the history of the Hutu and Tutsi, *see* **Burundi (Peoples—Hutu** and **Tutsi)**.

TWA

For information about the history of the Twa people, *see* **Burundi (Peoples—Twa)**.

War orphan
This child was a casualty of the 1990s conflict in Rwanda, and more recently Burundi, between the Tutsi-dominated rebels and the majority Hutu people. Large numbers of Hutu refugees fled to neighboring countries, while many Tutsi families found themselves the victims of retaliation.

Rwanda timeline

Pre 19th century

7th-10th centuries CE Hutu farmers migrate to the Rwanda region

15th century The Tutsis invade Rwanda from the north and conquer the Hutus

19th century

1897 The Germans conquer Ruanda-Urundi (the region of modern Rwanda and Burundi)

1900-49 CE **1916** Belgian troops occupy Ruanda-Urundi

1923 The League of Nations mandates Ruanda-Urundi to Belgium

1946 Ruanda-Urundi becomes a UN trust territory administered by Belgium

1950-59 CE **1959** Gregoire Kayibanda forms the Party for Hutu Emancipation (PARMEHUTU)

1959 Hutu-Tutsi violence breaks out after the mysterious death of King Mutara III

1960-69 CE **1960** The Hutus win control of local legislature in elections

1961 Ruanda votes to become an independent republic, Urundi to become an independent kingdom (Burundi)

1962 July 1 Rwanda becomes independent. The Hutu leader Kayibanda, becomes president

1965 Kayibanda is re-elected president

1969 Kayibanda is elected to a third term as president

1970-79 CE **1973** Kayibanda is ousted by a military coup: Hutu Maj. Gen. Juvenal Habyarimana becomes president

1978 Rwanda becomes a one party state

1980-89 CE **1980** Habyarimana purges the ruling party, PARMEHUTU

1983 President Habyarimana is re-elected unopposed

1990-99 CE **1990** The Rwandan Patriotic Front (RPF), a Tutsi rebel movement based in Uganda, begins attacks on the government

1991 A multiparty constitution is introduced after another RPF invasion

1992 Hutu militias forcibly relocate members of the Tutsi minority

1993 Habyarimana repudiates a peace treaty signed by his prime minister and the RPF

1994 Apr President Habyarimana and President Ntaryamira of Burundi are killed when their plane is shot down by Hutu extremists

1994 May Hutu extremists kill 750,000 Tutsi in a campaign of genocide

1994 Jun Despite the genocide, France supports the French-speaking Hutus against the English-speaking RPF

1994 Jul The RPF defeats Hutu forces and forms a government of national unity under a moderate Hutu president and prime minister: two million Hutus flee, most of them to Zaire (now Dem. Rep. of Congo)

1995 The government begins holding war crimes trials

1996 Many Hutus return to Rwanda after attacks on their refugee camps by Zairian Tutu rebels

1998 After being convicted of genocide, 22 Hutus are executed

Rwandan presidents

Jan 28 1961–Oct 26 1961 CE
Dominique Mbonyumutwa

Oct 26 1961–Jul 5 1973 CE
Grégoire Kayibanda

Jul 5 1973–Apr 6 1994 CE
Juvénal Habyarimana

Apr 9 1994–Jul 19 1994 CE
Théodore Sindikubwabo (acting)

Jul 19 1994–Mar 23 2000 CE
Pasteur Bizimungu

Mar 24 2000 CE–
Paul Kagame
(acting to Apr 22 2000)

Rwanda's major political figures

Mutara III Rutahigwa (1913–1959 CE)

Mutara III served as *mwami* (traditional king) of Rwanda from 1931 until his death. Despite opposition by the Belgian colonial rulers, who wanted to introduce a democratic form of government, Mutara III continued to maintain the traditional Tutsi domination over the Hutu. He was succeeded by Kigeri V, but in a referendum in 1961, the people voted to make Rwanda a republic and Kigeri V fled the country.

Habyarimana, Juvénal (1937–1994 CE)

Juvénal Habyarimana, an army officer, took power in Rwanda in a bloodless coup that ousted President Grégoire Kayibanda in 1973. He ruled the country until he was killed, together with President Cyprien Ntaryamira of Burundi, when their plane was shot down in April 1994. Both presidents were Hutu and their deaths provoked terrible conflict between the Hutu and Tutsi in Rwanda, Burundi, and Congo (Dem.Rep.).

Kayibanda, Grégoire (1924 CE –)

Grégoire Kayibanda, a Hutu, became the first president of Rwanda when the country became independent in 1962. He was reelected in 1965 and 1969, but he was overthrown by a military group in 1973 and replaced by Juvénal Habyarimana.

Saguia el Hamra

Saguia el Hamra (sometimes also called Spanish Sahara) was the name of the northern half of the Spanish Sahara province. It was united with Río de Oro in 1958 CE to form Spanish Sahara. *See also* **Spanish Sahara**; **Western Sahara**.

Saint Helena

The island of Saint Helena is a British colony in the South Atlantic Ocean, 1,200 miles (1,950 km) west of the Southwestern coast of Africa. The island was discovered in 1502 CE by João da Nova, a Spanish navigator in the service of Portugal. The day that he discovered the island was the feast day of the Eastern Orthodox Church Saint Helena and so he named it for her. The island became an important staging post for ships traveling between Europe and India and Southeast Asia. The Dutch might have occupied St. Helena briefly in the mid-seventeenth century but the English East India Company took possession of it in 1659 CE. Another brief Dutch occupation followed in 1673 CE.

The defeated French emperor Napoleon was imprisoned there from 1815 CE until his death in 1821 CE. The East India Company relinquished control of the island to the British government in 1834 CE. In the latter half of the twentieth century St. Helena's role as a staging post on trade routes declined. The island won a degree of autonomy in 1966, followed by the 1988 CE constitution that came into force in 1989 CE. While authority still resides with the British Crown and is exercised through an appointed governor, the people of St. Helena and its island dependencies (Ascension Island and Tristan da Cunha) elect twelve members of the legislative council.

Sakalava kingdom

The first major civilization to arise on the island of Madagascar was the Sakalava kingdom. It arose on the west coast in the sixteenth century from an amalgamation of several smaller states. By the middle of the nineteenth century, it controlled nearly half of the island. After the death of Queen Ravahiny in 1808 CE, however, the kingdom began to disintegrate. *See also* **Madagascar**.

SÃO TOMÉ AND PRÍNCIPE
Democratic Republic of São Tomé and Príncipe

In 1470 CE, when Portuguese mariners first reached what is now São Tomé and Príncipe, these islands off the coast of west-central Africa were probably uninhabited. In 1485 CE, the first European settlers, together with convicts and Portuguese exiles, began to arrive. Their economy was based on sugar, but, because the population was too small to sustain this labor-intensive industry, African slaves were soon used as plantation workers. With a enlarged labor force, sugar production increased and the islands achieved a degree of prosperity. Also, the intermingling of Europeans and Africans led to the creation of the Creole community which forms the majority group in the country today. In 1522 CE, the Portuguese government took control of the islands, but, in the mid-sixteenth century, following a slave revolt, some sugar plantation owners left the territory. Sugar production declined and the economy deteriorated. However, before long, the islands became a center of the slave trade, handling slaves from the mainland before they were shipped to the Americas and elsewhere.

In the seventeenth and eighteenth centuries, the Dutch and French ruled the islands intermittently, but the Portuguese regained full control in the nineteenth century, when cocoa and coffee were grown using slave labor. Portugal officially banned slavery in 1875 CE, but contract laborers were brought in, mainly from Angola, Mozambique, and Cape Verde, and they were used virtually as slaves. The harsh treatment received by the plantation workers led to periodic revolts, the most violent of which occurred in 1953 CE, when the Portuguese killed hundreds of workers during the so-called Batepa massacre.

Recent history

In 1960 CE, when the two islands were being governed as a Portuguese overseas province, a group of nationalists, including Manuel Pinto Da Costa and Miguel Trovoada, set up the Movement for the Liberation of São Tomé and Príncipe (MLSTP). However, they were unable to act as officers of the movement on the islands and their main base from 1961 CE was in Gabon. In 1970 CE, Portugal introduced some reforms, namely the setting up of a 16-member legislative council and a provisional consultative council. But dissatisfaction with Portuguese rule continued. The MLSTP was reorganized in 1972 CE and it won recognition by the Organization of African Unity. A coup in Portugal in April 1974 CE which overthrew the government of the dictator Marcello Caetano led the new military regime to concede autonomy to the islands. Following disturbances caused mainly by independence tensions, the Portuguese set up a transitional government and full independence was achieved on July 12, 1975 CE.

The first president was Manuel Pinto Da Costa of the MLSTP, while Miguel Trovoada became prime minister. Most of the 2,000 or so Portuguese living on the islands left the country at independence, depriving it of skilled civil servants, professionals, and traders. The new government began to pursue socialist policies. It nationalized the plantations, took control of all retail businesses, and introduced a planned economy, although private property and investment were still permitted. The MLSTP became the sole legal party and the government set up a secret police force to maintain control. However, because the new country remained unaligned in foreign affairs, it continued to enjoy good relations with Portugal, which supplied aid.

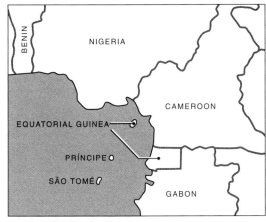

Location of São Tomé and Príncipe

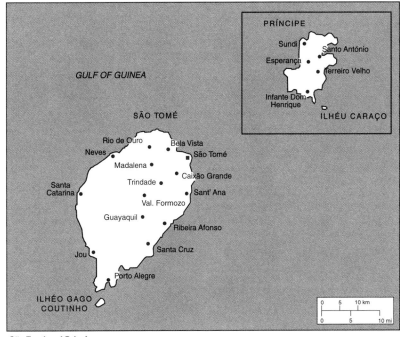

São Tomé and Príncipe

In the 1970s, differences within the MLSTP, especially over economic policies. led to plots against Da Costa. Da Costa brought charges against Trovoada, who was removed from the premiership in 1979 CE and imprisoned for two years. In 1988 CE, with the economy in decline and shaken by the divisions in his own party, Da Costa modified his socialist policies and accepted a tough package for economic reform imposed by the International Monetary Fund (IMF). A new constitution was introduced in 1990 CE, enabling the country's first multiparty elections to be held in 1991 CE. In these elections, Trovoada, who had returned from exile in France, stood as the candidate for the Democratic Convergence, a party which had been founded in 1987 CE. Trovoada was victorious after Da Costa, sensing defeat, withdrew. Trovoada continued the stringent policies of economic reform advocated by the IMF and his government abolished the secret police. In 1995 CE, the government granted self rule to the island of Príncipe. Following an attempted coup in 1995, Trovoada was reelected president in 1996 CE, defeating Da Costa in a second ballot.

Peoples

CREOLES

Most of the people of São Tomé and Príncipe are Creoles–that is, they are of mixed African and European ancestry. Africans and Europeans make up smaller groups. This complex mixture of people arose from the days when Portugal began to send convicts and settlers to the islands in the late fifteenth century and also, later, to the days when São Tomé became a major center of the slave trade. After slavery was ended in the nineteenth century, the Portuguese continued to bring Africans to the islands as contract laborers.

Flag of the people
This post-independence stamp shows the flag of São Tomé and Príncipe.

São Tomè and Príncipe timeline		
Pre 19th century CE		
	1470	The Portuguese discover the islands of São Tomé and Príncipe
	1485	Portuguese colonization begins: sugar cane plantations are created
	1522	São Tomé and Príncipe are taken over by the Portuguese crown
19th century CE		
	1875	Slave labor is officially abolished
1950–59 CE	1953	The Batepa massacre: troops kill hundreds of plantation workers who are on strike
1960–69 CE	1960	The Committee for the Liberation of São Tomé and Príncipe is formed
1970–79 CE	1975 July 12	São Tomé and Príncipe become independent: Manuel Pinto da Costa becomes president
1990–99 CE	1990	Da Costa resigns. Miguel Trovoada becomes president after the first multiparty presidential election since independence
	1995	Príncipe is granted autonomy. An attempted military coup is defeated
	1996	São Tomé and Príncipe join the Community of Portuguese-speaking Countries. President Miguel Trovoada is re-elected

São Tomé and Príncipe presidents
Jul 12 1975–Apr 3 1991 CE Manuel Pinto da Costa
Apr 3 1991–Aug 15 1995 CE Miguel Trovoada (1st time)
Aug 15 1995–Aug 21 1995 CE Manuel Quintas de Almeida (chairman of military junta)
Aug 21 1995 CE – Miguel Trovoada (2nd time)

© DIAGRAM

São Tomé and Príncipe's major political figures

Da Costa, Manuel Pinto (1937 CE–)

Manuel Pinto Da Costa was one of the founders of the nationalist Movement for the Liberation of São Tomé and Príncipe (MLSTP) in 1960 and, in 1975, he became the country's first president. In office until 1991, he pursued socialist policies, but later he accepted severe economic measures advocated by the International Monetary Fund (IMF). He also restored multiparty rule to his country in 1990.

Trovoada, Miguel Anjos da Cunha (1937 CE –)

Trovoada, one of the founders of the nationalist Movement for the Liberation of São Tomé and Príncipe in 1960, became prime minister when his island country became independent in 1975. He was dismissed in 1979 and served two years in prison. However, on his return from exile in 1991, he was elected president. Despite the country's economic problems, he was reelected in 1996.

Second Mandinka Empire

See **Mandinka Empire**.

Segu

According to tradition, the brothers Barama and Nia Ngolo were robber barons who founded the Bambara kingdoms of Kaarta and Segu in 1650 CE. The Bambara are a Manding-speaking people of West Africa. Segu was the more powerful of the two states, but both were politically influential in West Africa until the mid-eighteenth century. Segu's center was what is now the town of Ségou in central Mali on the Niger River.

Mamari Koulibali is more often credited with the founding of the Segu state. Koulibali was a strict ruler who made all the men in his kingdom his personal slaves. The *ton-dyon* were a group of slaves who helped the king govern. From Koulibali's death in 1755–1766 CE, successive rulers found it hard to control the *ton-dyon*, and many were assassinated. Ngolo Diara was a powerful military leader who managed to return Segu to stability. In the early nineteenth century Segu fell to the Muslim *jihads* (holy wars of conquest) that swept West Africa. Seku Ahmadu of Macina took Jenne and Timbuktu from Segu then Al Hajj Umar, the founder of the Tukulor empire, conquered Segu. *See also* **Kaarta**; **Mali**.

SENEGAL Republic of Senegal

The area that is now Senegal has formed part of a long series of African kingdoms and empires. For example, eastern Senegal came under the rule of ancient Ghana, ancient Mali, and Songhay, while the Wolof kingdom dominated central Senegal between the fifteenth and eighteenth centuries.

DAKAR-MERS EL-KEBIR

German propaganda
A World War II poster that celebrated the defeat of the British and Free French forces. They had attempted to gain control of Senegal from the port of Dakar, the capital of Vichy French West Africa.

Portuguese mariners, in search of a route from Europe to Asia around Africa, reached the Senegal coast in about 1445 CE. They sailed up the Sénégal, Gambia, and Casamance Rivers, trading with the local people. In the sixteenth century, rival Dutch, French, and English traders competed for the region's trade, including slaves, along the coast. The Dutch set up a trading post on an island opposite the site of present-day Dakar, Senegal's capital, in 1617 CE, while the French established a post at the mouth of the Sénégal River in 1626 CE. In 1677 CE, the French drove out the Dutch, but the French were in turn pushed out by the English in 1763 CE. French rule was restored in the late eighteenth century and, in 1848 CE, France abolished slavery in Senegal. From the mid-nineteenth century, French troops gradually conquered the independent African kingdoms which ruled the interior and, in 1882 CE, Senegal became a French colony. In 1895 CE, Senegal became part of French West Africa, which also included Benin, Burkina Faso, Guinea, Ivory Coast, Mauritania, Mali, and Niger. Dakar became important as the capital of this vast territory. However, many Senegalese favored independence and, in 1946 CE, Senegal became an overseas territory of France, with its own assembly. All Senegalese became French citizens.

Recent history

In April 1959 CE, Senegal joined with Mali to form the Federation of Mali, which became fully independent from France on June 20, 1960 CE. However, two months later, Senegal seceded from the federation and declared itself the Republic of Senegal on August 20, 1960.

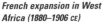

French expansion in West Africa (1880–1906 CE)

From the sixteenth century French traders competed with the Dutch and English for trade, including slaves, along the coast of West Africa. In 1677 CE the French drove out the Dutch, but the French were pushed out by the English in 1763 CE. French rule was restored in the late eighteenth century and, in 1898 CE, France abolished slavery in Senegal. From the mid-nineteenth century, French troops gradually conquered the the independent African kingdoms which ruled the interior. In 1882 CE, Senegal became a part of French West Africa, and Dakar became important as the capital of this vast territory. However, many Senegalese favored independence and, in 1946 CE, Senegal became an overseas territory of France with its own assembly.

The maps show the extent of French expansion in the area at the following dates:

1 *1880 CE* **4** *1895 CE*

2 *1885 CE* **5** *1897 CE*

3 *1890 CE* **6** *1906 CE*

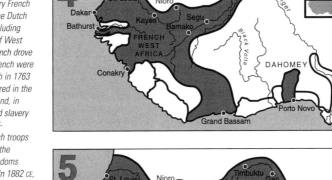

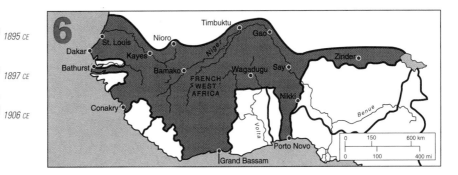

Senegal's first president was Léopold Sédar Senghor, who had founded the socialist Senegalese Progressive Union (UPS) in 1948 CE. The government, led by the prime minister Mamadou Dia launched a program of economic development aimed mainly at the rural sector. However, in 1962 CE, Dia tried to overthrow Senghor, and he was arrested and imprisoned.

In 1963 CE, Senghor increased the power of the president by abolishing the post of prime minister. His constitutional changes were approved in a referendum and, later that year, his party won a decisive victory in parliamentary elections. But protests by rioters, alleging electoral fraud, caused much tension. In 1966 CE, Senegal became a one-party state, although opposition persisted within the ruling party. Several attempted coups occurred and the country's problems were compounded by long droughts, which seriously damaged the economy in the late 1960s and 1970s. However, Senghor cautiously restored multiparty democracy in the 1970s. First, in 1970 CE, he reestablished the post of prime minister and appointed one of his protégés, Abdou Diouf, as prime minister. In 1974 CE, political parties were legalized and, in 1978 CE, he was reelected president, defeating Abdoulaye Wade, leader of the Senegalese Democratic Party. Finally, in 1981 CE, Senghor announced his retirement–he was the first

African president to do so freely. Senghor was succeeded by Abdou Diouf.

In 1981 CE, Senegal won the gratitude of Gambia's government by intervening and putting down a rebellion. In 1982 CE, the two countries established the Confederation of Senegambia. But this defensive and economic alliance did not work, largely because the two countries were not equal, and the confederation was abandoned in 1989 CE. In 1990 CE, Diouf had to handle racist violence in the north, where there were border clashes with Mauritania and the expulsion of expatriates from each country. The government also took a firm line with an urban Muslim fundamentalist movement and a secessionist movement in the southern province of Casamance. Diouf, who was re-elected in 1993 CE, maintained good relations with France, from which it received much aid. France also provided military advisers to Senegal.

In 2000 CE, Diouf was defeated in presidential elections by the 74-year-old Abdoulaye Wade, an economist, who ended 40 years of uninterrupted socialist rule. Wade argued that earlier elections had been rigged and that Diouf's government had become inefficient and increasingly corrupt. He declared that, in order to democratize the country, he planned to cut the president's term in office from seven to five years.

Seku Ahmadu

He was the ruler of the Tukulor empire from 1864–93 CE, and was the son, and successor, of Al-Hajj Umar, the founder of the empire which today covers much of the area of modern Senegal.

Senegal presidents

Senegal presidents	
Sep 6 1960–Dec 31 1980 CE	Léopold Sédar Senghor
Jan 1 1981–Apr 1 2000 CE	Abdou Diouf
Apr 1 2000 CE –	Abdoulaye Wade

Anniversary
A 1970 CE stamp marking the twenty-fifth anniversary of the UN.

Senegal timeline

Pre 19th century CE

c. 800–1100 CE Senegal region is dominated by the Fulani Takrur empire
c. 1240–1400 The empire of Mali dominates the Senegal region
15th–18th centuries The Fulani Wolof kingdom dominates much of Senegal
1445 Portuguese navigators explore the coast of Senegal
1617 The Dutch establish a trading post on Gorée island
1626 The French build a trading post at the mouth of the Senegal River
1677 The French take over Gorée Island from the Dutch
1763 Britain expels the French from Senegal
1765 Britain creates the colony of Senegambia, incorporating parts of Senegal and Gambia
1783 Britain cedes Senegal back to France late eighteenth century. The reformist Islamic kingdom of Futa Toro dominates inland Senegal

19th century CE

19th century Islam becomes the main religion in Senegal
1848 France abolishes slavery in Senegal
1854 France begins to establish control over inland areas but comes into conflict with al-Hajj Umar of the Tukulor caliphate
1857 France agrees a truce with al-Hajj Umar
1865 French control established over most of present-day Senegal
1882 Senegal becomes a French colony
1889 Borders of Senegal agreed by treaty with Britain
1895 Senegal is incorporated into the French West Africa colony
1933 Léopold Sédar Senghor and others develop the idea of négritude (resistance to French cultural influence)

1900–49 CE **1940** Senegal supports the collaborationist Vichy French regime
1942 Free French gain control of Senegal
1946 Senegal becomes an overseas territory of France
1948 Senghor founds the Senegalese Progressive Union to campaign for greater autonomy

1950–59 CE **1956** Senegal is granted internal self-government
1959 Senegal and the French Sudan join to form the federation of Mali

1960–69 CE **1960 Jun 20** The federation of Mali becomes independent
1960 Aug 20 Senegal withdraws from the federation and becomes the republic of Senegal: Senghor is the first president
1962 The prime minister Mamadou Dia attempts unsuccessfully to overthrow president Senghor
1963 Senghor abolishes the office of prime minister
1966 Senegal becomes a one-party state

1970–79 CE **1970** The office of prime minister is restored by a referendum
1974 Political parties are legalized

1980–89 CE **1981** President Senghor resigns: the prime minister Abdou Diouf becomes president
1982 Senegal and Gambia form the confederation of Senegambia
1983 Diouf is re-elected to the presidency
1989 Gambia withdraws from Senegambia. Fighting breaks out on the border with Mauritania

1990–99 CE **1991** Renewed fighting on the border with Mauritania
1992 Armed clashes with Casamance separatists in southern Senegal
1993 Diouf is re-elected to the presidency for the third time. A cease-fire is agreed with the Casamance separatists
1995 The Casamance breach the cease-fire
1998 In a visit to Dakar, US president Clinton proposes the creation of an "African peace maintaining force"

Peoples

DYULA

For information about the history of the Dyula people, *see* **Burkina Faso (Peoples—Dyula)**.

FULANI

For information about the history of the Fulani people, *see* **Fulani states**.

MANDING

For information about the history of the Manding people, *see* **Mali (Peoples—Manding)**.

SERER

The Serer, one of Senegal's largest ethnic groups, are also found in smaller numbers in Gambia and Guinea-Bissau. Together with the Wolof, the Serer were the primary inhabitants of the Wolof Kingdom, and later empire, which became powerful in the fifteenth century. The Wolof introduced the Serer to Islam, which was, at first, violently resisted. However, since the nineteenth century, Islam has spread increasingly among the Serer.

Senegal's major political figures

Wade, Abdoulaye (1927 CE–)
Abdoulaye Wade. a lawyer and economist, became one of Senegal's leading opposition figures from 1978. In 2000, he won presidential elections, defeating Abdou Diouf. Wade became known for his support for human rights and a free market economy. He also condemned corruption in government and advocated a reduction in presidential powers as part of a program to make Senegal more democratic.

Al Hajj Umar (1794–1864 CE)
Al Hajj Umar, born Umar Said Tall in Futa Toro, northern Senegal, was the Fulani Muslim leader who founded the Tukolor Empire. In the 1840s, he established a fortress in the the town of Dinguiray (in present-day Guinea), where he trained and armed a powerful army. From there, in 1852, he began a *jihad* (Islamic holy war) during which he conquered the West African states of Kaarta, Segu, and Macina, but was driven out of Futa Toro by the French. In 1864, he was killed during a battle with Fulani, Bambara, and Tuareg forces who had rebelled against his rule and besieged the Macina town of Hamdullahi.

Diouf, Abdou (1935 CE –)
Abdou Diouf became Senegal's first prime minister from 1970 until 1981, when he succeeded Léopold Sédar Senghor as president. Diouf set about reorganizing Senegal's political system and allowed opposition parties to proliferate. In 1981, he used Senegalese troops to reinstate the Gambian president, Alhaji Sir Dawda Jawara, who had been ousted by a military coup. In 1982, Diouf and Jawara united their countries to form the confederation of Senegambia, with Diouf as president. He was elected president of Senegal in his own right in l983 and reelected in 1988 and 1993. The Senegambia confederation dissolved in 1989.

Senghor, Léopold Sédar (1906 CE –)
A distinguished poet, Léopold Senghor became the first president of Senegal in 1960. He favored moderate "African socialism" and restricted political activity – by 1966, Senegal was a one-party state. He worked to modernize agriculture, prevent corruption, and establish close ties with neighboring countries. He also developed a philosophy called "negritude" that celebrated African culture and values. A declining economic situation and pressure for political reforms led to Senghor's resignation in late 1980. He was succeeded by Abdou Diouf.

Léopold Senghor
He became the first president of Senegal in 1960, and served in this office until a declining economic situation, and pressure for economic reforms, led to his resignation in late 1980.

Senegambia

From 1982–1989 CE the independent countries of Senegal and The Gambia merged to form Senegambia. While military, economic, foreign, and other policies were to be integrated, the two countries were to remain independent. The much larger Senegal was the more powerful of the two countries, however, and The Gambia grew increasingly concerned over its loss of influence. In 1989 CE the confederation was dissolved for that reason. *See also* **Gambia, The**; **Senegal**.

SEYCHELLES Republic of Seychelles

Arabs may have visited the Seychelles in ancient times, but Portuguese mariners made the first recorded sighting in 1505 CE. In 1609 CE, an expedition launched by the English East India Company made the first known landing and it reported that the islands were uninhabited. In the early eighteenth century, pirates used the islands as a source of fresh water and food, including fruit.

In 1742 CE, the French colonial rulers of the Île de France (now Mauritius) sent an expedition to explore the islands, but they did not try to annex them until 1756 CE, when they wanted to forestall an English occupation. The French named the islands the "Séchelles," which the British changed to "Seychelles." The first French colonists arrived in 1770 CE, together with African slaves, and they created a supply station for French ships sailing to southern Asia. But they cut down the forests and killed the wildlife, including the giant tortoises, greatly damaging the environment. Controls were put on this destruction in the early 1790s.

In 1794 CE, Britain demanded the surrender of the islands, which were officially ceded to Britain in 1815 CE. The British made the Seychelles a dependency of

Mauritius, which they had also taken from France. In the 1830s, with the abolition of slavery, the settlers began to cultivate such crops as coconuts, cinnamon, and vanilla, which were less labor-intensive than the crops grown earlier. Britain made the Seychelles a separate colony in 1903 CE and, in 1948 CE, they set up the islands' first legislative council.

Recent history
In 1964 CE, two political parties were formed. One, led by James Mancham, was the right-wing Seychelles Democratic Party (SDP), which opposed independence, favoring some kind of association with Britain. The other was the leftwing Seychelles People's United Party (SPUP), led by France-Albert René. The SDP won a majority in the 1970 CE elections and Mancham became prime minister. It increased its majority in 1974 CE, when it adopted a pro-independence policy, following a strong swing in public opinion against continuing British rule. The Seychelles achieved internally self-government on October 1, 1975 CE and full independence as a republic within the British Commonwealth on June 29, 1976 CE.

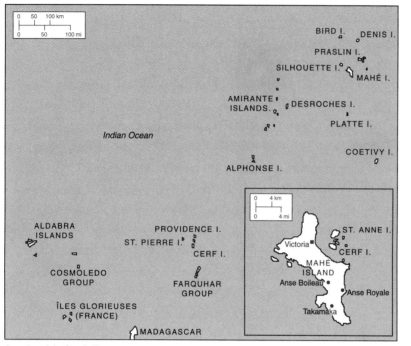

Location of the Seychelles

A double celebration
A stamp issued in 1976 CE marking the independence of Seychelles and the US Bicentenary.

Progressive Front (SPPF) the country's sole legal party. In 1980 CE, an attempt by South African mercenaries to restore Mancham to power, was put down only with the help of Tanzanian troops. This was followed by an army mutiny in 1982 CE, which was also suppressed, as were other subsequent coups. In 1979 CE, 1984 CE, and 1991 CE, René was the only candidate in the presidential elections, but he gradually began to feel more secure and, under pressure from aid donors and foreign creditors, his government legalized other parties.

A new constitution was approved by the electorate in 1993 CE, when elections were held. Mancham returned to the Seychelles to stand as opposition candidate, but he and another candidate were defeated by René in what was considered to be a fair election. Presidential and parliamentary elections were held in 1998 CE, when René was reelected to a fifth term, taking 66 percent of the vote, while the SPPF increased its majority in the People's Assembly. The constitutional changes improvemed freedom of speech, although René's opponents argued that his domination of the country's politics still contributed to a repressive atmosphere. However, under René, the country's economy has developed quickly. Much of his government's economic success has been based on tourism, which has become the country's leading source of income.

Peoples
Almost 90 percent of the people of the Seychelles are Creoles–that is, people of mixed African, Asian, and European ancestry. Other groups include people of Indian, Malagasy, Chinese, and English origin. The islands were uninhabited when they were discovered by the Portuguese in the early sixteenth century, but they were later populated by white settlers and African slaves. In the nineteenth century, they were joined by deportees from France and by some British people. Later still, Asians from China, India, and Malaya arrived and widespread intermarriage led to the complex intermix of peoples in the Seychelles today.

The first president was James Mancham, who appointed René as his prime minister. However, Mancham, who had developed a reputation for flamboyancy, was deposed by an armed group of René's supporters in June 1977 CE, when Mancham was out of the country. Although bloodless, the coup led to the departure from the islands of about 10,000 people. René, who denied that he had backed the coup, became president. He suspended the constitution and dissolved the national assembly. He introduced moderate socialist policies, including measures to help the poor obtain a greater share in the country's wealth. But he felt insecure and feared that a coup would be mounted to depose him. In 1979 CE, René introduced a new constitution, making his reconstituted Seychelles People's

Seychelles timeline		
Pre 19th century CE		
	1505	The Seychelles are discovered by the Portuguese
	1742	A French expedition explores the islands
	1756	France claims the islands
	1770	French planters and African slaves settle on Mahé
	1794	The British occupy the Seychelles
19th century CE		
	1814	France formally cedes the Seychelles to Britain
1970–79 CE	1976 Jun 29	The Seychelles become independent: James Mancham is the first president
	1977	France Albert René becomes president after a military coup
	1979	René's Marxist Seychelles People's Progressive Front (SPPF) becomes the only legal party
1980–89 CE	1981	A coup attempt by foreign mercenaries is defeated
1990–99 CE	1991	Opposition parties are legalized and Marxism is abandoned
	1993	René defeats Mancham in the first multiparty presidential elections
	1998	René and the SPPF are again re-elected

Mancham, James Richard (1929 CE–)
James Mancham became the first president of the Seychelles when the country became independent in 1976, but he was deposed by his prime minister France-Albert René in 1977. He had earlier served as chief minister, from 1970 until 1974.

René, France-Albert (1935 CE–)
France-Albert René, prime minister of Seychelles, seized power in 1977 to become the country's second president, replacing James Mancham. René created a one-party state and followed policies of nonalignment. He was reelected in multiparty elections in 1993 CE.

Seychelles presidents
Jun 29 1976–Jun 5 1977 CE Sir James R. Mancham
Jun 5 1977 CE– France-Albert René

SIERRA LEONE Republic of Sierra Leone

Sierra Leone was once divided into small kingdoms, or chiefdoms, each with its own ruler. These kingdoms, including those of the Mende and Temne, came into conflict with the British during the colonial era. The first Europeans who reached the coast of what is now Sierra Leone were Portuguese mariners in 1460 CE. The coast soon became important for trade in ivory and slaves. Although Britain established some trading posts in the seventeenth century, no European power made claims on the area, and the traders operated under the protection of local African rulers.

In 1787 CE, a group of freed slaves arrived from England and Canada to establish a settlement, sponsored by the leading English abolitionist, Granville Sharp. The abolitionists hoped to make the settlement an antislavery base, but the Temne nearly destroyed it in 1789 CE. The settlement was revived in 1791 CE, rebuilt and named Freetown. After 1807 CE, when Britain abolished slavery, Freetown became a British protectorate (colony). It became a naval base, where many slaves freed from the ships of other nations, called recaptives, were landed. The intermingling of the original settlers and the recaptives led to the creation of Sierra Leone's modern Creole community.

British influence gradually spread inland and the interior of what is now Sierra Leone was made a British protectorate in 1896 CE. Freetown and the interior were united in 1951 CE and Sierra Leone achieved internal self-government. The government elected in 1951 CE was led by Milton (later Sir Milton) Margai, leader of the Sierra Leone People's Party (SLPP).

Recent history
Sierra Leone became fully independent on April 27, 1961 CE, with Milton Margai as its prime minister. Margai worked to defuse ethnic tensions, but, after his death in 1964 CE, his brother Albert became prime minister and he failed to maintain national unity. Army officers took power in 1967 CE, after they refused to accept indecisive election results. Army rule under the military National Reformation Council was shortlived and, in 1968 CE, lower ranking soldiers overthrew the military regime and restored democracy. Siaka Stevens, leader of the All-People's Congress (APC), became prime minister, heading a coalition government. In 1971 CE, a new constitution made the country a republic and, in 1976 CE, the APC became the sole legal party. Political unrest and economic problems marked Siaka's period in office, but, in 1985 CE, as his popularity began to wane, he handed over power to his favored successor Major

General Joseph Momoh. Momoh failed to maintain stability and Sierra Leone faced mounting economic and political problems, including government corruption.

A new problem arose in 1990 CE when rebels from Liberia invaded in an attempt to overthrow Momoh who had favored a West African peacekeeping force to govern wartorn Liberia. The rebels called themselves the Revolutionary United Front (RUF). Led by Corporal Foday Sankoh, they were driven back with support from Guinea and Nigeria, although they later gained strength by recruiting members of the Sierra Leonean army. By the mid-1990s, the RUF controlled many of the country's diamond-mining areas. In 1990 CE, Sierra Leone adopted a new constitution allowing for multiparty elections in 1992 CE. But before elections could be held, Momoh fled the country and was replaced by Captain Valentine Strasser, who led a National Provisional Ruling Council. Strasser was deposed in 1996 CE and elections were held, despite intimidation by the RUF, which wanted the elections delayed. Ahmad Tejan Kabbah was elected president, but a group of junior officers led by Major Johnny Koroma deposed him in 1997 CE. Koroma suspended the constitution and set up an Armed Forces Revolutionary Council.

In 1998 CE, following a Nigerian-led intervention against the military regime, Kabbah returned from exile. However, in 1999 CE, the country was again plunged into civil war. Following a CEasefire, a new government was formed with Foday Sankoh, the RUF leader, as vice-president. Fighting again broke out in 2000 CE, when rival rebel groups struggled for control of the diamond-producing areas. British troops intervened and Sankoh was arrested and accused of war crimes. In an attempt to stop the funding of rebel groups, the UN Security Council imposed a ban on diamonds from Sierra Leone. Another ceasefire was signed in November 2000 CE, when the RUF controlled about two-thirds of the country.

Peoples
CREOLES
The Creoles, or Krio, of Sierra Leone are the descendants of former slaves, who settled in Freetown in the late eighteenth century. Their culture mixes elements of African and European origin and their language–Creole or Krio–has evolved from African languages and English. Freetown was established on the coast of Sierra Leone by freed slaves from Britain,

Mano River Union
A stamp issued in 1974 CE marking the first anniversary of the Mano River Union.

Centre of learning
Fourah Bay College in Freetown (now part of the University of Sierra Leone) was founded in 1827 CE, and has been attended by many notable Creoles.

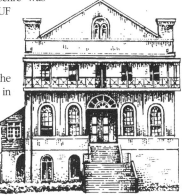

© DIAGRAM

some of whom had European wives. By 1800 CE, they had been joined by former slaves from the then British colony of Nova Scotia in Canada, as well as Maroons–former slaves from Jamaica who had been deported to Nova Scotia after a successful revolt against their owners 100 years earlier. Later still, the British brought Africans from illegal slaving ships to Sierra Leone. Many of these so-called recaptives were of Yoruba descent—*see also* **Nigeria (Peoples—Yoruba)**. By the mid-nineteenth century, this mixture of settlers and recaptives had blended into the distinctive ethnic group now known as the Creoles.

FULANI

For information about the history of the Fulani people, *see* **Fulani states.**

MENDE

Most Mende live in central and southeastern Sierra Leone, though a few also live in western Liberia. During the thirteenth and fourteenth centuries, the ancestors of the Mende lived around the upper reaches of the Niger and Sénégal rivers, in what is now Guinea. These lands formed part of the ancient Empire of Mali. When Mali was in decline in the fifteenth century, the Mende moved slowly south as part of a wave of Mande-speaking migrants who spread across West Africa.

At the beginning of the sixteenth century, according to Mende oral history, a group of Manding (another Mande language) speakers, called the Mani, were exiled from the Empire of Mali. Under their queen, Mansarico, they traveled southwest, finally settling in the Cape Mount area of Liberia around 1540 CE. From there, the Mani conquered much of present-day Sierra Leone, establishing many subkingdoms. The resulting peoples of mixed Mani and local descent formed new ethnic groups, the largest of which was the Mende. In the early eighteenth century, the Mende began migrating west of the Sewa River. They gained control of the southern

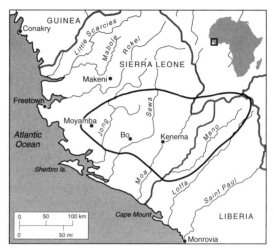

Modern extent of the Mende peoples

half of modern Sierra Leone by the early nineteenth century. However, by 1896 CE, they were conquered by the British. The Mende people were among the most active in the fight for independence from colonial rule, which culminated in 1961 CE when Sierra Leone became independent.

TEMNE

The Temne, Sierra Leone's second largest group, live in the northwest of the country, in the coastal hinterland around Port Loko. Historically, the Temne were ruled by local chiefs and played an important role in the trade with Europeans on the coast at least 500 years ago. In the late eighteenth century, free blacks and former slaves from Britain and Canada settled on the coast of what is now Sierra Leone. The Temne were hostile to the colonists and invaded the colony, nearly destroying it. The British then established a colony in the region and large numbers of freed slaves, the ancestors of the modern Creoles, were settled in the region. Expeditions were launched against the Temne. Since 1991 CE, the Temne have taken part in Sierra Leone's civil war.

Mende attire

This man is wearing the attire of a Mende chief. The shirt has been woven from locally grown cotton and is also richly embroidered; thread for weaving is more likely to be imported than locally produced today.

Sierra Leone's major political figures

Kabbah, Alhaji Ahmad Tejan (1932 CE–)

A former civil servant and diplomat, Kabbah was elected president of Sierra Leone in 1996. He was overthrown in 1997 by a military junta but, in 1998, a Nigerian-led force overthrew the military regime and Kabbah returned to Sierra Leone as president on March 10.

Mende script (below)

The Mende language utilizes the Roman alphabet nowadays, but in the past the language was written in its own script.

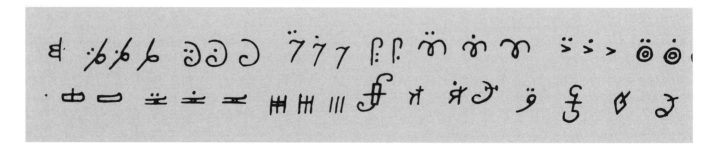

Sierra Leone timeline

Pre 19th century CE
1460 Portuguese navigators explore the coast of present-day Sierra Leone
16th century Ancestors of the modern Mende and Loko peoples arrive in Sierra Leone from the east
1787 Granville Sharp of the Anti-Slavery Society buys land on Cape Sierra Leone for a settlement of freed slaves
1792 The first 400 freed African-American slaves are settled on the site of present-day Freetown

19th century CE
1807 Britain abolishes the slave trade
1808 Britain makes Freetown a crown colony
1815 Britain starts settling slaves freed from captured slave ships at Freetown
1864 The last of over 50,000 freed slaves are settled at Freetown.
1876 The Church Missionary Society founds a teacher training college in Freetown
1896 Inland areas of Sierra Leone become a British protectorate
1898–1899 Bai Buré leads a rebellion of indigenous tribes against British taxes

1900–49 CE
1924 The first elected representatives join the Sierra Leone legislative council

1950–59 CE
1951 Freetown is united with Sierra Leone and the colony is granted internal self-government
1952 Milton Margai becomes prime minister of Sierra Leone

1960–69 CE
1961 Apr 27 Sierra Leone becomes independent with Milton Margai as prime minister
1964 After the death of Margai, political instability sets in
1967 An indecisive general election is followed by a military coup
1968 The military government is overthrown: Siaka Stevens becomes head of government

1970–79 CE
1971 Sierra Leone becomes a republic with Stevens as president
1978 Sierra Leone becomes a one party state

1980–89 CE
1981 The Sierra Leone Labor Congress calls a general strike against government economic policy
1985 Stevens retires and is succeeded by Maj. Gen. Joseph Momoh
1987 The government declares a state of economic emergency

1990–99 CE
1991 Corporal Foday Sankoh leads an uprising against Momoh
1992 Capt. Valentine Strasser overthrows Momoh and cancels planned elections: Sankoh leads a second uprising
1993 The rebels refuse a government offer of a cease-fire and amnesty
1996 Ahmad Tejan Kabbah of the Sierra Leone People's Party is elected president: he signs a peace deal with Sankoh
1997 Maj. Johnny Paul Koromah ousts Kabbah in a military coup
1998 Troops from Nigeria overthrow Koromah and restore Kabbah to power
1999 A peace agreement is signed and Foday Sankoh becomes vice president

Sierra Leone presidents and chairmen

Presidents

Apr 19 1971–Apr 21 1971 CE
Christopher Cole

Apr 21 1971–Nov 28 1985 CE
Siaka Stevens

Nov 28 1985–Apr 30 1992 CE
Joseph Saidu Momoh
Chairman of the national provisional defense council

Apr 30 1992–May 1 1992 CE
Yahya Kanu

Chairmen of the national provisional ruling council (from Jul 1992, supreme council of state) (from May 6 1992 also heads of state)

May 1 1992–Jan 16 1996 CE
Valentine Strasser

Jan 17 1996–Mar 29 1996 CE
Julius Maada Bio

President

Mar 29 1996–May 25 1997 CE
Ahmad Tejan Kabbah (1st time)

Head of the armed forces revolutionary council

May 25 1997–Feb 12 1998 CE
Johnny Paul Koroma

President

Mar 10 1998 CE–
Ahmad Tejan Kabbah (2nd time)

Sir Milton Margai (above)
He was the chief minister of Sierra Leone from 1954–1958 CE, and prime minister from 1958 until his death in 1964 CE.

Siaka Stevens (below)
He became the head of government in Sierra Leone in 1968 CE, and was president from 1969–1985 CE.

Margai, Sir Milton Augustus Stiery (1895–1964 CE)
Milton Margai was chief minister of Sierra Leone from 1954 to 1958, and the country's first prime minister from 1958 until his death in 1964. He was succeeded as prime minister by his half-brother Albert Margai.

Momoh, Joseph Saidu (1937 CE –)
Joseph Momoh became commander of the Sierra Leone army in 1983, and in 1985, he was the sole presidential candidate of Sierra Leone's only political party, the All-People's Congress (APC). Initially popular, Momoh used tough measures to crack down on the corruption that had flourished under his predecessor, Siaka Stevens. He refused to consider adopting multiparty politics, however, and was removed from office in 1992 by a military coup led by Valentine Strasser.

Stevens, Siaka Probyn (1905–1988 CE)
Stevens was active in the struggle for independence in Sierra Leone, but in 1957 he fell out with the main nationalist leader, Milton Margai, and set up the All-People's Congress (APC). He was an opposition leader until the APC won the elections in 1967. The army then seized power and Stevens fled, but in 1968, he returned to become the head of government. From 1969 he served as president until he voluntarily gave up power in 1985.

© DIAGRAM

Sofala

Sofala is an important and historic trading port on the east coast of Africa in what is now Mozambique. It was established by African, Arabian, and Indian settlers several centuries before it was occupied by the Portuguese in 1505 CE. It was an important outlet for gold from the Zambezi River Basin. From Sofala, goods were mostly shipped to Mozambique (a port farther north) and then to Goa, western India. *See also* **Mozambique**.

Sokoto Caliphate

See **Fulani Empire**.

Solomonid empire

A dynasty of kings that claimed descent from King Solomon and Queen Sheba ruled in the central Ethiopian region called Shoa (Shewa or Showa) from the mid-tenth century to the end of the fourteenth century. One of these Christian Amhara kings, Yekuno Amlak (reigned 1270–1285 CE) overthrew the ruler of the Zagwe dynasty, which had taken control of the Christian Axumite kingdom. Yekuno's claim to the throne was supported by influential church officials. Unlike their predecessors, the Zagwes were not of pure "Solomonid" stock, so the succession of Yekuno Amlak was seen as the reinstatement of the true Ethiopian kings. The Solomonid kings established their capital in the Shoa region.

In 1528 CE Shoa was overrun by the Muslim state of Adal, which lay to the east. Adal was defeated by Shoa two years later, however, and incorporated into the Solomonid empire. The base of the empire was moved to Gondar in 1632 CE, and the Shoan kings lost control of the empire as Muslim Oromo peoples increasingly migrated into their land. In the late eighteenth century the highlands broke up into feudal states and the southern regions were ruled by Muslim Oromo people. For the succeeding centuries the Shoa region was dominated by Oromo people until, in 1856 CE, it was reincorporated into the Ethiopian Empire being reestablished by Tewodros (Theodore) II (reigned 1855–1868 CE). His successor, Yohannes IV (reigned 1872–1889 CE) stopped Egyptian and Mahdist expansion into Ethiopia. In 1889 CE a Shoan king, Menelik II, was made Emperor of Ethiopia. The empire expanded under Menelik II, and succeeded in keeping his country free of European rule. After Ethiopia defeated the Italians at the Battle of Adowa in 1896 CE, Menelik signed treaties with the European countries that had colonies surrounding his empire. *See also* **Axum; Ethiopia**.

The Solomonid empire

From the middle of the tenth until the end of the fourteenth centuries, a dynasty of kings that claimed descent from Solomon and Sheba ruled the central Ethiopian region of Shoa. Documents dating from the fourth century CE reveal the story that Solomon, the ruler of Israel, fell in love with Sheba, an Ethiopian, when she visited Jerusalem at a time when Israel was at the height of its power. When she returned to her own country, she gave birth to a son whom the Ethiopians claim was their first king, called Menelik I.

Solomon and Sheba (right)
A modern manuscript from Ethiopia depicts Solomon and Sheba telling riddles to each other. Solomon was known as the wisest person of his time, and Sheba is said to have been suitably impressed by his erudition.

King Yohannes IV (left)
Yohannes served as the King of Ethiopia from 1871–1879 CE. He defeated Egyptian invaders in 1875–76 CE; the Italians in 1887 CE; and was killed in 1897 CE while trying to repel a Dervish attack on the border with Sudan.

Seltan Sagad Susenyos (left)
He was Emperor of Ethiopia from 1605 –1632 CE. He is shown here at an official reception for the Patriarch Mendes, a high-ranking member of the Jesuit religious order.

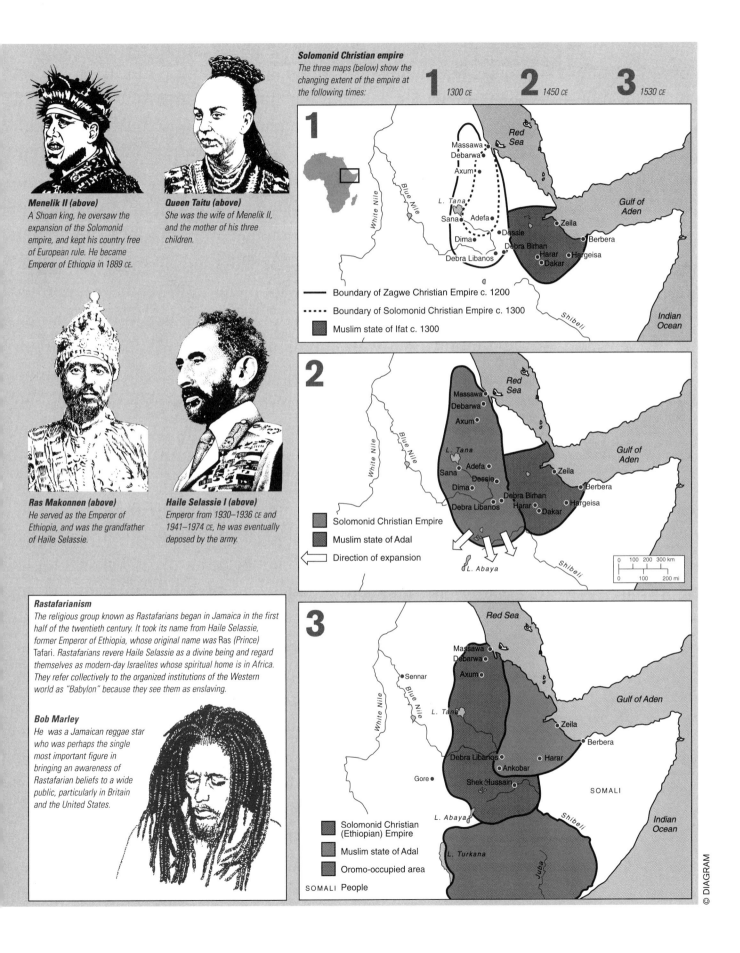

Menelik II (above)
A Shoan king, he oversaw the expansion of the Solomonid empire, and kept his country free of European rule. He became Emperor of Ethiopia in 1889 CE.

Queen Taitu (above)
She was the wife of Menelik II, and the mother of his three children.

Ras Makonnen (above)
He served as the Emperor of Ethiopia, and was the grandfather of Haile Selassie.

Haile Selassie I (above)
Emperor from 1930–1936 CE and 1941–1974 CE, he was eventually deposed by the army.

Rastafarianism
The religious group known as Rastafarians began in Jamaica in the first half of the twentieth century. It took its name from Haile Selassie, former Emperor of Ethiopia, whose original name was Ras (Prince) Tafari. Rastafarians revere Haile Selassie as a divine being and regard themselves as modern-day Israelites whose spiritual home is in Africa. They refer collectively to the organized institutions of the Western world as "Babylon" because they see them as enslaving.

Bob Marley
He was a Jamaican reggae star who was perhaps the single most important figure in bringing an awareness of Rastafarian beliefs to a wide public, particularly in Britain and the United States.

Solomonid Christian empire
The three maps (below) show the changing extent of the empire at the following times:

1 1300 CE   **2** 1450 CE   **3** 1530 CE

1
— Boundary of Zagwe Christian Empire c. 1200
···· Boundary of Solomonid Christian Empire c. 1300
▨ Muslim state of Ifat c. 1300

2
▨ Solomonid Christian Empire
▨ Muslim state of Adal
⇦ Direction of expansion

3
▨ Solomonid Christian (Ethiopian) Empire
▨ Muslim state of Adal
▨ Oromo-occupied area
SOMALI People

© DIAGRAM

SOMALIA Somali Democratic Republic

At the time of ancient Egypt, the Somali coast probably formed part of the region known as Punt, which produced incense and perfumes. Between the seventh and tenth centuries CE, Arabs and Persians founded trading stations along the northern and eastern coasts. But the European exploration of the interior, which had been occupied by Somali people for around 1,100 years, did not begin until the mid-nineteenth century. Britain established a protectorate (colony) in what is now northern Somalia between 1884–1886 CE. while Italy made southern Somalia a colony between 1889–1905 CE. Italian influence included the Ogaden region, which was occupied by Somali people, but in 1897 CE the Italians ceded this region to Ethiopia. The colonizers met with resistance, especially in northern Ethiopia in the early twentieth century.

In 1936 CE, Italy, under its dictator Benito Mussolini, invaded Ethiopia and, for a few years, Italian Somaliland was ruled from Ethiopia's capital, Addis Ababa. In 1940, during World War II, Italy also invaded British Somaliland. However, in 1941 CE, British forces defeated the Italians, driving them out of Ethiopia and British Somaliland, and occupying Italian Somaliland, where a British military administration was set up. In 1950 CE, the UN asked Italy to return to eastern Africa and prepare Italian Somaliland for independence within ten years. British Somaliland became independent on June 26 CE, 1960 CE and, on July 1, 1960, it united with the former Italian Somaliland. The two territories together formed the independent Republic of Somalia.

Africa General Service Medal
A medal issued from 1902–04 CE with a bar honoring Somaliland.

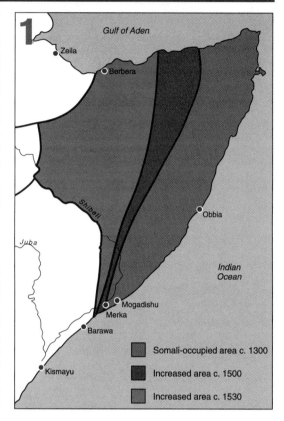

Somali expansion
From 1526 CE the Somalis allied with Muslim Adal in a holy war against Christian Ethiopia. The defeat of Adal by Ethiopia in 1543 CE allowed the Somalis to expand into its territory and that of other Muslim provinces. By the seventeenth century the Somalis controlled the region from Zeila to Barawa. They expanded as far as the Tana River in modern-day Kenya before they were halted by European colonialists in 1909 CE.

The maps show the extent of expansion at the following dates:

1 *1530 CE* **3** *1909 CE*

2 *c.1600 CE*

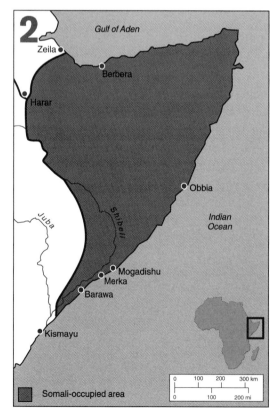

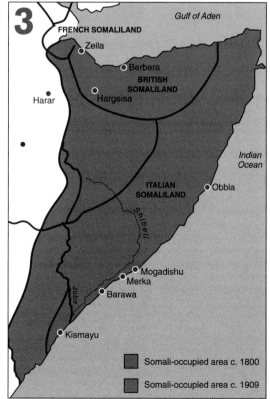

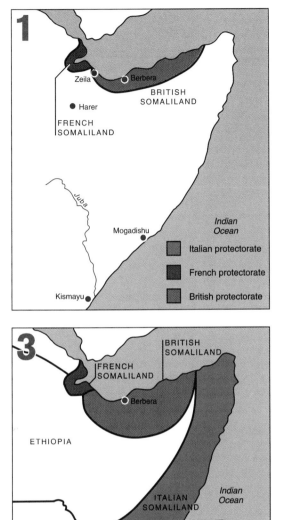

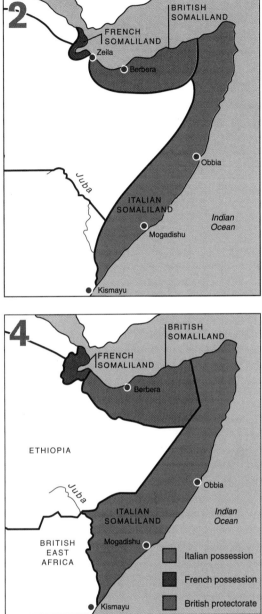

Colonial expansion in East Africa

European exploration of the interior of Somaliland began in the middle of the nineteenth century. Britain established a protectorate in northern Somalia between 1884–86 CE, while Italy made southern Somalia a colony between 1889–1905 CE. Italian influence extended into the Ogaden region, but in 1897 CE the Italians ceded this region to Ethiopia. The colonizers met with resistance, especially in the north of the country in the early years of the twentieth century.

The maps show the extent of expansion of these three colonial powers at the following dates:

1 *1885 CE*   **3** *1892 CE*

2 *1889 CE*   **4** *1908 CE*

Governor L. Lagarde
A stamp issued in 1938 CE when Somalia was under Italian control.

Recent history

Somalia's first president, Aden Abdullah Osman, supported the creation of a Greater Somalia, including Djibouti, the Ogaden (Somali-speaking) region of Ethiopia, and a slice of territory in northeastern Kenya. In 1967 CE, Osman resigned, following a clan conflict, and was succeeded by Abder-Rashid Shermarke, the former prime minister. Shermarke rejected Osman's confrontational policy and stressed the right of self-determination for Somalis everywhere. But tensions between the south and north mounted and, in 1969 CE, the army, led by Major General Muhammad Siad Barre staged a coup and abolished parliament. Shermarke was assassinated and Somalia, which from 1976 was a one-party state, came under Barre's personal control.

Due to Somalia's strategic importance, Barre received foreign economic and military support, at first from the

former Soviet Union, and later from the United States. The weapons that these superpowers poured into the region enabled Somalia and Ethiopia to enter into disastrous wars with each other in 1964 CE and again in 1977 CE. It also helped to create a "gun culture" in the country and provided Barre with the means to persecute rival clans. The late 1970s were marked by food shortages caused by drought. In the late 1980s, Barre met with organized opposition and, with the end of the Cold War, the United States ceased to support him. In January 1991 CE, Mogadishu fell to rebels and Barre was deposed and fled the country.

The rebels created political chaos and civil conflict caused great destruction in the south. Meanwhile, in the north, the Somali National Movement announced its secession from Somalia and declared itself the independent "Somaliland Republic". However, this

Royal visit
A 1967 CE stamp marking the visit of King Faisal of Saudi Arabia.

secessionist state has never received recognition internationally. Somalia's civil and political institutions collapsed, with opposition leaders unable to exert control. Into this power vacuum stepped armed factions, loosely allied to clans or subclans. The largest of the factions was led by led by General Muhammad Farah Aidid, who did much to undermine attempts to restore order. The breakdown of order in Somalia led to famine and, with food deliveries from abroad interrupted by armed gangs, the UN attempted unsuccessfully to impose order between 1992–1995 CE. By the turn of the twenty-first century, a fragile peace had returned, but the country was effectively divided into three parts: the divided south; the northeast, called Puntland; and the northern "Somaliland Republic".

In 2000 CE, some hope emerged when a peace conference held in Djibouti established a three-year transitional Assembly to operate in Mogadishu. The new president was Abdikassim Salad Hassan, but the new institution applied only to the south. The northeast promised that it would rejoin a reconstituted Somalia, but the north seemed likely to remain a separate entity.

Child soldiers
During Somalia's long civil war, arms poured in from both the former USSR and US, creating a culture of violence in which even children were involved.

Peoples

ISSA

For information about the history of the Issa, *see* **Djibouti (Peoples—Issa)**.

SOMALIS

Most Somalis live in Somalia, but smaller groups are found in Djibouti, Ethiopia, and Kenya. Because of the political turbulence in the 1980s and 1990s, many Somalis have sought refuge in neighboring countries, as well as in Yemen, Saudi Arabia, Italy, and Britain.

The origins of the Somalis are uncertain. However, by 1000 CE, the area that is now Somalia was home to Cushitic people who had migrated from the Ethiopian Highlands. These people developed close contacts with Arabs and Persians who had settled along the coast. Through marriage and cultural and commercial ties, the Somali people gradually emerged from these groups. Between the eleventh and thirteenth centuries, the Somalis converted to Islam. During this period, their influential clans (several extended families who claim descent from a common ancestor or ancestors) originated. According to tradition, the founding fathers of the clans were related to the prophet Muhammad and came from Arabia. By 1500 CE, Somalis were raiding eastern Ethiopia, where they pushed the Oromo people out of the Ogaden region, and were expanding southward. They gradually consolidated their position but, in the late nineteenth century, Britain, France, Italy, and Ethiopia divided Somali territory into separate areas. In recent times, Somalia has been divided into three main areas: the "Somaliland Republic" in the north, Puntland in the northeast, and southern Somalia, which has been beset by clan rivalries. In 2000 CE, a transitional Assembly was set up in Mogadishu, in the south, though clan warlords refused to recognize its authority.

The Ethiopian Somalis, backed by the Somali government, have agitated for union with Somalia for many years, but armed resistance to Ethiopia ended in 1988 CE. The situation improved in 1994 CE, when the Ethiopian government established a Somali state within the republic. Kenya's Somalis have often found themselves used as political pawns between the Kenyan and Somali governments. The situation improved in 1981 CE, when Somalia's president Muhammad Siad Barre renounced his claim to northeastern Kenya. However, in 1989, the Kenyans accused Somalis of poaching elephants. Thousands of Somalis were evicted from areas around game parks, while others had their Kenyan nationality questioned.

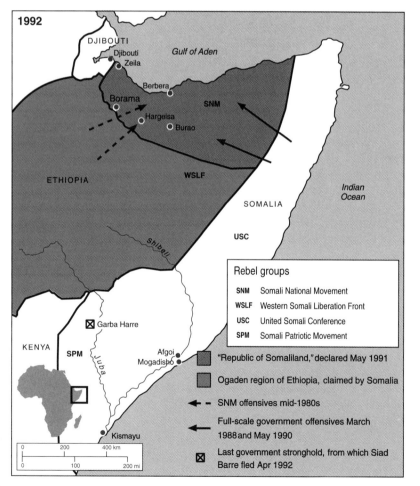

Rebel groups

SNM	Somali National Movement
WSLF	Western Somali Liberation Front
USC	United Somali Conference
SPM	Somali Patriotic Movement

"Republic of Somaliland," declared May 1991

Ogaden region of Ethiopia, claimed by Somalia

SNM offensives mid-1980s

Full-scale government offensives March 1988 and May 1990

Last government stronghold, from which Siad Barre fled Apr 1992

Somali Civil War
Following a coup in 1969 CE, Somalia was ruled by the Supreme Revolutionary Council, headed by Major General Siad Barre. Famine, war with Ethiopia, and internal strife led, in 1981 CE, to civil war. The Somali National Movement declared a "Republic of Somaliland" in northern Somalia, which has yet to be recognized by the international community. Other rebel groups emerged towards the end of the 1980s. Siad Barre fled in 1992 CE, but the existence of 15 opposing factions has made consensus difficult to achieve. The map (left) shows the situation in Somalia in 1992. The internal conflict continues to this day.

Somalia timeline

Pre 19th century
c. 1400 BCE Egyptian trading expeditions reach the Somali coast
c. 750 CE The Somalis settle the north of modern Somalia
920 The Omani Arabs capture Mogadishu
11th century CE The Somalis convert to Islam
13th century Somali kingdom of Ifat (later Adal) develops in the northwest
16th century The Somalis have settled most of modern Somalia
1506–1542 Ahmed Gran of the Somali kingdom of Adal occupies most of Ethiopia
1543 Ahmed Gran is killed in battle with a Portuguese-Ethiopian army

19th century CE
1870 Egypt occupies northern Somalia
1871 Mogadishu comes under the control of the sultan of Zanzibar
1877 Egypt withdraws from Somalia
1884-1886 Britain establishes a protectorate in northern Somalia
1885 The Somalis defeat the Gallas of eastern Ethiopia
1889-1905 Southern Somalia becomes an Italian colony
1892 The sultan of Zanzibar leases Mogadishu to Italy (and sells it outright in 1905)
1897 Italy cedes the Somali Ogaden to Ethiopia
1899–1920 Mohammad Abdullah Hassan wages an intermittent guerrilla war against the British

1900–49 CE
1912 The British build border posts to halt Somali infiltration into Kenya
1936 After Italy conquers Ethiopia, Italian Somaliland is ruled from Addis Ababa
1940 Italy occupies British Somaliland
1941 Britain recaptures British Somaliland and occupies Italian Somaliland

1950–59 CE
1950 The UN returns Italian Somaliland to Italy for a ten year period to prepare it for independence

1960–69 CE
1960 Jun 26 British Somaliland becomes independent
1960 Jul 1 The two Somali territories unite to form the independent republic of Somalia
1969 President Shermarke is assassinated during a military coup: Maj. Gen. Mohammad Siad Barre becomes president

1970–79 CE
1974 War breaks out between Somalia and Ethiopia over the Ogaden region
1976 Siad Barre sets up the Somali Revolutionary Socialist Party as the only legal political party
1977 Somalia occupies the Ogaden
1978 Ethiopia recovers the Ogaden
1979 Drought results in food shortages

1980–89 CE
1980 US is granted the use of a naval base at Berbera
1988 Somalia and Ethiopia sign a peace treaty
1989 Anti-government rioting breaks out in Mogadishu

1990–99 CE
1991 The rebel United Somali Congress overthrows the military government and captures Mogadishu. Civil war breaks out between rival clans and in the north the Somali National Movement declares the independent Somaliland republic
1992 A US-led force arrives to secure the distribution of food aid after famine breaks out
1993 May A UN peace keeping force is sent into Somalia
1993 Jun Warlord Gen. Mohammad Farah Aidid attacks Pakistani UN peace keepers
1993 Oct A bungled attempt to capture Aidid leaves 18 US soldiers and hundreds of Somali civilians dead
1994 Mar US troops are withdrawn from Somalia
1995 Remaining UN forces pull out after the peace settlement fails. Aidid pronounces himself president
1996 Gen. Aidid is killed fighting a rival faction
1997 The UN begins a new aid program after southern Somalia is devastated by floods
1998 Rival clan leaders declare their commitment to peace and unity

Somalia's major political figures

Osman, Aden Abdullah (1908 CE–)
Osman became the first president of Somalia when British Somaliland and Italian Somaliland were united in 1960. He served until 1967, when he resigned. Osman supported the concept of a "Greater Somalia," which would unite all territory occupied by Somali-speaking people, including Djibouti, and parts of Ethiopia and Kenya.

Siad Barre, Muhammad (1919 CE–)
Muhammad Siad Barre became president of Somalia in 1969, following a military coup. His rule was marked by civil war and war with Ethiopia, and he was overthrown by rebel forces in January 1991.

Abdar-Rashid Shermarke
A former prime minister and president, he stressed the right of self-determination for Somalis everywhere, but was assassinated in a military coup in 1969 CE.

© DIAGRAM

Sankoré Mosque
The Sankoré Mosque in Timbuktu was built by the Muslim kings of Mali. It became the center of Islamic worship during the era of the Songhay Empire, and West Africa's first university was established within its walls. Built of mud bricks, it is the oldest surviving mosque in West Africa.

Songhai

See **Songhay empire**.

Songhay empire

The Songhay empire was a powerful trading state of West Africa. It was based around the middle parts of the Niger River, in what is now Mali. At its height, it extended west to the Atlantic Ocean and covered parts of Niger and Nigeria in the east. Songhay was originally a small state founded by the Songhay people c.750 CE. It lay on the Niger River across an important trading route and had its capital at Gao. About 1240 CE, the Mali empire absorbed Songhay, but it had regained its freedom by the 1340s. Songhay rose to greatness during the 28-year reign of Sunni Ali (reigned 1464–92 CE). He began by seizing Timbuktu from the Tuareg, who had wrested it from Mali. Four years later he captured Jenne, previously part of the Mali empire. Be the time of his death, Sunni Ali had made Songhay the most powerful empire in west Africa. Songhay reached the height of its power during the reign of Askia Muhammad (1493–1528 CE). He was a devout Muslim who organized his large empire into provinces, each with a governor. Through military might and religious zeal, Songhay remained powerful until 1591 CE, when Moroccans conquered it. In 1618 CE the Moroccans set up a puppet state in Songhay, which was governed by the rulers of Timbuktu. This state lasted until 1787 CE, when it was taken over by the Tuareg.

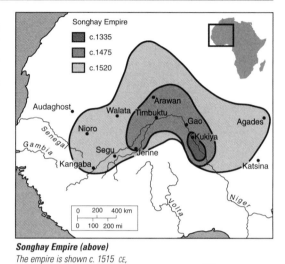

Songhay Empire (above)
The empire is shown c. 1515 CE, when it took over much of historic Mali's former territories.

Tomb of a mighty ruler (right)
The tomb of Askia Muhammad of Songhay still survives. This is a view of the exterior.

Soudain

Soudain was the French name for the French Sudan, now the independent republic of Mali. *See also* **French Sudan**; **Mali**.

SOUTH AFRICA Republic of South Africa

South Africa's first known inhabitants were the ancestors of the Khoisan people, who lived by hunting and gathering plant foods. However, from around 1,700 years ago, Bantu-speaking people from the north began to arrive in southern Africa. These farming people, who used iron tools, gradually displaced the indigenous people.

Portuguese mariners reached the coast of present-day South Africa in 1488 CE, but the first settlement was established in 1657 CE by the Dutch East India Company on the site of modern Cape Town. The settlement was a supply station for Dutch ships. But Dutch people called Boers (farmers), and later Afrikaners, began to settle and work the land. British forces occupied the Cape in 1795 CE and, in 1814 CE, the Netherlands ceded the territory known as Cape Colony to Britain.

Many Boers resented British rule and, from 1836 CE, many of them joined the Great Trek into the interior. There, they met with opposition from the Bantu-speaking peoples, but they established new states in Natal, Orange Free State, and Transvaal. Britain annexed Natal in 1843 CE, but it recognized the independence of Transvaal in 1852 CE and Orange Free State in 1854 CE. Rivalries between the Afrikaners and the British were heightened when diamonds, gold and other valuable

Anniversary
A stamp issued in 1986 CE to mark the twenty-fifth anniversary of the Republic of South Africa,

'The Cape of Storms'
In 1488 CE, the Portuguese sailor Bartholomeu Dias and his crew were the first Europeans to round the Cape of Good Hope, which Dias named the Cape of Storms. King John of Portugal later renamed it the Cape of Good Hope because its discovery indicated that a sea route to India would, hopefully, soon be found.

mineral deposits were discovered in the interior. Anglo-Boer wars were fought in 1880–1881 CE and 1899–1902 CE. Britain was finally victorious and, in 1910 CE, it united the four territories (Cape Colony, Natal, Orange Free State, and Transvaal) to form the Union of South Africa, a self-governing country in the British Empire.

Indigenous communities

From a very early date (c.2600 BCE and probably before), southern Africa was inhabited by communities of Khoikhoi pastoralists and San hunter-gatherers (the Khoisan). Gradually, Bantu-speaking peoples using iron-and copper-based technology spread into southern Africa between the fourth and eighth centuries CE. They settled as specific groups and some formed states. For example, the Rozwi, a Karanga people, had destroyed the Mutapa Empire, settled in Shona lands, and created the powerful Changamire state in the seventeenth century.

The gold trade between the interior and the east coast was first dominated by the Arabs, who had settled on the east coast in the tenth century, and then by the Portuguese from c.1506 CE. The Dutch began to settle the Cape of Good Hope in 1652 CE. They did not begin to make a truly harmful impact on the indigenous communities until the 1770s.

The map (right) shows the locations of the peoples, states and kingdoms in Southern Africa c.1790 CE.

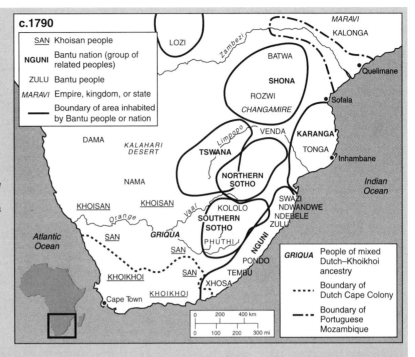

c.1790

SAN	Khoisan people
NGUNI	Bantu nation (group of related peoples)
ZULU	Bantu people
MARAVI	Empire, kingdom, or state
———	Boundary of area inhabited by Bantu people or nation

GRIQUA	People of mixed Dutch–Khoikhoi ancestry
······	Boundary of Dutch Cape Colony
–·–·–	Boundary of Portuguese Mozambique

The Coldstream Stone
Painted 2,000 years ago by a Khoisan artisan, this quartzite stone was excavated from Coldstream Cave on the southern Cape coast. It was found placed on the shoulder of a skeleton and is thought to have played a role in funeral rites.

Bushman rock art
Roughly 27,000 years ago, Bushman rock art was created throughout Southern Africa at around 15,000 different sites. The painting (left) probably shows a group of hunters. The painting (above) is relatively recent (probably from within the last 1,500 years) as the larger people on the right of the scene are most likely Bantu-speaking herders, who did not appear in Southern Africa until the first millennium CE. It seems the Bushmen (in the center of the scene) have stolen cattle from the herders.

Recent history

In 1912 CE, African opposition to white rule in South Africa was expressed in the formation of the African National Congress (ANC). Another significant event was the formation of the National Party in 1914 CE. This party was set up to protect the interests of the Afrikaners, who still resented the British victory in the Second Boer War.

In World War I, South Africa occupied Southwest Africa (now Namibia) and, after the war, the League of Nations mandated South Africa to rule the territory (*see also* **Namibia**). South Africa also fought alongside the

Expansion in Southern Africa
The first settlement by a colonial power was set up in 1657 CE by The Dutch East India Company on the site of modern Cape Town. British forces occupied the Cape in 1795 CE and, in 1814 CE, the Netherlands ceded the territory known as Cape Colony to Britain. The maps show the situation in the region at the following dates:

1 *1652–1700 CE* **2** *1700–1750 CE* **3** *1795 CE* **4** *1835*

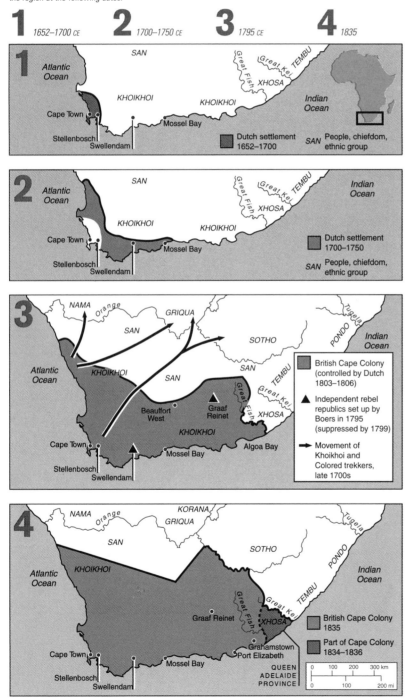

Allies against Germany in World War II. In 1948 CE, the National Party won power in the parliamentary elections, in which the voters were all white. Under prime minister Daniel Malan, the National Party introduced apartheid (the racist doctrine of "separate development"). The ANC, together with other black, Colored, Asian, and white liberal groups, strongly opposed the discriminatory laws introduced by the National Party and international opposition began to mount. In 1961 CE, South Africa, stung by the widespread criticisms, became a republic and left the Commonwealth (a free association of independent countries which had formerly been part of the British Empire).

In 1984 CE, South Africa set up a three-house parliament, with one house each for the whites, Coloreds, and Asians. Blacks had no part in this new constitution. They were supposed to vote in their "homelands," some of which were given "independence." However, this independence was fictional and never recognized outside South Africa. Pressure on South Africa mounted when the Commonwealth, the European Community, and the United States imposed sanctions which damaged South Africa's economy.

In 1989 CE, Frederik Willem de Klerk was elected president, and he began talks with the ANC. In 1990 CE, Namibia was made independent, while, in South Africa, de Klerk legalized the ANC. The government then released the ANC's leader, Nelson Mandela, who had been imprisoned since 1962 CE. Apartheid laws were repealed and a new constitution was approved by a referendum in 1992 CE. In 1994 CE, South Africa held its first nonracial elections. The ANC won a majority and Nelson Mandela became president. Mandela's leadership was marked by his policies of "reconciliation" between former enemies and ethnic groups and his moderation isolated extremists on the right and left.

In 1999 CE, Mandela retired as president and, following parliamentary elections in which the ANC won 66.4 percent of the votes, Thabo Mbeki succeeded Mandela and became president. Mbeki faced many problems, including the continuing poverty experienced by most of the black population, the high crime rate, and the high incidence of HIV and AIDS–in 2000 CE, a UN report stated nearly 10 percent of the country's population was infected.

Peoples

AFRIKANERS

In 1652 CE, the Dutch East India Company founded a garrison and supply station on the Cape of Good Hope for ships sailing between Holland and Asia. In 1688 CE, 156 French Protestant refugees (Huguenots) arrived in the Cape. The Company encouraged the establishment of farms around Cape Town to supply the garrison and passing ships. The African-born children of the settlers became known as "Afrikaners"–the first recorded use of the term was in 1707 CE. Until the early nineteenth century, "Afrikaner" carried few racial connotations, being applied to people of mixed European, African, and Malay origin, as well as those of sole European ancestry. Later, the term was used for 'Whites", with people of mixed ancestry being designated "Coloreds". Many Afrikaners are descendants of interracial unions, although few admit that this is so.

Over the years, tension developed between the Dutch authorities and the Boers (the Dutch word for "farmer" and the historical name for the Afrikaners). Many farmers moved inland to escape what they felt was oppressive rule. In the interior, away from Dutch East India Company influence, the Afrikaners became a distinct group. In 1806 CE, the British took permanent control of Cape Town. Unwilling to live under British rule, many more Afrikaners journeyed north and east into the interior in the Great Trek of the 1830s. These migrants, the *Voortrekkers*, met with fierce resistance from Bantu-speaking peoples. Many battles between the Boers and the indigenous people took place. Boer victories in these battles are still celebrated by the Boers' descendants as proof of divine intervention. The 1838 CE victory at Blood River, when 500 Boers defeated 10,000 Zulu, is especially remembered and is claimed to the result of a pact with God–although the pact was never mentioned until after the event.

The *Voortrekkers* established independent republics that became Transvaal, Orange Free State, and Natalia. The British annexed these republics, but later returned them to independence, except for Natalia which became Natal. In 1886 CE, gold was discovered in Transvaal, leading to the arrival of thousands of fortune seekers. When the British sent troops into Transvaal, they met with fierce resistance, resulting in the Anglo-Boer War (1899-1902 CE). Even today, bitterness towards the British remains about the loss of some 7,000 men in battle, and of the 18,000 to 28,000 women and children who died in British concentration camps.

In 1948 CE, the National Party came to power in South Africa–mainly thanks to the support of poor and rural Afrikaners. Apartheid (the racial doctrine of "separate development") was the government's main political platform, while many of its ideals were inspired by

Trekboers (above)
A group of Afrikaner farmers (Boers) is shown, accompanied by their Khoikhoi herdsmen and herds of sheep and cattle. During the eighteenth century, such trekboers *(migrant farmers) led the colonization of areas inland as they moved farther away from the Cape in search of new pastures.*

Stephanus du Toit (left)
He was a leading exponent of Afrikaner nationalism, which was based on developing a common language, religion, and history. His pioneering treatise, History of Our Land in the Dialect of Our People, *was published in 1877 CE.*

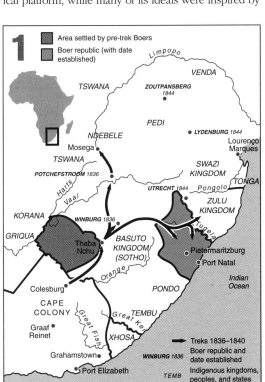

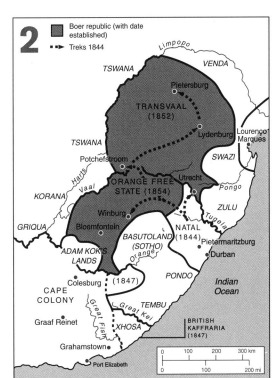

The Boer Republics
In 1814 CE the Netherlands ceded the territory know as Cape Colony to Britain. Many Boers resented British rule and, from 1836 CE, joined the Great Trek into the interior. Despite opposition from the Bantu-speaking peoples, they established new states in Natal, Orange Free State and Transvaal. Britain annexed Natal in 1843 CE, but it recognized the independence of Transvaal in 1852 CE, and Orange Free State in 1854 CE. The two maps show the situation in the region at the following dates:

1 *1836–44 CE*

2 *1854 CE*

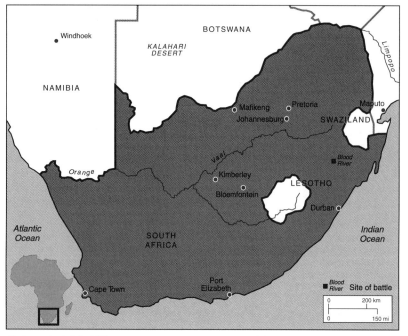

Modern extent of the Afrikaner peoples

Nazi Germany. Most Afrikaners supported apartheid, but some were fierce critics and joined nonracial churches, the illegal Communist Party, or the African National Congress (ANC). Branded as traitors, some were forced into exile, imprisoned, or put under house arrest.

In 1991 CE, a reformed National Party government ended all apartheid laws and, in 1994 CE, South Africa's first nonracial elections were held, bringing to an end Afrikaner-dominated rule. However, Afrikaners consider themselves to be Africans and, in the immediate future, they are likely to remain an economically privileged minority in South Africa.

ASIANS

In 1996 CE, Asians made up about 2.6 percent of the population of South Africa. The ancestors of the Asian community began to arrive in 1860 CE, when Indians were brought to the country to work on the sugar plantations in Natal and, even today, about 75 percent of Asians are found in the province of KwaZulu-Natal, with the remainder concentrated in the Johannesburg-Pretoria area.

Mohandas Karamchand Gandhi

An Indian lawyer, Gandhi came to South Africa at the end of the nineteenth century and stayed until 1914. CE By using peaceful means of resistance, such as boycotts and civil disobedience, he highlighted the often ridiculous and illogical nature of racial laws. His tactics were adopted by many later civil rights movements. Gandhi returned to India in 1914 CE and led the campaign for independence there.

By 1911 CE, when the recruitment of Indian laborers was suspended, about 152,000 Indians had arrived in South Africa. Besides the sugar plantations, Indians were also contracted to work in the mines, on the railroads, and on tea plantations, often enduring slavelike conditions. Contracts were for five years, followed by an additional two years. After a further five years as "free" workers, laborers were given the choice of a free passage to India, or of remaining in South Africa with a small land grant. Most of the immigrants were men, but one-third were women–to the objection of many white settlers who argued that this might encourage the creation of a stable Indian community..

Most Indians arrived in South Africa on contracts, but about ten percent were there at their own expense.

Indian South Africans' timeline			
1652 CE Dutch garrison established on the Cape of Good Hope	**1910** Boers and British form white-ruled Union of South Africa	**1949** Rioting South Africans attack Indian businesses	**1983** Separate House of Representation established for Indian voters
1806 British annex Cape Colony	**1911** Recruitment of indentured laborers suspended	**1950** Population Registration Act restricts people to certain jobs and areas according to their officially-designated "race"	**1984–1989** Many people refuse to vote in elections for new House
1843 British annex Natal (present-day KwaZulu/Natal)	**1914** Gandhi leaves South Africa		**1991** End of all apartheid legislation
1860 First indentured (contract) laborers arrive from south Asia	**1934** South Africa approves independence from Britain	**1952** Indian and other antiapartheid movements organize the nonviolent Defiance Campaign	**1994** First nonracial elections held
1893 Mohandas K. Gandhi arrives in South Africa from India	**1946** Asiatic Land Tenure Act	**1961** South Africa accepts Indians as legitimate citizens	**1996** New constitution adopted
	1948 Apartheid officially introduced		**1999** Second multiracial elections result in massive victory for the ANC

Sikh soldier (left)
This late nineteenth-century Sikh soldier was a member of the British colonial army. His uniform of black, yellow, and white was intended to express racial harmony, though by this time racist polices were in effect in many parts of white-ruled Southern Africa.

Soofie Mosque (below)
This beautiful mosque is a fine example of Islamic architecture in Southern Africa.

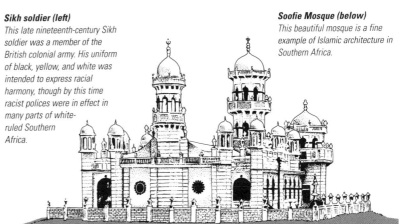

Modern extent of the South African Asian peoples

Cape Malays at prayer (below)
Most Cape Malays are Muslim, their religion being the prime factor that distinguishes them from the Cape Colored population. As required by Islam, Cape Malays typically dress in what they consider to be a "modest" manner, the severity of interpretation of which is a matter of personal choice. Women generally wear long dresses or skirts, long sleeves and a headscarf. Men dress as other urban South Africans though many wear a fez (a brimless felt hat) or a small, white prayer cap.

Most of them were traders from Gujarat in western India. These often wealthy immigrants–known as "Passengers"–formed an elite group that campaigned vigorously for political and civil rights, but their economic strength often undermined the few advances ex-indentured (contracted) laborers were making. In 1893 CE, a young Indian lawyer. Mohandas Karamchand Gandhi, arrived in South Africa to work in what was then Transvaal. It was in South Africa that Gandhi–the founder of the Indian independence movement—developed and first practiced nonviolent resistance and civil disobedience. Within a few years, Gandhi was regarded as an important leader of Indian South Africans, though he essentially represented the interests of the "Passengers."

In 1946 CE, just as Indians were gaining political and economic strength in South Africa, the Asiatic Land Tenure Act was introduced, restricting where they could live and trade. The 1948 CE electoral victory of the Afrikaner-dominated Nation Party led to even more restrictions on Indians. Indians–whether born in South Africa or not–were officially regarded as immigrants. "Repatriation" was official policy, and the limited parliamentary representation held by Indians ceased. The following year, rioting by Zulus directed at Indian businesses resulted in 142 deaths, but led to an agreement between Indian and other civil rights movementsthe African National Congress and Natal Indian congresses–to coordinate their resistance to apartheid, the racist doctrine of "separate development."

In 1961 CE, the South African government officially accepted Indians as a permanent part of the country's population. In 1983 CE, in an attempt to divide apartheid's opponents, a new constitution was introduced giving "Colored" people and Indians limited parliamentary representation. However, in the following year's elections, only 18 percent of Indians voted. The 1989 CE elections were also boycotted. The abolition of apartheid laws in 1991 CE led to all South Africans being given the right to vote, regardless of race and, in 1994 CE, South Africa celebrated its first nonracial elections.

CAPE COLORED AND MALAY

Of the 3,600,000 people of mixed origin in South Africa, about 3,050,000 live in the provinces of Western Cape, Eastern Cape, and Northern Cape. Most of them are of Cape Colored ancestry, although many South Africans reject the term "Cape Colored" believing the term to be a legacy of apartheid. Others feel that the Cape Colored people do form a genuine group that has developed over time a rich cultural and ethnic heritage

Cape Colored and Cape Malays' timeline			
25,000 BCE Oldest examples of Khoisan rock art in Southern Africa	**1807** British ban slave trade	**1934** South Africa approves independence from Britain	**1983** Separate House of Representation given to Cape Colored voters
c. 400s Some Khoisan begin to keep livestock: Khoikhoi emerge	**1819–1839** Mfecane/Difaqane: period of mass migrations and wars	**1948** Apartheid officially introduced	**1984–1989** Many people refuse to vote in elections for new House
1652 CE Dutch garrison established on the Cape of Good Hope. Dutch and Khoikhoi mix	**1833** British abolish slavery	**1949** Second Immorality Act bans interracial marriages	**1991** Apartheid legislation repealed
1600s–1800s African and Asian slaves brought to Cape; Cape Colored population emerges	**1910** Boers and British form white-ruled Union of South Africa	**1950** Population Registration Act	**1994** First nonracial elections held
1806 British annex Cape Colony	**1927** First Immorality Act bans extramarital intercourse between "Europeans" and "natives"	**1951** Colored voting rights removed	**1996** New constitution adopted
		1961 South Africa becomes a republic; leaves Commonwealth	**1999** Second multiracial elections held

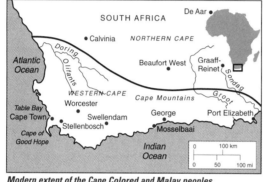

Modern extent of the Cape Colored and Malay peoples

first known inhabitants of southern Africa, the Khoisan probably originated in what are now western Zimbabwe and northern Botswana, where they lived as hunter-gatherers in widely scattered bands at least 20,000 years ago. Around 2,300 years ago, some Khoisan in northern Botswana began to keep livestock. Over the course of generations, these people migrated south, reaching the Cape about 2,000 years ago and gradually developed into the pastoralist (livestock-rais-

that is completely individual. Cape Malays are of mixed Malay, Indian, Sinhalese, Arab, Madagascan, and Chinese origin. Most of the 90,000 or so Cape Malays live in or around Cape Town.

In 1652 CE, the Dutch East India Company founded Cape Town as a garrison and supply station for ships sailing between Holland and Asia. Relationships between Dutch sailors and Khoikhoi women were common (*see also* **Khoisan**, below). During the seventeenth and eighteenth centuries, slaves were introduced into the region from Asia and other parts of Africa. Interracial marriages were common and the Cape Colored and Cape Malay peoples gradually emerged from this mix. By the late nineteenth century, the Cape Coloreds formed a distinct group. Like other nonwhite people, the Cape Coloreds suffered under apartheid and its legacy means that many of them are unskilled or semiskilled workers. Cape Malays are renowned as artisans, small traders, and fishermen.

GRIQUA

The Griqua are a Southern African people descended from the Khoikhoi, San and European ancestors (*see also* **Khoisan**, below). The Khoikhoi (now largely a historical grouping) and the San are also known as the Hottentots and Bushmen respectively. Besides South Africa, the Khoisan also live in Botswana, Namibia, Angola, Zambia, and Zimbabwe.

KHOISAN

The name "Khoisan" is a linguistic term for the closely related Khoikhoi and San peoples. Descendants of the

Adam Kok III (1811–75) CE

The Griqua are a Southern African people with Khoikoi, San and European ancestors, and Adam Kok III ruled the eastern part of Griqua at Philippolis from 1837 CE until the early 1860s. Kok and his people trekked across the Drakensberg Mountains to set up a new state that subsequently became known as Griqualand East. Their independence proved to be short-lived as the British took control of the region in 1874 CE, leaving Kok with only minimal power. He died at the end of the following year.

ing) Khoikhoi people. The Khoikhoi first encountered Europeans in the late fifteenth century, when Portuguese mariners reached the Cape. During the course of the sixteenth century, they regularly traded cattle and sheep for iron goods and beads brought by the sailors. In the seventeenth century, Dutch settlers began expanding onto Khoikhoi grazing lands. Without access to land for their livestock, many Khoikhoi became hunter-gatherers, or they settled on European farms as laborers. Although technically free, many Khoikhoi had no choice but to work on Boer farms. Now extinct as a separate ethnic group, descendants of the Khoikhoi and Europeans helped to form the present-day Cape Colored population.

The San faced similar pressures to those experienced by the Khoikhoi. Throughout southern Africa, they were gradually dispossessed of their hunting grounds–first by the migrations of the Bantu-speaking peoples, who began to move into southern Africa in the early part of the first millennium CE, and, later, by European settlers. The Bantu-speaking peoples forced the San into isolated arid regions. The Europeans were harsher, and some white settlers killed San people on sight. By the nineteenth century, only small bands of San remained in South Africa, living in some of the most arid parts of what is now Northern Cape. Some San escaped into Botswana and Namibia, where they joined long-established San communities. But there they found themselves in competition for land with the cattle-raising Tswana, Herero, and other peoples.

In more recent times, many Khoisan were recruited into the Portuguese colonial army in Mozambique and the South African army in Namibia. However, after Namibia became independent in 1990 CE, about 4,000 Khoisan moved to South Africa. In recent decades in Botswana, the government and cattle herders systematically drove the Khoisan from most of their territories into the Kalahari Desert. However, the establishment of the Central Kalahari Game Reserve in 1961 CE helped to safeguard the land rights of some of the local Khoisan–the Khwe. However, long periods of drought and plans to encourage tourism led the government of Botswana to induce the Khwe to leave the reserve in 1996 CE.

NDEBELE

The Ndebele, who live in Northern Province, South Africa, are commonly divided into two groups: the Northern Ndebele and the Southern Ndebele. However, the Northern Ndebele have been absorbed into the Sotho population and are no longer regarded as a distinct ethnic group. The Matabele of southern Zimbabwe are also sometimes, confusingly, called Ndebele. The histories and cultures of the Ndebele and Matabele are closely connected and the two groups are often treated as branches of the same, Ndebele, people. *See also* **Zimbabwe (Peoples–Matabele)**.

Ndebele history begins with the Nguni, a Bantu-speaking people who arrived in southern Africa around 1,800 years ago. The Ndebele are one of the many ethnic groups descended from the original Nguni ("Ndebele" is the Sotho name for "Nguni"). History suggests that the Ndebele probably separated sometime in the late sixteenth century under a chief named Musi into two groups–Northern and Southern–most of

Modern extent of the Ndebele peoples

whom migrated from present-day KwaZulu-Natal northward to modern Northern Province, where the Northern Ndebele gradually became absorbed by the Sotho neighbours. In the eighteenth century, the Southern Ndebele fragmented into several groups. Two branches survived this fragmentation into the present-day: a smaller group led by Manala, and a larger group led by Ndzundza. The Ndzundza Ndebele reached a height of prosperity in the mid-nineteenth century under the rule of King Mabhogo, but they were finally conquered by the Boer's South African Republic (Transvaal) in 1883 CE. All the Ndzundza lands were confiscated and the people were forced to work for the Boers (Afrikaner farmers) virtually as slaves.

In 1973 CE, under apartheid, the Ndebele were given a homeland called KwaNdebele, which was located in lands completely strange to them. Great conflict arose in the 1980s between the homeland's government-appointed regime and supporters of the Ndebele monarch. The conflict resulted in 160 deaths, while 300 people were detained, and hundreds disappeared. The homelands were abolished in 1994 CE, when the country's first nonracial government took office.

NGUNI

The ancestors of the Bantu-speaking Nguni peoples arrived in South Africa around 1,800 years ago and it is possibly from the Tsonga of Mozambique that the earliest Nguni trace their origins. The larger Nguni groups include the Swazi, Xhosa, and Swazi. Other groups, including the Ndebele and Matabele, were pushed north by the Mfecane. The Ngoni of East Africa are another Nguni people.

SOTHO

The Sotho (or Basotho) are divided into two groups in the northern part of South Africa. The two main groups are the Northern Sotho, who live in South Africa's Northern Province, and the Southern Sotho, who live in modern Free State and Lesotho. For information about the Southern Sotho, *see also* **Lesotho (Peoples—Sotho)**. By about 1000 CE, Bantu-speaking peoples had settled on the High Veld–the arid plains west of the Drakensberg Mountains–and in the valleys of the

Mzilikazi (1795–1868 CE)

He was the founder of one of the most formidable African states in Southern Africa in the nineteenth century. It was located first in the area now known as the Transvaal, and then north of the Limpopo River in what is now called Zimbabwe. The illustration (above) is based on an illustration by a European artist in 1836 CE.

Moshoeshoe (above)
He was widely credited with being the creator of the Sotho nation, and is pictured here in 1860.

Mashopa (right)
The third son of Moshoeshoe, he became leader of the southern Sotho. While his father was still alive, he fought against both Africans and Africaners and, in the 1870s, he opposed the Cape administration in Basutoland. His resistance played a major part in forcing the Cape to hand the territory back to the British, and he continued to oppose their rule until he was defeated in battle in 1898.

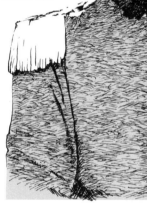

Orange, Vaal, and Tugela rivers. They slowly absorbed the local Khoisan people and adopted many aspects of their culture. By about 1400 CE, the Sotho had established their main clans—several families who share the same ancestor. Groups of these clans eventually came together to form three main divisions of the Sotho people: the Northern Sotho, the Southern Sotho, and the Tswana (or Western Sotho). *See also* **Botswana (Peoples—Sotho)**.

During the seventeenth century, the Pedi group of clans became dominant among the Northern Sotho and established the Bapedi Empire. Bapedi lasted for more than 200 years and expanded the Pedi clan into a wider political and then ethnic grouping made up of people who joined or were conquered by the Bapedi Empire.

However, from the 1820s, the lives of all the Sotho peoples were disrupted by the Mfecane/Difaqane – two decades of invasion, warfare, and famine triggered by the Zulu upheavals east of the Drakensberg Mountains. After the Mfecane, Bapedi became a popular destination for Africans seeking to escape the harsh labor laws of the newly formed South African Republic. In the 1860s, open war broke out between the Afrikaners, or Boers, and the Pedi, led by their king Sekhukhuni. The Boers were defeated at this time, but, three years later, the British forces, with the help of the Swazi, defeated the Pedi.

When the racist doctrine of apartheid, or "separate development", was introduced in 1948 CE, it made the Northern Sotho third-class citizens in their own land. In 1959 CE the South African government attempted to divide the black population from the whites by creating homelands, or Bantustans, in which the black people were forced to live. The Northern Sotho were allocated a number of separate regions in the north, collectively known as the Lebowa homeland. Lebowa was abolished in 1994 CE by South Africa's first nonracial government.

Modern extent of the Sotho peoples

VENDA

The Venda (or Vhavenda: "the People of Venda") live in northeastern South Africa in a region which is also known as Venda. The Venda migrated from East Africa's great lakes region to the north in several waves. The first arrivals, the Vhangona, reached the Limpopo River by the twelfth century. A Venda group led by Thoho ya Ndou was the first to cross the Limpopo and enter the northern region of present-day South Africa, most likely in the seventeenth century. Large, powerful

Sekhukhuni (left)
He was the king of the Pedi people, and led them in their war against the Boers in the 1860s. The Boers were defeated, but three years later the British defeated the Pedi with the help of the Swazi. This illustration is based on a photograph taken in 1879 CE.

The captive king (above)
Sekhukhuni, the Pedi king, is shown here being carried on a litter after his defeat by the British in 1879 CE.

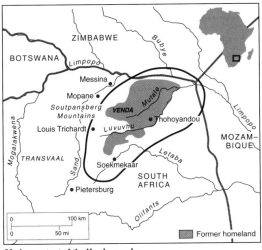

Modern extent of the Venda peoples

bows probably gave the Venda a military edge over the previous inhabitants and, for a time, they controlled much of eastern South Africa. However, rivalries between Thoho ya Ndou's descendants lost the Venda their supremacy and kept them divided into a number of chiefdoms. During a Swazi invasion in 1839 CE, the decentralized structure of the state and its mountain refuges helped to save the Venda from being wiped out. But later that century, they suffered from famines and wars of succession. In the 1840s, Afrikaners established the Soutpansberg republic in Venda. At first, it was basically a hunting settlement, employing Venda men to hunt for ivory, but the Boers (Afrikaner farmers) established a large army to carry out slave raids on Venda villages. The Venda rebelled and by 1867 CE had ousted all the white settlers from their land. Gradually, however, Boer commandos isolated and defeated the Venda chiefdoms one by one. An onslaught in 1898 CE finally drove the Venda north of the Limpopo River. The Venda lands were then incorporated into the Boers' South African Republic (later the Transvaal).

Under white rule, the Venda suffered from racial discrimination. From 1948 CE, the introduction of apartheid (the racist doctrine of "separate development") made matters worse. In 1973 CE, the South African government turned the reserves allocated to the Venda into a "self-governing" homeland, which was given "independence" in 1979 CE. The independence was fictional and never recognized outside South Africa. The homelands were abolished in 1994 CE by South Africa's first nonracial government.

Xhosa

Most Xhosa live in rural areas in southeastern South Africa. Many also live in the cities of Cape Town, Nelson Mandela Metropolis (formerly Port Elizabeth), East London, and also around Johannesburg. The Xhosa, who are sometimes referred to as the Southern Nguni peoples, belong to a variety of groups, including the Gealeka, Hlubi. Mpondo, Ngqika, and Thembu. (Nelson Mandela, the first South African president to be elected in a nonracial election, is a Thembu, although, like many black Africans, regards himself, not as a tribalist, but first and foremost a South African.)

The Xhosa are descended from Bantu-speaking peo-

ples from present-day eastern Nigeria who arrived in Southern Africa around 1,800 years ago. The Xhosa are one of the groups who emerged from the Nguni peoples. They originally consisted of three main groups: the Mpondo, the Thembu, and the Xhosa. These groups share the same language and hold the belief that their cultures originate from the same source. Over the course of many centuries, internal friction, migration, and contact with the Khoisan peoples created subdivisions within the original Xhosa groups, which fragmented into numerous clans (extended families who share a common ancestor, or ancestors). Sons of chiefs established new chiefdoms of their own and this was the way in which the Xhosa gradually expanded their territory. Eventually, they occupied an area along the eastern coast that reaches roughly from the Groot-Vis River to present-day KwaZulu-Natal, spreading inland to the Drakensberg Mountains. The various Xhosa groups remained linked through marriage and political and military alliances.

Between 1779–1878 CE, a series of nine frontier wars occurred. These were the Cape-Xhosa wars between the Xhosa and the Boers (Afrikaner farmers) and British of Cape Colony. In addition, in the early nineteenth century, many Xhosa fled from the northeast of their territory (in what is now KwaZulu-Natal) to escape the armies of the great Zulu leader, Shaka. The Xhosa suffered their most traumatic blow in the "cattle killings" of 1856 to 1857 CE. A young girl called Nongqawuse–said to be possessed by their spirits of the ancestors–had a vision that the white invaders would be swept into the sea, that the great Xhosa chiefs would return from the dead, and the land would be filled with cattle and crops. For this to happen, Nongqawuse said, all existing cattle and food supplies must first be destroyed. Coming at a time of great conflict for the Xhosa, many people saw this as a way out of the turmoil. However, despite the slaughter of 200,000 cattle, the prophecy was not fulfilled and defeat resulted. Survivors of this desperate act of resistance were compelled to work on the invaders' farms and the Xhosa were finally defeated in 1878 CE.

Under apartheid (the racist doctrine of "separate development"), the South African government created homelands for the country's black population. The

Ngqika (1779–1829 CE)
He was a leader of the Xhosa people who, during his lifetime, saw much of their territory lost to the onslaught of European settlers, trade and religion. Ironically, all his actions were intended to place him at the head of a strong Xhosa nation, and possibly his gravest miscalculation was to ally himself with the Cape against his internal enemies within the Xhosa, namely the Ndlambe and Hintsa.

Tiyo Soga and his wife, Janet
An ordained minister of the United Presbyterian Church in 1856 CE, Tiyo Soga returned with his Scottish wife, Janet, to work among his own people, the Xhosa, in Southern Africa. He was caught between two different cultures: his African heritage on the one side, and his Christian upbringing in the West on the other. He died at the early age of only 42 from tuberculosis.

© DIAGRAM

Xhosa homelands of Ciskei and Transkei were later declared "independent" by the South African government, which then withdrew South African citizenship from all Xhosa. The homelands were abolished in 1994 CE by South Africa's first nonracial government.

ZULU

For information about the history of the Zulu people, who emerged from the Nguni group of Bantu-speaking people, *see also* **Zulu kingdom**.

In the twentieth century, the Zulu have suffered racial discrimination, especially under the policy of apartheid (the racist doctrine of "separate development"). A homeland for the Zulu, called KwaZulu, was established in the 1970s, but in 1994 CE, under South Africa's first nonracial government, all the homelands were abolished. However, in the run up to the 1994 elections, the Zulu Inkatha Freedom Party (IFP), led by Chief Mangosuthu Gatsha Buthelezi, claimed that the African National Congress (ANC) did not represent Zulu interests. This led to violent clashes between IFP and ANC supporters.

John Tengo Javabu (1859–1921 CE)

Of Mfengu origins, Javabu was the son of Christian converts and became a modern leader among the Xhosa-speaking peoples in the Cape colony. Although he was a teacher, a preacher and a political agent, it is as a newspaper journalist and proprietor that he is most renowned; his paper was founded in 1884 CE, and called Invo Zabantsundu.

Modern extent of the Xhosa peoples

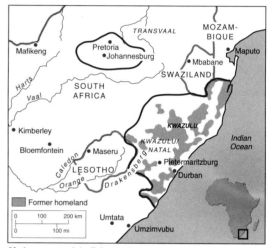

Modern extent of the Zulu peoples

South African Native National Congress

The first organized resistance to apartheid was led by Mohandas Gandhi, an Indian lawyer who came to Natal in 1873 CE and stayed until 1914 CE. Using nonviolent methods and recourse to the law Gandhi was an inspiration to later movements. The South African Native National Congress, which later became the African National Congress (ANC) in 1923 CE, was set up in January 1912 CE. Its first leaders were John Langalibalele Dube (president), Walter Benson Rubusana (vice-president), Solomon Tshekisho Plaatje (secretary), and Pixley Kalsaka Seme (treasurer). The Congress sought to effect changes by appealing to Britain and challenging unjust laws in court. The government's refusal to reform led to more militant methods.

Solomon Tshekisho Plaatje (1875–1932 CE)

He worked as a court interpreter, and also as a mediator between the black and white factions at the siege of Mafikeng. Plaatje was also the editor for seven years of the Mafeking newspaper Koranta ea Becoana.

Pixley Kalsaka Seme (1880–1951 CE)

Educated in both Columbia University in New York and Oxford University in England, he went on to practice as a lawyer, and was called to the bar in London.

Walter Benson Rubusana (1858–1936 CE)

Ordained as a minister in the Congregationalist church in 1884, Rubuana was awarded degrees by McKinley University in the United States for his writings on the situation of the indigenous peoples in South Africa.

John Langalibalele Dube (1871–1946 CE)

Dube was educated in the United States and was greatly influenced by the African-American educationalist, Booker T. Washington. He founded the Ohlange Institute in Natal in 1889 on the model of Washington's ideas on industrial education.

South Africa's major political figures

Biko, Steve (Stephan Bantu) (1946–1977 CE)
A founder of South Africa's Black Consciousness movement, Steve Biko was the first president of the all-black South African Students' Organization. He was also an organizer of the Black Community Program, which encouraged black pride and opposition to apartheid, and the government banned him from political activity in 1973. He died of head injuries while in police custody.

Botha, P. W. (Pieter Willem) (1916 CE –)
Botha was prime minister (1978–84) and then president (1984–89) of South Africa. His attempts to modify apartheid while maintaining white supremacy alienated the right wing of his National Party, while failing to satisfy black or international opposition to apartheid. He resigned, unwillingly, in 1989 and was replaced by F. W. de Klerk.

Buthelezi, Chief Mangosuthu Gatsha (1928 CE –)
A member of Zulu nobility, Chief Buthelezi became chief executive in the KwaZulu "homeland" in South Africa in the early 1970s. At first a supporter of the African National Congress (ANC), he later formed the Zulu Inkatha movement, which developed into the Inkatha Freedom Party (IFP). This party, which favors maximum autonomy for KwaZulu/Natal (formerly KwaZulu) province, won the provincial elections in 1994, but it finished third in the national elections. Buthelezi then became Minister for Home Affairs in the new South African government.

de Klerk, F. W. (Frederik Willem) (born 1936 CE)
F. W. de Klerk succeeded P. W. Botha as president of South Africa in 1989. Under his leadership, the racial policies of apartheid were swiftly dismantled. The release of Nelson Mandela in 1990 led to multiracial negotiations and elections in 1994, when a multiparty government was set up. Mandela became president and Thabo Mbeki and de Klerk became deputy presidents. De Klerk shared the 1993 Nobel Peace Prize with Nelson Mandela.

Luthuli, Chief Albert John (1898–1967 CE)
Chief Luthuli, a leading Zulu figure in the struggle against apartheid in South Africa, was awarded the 1960 Nobel Peace Prize. President-general of the African National Congress (ANC) from 1952 until it was banned in 1960, he was arrested in 1956 and charged with treason, but released in 1957. His autobiography, *Let My People Go*, appeared in 1962.

Malan, Daniel François (1874–1959 CE)
Daniel Malan became prime minister of South Africa after defeating Jan Smuts in the 1948 elections. He is best known for the official introduction of apartheid. He retired from office in 1954.

Mandela, Nelson Rolihlahla (1918 CE –)
Nelson Mandela, leader of the African National Congress (ANC), was elected president of South Africa in the country's first multiracial elections in 1994. Mandela qualified as a lawyer and worked with Oliver Tambo. He became a leader of the ANC before it was banned in 1960 and founded *Umkonto we Sizwe* (the military wing of the ANC) in 1961. He was one of the defendants in the so-called Treason Trial (1956–61) of 156 antiapartheid activists, every one of whom was acquitted. Mandela continued his antiapartheid activities and in 1962, along with Walter Sisulu and seven others, he was arrested and charged with sabotage and terrorism. All except one were sentenced to life imprisonment. Mandela was released in 1990, having become an international symbol of the struggle against apartheid. During his imprisonment, his wife Winnie Mandela did much to ensure that his plight was not forgotten by the outside world. After his release, he successfully led negotiations for a new, nonracial constitution for South Africa. He shared the 1993 Nobel Peace Prize with F. W. de Klerk, and retired in June 1999.

Mandela, Winnie (1934 CE –)
Winnie (Nomzano Zaniewe Winnifred) Mandela emerged as a major opponent of apartheid and a controversial figure in her own right during her husband Nelson Mandela's twenty-eight-year imprisonment. After qualifying as a social worker, she married him in 1958. Her first arrest took place three months later, and in 1962 she was banned from political activity for the first time. For the next twenty years she was banned, restricted, detained, and jailed a number of times. In 1990, after her husband's release from prison, she took a prominent role in the African National Congress (ANC) until her 1991 ceconviction for assault and kidnapping. She was divorced from Nelson Mandela in 1996.

Mbeki, Thabo (1942 CE –)
Thabo Mbeki became First Deputy President of South Africa in 1994 and succeeded Nelson Mandela as leader of the African National Congress (ANC) and president of South Africa following the elections of 1999. Born in Transkei, Mbeki studied economics in Britain and became active in the ANC. In 1975, he became the youngest member of the ANC executive, and in 1993, he became ANC chairperson.

Steve Biko
Medical student Steve Biko was the leading thinker of the Black Consciousness Movement which emerged in the 1970s. He believed that oppression had caused many to feel that they were really inferior to whites, and argued that pride in being black should be cultivated instead. He was arrested in 1977 CE, and died in police custody.

Dr Daniel François Malan
He was prime minister from 1948–1954 CE, and was a fierce Afrikaner nationalist, His cabinet was the first to consist entirely of Afrikaners, and to speak only Afrikaans. He also promoted Afrikaner iinterests above those of any other group.

Nelson Mandela
He was the leader of the ANC and, in 1994 CE, he was elected president in South Africa's first non-racial elections.

© DIAGRAM

Naidoo, Jay (Jayaseelan) (1954 CE–)
A leading trade unionist and opponent of apartheid, Jay Naidoo was elected general secretary of the Congress of South African Trade Unions (COSATU) in 1985. He played a major role in organizing the mass protests against apartheid policies during the 1980s. After the democratic elections in 1994, he was appointed as Minister for Reconstruction and Development.

Plaatje, Solomon Tshekiso (1876–1932 CE)
In 1912, Sol Plaatje was a cofounder of the South African Native National Congress, which became the African National Congress (ANC) in 1923. His book *Native Life in South Africa* (1916) was an indictment of the misery caused by the Natives Land Act of 1913, while his novel *Mhundi* celebrates the importance of African culture and African history. Largely self-educated, Plaatje also translated several of Shakespeare's plays into the Setswana language.

Retief, Piet (1780–1838 CE)
Piet Retief was a leader of the Voortrekkers, the South African Boer farmers who migrated north on the Great Trek to escape British rule in the Cape. In 1837, he published a declaration listing the grievances of the Boers against the British, and led a party into Natal, stronghold of the Zulu. The Zulu king, Dingane, refused to grant him land and in 1838 killed Retief and his followers.

Sisulu, Nontsikelelo Albertlna (1918 CE –)
Albertina Sisulu and her husband Walter Sisulu were leading figures in the struggle against apartheid in South Africa and were imprisoned or placed under house arrest for long periods. She was a leader of the African National Congress (ANC) Women's League, became president of the Federation of African Women in 1984, and was elected a member of parliament in 1994.

Sisulu, Walter Max Ulyate (1912 CE –)
Walter Sisulu, like his wife Albertina Sisulu, was a prominent South African antiapartheid campaigner. Together with Nelson Mandela, he was one of the 156 black activists tried and acquitted in the so-called Treason Trial (1956–61). In 1962, Sisulu and Mandela were arrested again, along with seven others, and charged with sabotage and terrorism. All except one were sentenced to life imprisonment in 1964. Sisulu was released in 1989, and in 1991 cehe became deputy president of the African National Congress (ANC).

***Prime ministers 1910–1960** CE*
A stamp depicting six former prime ministers of South Africa: Botha, Smuts, Hertzog, Malan, Strijdom, and Verwoerd.

Slovo, (Yossel) Joe Mashel (1926–1995 CE)
Born in Lithuania, Joe Slovo became a leading South African opponent of apartheid. A member of the Communist Party of South Africa (CPSA), he was barred from political activity in 1954. He later helped to found the military wing of the African National Congress (ANC), but he spent many years in exile before returning to South Africa in 1990. He was appointed minister for housing in South Africa's first multiracial government in 1994.

Smuts, Jan Christiaan (1870–1950 CE)
A South African politician and prime minister, Jan Smuts fought against the British in the Anglo-Boer War (1899–1902), becoming a general. Later, he worked to reconcile the Boer and British populations. He served as South Africa's prime minister from 1919 until 1924, and again from 1939 until 1948.

Sobukwe, Robert Mangaliso (1924–1978 CE)
A founder of the antiapartheid Pan-Africanist Congress (PAC) in South Africa, and its president from 1959, Robert Sobukwe helped to organize demonstrations against the Pass Laws in 1960. During one of these, at Sharpeville, the police opened fire on demonstrators and 69 people were killed and 180 wounded. This event, which became known as the Sharpeville massacre, focused world attention on the antiapartheid struggle. Sobukwe was banned from political activity and imprisoned–under a law used only against him and nicknamed the "Sobukwe clause"–from 1960 until 1969.

Suzman, Dame Helen (1917 CE –)
Between 1953 and her retirement in 1989, Helen Suzman was the chief voice of liberalism in South Africa's parliament. Daughter of a Lithuanian Jewish immigrant, she was first elected to parliament in 1953 as a member of the United Party. After the United Party split in 1959, she became a member of the antiapartheid Progressive Party, and from 1961 ceuntil 1974, she was its sole representative in parliament. She was awarded the UN Human Rights Award in 1978.

Tambo, Oliver Reginald (1917–1993 CE)
Oliver Tambo directed the activities of the African National Congress (ANC) while in exile from South Africa from 1960 until his return in 1990. He had joined the ANC in 1944 and, like Nelson Mandela, was one of the defendants in the so-called Treason Trial (1956–61). He became acting president of the ANC in 1967 and was president from 1977 until 1991, when Mandela succeeded him. In July 1991, he was named ANC vice-president.

Tutu, Desmond Mpilo (1931 CE –)
Desmond Tutu was a powerful and eloquent antiapartheid campaigner. His emphasis on nonviolent resistance to the apartheid regime earned him the 1984 Nobel Peace Prize. His appointment as Archbishop of Cape Town in 1986 made him head of the Anglican Church in South Africa, Lesotho, Mozambique, Namibia, and Swaziland; he retired in 1996. After the downfall of the apartheid regime, he set up the Truth and Reconciliation Commission to give the enforcers of apartheid the opportunity to confess their crimes and seek forgiveness. This has been opposed by many of apartheid's victims and their families, who feel that the guilty should be tried for their crimes. His demand that the African National Congress (ANC) also seek amnesty for its past human rights abuses has sparked controversy.

van Riebeeck, Jan (1618–1677 CE)
Jan van Riebeeck, an official in the service of the Dutch East India Company, headed the first Dutch settlement at the Cape of Good Hope, in 1652. In 1657, he allowed some of the soldiers under his command to set up farms on Khoikhoi grazing lands. These soldiers became the first of South Africa's Boers – "boer" is the Dutch word for "farmer" and the historical name of the Afrikaners.

Verwoerd, Dr Hendrik Frensch (1901–1966 CE)
Hendrik Verwoerd was prime minister of South Africa from 1958 until his assassination in 1966; he was succeeded by John Vorster. He favored the breaking of his country's ties with the Commonwealth, which it left in 1961. He had earlier served as minister of "native affairs," when he developed strict apartheid policies with the support of the premier, Johannes Strijdom, whom he succeeded. His administration was marked by further development and ruthless application of the highly controversial apartheid policy. In fact, he has been called the architect of apartheid for his efforts to enforce it.

Dr. H. F. Verwoerd
He was minister of native affairs from 1950–1958 CE, and prime minister from 1958–1966 CE. He introduced the policies needed to make apartheid a reality, trying to justify it on the grounds that it was a 'separate development of the races.' He was subsequently assassinated in 1966 CE.

Vorster, John (1915–1983 CE)
John (formerly Balthazar Johannes) Vorster was the prime minister of South Africa following the assassination of Hendrik Verwoerd in 1966 until 1978. He was elected president in 1978, but resigned in 1979 following a political scandal. He enforced apartheid policies, but sought to make contacts with other African governments.

Apartheid, a 'separate development of the races'

Apartheid (the Afrikaans word for 'apartness') was the name given to South Africa's policy of racial segregation, discrimination, and white domination that was in force from 1948–1991 CE.
By the time apartheid was officially introduced, racist policies had been practiced for over 300 years in South Africa. The Dutch who settled on the Cape in the seventeenth century soon established semi-slave relationships with the local Khoikhoi population, whose way of life became dependent on employment by Afrikaners (the name the Dutch settlers later adopted). The Boers (the Dutch word for farmers) then began to import slaves from other parts of Africa, and elsewhere, to provide cheap labor for building and farming work.

In the nineteenth century, Britain took Cape Colony from the Dutch. In 1807 CE, they outlawed slave trading, although slaves could still be kept legally, and in 1820 CE about 4,000 Britons settled in the Cape. Unable to purchase slaves legally and with no free labor available, the new settlers set about wresting the Afrikaners' slaves from them by decreeing that nobody, of whatever color, could be forced into service. This was followed by the abolition of slavery throughout the British Empire in 1833 CE. Combined with other changes, this threatened to destroy the Afrikaners' lifestyle, and, in 1836 CE, they began to trek to the interior of Africa where they planned to live unhampered by British bureaucrats. The Afrikaner republics that were set up en route during this Great Trek had constitutions that included as a central element the right of Afrikaner self- determination, and the "right" to rule the "natives."

To secure huge diamond and gold reserves discovered in the 1870s and 1880s in Southern Africa, the British conquered the whole of what is now South Africa by force. The Afrikaners were defeated during the Anglo-Boer War (1899–1902 CE). However, a liberal backlash in Britain over British cruelty during the war promoted Anglo-Boer conciliation. In 1910 CE, the British colonies and the Afrikaner republics (most of which had been made independent in 1907 CE) united to form the white-ruled Union of South Africa. Louis Botha, an Afrikaner, was the first prime minister.

Over the years, the Afrikaners–who were mainly farmers or, later, part of the underclass of urban workers–came to resent the British, who dominated the lucrative mining industry, skilled professions, the military, and the civil service. Indeed, the strident Afrikaner nationalist sentiment that emerged had developed largely as a result of British imperialism and domination. This nationalism was turned on the black population in force after the National Party (NP), which was formed in 1912 CE to further Afrikaner interests, came to power in 1924 CE. This does not mean, however, that English-speaking South Africans were not in collusion with the Afrikaners in the creation of apartheid.

The NP merged in 1934 CE with another party to form the United Party, which addressed the interests of both English-speakers and Afrikaners. The remnants of the NP were resurrected by the *Broederbond* (an influential, secret, nationalist Afrikaner society) and other Afrikaner extremists led by Dr Daniel François Malan. This "purified" National Party came to power in 1948 promising to create apartheid. Malan promised to send all black people to reserves, run a white-only economy, and "to save civilization from black hordes," a task he claimed to be ordained by God. This message appealed to many white industrial workers who feared competition from the black majority for their jobs. Apartheid was also welcomed by the mine owners and white farmers as it allowed them to maintain the–for them–profitable status quo. In order to provide themselves with cheap labor, mine owners had long been employing black workers and installing them in cramped, single-sex barracks.

Apartheid was different from theracial segregation practised historically in South Africa because it was enshrined in, and enforced by, the law. Under J. B. M. Hertzog, the Ministry of Native—later, Bantu—Affairs (created in 1910 CE) began drafting some of the laws and policies that formed the bones of apartheid. Although many policies were in place before 1948 CE, they were extended and enforced to a greater extent after this date.

J. B. M. Hertzog
A Boer general in the Anglo-Boer War (1899–1902 CE), Barry Hertzog was prime minister from 1924–1939. Hertzog created the Ministry of Native–later, Bantu–Affairs in 1910 CE, and founded the Afrikaner-based National Party in 1912 CE, two institutions that were central to apartheid.

Apartheid, a "separate development of the races" (cont.)

At the heart of apartheid was the denial of voting rights to all but the white population. Like other apartheid policies, this had a long history. The first Afrikaner republics of the nineteenth century had only allowed Afrikaner men to vote. Also, the British passed a law to deny black people the right to vote outside the Cape. Within the Cape, few could meet the strict educational and financial requirements needed to qualify. Indian and "Colored" voters were given separate houses of representation in 1983 CE, but in a ratio that ensured continued white domination. In protest, many did not exercise their right to vote.

Relocation policies aimed to limit the number of black people staying overnight in "white" towns, and to segregate people within urban areas. After the 1913 CE Native Land Act, black South Africans were allowed to buy or rent land only in "native reserves." Over 60 percent of the population was restricted to living in only 7.3 percent of the land (later increased to 13 percent). Denied access to land, black South Africans had to work for the white population, who needed their labor on farms, in towns, and down the mines. The 1948 CE Group Areas Act created separate residential and business areas for each officially-designated race into which people could be forcibly moved.

By the 1960s, it was obvious that the reserves were not viable; they were overpopulated and under-resourced, and starvation was widespread. Nevertheless, in 1959 CE the 260 reserves were organized into several homelands, or Bantustans. Despite segregationist policies, 60 percent of the black population lived in "white" areas in 1948 CE. Between 1960–1983 CE, however, over three million people were evicted to live in the homelands.

Color bars prevented the majority of South Africans from doing many things, such as working as skilled professionals. Unofficial color bars had long been in existence in the mining industry, for example. White workers filled supervisory and skilled positions while black workers were left to do the lower-paid manual jobs. When the mines tried to promote black workers to supervisory positions in 1922 CE, simply to save money on wages, strikes and demonstrations by white miners nearly caused a civil war. Two years later the NP came to power with the support of the white-only trade unions and immediately legalized color bars.

In 1955 CE, the Bantu Education Act was passed. After this date, many students were denied the right to a high-standard academic education. Instead, a poor-quality education was provided as approved by the Department of Native (Bantu) Affairs. Schools that refused to conform were closed down and reluctant teachers fired.

Under this act, every South African was required to register and be classified by "race," which would then be stamped in his or her identity pass. This would then be used to determine, for example, where people could live, what job they could do, and who they could marry.

The first pass law—the Hottentot Code—was introduced by the British to the Cape Colony in 1809. It required that all Khoikhoi have a fixed place of abode and a pass with an employer's stamp if they needed to travel. This law forced the Khoikhoi to work for the Afrikaners in order to obtain a pass. Although repealed a few years later to create a mobile supply of workers for the British settlers, it was the first of many similar laws. Pass laws gave the authorities power to restrict people's access to towns, send others back to their homelands, and ensured a continual supply of labor to the white population.

Wealthy and heavily armed, South Africa was able to dominate neighboring countries, the front-line states in the fight against apartheid, in order to protect its own policies. Intimidation, sabotage, military action, and subversion were all used to destabilize the regimes that South Africa found threatening, and to prop up those that supported it, such as the illegal white-minority regime in Rhodesia (present-day Zimbabwe). Using the excuse of trying to eliminate its enemies' guerrilla bases, South Africa invaded many front-line states. Angola was invaded, bombed and, together

with Mozambique, was subjected to a prolonged civil war due, in part, to South Africa's funding of rebel groups. Other East and Central African countries suffered from these problems because of the influx of refugees from war zones. Namibia was illegally occupied by South Africa (as Southwest Africa) until 1990 CE, and a form of apartheid was introduced. South Africa easily pressured Lesotho and Swaziland, which were economically reliant on the goodwill of South Africa, into supportive roles. Border blockades were often used to force Lesotho's policies into line.

Opposition to apartheid was widespread, involved people of all colors, and took many forms. The first organized resistance was led by Mohandas Karamchand Gandhi, an Indian lawyer who came to Natal in 1893 CE and stayed until 1914 CE. Using nonviolent methods and recourse to the law, Gandhi was an inspiration to later movements. The South African Native National Congress—it became the African National Congress (ANC) in 1923—was formed in 1912. Its first leaders—John L. Dube, president, and Sol Plaatje, secretary—attempted to effect changes by appealing to Britain and challenging unjust laws in court. The government's stubborn refusal to reform, however, led to the development of more militant methods. The ANC really became a mass movement only in 1944 CE with the founding of the ANC Youth League by Anton Lembede. His colleagues included Nelson Mandela, Walter Sisulu, and Oliver Tambo.

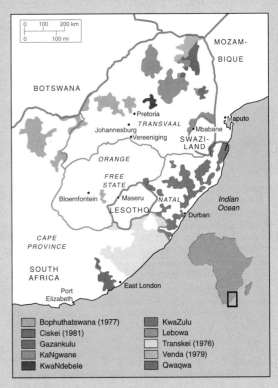

Bophuthatswana (1977)	KwaZulu
Ciskei (1981)	Lebowa
Gazankulu	Transkei (1976)
KaNgwane	Venda (1979)
KwaNdebele	Qwaqwa

Homelands
At first self-governing, some homelands were given their "independence" after 1970 CE. This independence was not recognized anywhere but inside South Africa as it was simply an excuse for the government not to concern itself with the provision of facilities. More importantly, the inhabitants of homelands could be denied any rights in the rest of South Africa as they were now "foreign" nationals. Homelands were wholly dependent on external areas for work: industries were encouraged to set up on the edge of homelands but not inside. Most homeland leaders, with the exception of Chief Buthelezi, Prime Minister of KwaZulu, were supporters of apartheid.

Segregation of amenities
After the Defiance Campaign of civil disobedience in 1952 CE, the government introduced The Separate Amenities Act. Separate facilities had to be provided for different races, and these included public benches, beaches, and even stairways. The Act also stated that the facilities did not have to be of an equal standard.

Pass laws
During apartheid, pass laws were used to enforce racial segregation. Every black person had to carry a pass with an employer's stamp if they were in a "white" town. Police could stop people at any time to check their passes.

One of the first examples of successful mass political mobilization was the Defiance Campaign of 1952 CE. With Indian and other groups, and using trained volunteers, the ANC orchestrated local defiance of unjust laws all over the country. The campaign was called off after outbreaks of violence occurred. Reprisals by the government were often severe. Police powers were increased to deal with the growing unrest caused by apartheid. Torture and informers were widely used, and many died in police custody. More "humane" methods included the banning and restraining orders put on political activists in order to halt their activities.

In 1961 CE, as president of the ANC, Oliver Tambo left South Africa to open overseas offices of the ANC. From Lusaka, Zambia, he organized guerrilla forays into South Africa and raised funds. In the same year, Mandela formed the *Umkonto we Sizwe* (Spear of the Nation) movement, which was to perform sabotage on economically important facilities, but to avoid harming people, in order to pressurize the government into talks. The initial result was that Mandela and Sisulu, among others, were imprisoned for life in 1964 CE.

Huge uprisings led by the schoolchildren of Soweto (the southwestern townships of Johannesburg) followed the announcement in 1976 CE that Bantu education would be in Afrikaans. Protests escalated and strikes paralyzed Johannesburg. Police response was harsh, and by the end of the year over 500 people, including many children, had been killed.

Most opposition leaders were committed to non-violent methods (Desmond Tutu won the Nobel Peace Prize for his non-violent campaigning), but this fact was sometimes ignored by others. Apartheid policies of segregation, not only by race but also by ethnic group, inevitably led to outbreaks of what came to be called "black-on-black" violence, although many incidents were no doubt incited by government agents. Although Chief Buthelezi's Zulu Inkatha movement (originally formed in 1928 CE, and reconvened in 1975 CE) and Mandela's *Umkonto* were mutually supportive, their members often clashed on a number of issues.

Deaf to moral arguments, economic reasons for the government to end apartheid brought matters to a crisis point. Even before the 1948 elections, serious drawbacks to segregationist policies had become obvious. The government soon discovered that labor provided by the excluded majority was vital for the fastest-growing sector of the economy: manufacturing

industries. This labor force also needed to be well-educated and mobile enough to be efficient, which was impossible within apartheid. Employers, especially in the construction sector, often had to ignore color bars just to fill vacancies. After the Sharpeville massacre in 1960 CE and the 1970s Soweto uprisings, foreign investment halted, capital flowed out of the country, house prices and the share market slumped, and businesses collapsed. In many ways, apartheid did not make sound economic sense. Pressure at home and from abroad was also making the system increasingly unworkable. As increasing numbers of African and Asian countries joined the United Nations, calls for sanctions against South Africa grew. Anti-apartheid movements had been arguing for sanctions for years and, in 1985 CE many international banks paid heed. Loans were not renewed and the promise of future ones withdrawn. In 1990 CE, Mandela was released from prison and, from 1991 CE, all apartheid legislation was repealed. Finally, in 1994 CE, the first non-racial elections were held in South Africa and Mandela was elected president. The inequalities that apartheid created over many years will not disappear overnight, however.

The right not to vote (above)
Apartheid, in effect from 1948–1991 CE in South Africa, used force and official classifications of "race" and ethnicity to oppress the majority of the population. Separate houses of representation were created for "Colored" and Indian voters in 1983 CE, but in a ratio that kept the balance of power in the hands of the whites. Many people chose not to vote, as the author of this graffiti in Johannesburg demanded.

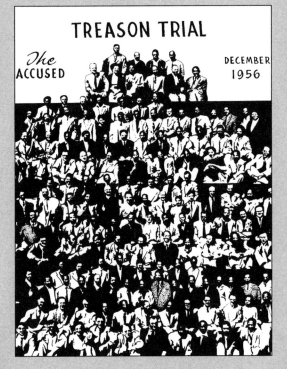

Treason Trial (left)
The 1956 CE "Treason Trial" of 156 people involved in the 1952 CE Defiance Campaign, including Nelson Mandela, lasted until 1961 CE. All charges were eventually dismissed as the defendants' non-violent principles contradicted the government's claim that they had incited violence. The trial attracted worldwide attention, which enabled the International Defense and Aid Fund to be established to fund anti-apartheid activities.

Patrolling the townships (above)
Regular patrols by armed police made townships seem like war zones. Many people were moved to these government-built townships out of sight of the "white" cities.

Sharpeville Massacre (right)
In 1960, a demonstration organized by the newly-formed Pan-African Congress (PAC) outside a police station in Sharpeville was fired on by the police. Sixty-nine people were killed, and over 100 were injured. Most of these people were shot in the back.

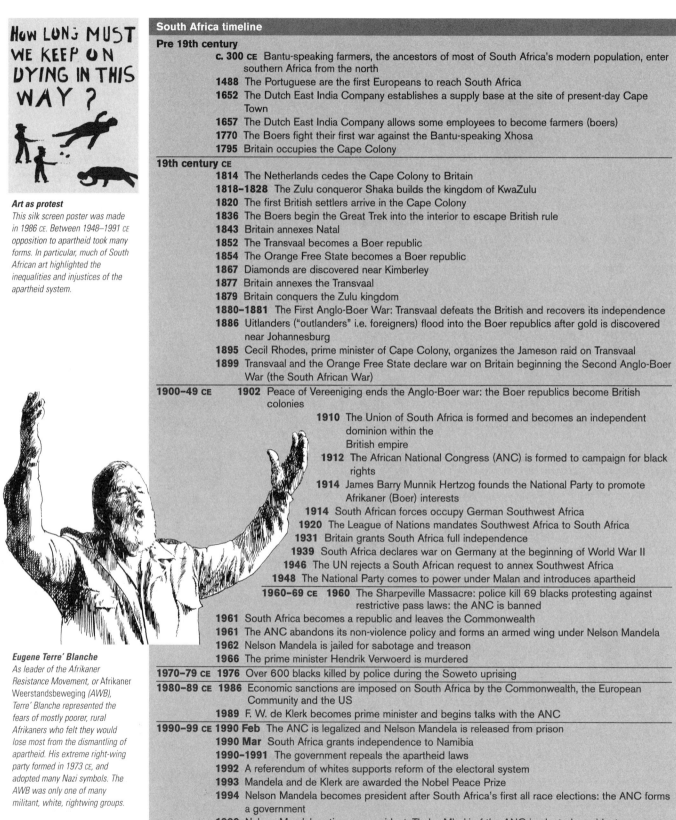

HOW LONG MUST WE KEEP ON DYING IN THIS WAY?

Art as protest
This silk screen poster was made in 1986 CE. Between 1948–1991 CE opposition to apartheid took many forms. In particular, much of South African art highlighted the inequalities and injustices of the apartheid system.

Eugene Terre' Blanche
As leader of the Afrikaner Resistance Movement, or Afrikaner Weerstandsbeweging (AWB), Terre' Blanche represented the fears of mostly poorer, rural Afrikaners who felt they would lose most from the dismantling of apartheid. His extreme right-wing party formed in 1973 CE, and adopted many Nazi symbols. The AWB was only one of many militant, white, rightwing groups.

South Africa timeline

Pre 19th century

c. 300 CE Bantu-speaking farmers, the ancestors of most of South Africa's modern population, enter southern Africa from the north
1488 The Portuguese are the first Europeans to reach South Africa
1652 The Dutch East India Company establishes a supply base at the site of present-day Cape Town
1657 The Dutch East India Company allows some employees to become farmers (boers)
1770 The Boers fight their first war against the Bantu-speaking Xhosa
1795 Britain occupies the Cape Colony

19th century CE

1814 The Netherlands cedes the Cape Colony to Britain
1818–1828 The Zulu conqueror Shaka builds the kingdom of KwaZulu
1820 The first British settlers arrive in the Cape Colony
1836 The Boers begin the Great Trek into the interior to escape British rule
1843 Britain annexes Natal
1852 The Transvaal becomes a Boer republic
1854 The Orange Free State becomes a Boer republic
1867 Diamonds are discovered near Kimberley
1877 Britain annexes the Transvaal
1879 Britain conquers the Zulu kingdom
1880–1881 The First Anglo-Boer War: Transvaal defeats the British and recovers its independence
1886 Uitlanders ("outlanders" i.e. foreigners) flood into the Boer republics after gold is discovered near Johannesburg
1895 Cecil Rhodes, prime minister of Cape Colony, organizes the Jameson raid on Transvaal
1899 Transvaal and the Orange Free State declare war on Britain beginning the Second Anglo-Boer War (the South African War)

1900–49 CE

1902 Peace of Vereeniging ends the Anglo-Boer war: the Boer republics become British colonies
1910 The Union of South Africa is formed and becomes an independent dominion within the British empire
1912 The African National Congress (ANC) is formed to campaign for black rights
1914 James Barry Munnik Hertzog founds the National Party to promote Afrikaner (Boer) interests
1914 South African forces occupy German Southwest Africa
1920 The League of Nations mandates Southwest Africa to South Africa
1931 Britain grants South Africa full independence
1939 South Africa declares war on Germany at the beginning of World War II
1946 The UN rejects a South African request to annex Southwest Africa
1948 The National Party comes to power under Malan and introduces apartheid

1960–69 CE

1960 The Sharpeville Massacre: police kill 69 blacks protesting against restrictive pass laws: the ANC is banned
1961 South Africa becomes a republic and leaves the Commonwealth
1961 The ANC abandons its non-violence policy and forms an armed wing under Nelson Mandela
1962 Nelson Mandela is jailed for sabotage and treason
1966 The prime minister Hendrik Verwoerd is murdered

1970–79 CE

1976 Over 600 blacks killed by police during the Soweto uprising

1980–89 CE

1986 Economic sanctions are imposed on South Africa by the Commonwealth, the European Community and the US
1989 F. W. de Klerk becomes prime minister and begins talks with the ANC

1990–99 CE

1990 Feb The ANC is legalized and Nelson Mandela is released from prison
1990 Mar South Africa grants independence to Namibia
1990–1991 The government repeals the apartheid laws
1992 A referendum of whites supports reform of the electoral system
1993 Mandela and de Klerk are awarded the Nobel Peace Prize
1994 Nelson Mandela becomes president after South Africa's first all race elections: the ANC forms a government
1999 Nelson Mandela retires as president, Thabo Mbeki of the ANC is elected president

South African presents

South African presidents	
State presidents	**Sep 3 1984–Aug 15 1989** CE
May 31 1961–Jun 1 1967 CE Charles Robberts Swart	Pieter Willem Botha (acting to Sep 14 1984)
Jun 1 1967–Apr 10 1968 CE Jozua François Naudé (acting)	**Jan 19 1989–Mar 15 1989** CE J. Christian Heunis (acting for Botha)
Apr 10 1968–Apr 9 1975 CE Jacobus Johannes Fouché	**Aug 15 1989–May 10 1994** CE Frederik W. de Klerk (acting to Sep 20 1989)
Apr 9 1975–Apr 19 1975 CE Johannes de Klerk (acting)	**Presidents**
Apr 19 1975–Aug 21 1978 CE Nicolaas J. Diederichs	**May 10 1994–Jun 16 1999** CE Nelson Mandela
Aug 21 1978–Oct 10 1978 CE Marais Viljoen (1st time acting)	**Jun 16 1999** CE– Thabo Mbeki
Oct 10 1978–Jun 4 1979 CE B.J. Vorster	
Jun 4 1979–Sep 3 1984 CE Marais Viljoen (2nd time acting to Jun 19 1979)	

Mangosthutu Buthelezi
In 1994 CE, former prime minister of KwaZulu homeland and leader of Inkatha, Chief Mangosthutu Gatsha Buthelezi, became Minister for Home Affairs in South Africa's first democratically-elected government.

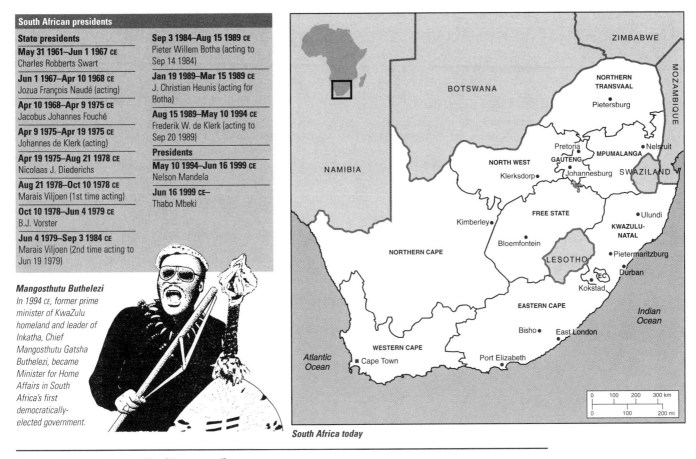

South Africa today

South African Republic (Transvaal)

In the nineteenth century Afrikaners (Boers) from the Cape region undertook mass treks northeastward to inland Southern Africa. On the highveld Transvaal region of what is now northeastern South Africa, several independent republics were established by the Boers. One of these was founded in Potchefstroom in 1838 CE. By the second half of the nineteenth century, the Potchefstroom Boers were calling their state the South African Republic. The Boer republics of Lydenburg, Soutpansberg, and the Potchefstroom Boers united as the South African Republic in 1860 CE, but remained engaged in civil war until 1864 CE. The Boers attempted to bring Africans under their control, but met

Independant Boer republics in 1894

A krugerrand
The discovery of gold in Southern Africa in the late ninetenth century caused a huge gold rush, and eventually led to the establishment of colonial rule. This krugerrand, a South African coin, contains 1 oz (28 g) of pure gold.

Paul Kruger
President of the Transvaal Republic (1883–1902 CE), Kruger had no formal education but established himself as a leader by fighting heroically in a commando unit against other Africans and the British. He was a strong and forceful champion of Afrikaner interests and tried to free his republic from British domination.

The "Star of Africa" (above)
In 1905 CE, the world's largest uncut diamond, the "Cullinan" was found in Transvaal. The "Star of Africa" stone that was cut from it in 1908 CE was then incorporated into the British crown jewels.

with strong resistance. They assembled a 5000-strong army to battle with the Pedi in 1876 CE but were defeated; one year later they were annexed by Britain as the Crown Colony of Transvaal. In 1880 CE the Boers rebelled against British rule, and the British withdrew in 1881 CE. The Boers ruthlessly exerted their control over the Africans living on the highveld, as their president pursued a policy of "Africa for the Afrikaners." The development of gold mining made the South African Republic one of the richest states in Southern Africa. The Boers of the Orange Free State and the South African Republic (Transvaal) declared war on Britain in 1899 CE. The South African, or Anglo–Boer,

War lasted until 1902 CE, and it was the largest war the region had ever seen. Around 500,000 British troops were pitted against around 100,000 Boer troops. Many Africans were involved as soldiers in the war. The South African Republic was annexed in 1900 CE, but the Boers continued to fight. A treaty in 1902 CE ended the war and imposed British rule over the South African Republic as well as the Orange Free State. The republic once more became the Crown Colony of Transvaal, and (after 1910), the province of Transvaal. *See also* **South Africa**.

The Anglo-Boer War (1899–1902 CE) (left)
These Afrikaner women are being taken to a British concentration camp. After the discovery of gold and diamonds in the region, the British set about conquering most of present-day South Africa including the Boer republics. In an attempt to wipe out Boer resistance, the British adopted a "scorched earth" policy. Afrikaner women and children were forcibly moved to concentration camps, and their farms were destroyed in order to deny the Boer guerrillas access to food and supplies. Housed in wooden huts or tents with inadequate food and water supplies, many camp internees died from disease or starvation.

Voortrekker *Monument (above)*
Opened in 1949 CE by Prime Minister Malan, the Voortrekker Monument near Pretoria commemorates the Great Trek of the mid-nineteenth century. It has become an important symbol for the Afrikaner people.

Southern Nigeria

Southern Nigeria is the name of a British colony that came into being in 1894 CE. It was formed by the merging of the Niger Coast Protectorate (established as the Oil Rivers Protectorate in 1885 CE) and the southern

areas of the former Royal Niger Company's territories. Southern and Northern Nigeria were joined as the Colony and Protectorate of Nigeria in 1914 CE. *See also* **Nigeria**.

Southern Rhodesia

Coat of arms
This stamp celebrates the existence of the British South Africa Company (BSAC) from 1890–1923 CE.

Zimbabwe was once a British-ruled colony called Southern Rhodesia. The land had been colonized by white settlers in the late nineteenth and early twentieth centuries, and it became part of the British Empire. Before that time, the region had a long history of empire building, and it was the center of many great civilizations, including Great Zimbabwe, Mwene Mutapa empire, and the Rozvi empire. At the time of conquest by the British the dominant people were the Ndebele from Southern Africa, or the Matabele as they came to be known in their new home. The discovery of gold in their lands excited the interest of the British South Africa Company (BSAC), a commercial venture established by the wealthy businessman Cecil Rhodes. The BSAC defeated the Ndebele in 1893 CE, and their land became part of white-ruled Southern Rhodesia. The colony was handed over to the British government. In 1964 CE, the neighboring colony of Northern Rhodesia became independence as Zambia, and Southern Rhodesia was thereafter commonly known as Rhodesia. *See also* **Rhodesia**; **Rhodesia and Nyasaland, Federation of**; **Zimbabwe**.

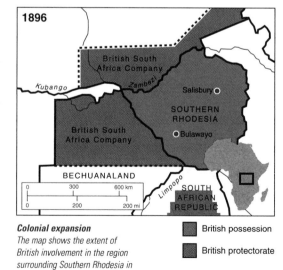

Colonial expansion
The map shows the extent of British involvement in the region surrounding Southern Rhodesia in 1896 CE.

■ British possession
■ British protectorate

South West Africa

What is now Namibia was colonized by Germany as South West Africa in 1884 CE. The port of Walvis Bay and some offshore islands were already controlled by Britain. At the start of World War I, South Africa occupied South West Africa. The United Nations granted a mandate to South Africa to administer South West Africa. South Africa instituted an apartheid-style regime in the territory, allowing only Europeans any power. In 1946 CE the UN rejected South Africa's appeal to annex South West Africa, and in following years the UN declared South Africa's occupation of South West Africa illegal. Lengthy uprisings against South African rule followed, and harsh repression was the norm. Southwest Africa gained independence as Namibia in 1990 CE. *See also* **Namibia**; **South Africa**.

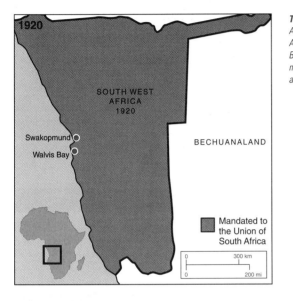

1920

SOUTH WEST
AFRICA
1920

Swakopmund

Walvis Bay

BECHUANALAND

Mandated to
the Union of
South Africa

0   300 km

0   200 mi

The aftermath of war (left)
At the start of World War I South Africa occupied Southwest Africa. By 1920 the UN had granted a mandate to South Africa to administer Southwest Africa.

An oath of allegiance (below)
Boer soldiers are here shown swearing an oath of allegiance to the German Army. The Boers helped them defeat a series of uprisings by black Africans in South West Africa from 1904–07 CE.

Soutpansberg

Dutch settlers first came to Southern Africa in the seventeenth century. Their descendants, the Afrikaners or Boers (from the Dutch for "farmer"), were trekking inland 200 years later to found independent republics away from increasing British control of the Cape. One of these Voortrekker groups founded the Soutpansberg republic in lands inhabited by the Venda people, who long resisted the Boer newcomers. The Boer republics of Lydenburg, Soutpansberg, and the Potchefstroom Boers united together as the South African Republic in 1860 CE, but remained engaged in civil war until 1864 CE. The Venda drove all the whites from the Soutpansberg in the 1860s. From the 1880s to 1898 CE, the regenerated South African Republic–which had formed the British Crown Colony of Transvaal from 1877 to 1881–finally defeated the Venda. *See also* **South Africa**; **South African Republic (Transvaal)**.

Spanish Guinea

Spanish Guinea was the name given to Equatorial Guinea when it was a Spanish colony. The country was within the area CEded by the Portuguese to the Spanish in 1778 CE. Fernando Po (now Bioko), Annobon and other islands along with the mainland province of Rio Muni became part of Spanish Guinea; although Bioko was administered by the British from 1827–1858 CE. The Spanish did not truly control the mainland until 1926 CE, however. Spanish Guinea gained independence as Equatorial Guinea in 1968 CE. *See also* **Equatorial Guinea**; **Fernando Po**; **Rio Muni**.

Spanish Morocco

The Spanish enclaves of Ceuta in Melilla and surrounding area on the north coast of Morocco once formed the territory known as Spanish Morocco, or the Spanish Zone. The ports themselves were occupied by the Spanish several centuries ago, but the surrounding lands only came under Spanish control toward the start of the twentieth century. The colonial borders of French- and Spanish-controlled Morocco were established in 1912 CE. Much of the Spanish Zone was returned to Morocco on independence in 1956 CE, but the ports of Ceuta and Melilla remain under the control of Spain to this day. *See also* **Ceuta**; **Melilla**; **Morocco**.

Spanish Sahara

Spanish Sahara was created in 1958 CE by the union of the Spanish-ruled Río de Oro (established 1885 CE) and its northerly neighbor Saguia el Hamra (established 1912 CE) as a province of Spain. The Spanish withdrew in 1976 CE, and the region was under nominal Mauretanian administration in the south and Moroccan occupation in the north. In 1979 CE the Mauretanian government abandoned any claim to the area, and the entire territory was occupied by Morocco. *See also* **Río de Oro**; **Western Sahara**.

Spanish Zone

See **Spanish Morocco**.

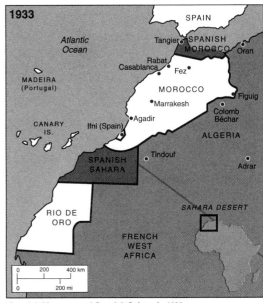

Spanish Morocco and Spanish Sahara in 1933 CE

SUDAN Republic of Sudan

The Nile valley in northern Sudan, a region called Nubia, was populated around 6,000 years ago by farmers, much like the *fellahin* in Egypt. Around 2,600 years ago, Nubia was incorporated into ancient Egypt. However, in around 1700 BCE, the Nubian Kingdom of Kush, which was strongly influenced by ancient Egyptian culture, developed in northern Sudan. In 712 BCE, Nubians invaded ancient Egypt, but they were driven out in 671 BCE by the Assyrians. In 590 BCE, the center of Nubian power moved south to Meroë, in central Sudan, but Meroë was conquered in about 350 CE by the Ethiopian Kingdom of Axum (*see also* **Axum, kingdom of**).

Christianity was introduced into Sudan in about 540 CE and, despite mounting pressure from Muslim peoples, it survived until 1505 CE, when Alwa, the last Christian kingdom in the region was conquered by the Muslim Funj people. Egypt conquered the Funj in 1821 CE and the Egyptians gradually extended their rule over most of this vast country. In 1887 CE, a religious leader, Muhammad Ahmad, proclaimed himself the *Mahdi* (Muslim messiah) and he led a successful revolt against the Egyptians over the following four years. During the uprising, the British soldier Charles Gordon was killed while defending Khartoum against the Mahdi's forces.

In 1896 CE, a joint British and Egyptian force was established and it invaded Sudan, ending the Mahdi's revolt. In 1899, a joint Anglo-Egyptian government was established. In 1948 CE, Sudan was given its own legislative council and, the early 1950s, Britain and Egypt prepared Sudan for independence.

Recent history

In 1955 CE, Sudan's parliament voted for independence, which was achieved on January 1, 1956 CE. However, the civilian government proved unable to tackle the country's most intractable problem, namely reconciling the interests of the Muslim Arabs in the north with those of the black southerners, who practice either traditional African religions or Christianity. In 1958 CE, General Ibrahim Abboud led a military coup, abolishing all political parties, and heading a military regime. Abboud's view that the problem of the southerners

Colonel Gaafar Muhammad el Nimeri
He seized power in 1969 CE, abolished all political parties and, in 1972 CE, became the president of Sudan. While in office he gave the southern provinces autonomous regional government (1972 CE), imposed Islamic law throughout the country (1983 CE), and was eventually deposed in a military coup (1985 CE). He was often regarded as the architect of an Islamic state.

could be solved by military, rather than political, action angered many people. Especially criticized by people outside Sudan was the expulsion of Christian missionaries. In 1964 CE, the problem of the south, combined with economic setbacks, led to a general strike. This strike, which was supported by professional people, succeeded in restoring civilian rule, but the new government was also unable to solve the country's problems. In 1969 CE, Colonel Gaafar Muhammad Nimeri seized power. He abolished all political parties and, in 1972 CE, he became Sudan's president. In 1973 CE, Sudan became a one-party state.

In 1972 CE, Nimeri appeared to solve the problem of the south by giving the southern provinces autonomous regional government. However, in 1983 CE, he imposed Islamic law throughout the country and ended regional government in the south. His actions sparked off a rebellion and the rebel Sudanese People's Liberation Army launched guerrilla attacks on government installations in the south. In 1985 CE, a group of officers deposed Nimeri. However, the coup leader, General Abdul Rahman Suwar Al-Dahab, soon set up a transitional government which included civilians. In 1986 CE, multiparty elections were held and Sadiq al-Mahdi became prime minister. Civilian rule did not last long. In 1989 CE, Brigadier General Omer Hassan Ahmed al-Bashir seized power dissolved parliament, and ruled through a military council.

Sudan's new regime made attempts to restore peace in the south, but the fighting continued. Many people suffered not only from the conflict, but also through starvation caused by the disruption of the production and distribution of food. In 1996 CE, elections were held in Sudan. This led to the lifting of the ban on opposition political parties in 1998 CE. Also in 1998, the government announced its willingness to hold a referendum on the secession of the south, although no date was suggested and it was clear that northerners and southerners would find it hard to agree on a definition of "the south." The government also gave no indication that it might compromise on the imposition of Islamic law on the south as well as the north. In October 2000 CE, the United States prevented Sudan, which it believes has fostered international terrorism, from gaining a seat on the United Nations Security Council.

Peoples

ACHOLI

The Acholi live in a region that includes southern Sudan, northwestern Kenya and northern Uganda. They are descended from Lwo-speaking ancestors, a branch of the River-Lake Nilotes, who migrated into Eastern Africa from their homeland in southern Sudan several centuries ago. The Acholi began to emerge as a distinct ethnic group in the seventeenth century from the melding of three main ethnic groups: the Patika (the Lwo ancestors who first migrated into what is now Acholiland), the local Ateker-speaking people, who had migrated there earlier, and Sudanic-speaking people coming in from the west. In the nineteenth century, slave raiders reached Acholi land from the east coast, and the Acholi suffered greatly from the slave trade.

ANUAK

The Anuak occupy an area that straddles the border of southern Sudan and western Ethiopia, although the civil war in Sudan has led many Anuak to move into Ethiopia. The Anuak are Nilotes who originated in the cradleland of the so-called River Nilotes–southern Sudan. Sometime after 1000 CE, the ancestors of the Anuak migrated from their cradleland, reaching present-day Juba in southern Sudan. From Juba, the Anuak returned north, settling in their present lands.

AZANDE

For information about the history of the Azande people, *see*: **Congo, Democratic Republic of (Peoples—Azande)**.

BAGGARA

The Baggara (or Baqqara) of southwestern Sudan are descended from Bedouin Arabs and black Africans with whom the Bedouin intermarried. There are over one million Baggara divided into more than twenty subgroups; some of the major subgroups are the Messirya, Habbania, and Reizegat of Darfur province and the Humr of the Bahr al Arab region.

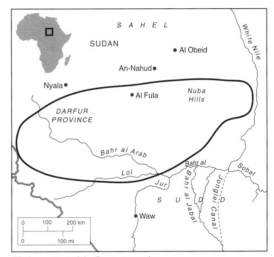

Modern extent of the Baggara peoples

Baggara timeline		
c.1000s CE Bedouin Arabs enter North Africa from Arabia	**1882** Anglo-Egyptian forces conquer Sudan	**1972** South granted regional autonomy; civil war ends
1500s Baggara migrate into present-day eastern Sudan	**1882–1883** Mahdist revolution overthrows Anglo-Egyptian rulers	**1983** Sudan adopts *Sharia* (Islamic holy) law against wishes of non-Muslim south; civil war erupts again
1700s Baggara settled in present-day southern Sudan	**1885** Mahdists take Khartoum. Abdullah ibn Muhammad succeeds Mahdi as Khalifa	**1985** Government begins training and arming Baggara militia
1821 Trade routes opened from north to south Sudan	**1898** Anglo-Egyptian force conquers Mahdist State; Khalifa killed	**1988** Formation of Baggara Popular Defense Front (PDF)
1840s Arab slave trade develops; Baggara active as traders	**1955** First civil war between south and north Sudan begins	**1990s** PDF accused of "ethnic cleansing" of Nuba people as civil war continues
1881 Muhammad Ahmad declares himself *Mahdi*	**1956** Sudanese independence	

© DIAGRAM

The Anglo-Sudanese War

The advance of the European colonial powers into Africa during the last quarter of the nineteenth century was relentless. The most successful revolt against this tide of colonialism was made by Mohammad Ahmed, who was better known as the Mahdi, or Guided One, in the Sudan. Two Egyptian forces sent to capture him in 1881 CE and 1882 CE failed, and his army then went on the offensive. A further Egyptian force, under the command of an English general, was also defeated. When General Gordon arrived in 1884 CE he offered the Mahdi peace, but this offer was refused. The garrison at Khartoum, under Gordon's command, was then attacked by the Mahdist forces and it fell in January 1885 CE. Gordon was killed in the massacre that ensued. The Mahdi then moved on to Omdurman and established his capital there: he died from typhus in 1885. The state he created lasted until the Battle of Omdurman in 1898, CE in which thousands of Mahdists were killed in a battle against an Anglo-Egyptian army.

Muhammad Ahmad
A religious leader, he proclaimed himself the Mahdi (or messiah) in 1887 CE, and led a successful revolt against Egyptian rule in the Sudan. The Mahdist state survived until 1898 CE when its forces were defeated by a joint British and Egyptian force under "Kitchener of Khartoum."

General Charles Gordon
Gordon was appointed by the British cabinet of the time, led by prime minister Gladstone, to organize the evacuation of the Egyptian forces in the Sudan. However, once he arrived in the Sudan, he disobeyed his orders and tried to hold the territory against the Mahdist forces who were in control. An expedition which had been sent to rescue him at Khartoum, under the command of Lord Wolseley, unfortunately arrived two days after his death in the siege.

The spoils of victory
Despite the instruction given by the Mahdi, allegedly, that General Gordon was not to be harmed, he was killed in the general massacre that followed the siege of Khartoum, which lasted from September 1884 CE until January 1885 CE. This illustration graphically recreates the victorious Mahdists displaying the decapitated head of General Gordon.

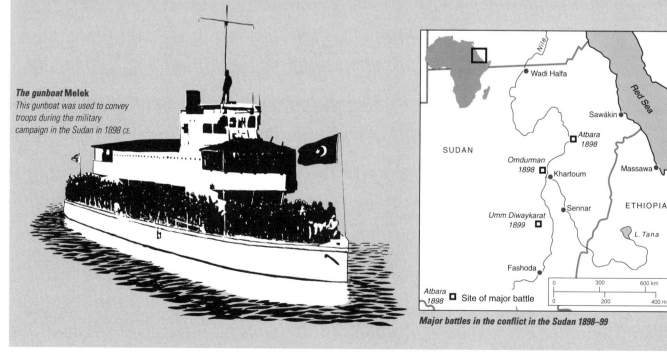

The gunboat Melek
This gunboat was used to convey troops during the military campaign in the Sudan in 1898 CE.

Major battles in the conflict in the Sudan 1898–99

Lord Wolseley
He was sent to the Sudan in August 1884 CE in an attempt to rescue General Gordon at the siege of Khartoum; but he arrived too late to save him.

'Kitchener of Khartoum'
Partly in revenge for the death of General Gordon, and also from fear that the French might invade the Sudan from the west, an Anglo-Egyptian force, under the command of Lord Kitchener, invaded the Sudan in 1896 CE. In 1898 CE this force defeated the Mahdist army at the battle of Omdurman. Primarily in recognition of his victorious military campaign in the Sudan, he was subsequently given the title of Lord Kitchener.

Fleeing the battlefield
This dramatic illustration is based on the painting entitled: The Flight of the Khalifa After his Defeat at the Battle of Omdurman 1898 by the artist Robert Talbot-Kelly. The Khalifa Abdullah succeeded the Mahdi as leader of the Mahdist state upon the Mahdi's death in 1885 CE. The painting dramatically recreates the aftermath of the defeat of the Mahdist forces under Abdullah by an Anglo-Egyptian army led by Lord Kitchener at the Battle of Omdurman in 1898 CE.

The Fashoda Crisis
Captain Jean-Baptiste Marchand was given the task by the French government of the day of establishing an east-west French route from Dakar to Djibouti, thus cutting the existing English route south from Cairo to the Cape. He arrived in Africa in 1896 CE, quelled all opposition as he moved toward the Upper Nile, and reached Fashoda in the Sudan in July 1898 CE. Lord Kitchener then arrived on the scene backed by an Anglo-Egyptian army of 20,000 men. The diplomatic crisis that ensued ended in November of that same year with the withdrawal of Marchand and his troops. In spite of the retreat, France still managed to turn the crisis into a propaganda exercise, as exemplified by this patriotic illustration of the time.

The Mahdi's tomb
When the British Army occupied Omdurman after the battle in 1898 CE, the Mahdi's tomb was destroyed, his body was burned, and the ashes were thrown into the Nile River.

Il est l'espoir de la France
Vive Marchand!

ONNEUR ET PATRI

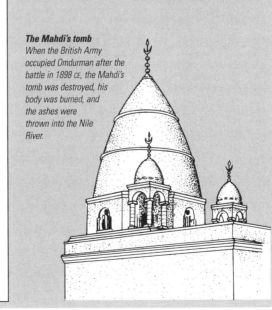

Beja

The Beja live in northeastern Sudan and northern Eritrea, between the Red Sea and the Nile River. They have probably lived in this region for at least 5,000 years and are mentioned in ancient Egyptian, Greek, and Roman writings.

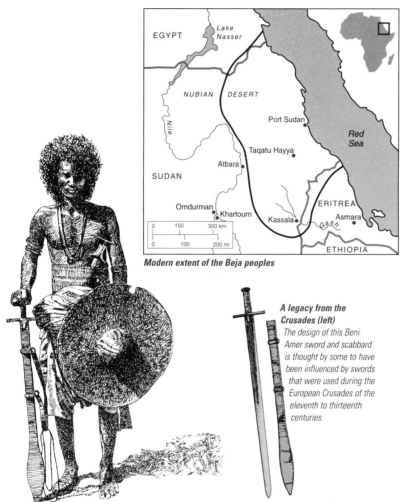

Modern extent of the Beja peoples

A legacy from the Crusades (left)
The design of this Beni Amer sword and scabbard is thought by some to have been influenced by swords that were used during the European Crusades of the eleventh to thirteenth centuries.

Beja warrior (above)
Pictured in the early twentieth century, the look of this Amarar man recalls the reputation the Beja had for being great warriors.

Beja timeline
c. 3000–2000 BCE Ancient Egyptians mine gold in northern Beja territories
100s CE Axumite Kingdom emerges in Tigre lands: southern Beja adopt Tigrean class structure and language, Tigrinya
600s Beja convert to Christianity. Decline of Axumite Kingdom
640 Arab conquest of North Africa begins: Islam introduced
c. 1150–1300s The vast majority of Beja convert to Islam
1882 Mahdist revolution in Sudan begins; many Hadendowa become Mahdist warriors
1885 Battle at Tofrek between Anglo-Egyptian force and Mahdists. Anglo-Egyptian force supported by Bisharin and Amarar is defeated
1898 Britain and Egypt conquer Mahdist State

Dinka

The Dinka are a Nilotic people who live in southern Sudan. Little is known of their history before 1500 CE, when they are known to have settled in their present location.

As the largest of the non-Muslim, non-Arab peoples of southern Sudan, the Dinka have often been involved in the civil war in Sudan, which broke out in 1983 CE, when the government imposed Islamic law throughout the country. Furthermore, the government divided the south into three regions to break up the power base of the Dinka. The Dinka gave much support to the southern-based rebel groups. In 1988 CE, the Sudanese People's Liberation Movement and international human rights organizations accused the Sudanese government of attempted genocide (extermination) of the Dinka.

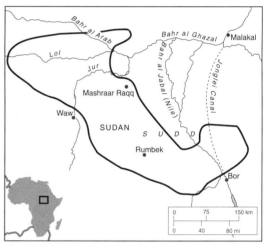

Modern extent of the Dinka peoples

Funj

The Funj (or Fung) are a mainly Arab but partly black African people who live in southern Sudan between the White and Blue Nile rivers. From the sixteenth to the nineteenth centuries, the Funj formed the most powerful state in the region. In the fifteenth century, Funj herders migrated north from the Blue Nile and occupied the Christian kingdom of Alodia by about 1500 CE. In the same century, the Funj became Muslims, and their state was ruled by a sultan. Their capital was at Sennar, a now deserted town on the west bank of the Blue Nile. The modern town of Sennar is located about six miles (10 km) farther south, where it stands near the Sennar Dam across the Blue Nile. Old Sennar was crossed by a north-south trade route. Here, cloth, dates, and other goods from the north were exchanged with ebony, ivory, gold, and other goods from the south.

Fur

The Fur are a people of northern Sudan, who live in the westernmost province of Darfur–the land of the Fur. The Fur have long lived in a centralized state, perhaps for as long as 2,000 years. Darfur became especially important in the eighteenth century, when it expanded to the south and east. Much of its power at this time relied on maintaining control over trade routes. Darfur's main "commodity" was slaves, taken from the Bahr al Ghazal region of southern Sudan. An important route for West African Muslims journeying to Mecca still passes through Darfur, although the recent civil war in Sudan has seen its use decline. The Fur have been Muslim since the seventeenth century.

NUBA

The Nuba live in the Nuba Hills of Kordofan province, southern Sudan. Although little is known about Nuba history until the Arab invasion of North Africa in the seventh century, it seems that the Nuba had lived in the present location for centuries before the Arab invasion. About 300 years before the Arab invasion, references had been made to the presence of a people called the "Black Nuba," who were probably ancestors of the modern Nuba. Some Nuba groups claim that they have always lived in the Nuba Hills. Since the eighteenth century, others have moved into the inaccessible hills in retreat from Baggara raids or, in the nineteenth century, Mahdist troops.

During the modern Sudanese civil war between the Islamic north and the mainly non-Muslim south, the Nuba have been drawn into conflicts with their Islamic neighbors, the Baggara. The government has armed the Baggara and this resulted in the deaths of thou-

Nuba timeline
300s CE "Black Noba," probable ancestors of present-day Nuba, recorded in southern Sudan
640 Arabs begin conquest of North Africa; Islam introduced
1700s Arab slave raids against the Nuba. Baggara raids begin; more Nuba retreat into hills
1821 Trade routes opened from north to south Sudan – as a result, southern population is reduced by disease and slave trading
1882 Anglo-Egyptian forces conquer Sudan; Mahdi begins campaigns; more Nuba retreat into hills
1898 Anglo-Egyptian force conquers Mahdist State
1955 First civil war between south and north Sudan begins
1956 Sudanese independence
1972 South granted regional autonomy; first civil war ends
1975 The oil group Chevron begins drilling for oil in southern Sudan
1983 Sudan adopts Sharia (Islamic holy) law against wishes of mainly non-Muslim south; civil war breaks out again
1983– 1996 Many Nuba join Sudanese People's Liberation Army (SPLA), a southern-based rebel group
1986 The oil group Chevron pulls out of Sudan
11990s Famine hits Nuba Hills. Reports of "ethnic cleansing" of the Nuba by Baggara militias
1992 Relocation camps for Nuba, so-called "peace villages," set up by government

sands of Nuba. Many thousands more have been deported from the hills to government-run "peace villages", where they were under pressure to convert to Islam or to join government forces fighting the southern rebels. Reports of rebel groups forcibly conscripting civilians have also been made.

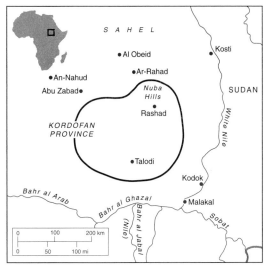

Modern extent of the Nuba peoples

NUBIANS

For information about the history of the Nubians, *see*: **Egypt (Peoples—Nubians)**.

NUER

The Nuer, a Nilotic people of the southern Sudan, are closely related the Dinka. Along with other Nilotic peoples, the Nuer originated in a region to the southwest of their present location. This gradual process of migration was brought to a halt when the British and Egyptians conquered Sudan in 1898 CE. The Nuer have also been greatly affected by the modern civil war in Sudan and the Nuer-dominated South Sudan Independence Movement (SSIM) has been in conflict with the mainly Dinka Sudanese People's Liberation Army (SPLA). Attacks on civilians have been common and Nuer civilians have been forcibly conscripted into both rebel and government troops.

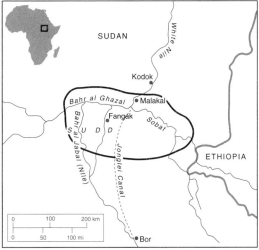

Modern extent of the Nuer peoples

Sudanese Civil War 1983–93 CE
In September 1983 CE, relations between Muslim northerners and Christian southerners flared into fighting after the adoption of Sharia (Islamic) law, renewing civil war (the original war was fought from 1955–1972 CE). The Sudanese People's Liberation Army (SPLA), the southern rebel force formed in 1982 CE, engaged government troops in a series of battles throughout the 1980s. There were reports of government atrocities against, and "ethnic cleansing" of, the Nuba people from the Nuba Mountains in central Sudan, where fighting was said to be heavy. In 1991 CE, the SPLA split into factions: the two major ones were SPLA "united" and SPLA "mainstream." There was fierce fighting between the two, compounding an already hopeless situation. Even so, by 1992 CE, rebel forces were in control of most of southern Sudan.

The fighting continues and so does the misery. Those who suffer are refugees and civilians, the victims of famine (a result of farmers being displaced by the war) and disease.

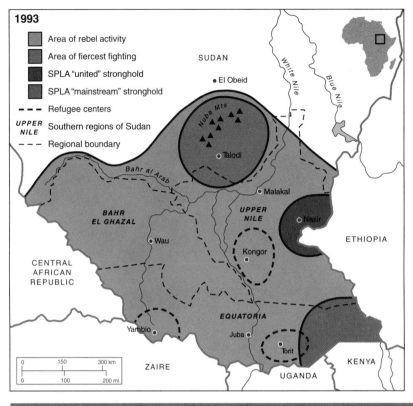

1993

- Area of rebel activity
- Area of fiercest fighting
- SPLA "united" stronghold
- SPLA "mainstream" stronghold
- --- Refugee centers
- **UPPER NILE** Southern regions of Sudan
- --- Regional boundary

Sadiq al Mahdi
In 1986 CE, nearly a century after the Mahdi was defeated by Anglo-Egyptian forces, one of his descendants, Sadiq al Mahdi, became prime minister of Sudan.

Sudan's major political figures

Abboud, Ibrahim (1901–1983 CE)
Abboud became president of a military government in Sudan in 1958, when he seized power and ended all democratic institutions. However, he never realized how deep was the cultural gulf between the people of the north and south, and his military policies against the south were strongly disliked by many professional people. A general strike in 1964 toppled him from power.

Bashir, Omar Hassan Ahmad al- (1944 CE–)
Brigadier-General (later Lieutenant-General) Omar al-Bashir overthrew Sudan's civilian government led by Sadiq al-Mahdi in June 1989. He served as president of the Revolutionary Command Council for National Salvation and, in 1993, he was appointed president of Sudan. He was reelected in 1996.

Emin Pasha, Mehmed (1840–1892 CE)
Emin Pasha was born in Germany and originally named Eduard Schnitzer. He adopted the name Mehmed Emin in Albania in 1865, when he became a Muslim, and later became Pasha (administrator) of Equatorial Province in Sudan. An explorer and physician, Emin Pasha was also a skilled linguist and his studies added enormously to the knowledge of African languages. He also wrote valuable geographical papers and collected many specimens of African flora and fauna. He fought against slavery and was murdered by Arab slave traders at Stanley Falls (now Boyoma Falls, Democratic Republic of Congo).

Garang de Mabior, John (1945 CE–)
In 1983, John Garang, a Dinka from southern Sudan, became leader of the rebel Sudanese People's Liberation Movement (SPLM) and its military wing, the Sudanese People's Liberation Army (SPLA). His movement opposes such government policies as the use of Arabic in schools and the imposition of Sharia (Islamic holy) law.

Mahdi, Sadiq al- (1936 CE–)
Sadiq al-Mahdi, great grandson of Muhammad Ahmad al Mahdi, or the "Mahdi," served as prime minister of Sudan from 1966 until 1968 and again from 1986. In his second term, his attempts to negotiate with southern leaders failed and he was forced to seek support from Muslim fundamentalists, who demanded full application of Islamic law in southern Sudan. He was overthrown in 1989.

Muhammad Ahmad al Mahdi (1848–1885 CE)
Muhammad Ahmad, who assumed the title of Mahdi (Muslim Messiah) in 1881, was a former civil servant turned slave trader who went on to lead the Sudanese rebellion against Anglo-Egyptian rule in 1882. He captured east-

ern Sudan in 1883, made Al Obeid his capital, and annihilated an Egyptian army that had been sent to retake it. In 1885, he captured Khartoum after a five-month siege and moved his capital to Omdurman, where he died later that year. The Islamic state he had established lasted until 1898 CE, when the Mahdist forces were defeated by General Kitchener's Anglo-Egyptian army at the Battle of Omdurman. His great-grandson, Sadiq al Mahdi, has been prime minister of Sudan two times.

Sudan timeline

Pre 19th century
c. 1700 BCE The kingdom of Kush (Nubia) develops
1504–1492 BCE Kush is conquered by Tuthmosis I of Egypt
712 BCE The Nubians conquer Egypt
671 BCE The Nubians are driven out of Egypt by the Assyrians.
590 BCE The center of Nubian power shifts south to the city of Meroë in central Sudan
c. 300 BCE The kingdom of Meroë is at its peak
c. 350 CE Meroë is conquered by the Ethiopian kingdom of Axum
c. 540 The Nubians are converted to Christianity
652 The kingdom of Makkura repels an Islamic Arab invasion
1317 Islamic Arab nomads conquer the kingdom of Makkura
1505 Alwa, the last Christian kingdom in present-day Sudan, is conquered by African Funj tribes
17th century Funj kingdom is at the peak of its power

19th century CE
1821 Egypt conquers the Funj
1869 Khedive Ismail of Egypt sends Samuel Baker on an expedition up the White Nile
1873 Baker establishes Egyptian control on the upper Nile and undermines the local slave trade
1874 Ismail appoints the British general Charles George Gordon governor of Sudan
1876 Egypt has control of most of present-day Sudan
1881 Muhammad Ahmad proclaims himself the Mahdi ("messiah") and leads a revolt against Egypt
1885 The Mahdi captures Khartoum after a long siege in which Gordon is killed
1896 Anglo-Egyptian force under Kitchener invades Sudan
1898 Anglo-Egyptians defeat the Sudanese at Omdurman
1898 Fashoda incident: Britain forces a French military expedition to withdraw from Sudan
1899 Joint Anglo-Egyptian government of the Sudan established

1900–49 CE
1924 Britain expels Egyptian officials from Sudan after they incite an army mutiny
1936 Britain permits Egypt to resume joint control of Sudan
1948 Sudan is granted a legislative council

1950–59 CE
1951 King Farouk of Egypt declares himself King of Sudan
1953 Britain and Egypt grant self-government to Sudan
1955 The Sudanese parliament votes for independence
1956 Jan 1 Sudan becomes an independent republic
1958 Gen. Ibrahim Abboud becomes president after a military coup

1960–69 CE
1964 General strike forces the military government to step down. A rebellion breaks out in the Christian southern provinces
1969 Col. Gaafar Nimeiri seizes power after a military coup

1970–79 CE
1971 Nimeiri becomes president of Sudan
1972 Nimeiri gives the southern provinces an autonomous regional government ending the rebellion
1973 Nimeiri's Sudanese Socialist Union (SSU) becomes the only legal political party

1980–89 CE
1983 Rebellion breaks out in the Christian south after Nimeiri imposes Islamic law throughout the country
1985 Nimeiri ousted by a military coup and the SSU is disbanded
1986 Elections are held for a new legislature, Sadiq al-Mahdi becomes prime minister
1989 Brig. Gen. Omer Hassan Ahmed al-Bashir overthrows al-Mahdi in an Islamic fundamentalist inspired military coup

1990–99 CE
1991 Southern rebels split over whether to seek independence or a united secular Sudan
1993 The military appoint al-Bashir president
1995 Sudanese conspiracy to assassinate president Mubarak of Egypt fails
1996 In presidential and parliamentary elections, al-Bashir is re-elected president and the fundamentalist National Islamic Front wins control of the legislature
1997 Rebel Sudanese Peoples Liberation Army makes big gains in the south
1998 Government declares its willingness to hold a referendum on the secession of the south
1998 Aug US missiles destroy pharmaceutical plant at Khartoum in retaliation for bombing of US embassies in Kenya and Tanzania
1999 Sudan and Uganda sign a peace agreement

THE DEMOCRATIC REPUBLIC OF THE SUDAN

African Development Bank
A stamp issued in 1969 CE to celebrate the fifth anniversary of the African Development Bank.

© DIAGRAM

Nimeri, Gaafar Muhammad (1930 CE–)

Gaafar Nimeri was president of Sudan from 1969 until 1985. A professional soldier, he seized power in a coup in 1969. He was elected president in 1971 CE and worked to raise food production throughout the country, but his attempts to introduce Sharia (Islamic holy) law alienated many people in the non-Muslim, largely Christian south. He was deposed by a coup in 1985.

Piankhy (died c.712 BCE)

From 751–712 BCE, Piankhy was the Nubian king of Kush (part of modern Sudan). He was a brilliant general, and he conquered Egypt and became its pharaoh (king). When he invaded Egypt, his forces were moving down the Nile while a Libyan chief, Tefnakht, was advancing upriver. Piankhy defeated Tefnakht and some Egyptian forces, seized the throne, then sailed back up the Nile to Kush with a large hoard of spoils from the battle.

Sudanese presidents			
Jan 1 1956–Nov 17 1958 CE Sovereignty Council –`Abd al-Fattah Muhammad al-Maghrabi –Muhammad Ahmad Yasin –Ahmad Muhammad Salih –Muhammad `Uthman ad-Dardiri –Siricio Iro Wani	–Tijani al-Mahi –Mubarak Shaddad –Ibrahim Yusuf Sulayman –Luigi Adwok Bong Gicomeho (1st time)	**May 25 1969–Jul 19 1971 CE** Gaafar Nimeiry (1st time) (chairman of the revolutionary command council)	**May 6 1986–Jun 30 1989 CE** Ahmad al-Mirghani (chairman of the supreme council)
Nov 18 1958–Nov 16 1964 CE Ibrahim Abboud (chairman Supreme Council to Oct 31 1964)	**Jun 10 1965–Jul 8 1965 CE** Committee of Sovereignty –Isma`il al-Azhari –`Abd Allah al-Fadil al-Mahdi –Luigi Adwok Bong Gicomeho (2nd time) –`Abd al-Halim Muhammad (2nd time) –Khidr Hamad	**Jul 19 1971–Jul 22 1971 CE** Abu Bakr an-Nur `Uthman (chairman of the revolutionary council) **Jul 22 1971–Apr 6 1985 CE** Gaafar Nimeiry (2nd time) (chairman of the revolutionary command council to Oct 12 1971)	**Jun 30 1989 CE –** Omar Hassan Ahmad al-Bashir (president of the revolutionary command council for national salvation to Oct 16 1993)
Nov 16 1964–Dec 3 1964 CE Sirr al-Khatim al-Khalifah (acting)			
Dec 3 1964–Jun 10 1965 CE Committee of Sovereignty –`Abd al-Halim Muhammad (1st time)	**Jul 8 1965–May 25 1969 CE** Isma`il al-Azhari (chairman of the sovereignty council)	**Apr 6 1985–May 6 1986 CE** `Abd ar-Rahman Siwar ad-Dahab (commander-in-chief to Apr 9 1985, then chairman of the transitional military council)	

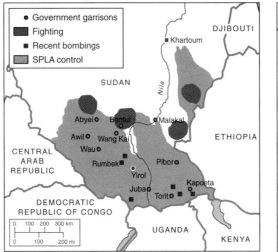

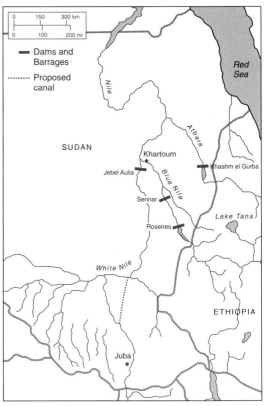

The disputed South (above)
Periodic fighting between the Dinka and Nuer tribes, and shifting alliances with the government and the SPLA (Sudanese People's Liberation Army), have led to recent conflict in the southern part of the Sudan. This map shows the disposition of forces at the beginning of October 2000 CE.

Reducing drought (right)
Better use of the Nile River's constant water supply would drastically reduce the threat of drought in those areas, such as the Sudan, that fall within the Nile's watershed. This map shows the locations of dams and barrages, together with the route of a proposed canal.

Sudanese Republic

In 1958 CE French Sudan was proclaimed the Sudanese Republic, which a year later united with Senegal to form the Mali Federation. *See also* **French Sudan**; **Mali**.

SWAZILAND Kingdom of Swaziland

The Swazi people are descendants of Bantu-speaking people, called the Nguni, who settled in what is now southern Mozambique more than 500 years ago. Around 1750 CE, a group of Nguni migrated from Mozambique into what is now southeastern Swaziland. There they developed into the Swazi nation, absorbing the people already living in the area. Similarly, the refugees from the Zulu Mfecane between 1819–1839 CE were also absorbed into the Swazi nation. (The Mfecane was the period of Zulu expansion in Southeastern Africa that led to mass migrations and wars).

British traders and Boer farmers (Afrikaners) first reached Swaziland in the 1830s. From the late 1870s, the discovery of gold led to an influx of hundreds of prospectors looking for mining concessions from the Swazi king Mbandzeni. In 1890 CE, Britain and the Afrikaner South African Republic (Transvaal) established a provisional government, including representatives of Britain, the South African Republic, and the Swazi people. In 1893 CE, Britain signed another convention permitting the South African Republic to take control, without incorporating the territory. The Swazi refused to sign that convention, but, in 1894 CE another convention allowed the South African Republic to rule Swaziland as a colony.

In 1902 CE, at the end of the Second Boer War, Britain took control of Swaziland and, in 1906 CE, it passed responsibility for the territory to the British High Commissioner for Basutoland (now Lesotho), Bechuanaland (now Botswana), and Swaziland. These three countries became known, collectively, as the High Commission Territories.

King Mswati I (left)
King Mswati I, who reigned from1839–65 CE, is shown here with Swazi chiefs in full ceremonial dress. Skilfully using both warfare and diplomacy, Mswati forged a powerful kingdom at a time when the region was under threat from Boer, British, Portuguese, and Zulu aggressors.

Sobhuza II (right)
First made king of Swaziland in 1921 CE, and then head of state in 1968 CE when the country became independent of Britain. During his long reign, Swaziland became a strong and relatively prosperous nation.

Location of Swaziland

A Swazi deputation, 1925 CE
Sobhuza II, king of Swaziland, and his supporters visited London to appeal to the Privy Council to uphold what they believed to be their superior claim in a dispute over ownership of land. However, the Privy Council ruled that British sovereignty was in no way limited by Swazi royal claims to land previously leased to whites by Sobhuza's grandfather, Mbandzeni.

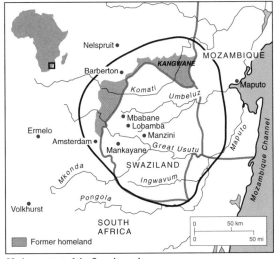

Swazi warrior
A 1968 CE stamp depicting a Swazi warrior armed with a shield and an assegai (spear).

Swaziland kings and queens
Nkosi Dlamini dynasty
Sep 6 1968–Aug 21 1982 CE Sobhuza II
Aug 21 1982–Aug 9 1983 CE Queen Dzeliwe (regent)
Aug 9 1983–Aug 18 1983 CE Sozisa Dlamini ("Authorized Person")
Aug 18 1983–Apr 25 1986 CE Queen Ntombi (regent)
Apr 25 1986 CE– Mswati III

Recent history

Swaziland became internally self-governing in 1967 and it achieved full independence as a constitutional monarchy on September 6, 1968 CE. However, the Swazi monarch, Sobhuza II, and other conservative Swazi leaders were opposed to the independence constitution, which they regarded as a departure from Swazi tradition because it placed some checks on royal power. In 1973 CE, Sobhuza suspended the constitution, and abolished all political parties and other political organizations, which were denounced as "alien" to Swazi traditions. Sobhuza then began to rule directly, with the assistance of personal advisers and a Swazi National Council, the members of which he had appointed. Under a new constitution, the king appointed a new legislature in 1979 CE, though he retained the power of veto.

Sobhuza died in 1982 CE and a regency was set up under Queen Ntombi until a successor was crowned. In 1983 CE, one of Sobhuza's many sons, Makhosetive, was named heir and he was crowned Mswati III in 1986 CE. He was only 19 when he became king, but he soon showed that he had the authority to rule his country by dissolving the Liqoqo, the Supreme Council of State set up by his father to advise the regent, and by dismissing the prime minister. In 1992 CE, he suspended the constitution and ruled by decree, although, in 1993 CE, he allowed directly elected members to be appointed to the legislature. He also introduced other reforms, including elections by secret ballot instead of by a show of hands. But such changes failed to satisfy those who favored democracy. In 1995 CE, protesters, claiming to belong to the Swazi Youth Congress, burned down the national House of Assembly. Political tension continued to mount, with the Swaziland Federation of Trade Unions calling for an end to the absolute monarchy and the establishment of a multiparty democracy. After receiving no response, the unions staged a three-week-long strike in 1997 CE.

Mswati's response was to set up a 30-member commission to review the constitution, but critics pointed out that the commission was packed with members of the royal family and others who had much to lose should reforms ever take place. Elections were held in 1998 CE, but the turnout was very low, partly because political parties were banned and also because candidates were not allowed to campaign or discuss major issues. By the beginning of the twenty-first century, Swaziland remained an absolute monarchy. Mswati showed little enthusiasm for sharing power and continued to rule by decree. Freedom of expression was severely restricted; criticism of the king was banned. Swaziland also faced many other economic and social problems; for example, about a quarter of the population was believed to be HIV-positive.

Peoples

SWAZI

The Swazi form the main group of people in Swaziland. Other Swazis live in neighboring areas in South Africa, especially in the former homeland of KaNgwane, and Mozambique. The Swazi are descended from a group of Bantu-speaking peoples called the Nguni who migrated from present-day eastern Nigeria to what is now Mozambique before the late fifteenth century. Dlamini I was their leader and his descendants became the Swazi kings. About 1750 CE, Ngwane II, the earliest king commemorated in Swazi ritual, led his people into what is now Swaziland. At this time, both the kingdom and people were known as Ngwane.

In 1839 CE, Mswati I succeeded to the Ngwane throne at the age of 13, so his mother Thandile, ruled as regent until he came of age in 1845 CE . Thandile set the foundations for the success of Mswati's reign by centralizing the kingdom and introducing age-regiments (groups who could be called upon for work or warfare) and establishing royal villages around the country to control them. The previous king Sobhuza I, who reigned from about 1815–1839 CE, and the powerful Mswati I, who reigned until 1865 CE, extended their territory and effectively created Swaziland by integrating local peoples and refugees from the Zulu Mfecane into a nation powerful enough to resist Zulu pressure. Swazi means "the people of Mswati" and, since the nineteenth century, the name has been given to both the people and the nation.

In the late nineteenth century, the Swazi kings pursued friendly relations toward the Boers (Afrikaner farmers). However, by granting the Boers concessions they lost their land, resources, and finally their independence when their country became a British colony, administered by the Boers.

Modern extent of the Swazi peoples

Mswati I (c.1820–1865 CE)

Mswati I founded the Swazi nation, which was named after him. He was the king of the Ngwane kingdom that had been united by his father, Sobhuza I. Mswati, who ruled from 1845–1865, was a great general and made his kingdom one of the most powerful in the region.

Mswati III (1968 CE–)

Mswati III, son of Sobhuza II, is the king of Swaziland. Educated in Britain, he was formerly named Prince Makhosetive. He was chosen as heir to the throne following the death of his father in 1982, and was officially installed as king when he reached the age of eighteen in 1986. He reorganized the government, but public dissatisfaction with the political system has grown, with many opposition groups demanding change.

Sobhuza II (1899–1982 CE)

Sobhuza II was king of Swaziland from 1921 and made his country strong and prosperous. As head of state from 1968, when Swaziland became independent from Britain, he regained large areas of land that had been taken by European settlers. He abolished the country's democratic constitution in 1973 and ruled the country with a council of ministers, but introduced a new constitution in 1979, allowing for a partly elected parliament and a "traditional" Swazi National Council. After his death, he was succeeded by his son Mswati III.

Swaziland timeline		
Pre 19th century		
	c. 1 CE	Bantu-speaking herders arrive in the Swaziland region
	c. 1770	Chief Ngwane II leads his Dlamini clan into present-day Swaziland
19th century CE		
	1830s	British traders and Boer farmers visit Swaziland
	1836	Ngwane's successor, Mswati (Mswazi) II, names his people "Swazi" after himself
	1865	Mswati II allies with the British against the Boers
	1878	Influx of Europeans after gold is discovered in Swaziland
	1881	Britain guarantees the independence of Swaziland
	1884	The Boer republic of Transvaal guarantees the independence of Swaziland
	1888	The Swazi give European settlers conditional self-government
	1890	A provisional government of Swazi, British and Boer representatives is formed
	1894	Britain agrees that Transvaal should establish a protectorate over Swaziland
	1899	The infant Sobhuza II becomes king under a regency
1900–49 CE	**1902**	Following their victory in the Anglo-Boer War, the British take control of Swaziland
	1903	Swaziland is declared a British protectorate
	1921	King Sobhuza II begins personal rule
	1944	The king is granted power to issue legally enforceable decrees
1960–69 CE	**1964**	The royalist Imbokodvo party wins elections to a newly created legislature
	1967	Swaziland is granted internal self-government
	1968 Sept 6	Swaziland becomes an independent constitutional monarchy under king Sobhuza II
1970–79 CE	**1973**	King Sobhuza suspends the constitution and assumes direct rule
	1979	King Sobhuza appoints a new legislature but retains the power of veto
1980–89 CE	**1982**	Death of King Sobhuza after a reign of 82 years
	1983	Sobhuza II's son Makhosetive is named heir to the throne
	1984	State university is closed by the government after student protests
	1985	Prince Clement Dlamini, leader of the opposition Swazi Liberation Movement, is exiled
	1986	Makhosetive is crowned king, assuming the name Mswati III
1990–99 CE	**1992**	King Mswati suspends the legislature and rules by decree
	1993	For the first time directly elected members of parliament are appointed to the legislature
	1995	Democracy protesters from the Swaziland Youth Congress burn down the parliament building
	1996	A constitutional committee is appointed to consider plans to democratize the country
	1997	Labor unions call for the constitutional committee to be dissolved
	1998	King Mswati announces a major environmental restoration program

Takrur

Takrur, perhaps the first Islamic state in West Africa, developed in the eleventh century toward the center of the Sénégal River Valley. Subject to Ghana and Mali for periods, Fulani settlers in Takrur evolved over generations into the Tukulor Fulani people, later the citizens of a great empire. *See also* **Senegal**; **Tukulor empire**.

Tanganyika

In 1890 CE the Anglo-German agreement established that lands north of 1° South in East Africa would fall into the British sphere of influence, and lands to the south would fall under German influence. This defined the northern border of what is now mainland Tanzania, while its eastern borders were set by the Congo Free State, British Central African possessions, and Portuguese Africa to the south. A guerilla war was fought

British mandate
A stamp issued in 1927 CE marking Tanganyika's status as a mandated territory of Britain.

© DIAGRAM

Tanganyika's origins

During the period 1892–1908 CE no less than five colonial powers had an interest in the area that became known as Tanganyika. During World War I, German forces at first effectively resisted the Allies. However, more Allied troops became available once the Germans had surrendered in other parts of Africa, leading to a series of Allied victories in 1916 CE. By November 1917 CE the British occupied the whole coast as far as the border with Mozambique. Two months later, German forces retreated into German East Africa and invaded Northern Rhodesia. There, they surrendered on November 25, 1918 CE after hearing of the Armistice. After the war, the rule of German territories was transferred by the League of Nations to neighboring colonial powers, underlining the inequality of African lives having been lost solely for European gain.

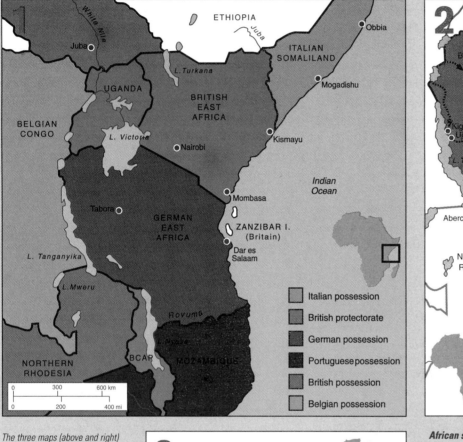

Italian possession

British protectorate

German possession

Portuguese possession

British possession

Belgian possession

The three maps (above and right) show the extent of colonial control in Tanganyika at the following dates:

1 1892–1908 CE   **3** 1920 CE

2 1916–1918 CE

◄--- British movements from Mar 1916

◄····· Belgian movements May–Sep 1916

◄── German movements Nov 1917–Nov 1918

■ Point of German surrender Nov 2, 1918

Belgian

British

African soldiers
African soldiers fought for both the Germans and the British in West Africa at the turn of the century. A soldier is shown in German uniform in the 1890s (right), and another in British uniform in the 1920s (below).

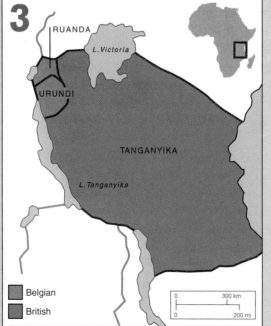

against German occupation for several years, especially by the Hehe people of southern Tanzania. The Maji Maji uprising of 1905 CE severely threatened the German's hold on its German East Africa colony, but was soon suppressed. After Germany's defeat in World War II (1939–45 CE), German East Africa was handed over to Britain, who renamed the colony Tanganyika. Tanganyika gained independence in 1961 CE. In 1964 CE Tanganyika and the former sultanate of Zanzibar united to form Tanzania. *See also* **Tanzania**; **Zanzibar**.

Tangier Zone

At the start of the twentieth century France, Britain, and Germany were in conflict over who controlled which parts of North Africa, Morocco in particular. After two "Moroccan crises" that almost led to war, agreements were made in 1911–12 CE, of which the international Tangier Zone was one result. Tangier and its environs formed this internationally controlled zone in 1923 CE. Its international status was abolished in 1956 CE, and Tangier returned to Morocco. *See also* **Morocco**.

TANZANIA United Republic of Tanzania

Archaeological evidence shows that, by the first century CE, the coast of what is now Tanzania had become important in Indian Ocean trade and, in 695 CE, Prince Hamza of Oman founded a settlement on the island of Zanzibar. From the tenth century, the mainland was settled by Bantu-speaking farmers, using iron tools. These people displaced the original people, who lived as hunter-gatherers.

Portuguese mariners reached the coast in the late fifteenth century and Portugal soon won control of the area. Arabs regained control in the late seventeenth century, when the sultanate of Oman took control of Zanzibar. The Arabs developed trade with such groups as the Nyamwezi and Yao in the mainland interior, exchanging such things as ceramics, cloth, and glassware for gold, ivory, and slaves. Zanzibar soon became a major center of the slave trade.

European explorers began to map the interior in the nineteenth century and, later, European powers began to compete for control of the area. In the 1880s, Germany began to take control of the mainland, making it a colony with the name of German East Africa in 1891 CE. Meanwhile, Britain made Zanzibar a protectorate (colony) in 1890 CE. Germany's rule was harsh and thousands of Africans were killed during the so-called Maji Maji rebellion in 1905 CE. During World War I, Britain gained control of the mainland, which it renamed Tanganyika. After the war, the League of Nations mandated Britain to rule Tanganyika, and, following World War II, the UN made the mainland a trusteeship territory.

Recent history

Opposition to colonial rule mounted in the 1950s, especially after the formation by Julius Nyerere and others of the Tanganyika African National Union (TANU) in 1954 CE. In 1958 CE, Tanganyika was granted internal self-government, while full independence was achieved on December 9, 1961 CE. Nyerere, the country's first prime minister, was elected president in 1962 CE, when Tanganyika became a republic. Nyerere established a one-party state, believing that a multiparty system might lead to ethnic conflict in African countries with different ethnic groups. He further argued that a one-party system maintained national unity, but did not rule out democratic debate.

The British territory of Zanzibar, where tensions existed between Africans and Arabs, achieved its independence on December 10, 1963 CE and, on April 26, 1964 CE, Tanganyika and Zanzibar merged to form the United Republic of Tanzania. In 1964 CE, TANU united with Zanzibar's Afro-Shirazi Party to form the *Chama Cha Mapinduzi* (CCM). The CCM became the sole legal party. Nyerere's objective was the creation of "African socialism," as defined in a famous policy document called the Arusha Declaration. At the heart of Nyerere's policies was *ujamaa*, a Swahili term meaning familyhood and self-reliance. The government set up large ujamaa villages and encouraged farmers on scattered farms to move into them, so that they could benefit from centralized services, such as education and health. At first, many people settled voluntarily in the *ujamaa* villages, working on collective and cooperative farms. However, in the 1970s, several million people were forced to move because they did not want to leave their traditional areas. The government's policies led to improvements in social services, but agricultural output declined.

Tanzania also faced other problems. Mainly because of political differences, the East African Community, which had been established to promote economic cooperation between Tanganyika, Kenya, and Uganda collapsed in 1967 CE, although it was revived in 1999 CE. Tanzania was also embroiled in the politics of its neighbors. In 1975 CE, with Chinese aid, a railway was built from Tanzania into Zambia, to give landlocked Zambia an outlet to the sea through a friendly country. Then, in 1978 CE, Tanzanian troops helped to

Year of the child
A stamp marking the International Year of the Child, 1979 CE.

Female recruits
Many women joined the Tanzanian People's Militia, some of whom can be seen in this illustration of a march-past.

© DIAGRAM

overthrow Idi Amin, the military dictator of Uganda. The war proved highly costly for Tanzania.

The economy was in decline in 1985 CE, when Nyerere retired as president. His successor, Ali Hassan Mwinyi dropped many of Tanzania's socialist policies and introduced more pragmatic policies to revive the economy. Opposition parties were made legal in 1992 CE. The first multiparty elections, held in 1995 CE, were won by the CCM and Benjamin Mkapa became president. Mkapa was reelected in 2000 CE.

Peoples

BONDEI

The Bondei are part of a larger grouping of Shambaa peoples, who inhabit the coastal lowlands of Tanzania, especially the rich plains between the northern coast of Tanzania around Tanga and the Usambara (or Shambaa) Mountains in northeastern Tanzania. The region they inhabit is called Bonde.

The Bondei probably emerged as a distinct group as recently as the mid-nineteenth century. At that time, the Bondei ancestors were ruled by the powerful Shambaa kingdom, but the Shambaa representative in Bonde exercised less and less power. Historians believe that the concept of the Bondei as a distinct ethnic group emerged during this period. In fact, this idea was actively encouraged by local settlement leaders in the area, who thought that they could lessen the impact of Shambaa rule if they could be seen as a unified group. During the late nineteenth century, the Bondei declared themselves independent from the Shambaa kingdom, and, over the following decades, the Bondei have come to be regarded as a separate ethnic group.

CHAGGA

The Chagga live on the slopes of Mount Kilimanjaro in northern Tanzania, where they have developed an intensive farming system. The Chagga's Bantu-speaking ancestors probably came to Mount Kilimanjaro at least 500–600 years ago, establishing several chiefdoms on its slopes. However, in recent decades, many Chagga have moved away from the area to the cities.

EAST AFRICAN ASIANS

For an account of the history of East African Asians, *see* **Kenya (Peoples—East African Asians)**.

FIPA

The Fipa live on the high plateau between Lake Rukwa and Lake Tanganyika in eastern Tanzania. Historically, the Fipa were divided into two states–Nkansi and Lyangile, with related ruling dynasties known as a *Twa*. History portrays the Fipa states as being wealthy and peaceful. Many powerful political positions in the Fipa states were open to anybody, irrespective of their social positions as long as they had the necessary abilities. Only the kingship and a few other symbolic roles were handed down through particular families.

HADZA

The Hadza are a small ethnic group who live mostly around Lake Eyasi in northern Tanzania. With the Sandawe (*see below*), they are perhaps the last remaining descendants of the first inhabitants of East Africa. They are historically associated with a hunting and gathering lifestyle. They are sometimes counted as descendants

of Khoisan people, but some experts have suggested that their language belongs to a different language family. As a result, the Hadza and Khoisan could be unrelated.

HAYA

The Haya are a large Bantu-speaking group who live in northern Tanzania, west of Lake Victoria. They formed several powerful kingdoms, all of which were abolished in 1962 CE.

IRAQW

Also known as the Mbulu (or Wambulu), the Iraqw live in northern Tanzania, largely in the Mbulu district south of Arusha. Beginning in the late nineteenth century, the Iraqw probably expanded outward from their mountainous homeland at the center of the Mbulu plateau. Cattle epidemics and colonial rule had weakened their neighbors, the Maasai, allowing the Iraqw to colonize more land.

LUO

For information about the history of the Luo people, *see*: **Kenya (Peoples—Luo)**.

MAASAI

For information about the history of the Maasai people, *see*: **Kenya (Peoples—Maasai)**.

NYAMWEZI

The Nyamwezi live in west-central Tanzania. Their name, originally *Wanyamwezi*, meaning "People of the Moon," was given because they came from the west, where the new Moon is first seen. Their homeland is called Unyamwezi.

Modern extent of the Nyamwezi people

Oral history holds that Unyamwezi was uninhabited until the seventeenth century. Then chiefly families began to arrive from various directions. The earliest records are from the late seventeenth century and concern the Galagansa, a western group. The Nyamwezi formed a number of semi-independent, self-governing units called *ntemi* (chiefdoms). A few powerful *ntemi* dominated the others. By about 1800 CE, traders from these groups were visiting the east coast–whose

Julius Nyerere
He was a leading campaigner for independence from colonial rule, and the president of Tanzania from 1964–1985 CE. Nyerere introduced policies of socialism and self-reliance to Tanzania between the 1960s and the 1980s.

Chief's stool
One of the most famous pieces of Nyamwezi art, this high-backed stool is typical of those made for chiefs. It was made for the chief of Buruku in the nineteenth century, and has a human figure on the backrest. The three legs are carved in the characteristic, curved Nyamwezi style.

Ntemi chiefs
These two men were the chiefs of Kahima and Karitu chiefdoms in 1959 CE. They are shown wearing their ceremonial robes, which are rarely seen today.

inhabitants gave them the name Wanyamwezi. The Nyamwezi gained a reputation as pioneers of long-distance trade in East and Central Africa by organizing trading caravans (companies of travelers journeying together). The principal trade was in iron—made and worked by the northern Nyamwezi—and salt. Later, copper and ivory became the main commodities. There was also some slave trading. During the nineteenth century, the Nyamwezi bought guns and some groups established standing armies. Several wars took place between the chiefdoms and armed conflict took place with Arab traders from the coast.

In the nineteenth century, a *ntemi* chief named Mirambo managed to establish his dominance over several chiefdoms. Mirambo's short-lived empire came into conflict with Arab traders, but broke up soon after his death in 1884 CE. By the 1890s, German colonists had taken control of mainland Tanzania, which they ruled as German East Africa. Britain took over after World War I.

PARE

The Pare are part of the larger grouping of Shambaa peoples, who inhabit the coastal lowlands of Tanzania. The Shambaa are descended from both Bantu and Cushitic ancestors, who migrated into East Africa hundreds of years ago. The first Bantu-speaking settlers reached the Pare region some time before the sixteenth century. From the eighteenth century, Bantu-speakers steadily moved into the Pare region, where they intermingled with other groups and eventually organized themselves into lineage (family-based) groups. The northern Pare state of Gwena, ruled by the Wasuya lineage, was a stable and well-organized union that survived well into the nineteenth century. The leader, or Mangi Mrwe, ruled with the help of *chila* (councils), *wanjama* (ministers), and *wamgani* (local chiefs).

SANDAWE

The Sandawe live in the northern regions of Tanzania's central highlands, south of lakes Eyasi and Manyara in northern Tanzania. With the Hadza (*see above*), they are perhaps the last remaining descendants of the first human inhabitants of East Africa. They may have been the ancestors of the modern Khoisan.

SHAMBAA

The Shambaa are a cluster of closely related ethnic groups, including the Bondei, Pare, and Shambala, who inhabit the coastal lowlands of Tanzania. Although they are what is known as an Eastern Bantu people, the Shambaa are descended from both Bantu and Cushitic ancestors. Early in the first millennium, Bantu speakers migrating into East Africa from Central Africa mingled with Cushitic peoples, who had already moved into that region. Interaction between the two cultures led to the development of the Shambaa and other groups, such as the Kikuyu in what is now Kenya. At first, the Shambaa's ancestors lived in widespread, independent settlements. However, after experiencing Maasai raids in the early eighteenth century, the different family-based groups began to form closer political unions. Under Mbegha, who perhaps came from areas in western and central Tanzania that had already established chieftaincies, the Shambaa began to develop a powerful, centralized state. Ruled by a group known as the Kilindi, the Shambaa kingdom reached its heights in the nineteenth century under the famous Kimweri ye Nyumbai.

SUKUMA

The Sukuma, who are closely related to the Nyamwezi people, live in lands north of the Nyamwezi in west-central Tanzania. Like other Bantu-speaking peoples of what is now western and central Tanzania, the Sukuma formed semi-independent, self-governing units, called *ntemi*. The *ntemi* system of political organization was in use by the Sukuma and Nyamwezi people by the fourteenth century, and it was adopted by other peoples in the region who came into contact with them.

SWAHILI

The Swahili people live in coastal regions and on the small offshore islands of Tanzania and Kenya. Their name is derived from an Arabic word, meaning "coast dwellers". The Swahili are of mixed black African, Arab, and Persian descent. The coastal black Africans were mainly Bantu and Cushitic groups, who had migrated into the area from the northwest, and some Bantu from the south, before 1000 CE. Arabs and Persians arrived from Southwest Asia after the Bantu-speaking people. Most were attracted by the trade in ivory, skins, and slaves, though some were seeking refuge from political or religious persecution. The Arabs established settlements at Mogadishu, Lamu, Malindi, Zanzibar, and Kilwa. Arabs ruled some of the settlements, while Africans ruled others. Around 1200 CE, Persians from Shiraz established the Shiraz dynasty on the Banadir coast around Mogadishu.

Swahili culture emerged from the intermingling–mainly through marriage and trade–of these Arab, African, and Persian groups. By the twelfth century at the latest, the Swahili had emerged as a distinct people. They had a number of small kingdoms based on trading cities up and down the coast. One of the most important was Kilwa. Here, gold, gum, ivory, slaves, and lumber from inland were traded for cotton, glass, porcelain, and pottery supplied by the Arabian, Chinese, and Indian merchants. Kilwa was just one of about 40 such ports along the East African coast and on the islands of Pemba and Zanzibar, which are now part of Tanzania. The ruins of their stone buildings and palaces still survive. The golden age of Swahili culture came to an abrupt end when Portuguese adventurers arrived on the coast, at first in 1498 CE. By 1509 CE, the Swahili had lost their independence to the Portuguese. In the seventeenth century, Omani Arab traders began to settle on the East African coast, driving out the Portuguese. They controlled most of the region by 1699 CE and, between 1822–1837 CE, the coast was ruled as part of the Omani empire. During this period, the Omani sultan, Seyyid Said, transferred his capital from Muscat in Oman to the island of Zanzibar, in order to gain control of the trade routes. Zanzibar dominated East African trade and became an international trading depot during the nineteenth century. Much of its prosperity was owed to the slave trade. This was stimulated by the development of Arab plantations of cloves and coconuts on the East African coast and its islands, and French sugar plantations on islands in the Indian Ocean. Caravans (companies of travelers journeying together) began to enter the interior of East Africa to collect slaves from as far

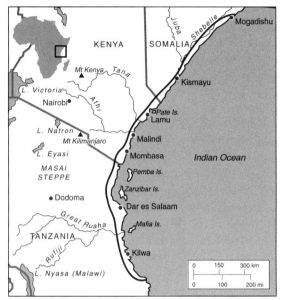

Visitors' chair

Chairs such as this one were used in many Swahili royal courts from the fourteenth to the nineteenth centuries. Elaborately carved in ebony and inlaid with ivory, the chair was a symbol of power and would be offered as a sign of respect to visiting notables.

Modern extent of the Swahili people

south as present-day Malawi, and many Arab and Swahili traders made their fortunes in this destructive trade. By the 1860s, 70,000 people a year were being sold as slaves at the Zanzibar slave market. Zanzibar declined with the abolition of the slave trade and the advent of German and British colonists.

YAO

For information about the history of the Yao people, *see*: **Malawi (Peoples—Yao)**.

ZARAMO

The Zaramo occupy a 100-mile (160-km) strip of Tanzanian coastline centered on Dar es Salaam, Tanzania's largest city. Their language is called Kizaramo, although most of them also speak Swahili, East Africa's most common language.

The Zaramo migrated into their present lands more than 200 years ago. They share a common ancestry with the Luguru of the Uluguru Mountains, about 125 miles (200 km) west of Dar es Salaam. The name Luguru simply means "people of the mountains," and, when the people migrated eastward, they developed into new ethnic groups. There are only slight differences between the Kizarama and Luguru languages.

Tanzania's major political figures

Mkapa, Benjamin William (1938 CE–)

Mkapa, a former civil servant and journalist, was elected president of Tanzania in 1995, winning 61.8 percent of the total votes cast. He is chairman of the *Chama Cha Mapinduzi* (Revolutionary Party).

Tanzania timeline

Pre 19th century

1st century CE Egyptian and Greek merchants sail to Tanzanian coast to buy ivory and hardwood

695 Prince Hamza of Oman settles at Zanzibar

10th century Bantu-speaking peoples settle in Tanzania region

975 According to tradition, prince Ali bin Sultan al Hassan of Shiraz (Iran) settles at Kilwa

c. 1200 Kilwa becomes the first state in sub-Saharan Africa to issue its own coinage

1499 Portuguese navigator, Vasco de Gama, visits Tanzania on his way to India

1698 The sultanate of Oman wins control of Zanzibar

19th century CE

1840 Sultan Sayyid Said of Oman moves his court to Zanzibar

1844 The Anglican Church Missionary Society sets up a mission station in Zanzibar

1848 Johannes Rebmann becomes the first European to see Mt Kilimanjaro, the highest mountain in Africa

1850s Trading caravans from Zanzibar reach as far as the Congo River basin

1858 Richard Burton and John Hanning Speke reach Lake Tanganyika and lake Victoria

1867 Britain begins a campaign to destroy Zanzibar's slave trade

1871 Henry Morton Stanley meets David Livingstone at Ujiji on Lake Tanganyika

1873 The Sultan of Zanzibar abolishes the slave trade

1884 German explorer Karl Peters signs treaties with several chiefs in the Tanzania region

1890 The Sultanate of Zanzibar becomes a British protectorate

1891 The German East Africa colony is established

1900–49 CE

1905 The Maji Maji rebellion against German rule is crushed

1907 Germany has full control of the territory of modern Tanzania

1914–1918 The German commander in East Africa Gen. Paul von Lettow-Vorbeck fights a skillful guerrilla war against allied forces throughout World War I

1918 British forces occupy the Tanganyika portion of German East Africa

1919 Disruption caused by fighting in World War I leads to a serious famine

1920 Tanganyika is mandated to Britain by the League of Nations

1926 Legislative councils appointed for Tanganyika and Zanzibar

1930s Nazi party becomes popular among German settlers in Tanganyika

1945 The first Africans are appointed to the legislative councils

1946 Tanganyika becomes a UN Trust Territory

1950–59 CE

1954 Julius Nyerere forms the Tanganyika African National Union (TANU)

1958 Tanganyika is granted internal self-government

1960–69 CE

1961 Dec 9 Tanganyika becomes independent

1962 Julius Nyerere is elected president

1963 Dec 10 Zanzibar is granted independence

1964 Apr 26 Tanganyika and Zanzibar merge to form the United Republic of Tanzania

1965 Nyerere merges TANU with Zanzibar's Afro-Shirazi party to form the *Chama Cha Mapinduzi* (CCM) party: it becomes the only legal political party

1967 Tanzania, Kenya and Uganda form the East African Community

1975 Tan-Zam (Tanzania-Zambia) railroad is completed

1970–79 CE

1977 Internal differences cause the collapse of the East African Community

1978 Tanzania defeats a Ugandan invasion

1979 Tanzanian troops help overthrow the Ugandan dictator Idi Amin

1980–89 CE

1981 Tanzanian troops are withdrawn from Uganda

1985 Nyerere retires from the presidency: he is succeeded by Ali Hassan Mwinyi

1990–99 CE

1990 Mwinyi is re-elected president

1992 Opposition parties are legalized

1994 Around 800,000 refugees from ethnic violence in Rwanda and Burundi flee to Tanzania

1995 Benjamin Mkapa of the CCM becomes president after the first multiparty elections

1996 Government expels 540,000 Rwandan refugees

1998 Eleven killed and 80 injured in Islamic fundamentalist bomb attack on US embassy in Dar-es-Salaam

1999 Nyerere dies; Tanzania, Kenya and Uganda sign a framework agreement establishing a new East African Community, aimed at creating a common market

Tanzanian presidents

Dec 9 1962–Nov 5 1985 CE
Julius Nyerere

Nov 5 1985–Nov 23 1995 CE
Ali Hassan Mwinyi

Nov 23 1995 CE–
Benjamin Mkapa

Stanley meets Livingstone
Henry Morton Stanley meets David Livingstone on November 10, 1871 at Ujiji on Lake Tanganyika. Livingstone had been missing for several years and the New York Herald *paid Stanley to find him as a journalistic enterprise.*

© DIAGRAM

Mwinyi, Ali Hassan (1925 CE–)

Ali Hassan Mwinyi became president of Tanzania in 1985, after President Julius Nyerere retired. He was reelected in 1990 and served until 1995, when, having completed the maximum of two terms in office, he was replaced by Benjamin Mkapa. Mwinyi pursued liberal economic policies and introduced a multiparty constitution in 1993.

Nyerere, Julius Kambarage (1922–1999 CE)

Julius Nyerere, leader of the Tanganyika African National Union (TANU)–later named *Chama Cha Mapinduzi* (CCM)–became Tanganyika's first prime minister in 1961 and its first president in 1962. In 1964, he became president of the united Tanzania (Tanganyika and Zanzibar). He retired in 1985, but remained chairman of the CCM until 1990. A pioneer of *ujamaa* (self-help) policies and African socialism, Nyerere was successful in introducing social reforms, but his economic policies were less successful. In the mid 1990s, he acted as mediator in the Burundi peace talks.

Tourism in Tanzania

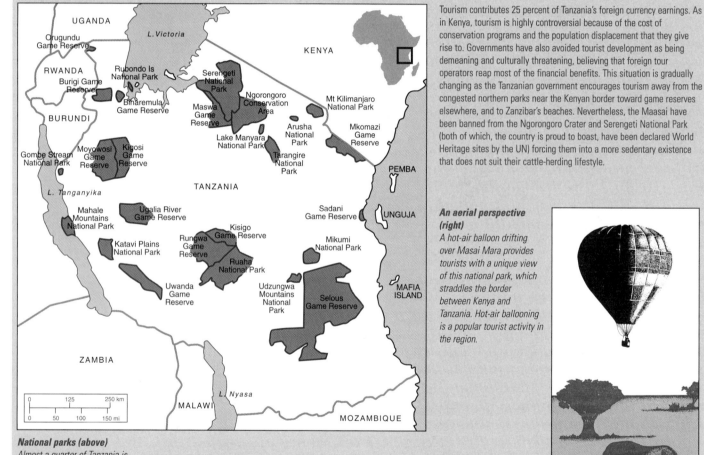

Tourism contributes 25 percent of Tanzania's foreign currency earnings. As in Kenya, tourism is highly controversial because of the cost of conservation programs and the population displacement that they give rise to. Governments have also avoided tourist development as being demeaning and culturally threatening, believing that foreign tour operators reap most of the financial benefits. This situation is gradually changing as the Tanzanian government encourages tourism away from the congested northern parks near the Kenyan border toward game reserves elsewhere, and to Zanzibar's beaches. Nevertheless, the Maasai have been banned from the Ngorongoro Crater and Serengeti National Park (both of which, the country is proud to boast, have been declared World Heritage sites by the UN) forcing them into a more sedentary existence that does not suit their cattle-herding lifestyle.

An aerial perspective (right)
A hot-air balloon drifting over Masai Mara provides tourists with a unique view of this national park, which straddles the border between Kenya and Tanzania. Hot-air ballooning is a popular tourist activity in the region.

National parks (above)
Almost a quarter of Tanzania is protected land designated as national parks, game reserves, and conservation areas.

Tema

See **Ga towns**.

Teshi

See **Ga towns**.

TOGO Republic of Togo

Historians believe that the ancestors of many of the people of what is now Togo were either invaders from the north or refugees from wars in Asante and Dahomey—*see also* **Asante empire**; **Benin (Peoples—Fon)**. Portuguese mariners, seeking a route to Asia around Africa, reached the area in the late fifteenth century. The slave trade soon developed and southern Togo became part of the so-called "Slave Coast," which stretched from southwest Nigeria to around the mouth of the Volta River in present-day Ghana.

From the mid-nineteenth century, German traders and missionaries became established in Togo. In 1884 CE, Germany set up a protectorate (colony) on the coast and, in 1899 CE, they established a colony called German Togoland. During World War I, British and French troops occupied German Togoland and, in 1922 CE, the League of Nations mandated Britain to administer the western third of the territory and France to rule the eastern two-thirds. In 1946 CE, the UN made British and French Togoland trust territories.

In 1956 CE, the people of British Togoland voted in a referendum to join Gold Coast and it was incorporated when Gold Coast became independent as Ghana in 1957 CE. However, in 1956, French Togoland became an internally self-governing republic within the French Union. The French appointed as prime minister Nicolas Grunitzky, leader of the Togolese Progressive Party, who wanted Togo to remain within the French Union. But in 1958 CE, Sylvanus Olympio, leader of the Togolese Unity Party, was elected prime minister. Olympio demanded complete independence, which was achieved on April 27, 1960 CE.

Recent history

Sylvanus Olympio, Togo's first president, sought to develop the economy, encouraging foreign investment and developing the phosphate industry–with phosphates becoming a major export. However, his strict budgets and his failure to meet the needs of the unemployed made him unpopular. Eventually, he aroused the enmity of many soldiers by reducing the size of the army and, in 1963 CE, demobilized veterans who had served in the French Army attacked Olympio's palace. Olympio fled seeking sanctuary and was killed by a junior officer, Gnassingbé Eyadéma, outside the gates of the United States embassy.

Olympio was succeeded by his rival Nicolas Grunitzky, who returned to the country from Ivory Coast to become president. Grunitzky sought to rule with a coalition government, but he met with much opposition. In 1967 CE, the army intervened and Eyadéma, who by then was a general, seized power in a bloodless coup. Grunitzky returned to Ivory Coast and Eyadéma ruled as a military dictator. In 1969 CE, he declared the Rally of Togolese People as Togo's only legal party. In the 1970s, the country's stability and economic success made Eyadéma popular. He nationalized the French phosphate mines in 1974 CE, developed the road system, and modernized the capital city of Lome. But his measures were accompanied by harsh methods that flouted human rights–with corruption and torture becoming common.

In the early 1980s, the economy began to decline and, in 1985 CE, the country's stability was disrupted by a series of bombings in Lome and an attempted coup, which was put down with the assistance of French troops. Togo accused Ghana and Burkina Faso of involvement in the failed coup. Demands for democracy mounted and, in 1991 CE, Eyadéma agreed to divide power with a transitional administration and political parties were legalized. In 1992 CE, a new constitution was approved. Eyadéma was elected president in 1993 CE, though allegations were made of electoral fraud. Also in 1993, France, Germany, and the United States suspended aid to Togo because of mounting evidence of state terrorism. Eyadéma was reelected president in 1998 CE, although more allegations of irregularities clouded the outcome. In 2000 CE, a UN report alleged that Burkina Faso's president Blaise Compaoré and Eyadéma had helped the rebel UNITA group in Angola to obtain arms and fuel in exchange for diamonds mined in the areas occupied by UNITA forces.

Endangered animals
The African crocodile, one of several endangered species featured on Republic of Togo stamps issued in 1977 CE.

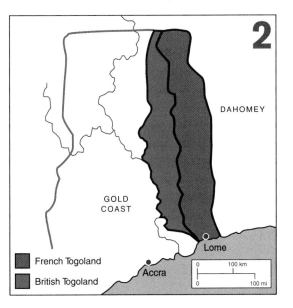

Concentration of German forces
British forces
French forces

Sansana-Mangu
TOGOLAND
DAHOMEY
GOLD COAST
Atakpame
Lome
Accra

1

DAHOMEY
GOLD COAST
Lome
Accra

French Togoland
British Togoland

0 100 km
0 100 mi

2

World War I and its aftermath
In 1884 CE Germany set up a protectorate on the Gold Coast and, in 1899 CE, they established a colony called German Togoland. During World War I British and French troops occupied German Togoland and, in 1922 CE, the League of Nations mandated the British to administer the western third of the territory, and France to govern the eastern two thirds. The maps show the extent of the allied invasions and the subsequently mandated territories.

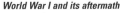

1 1914–16 CE

2 1919–1922 CE

© DIAGRAM

Both Burkina Faso and Togo denied the charges of breaching sanctions and helping UNITA's war effort. Also in 2000 CE, a joint UN–Organization of African Unity (OAU) panel was set up to investigate allegations made by Amnesty International that Togo's armed forces had executed hundreds of people in the runup to the 1998 CE presidential election.

Peoples

EWE

For information about the history of the Ewe people, *see* **Ghana (Peoples—Ewe)**.

YORUBA

For information about the history of the Yoruba people, *see* **Nigeria (Peoples—Yoruba)**.

Togo presidents
Apr 27 1960–Jan 13 1963 CE Sylvanus Olympio (acting to Apr 12 1961)
Jan 13 1963–Jan 15 1963 CE Emmanuel Bodjollé (chairman Insurrection Committee)
Jan 15 1963–Jan 13 1967 CE Nicolas Grunitzky (acting to May 5 1963)
Jan 13 1967–Apr 14 1967 CE Kléber Dadjo (chairman National Reconciliation Committee)
Apr 14 1967 CE– Etienne Eyadéma (from May 8 1974, Gnassingbe Eyadéma)

Togo timeline

19th century CE
1884 Germany sets up a protectorate on the coast
1899 The German Togoland colony is created

1900–49 CE 1914 British and French troops occupy German Togoland
1922 The League of Nations mandates the western third of German Togoland to Britain, the eastern two-thirds are mandated to France
1946 British and French Togolands become UN trust territories

1950–59 CE 1956 British Togoland votes to join Gold Coast (now Ghana)

1960–69 CE 1960 Apr 27 French Togoland becomes the independent republic of Togo: Sylvanus Olympio becomes the first president
1963 Olympio is assassinated by rebel army officers who make Nicolas Grunitzky president
1967 Grunitzky is overthrown by a military coup led by Gnassingbé Eyadéma
1969 Eyadéma creates the Rally of Togolese People (RPT) and makes it Togo's only legal party

1990–99 CE 1993 Eyadéma is re-elected under a new multiparty constitution
1994 The RPT forms a coalition government with opposition parties
1998 Eyadéma is re-elected president

Gnassingbe Eyadéma
He first became president of Togo in 1967 CE following a bloodless coup, and was reelected in 1993 CE under a new constitution.

Togo's major political figures

Eyadéma, Gnassingbe (formerly Etienne) (1937 CE–)
Following a bloodless coup in 1967, Gnassingbe Eyadéma–who had served in the French Army–became president of Togo, ousting Nicolas Grunitzky. In 1969, he set up the *Rassemblement du Peuple Togolais* (RPT), which later became the sole political party. He was reelected president under a new constitution in l993. An unpopular leader, he has begun to make Togo's political system more democratic but there have been many attempts to overthrow him.

Grunitzky, Nicolas (1937–1994 CE)
Nicolas Grunitzky served as prime minister of Togo (1956–68) and became president of Togo in 1963 after the overthrow of Sylvanus Olympio. Dependence on France increased under him and, in 1967, he was ousted in a bloodless coup by Gnassingbe Eyadéma and exiled.

Olympio, Sylvanus (1902–1963 CE)
Sylvanus Olympio was prime minister of Togo (1958–60) and became the country's first president when it gained independence in 1960. Olympio was a prominent campaigner for reunification of the Ewe people, who are divided between Togo and Ghana. He was killed in a military coup in 1963 and replaced by Nicolas Grunitzky.

Togoland

Togoland was created in 1884 CE when Germany declared a protectorate the region between British Gold Coast Colony to the west, and French Dahomey to the east. During World War I, France and Britain occupied Togoland, which was then officially divided between the two European nations in 1922 CE. The eastern two-thirds became French Togoland; the remainder British Togoland. The British part became part of independent Ghana in 1957 CE. French Togoland gained independence as Togo in 1960 CE. *See also* **Ghana**; **Togo**.

Toro kingdom

A prince of the Bunyoro kingdom (Uganda) established his own kingdom called Toro in the nineteenth century. After this prince, Kaboyo, died in the 1850s the kingdom was divided by successive civil wars. Nyaila I emerged as the ruler, but the kingdom was invaded by Bunyoro in 1876 CE. British forces restored Toro to independence and installed Kasagama as their puppet in the 1890s. Toro joined the Uganda Protectorate, along with Ankole, Bunyoro, and Buganda. *See also* **Uganda Protectorate**; **Uganda**.

Transkei

Transkei was the first of the ten homelands established during South Africa's apartheid era. In 1959 CE Europeans gave the name "Ciskei" to the Xhosa lands between the Great Fish and Great Kei rivers; Xhosa lands east of the Great Kei were named "Transkei." The Transkei homeland was created, along with Ciskei, for the Xhosa people to live in. The white-controlled South African government forced black South Africans to live in these areas, which often bore no relation to their true home lands. The vast majority of Transkei's inhabitants were Xhosa people. Transkei was declared "independent" in 1976 CE, but its independence was not genuine and never recognized internationally. After the first multiracial elections held in 1994 CE, Transkei was officially reincorporated into South Africa as part of Eastern Cape and KwaZulu/Natal provinces. *See also* **South Africa.**

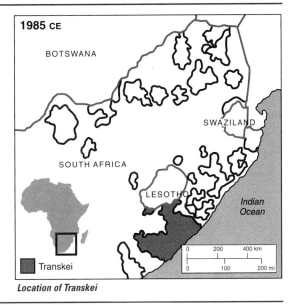

Location of Transkei

Transvaal, Crown Colony of

From 1877–1881 CE the British-ruled Crown Colony of Transvaal was established over the Boer South African Republic. After a short period of independence, the Crown Colony was reestablished over the Boer republic in 1900 CE, and the colony became a province after the creation of the Union of South Africa. *See also* **South African Republic (Transvaal)**.

Tripolitana

Tripolitana was an ancient region of north Africa that lay between Tunis and Cyrenaica. It included the three cities Oea, Leptis Magna (now Lebda), and Sabrata. Tripolitana was under Turkish control from the sixteenth century until 1911 CE, then under Italian control until 1943 CE, and finally British control until 1952 CE.

Tristan da Cunha

Several small islands (Tristan da Cunha, Inaccessible, Nightingale, Middle, Stoltenhoff, and Gough) together form Tristan da Cunha, a dependency of St. Helena, which is, in turn, a dependency of Britain. Tristan da Cunha lies 1,500 miles (2,400 km) west of Cape Town in the South Atlantic Ocean. St. Helena is 1,300 (2,100 km) miles to the northeast. The islands were discovered in 1506 CE by a Portuguese admiral, Tristão da Cunha.

Tristan da Cunha has a population of around 300, and Gough has a crewed weather station, but all the other islands are uninhabited. Tristan da Cunha was annexed by Britain in 1816 CE, and a garrison was stationed there. The garrison was withdrawn the following year, but three members decided to stay. By 1886 CE, nearly 100 people lived on the island: the original settlers had been joined by shipwrecked sailors, women from St. Helena, and European settlers. In 1938 CE all six islands were made dependencies of St. Helena. In 1961 CE Tristan da Cunha was evacuated after a volcanic eruption, but most inhabitants returned in 1963 CE. *See also* **St. Helena**.

Tsitambala confederation

The Tsitambala confederation was a seventeenth century alliance of chiefdoms along the east coast of Madagascar. This confederation was taken over and expanded in the early eighteenth century by Ratsimilaho, the English-educated son of an English pirate. From this confederation, Ratsimilaho created the Betsimisaraka kingdom. Although the kingdom extended along more than 200 miles (320 km) of coast, it disintegrated after Ratsimilaho's death in 1750 CE.

Tukulor empire

The Tukulor empire was founded by the al-Hajj Umar (c.1795–1864 CE), a Muslim cleric of Fulani birth. In 1848 CE he settled with his followers near Futa Djallon, intending to found a strict Muslim state. By the 1850s, they were ready to launch *jihads* (holy wars) to achieve this aim. The first to be attacked were the Bambara kingdoms to the north, such as Kaarta and Segu. Soon, Umar's kingdom reached as far north as Timbuktu. The Tukulor empire, although vast, was not stable and uprisings were common. Eventually, the French conquered their lands, from 1890 CE on. The Tukulor people fought the French until 1894, but were defeated by their superior firepower. *See also* **Mali**; **Niger**.

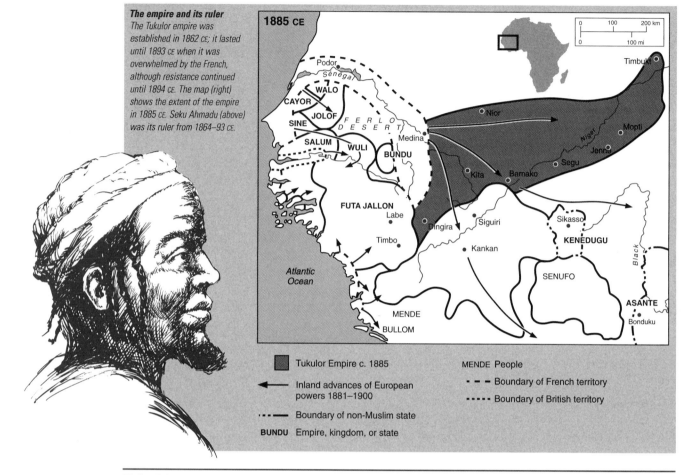

The empire and its ruler
The Tukolor empire was established in 1862 CE; it lasted until 1893 CE when it was overwhelmed by the French, although resistance continued until 1894 CE. The map (right) shows the extent of the empire in 1885 CE. Seku Ahmadu (above) was its ruler from 1864–93 CE.

1885 CE

	Tukulor Empire c. 1885	MENDE People
←	Inland advances of European powers 1881–1900	- - - Boundary of French territory
∙-∙-∙	Boundary of non-Muslim state	∙∙∙∙∙ Boundary of British territory
BUNDU	Empire, kingdom, or state	

Tulunids

The Tulunid dynasty ruled Egypt and Syria from 868–905 CE. It was founded by a Turk, Ahmad ibn Tulun, who arrived in Egypt as a vice-governor for the 'Abbasids. Under the Tulunids, Egypt first emerged as an independent Arabic state but it was retaken by the Abbasids in 905 CE. *See also* **Egypt**.

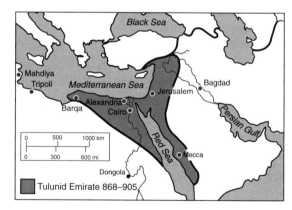

The Tulunids
This dynasty ruled Egypt and Syria from 868–905 CE after which they were retaken by the 'Abbasids.

Tulunid Emirate 868–905

TUNISIA Republic of Tunisia

The earliest people known to have inhabited what is now Tunisia were Berbers, However, from ancient times, the area received waves of immigrants, including Phoenicians from the coasts of what are now Syria, Lebanon, and Israel. According to tradition, the Phoenicians founded Carthage, near present-day Tunis, in 814 CE BCE. The Romans destroyed Carthage in 146 BCE and ruled the area for nearly 600 years. The Vandals, a Germanic tribe, overran Tunisia in 439 CE, but the Eastern Roman Empire regained control in 534 CE. In 670 CE, Arabs invaded Tunisia, introducing the Arabic

language and Islam. The region became part of the Arab-Muslim world, and was ruled by a series of Arab and Berber dynasties.

In 1574 CE, the Ottoman Turks conquered Tunisia and made it part of their empire, which they governed through local rulers called *beys*. After Tunisia became a French protectorate (colony) in 1881 CE, *beys* continued to hold office, but their responsibilities were extremely limited. Opposition to colonial rule developed before World War I and, in 1920 CE, nationalists called for the creation of a national assembly. In 1934 CE, a leading

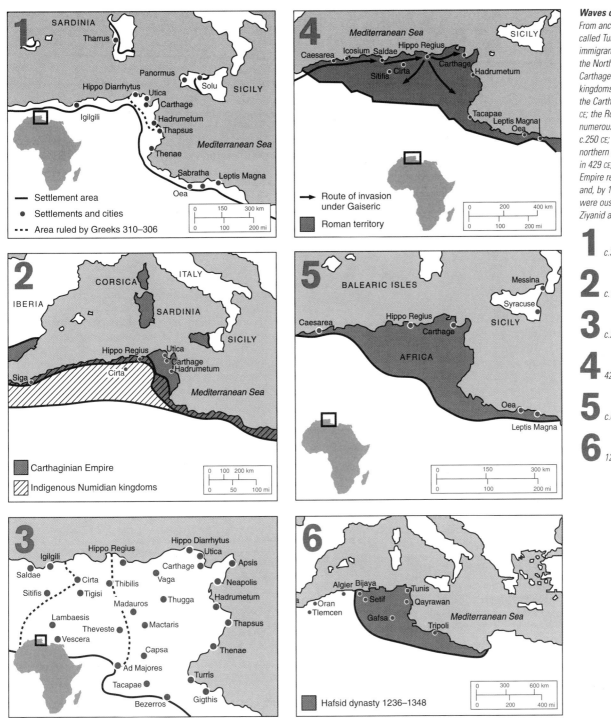

nationalist, Habib Bourguiba, founded the *Neo-Destour* (New Constitution) party. During World War II, Tunisia was at first governed by a French collaborationist regime but, in 1942 CE, it was invaded by German and Italian troops. In the following year, British, Free French, and United States forces liberated Tunisia. After the war, France tried to maintain its control, but nationalist activities increased and, after Bourguiba was arrested in 1952 CE, outbreaks of violence occurred.

Tunisia in World War II
In 1942 CE Tunisia was invaded by German and Italian troops but, in the following year, it was liberated by British, Free French, and United States forces. The illustration (top) graphically captures a scene from one of the battles fought, while a stamp, issued in 1943 CE, celebrates the bond between the allied soldiers.

Habib ibn Ali Bourguiba
He was Tunisia's first prime minister (1956-7), and its first president (1957-87). Declared president for life, he was deposed by his prime minister in 1987.

Recent history

Internal self-government was achieved in 1955 CE and Tunisia became fully independent on March 20, 1956 CE. At first, the French kept military bases in the country until the early 1960s, when relations with France improved. Meanwhile, in July 1957 CE, the *bey*, who had been criticized for not identifying himself with the independence struggle, was deposed. Tunisia then became a republic, with Habib Bourguiba, the former prime minister, as president. Bouguiba's ruling *Neo-Destour* party, (which was renamed the Destourian Socialist Rally in 1964 CE and the Democratic Constitutional Rally in 1988 CE), launched a series of reforms. They included the emancipation of women and compulsory free education.

However, the party's opposition to Islamic fundamentalism led to a concern that the country might lose its Arab-Muslim heritage. Bourguiba, therefore, had to keep Islamic fundamentalists under control–a policy that led him to adopt an increasingly dictatorial manner. In 1975 CE, the constitution was amended so that the National Assembly could proclaim Bourguiba "president-for-life." In 1981 CE, a multiparty system was introduced, but it had little liberalizing effect in the 1981 elections, because an alliance of the Destourian Socialist party and the trade unions won every parliamentary seat.

In 1987 CE, the 84-year-old and infirm Bourguiba was removed from office in a bloodless coup by General Zine al Abidine Ben Ali, who had become prime minister one month earlier. Ben Ali, who declared that

Bourguiba was senile and unfit to continue in office took over the presidency. Ben Ali was fortunate to inherit a stable economy, with a fast-growing tourist industry. In 1988 CE, he amended the constitution. abolishing the office of "president-for-life," and holding presidential elections every five years. He also ordered the release of all political prisoners. He introduced some political reforms, including an increase in press freedoms, but he continued Bourguiba's hardline policy against Islamic fundamentalism, regarding it as a threat to national unity.

In 1992 CE, the Islamic Nahda party was accused of plotting against the government and banned. This was followed in 1994 CE by further action when Ben Ali prevented Islamic fundamentalist parties from participating in the national elections and ran unopposed for the presidency. He was again reelected in 1999 CE, taking 99 percent of the vote despite the fact that he ran against two other candidates. His Democratic Constitutional Rally also dominated in the parliamentary elections, although a new constitutional amendment reserved 20 percent of the parliamentary seats for opposition parties, whatever their public support. The 1990s were marked by occasional outbreaks of violence, the arrests of many Islamic fundamentalists, and the suspension of human rights. However, Tunisia managed to control the situation and prevented the strife reaching the scale of the similar conflict in neighboring Algeria.

Peoples
ARABS
The Arabs, who originated in Arabia, conquered the Berbers of North Africa in the late seventh century, introducing their language, Arabic, and their religion, Islam. Today Arabs make up more than 98 percent of Tunisia's population.

BERBERS
Berbers are the earliest known inhabitants of Tunisia. They were settled along the North African coast by 3000 BCE, but little is known about their history before the third century BCE. For an account of the early history of history of the Berber peoples, *see also* **Berber kingdoms**.

The modern history of the Berbers begins with their conversion to Islam in the late seventh century CE. Over the years, Arab invasions forced many Berbers out of coastal regions and into the mountains and desert. But many others were absorbed into the Arab population. Today, only about one percent of Tunisians are classified as Berbers.

Tunisia's major political figures

Ben Ali, Zine al Abidine (1936 CE–)
In a peaceful takeover in November 1987, Zine al Abidine Ben Ali, prime minister of Tunisia since early October, replaced former President Habib Bourguiba as head of state. He was reelected in 1989, 1994 and 1999. His government has been criticized for abuses of human rights, but praised for its economic reforms.

Bourguiba, Habib ibn Ali (1903–2000 CE)
A radical nationalist, Habib Bourguiba was Tunisia's first prime minister (1956–57) and its first president (1957–87). He attempted to curb Islamic fundamentalists during his years as president and maintained moderate, pro-Western foreign policies. He was declared president-for-life in 1975, but was deposed by his prime minister, Ben Ali, in 1987 on the grounds that he was unfit to continue, because of senility and ill-health.

Tunisia timeline

Pre 19th century

814 BCE Phoenicians found the city of Carthage near present-day Tunis

c. 264 BCE Carthaginian Empire at its peak

146 BCE Carthage is conquered by the Roman Empire: all of present-day Tunisia comes under Roman rule

439 CE The Vandals, a Germanic tribe, capture Carthage

534 Carthage is recaptured by the Eastern Roman Empire (Byzantine Empire)

670 The Islamic Arabs invade Tunisia and found Kairouan

698 The Arabs capture Carthage: the city is abandoned in favor of nearby Tunis

800–909 Tunisia becomes independent under the Arab Aghlabid dynasty

909 The Aghlabids are replaced by the Arab Fatimid dynasty

969 The native Berber Zirid dynasty replaces the Fatimids when they move their capital to Cairo

1236–1574 The Hafsid dynasty rules Tunisia

1270 The Eighth Crusade attacks Tunis

1535 The Spanish capture Tunis

1573–1574 The Spanish again occupy Tunis

1574 The Ottoman Turks conquer Tunisia

1705 The *beys* (regents) of Tunis become effectively autonomous within the Ottoman empire

19th century CE

1869 A financial crisis forces the *bey* to accept Anglo-French financial supervision

1878 Tunisia is recognized as a French sphere of influence at the Congress of Berlin

1881 Tunisia becomes a French protectorate

1900–49 CE

1920 The *Destour* party calls for the creation of a national assembly

1934 Habib Bourguiba founds the *Neo-Destour* (New Constitution) party

1940 Tunisia supports the collaborationist Vichy regime after France surrenders to Germany in World War II

1942 German and Italian troops occupy Tunisia

1943 British, US and Free French troops drive the Germans and Italians out of Tunisia

1950–59 CE

1955 France grants Tunisia internal self-government

1956 Mar 20 Tunisia becomes independent under the *bey* of Tunis

1957 Tunisia becomes a republic when the *bey* abdicates, Bourguiba is elected the first president of Tunisia

1960–69 CE

1961 Fighting breaks out when France attempts to expand its naval base at Bizerte without Tunisian permission

1962 France withdraws from its bases in Tunisia

1963 Bourguiba's Democratic Socialist Rally (formerly the *Neo-Destour* Party) becomes the only legal party

1964 Land owned by Europeans is nationalized

1970–79 CE

1975 Bourguiba becomes president for life

1978 A general strike is broken by the army

1980–89 CE

1982–1986 Tunis is the HQ of the Palestine Liberation Organization (PLO)

1983 Mass protests follow the withdrawal of government food subsidies

1987 Prime minister Zine el-Abidine Ben Ali removes Bourguiba from office and becomes president in his place

1988 Opposition parties are legalized

1989 Tunisia joins Algeria, Libya and Morocco in the Arab Maghrib Union

1990–99 CE

1992 The Islamic fundamentalist Nahda party is banned

1994 Islamic fundamentalist political parties are banned from participating in the first multiparty elections. Ben Ali is re-elected to the presidency

1999 Ben Ali is re-elected to the presidency

Muhammad es Sadek (above)
He was the bey, or regent, of Tunis in the middle of the nineteenth century when the country was in such a difficult financial situation that it had to seek support from Britain, Italy and, more significantly, French creditors.

A French protectorate (above)
French soldiers are shown hoisting the tricolor aloft at Tunis in May, 1881 CE when the country became a French protectorate.

Tunisian presidents

Aug 30 1957–Nov 7 1987 CE
Habib Bourguiba

Nov 7 1987 CE–
Zine al-Abidine Ben Ali

© DIAGRAM

Ubangui–Shari

See **Oubangui–Chari**.

Ubangui–Shari–Tchad

See **Oubangui–Chari–Tchad**.

UGANDA Republic of Uganda

More than a 1,000 years ago, Bantu-speaking peoples settled in what is now Uganda, where they established farming communities. They were later joined by Nilotic and Nilo-Hamitic people who came from the north. Several medieval kingdoms developed. The most powerful was that of the Bunyoro-Kitara, which was founded by the Nyoro people. By the nineteenth century, when the Bunyoro kingdom was breaking up, another kingdom, Buganda, grew in power. Developed by the Ganda people, it dominated the lands north and west of Lake Victoria.

In the 1840s, the arrival of Arabs seeking to trade in ivory and slaves caused disruption in the region, especially in Acholiland in the north. However, in the 1870s, British and French Roman Catholic missionaries arrived in Buganda. In 1888 CE, the *kabaka* (king) of Buganda, Mwanga, was briefly deposed when he tried to drive missionaries from his lands. Buganda became a British protectorate (colony) in 1894 CE and, in 1896 CE, the British, with the support of the Ganda people, expanded the protectorate, taking over Ankole, Bunyoro, Busoga, and Toro. In 1897 CE, Mwanga rebelled and was deposed, but Buganda finally signed a treaty accepting British protection in 1900 CE.

After World War I, Britain began to develop Uganda's economy, which was based on two cash crops, coffee and cotton. After World War II, Africans played an increasing part in the administration of Uganda. However, problems arose when some people in Buganda requested independence for their kingdom. This led to conflict between the *kabaka*, Mutesa II, and the British.

Recent history

Uganda became independent on October 9, 1962 CE. Its first prime minister was Apollo Milton Obote, a northerner. In 1963 CE, the *kabaka* of Buganda, Mutesa II, was elected president of Uganda, but disputes with Obote led to his dismissal in 1966 CE. Under a new constitution adopted in 1967 CE, Obote became president and the traditional kingdoms were abolished. They were restored in 1992 CE, though their powers were strictly limited.

In 1971 CE, army officers mounted a coup to over-

An expanding protectorate
Bunyoro was annexed to the Uganda protectorate in 1896 CE. However, the people were still ruled by their own king and a Sacred Guild of great chiefs under the control of the British.

throw Obote and Major General Idi Amin Dada became president. In 1972 CE, he ordered an estimated 50,000 Asians to leave the country. Many Asians ran businesses that formed an important part of the economy, which soon declined. Amin also launched a reign of terror and thousands of his opponents were murdered. In 1978 CE, during a boundary dispute, Ugandan troops crossed the southern border into Tanzania. In 1979 CE, Ugandan rebels led by Yoweri Museveni and aided by Tanzanian troops, defeated the Ugandan army and deposed Amin, who fled into exile. In 1980 CE, Obote was reelected president but, following charges of electoral fraud, Museveni founded the National Resistance Movement (NRM) and launched a guerrilla war against the government. In 1985 CE, Obote. whose rule had become increasingly repressive, was removed by a military coup. General Tito Okello became president but, in 1986 CE, the NRM seized power and Museveni became president.

Mutesa
In 1890 CE an Anglo-German agreement recognized Buganda as a British sphere of influence and, four years later, Buganda became a British protectorate. This illustration shows Mutesa, the country's king.

By the end of 1986 CE, peace had been restored in most of Uganda, though conflict continued in parts of the north and east. A National Resistance Council served as the legislature until 1994 CE, when it was replaced by a 276-member Constituent Assembly. In 1995 CE, a new constitution was introduced, extending the nonparty system which Museveni believed was the only way to achieve stability. In 1996 CE, Museveni was reelected president in nonparty elections. Uganda faced many problems in the 1990s. Insurgent groups, such as the Lord's Resistance Army in the north, conducted guerrilla campaigns, while, in 1998 CE, Uganda became involved in the civil war in the Democratic Republic of Congo. However, by the mid-1990s, the economy had improved, and the revival of the East African Community with Kenya and Tanzania in the late 1990s held out hope for regional development. (The first East African Community collapsed in 1977 CE because of political differences between the countries.)

Another major achievement made by Uganda in the 1990s was its educational campaign to combat the spread of HIV-AIDS. As a result, the national rate of infection fell from 14 percent in the early 1990s to 8 percent in 2000 CE. Uganda and Senegal were the only countries in Africa south of the Sahara to make real progress in reducing the spread of this disease.

Peoples

ACHOLI

For information about the history of the Acholi people, *see* **Sudan (Peoples—Acholi)**.

ALUR

The Alur live in northwestern Uganda and neighboring parts of the Democratic Republic of Congo. The historical Alur homeland is around the northwestern shores of Lake Albert and the Albert Nile, though many Alur now live in Uganda's cities. The Alur are Nilotes who came originally from the cradleland of the so-called River-Lake Nilotes, that is, southern Sudan. The ancestors of the Lwo-speaking River-Lake Nilotes migrated sometime after 1000 CE, settling at Pubungu on the northernmost tip of Lake Albert. From about 1450 CE, a group led by a man called Nyipir moved west across the Nile, founding several chiefdoms. The followers of Nyipir and the people they colonized came to be called the Alur.

EAST AFRICAN ASIANS

For an account of the history of East African Asians, *see* **Kenya (Peoples—East African Asians)**.

GANDA

The Ganda (or Baganda) occupy a large area to the north and west of Lake Victoria in Uganda. The islands in Lake Victoria are inhabited by a people known as the Basese, who are part of the Ganda.

Abundant information exists about the history of the Ganda because each clan (extended families who share an ancestor or ancestors) kept its own oral history, while court historians preserved royal accounts. The Ganda are descendants of Bantu-speaking people, who migrated to East Africa from Central Africa around 1000 CE. Some settled on the northwest corner of Lake Victoria around the Kyadondo region. By the fourteenth century, this region was the heart of a small state, the

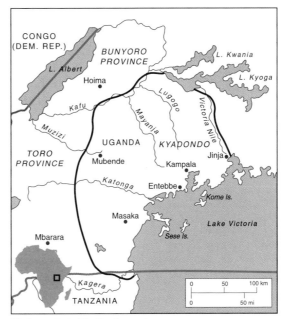

Modern extent of the Ganda people

Buganda Kingdom. The head of state was the *kabaka*, whose role initially was one of arbiter rather than ruler. His power was limited by that of the *batakas*, or clan heads. However, during the eighteenth century, successive *kabakas* skilfully increased their powers at the expense of the *batakas*. Buganda eventually became a centralized monarchy with the *kabaka* acting as king.

Despite clashes with the dominant, northerly kingdom of Bunyoro, Buganda increased in size from the sixteenth century onwards. By 1870 CE, Buganda was a wealthy and influential nation state, with a highly organized system of government led by the *kabaka* with help from his *Lukiko* (council of ministers). A currency of cowrie shells, their value denoted by the holes drilled in the shells so that they could be suspended on strings, was in use. The Basese provided the *kabaka* with a useful naval capacity, and could sometimes muster fleets of as many as 100 vessels, each crewed by up to 30 men. This growing economic, political, and military strength had an effect on neighboring areas, particularly Bunyoro. Buganda supplanted Bunyoro and dominated the region throughout the nineteenth century, helped by several factors. Prime among these was the absence of a Ganda caste system, their military superiority, and their talent for administration.

In 1900 CE, the Buganda Agreement between the British and Bugandan regents (the reigning *kabaka* was still a boy at this time) made the kingdom a province of the Uganda Protectorate (colony). Its territory was reorganized and numerous counties and parishes were created, each with its own head. In 1955 CE, a second Buganda Agreement made the *kabaka* a constitutional monarch and the *Lukiko* became an elected body. As the identity of the wide state of Uganda began to emerge, the solidarity of the Ganda became a block to national unity. Following Uganda's independence in 1962 CE, *Kabaka* Mutesa II became the country's first president in 1963 CE. However, he was arrested and dismissed in 1966 CE–an act that led to widespread rioting in Buganda. In 1967 CE, traditional kingdoms were abolished in Uganda. However, the Bugandan monarchy and other traditional kings were restored in 1993 CE, though they had a purely ceremonial and cultural role.

ITESO

The Iteso people of northern and eastern Uganda and western Kenya are often grouped together with the Karamojong, forming the so-called Karamojong-Teso cluster of related people. These people are Plains Nilotes, who emerged as a powerful force in East Africa sometime after 1000 CE and who also include the Maasai—*see also* **Kenya (Peoples—Maasai)**.

During the second millennium BCE, the Plains Nilotes began dispersing from a region around Lake Turkana (northern Kenya). The Karamojong-Teso moved west toward Mount Elgon (on the present-day border between Uganda and Kenya) from where they have since dispersed farther. The Iteso were settled in their present lands by the first half of the nineteenth century. Like other Nilotes, the Iteso originally practiced pastoralism (livestock raising), but, after reaching their present territory, they gradually turned to settled farming.

KARAMOJONG

The Karamojong live in Karamoja, a semiarid plateau in northeast Uganda on the border with Kenya. The Turkana, who live across the border in Kenya, are sometimes considered to be Karamojong—*see also* **Kenya (Peoples—Karamojong)**.

The Karamojong moved into Karamoja hundreds of years ago. They and related groups are Nilotic in origin—some of their ancestors originally came from the Nile River region in present-day southern Sudan. Drought and famine have affected the history of the Karamojong since the eighteenth century and they have led to widespread dispersal. Until fairly recently, the Karamojong were isolated and they were able to maintain their own ways of life, including cattle rustling. But the British tried to encourage them to settle in one place. "Modernization" policies aimed at controlling the Karamojong continued after Uganda became independent. Under the dictator Idi Amin, around 30,000 Karamojong were executed "for being too primitive." When Amin's troops fled in 1979 CE, the Karamojong armed themselves from abandoned army

barracks. The availability of automatic rifles disrupted Karamojong society, greatly increasing the crime rate. In the 1990s, a group of Karamojong elders, government officials, and other concerned parties attended a "Peace Forum" to resolve the problem.

LANGO

The Lango (or Langi) live in central and northern Uganda. They are perhaps descended from Karamojong ancestors who split away from the main group some 500 years ago. The Lango are Nilotes, belonging to the so-called River-Lake Nilotes, who originated in a region in what is now southern Sudan. The ancestors of the Lango, a Lwo-speaking people, migrated south probably during the fifteenth century, traveling along the Nile River to the lakes region of central Uganda. They settled in an area inhabited by Ateker-speaking peoples. The present-day Lango evolved out of the two cultures. The Lango have often been in conflict with other Ugandans, including the Ganda and Nyoro.

LUGBARA

Most Lugbara live in northwestern Uganda, with some in the northeastern Democratic Republic of Congo. In the 1950s, the Lugbara numbered about 250,000 people. However, in the late 1970s and 1980s, they were persecuted by the regime of Milton Obote, after having been treated favorably by his predecessor Idi Amin, who came from the Lugbara region. As a result, the Lugbara suffered near-genocide (extinction) and their population is now far lower than it was in the mid-twentieth century.

LUYIA

The Luyia (also called Luhya or Abaluyia) live in eastern Uganda and southwestern Kenya, between the northern shores of Lake Victoria and Mount Elgon in the north. The Luyia are descended from Kalenjin, Bantu-speaking, and Maasai ancestors, who probably emerged sometime in the seventeenth century. The dominant influence on the Luyia was Bantu and the Luyia language, LuLuyia, is a Bantu language.

NYORO

The Nyoro (or Bunyoro) people live in the great lakes region of northwestern Uganda. The main area they inhabit is bounded on its western side by Lake Albert, on the northeast by the Victoria Nile River, and to the southeast by the Muzizi River. Nyoro history is centered around that of the medieval empire of Bunyoro-Kitara and later the Bunyoro Kingdom. Oral history attributes the founding of the first Bunyoro-Kitara Empire to the mythical Abatembuzi (or Tembuzi) people. They were succeeded by the Bachwezi (or Chwezi) dynasty (between about 1350–1500 CE), about whom little is certain except that they were an immigrant, cattle-herding people. The Bachwezi established a centralized monarchy over the local Bantu-speaking peoples. They had a hierarchy of officials and also maintained an army. After the death of the last Bachwezi *bakama* (king), Wamara, the Bunyoro-Kitara Empire broke up into several separate states, one of which was Bunyoro.

The Babito dynasty took control of Bunyoro around the start of the sixteenth century. The Babito were originally Lwo-speaking River-Lake Nilotes–people who migrated from the Nile River in present-day southern

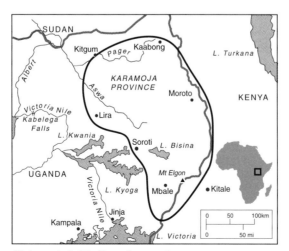

Modern extent of the Karamojong peoples

Sudan to the lakes region of modern Uganda, Under their first *omukama* (ruler), Mpuga Rukidi, the Babito took over the country from the Bachwezi, but kept many of the previous dynasty's rituals and customs. Raids against neighboring peoples expanded Bunyoro. By 1870 CE, it extended north and east of the Nile and to the west of Lake Victoria.

Bunyoro was governed as a loose federation of *saza* (provinces), each under a chief appointed by the *omukama*. These *saza* were semiindependent, and some on the edges of Bunyoro territory broke away to form independent states. For example, during the long reign of Omukama Kyebambe Nyamutukura III (1786-1835 CE), four of his sons turned against him. One of them, Kaboyo Omuhanwa, took the *saza* of Toro and established his own kingdom. Toro then became one of the border regions in dispute between the various Nyoro factions.

Omukama Kabalega (reigned 1870-1898 CE) tried to unite the Bunyoro once again and regain the ascendancy it had lost on the rise of Buganda, a kingdom to the southeast. Kabalega created the Abarusa, a standing army of 20,000 men in ten divisions, each with its own commander. One division went to the capital Masindi to maintain law and order, under Kabalega's greatest general, Rwabudongo. Omukama Kabalega defeated the British in 1872 CE at the battle of Baligota Isansa, when they tried to set up an Egyptian protectorate (colony) in the northern part of Bunyoro. Kabalega later led a guerrilla war against the British for seven years until the British deported him to the Seychelles in 1897 CE. Toro and Bunyoro had already been made British protectorates in 1896 CE and, in 1900 CE, they became part of the British Uganda Protectorate.

After Uganda became independent, the existence of traditional kingdoms proved an obstacle to national unity. In 1967 CE, President Milton Obote abolished all of Uganda's kingdoms. However, they were restored in 1993 CE, though the monarchs had ceremonial and cultural roles only.

Toro

The Toro, a Bantu-speaking people who live in western Uganda, share a common ancestry with the Nyoro people. In the first half of the nineteenth century, the Toro *saza* (province) of Bunyoro became an independent kingdom in its own right under the rule of the first Toro *omukama* (ruler), Kaboya, who was the rebellious son of the Bunyoro *omukama*. After Kaboya's death in the 1850s, Toro nearly lost its new-found independence. However, when British forces overthrew the Bunyoro *omukama*, Toro independence was restored. In 1967 CE, the Ugandan government abolished all the Ugandan kingdoms and it was not until 1993 CE that the Toro kingdom was restored. It functions as a cultural institution and the *omukama* has limited powers.

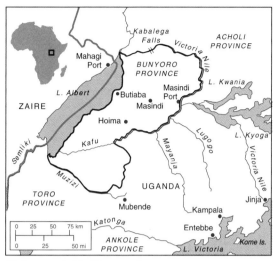

Modern extent of the Nyoro peoples

Kabaka Mutesa II
He was the first president of the Republic of Uganda and, until 1993 CE, the last king of the Bugandan dynasty. Mutesa II ruled over Buganda from 1939–1967 CE, but the kingdom was never fully independent. It was a province of the British Uganda Protectorate, which had some autonomy, and he kept his status, if not his power, until 1962 CE.

Royal appearance
An omukama, or king, of Bunyoro is shown here outside his palace accompanied by his royal retinue.

cordia abyssinica 5c

Cordia abyssinica
*A 1969 CE Ugandan stamp
showing the white cordia, a
tropical African tree that produces
white, bellshaped flowers and
yellow fruit.*

Uganda timeline

19th century CE

1840s	Arab slave traders begin operating in the Uganda region
1862	John Hanning Speke reaches Buganda during his search for the source of the Nile
1875	Henry Morton Stanley visits *kabaka* (King) Mutesa I of Buganda
1877	British Anglican missionaries arrive in Buganda
1879	French Catholic missionaries arrive in Buganda
1888	Kabaka Mwanga is briefly deposed after attempting to drive missionaries from his country
1889	The German explorer Karl Peters agrees a protection treaty with kabaka Mwanga
1890	Anglo-German treaty recognizes Buganda as a British sphere of influence
1894	Buganda becomes a British protectorate and helps the British conquer the rest of Uganda
1896	The British protectorate is extended to Bunyoro, Toro, Ankole, and Busoga
1897	Mwanga is deposed after rebelling against the British

1900–49 CE

1900	Buganda's chiefs sign a treaty accepting British protection in return for freehold rights to their land and other privileges
1904	Cotton is introduced to Uganda and quickly becomes a major cash crop
1921	A colonial legislative council is set up
1925	An education department is set up to provide basic schooling
1926	Uganda's present borders are established
1931	railroad between Kampala and the Indian Ocean at Mombasa is completed
1945	The first Africans are appointed to the legislative council

1950–59 CE

1953	*Kabaka* (King) Mutesa II of Buganda is exiled to Britain for refusing to support British constitutional plans
1954	A hydroelectric dam is built at Owen Falls
1955	Mutesa is allowed to return to Uganda after Britain shelves its constitutional plans
1956	Copper mining begins at Kilembe

1960–69 CE

1962 Oct 9	Uganda becomes independent: Apollo Milton Obote becomes prime minister
1963	Mutesa II is elected president
1966	Obote dismisses Mutesa and makes himself president under a new constitution
1967	Uganda becomes a republic and the traditional kingdoms are abolished. Uganda, Kenya and Tanzania form the East African Community

1970–79 CE

1971	Obote is overthrown by a military coup: Maj. Gen. Idi Amin Dada becomes president
1972	Amin expels 50,000 Asians and confiscates their assets
1978	Uganda invades Tanzania following a border dispute
1979	Ugandan rebels, aided by Tanzanian troops, overthrow Amin's government

1980–89 CE

1980	Obote returns from exile and is re-elected to the presidency
1981	Yoweri Museveni founds the National Resistance Movement (NRM) and starts a guerrilla war against Obote
1985	Obote is overthrown by another military coup: Gen. Tito Okello becomes president
1986	The NRM captures Kampala and overthrows the military government: Museveni becomes president
1986–1994	The National Resistance Council (NRC) serves as Uganda's legislature

1990–99 CE

1993	Uganda's four traditional kingdoms are restored
1994	A Constituent Assembly replaces the NRC
1995	A new constitution is approved extending nonparty government for five years
1995–1996	Terrorist campaign in northern Uganda by the Lord's Resistance Army
1996	Museveni is elected president in nonparty elections
1998	Uganda supports rebel forces in the civil war in the Congo
1999	Uganda Kenya and Tanzania sign a framework agreement to establish a new African Community, aimed at creating a common market. Uganda and Sudan sign a peace agreement

Ugandan presidents

Oct 9 1963–Mar 2 1966 CE Sir Edward Muteesa	**Jun 20 1979–May 11 1980** CE Godfrey L. Binaisa	–Polycarp Nyamuchoncho –Yoweri Hunter Wacha-Olwol	**Jul 29 1985–Jan 26 1986** CE Tito Okello (chairman of the military council)
Apr 15 1966–Jan 25 1971 CE Milton Obote (1st time)	**May 11 1980–May 22 1980** CE Paulo Muwanga (chairman of the military commission)	**Dec 17 1980–Jul 27 1985** CE Milton Obote (2nd time)	**Jan 26 1986** CE– Yoweri Museveni (commander of the national resistance army to 29 Jan 1986)
Jan 25 1971–Apr 13 1979 CE Idi Amin	**May 22 1980–Dec 15 1980** CE Presidential commission –Saulo Musoke	**Jul 27 1985–Jul 29 1985** CE Basilio Olara Okello (chairman of the military council)	
Apr 13 1979–Jun 20 1979 CE Yusufu K. Lule			

Uganda's major political figures

Amin Dada, Idi (1925 CE–)
Commander of Uganda's army from 1968, Idi Amin seized power in January 1971. On becoming president of the country, he declared himself ruler for life. His regime was harsh and brutal, and he murdered thousands of his opponents and expelled Uganda's Asian population. Amin was deposed by rebels led by Yoweri Museveni and backed by the Tanzanian army in 1979 and fled into exile, finally settling in Saudi Arabia. Amin was once the heavyweight boxing champion of Uganda, a title he held from 1951 to 1969.

Museveni, Yoweri Kaguta (1945 CE –)
Yoweri Museveni took part in the overthrow of Uganda's dictator Idi Amin Dada in 1979. Museveni became president of Uganda in 1986 after his National Resistance Army had defeated government forces, ending a five-year conflict. He has been criticized for his ban on political parties which, he claims, encourage tribal divisions.

Mutesa I (1838–1884 CE)
Mutesa I became *kabaka* (king) of Buganda in 1856. He made contacts with the first Europeans who arrived in Uganda, including the explorers John Hanning Speke in 1862 and Henry Morton Stanley in 1875. He was succeeded by his son Mwanga II (1866-1903).

Mutesa II, Edward Frederick (1924–1969 CE)
Mutesa II became *kabaka* of Buganda in 1939. In 1963, he was elected president of Uganda, but he was forced into exile in 1966, after clashing with the prime minister Apollo Milton Obote. He had earlier been deported from Uganda by the British between 1953 and 1955, because of his support for the independence of Buganda and its separation from the rest of Uganda.

Obote, Apollo Milton (1924 CE–)
Milton Obote led Uganda to independence in l962, serving as its first prime minister. In 1966, he deposed the head of state, King Mutesa II of Buganda, and made himself executive president. In 1971, he was himself deposed, by Idi Amin Dada. Obote returned from exile in Tanzania to regain the presidency in 1980 but was again deposed in 1985.

Uganda Protectorate

The British Uganda Protectorate was formed after the 1890 CE Anglo-German agreement declared the region north of latitude 1º South to be in the British sphere of influence. Buganda was declared a protectorate in 1894 CE, and within two years the kingdoms of Ankole, Bunyoro, and Toro were also British protectorates. At first the Imperial British East Africa Company administered the colonies but the British government soon took over. It allowed the rulers to retain their status as long as they still acknowledged Britain's supremacy. By 1914 CE the boundaries of Uganda had been established. *See also* **Buganda**; **Bunyoro–Kitara**; **Uganda**.

Umayyads

See **Omayyads**.

United Arab Republic

In 1958 CE Egypt and Syria joined to form the United Arab Republic (UAR). The president of the state was Gamal Abd an-Nasser, prime minister of Egypt. After a military coup in Syria in 1961 CE, the union ended. Egypt, however, kept the name until 1971 CE, when it was renamed the Arab Republic of Egypt. *See also* **Egypt**; **United Arab States**.

United Arab States

In 1958 CE the United Arab Republic and Yemen formed a short-lived federation called the United Arab States, which dissolved in 1961 CE. *See also* **Egypt**; **United Arab Republic**.

Upper Volta

Upper Volta is the former name of Burkina Faso. The lands were conquered in the later years of the nineteenth century, and attached to French Sudan from 1904–1920 CE. Upper Volta was formed as a separate colony in 1919 CE, but partitioned between Ivory Coast, Niger, and French Sudan in 1932 CE. In 1947 CE Upper Volta reemerged, this time as a French overseas territory. Upper Volta gained complete independence from French rule in 1960 CE but retained its name until 1984 CE. *See also* **Burkina Faso**.

Idi Amin
In 1971 CE Colonel Idi Amin Dada seized power in Uganda. Initially a popular leader, he went on to create a repressive regime under which many thousands were exiled or, even worse, executed.

Mutesa I
He became king in 1856 CE and during his reign welcomed John Hanning Speke and Henry Morton Stanley, the first European explorers, to Uganda.

Milton Obote
He became the first prime minister of a newly independent Uganda in 1962 CE, but was deposed by Idi Amin in 1971 CE. He returned as president in 1980 CE, but was again deposed in 1985 CE.

Defense Force
A regimental sergeant-major of
the Witwatersrand Rifles is shown
against a background of
Johannesburg.

South African flag
The old flag of South Africa
included the flags of Britain and
the Boer Republics, which united
with the British colonies in 1910 CE
to form the Union of South Africa.
In 1934 CE South Africa became
independent from Britain. It left the
Commonwealth in 1961 CE, but the
flag did not change until 1994 CE.

Union of South Africa

In 1910 CE the Union of South Africa came into being. It united the British colonies of the Cape, Natal, Transvaal, and Orange River. *See also* **Cape**; **Natal**; **South Africa**; **South African Republic**.

Urundi kingdom

See **Ruanda–Urundi**.

Venda

Venda was one of the homelands established during South Africa's apartheid era in which Africans were forced to live. The Venda people of the northeastern corner of South Africa had been restricted to three small "native reserves" soon after the establishment of the Union of South Africa in 1910 CE. In 1973 CE, during the racist apartheid era, Venda was declared a self-governing homeland, which was granted independence in 1979 CE. This independence was never officially recognized, however, because it was largely a ruse to deprive the Venda of their rights and citizenship in South Africa. After the end of white-minority rule in 1994 CE, the Venda homeland was reabsorbed into South Africa. *See also* **South Africa**.

Wadai

Wadai, originally a kingdom founded in the sixteenth century, became a sultanate in c.1630 CE when a Muslim dynasty was established there. Wadai lay to the east of Lake Chad, in what is now eastern Chad. For many years it was tributary to Darfur, finally becoming independent in the 1790s. Situated on a profitable trade route, Wadai expanded rapidly–often at the expense of Borno. Wadai was conquered by France in 1906 CE. *See also* **Kanem–Borno**; **Chad**.

Sultanate of Wadai
Originally an offshoot of Darfur,
the Muslim sultanate of Wadai
was founded in the mid-
seventeenth century in what is
now Chad. It warred with Darfur
until the mid-eighteenth century,
when it began to expand
westward and southward. Wadai
conquered the Bagirmi in 1805 CE.
It took Kanem from Borno in 1808
CE and expanded south into Dar
Kuti. By the 1850s, vast areas
north and south of Wadai were
tributary to it.
From c. 1880 CE Wadai was
threatened by the Darfurian slave
trader, Rabih bin Fadl Allah. In
1893 CE, Rabih conquered the
territory of the Bagirmi and
invaded Borno, reducing Wadai's
influence. Rabih's incursions,
together with French colonial rule
in the Lake Chad area, weakened
Wadai. The sultanate continued to
resist the French until 1912 CE,
when it was formally abolished by
its colonial masters. The maps
show the extent of the sultanate
at the following times:

1 *1750 CE* **2** *1880 CE*

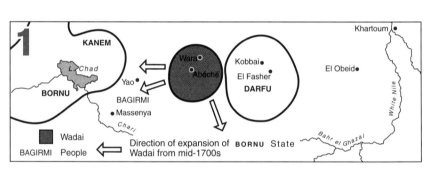

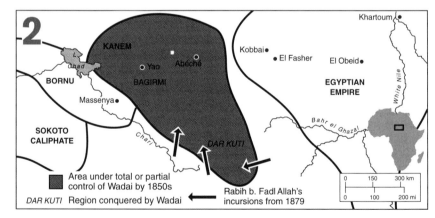

Wagadugu

Today the capital of Burkina Faso, Wagadugu (now spelled Ouagadougou) was once the base of an important West African kingdom. It was founded in the fifteeenth century, according to tradition by invaders from northern Ghana, and became the seat of the Mossi king, or *mogho naba*. The king still lives in the capital but has no real power. *See also* **Burkina Faso**.

Walvis Bay

Until 1992 CE Walvis Bay, which is surrounded by Namibia, was an exclave of South Africa. In the middle of the nineteenth century there was great demand for the dried droppings of fish-eating sea birds (guano), which could be found on adjacent islands. The British annexed the bay and hinterland in 1878 CE, and it was joined to the Cape Colony in 1884 CE. When the Union of South Africa was formed in 1910 CE, Walvis Bay was included although it was administered as part of Southwest Africa (Namibia) from 1922–1977 CE. On gaining independence from the illegal South Africa regime, Namibia immediately called for the return of Walvis Bay. In 1994 CE South Africa returned Walvis Bay to Namibia. *See also* **Namibia**; **South Africa**.

Wanga kingdom

The Luhya people of Kenya were united in the seventeenth century by Wanga, who founded the kingdom named after him. Many Luhya came from the rich Ugandan kingdoms to the west of Lake Victoria, and legend says this is where Wanga was from. The Wanga kingdom flourished until the final years of the nineteenth century, when it became part of British East Africa during the reign of Mumia. *See also* **Kenya**.

Warri kingdom

The Itsekiri kingdom of Warri (Ouwerre) was founded by Prince Ginuwa from Benin in the late fifteenth century. It was based along the Warri River, western Nigeria, upstream from the Bight of Benin. Like the rulers of Benin, its kings were called *obi*. The town itself was the trading capital of the region, growing rich from the slave trade on the Ethiope and Warri Rivers. Warri switched to the export of palm oil and kernels in the mid-nineteenth century. The kingdom came under British control in 1884 CE. *See also* **Nigeria**.

Western Sahara

See **Morocco**.

Wolof empire

Soon after 1200 CE the Wolof state was founded, and by the fifteenth century it was an empire controlling much of modern Senegal. The ruler of the Wolof state was called the *burba*, and he was elected by officials. Wolof was in a good position to control both transSaharan trade routes and those going to the Atlantic coast. As trade with Europeans on the coast became increasingly important, however, the Wolof empire began to disintegrate. The original Wolof state remained, at times tributary to others, until the French colonized Wolof territory in the mid-nineteenth century. *See also* **Senegal**.

Yoruba states

The Yoruba people of west Africa have a long history of urbanization. Centuries ago they were living in walled towns surrounded by farmlands. Many of these independent towns developed into important and powerful states. *See also* **Benin**; **Ife**; **Ilorin**; **Oyo**.

Zagwe

The Zagwe was a dynasty of Christian kings who ruled in northern and central Ethiopia during the twelfth and thirteenth centuries. Many of Ethiopia's famed churches were made during this era. The last Zagwe king, Lalibela (reigned c.1185–1225 CE), is famous for the many churches that he commissioned. These churches were literally carved out of the rock in and around the capital city, Roha (since renamed Lalibela). The Zagwe were overthrown by Yekuno Amlak, founder of the Solomonid empire, at the end of the thirteenth century. *See also* **Ethiopia**; **Solomonid empire**.

Zaire

See **Congo, Democratic Republic of**.

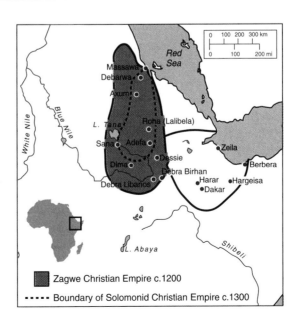

Zagwe Christian Empire c.1200

- - - - Boundary of Solomonid Christian Empire c.1300

The Zagwe Christian Empire
The Zagwe were a dynasty of Christian kings who ruled in northern and central Ethiopia during the twelfth and thirteenth centuries. The dynasty was renowned for the number of churches built during its existence.

© DIAGRAM

National pride
A 1967 CE stamp marking the inauguration of the National Assembly Building.

ZAMBIA Republic of Zambia

Bantu-speaking farmers using iron tools began to settle in what is now Zambia perhaps 2,000 years ago, gradually displacing the original hunter-gatherer people. The ancestors of the Tonga people arrived around 1,000 years ago, but most of the other main groups, including the Bemba and the Lozi, migrated into the area from the north from the seventeenth century. The Bemba and Lozi founded powerful kingdoms. In the nineteenth century, other waves of immigrants reached southern and western Zambia in flight during the Mfecane (the mass migrations and wars triggered by the rise of the Zulu kingdom).

In the late eighteenth century, Portuguese traders founded a trading post on the border of present-day Zambia, while the Scottish explorer, David Livingstone, reached the Victoria Falls in 1851 CE. In the 1880s, the British South Africa Company, led by the imperialist Cecil Rhodes, made treaties with local chiefs and, in 1911 CE, the territories were united to form a territory called Northern Rhodesia. In 1924 CE, the British government took over administration of Northern Rhodesia. The discovery of rich copper deposits attracted many European immigrants and copper production soon became Northern Rhodesia's chief industry.

After World War II, many Europeans wanted to unite with Southern Rhodesia (now Zimbabwe), and have greater control over their own affairs. In 1953 CE, against much African opposition, Britain created the Central African Federation of Northern Rhodesia, Southern Rhodesia, and Nyasaland (now Malawi). But this federation was shortlived and it was dissolved in 1963 CE.

Recent history

Northern Rhodesia achieved internal self-government in January 1964 CE. Elections based on universal suffrage enabled Kenneth Kaunda, who had been imprisoned for his activities in opposing the Central African Federation, to form a government with his party, the United National Independence Party (UNIP), which had been formed in 1960 CE. Finally, the country became fully independent as the Republic of Zambia on October 24, 1964. with Kaunda as president. The new government faced many problems. At independence, the country had less than 100 Zambian African graduates. Copper mining, on which the economy was based, provided much of the revenue for the government's social programs, including free education and health; but when copper prices fell, the economy came close to collapse. Kaunda's socialist policies also did little to encourage foreign investment, while the large government-owned companies, called *parastatals*, proved inefficient and became riddled with corruption.

Zambia also faced mounting problems with its southern neighbor Rhodesia (as Southern Rhodesia was then known), which had declared itself independent from Britain, an act which Britain declared to be illegal, in 1965 CE. Relations between the countries became strained because of Rhodesia's refusal to allow Africans more representation in Rhodesian government. In 1973 CE, Rhodesia refused to allow Zambia to ship goods through its territory, and so Tanzania, with Chinese help, built a new railroad from Dar es Salaam, giving Zambia a trade route through friendly territory. However, after 1980 CE, when white minority rule ended in Rhodesia, which was renamed Zimbabwe, relations with Zambia improved.

"Copperbelt" of Zambia (left)
Minerals such as diamonds, manganese, uranium, cobalt, and copper are abundant in Central Africa, as are energy resources such as oil and natural gas. This is a mine in the "Copperbelt" of Zambia, one of the world's largest copper producers since the 1930s.

Kariba Dam (above)
The Kariba Dam was built in the 1950s at a cost of many millions of dollars. Thousands of Zambians were forced to move their homes to make way for the dam which was built to supply hydroelectric power.

In 1972 CE, when the country's economic problems had caused a split in UNIP, Zambia became a one-party system, with UNIP as the sole legal party. Kaunda also extended his control over the army, the media, and the trade unions. In the late 1980s, the economic situation worsened and food riots occurred in 1990 CE. Kaunda, under great pressure, legalized opposition parties in 1990 CE. In the 1991 CE multiparty elections, Frederick Chiluba, a trade union leader and president of the Movement for Multiparty Democracy (MMD) defeated Kaunda and became president. The MMD also won a majority in the National Assembly. The government's austerity policies were unpopular and the government declared a shortlived state of emergency in 1993 CE, following an alleged plot by opposition leaders.

Chiluba was reelected president in 1996 CE and the MMD won an overwhelming victory in the National Assembly in 1997 CE. A coup was put down in 1997 and Kaunda was arrested for his alleged involvement in the coup attempt. Kaunda's desire to return to active politics was made difficult by a constitutional amendment, making it necessary for both parents of a presidential candidate to be Zambians by birth. Kaunda's parents were Malawians.

Peoples

BEMBA

Most Bemba live on the high, forested plateau of northern Zambia. The Bemba are descended from Luba-Lunda people, who migrated from what is now Katanga (formerly Shaba) province in the Democratic Republic of Congo, more than 300 years ago. Gradually, they conquered or absorbed the original inhabitants of the region. One of the most important of the migrant groups was the Bena Yanda (the Crocodile Clan), possibly descendants of Lunda chiefs, who settled on the banks of the Chambeshi River in the second half of the seventeenth century. They were led by a chief called Chiti. Bemba kings have adopted the name *Chitimukulu*, which means "Chiti the Great," ever since. This small kingdom steadily expanded during the eighteenth and nineteenth centuries. It became one of Central Africa's most important kingdoms and the name *Bemba* was applied to all people who acknowledged the rule of the current *Chitimukulu*.

By 1889 CE, the British government authorized Cecil Rhodes's British South Africa Company (BSAC), which was basically a mining company with its own army, to administer territories north of the Limpopo River and to control their mineral resources and trade. As a result, the Bemba kingdom became part of Northern Rhodesia. In 1924 CE, control of Northern Rhodesia was transferred from the BSA to the British government and the country became a British colony until its independence in 1964 CE. The Bemba played a major part in the struggle for independence.

LOZI

The Lozi (or Barotse) live mainly on the floodplains of the Zambezi River in western Zambia. The Lozi are descended from the Luyi, a people who migrated from the north in around the seventeenth century or earlier. These Luyi migrants were led by a woman, Mwambwa, who was succeeded first by her daughter, Mbuywamwambwa, and then by Mbuywamwambwa's son, Mboo, the first *litunga* (king) of the Lozi. During Mboo's reign, the Lozi kingdom expanded by conquering and absorbing neighboring peoples. At that time, the kingdom was not so much a centralized state as a collection of semi-independent chiefdoms ruled by Mboo and his relatives. The unification of these chiefdoms into a single kingdom began in the rule of the fourth *litunga*, Ngalama, in the early eighteenth century, and was completed by Mulambwa, who ruled from about 1780–1830 CE. Mulambwa was able to establish direct rule over the peoples conquered by the Lozi and over the numerous immigrant groups arriving in the kingdom from the north and south.

The most important of these immigrant groups was the Mbunda, who had been driven from their homes in Angola. Mulambwa allowed them to settle in the border areas, where they could help defend the kingdom from raids by neighboring people, such as the Luvale and the Nkoya. As well as helping the Lozi in this way, the Mbunda played a big part in the military and economic development of the kingdom. They

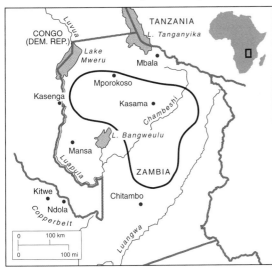

Modern extent of the Bemba peoples

Modern extent of the Lozi peoples

brought with them military innovations–such as the bow and arrow and an improved type of battleax–and new crops, including cassava, millet, and yam, as well as medical and artistic skills.

The Lozi prospered under Mulambwa's rule. But, after his death, the country was torn apart by a civil war between the army of his eldest son, Silumelume, and the supporters of his younger son, Mubukwanu. This war was won by Mubukwanu, supported by the Mbundu. But before he could reunite the kingdom, it was attacked and conquered by the Kololo, a Sotho people from southern Africa. The Kololo ruled the country (and introduced their language) from about 1840–1864 CE, when they were defeated by the armies of an exiled Lozi leader, Sipopa. For the next 4 ce0 years or so, the kingdom continued to prosper, despite a series of leadership disputes, but its power began to wane when treaties with the British in 1890 CE and 1900 CE placed it under the control of Cecil Rhodes's British South Africa Company (BSAC).

LUNDA
For information about the history of the Lunda people, *see* **Congo, Democratic Republic of (Peoples—Lunda)**.

NDEMBU
For information about the history of the Ndembu people, *see* **Congo, Democratic Republic of (Peoples—Ndembu)**.

TONGA
The Tonga live in a region called Butonga in southern Zambia. They also live across the border in the middle of the Zambezi plain in northern Zimbabwe. Archaeologists have discovered remains that suggest the Tonga have been in their present location for about 1,000 years. The early Tonga were farmers and fishermen who raised cattle and goats. Bones found in waste dumps show that they also hunted antelopes. The Scottish explorer David Livingstone visited Butonga in the 1850s and found the Tonga living in small, scattered settlements. In the earlier nineteenth century, they had been subjected to raids from other groups, including the Lozi, Kololo, and Matabele, who had taken many of their cattle. The Tonga were not a warlike people, although they had such weapons as spears and clubs. They had a simple system for dealing with raids. They hid grain in their long hair, so that, if they had to flee to fresh territory, they had the seeds to plant fresh crops and begin again. In the 1890s, Cecil Rhodes's

British South Africa Company (BSAC) occupied the area and white settlers soon took control of Butonga. Under colonial rule, the Tonga were grouped into three small "native reserves," leaving the better land for white settlers. The first group was the Plateau Tonga in what is now Zambia. The Toka Tonga of Kalomo and Livingstone districts were allocated land with poor soils, while the Gwembe Tonga were in the more isolated Zambezi valley. As a result, the Toka Tonga and the Gwembe Tonga could not survive by farming and were forced to work mainly as migrant laborers for the whites. In the late 1950s, more than 50,000 Gwembe Tonga were displaced by the building of the Kariba Dam. They were forcibly evicted to the hills above Lake Kariba or to more arid lands below the dam. However, their lot improved after the independence of Zambia and Zimbabwe, because they were no longer confined to reserves.

Modern extent of the Tonga peoples

Kenneth Kaunda
A leader in the fight against colonial rule, he became president of the newly-independent Zambia, formerly the British colony of Northern Rhodesia, in 1964 CE.

Zambia's major political figures

Chiluba, Frederick (1943 CE–)
Frederick Chiluba, a former labor leader, became the second president of Zambia by defeating Kenneth Kaunda in multiparty presidential elections in 1991. His Movement for Multiparty Democracy (MMD) party also won the majority of seats in the National Assembly elections. He was re-elected in 1996.

Kaunda, Kenneth David (1924 CE–)
The first president of Zambia, Kenneth Kaunda was born in Nyasaland (now Malawi). He became a world-famous figure in the late 1950s for his opposition to the white-minority ruled Central African Federation. Kaunda served as president of Zambia from 1964–1991, when he was defeated in multiparty elections. He gave help and support to many black nationalist groups in the formerly white-minority ruled countries of Southern Africa.

Zambia timeline

Pre 19th century
c. 1000 CE Bantu-speaking peoples settle in the area of modern Zambia
1514 Portuguese explorers are the first Europeans to enter the Zambia region
1740 The Lunda people invade Zambia from the west
1762 Portuguese traders from Mozambique found a trading post on the border of present-day Zambia

19th century CE
1835 Zambia is settled by Nguni people fleeing from Zulu expansion in southern Africa
1855 David Livingstone discovers the Victoria falls
1889 Cecil Rhodes' British South Africa Company (BSAC) is given responsibility for Barotseland (the area of present-day southern Zambia) by British government charter
1890 Agents of the BSAC take possession of Barotseland
1898 The Ngoni rebel against the BSAC

1900–49 CE
1900 The BSAC acquires mineral and trading rights from king Lewanika in the area of northern Zambia
1902 Vast copper deposits are discovered at Broken Hill
1909 A railroad links Zambia with the Indian Ocean
1911 Barotseland and other BASC territories are united to form the territory of Northern Rhodesia
1924 The British government takes over the administration of Northern Rhodesia
1927–1939 Rapid expansion of the copper mining industry
1935 Lusaka becomes the capital of Zambia
1940 A general strike by African copper miners achieves major improvements in pay and conditions

1950–59 CE
1953 Britain forms the Central African Federation of Northern Rhodesia, Southern Rhodesia (now Zimbabwe) and Nyasaland (now Malawi)
1959 Kenneth Kaunda is jailed for nationalist activities

1960–69 CE
1960 Kaunda becomes leader of the United National Independence Party (UNIP)
1961 UNIP is outlawed
1963 Britain dissolves the Central African Federation
1964 Oct 24 Northern Rhodesia becomes independent as Zambia: Kenneth Kaunda becomes president

1970–79 CE
1970 The Zambian government acquires a controlling interest in the copper mining industry
1972 UNIP becomes the only legal party
1973 The white government of Rhodesia (Zimbabwe) closes its border with Zambia
1975 A railroad from the Copperbelt to the Indian Ocean at Dar-es-Salam (Tanzania) is built with Chinese help

1980–89 CE
1986 Widespread rioting breaks out after austerity measures are introduced by the government

1990–99 CE
1990 Opposition parties are legalized
1991 Frederick Chiluba of the Movement for Multiparty Democracy (MMD) defeats Kaunda in the first multiparty elections
1993 A state of emergency is declared to undermine a campaign of civil disobedience by supporters of UNIP
1996 Chiluba is re-elected president
1997 Kaunda is barred from standing for election after a failed coup attempt

Zambian presidents
Oct 24 1964–Nov 2 1991 CE
Kenneth Kaunda

Nov 2 1991 CE–
Frederick Chiluba

Zanzibar

Zanzibar is an island off the east coast of Tanzania that has long been an important depot for the intercontinental trade routes of the Indian Ocean. The first settlers came from mainland Africa, and they were joined by people from Arabia, Persia, and Indians. Many of the Persian settlers came from Shiraz, Persia (Iran), and Zanzibaris often refer to themselves as Shirazi. The distinct groups merged to form the Swahili people, and for many years Zanzibar was an independent Swahili city-state. Then Zanzibar fell under Portuguese and Omani Arab control in the sixteenth and seventeenth centuries respectively. At the beginning of the

A trading center
An island situated off the east coast of Tanzania, Zanzibar has historically been an important place on the intercontinental trade routes of the Indian Ocean.

© DIAGRAM

Zanzibar's trade with Asia

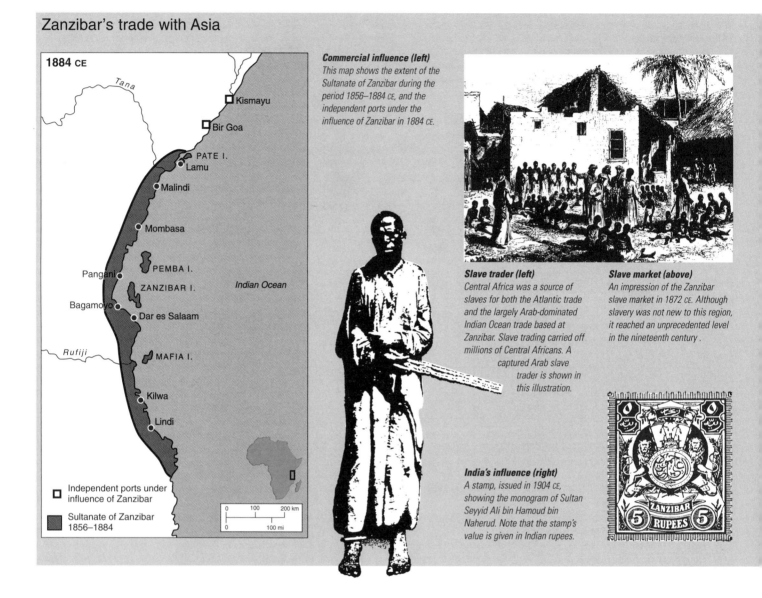

1884 CE

Tana

☐ Kismayu

☐ Bir Goa

● PATE I.
● Lamu

● Malindi

● Mombasa

PEMBA I.

Pangani ●

ZANZIBAR I.

Bagamoyo ●

● Dar es Salaam

Rufiji

● MAFIA I.

Indian Ocean

● Kilwa

● Lindi

☐ Independent ports under
influence of Zanzibar

■ Sultanate of Zanzibar
1856–1884

0   100   200 km
0   100 mi

Commercial influence (left)
This map shows the extent of the Sultanate of Zanzibar during the period 1856–1884 CE, and the independent ports under the influence of Zanzibar in 1884 CE.

Slave trader (left)
Central Africa was a source of slaves for both the Atlantic trade and the largely Arab-dominated Indian Ocean trade based at Zanzibar. Slave trading carried off millions of Central Africans. A captured Arab slave trader is shown in this illustration.

Slave market (above)
An impression of the Zanzibar slave market in 1872 CE. Although slavery was not new to this region, it reached an unprecedented level in the nineteenth century .

India's influence (right)
A stamp, issued in 1904 CE, showing the monogram of Sultan Seyyid Ali bin Hamoud bin Naherud. Note that the stamp's value is given in Indian rupees.

nineteenth century the Omani ruler made Zanzibar his capital and reconquered many other coastal islands and parts of the mainland. In 1861 CE Zanzibar was separated from Oman and became an independent sultanate. In the 1890 CE Anglo-German agreement most of Zanzibar's territory on the mainland was divided between the two countries and economic control over the remaining coastal strip was secured. Zanzibar and Pemba became a British Protectorate in 1890 CE. In 1963 CE the Zanzibar sultanate regained its independence. In 1964 CE Tanganyika and Zanzibar united to form Tanzania while a revolt overthrew the sultan of Zanzibar and established a republic. *See also* **Omani Arabs**; **Pemba**; **Tanganyika**; **Tanzania**.

Zaria

Zaria is one of the seven "true" Hausa states, or Hausa *Bakwa,* that existed in what are now northwestern Nigeria and southwestern Niger. According to tradition it was founded in the 11th century as Zazzau (or Zegzeg) by King Gunguma. Islam was introduced in the fifteenth century and by the next century the rulers of Zaria were Islamic. In 1512 CE, however, Songhay conquered Zaria. After a period of independence and expansion under Queen Amina at the end of the sixteenth century, Zaria lost its independence to Kororofa and then Bornu in the eighteenth century. Zazzau was then conquered in 1808 CE by the Fulani empire and became known as Zaria. It became an emirate in 1835 CE. Although many of the emirate's satellite towns and dependencies were stripped from it by the British during the era of colonial rule, Zaria remains one of the largest emirates in Nigeria today. Based around Zaria city, the emirate is located in Kaduna state, Nigeria. *See also* **Hausa states**; **Nigeria**; **Northern Nigeria**.

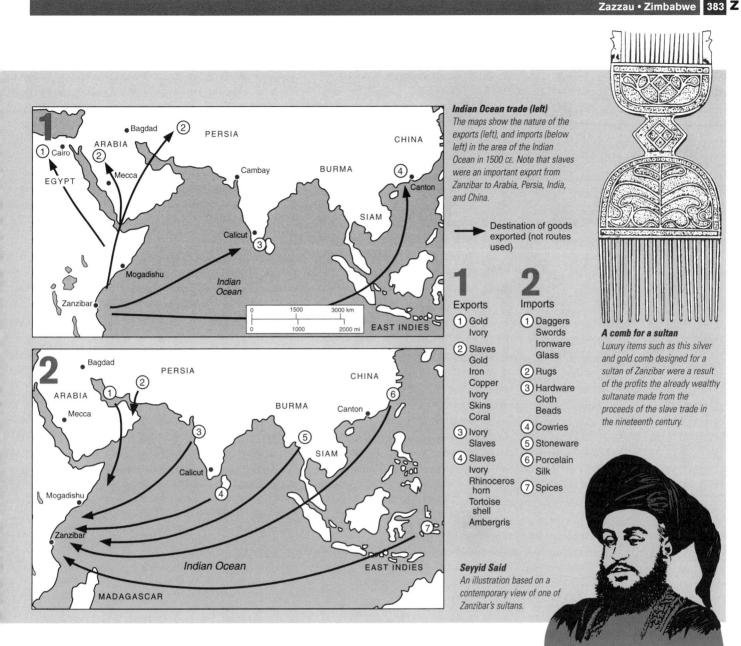

Indian Ocean trade (left)
The maps show the nature of the exports (left), and imports (below left) in the area of the Indian Ocean in 1500 CE. Note that slaves were an important export from Zanzibar to Arabia, Persia, India, and China.

→ Destination of goods exported (not routes used)

1 Exports
1. Gold
   Ivory
2. Slaves
   Gold
   Iron
   Copper
   Ivory
   Skins
   Coral
3. Ivory
   Slaves
4. Slaves
   Ivory
   Rhinoceros
   horn
   Tortoise
   shell
   Ambergris

2 Imports
1. Daggers
   Swords
   Ironware
   Glass
2. Rugs
3. Hardware
   Cloth
   Beads
4. Cowries
5. Stoneware
6. Porcelain
   Silk
7. Spices

A comb for a sultan
Luxury items such as this silver and gold comb designed for a sultan of Zanzibar were a result of the profits the already wealthy sultanate made from the proceeds of the slave trade in the nineteenth century.

Seyyid Said
An illustration based on a contemporary view of one of Zanzibar's sultans.

Zazzau
See **Zaria**.

Zegzeg
See **Zaria**.

ZIMBABWE Republic of Zimbabwe

Bantu-speaking farmers began to settle in what is now Zimbabwe around 1,800 years ago. From around the tenth century, some of their descendants, the Shona, began to develop a metalworking culture. From around 1100 CE, the Shona began to build dry-stone wall enclosures, such as Great Zimbabwe. A Shona subgroup, the Karanga, later established the Mwene Mutapa empire, while a southern Karanga group, the Rovzi, founded the Changamire empire in about 1600 CE. The Changamire empire remained strong until an influx of the Matabele (or Ndebele) in the early nineteenth century. The Matabele were refugees from the period of wars and migrations triggered by the rise of the Zulu kingdom to the south.

Portuguese explorers reached the area in the sixteenth century, but European influence did not become important until the nineteenth century. In 1888 CE, the British South Africa Company (BSAC), headed by the British imperialist, Cecil Rhodes, gained mineral rights from the Matabele king Lobengula. In the 1890s, the BSAC defeated African uprisings and won control over an area that was named Rhodesia for Cecil Rhodes. In

The Shona Rebellion
European influence in the area now known as Zimbabwe only became widespread in the nineteenth century. In 1888 CE the British South Africa Company (BSAC), headed by the British imperialist, Cecil Rhodes, acquired mineral rights from the Matabele king Lobengula. In the 1890s the BSAC defeated various African uprisings, one of which was the Shona Rebellion in July, 1896 CE, and seized the area, which was named for Cecil Rhodes. In 1897 CE the territory was divided into Southern Rhodesia (now named Zimbabwe) and Northern Rhodesia (now named Zambia).

Independence medal
This medal was struck in both silver and bronze when Southern Rhodesia became the independent Republic of Zimbabwe in 1980 CE.

1897 CE, the territory was divided into Southern Rhodesia (now Zimbabwe) and Northern Rhodesia (now Zambia). White settlement was encouraged and, in 1923 CE, Southern Rhodesia became a self-governing colony. With its sizeable white population, the government passed many laws that discriminated against the black majority. In 1953 CE, Britain set up the Central African Federation, linking Southern Rhodesia, Northern Rhodesia, and Nyasaland (now Malawi). But African opposition proved so strong that the federation was dissolved in 1963 CE.

Recent history

In 1964 CE, after Northern Rhodesia and Nyasaland had become independent as Zambia and Malawi, respectively, Southern Rhodesia became known simply as Rhodesia. Britain pressed Rhodesia's white government to increase the rights of the black Africans. But when talks finally broke down, the Rhodesian prime minister, Ian Smith, declared his country independent on November 11, 1965 CE. Britain declared Smith's unilateral action illegal. It imposed a trade ban on Rhodesia and, in 1966 CE, the United Nations followed Britain by

imposing economic sanctions. In the same year, a guerrilla war broke out between the black nationalists and government troops. The two main nationalist groups were the Zimbabwe African People's Union (ZAPU), led by the veteran nationalist, Joshua Nkomo, and the Zimbabwe African National Union (ZANU), which was led, from 1976 ce, by Robert Mugabe. In 1976 ce, ZAPU and ZANU united to form the Patriotic Front (PF).

From the mid-1970s, the white government made plans to introduce a new constitution which would lead to a government which included moderate black leaders. This objective was reached in 1979 CE, when Abel Muzorewa, a Methodist bishop, was elected prime minister. But the government was unable to end the guerrilla war and, in 1980 CE, new elections resulted in victory for ZANU-PF. Robert Mugabe then became prime minister and head of the government. Rhodesia finally became independent as the Republic of Zimbabwe on November 11, 1980. In 1985 CE, after ZANU-PF won the elections, the office of prime minister was abolished and an executive president was created to replace it. Parliament then elected Robert Mugabe to serve as executive president. In 1988 CE, ZANU and ZAPU merged and, in 1990 CE, Nkomo, who had been dismissed from the cabinet in 1983 CE, became vice-president.

Following independence, many Europeans left Zimbabwe, while the country's white farmers soon faced problems. In colonial times, the Europeans had taken over the best farmland and land reform was a central issue for newly independent Zimbabwe. Under the Land Apportionment Act of 1992 CE, the government began to purchase European-owned land, with Britain providing the money, and redistributed the farms to landless Africans.

In the late 1990s. Zimbabwe's government lost popularity as inflation and unemployment rates soared. Mugabe's policy of sending troops to the Democratic Republic of Congo to support the government there also came under criticism. In a referendum in 2000 CE, the electorate defeated proposals that the constitution should be changed giving the president more power and the right to take over European-owned farms without compensation, a policy which had already begun in early 2000, leading to violence and the murder of some European CE farmers. However, ZANU-PF won 62 of the 120 seats in the June parliamentary elections and the confiscation of white-owned farms continued.

President Mugabe's reelection campaign 2001 CE
The illustration is an example of the military force the Zimbabwean leader brought to bear to ensure that he was reelected for another term of office. Intimidation proved effective in the past, and a new campaign of repression was undertaken to silence any potential critics of his regime.

Peoples

MATABELE

The Matabele of southern Zimbabwe are also sometimes, confusingly, called Ndebele. The histories and cultures of the Ndebele of South Africa and Matabele are closely connected and the two groups are often treated as branches of the same, Ndebele, people. *See also* **South Africa (Peoples—Ndebele)**.

Like the Ndebele people of South Africa, the Matabele are descended from early Nguni settlers, but did not emerge as a separate people until the nineteenth century. In the early eighteenth century, South Africa was dominated by the Zulus under the great military strategist, Shaka. His lieutenant, Mzilikazi, was one of the Khumalo, an Ndebele group who had not migrated into what is now northern South Africa but had remained in present-day KwaZulu-Natal. In 1823 CE, Mzilikazi rebelled against Shaka during the violent Mfecane/Difaqane era, and led the Khumalo northward for safety. Mzilikazi settled north of the Vaal River and established a powerful Ndebele kingdom near present-day Tshwane (formerly Pretoria). This empire came under repeated attacks by the Zulu, Griqua, and Kora peoples, and finally by the Boers (Afrikaner farmers) on the Great Trek. In 1837 CE, Mzilikazi led his people to a new settlement that he called Bulawayo ("Great Place"). It was there that they became known as the Matabele.

The Matabele came into conflict with the British in the late nineteenth century, when the British South Africa Company (BSAC), headed by the imperialist Cecil Rhodes, occupied most of the region. Under colonial rule, the Matabele experienced years of oppression and they were active in the nationalist opposition to white rule. Even after the establishment of majority rule, the Matabele suffered the effects of a power struggle between the leaders of two former rebel guerrilla groups–Robert Mugabe, the new prime minister, and Joshua Nkomo, who drew most of his support from the Matabele. The difficult situation eased in the late 1980s.

SHONA

The lands of the Shona people cover most of Zimbabwe and also extend into Mozambique. Shona people are also found in Botswana, South Africa, and Zambia. The Shona are descended from Iron Age, Bantu-speaking farmers who settled on the Zimbabwe plateau around 200 CE. Little is known of these early settlers, except that they worked with iron. However, from about the tenth century, the Shona civilization that had developed in the area became adept at working gold and copper, both of which were found on the plateau, and traded those metals with coastal cities. The people who ruled this trade became the wealthy elite. Their graves were found to contain gold ornaments and imported beads and cloth.

From around the late twelfth century, the Shona began to construct impressive dry-wall (built without mortar) structures. Called *zimbabwes* (literally "stone houses"), they served as palaces. This building system was perfected at the site of Great Zimbabwe (south of modern Masvingo) from the fourteenth century onward. By the end of the fifteenth century, Shona kings had abandoned Great Zimbabwe as a palace, but it continued as a religious and commercial site. The capital was moved north to the area around the Zambezi River. This marked the beginning of a new Shona dynasty, the Mwene Mutapas. The first Mwene Mutapa was Nyatsimba Mutota, who conquered territory from the Kalahari Desert to the Indian Ocean. After the death of his successor Matope, the kingdom split, the southern part being dominated by the Rovzi peoples, a Shona subgroup.

When the Rovzi Empire finally collapsed in the early nineteenth century, more than 100 small Shona states took its place. Many of these were disrupted after 1820 CE by the wave of emigration emanating from Shaka's Zulu Mfecane expansion, which brought the Matabele people into southern Zimbabwe. It was the Matabele who gave these many groups the name "Shona". Previously, each of the groups had its own name, even though they were all Shona-speaking peoples. In the

Modern extent of the Matabele peoples

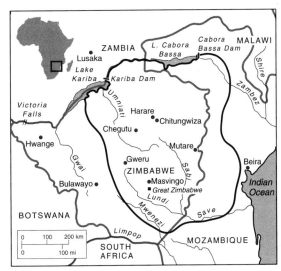

Modern extent of the Shona peoples

late nineteenth century, the British South Africa Company (BSAC), headed by the imperialist Cecil Rhodes, occupied most of the region. The Shona came under colonial rule until 1980 CE, when majority rule was finally achieved, following a prolonged civil war in which the Shona and Matabele fought against government troops.

SOTHO

For information about the Sotho peoples, *see also*

Lesotho (Peoples—Sotho); South Africa (Peoples—Northern Sotho).

TONGA

For information about the history of the Tonga people, *see* **Zambia (Peoples—Tonga)**.

VENDA

For information about the history of the Venda people, *see* **South Africa (Peoples—Venda)**.

Reverend Canaan Banana
He was the first president of the Republic of Zimbabwe when it achieved independence on November 11, 1980 CE.

Mzilikazi
He established the Matabele (or Ndebele) kingdom in what is now known as Zimbabwe in the early nineteenth century. The Matabele were refugees from the period of wars and migrations triggered by the rise of the Zulu kingdom to the south of the country.

Zimbabwe's major political figures

Banana, Reverand Canaan Sodingo (1836 CE–)
Banana, who had been active in the struggle for independence, became the first president of Zimbabwe when the country achieved majority rule in 1980. His duties were largely ceremonial. He stepped down in 1987 when, under a new constitution, he was replaced by former prime minister Robert Mugabe, who became the executive president. During his period in office, Banana worked to unite the various factions in his country.

Lobengula (1836?–1894 CE)
Lobengula. the last independent chief of the Matabele (Ndebele) nation, was proclaimed chief following the death of his father Mzilikazi in 1868. He welcomed early European missionaries and traders and, in 1888, he granted Cecil Rhodes's British South Africa Company (BSAC) extensive mineral rights. This led to the annexation of what is now Zimbabwe in the 1890s.

Mugabe, Robert Gabriel (1924 CE–)
Robert Mugabe, president of Zimbabwe, was a largely self-educated teacher who founded the anticolonialist Zimbabwe African National Union (ZANU) with Ndabaningi Sithole in 1963. He was detained by the then ruling British authorities in Southern Rhodesia (now Zimbabwe) in 1964, and imprisoned until 1974 for his nationalist, anti-colonial activities. From 1976 until 1979, Mugabe was joint leader–with Joshua Nkomo–of the Patriotic Front guerrilla movement, which fought Ian Smith's illegal white-minority regime in Rhodesia. As leader of ZANU, Mugabe was elected prime minister of Zimbabwe (defeating Bishop Abel Muzorewa) when it became fully independent in 1980. In 1988, ZANU merged with the main opposition party–Joshua Nkomo's Zimbabwe African People's Union (ZAPU)–and Zimbabwe effectively became a one-party state. Mugabe became executive president in 1987 and was reelected in 1990 and 1996.

Muzorewa, Bishop Abel Tendekayi (1925 CE–)
Abel Muzorewa became the first black bishop of the United Methodist Church, in 1968. He was a prominent opponent of Ian Smith's illegal white-minority government in Zimbabwe in the 1970s. In elections in 1979, Muzorewa became the country's first black prime minister, but he was heavily defeated by Robert Mugabe in 1980. Muzorewa returned to politics in 1994, but he withdrew his candidacy in the l995 presidential elections, criticizing the way in which they had been conducted.

Mzilikazi (c. 1790–1868 CE)
Mzilikazi established the Ndebele/Matabele kingdom around Bulawayo, in what is now Zimbabwe. His territory became known as Matabeleland. Mzilikazi led a number of Ndebele north from Natal to Transvaal to escape from the Zulu under Dingane, and then farther north still to escape from the Boer settlers.

Nkomo, Joshua Mqabuko Nyongolo (1917–1999 CE)
Joshua Nkomo was the leader of the nationalist Zimbabwe African People's Union (ZAPU) from the 1960s. Nkomo and Robert Mugabe were joint leaders of the Patriotic Front guerrilla movement which campaigned against Ian Smith's illegal white-minority government of Rhodesia from 1976–1979. In the 1980 elections, however, Nkomo's ZAPU was defeated by Mugabe's Zimbabwe African National Union (ZANU). Nkomo was given a cabinet position in Mugabe's government but was dismissed in 1982 after conflicts between ZAPU and ZANU. In the 1980s, Nkomo's native Matabeleland harbored dissidents from Mugabe's rule and this led to further tensions between ZAPU and ZANU. In 1988, however, the two parties merged and Nkomo became one of Zimbabwe's two vice-presidents. He died in office in 1999.

Rhodes, Cecil John (1853–1902 CE)
Rhodes was a major British imperialist, politician, founder of southern Africa's diamond industry, and a noted philanthropist. Rhodes was elected to the assembly of Cape Colony in 1881 and served as the Colony's prime minister from 1890–1895. He helped to shape the history of southern Africa, especially when, in the 1890s, his British South Africa Company (BSAC) took over the vast territory that is now Zambia and Zimbabwe.

Zimbabwe timeline

Pre 19th century CE
5th century CE Bantu-speaking peoples settle in the Zimbabwe region
c.1100 The Karanga people found a state centered on the city of Great Zimbabwe
c.1200 The "Great Enclosure" is built at Great Zimbabwe
c.1400 The Torwa kingdom is founded near present-day Bulawayo
c.1450 Great Zimbabwe is abandoned when it is superseded by the Mwenemutapa kingdom to the north c.1600 The Rozvi people conquer Torwa and establish the Changamire state

19th century CE
1840s The Ndebele under Mzilikazi conquer the Changamire kingdom and establish a capital at Bulawayo
1888 Cecil Rhodes' British South Africa Company (BSAC) obtains extensive mineral rights from the Ndebele king Lobengula
1889 The BSAC gains responsibility for the Zimbabwe area by a British government charter
1890 The BSAC's Pioneer Column establishes Fort Salisbury on Harare Hill
1893 BSAC forces defeat Lobengula and destroy the Ndebele kingdom
1895 The BSAC territory is named Rhodesia after Cecil Rhodes
1897 Rhodesia is divided into two separate territories, Southern Rhodesia (now Zimbabwe) and Northern Rhodesia (now Zambia)

1900–49 CE
1900 The BSAC begins to encourage white settlement in Southern Rhodesia
1922 In a referendum, the white settlers vote to become a self-governing colony rather than join South Africa
1923 Southern Rhodesia becomes a self-governing British colony
1930 The Land Apportionment Act divides the land between whites and Africans, much in favor of the whites
1934 The Industrial Conciliation Act restricts African competition in the labor force

1950–59 CE
1953 Britain forms the Central African Federation from Southern Rhodesia, Northern Rhodesia and Nyasaland (now Malawi)
1958 The prime minister Garfield Todd is forced from office after he attempts to end segregationist policies

1960–69 CE
1960 Africans form the National Democratic Party (NDP)
1962 The white supremacist Rhodesian Front (RF) wins control of the legislature in whites-only elections
1963 The Central African Federation is dissolved
1963 The NDP splits into Zimbabwe African Peoples' Union (ZAPU) under Joshua Nkomo and the Zimbabwe African national Union (ZANU) under Ndabaningi Sithole
1964 Ian Smith becomes leader of the RF
1965 11 Nov Smith issues a unilateral declaration of independence (UDI), proclaiming "Rhodesia" independent
1966 The battle of Chinhoyi begins a guerrilla war by Africans

1970–79 CE
1971 Bishop Abel Muzorewa forms the United African National Council (UANC)
1976 Nkomo and Robert Mugabe, the new leader of ZANU, unite to form the Patriotic Front (PF)
1979 After a RF alliance with the UANC fails to bring peace, Rhodesia reverts to colonial status

1980–89 CE
1980 Feb ZANU-PF win British supervised elections: Mugabe becomes prime minister
1980 18 Apr Rhodesia becomes independent as the republic of Zimbabwe
1982 Mugabe dismisses Nkomo from the government
1987 Mugabe becomes president
1988 ZANU and ZAPU formally merge and Zimbabwe becomes a one-party state

1990–99 CE
1991 Opposition parties are legalized but under conditions which prevent them campaigning effectively
1992 The Land Acquisition Act provides for government purchase of white-owned lands for redistribution to poor Africans
1996 Mugabe is re-elected president in elections boycotted by opposition parties
1998 Mugabe sends troops to support the government in the Congo civil war
1999 Demonstrations break out over Zimbabwe's involvement in the Congo war

2000 CE–
2000 Electors reject proposals for Mugabe to change the constitution

Endangered species
A stamp issued in 1989 CE depicting the black rhinoceros, one of the most endangered species in the world.

© DIAGRAM

Ian Smith

He was the prime minister of Rhodesia (now Zimbabwe) when a Unilateral Declaration of Independence (UDI) from Britain was made in 1965 CE, and continued to serve in office until 1979 CE.

Sithole, Rev. Ndabaningi (1920 CE–)

Ndabaningi Sithole, a clergyman, politician, and influential writer, was a major figure in the nationalist struggle in Rhodesia (now Zimbabwe) in the 1960s and 1970s. He founded the anticolonialist Zimbabwe African National Union (ZANU) with Robert Mugabe in 1963. He was imprisoned from 1965 until 1974, but in 1978 he helped to achieve an agreement with Ian Smith's white-minority government for constitutional change. This agreement was considered inadequate by the other leading nationalists, Robert Mugabe and Joshua Nkomo, and Sithole's political influence declined when a new agreement was negotiated in 1979. In November 1996, he was taken to court charged with planning to assassinate Mugabe and overthrow the government.

Smith, Ian Douglas (1919 CE–)

Ian Smith became prime minister of the white-dominated Rhodesia (now Zimbabwe) in 1964 and in 1965 he made an illegal Unilateral Declaration of Independence (UDI) from Britain in order to maintain white domination of the government. This eventually led to civil war between Smith's government forces and those of Robert Mugabe and Joshua Nkomo. Smith continued to serve as prime minister until 1979, when an interim multiracial government led by Bishop Abel Muzorewa was established.

Great Zimbabwe

In the southeast of Zimbabwe, not far from the town of Masvingo, a small granite hill rises steeply to a height of about 350 ft (100 m) above the surrounding plains. At the top and to the south of the hill stand the massive granite walls that are the remains of the ancient Shona civilization of Great Zimbabwe.

Great Zimbabwe was the largest of about 200 similar *zimbabwes* (literally, stone houses), the palaces of Shona kings and chiefs, scattered throughout Zimbabwe and neighboring parts of Mozambique and South Africa. The Shona first began to construct these impressive dry-wall stone enclosures, built without mortar, in the late twelfth century. This system was perfected in the building of the Great Zimbabwe palace, which reached a peak in the fourteenth and fifteenth centuries. The quality of the stonework at the site is so impressive that for many years some people believed that no indigenous African people could possibly have been the builders.

For about 400 years, from the twelfth to the sixteenth centuries, the site of Great Zimbabwe, and the city that grew up around it, were the political, religious, and commercial center of a prosperous Shona civilization.

The great wealth of the Shona people that enabled them to build Great Zimbabwe, was based on agriculture, mining, and trade. They grew crops; raised cattle; mined and worked iron, copper, and gold; and controled the trade routes between the interior of Africa and the Arab/Swahili ports on the coast of what is now Mozambique. Through these coastal ports they exported gold, copper, and ivory and imported silks and porcelain from China; glass beads from Indonesia, India, and Europe; and faience (expensive, highly-colored glazed pottery) from Persia (modern Iran).

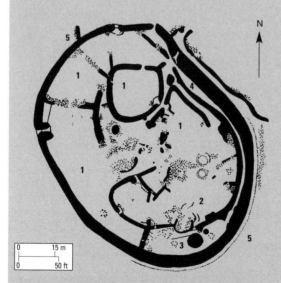

Plan of the Great Enclosure

The Great Enclosure, the finest of the Shona dry-wall zimbabwes (stone houses), was part of the main Great Zimbabwe site, which also included the Western and Eastern enclosures. Work on the site was begun in the late twelfth century and continued for over 300 years. All the walls were built without mortar, the earlier parts being undressed stone. Later parts feature dressed stone and beautiful, chevron-patterned friezes.

Key

1 Enclosure   3 Conical tower   5 Outer wall
2 Stone platform   4 Parallel passage

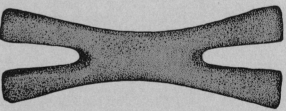

Ingot

The currency of Great Zimbabwe consisted of copper ingots (metal bars). Soapstone molds for making these ingots were found at Great Zimbabwe, and the ingots themselves turned up as far away as China.

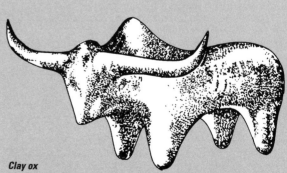

Clay ox

This clay model of an ox dates from the eleventh century and was found in the Western Enclosure of Great Zimbabwe.

Todd, Sir Reginald Stephen Garfield (1908 CE–)
Born in New Zealand, Garfield Todd went to Southern Rhodesia (now Zimbabwe) as a missionary in 1934. He was prime minister of the Federation of Rhodesia and Nyasaland from its formation in 1953 until 1958 when his party's policies were rejected as too liberal by the white-dominated electorate. An opponent of the illegal regime of Ian Smith, he was detained from 1965–1966, and again from 1972–1976.

Welensky, Sir Roland (Roy) (1907–1991 CE)
A former trade unionist and heavyweight boxing champion, Roy Welensky entered politics in 1938 and worked for the creation of the white-minority ruled Central African Federation (CAF). He was prime minister of the CAF from 1956 until it was broken up in 1963 to form Malawi, Zambia, and Rhodesia (now Zimbabwe). When the CAF collapsed, Welensky retired from politics.

Sir Roland (Roy) Welensky
He was the prime minister of the Central African Federation (CAF) from 1956–1963 CE.

The massive stone walls of Great Zimbabwe formed enclosures that contained mud-walled and thatched-roofed circular buildings, some up to 30 ft (9 m) or more in diameter. The largest buildings were often divided internally into separate rooms and had roofs about 20 ft (6 m) high. The stone walls themselves were up to 30 ft (9 m) high and about 16 ft (5 m) thick at the base. Their foundations were built in carefully prepared and leveled trenches.

To ontain the stones with which they built the walls, the Shona masons used a technique probably first developed by their miners. They built fires around boulders or outcrops of granite to heat them up, then doused the rocks with cold water. This sudden cooling split them into slabs 3 to 7 in. (7.5–17 cm) thick. These slabs were then dragged on sledges to the construction site, where they were cut into small blocks with stone hammers and iron chisels.

Great Zimbabwe lost its importance as a political center in the middle of the fifteenth century, when the Shona kings abandoned the site and moved their capital north to the area around the Zambezi River; it continued only as a religious and ceremonial site. The site was completely abandoned in the 1830s, when most of its inhabitants were driven out or taken prisoner by Nguni peoples fleeing from the Zulu Mfecane/Difaqane.

The Nguni ignored, or did not find, most of the treasures of Great Zimbabwe. In the late nineteenth century, the ruins were discovered by Europeans, and the buried riches were plundered by treasure hunters. Nearly all of the priceless gold artifacts that were found were melted down and so lost forever.

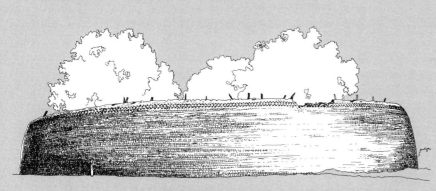

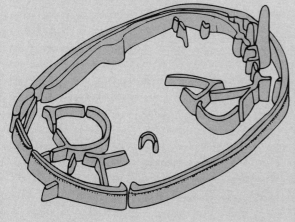

Great Zimbabwe: the outer wall (above)
This is the outer wall of Great Zimbabwe, the largest of the Shona zimbabwes (stone houses). Its stone walls were largely symbolic of the separation of ordinary citizens from nobility.

Stonework
These are two examples of stonework from Zimbabwe. The example on top is taken from earlier buildings, while the one below is a later example. Technical improvements can be seen in the quality of the later stonework.

Conical tower
This huge conical tower inside the Great Zimbabwe complex is regarded as the greatest architectural and technical achievement of the early Shona people. Originally thought to be hollow inside, it is now believed to be solid. It is 35 ft (10 m) high and 17 ft (5 m) across at the base.

The Great Enclosure (left)
A view of the Great Enclosure at the height of Great Zimbabwe's prosperity.

Zirid emirate

The Zirid emirate was a Muslim state that controlled what is now Tunisia in the eleventh and twelfth centuries. The Zirids took the region from Fatimid control in 1041 CE and remained in place until 1148 CE, when they lost power to the Berber Almohads. *See also* **Almohads**; **Fatimids**; **Tunisia**.

Zulu kingdom

Before 1818 CE, the Zulu people of southern Africa were part of the Mthethwa kingdom, which was ruled by Dingiswayo. Dingiswayo was killed in battle with the Ndwandwe, and his kingdom shattered, in 1818 CE. Long periods of drought and scarce resources had brought conflict to the whole eastern seaboard. From the ruins of the Mthethwa kingdom, the Zulu kingdom emerged. One of Dingiswayo's generals, a Zulu man named Shaka, reorganized the Mthethwa chiefdoms and brought them under Zulu control. When they came under renewed attack from the Ndwandwe, Shaka's military skills ensured they defeated the invaders. The Zulu took over the Ndwandwe lands and soon controlled the land between the Drakensberg and the sea. The rapid expansion of the Zulu nation triggered the Mfecane—a series of wars and mass migrations. This wave of conflict, which lasted from 1819–1839 CE, left an estimated five million people dead and made the region vulnerable to takeover by white settlers. After 1836 CE, the Zulu came into contact with the growing number of white settlers; first the Afrikaners (Boers) and then the British. In 1879 CE at Insandhlwana, a massive onslaught of Zulu warriors defeated the British, who retaliated later that year and defeated the 40,000 strong Zulu army led by Cetshwayo at Ulundi. In 1887 CE Britain annexed the Zulu kingdom. *see also* **Mthethwa**; **Ndwandwe**; **South Africa**.

Dingane and his dog
In 1828 CE, after he and his brother Mhlangane assassinated their half-brother Shaka, Dingane killed Mhlangane and proclaimed himself king of the Zulu. In 1838 CE he made a pact with Piet Retief, one of the Boer leaders of the Great Trek, then killed the Boers. A few months later, the Boers routed the Zulus at the Battle of Blood River and Dingane fled to Swaziland, where he was killed by his half-brother, Mpande.

Cetshwayo
He resisted British and Boer colonialism, and defeated the British at Isandhlwana in 1879 CE.

Zulu kingdom's major political igures

Cetshwayo (c.1826–1884 CE)
Cetshwayo, a nephew of the great Zulu leader Shaka, ruled the Zulu kingdom from 1872 and resisted British and Boer colonialism. In 1879, he defeated the British at Isandhlwana but was later defeated and captured at Ulundi. Part of his kingdom was restored to him in 1883, but soon after he was driven out by an antiroyalist faction.

Dingane (died c.1840 CE)
In 1828, after he and his brother Mhlangane assassinated their half-brother Shaka, Dingane killed Mhlangane and proclaimed himself king of the Zulu. In 1838 he made a pact with Piet Retief, one of the Boer leaders of the Great Trek, then treacherously killed the Boers. A few months later, the Boers routed the Zulus at the Battle of Blood River and Dingane fled to Swaziland, where his half-brother Mpande killed him.

Zulu timeline

200s Bantu-speaking peoples begin to arrive in Southern Africa	**1828** Shaka assassinated, Dingane succeeds him as Zulu leader	**1885–1887** Zululand divided between British Zululand and Transvaal	**1970s** KwaZulu homeland created
300s–400s Bantu-speakers reach present-day Kwazulu/Natal	**1838** Zulu defeated by Boers at the Battle of Blood River	**1910** White-minority ruled Union of South Africa created	**1975** Inkatha reconvened
1787 Birth of Shaka	**1840** After defeating Dingane, Mpande becomes Zulu leader	**1913** Zulu restricted to inadequate "native reserves"	**1980s–1990s** Fighting between Inkatha and ANC supporters
1816 Shaka becomes Zulu leader	**1872** Cetshwayo becomes Zulu king	**1920** Zululand joined to South Africa	**1991** Apartheid legislation repealed
1818–1819 Zulu-Ndwandwe War establishes Zulu supremacy	**1879** British conquer Zulu	**1928** Inkatha, Zulu nationalist movement, founded	**1994** First nonracial elections
1819–1839 Mfecane/Difaqane: period of mass migrations and wars	**1883–1884** Zulu Civil War after British partition Zululand	**1948** Apartheid in South Africa	**1999** ANC wins large majority in South African elections; the Inkatha Freedom Party comes third with 8% of the vote

Dingiswayo (c.1770–1818 CE)

Dingiswayo was ruler of Mthethwa, a kingdom that dominated present-day KwaZulu/Natal in the late eighteenth and early nineteenth centuries. He became overlord of 30 chiefdoms, including the Zulu chiefdom ruled by Shaka, one of his generals and military advisors. He was killed when his army was defeated by that of a neighboring kingdom, Ndwandwe, in 1818. This defeat led to the breakup of the Mthethwa kingdom and the rapid expansion of Zulu power.

Shaka (1787–1828 CE)

A brilliant military strategist, Shaka became a general in the army of Dingiswayo, king of Mthethwa, and founded the Zulu kingdom in 1818. He won many victories in what is now KwaZulu/Natal, practicing the strategy of total warfare–complete annihilation of the enemy. In 1828, he was murdered by his half-brothers Mhlangane and Dingane.

Battle formation (right)
As founder of the Zulu kingdom, Shaka devised an ingenious battle formation that helped the Zulus gain military supremacy. It involved four battalions of warriors: the central group would attack the enemy; the side battalions would encircle the enemy; and the last group were the reserves. The warriors would line up with their shields touching those of their comrades in arms.

Zulu warriors (below)
During the Mfecane (1819–39 CE) Zulu warriors formed the spearhead of Shaka's attacks on neighboring peoples. The rise of the Zulu kingdom had a huge impact on the whole of Southern Africa.

Modern extent of the Zulu peoples

Shaka (above)
Shaka, the founder of the Zulu kingdom, launched a series of attacks on neighboring peoples east of the Drakensberg Mountains in 1819 CE. The ensuing period of wars and migrations came to be known as the Mfecane (or Difaqane).

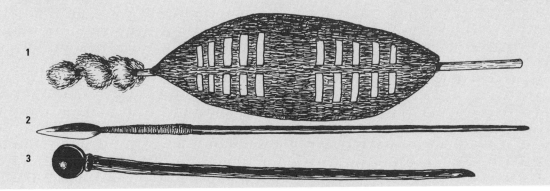

Zulu weapons (left)
Most of these highly effective weapons were developed during Shaka's reign and they ensured Zulu supremacy in battle.

1 A shield made from wood and animal skin.
2 An iron-bladed throwing spear.
3 A hardwood *knobkerrie* (or *iwisa*) sometimes thrown as a weapon.

© DIAGRAM

INDEX

Index of Personalities

A

Abacha, Sanni 59, 93, 283, 286–7
Abbas II, Khedive of Egypt 67, 157
Abbas, Ferhat 100
Abboud, Ibrahim 344–5, 350
Abd al Krim 82, 265
Abd al Mumim 265
Abd al Qadir 28, 82, 100
Abdallah, Ahmed 142–3
Abdessalam, Belaid 100
Abdille Hassan, Sayyid Muhammad 121
Abdullah, Khalifa 347
Abiola, Kudirat 287
Abiola, Moshood 287
Abu Yaqub Yusuf 67
Abubakar, Abdulsalam 283, 286
Acheampong, Ignatius 197, 199–200
Adjommani 211
Afewerki, Issias 175
Affonso I of Kongo 102, 226
Afonja of Oyo 210
Afrifa, Akwasi Amankwa 197–8
Agaja of Fon 113, 153
Aggrey, James Emman Kwegyir 199
Agostinho, Antoniu 102
Aguiyi-Ironsi, Johnson 283, 287
Ahidjo, Ahmadou 130–2
Ahmadu, Sekou 84, 242, 279, 310–11
Ahmed, Moussa 155
Aidid, Muhammad Farah 322
Akuffo, Frederick 197, 199
Akufo-Addo, Edward 197
Akwa 213
Alvaro II of Kongo 226
Amanitore 228
Amin Dada, Idi 83, 220, 370, 375
Amina 382
Amlak, Yekuno 318
Andersson, Karl 73
Andrianampoinimerina 242
Ankrah, Joseph 197, 199–200
Annan, Kofi 199
Anthony of Egypt 162
Arabi, Ahmad 157, 162
Ashmun, Jehudi 234
Askia Muhammad 252, 279, 324
Assoumani, Azali 142–3
Ateban 290
Aubame, Jean-Hilaire 190
Aubry, Augusto 236
Awolowo, Obafemi 287
Azikwe, Nnamdi 283, 287

B

Babangida, Ibrahim 283, 287
Bagaza, Jean-Baptiste 126, 128
Baikie, William 73
Baker, Sir Samuel 75
Balewa, Sir Abubakar Tafawa 93, 283, 287–8
Banana, Canaan 386
Banda, Hastings 12, 58, 247–9
Barbarossa 97
Barth, Heinrich 73
al-Bashir, Omer Hassan Ahmed 345, 350
Bédié, Henri Konan 211–13
Begin, Menachem 164
Behanzin of Dahomey 86, 114
Bello, Muhammad 188
Ben Ali, Zine al Abidine 368
Ben Bella, Ahmed 97, 100
Bendjedid, Chadli 100
Bennett, James Gordon 74
Berenger, Paul 259
Biko, Steve 335
Bilonda, Ngonda 146, 241
Binao 242
Biya, Paul 130, 132
Bizimungu, Pasteur 306
Blyden, Edward Wilmot 234
Boganda, Barthelemy 136
Bokassa, Jean-Bédel 16, 51, 92, 136–8
Bongo, Albert Bernard (later El Hadj Omar) 190–2
Borgnis-Desbordes, Colonel 84, 279
Botha, Louis 337
Botha, P.W. 335
Boumedienne, Houari 92, 97, 100
Bourguiba, Habib 92, 367–8
Bouteflika, Abdelaziz 100
Boutros-Ghali, Boutros 10, 162
Brand, J.H. 296
de Brazza, Pierre Savorgnan 149–51, 186, 190
Bruce, James 73
Buhari, Muhammadu 283, 287
Buller, Sir Redvers Henry 296
Burton, Sir Richard 73
Busia, Kofi 197, 200
Buthulezi, Mangosuthu 228, 334–5, 338–9, 341
Buyoya, Pierre 127–8

C

Cabral, Amilcar 134, 205–6
Cabral, Luiz 93, 205–6
Caetano, Marcello 102, 134, 268, 308
Caillié, René 73
Cameron, Verney 75
Campbell, John 73
Cão, Diego 72
Carey, Lott 234

Carter, Howard 171
Cetshwayo 390
Changa 305
Cheikh, Said Muhammad 142
Ch'eng Tsu 254
Chikura 281
Chilembwe, John 249
Chiluba, Frederick 379–80
Chinyanta 216
Chipenda, Daniel 104
Chissano, Joaquim 268, 270
Chiti of Bemba 110
Cholmondely, Hugh 224
Clapperton, Hugh 73
Cleopatra 65, 167, 170
Compaoré, Blaise 125–6, 363
Conrad, Joseph 110
Conté, Lansana 57, 93, 204–5
Coulibaly, Quezzin 125

D

da Costa, Manuel Pinto 308–10
da Covilhã, Pedro 72
Dacko, David 136, 138
Al-Dahab, Abdul Rahman Suwar 345
dan Fodio, Usman 188, 216, 242, 279, 282, 284
Darwin, Charles 223
de Klerk, F.W. 54, 326, 335
Déby, Idriss 139–40
Delamere, Lord 224
Denard, Bob 142
Denham, Dixon 73
Dhlakama, Afonso 268, 270–1
Dia, Mamadou 311
Diara, Ngolo 310
Dias, Bartholomeu 72, 324
Dias, Diogo 243
Dingane 336, 390–1
Dingiswayo 271, 391
Dinizulu 278
Diori, Hamani 280–1
Diouf, Abdou 311, 313
Djohar, Said Mohammed 142–3
Dlamini I of the Nguni 354
Doe, Samuel K. 53, 93, 233–5
dos Santos, José Eduardo 55, 103–5
Dube, John Langalibale 276, 334, 338

E

Emin Pasha, Mehmed 148, 350
Equiano, Olaudau 80
Ewuare the Great 112
Eyadéma, Gnassingbé 61, 93, 363–4
Ezana of Axum 176, 180

F

Faisal, king of Saudi Arabia 321
Farouk, king of Egypt 160–4

G

Gajemasu, king of Kano 215
Gaji, Ali 214
Galton, Sir Francis 73
da Gama, Vasco 72, 217, 225
Gandhi, Mohandas 328–9, 334, 338
Garang de Mabior, John 350
De Gaulle, Charles 41, 257
Gbagbo, Laurent 212
George VI, King 109
Gladstone, W.E. 346
Gordon, Charles, General 33, 83, 344, 346–7
Gordon, R.J. 73
Gouled Aptidon, Hassan 155–6
Gowon, Yakubu 45, 283, 287
Grant, Augustus 122
Grant, James 75
Grunitzky, Nicolas 363–4
Guei, Robert 212
Guelleh, Ismail Omar 155–6
Gunguma 382
Gungunyane 271

H

Habré, Hissène 139–40
Habyarimana, Juvénal 306–7
Haile Selassie 48, 93, 176–81, 210, 319
Al-Hajj Umar 84, 213, 310–11, 313
Haley, Alex 192
Hamilcar 135
Hamza of Oman 357
Hannibal 27, 65, 135
Hassan II of Morocco 45, 256, 264–7
Hassan, Abdikassim Salad 322
Hatshepsut 166, 170
de Herrera, Diego Garcia 209
Hertzog, Barry 336–7
Houphouët-Boigny, Félix 211, 213

I

Iala, Kumba 206
Ibn Battuta 265
Ibn Tumart 267
Idris I of Libya 208, 237
Ilo Makoko 150–1
Imhotep 165, 171
Ismail Pasha 157

J

Jaga 294
James I, King 192
Jammeh, Yahya 14, 193
Javabu, John Tengo 334
Jawara, Sir Dawda 192–3, 313

John, king of Portugal 324
John Paul II, Pope 213
Johnson, Prince 233
Jonathan, Chief Leabua
    230–1, 233
Juba II of Numidia 292
Jugnauth, Sir Aneerood
    259–60
Jugurtha 292
Julius Caesar 167, 170

K

Kabalega, Omukama 122–3,
    373
Kabbah, Ahmad Tejan
    315–16
Kabila, Joseph 16, 145
Kabila, Laurent 16, 103,
    144–5, 306
Kaboya 373
Kaboyo Omuhanwa 123
Kagame, Paul 306
Kala Ilunga 146, 240
El-Kanemi 214
Kanta, Muhammad 217
Kasavubu, Joseph 43, 144,
    149
Kassa 180–1
Kata Mbula 227
Kaunda, Kenneth 16, 47,
    378–80
Kayibanda, Grégoire 306–7
Kazembe II 241
Kazembe IV 144
Keita, Modibo 93, 249, 252
Kenyatta, Jomo 40, 217, 224
Kenyatta, Margaret 224
Kérékou, Mathieu (later
    Ahmed) 111, 114
Khama III of the Ngwato
    118–19
Khama, Sir Seretse 43,
    118–19
Khufu 171
Kibinda Ilunga 146, 241
Kigeri V of Rwanda 306–7
Kimathi, Dedan 224
Kitchener, Lord 347, 351
Kok, Adam III 330
Kolelas, Bernard 150
Kolingba, André 56, 136–8
Konaré, Alpha Oumar 250,
    252
Koroma, Johnny 315
Kot aPe, king of Kuba 228
Koulibali, Mamari 310
Kountché, Seyni 280–2
Kruger, Paul 341
Kufuor, John 198, 201
Kutako, Hosea 273
Kyebambe Nyamutukura III
    123, 373

L

Lagarde, L. 321
Lamizana, Sangoulé 124–6
Lander, John 73
Lander, Richard 73
Leakey family 223

Lekhanya, Justin 231, 233
Lembede, Anton 339
Léopold II, king of Belgium
    28, 87, 110, 143–7, 215–16,
    227–8, 241
Letsie III, king of Lesotho
    231–3
Lewanika, king of the Lozi
    240
Limann, Hilla 197
Lissouba, Pascal 150, 152
Livingstone, David 74, 117,
    148, 247, 361, 378, 380
Lobengula 276, 383–4, 386
Lueji 241
Lumumba, Patrice 43, 144,
    148–9
Lusengi of Lunda 146, 241
Luthuli, Albert John 335
Lyautey, Marshal 186, 263

M

Machel, Samora 49, 268–9,
    271
Maga, Hubert 111, 114
al-Mahdi, Muhammad
    Ahmad (The Mahdi) 33,
    83, 154, 246–7, 344, 346,
    350–1
al-Mahdi, Sadiq 54, 345,
    350–1
Maherero, Samuel 196, 274
Mai Idris Alloma 214
Mainassara, Ibrahim-Bare
    280, 282
Makanjila 248
Malan, Daniel 326, 335–7
Malloum, Félix 47, 139
Mamadou, Tandja 280
Mancham, James 313–15
Mandela, Nelson 18–19, 60,
    127, 326, 335–6, 339
Mandela, Winnie 335
Mane, Ansumane 206
Mansa Musa 25, 250–3
Mansarico 316
Marchand, Jean-Baptiste 347
Margai, Albert 315, 317
Margai, Sir Milton 315, 317
Mark Antony 167, 170
Marley, Bob 319
Mashopa 332
Masire, Sir Ketumile Joni
    118–19
Massamba-Débat, Alphonse
    150, 152
Massinisa of Numidia 115,
    290, 292
Massounde, Tadjiddine Ben
    Said 142–3
Matope 385
Mauch, Karl 75
M'Ba, Léon 190, 192
Mbandzeni 353
Mbeki, Thabo 19, 326, 335
Mbemba, Nzinga 102
M'Bida, André-Marie 132
Mbili Kiluhe 145–6, 240
Mbire 271
Mboo 239, 379

Mboya, Tom 217, 224
Mbuywamwambwa 239, 379
Mehemet Ali see
    Muhammad Ali
Menelik I of Ethiopia 318
Menelik II of Ethiopia 29,
    89, 173, 176, 181, 318–19
Mengistu, Haile-Mariam 57,
    93, 174–6, 179, 181
Mhlangane 390–1
Micombero, Michel 126, 128
Mikaila, Babban Gwani 207
Mirambo 359
Mkapa, Benjamin 358, 360,
    362
Mobutu, Joseph-Désire
    (later Mobutu Sese Seko)
    16, 144, 149
Mogae, Festus 118–19
Mohammed, Murtala 283,
    287
Moi, Daniel arap 217–18,
    224
Moisili, Pakalitha 231
Mokhehle, Ntsu 231–2
Momoh, Joseph 315, 317
Mondlane, Eduardo 271
Monteiro, António
    Mascarenhas 134
Moshoeshoe I 30, 109, 229,
    231–2, 332
Moshoeshoe II 230–3
Mpande 390
Mpuga Rukidi 123
Mswati I 278, 353–4
Mswati III 354–5
Mubarak, Hosni 56, 160, 164
Mubukwanu 240, 380
Mugabe, Robert 384–6, 388
Muhammad V of Morocco
    45, 264–5, 267
Muhammad VI of Morocco
    264, 267
Muhammad Ali, Pasha of
    Egypt 157, 164, 299
Mulambwa 239–40, 379–80
Muluzi, Bakili 12, 248–9
Museveni, Yoweri 220,
    370–1, 375
Mussolini, Benito 320
Mutara III Rutahigwa 306–7
Mutesa I 89, 122, 370, 375
Mutesa II 62, 121–2, 370–1,
    373, 375
Mutota Nyatsimba 271
Muzorewa, Abel 384, 386
Mwambutsa IV of Urundi
    126, 128
Mwambwa 239, 379
Mwami Rugamba 126
Mwana 146, 240
Mwanga I of Buganda 122,
    370
Mwanga II of Buganda 375
Mwata Yamvo 103
Mwene Putu Kasonga 87,
    147
Mwinyi, Ali Hassan 358, 362
Mzilikazi 276, 331, 385–6

N

Nachtigal, Gustav 75
Naidoo, Jay 336
Nana Kwako Dua 200
Napoleon 157, 159, 308
Narriman 163
Abd an-Nasser, Gamal 160,
    163–4
Naweji of Lunda 146, 241
Ndadaye, Melchior 127
Ndumba Tembo 103
Nefertiti 165, 171
Neguib, Muhammad 160,
    162, 164
Neto, Antoniu Agostinho
    104–5
Ngendandumwe, Pierre 126
Ngouabi, Marien 150, 152
Ngqika 333
Nguema, Macias 16, 172–3,
    184, 242
Ngwane II of the Nguni 354
Nigrita, Antonio 226
el Nimeiri, Gaafar 50, 93,
    344–5, 352
Nimi a Lukeni 103
Njoya of Cameroon 131
Nkomo, Joshua 384–6, 388
Nkrumah, Kwame 44, 92,
    197, 200–1, 204
Nongqawuse 333
Ntare V of Burundi 126
Ntaryamira, Cyprien 127–8,
    306–7
Ntibantunganya, Sylvestre
    13, 127–8
Ntombi 354
Nujoma, Sam 18, 59, 272–3
Nyatsimba Mutota 27, 385
Nyerere, Julius 46, 127,
    357–8, 362
Nzinga, Anna 104, 277

O

Obasanjo, Olusegun 283,
    287
Obiang Nguema Mbsango,
    Teodoro 172–3
Obote, Milton 93, 122, 370,
    373, 375
Ojukwu, Chukwuemeka 50,
    116, 287
Ojukwu, Odumegwu 283
Okello, Tito 370
Olympio, Sylvanus 363–4
Omuhanwa, Kaboyo 373
Opoku Ware, Lady Victoria
    200–1
Opoku Ware II 197, 200
Osei Bonsu 198, 201
Osei Tutu 198, 201
Osman, Aden Abdullah 321,
    323
Oudney, Walter 73
Oueddei, Goukouni 139–40
Ouédraogo, Jean-Baptiste
    124–6
Ould Daddah, Moktar 41,
    256–7
Outtara, Alassane 15, 212

Ovonramwon of Benin 113

P

Park, Mungo 25, 73, 281
Patassé, Ange-Félix 56, 136–8
Peregrino, Francis 240
Pereira, Aristides 134
Piankhy 290, 352
Plaatje, Sol 334, 336, 338
do Po, Fernão 184
Prempe I of the Asante 85, 106, 198, 201
Prempeh II of the Asante 201
Pretorius, Andre 275
Ptolemy 164

Q

al-Qaddafi, Muammar 53, 236–8

R

Rabemananjara, Jean-Jacques 245
Rabih bin Fadl Allah 83, 138, 141, 302
Radama I of Madagascar 242–5, 260
Radama II of Madagascar 243
Rainilaiarivony 242
Ramanantsoa, Gabriel 244–5
Rameamu, Elias 231, 233
Ramgoolam, Sir Navinchandra 259
Ramgoolam, Sir Seewoosagur 258–60
Ramses II 171
Ranavalona 88, 243, 245, 260
Ras Makonnen 319
Ratsimandrava, Richard 244
Ratsimiliaho 244
Ratsiraka, Didier 244–5
Ravahiny 244
Rawlings, Jerry 52, 93, 197, 201
René, France-Albert 313–15
Retief, Piet 117, 336, 390
Rhodes, Cecil 34, 240, 276, 289, 304, 378–80, 383–6
van Riebeeck, Jan 337
Roberto, Holden 102
Roberts, Joseph Jenkins 233–4
Rohlfs, Gerhard 75
Rommel, Erwin 237
Rubusana, Walter Benson 334
Rwabudongo 123

S

Saad Zaghlul 157
al Sadat, Anwar 52, 160, 163–4
es Sadek, Muhammad 369
Sagad Suseyos 318
Saibou, Ali 281–2
Saladin 157

Salazar, António de Oliviera 102
Samori Toure 84, 111
Sanhá, Malam Bacai 206
Sankara, Thomas 124–6
Sankosh, Foday 315
Saro-Wiwa, Ken 14, 286
Sassou-Nguesso, Denis 150, 152
Savimbi, Jonas 102–5
Sawyer, Amos 234
Sayé Zerbo 124
Sayf bin Dhu Yazan 214
Schnitzer, Eduard 350
Schweinfurth, Georg 75, 136
Schweitzer, Albert 186
Sekhukhuni 332
Seme, Pixley Kalsaka 334
Senghor, Leopold Sédar 311, 313
Septimus Severus 292
Seyyid Ali 382
Seyyid Said 229, 360, 383
Shagari, Shehu 283, 287–8
Shaka 32, 88, 194, 270, 279, 333, 385, 390–1
Shamba-Bolongongo 227
Sharp, Granville 315
Sheba, 23, 176, 180, 318
Shermarke, Abder-Rashid 321, 323
Siad Barre, Muhammad 321–3
Sidi Mohamed 265, 267
Sigcawu Mqikela 132
Silumelume 240, 380
Sipopa 240, 380
Sisulu, Albertina 336
Sisulu, Walter 335–6, 339
Sithole, Ndabaningi 388
Slovo, Joe 336
Smith, Ian 303–4, 384, 386, 388
Smuts, Jan 336
Sobhuza I 278, 354
Sobhuza II 353–5
Sobukwe, Robert 336
Soga,Tiyo and Janet 333
Soglo, Christophe 111
Soglo, Nicéphore 111
Soilih, Ali 142–3
Solomon 23, 176, 180, 318
Soshangane 194, 270
Speke, John Hanning 33, 73, 75, 122, 375
Stanley, Henry Morton 74–5, 136, 144, 148, 361, 375
Stevens, Siaka 93, 315, 317
Strasser, Valentine 315, 317
Strijdom, Johannes 336–7
Sumanguru 250
Sundiata 253
Sunni Ali 251
Suzman, Dame Helen 336

T

Taitu 181, 319
Taki, Mohammed 142–3
Talbot-Kelly, Robert 347
Tambo, Oliver 335–6, 339

Taya, Maaouiya Ould Sidi Ahmed 256–7
Taylor, Charles 233–4
Tefnakht 352
Terre' Blanche, Eugene 340
Tewodros II of Ethiopia 176, 183, 318
Thandile 354
Thoho ya Ndou 332
Todd, Garfield 389
du Toit, Stephanus 327
Tolbert, William 53, 233, 235
Tombalbaye, François (later Ngarta) 47, 139, 141
Toure, Samori 250, 254, 280
Touré, Sékou 93, 204–5
Traoré, Moussa 93, 249–50, 252
Trovoada, Miguel 308–10
Tshombe, Moise 144, 149, 215–16
Tsiranana, Philibert 244–5
Tubman, William 233, 235–6
Tutankhamen 168, 171
Tuthmosis III 166, 170
Tutu, Desmond 337, 339

U

Umaru Dallaji 216
Uteem, Sir Cassam 259

V

Verwoerd, Hendrik 46, 337
Victor Emmanuel I of Italy 210
Vieira, João Bernardo 206
Vorster, John 337

W

Wade, Abdoulaye 311, 313
Wanke, Daouda Malam 280, 282
Washington, Booker T. 199, 334
Waterboer, Nicholas 203
Welenski, Sir Roy 303, 389
Williams, Henry Sylvester 109
Williams, Ruth 118–19
Winyi Gafabusa, Sir Tito 123
Witbooi, Hendrik 196
Wolseley, Lord 346–7

Y

el Yachourtu, Caabi 142
Yaméogo, Maurice 124, 126
Yekuno Amlak 180
Yembe Yembe 216
Yhombi-Opango, Joachim 150
Yohannes IV of Ethiopia 174, 176, 318
Youlou, Fulbert 150, 152

Z

Zafy, Albert 244, 245
Zenawi, Meles 179, 183
Zéroual, Liamine 100
Zoser, king of Egypt 165, 171

Zubayr, Rabah 214
Zwangendaba 194
Zwide, king of the Ndwandwe 194

General Index

A

'Abbasid dynasty 96, 294
Abidjan 211–13
Abomey, kingdom of 111
Abu Simbel 160, 171
Abyssinia 96
Acholi people 345
Addo 32
Adowa, Battle of 29, 89, 176, 181, 318
Afar peoples 155
Afars and Issas, French Territory of 96
African Development Bank 351
African National Congress (ANC) 18, 60, 231, 326, 329, 334–8
    Women's League 336
    Youth League 339
'Africanization' policies 220
Afrikaner Resistance Movement 340
Afrikaners 326–8, 353
Aghlabid dynasty 96
AIDS 19, 118, 371
Aïr, sultanate of 96
Akan states and peoples 96, 198
Aksum see Axum
El Alamein, Battle of 237
Algeciras Conference (1906) 263
Algeria 10, 97–100
    chronology 28, 34, 39, 42, 47, 51, 55
    presidents 99
    timeline 98
Almohad empire 100–1
Almoravid empire 101
Alur people 371
Ambuila, Battle of 104, 227
Amchinga people 248
American Colonization Society 233–4
Americo-Liberians 233–4
Amhara people 180
Ammon, great temple of 169
Anglo-Egyptian Sudan 102
Anglo-Sudanese War 346–7
Angola 16, 18, 102–5, 338
    chronology 28, 34, 39, 42, 47, 51, 55
    presidents 104
    timeline 105
Anjouan 106, 142
Ankole 106
Annobón 171
Anuak people 180, 345
Anyi people 213
Apartheid 18, 42, 46, 54, 326–40

Arabs 99, 160, 236, 265, 293, 368
Asante empire and people 106, 198–9
Asante Wars 85, 106–7, 197–8, 202
Ascension 108
Asian communities in Africa 218–20, 328–9, 370, 375
Assyrian empire 64, 167
Aswan High Dam 160, 164
Australopithecus sites and finds 223
Axum, kingdom of 108, 173, 176, 180
Ayyubid sultanate 158
Azande people 145

B

Babito dynasty 123, 372–3
Bachwezi dynasty 123
Baganda people *see* Ganda
Baggara people 345
Bagirmi people 109, 139
Bakota people 191
Baligota Isansa, Battle of 123
Bambara people 250, 310
Bamum kingdom and people 109, 131
Banda people 137
Bandiagara Cliffs 251
Bantu migration 62–3
Bapedi empire 231, 332
Barotseland 109, 240
Basilica of Our Lady of Peace 69, 211, 213
Basuto, kingdom of 30
Basutoland 109, 229–31
Baulé kingdoms and peoples 109, 213
Baya people 136–7
Bechuanaland Protectorate 109
Bedouin people 160
Begemder, kingdom of 109
Beja people 348
Belgian Congo 109–10
Belgium 126, 147, 215, 241; *see also* Léopold II
Bemba kingdom and people 110, 379
Benin 111–15
    ancient kingdom of 284
    chronology 28, 34, 39, 42, 47, 51, 55
    presidents 111
    timeline 114
Berber kingdoms and peoples 97–9, 115, 236–7, 265, 368
Biafra 116, 283–4
Bioko 171, 184, 305
Black Panthers 53, 237
Blood River, Battle of 390
Boer republics 116–17, 241, 327, 376
Boer War 296–7, 324, 327, 337, 342
Bondei people 358

Bonny 117
Bophuthatswana 117
Borgu 117
Bornu 214
Botswana 19, 117–20
    chronology 28, 34, 39, 43, 47, 51, 55
    presidents 119
    timeline 120
Brazzaville 143
British Bechuanaland 120
British Cameroons 120
British Central Africa 120, 293
British East Africa 121
British Kaffraria 121
British Somaliland 121
British South Africa Company 240, 276–7, 289, 342, 378–80, 383–6
British Togoland 121
Broederbond, the 337
Bubi people 172
Buduma people 139
Buganda 89, 121–3, 370–1
Bunyoro 370–3
Bunyoro-Kitara 123
Burkina Faso 124–6
    chronology 28, 34, 39, 43, 47, 51, 55
    presidents 124
    timeline 126
Burundi 12–13, 126–9, 305–6
    chronology 28, 34, 39, 43, 47, 51, 55
    kings and presidents 129
    timeline 128
Bushongo people 227

C

Cabinda 129
Calabar 129
Cameroon 14, 129–32
    chronology 28, 34, 39, 43, 47, 51, 55
    presidents 132
    timeline 131
Camp David, peace treaty 52, 164
Cape Colony 132–3
Cape Colored and Cape Malay populations 329–30
Cape of Good Hope 133, 324, 326
Cape Juby 133
Cape Verde, Republic of 133–4, 205–6
    chronology 28, 34, 39, 43, 47, 51, 56
    presidents 134
    timeline 134
Carthage 27, 65, 135
Central African Federation 240, 289, 303–4, 378, 380, 384
Central African Republic 16, 136–8
    chronology 28, 34, 39, 43, 47, 51, 56

presidents and emperors 138
    timeline 137
Ceuta 138, 264, 343
Chad 138–41
    chronology 28, 34, 40, 43, 47, 51, 56
    presidents 141
    timeline 140
Chagga people 358
Cherr Baba War 257
Chokwe people 103
Christianity 31, 66, 68–9, 145, 173, 176, 180, 247, 272, 292, 344–5
Christiansborg 297
Ciskei 141, 334, 365
Civil wars 10–12, 14, 16, 116, 139–40, 145, 234, 240, 268, 283–4, 322, 350, 380
Cobras, the 150
Coldstream Stone 26, 325
Colonial occupation and independence 90–1
Commonwealth, the 14, 326
Comoros 141–3
    chronology 28, 35, 40, 43, 48, 51, 56
    presidents 143
    timeline 143
Congo Free State 143, 216, 228, 241
Congo, Democratic Republic of 12, 16, 144–9
    chronology 28, 35, 40, 43, 48, 51–2, 56
    presidents 149
    timeline 148
Congo, Republic of 149–52
    chronology 29, 35, 40, 43, 48, 52, 56
    presidents 151
    timeline 152
Copper mining 39, 215–16, 378, 380
Cordia abyssinica 374
Corisca 171
Côte d'Ivoire *see* Ivory Coast
Côtiers 244
Coups d'état 92–3
Creoles 259, 309, 315–16
Cullinan diamond 342
Cyrenaica 36, 153, 236

D

Dagomba kingdom 153
Dahomey 111, 153
Darfur 154
Daura 154
Diamond mining and trading 16, 19, 103, 118, 203, 315
Diego Garcia 258–9
Diégo-Suarez 154
Dinka people 348
Djenné, Great Mosque of 249
Djibouti 154–6
    chronology 29, 35, 40, 43, 48, 52, 56

presidents 156
    timeline 156
Dogon people 250–1
Dongola 156
Dyula people 125

E

East Africa 157
East African Community 157, 217, 371
East African Protectorate 157
East India Company
    Dutch 326–7, 330, 337
    English 308, 313
Economic Community of West African States (ECOWAS) 233–4
Edo people 284
Egypt 10, 157–71
    ancient civilization 164–71
    chronology 29, 35, 40, 43–4, 48, 52, 56
    presidents 163
    timeline 163
Egyptian Camel Corps 160
Elephantine, island of 169
Elizabeth II, Queen 304
Elobey 171
Equatorial Guinea 16, 171–3
    chronology 29, 35, 40, 44, 48, 52, 56
    presidents 173
    timeline 173
Eritrea 12, 173–5, 179
    chronology 29, 35, 40, 44, 48, 52, 57
    presidents 174
    timeline 174
Ethiopia 12, 176–83
    chronology 29, 35, 40, 44, 48, 52, 57
    heads of state and presidents 182
    timeline 182
Ethiopian empire 80
Evolution, theory of 223
Ewe people 198–9

F

Fang people 171–3
Fante people 198–9
Fashoda crisis 347
Fatimid dynasty 183
Fernando Po 184
Fezzan 184, 236
Finance Corporation of America 233
Fipa people 358
Firestone Tire and Rubber Company 233
FNLA (Frente Nacional de Libertaçào de Angola) 102
Fon kingdom and people 111–14, 153, 185
Fourah Bay College 315
France 154–5, 173, 204, 211, 245, 258
    colonial expansion 186–7, 311
Franco-Merino Wars 243

FRELIMO (Frente de
Libertação de
Moçambique) 49, 268,
270–1
French Cameroun 185
French Congo 185
French Equatorial Africa 186
French Guinea 186
French Morocco 186
French Somaliland 154–5,
186
French Sudan 187
French Togoland 187
French West Africa 187
Fulani empire and people
86, 125, 188–9, 207
timeline 188
Funj kingdom and people
189, 348
Fur people 348–9
Futa Djallon 190
Futa Toro 190

G
Ga towns 190
Gabon 16, 190–2
chronology 29, 35, 40, 44,
48, 52, 57
presidents 191
timeline 191
Gambia 14, 192–3
chronology 29, 35, 40, 44,
48, 52, 57
presidents 193
timeline 193
Game reserves 220
Ganda people 62–3, 121–2,
371
Gaza 194
Gazankulu 194
German Cameroons 194
German East Africa 195
German Southwest Africa
196
Germany 126, 172
Ghadames 197
Ghana 197–201
ancient empire of 201
chronology 29, 35–6, 40,
44, 48, 52, 57
presidents 199
timeline 200
Glele, king of Dahomey 114
Gobir 202, 207
Gold Coast 197–9, 202, 363
Gonja 202
Grain Coast 233
Grande Comore 202
Great Man-Made River 239
Great Pyramid of Khufu 168
Great Trek 116–17, 133, 295,
324, 327, 336–7, 342
Great Zimbabwe 202–3, 267,
271, 305, 385, 388–9
Greek Africa 64
Griqua people 330
Griqualand 203
Gross national product
(GNP) per capita 12, 14,
19

Guinea, Republic of 14,
204–5
chronology 29–30, 36, 40,
44, 48, 52, 57
presidents 204
timeline 205
Guinea-Bissau 205–6
chronology 30, 36, 40, 44,
49, 52, 57
presidents 206
timeline 206
Gusii people 220
Gwari 207

H
Hadza people 358
Hausa states and peoples
207, 280, 284
Haya people 358
Herero people 196, 272–4
High Commission Territories
208, 353
HIV 19, 118, 354, 371
Homelands 18–19, 326,
332–3, 338
Homo erectus sites and finds
223
Human rights 14, 155, 192,
204, 234, 336, 363
Husuni Kubwa 225
Hutu people 12–13, 126–7,
305–6

I
Ibadan 208
Ibibio people 284
Ibn Tulun, Mosque of 70
Idrisid state 208
Ifat 208
Ife 208–9
Ifni 209
Ifriqiyah 209
Igbo people 210, 284–5
Ijo states 210
Ilois of Diego Garcia 259
Ilorin 210
Independence, gaining of
90–1
Indian labour in Africa 219,
328–9
Indian Ocean trade 383
Inkatha Freedom Party
334–5, 339
International Anti-Apartheid
Year 238
International Court of
Justice 139, 256, 264, 272
International Monetary Fund
134, 204, 212, 217, 268,
309–10
International Year of the
Child 357
Invo Zabantsundu 334
Iraqw people 358
Irish Republican Army 53,
237
Islam, spread of 70–1
Islamic fundamentalism
10–11, 55, 98, 160, 163,
368

Islamic law 344–5, 350
Israel 48, 52
Issa people 155
Italian East Africa 210
Italian Somaliland 210, 320
Italy 89, 153, 176–8, 236,
320
Iteso people 220–1, 372
Ivory Coast 14–15, 211–13
chronology 30, 36, 40, 44,
49, 52, 57
presidents 213
timeline 212

J
Jammeh, Yahya 192
Jihads 86, 188, 207, 209,
213, 215–16, 242, 262, 313
Jubaland 213
Jukun 213

K
Kaarta 213
Kahima chiefdom 359
Kalenjin people 221
Kanem, empire of 214
Kanem-Borno 214
Kangaba, kingdom of 215
KaNgwane 215
Kano 215
Kanuri people 285
Karamojong people 372
Kariba Dam 378
Karitu chiefdom 359
Katanga 149, 215–16
Katsina 216
Kazembe kingdom 216, 241
Kebbi 207, 217
Kenya 12, 217–24
chronology 30, 36, 40, 44,
49, 52, 57
presidents 224
timeline 222
Khartoum 33, 83, 246, 346,
351
Khoisan people 330–1
Kikuyu people 63, 221
Kilaguni Lodge 220
Kilwa 224–5
Kimberley Regiment 276
King's African Rifles 120
Kinshasa 143
Kirijj War 208
Kirina, Battle of 253
Kololo people 240
Kong, Kingdom of 225
Kongo, kingdom 226–7
Kongo religion 145
Konso people 180
Kororofa 227
Kru people 234
Kuba kingdom 227–8
Kumasi 29
Kunda dynasty 146, 240–1
Kuomboka Festival 239
Kush, kingdom of 228
KwaNdebele 228, 331
KwaZulu 228, 334–5
Kwena clan 231
Kwi people 234

L
Labadi 229
Lagos 229
Lakhta, Battle of 83, 138,
302
Lalibela 176
Lambaréné 186
Lamu 229
Lango people 372
League of Nations 126, 129,
176, 196, 272, 326, 357,
363
Lebowa 229
Lesotho 229–33
chronology 30, 36, 40, 44,
49, 52, 57–8
kings 232
timeline 232
Liberia 14, 233–6
chronology 30, 36, 41, 44,
49, 53, 58
presidents 234
timeline 235
Libya 16, 236–9
chronology 30, 36, 41, 44,
49, 53, 58
Declaration of
Independence 81
kings, chairmen and
general secretaries 239
timeline 238
Lion Temple, Naqa 228
Lockerbie disaster 236
Lourenço Marques 239
Lozi kingdom and people
239–40, 379–80
Luba kingdom and people
145–6, 240–1
Lugbara people 372
Lunda empire and peoples
104, 146, 172, 241
Luo people 221
Luyia people 372
Lydenburg 241

M
Maasai people 221–2
Mabhogo 331
Macedonian Africa 64
Macias Nguema Biyogo 242
Macina 242
Madagascar 19, 242–7
chronology 31, 36, 41,
44–5, 49, 58
peoples 244–5
presidents 245
timeline 246
Mahdist state 246–7, 346
Maji Maji uprising 195
Makurra 247
Malagasy Republic 247
Malawi 12, 247–9
chronology 31, 37, 41, 45,
49, 53, 58
presidents 248
timeline 248
Mali 249–3
chronology 31, 37, 41, 45,
49, 53, 58
medieval empire of 253

presidents 252
timeline 252
Mali Federation 254
Malindi 254
Malinke (town) 253
Malinke people 250
Mamluk dynasty 158
Mamprusi state and people 199, 254
Manda 254
Manding people 251
Mandinka empire 254
Mangbetu people 146
Mano River Union 315
Mapungubwe 255
Maputo 255
Marinid dynasty 255
Marrakech 255
Masai Mara 362
Masallaci Jumaa 207
Mashonaland 255
Massiwa, Battle of 195
Matabele kingdom and peoples 276–7, 385
Matabeleland 256
Matapa 271
Mau Mau movement 217–18, 221
Mauritania 11, 256–8, 264
    chronology 31, 37, 41, 45, 49, 53, 58
    presidents and heads of state 257
    timeline 258
Mauritius 258–60
    chronology 31, 37, 41, 45, 49, 53, 58
    presidents 259
    timeline 259
Mayotte 260
Mazrui dynasty 229
Mbanza 226
Mbunda people 239, 379–80
Melilla 82, 260, 264, 343
Mende people 316
Mentuhetep, temple of 169
Merina kingdom and peoples 31, 88, 260
Meroitic kingdom and writing 260–1
Mfecane, the 32, 88, 231, 278–9, 294, 332, 353, 378, 385, 390–1
Middle Congo 150–1, 260
Mijikenda people 224
Mindelo 133
Missionaries 31, 130, 186, 194, 247, 272, 345, 370
Mogadishu 225, 261
Mohéli 142
Mombasa 262, 293
Mongo peoples 146–7
Monrovia 233–4
Moors 257
Moriuledegu, kingdom of 262
Morocco 11, 256–7, 262–7
    kings 266
    timeline 266

chronology 31, 37, 41, 45, 49, 53, 58
Mossi kingdom and people 125, 267
Mozambique 18–19, 267–71
    chronology 31, 37, 41, 45, 49, 53, 58–9
    presidents 269
    timeline 269
MPLA (Movimento Popular de Libertaçào de Angola) 102–3, 105
Mthethwa 271
Musi people 331
Muslim Africa 67
Mutapa 271
Mwene Mutapa state and dynasty 27, 271, 305

N
Nama people 274
Namibia 16, 18, 31, 272–5
    chronology 31, 37, 41, 45, 49, 53, 59
    presidents 273
    timeline 273
Natal 275
National parks 220, 362
Natural gas reserves 10, 16
Ndebele kingdom and people 276–7, 331
Ndembu people 147
Ndongo kingdom 277
Ndwandwe 277–8, 390
New Republic 278
Ngonde people 248
Ngoni states and peoples 270, 278
Ngorongoro Crater 362
Nguni chieftainships and peoples 63, 278, 331, 353–4
Ngwane 278
Niger, Republic of 279–82
    chronology 31–2, 37, 41, 45, 49, 53, 59
    presidents and chairmen 280
    timeline 281
Niger Coast Protectorate 282
Nigeria 14, 282–8
Nigeria
    chronology 32, 37, 41, 45, 50, 53–4, 59
    presidents and heads of state 288
    timeline 286
    see also Northern Nigeria; Southern Nigeria
Nigeria Regiment 282
Nile, river
    flooding 164
    kingdoms 291
    source 33, 75
Nkore, kingdom of 288
Nobatia 288
Nobel Peace Prize 164, 186, 335, 339
Nok people and culture 26, 288

Northern Nigeria 289
Northern Rhodesia 289
Nossi-Bé 290
Nuba people 349
Nubia 156, 160, 290, 344
nuclear tests 42, 98
Nuer people 349
Numidia 115, 290–2
Nungua 292
Nupe kingdom and people 292
Nyamwezi people 63, 358–9
Nyasaland 120, 247, 292–3
Nyoro people 63, 372–3

O
Ogaden conflict 155, 176
Ogoni activists 14
Oil reserves and revenues 10, 14, 16, 116, 236
Oil Rivers Protectorate 293
Omani Arabs 293
Omayyad dynasty 294
Omdurman, Battle of 83, 247, 347
Operation Torch 237
Opobo, kingdom of 294
Orange Free State 294–5, 297
Orange River Colony 296
Orange River Sovereignty 296
Organization of African Unity 11, 127, 142, 179, 200, 265, 308, 364
Oromo people 180–1
Osu 297
Ottoman empire 298–9
Ouagadougou 124
Oubangui-Chari 300
Oubangui-Chari-Tchad 300
Ovambo people 274–5
Ovimbundu people 104, 300
Oyo empire 285, 300–1

P
Palestine Liberation Organization 236
Pan-Africanism 197, 204
Pare people 359
Pass laws 338
Pate 301
Pedi people 231, 301, 332
Pemba 301–2
Pende people 147
Persian Africa 64
Phoenician Africa 65
Polisario (Popular Front for the Liberation of Saharan Territories) 256–7, 264–5, 304
Portugal 102–4, 129, 133–4, 171–2, 192, 225–6, 229, 262, 267–8, 308
Portuguese Guinea 302
Potchefstroom 302, 341
Prazos 302
Principe see São Tomè
Ptolemaic Africa 65
Puntland 12, 322

Q
Qwaqwa 302

R
Rabih's Empire 302
Ramileke people 131
Rano 303
Rastafarianism 319
RENAMO (Resistência Nacional Moçambicana) 268, 270–1
Resistance to Colonization 82–9
Réunion 303
Rhodesia 303–4, 383–4; see also Northern Rhodesia; Southern Rhodesia
Rhodesia and Nyasaland, Federation of 304
Rhodesia Medal 303
Rhodesia Regiment 289, 304
Ribeira Grande 133
Rif War 264
Río de Oro 304
Rio Muni 305
Roman Africa 66
Rovzi empire 305, 385
Ruanda-Urundi 305
Rukuba people 285
Rwanda 12, 16, 126, 306
    chronology 32, 37, 41, 45, 50, 54, 59
    presidents 307
    timeline 307

S
Saguia el Hamra 308; see also Spanish Sahara
Saharawi people 257
Sahrawi Arab Democratic Republic 11
Saint Helena 308
Sakalava kingdom 308
San people 331
Sandawe people 359
Sankoré Mosque 71, 324
São Tomé and Príncipe 308–10
    chronology 32, 38, 41, 45, 50, 54, 59
    presidents 309
    timeline 309
Sara people 139
Sefawa dynasty 214
Segu 310
Senegal 14, 310–13
    chronology 32, 38, 41, 45–6, 50, 54, 60
    presidents 312
    timeline 312
Senufo people 251
Serengeti National Park 362
Serer people 312
Seychelles 313–15
    chronology 32, 38, 41, 46, 50, 54, 60
    peoples 314
    presidents 315
    timeline 314
Seyyid Said 360

Shaba 16
Shambaa people 359
Shangaan people 194
Sharpeville massacre 336, 339
Shoa 89
Shona empire and peoples 27, 203, 385–6
Shona Rebellion 384
Sidama Stone 182
Sierra Leone 14, 315–19
  chronology 32, 38, 41, 46, 50, 54, 60
  presidents and chairmen 317
  timeline 317
Sikh soldiers 329
Six-Day War 160–1
Slavery and the slave trade 76–9, 382–3
  abolition of 80–1, 337
Sofala 318
Solomonid empire 318
Somali people 322
Somalia 12–13, 320–3
  chronology 32, 38, 41, 46, 50, 54, 60
  presidents 323
  timeline 323
Somaliland 12; see also British Somaliland; French Somaliland; Italian Somaliland
Somaliland Camel Corps 121
Songhay empire 207, 250–2, 324
Songye people 145, 147, 240
Soninke people 125
Soofie Mosque 329
Soso people 204
Sotho people 231, 331–2
Sotho people 63
South Africa 16, 18–19, 324–41
  chronology 32–3, 38, 42, 46, 50, 54, 60
  indigenous communities 325
  presidents 341
  timelines 328, 330, 340
South African Republic (Transvaal) 341–2
South West Africa 343
Southern Nigeria 342
Southern Rhodesia 342
Soutpansberg 343
Soviet Union 13
Soweto 339
Spain 11, 171–2
Spanish Guinea 343
Spanish Morocco 343
Spanish Sahara 256, 264, 344–52; see also Saguia el Hamra
'Star of Africa' 342
Sudan 10, 344
  chronology 33, 38, 42, 46, 50, 50, 54, 60
  presidents 352
  timelines 345, 348–9, 351

Sudanese Republic 353
Suez Canal 157
Suez crisis 160–1, 164
Sufi lodges 71
Suku people 147
Sukuma people 359
Susu people 204
Swahili peoples 359–60
SWAPO (South West Africa People's Organization) 59, 272–3, 275
Swazi kingdom and peoples 62–3, 354
Swaziland 353–5
  chronology 33, 38, 42, 46, 50, 54, 60–1
  kings and queens 354
  timeline 355
Syria 48

T
Takrur 355
Tanganyika 355–7
Tangier Zone 357
Tanzania 12, 357–62
  chronology 33, 38, 42, 46, 50, 54, 61
  presidents 361
  timeline 361
Tassili-n-Ajjer 99
Taureg people 280
Teda people 139
Teke people 149, 151
Tell al Kebir, Battle of 162
Temne people 316
Tigre people 174, 176
Timbuktu 71
Tiv people 285
Togo 363–4
  chronology 38, 42, 46, 50, 54, 61
  presidents 364
  timeline 364
Togoland 187, 197–9, 363–4
Tonga people 380
Toro kingdom and people 364, 373
Tourism 10, 118, 192, 220, 362
Transkei 334, 365
Trans-Saharan trade routes 184
Transvaal 341–2, 365
Treetops 220
Tripolitana 365
Tristan da Cunha 365
Truth and Reconciliation Commission 337
Tsitambala confederation 365
Tsonga people 194, 270
Tswana people 117–19
Tukulor empire 365–6
Tulunid dynasty 366
Tunisia 366–9
  chronology 33, 38–9, 42, 46, 50, 54, 61
  presidents 369
  timeline 369
Turkana people 224

Turkey 153
Tutsi people 12, 16, 126–7, 144, 305–6
Twa people 126–7, 305–6

U
Uganda 12, 16, 220, 370–5
  chronology 33, 39, 42, 46, 50, 54, 61
  presidents 374
  timeline 374
Uganda Protectorate 375
Uganda Railway 219
Umayyad dynasty 294
Union of South Africa 376
UNITA (União Nacional para a Independência Total de Angola) 16, 102–3, 105, 150, 363
United Arab Republic 375
United Arab States 375
United Nations 11, 126, 136, 173, 179, 204, 235, 281, 306, 322, 343, 363–4, 384
  Decolonization Committee 256, 264
  Educational, Scientific and Cultural Organization (UNESCO) 160, 246
  General Assembly 272
  Human Rights Award 336
  Security Council 315, 345
United States 13, 259, 345
Unyamwezi 358
Upper Volta 124, 375
Urundi 126, 305–6

V
Vandal Africa 66
Vegkop, Battle of 275
Venda and the Venda people 332–3, 376
Versailles Treaty (1919) 195, 305
Voortrekker Monument 342
Voortrekkers 116, 327

W
Wadai 376
Wagadugu 376
Walvis Bay 377
Wanga kingdom 377
Warri kingdom 377
Western Sahara 11
Wolof empire and people 193, 377
World Bank 134, 204
World Heritage Sites 362
World War I 120, 130, 139, 172–3, 195–6, 363
World War II 35, 38, 139, 160, 173, 178, 192, 221, 233, 236–7, 320, 326, 368

X
Xhosa people 63, 333–4, 365

Y
Yakurr people 285

Yam Festival 29, 202
Yamoussoukro 211, 213
Yao people 248, 270
Yom Kippur War 48, 160–1
Yoruba states and peoples 114, 285, 377
Yundum egg scheme 192

Z
Zagwe dynasty 176, 377
Zaire see Congo, Democratic Republic of
Zambia 16, 378–81
  chronology 33–4, 39, 42, 47, 50–1, 55, 61
  presidents 381
  timeline 381
Zangid empire 158
Zanizbar 293
ZANU (Zimbabwe African National Union) 384, 386, 388
Zanzibar 77–8, 357, 360, 381–2
ZAPU (Zimbabwe African People's Union) 384, 386
Zaramo people 360
Zaria 207, 382–3
Zazembe kingdom 146
Zerma people 280–1
Zimbabwe 16, 18, 383–9
  chronology 34, 39, 42, 47, 51, 55, 61
  presidents 387
  timeline 387
Zirid emirate 390
Zulu kingdom and people 32, 63, 88, 228, 334, 390–1
Zulu weapons 391